030
Ref.

The Yearbook of Agriculture 1965

THE

UNITED STATES

DEPARTMENT

OF

AGRICULTURE

CONSUMERS ALL
The Yearbook of Agriculture 1965

THE UNITED STATES GOVERNMENT PRINTING OFFICE

FOR SALE BY THE SUPERINTENDENT OF DOCUMENTS, WASHINGTON, D.C., 20402 - PRICE $2.75

FOREWORD

ORVILLE L. FREEMAN

Secretary of Agriculture

FOR MORE THAN 100 YEARS, the Department of Agriculture has been, in Lincoln's words, a "people's department"—a Department for producers and users of the essentials of living, for homemakers, for consumers. A Department, in short, for all of us.

This book presents practical results of the Department's efforts to make the lives of people healthier, happier, more fulfilling.

As an American, I am impressed by these accomplishments.

As Secretary of Agriculture, I am proud to be associated with the dedicated, highly trained men and women in laboratories and administrative offices, in marketplaces and processing plants, in fields and forest, all of them partners of our Nation's farmers, who have woven these services into the fabric of our daily living.

Here is a basic truth: Though a primary objective of the Department is service to United States farmers and ranchers, the real beneficiary of agricultural productivity and abundance has been, is now, and will continue to be the American consumer.

Consider these facts:

Today less than 19 percent of the average American's take-home pay is spent for food. Only about 15 years ago the proportion was 26 percent. In Russia today the average family spends half of its income for food; in Japan, more than two-fifths; in England and France, almost one-third.

During the past 15 years or so, retail prices of food produced on American farms rose 14 percent because of higher marketing costs. The farm price for food went down 15 percent. Meanwhile the cost of nonfood items increased 37 percent. Americans now pay 72 percent more for medical care, 37 percent more for housing, and 54 percent more for transportation than they did some 15 years ago.

Because of our great efficiency in agriculture, one farmworker in America now produces enough to feed 31 persons. In 1920 he fed 8 persons. The average farmer in Europe produces enough for 10 persons; in Russia, enough for 5 or 6.

These facts are a measure of the productive achievements of American farmers. They testify also to the work of the Department of Agriculture. Agriculture's present capacity could never have been attained without the Department's contributions in research, education, engineering, credit, technical guidance, and other fields.

Even those programs designed to adjust production to needs without wasting human or natural resources and to help equalize the prices farmers get for many of the commodities they sell—condemned by some as "subsidy"—help assure our abundance.

Yet only one dollar in three of the Department's expenditures goes for price support, income stabilization, and other programs in which farmers are the direct, primary beneficiaries.

Two dollars out of three are spent for services of primary benefit to all of us as consumers, such as inspection of meat and poultry to assure safety; grading of food and fiber to assure quality; control of pests and diseases that affect the health of plants and animals and people; protection of soil, water, and forest resources for the continued welfare of this and succeeding generations; and the development of new products, processes, and services that add remarkably to the convenience of living.

We have special aids also for those with special needs. More than 35 million people—schoolchildren, the elderly, the disabled, and those who are unemployed—are getting better diets through the School Lunch, Milk, and Direct Food Distribution programs. A million low-income consumers have been able to increase their food purchasing power a third because of the Food Stamp program. Eventually this program will serve all people with low incomes.

But there is much more that can and should be done to satisfy the people's needs. The impressive variety of moneysaving, health-preserving, comfort-producing consumer services now available from the "people's department" must be extended to many more Americans everywhere, assisting them to take better advantage of our Age of Abundance. Such services can help build the Great Society.

Yet the consumer must know what these services are, where they are, and how to obtain them. And the services themselves must be continually improved, made more effective, more responsive to the people's needs.

We are keenly aware that if these goals are to be accomplished, the major responsibility rests with the Department of Agriculture itself. We have developed a number of approaches to this end, and this book is one of them.

The total responsibility, however, cannot be ours alone. It rests also on all who seek to help—groups and organizations, agencies at all levels of Government, and consumers themselves. We offer many consumer services, but only informed people can profit by them.

There is, in short, an art to being a thoughtful and discerning consumer. This Yearbook of Agriculture is devoted to furthering that art.

PREFACE

ALFRED STEFFERUD

Editor of the Yearbook of Agriculture

THIS BOOK TELLS US—consumers all—many things about buying, using, or making food, clothing, household furnishings, and equipment; managing money; caring for yards, gardens, and houses; bettering communities; using leisure time; and staying healthy.

It is long on facts but short on sentiment. That may be a deficiency in a book, as in a household or an organization or society in general. As scientists, economists, or administrators (as all of us who prepared this book are), we tend to prefer facts, figures, and finite things and shy away from matters of spirit or sentiment.

But as homemakers (all of us are that, too) we know that a happy home is much more than a house; much more than opening cans and washing diapers and balancing budgets; much more than a place to sleep, dress, eat, and worry.

Here and there that point is hinted at, when social consciousness overcomes bureaucratic caution, but we have left it primarily to a reminder like this one: Man cannot live by bread alone.

This book reflects some—not all—of the many facets of the Department's work in behalf of consumers and homemakers. It may seem strange to persons who still think of the Department of Agriculture as concerned only with ways to grow more (or less) wheat and corn that we should be interested also in ways to improve communities, heat houses, and make bread.

But the step is not big, for example, between forests and the use of wood in homes, between crops and diets, between extension services and education, between farmers and the well-being of rural communities. Thus has the Department been given increased responsibilities since its establishment. And, as Secretary Freeman points out in his foreword, the Department of Agriculture always has been a people's department.

Many of the contributors to this book are in the Department or are connected with it, each writing from experience in his job, but we have called on others for some chapters that enlarge the usefulness of the book and are within its scope.

Some other matters belong in a volume on homemaking, but we considered them beyond the responsibilities given us by the Congress, and we did not want to duplicate materials in many fine, new books and magazines devoted to homemaking.

Nor did we wish to duplicate unduly the pamphlets the Department has prepared on many subjects of great interest to consumers. Some of them are cited in various chapters. Readers may find these bulletins especially useful: "A Consumer's Guide to USDA Services," Miscellaneous Publication No. 959, and "Popular Publications for the Farmer, Suburbanite, Homemaker, Consumer," List No. 5.

Single copies are available without charge on request to the Office of Information, the United States Department of Agriculture, Washington, D.C., 20250.

Previous Yearbooks of Agriculture also contain a wealth of information for homemakers and other consumers. We list those that are still in print and give the prices at which they may be obtained from the Superintendent of Documents: *Grass*, $2.00; *Trees*, $2.75; *Crops in Peace and War*, $2.50; *Insects*, $3.25; *Plant Diseases*, $3.00; *Marketing*, $1.75; *Water*, $2.25; *Animal Diseases*, $2.00; *Soil*, $2.25; *Land*, $2.25; *Food*, $2.25; *Power to Produce*, $2.25; *Seeds*, $2.00; *After a Hundred Years*, $3.00; *A Place to Live*, $3.00; *Farmer's World*, $3.00.

Requests for them should not be addressed to the Department of Agriculture, which has no copies for general distribution.

We acknowledge with gratitude the help given by the Government Printing Office, particularly its Division of Typography and Design, in the production of this and previous Yearbooks of Agriculture; the contributors, to whom this was a task outside the regular call of duty; and the members of the 1965 Yearbook Committee, who planned the book.

The members of the committee are:

Ruth M. Leverton, *Agricultural Research Service*, chairman;
Mary M. Hill, *Agricultural Research Service*, secretary;
Robert J. Anderson, *Agricultural Research Service;*
Margaret C. Browne, *Federal Extension Service;*
Sam R. Hoover, *Agricultural Research Service;*
Dorothy H. Jacobson, *Office of the Secretary;*
George M. Jemison, *Forest Service;*
Walter W. John, *Federal Extension Service;*
O. L. Kline, *Department of Health, Education, and Welfare;*
Harold C. Knoblauch, *Cooperative State Research Service;*
Roy W. Lennartson, *Consumer and Marketing Service;*
Lloyd E. Partain, *Soil Conservation Service.*

Herewith ends an editorship that began in 1945 and produced 18 Yearbooks of Agriculture, of which (at latest reckoning) 5,129,186 copies have been distributed. Forsan et haec olim meminisse iuvabit.

CONTENTS

FURNISHINGS

EQUIPMENT

FINANCES

SAFEGUARDS

PLANTS

OUTDOORS

ACTIVITIES

CLOTHING

FOOD

CONSUMERS ALL

HOUSES

The Choice

Is Yours

Most of us have not one but a number of homes in a lifetime.

Most of us therefore, as we move from country to city or city to suburb or job to job or status to status, have choices to make every time we move our lares and penates.

Let the choice be a good one or at least a thoughtful one, for—even if you stay in a place only a short time— it can influence your and your family's well-being, sometimes even involvement and identity, and happiness.

A mistake, if you make one, can be corrected, but a mistake almost always leaves some kind of mark.

First, THE COMMUNITY you choose.

Before you make your choice, compare the costs of commuting in money, time, and fatigue with the advantages and disadvantages of space, privacy, and quiet for yourself and your family.

Do not overlook differences in public amenities and governmental services and in taxes and the costs of insurance and utilities.

Wherever you decide to live, you will be concerned with the policies of local government—in the country, with the county and school district; in town, with them and also with the services and policies of city hall.

Choose, if you can, to live within the jurisdiction of a government that has a master plan of zoning and development, legislation to support it, and an active review procedure to keep it alive and fresh.

During any period of expansive physical development stimulated by the effects of increases in population and metropolitanization, it is hard to foresee the future of a community or to influence its development. Without a plan, growth is chaotic and unpredictable.

Many families have built houses in the country only to find the city at their doorsteps sooner than they had expected. Many others have built or rented in city neighborhoods whose residential character becomes eroded by conversion to incompatible uses.

My advice therefore is: Do not buy or build a house on land that has a potential for industrial, commercial, or multiple-housing development except as a calculated investment.

Rather, seek a site protected by zoning.

You will find other advantages in legislation for city or county planning. Visual quality—beauty and order—

depends on the good will and sensibility of each property owner and the competence of his architect, but laws can control some of the influences that have contributed to the deterioration of the American landscape—signs, billboards, gas stations, and utility structures.

Some communities limit the locations of billboards, refuse to accept standard designs for gas stations, and require that wires and pipes of utilities be put underground. Choose a community that does all that and is alert to the possibilities of more improvements like them.

LOCAL GOVERNMENT and public education are financed largely by taxes on real property.

Tax rates and sometimes assessment practices vary among communities. But do not assume that communities with low taxes therefore are more efficient. Usually they simply provide fewer or inferior services.

Some communities try to attract industry in the belief that new factories are another source of nonresidential tax income to help defray costs of government and schools. An economic analysis of the tax impact of each potential industry on the community, however, should be made to set forth the new costs as well as the new revenues.

New families that will accompany an industry to a community must be taken into account, because, ironically, most families are tax liabilities—their share of governmental and school costs is greater than their contributions.

In the final analysis, the property tax has inevitable shortcomings, because it penalizes quality by rewarding shoddy developments with low assessments.

When you attempt to estimate the fiscal soundness of a city or county or your future tax costs as an owner of real property within its jurisdiction, do not oversimplify the problem.

An example: Nothing is more important than excellent public schools. They are not easy to develop. They are built by the efforts of dedicated people over long periods. Your children of school age get no benefit from long-range improvements. They need good schools now.

Good schools are expensive. Usually they coexist with high real property taxes, but differences in tax rates in communities with good schools and those with poor schools are seldom great enough to influence one's choice and are never worth the "savings."

Communities with good schools usually are stimulating in other ways, too. So, when you are looking for a place to live, look into opportunities for intellectual activity, libraries, museums, theaters, concerts, a little-theater group, an amateur symphony. Mutual interests foster friendships more than geography does.

Look also for a beautiful place, or one that at least is not ugly.

Visual quality, like a good school system, is not achieved quickly. It depends on long traditions of pride and long-continued programs of responsible public works. Street trees take years to mature. Established visual elegance in a residential community is literally priceless.

Consider also convenience to work, shopping, and schools in terms of distance and methods of transport, for a house for most families in this day and age is a center from which to commute to work and to acquire goods and services. Children commute to school. If for no other reason, anticipate traveling costs in order to know how much you can afford to spend for housing.

The place you live often determines whether you need two automobiles, one, or none. A friend of mine kept records for a year, and demonstrated that he could not afford to own an automobile in New York City. He takes a taxi whenever he moves about the city and rents a car on weekends and holidays to go to the country, both at a lower total cost than the cost of owning an automobile.

The European lives in his city at large. Public and neighborhood gathering places—piazzas, parks, sidewalk cafes, coffeehouses—serve as extensions of his house into which some social parts of life are projected. Americans have 6-foot fences along property lines between suburban houses, yet we are experiencing a revival of interest in public amenities, especially in cities.

Consider then the relationship between the kind of urban situation in which you live and the kind of housing facilities you may need or are available.

In the older parts of established cities, you find multiple types—row houses or taller apartment buildings. These extend to outer parts of larger cities, where old townhouses, duplexes, and garden apartments (row houses scattered through the landscape rather than along streets), may be found. Suburbs now have duplexes, small apartments, and a renaissance of row houses, besides the traditional free-standing house, usually the only type found in the country.

Another recent house form is the mobile home, or trailer. Presumably it was developed to accommodate a mobile and space-loving society, but trailers usually are parked in crowded courts without privacy. Their occupants tend to be no more mobile than families in apartment houses; they move about once every 2 years. Actually, trailers used as tract houses are not inexpensive, but they do avoid or minimize tax contributions for the support of schools and local government.

Homeownership used to be possible only in a separate house, duplex, or row house. The mobile home and the extension of condominium to American apartments have extended the own-versus-rent choice.

It is possible to demonstrate that in a rising market it is more economical to own than to rent equivalent quarters. Owning, as opposed to renting, also has Federal (and sometimes State) income tax advantages, but renting and owning generally must be regarded as economic equivalents.

The choice should be made on other grounds—how long you expect to remain in a given locality and whether you wish to be involved in the maintenance, improvement, and accumulation of furnishings and equipment that accompany ownership.

How important are the intangibles of ownership? Much has been said about owned houses as prestige symbols. I do not assess the prestige value of houses or of locations, but assume that true value lies in utility and soundness and in the satisfactions that derive from compatibility, privacy, and the expression of personality.

SOMETIMES A NEIGHBORHOOD is so attractive that it determines one's choice of community, but usually the community is selected first.

Transportation may influence the second decision as well as the first. So, inevitably, will the housing situation. If you are interested in a particular kind of house or lot or one at a certain price, you may find it only in a limited number of places.

But, assuming there are alternatives, how to proceed?

Some Americans think that every man ought to own his house. On the other hand, many families rent because of mobility. As a matter of fact, when moving into a new community, there is an advantage in renting for a while.

Many qualities, especially the intangibles that have to do with sociability, common interests, and climate, cannot be understood without experience. Renting in an unfamiliar community will give you a clearer idea of the kind of house you want and the neighborhood in which you would like to live.

Whether renting or buying, look first for visual character. It is even more important in the neighborhood than in the community, because the neighborhood is closer to home.

Established neighborhoods have at least two advantages: You can examine the houses, and the landscape has had time to mature. Some of our best houses are very old, but middle-aged houses and neighborhoods tend to deteriorate.

Judge the viability of an established neighborhood before placing a new house there. If you don't trust your own evaluation, seek professional advice. New developments still under construction are harder to visualize, but plans can give some indication of their eventual completed appearance.

Houses for sale or rent and remaining lots in stable residential neighborhoods command higher prices. So does property in thoughtfully planned and sensitively designed new residential areas that can reasonably be expected to develop admirably.

Your choice is difficult: Whether to accept an area that is not and probably will not be developed attractively, or place a larger percentage of your investment in land and improvements to take advantage of a superior location, remembering that you will be able to do little to change the aspect of the neighborhood.

Look for a location where you can walk to stores and shops, school, and a park. That may be difficult, because much zoning legislation, in overreacting to 19th-century slums, has produced antiseptic neighborhoods, which by being unvaried are also unserviced. Well-designed and well-maintained multiple housing can be interspersed skillfully with smaller houses, and convenient shops are an advantage.

Incidentally, communities with too few service facilities often can improve their tax base simply by attracting the needed services.

Communities vary a good deal in the availability of facilities and programs for recreation. Do not overlook their importance for children.

Select a location that is free from unpleasant sources of noise, fumes, and dirt and not near a freeway, railroad, airport, or objectionable industry. Noise travels surprising distances on quiet nights. So do fumes and dust on breezy days.

Consider the views. If the terrain is hilly, the views are more extensive, but construction costs probably will be higher.

What does the street look like? Most streets are too wide. Narrower streets may be crowded now and then, but they hold down the scale of the neighborhood and so add to its character.

Streets are classified on the basis of expected traffic loads, and widths are proportional to the classifications. Select a site facing a street of the lowest classification, where the lightest traffic load is anticipated.

Purely local streets have advantages of relative quiet and safety. Subtly curved streets usually are more attractive than straight ones, but excessively curved patterns are puzzling to strangers and casual visitors.

What do the neighboring houses look like? Fences? Landscaping? What is the orientation of the lot?—can you take advantage of winter sunshine, yet keep out excessive summer sun? What is the direction of prevailing winds? Of prevailing storms? Are summer cooling breezes accessible? Is the lot readily drained? What is the character of the soil? Is it subject to movement, settling, slides?

After you have made a tentative on-site selection of neighborhood, find out at the city hall or county courthouse how it is designated on the master plan: Is it to be permanently residential and free from highways or overhead transmission lines? What will be its relationship to future developments—schools, libraries, transportation, recreation, and shopping and services facilities?

Look up the zoning regulations. Find out what you can and cannot do there, the restrictions on the house itself, and the kinds of activities that can take place in it. Can you have a separate house for your guests? Rent out a room? Practice a part-time profession or occupation? Build a swimming pool in the backyard?

Look into requirements for the setbacks of structures from lot lines so that you will understand possibilities for building or remodeling.

Ask whether there has been a recent flood in the neighborhood. If not, and if it has survived a severe rainy season, its drainage facilities are adequate unless subsequently overloaded by new developments.

Select a neighborhood that has underground electrical and telephone wires. Experience in California and elsewhere indicates that this can be done reasonably in new subdivisions.

Inquire about provisions for collecting trash and garbage.

Is there a water shortage, or is the supply adequate for house and garden? Are water softeners necessary?

In an expanding community within a society that regards land and buildings as fit objects for speculation (and where policies of Government encourage this attitude), everyone runs some risk of buying or building in a neighborhood that soon deteriorates.

The best protection lies in planning and zoning, but master plans and zoning legislation can be changed. You probably can improve your chances by selecting a location near an attractive and compatible development, such as a college campus, golf course, or public park, which, oftener than not, exert stabilizing influences on nearby residential property.

If you follow these criteria and acquire a sensitively designed and soundly constructed house, property values probably will be sustained. A house that is no more expensive than the average in the neighborhood and perhaps a little less so is a conservative investment. But who then will uphold the value of the neighborhood? Which comes first, responsibility or security?

Now, THE HOUSE itself.

When one acquires a house, he is inclined to think of the enterprise as an investment. It is true that a house can be ostentatiously out of place in its neighborhood or too expensive for a given market to support, especially in small communities without diversified demands. But be careful to distinguish superstition from sound assumption.

I know of one eastern bank that refused a loan for a house because it was to have only one story. How erroneous can such expert superstitions prove to be?

Experience does not support common assumptions about the effects of ethnic homogeneity. When a minority group begins to move into a neighborhood, property values do not automatically decline. Sometimes they increase.

Of course, one should consider all the economic factors involved in the venture: The relative advantages of renting and owning; indirect costs, such as transportation; and all direct costs—the land and improvements, building, landscaping, furnishing, and operation (amortization, maintenance, taxes, and insurance).

Land costs usually are lowest in the country and highest in the central city and vary with the desirability of the location and the extent of its improvement.

Do not overlook the costs of site improvements. As a prospective property owner, determine your liability to the city or county for current or future work.

In town you will usually be committed by law to a proportion of the neighborhood costs. In the country you are freer, but it is harder to anticipate total development costs accurately.

Grading, utilities, and streets are expensive. Their costs do not vary much from community to community for comparable developments, but some communities have higher standards of design and construction. Usually they are in more desirable urban locations and entail lower maintenance expenses.

All things considered, it is better to live in a community that requires first-class utilities, drainage facilities, street construction, and street lighting, but not in one that uses highway lighting standards in residential streets.

They do violence to residential quality.

At the other end of the process, think of landscaping and furnishing costs. Families often find themselves with inadequate funds for these items simply because they follow site and structure in the sequence of acquisition.

Insurance costs vary with the quality and proximity of fire and police protection, but differences in premiums do not measure the advantages of adequate protection.

The building itself represents the largest single expenditure. Many variables influence its cost. For families with reduced incomes, cost will be critical and the alternatives severely limited, but for many others, several choices will be available at similar prices.

At this point, turn to considerations other than price to find measures of value. Who else can understand precisely how important to you are an escape to an unspoiled stretch of wilderness or the sound of music or the company of friends?

The choice among house types and among individual examples of each is complex. Usually a single-family house offers the most privacy and an apartment the least. Duplexes and row houses fall between. However, tract houses with opposite bedroom windows at 10 feet are less private than row houses with well-built party walls. Some apartments are far more private than others, depending solely on qualities of design and construction.

Many people prefer the sense of a small private world, which is possible in a well-designed and well-maintained house (but hardly in an apartment) and believe that separate houses are better places for children.

A highway billboard near the town in which I live advertises "homes and apartments" in a new retirement community. Larger percentages of Americans are moving into apartments, but most of us apparently do not consider them homes. We reserve that concept for the freestanding house.

Retirement communities are a spe-cial subject. If you are interested in them, I suggest you read "Wake up and Live," by Calvin Trillin, in the April 4, 1964, issue of The New Yorker.

If you prefer not to live in an apartment or rent accommodations elsewhere, you face a number of alternatives: Whether to buy a lot and build a house, buy an existing house, or buy a new tract house.

Existing houses, new or old, can be examined before the purchase. Building a new house, on the other hand, presents the opportunity to achieve a uniquely personal environment, given competent professional design—at least an architect, and preferably also a landscape architect.

Many houses could have been conceived more economically had an architect designed them, but valid professional service entails costs and so does custom building. Select your architect carefully on the basis of his work—one who is interested and experienced in house design.

Select the builder carefully, too. Most people assume that competitive bidding is the only way to solicit a reasonable price. Sometimes it is, but limit the bidders to good contractors.

The best procedure, if you can manage it, and if your community is fortunate enough to have such men, is to select the best builder just as you selected the best architect. A man who takes a professional interest in his work usually quotes the same price whether he is bidding competitively or simply invited to build.

If your house is being designed for you, its form has limitless possibilities. Take advantage of the opportunities to make it truly original, but avoid exotic excesses, which disrupt visual harmony in the neighborhood and can make it difficult to sell in some unforeseen future.

Prefabricated houses are available in some localities for erection individually. Some are well designed by good architects and less expensive than custom-designed houses of comparable size and construction.

The term "prefabrication" does not describe the quality of design or structure but simply the building process. Quality must be judged separately, as it must for houses built by conventional methods.

Most people buy tract houses because repetitive construction processes reduce unit costs. If you buy a tract house, select one designed by a reputable architect. These are becoming prevalent and will be the rule if consumers insist upon quality; no builder puts up ugly houses he cannot sell. Complain about shortcomings in design to the salesmen and do your fellow consumer a good turn. Some enlightened zoning legislation has given professionally designed subdivisions advantages—freedom in space organization within buildings and within neighborhoods. Seek such a community, because the quality of future residential developments there will be relatively high.

In the final analysis, the value of a house can be judged only in terms of its success as a personal environment for each member of the family in an emotional as well as a functional sense.

As Robert Woods Kennedy remarked in his book, *The House and the Art of Its Design*, "Architecture is not for the ages; it is for the moment."

And as Frederic Heutte wrote in *A Place to Live*, the 1963 Yearbook of Agriculture, "A first principle of beauty is unity. . . . No community is so poor in natural resources or worldly goods that it cannot evolve a pattern of simple, inspiring, self-expression from its soil and surroundings, be it among desert sands or the deposit of a delta. Nature always provides a text, wherever we live."

In the case of a house, it is not a question of a penny saved, but of a penny thoughtfully spent and spent in large measure for intangibles. The values they return do not depreciate but are a constant source of renewal. Often they improve with the patina of age. (RICHARD D. CRAMER)

A Well-Built House

HOW CAN YOU TELL whether a house you are thinking of buying is well built?

First, get a copy of the plans and specifications. Compare what you can see of the house with what is shown on the plan. Often plans are revised during construction, for better or for worse.

Some general features are not structural but still may be important to you.

Among them are: Which way does the house face? Is the arrangement and size of rooms good? How about natural light and cross-ventilation? Do the rooms provide enough wallspace or storage space? Does the plan permit some flexibility of living arrangements?

These are partly matters of personal taste. If they satisfy your family's needs or preferences, they are good.

From this we go to the structural parts of the house—the foundation, walls, floors, ceilings, and roof.

START from the outside. Walk around the house.

Look at the foundation walls, which should extend at least 6 inches above the finish ground level. Watch for vertical cracks, which may indicate the structure has settled.

Hairline cracks in the concrete are due to volume changes and have no great significance.

If the concrete is uneven or honeycombed or has broken corners, it probably did not have enough cement or was carelessly placed in the forms—a sign of poor workmanship.

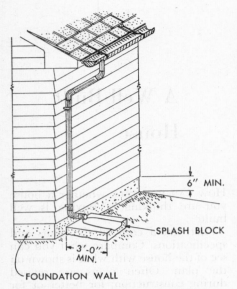

6" MIN.

SPLASH BLOCK

3'-0" MIN.

FOUNDATION WALL

Good drainage features include slope from the house, splash block, and good downspouts and gutters.

In block or stone walls, observe the character of the joints. Use a pocket-knife to pick at the mortar and see if it crumbles easily. If so, it is a sign that too much sand or a poor quality of cement was used. A nail driven into the joint will indicate whether the mortar is skimpy there.

If you wish to check the wall thickness, measure through a basement window.

Termites are a hazard to houses in much of the United States. Ask if there are termite shields or soil poison to protect against them.

If the house is built over a crawl space, look inside and check the girders and joists for signs of decay and for moisture stains on the floor framing.

Dampness in the crawl space may be due to lack of proper ventilation. The ventilators should be big enough and so placed that there is cross-circulation.

Whether there is a foundation wall or concrete slab on grade, the slope from the foundation at the grade line should be enough for rain to run off.

Basement window wells must drain readily. Water from the roof should be carried away by adequate gutters, conductors, and downspouts of non-corrosive material.

If downspouts are not connected to a storm sewer or other suitable outlet, splash blocks at the outlet will divert the roof water away.

Check basement window jambs and trim to see if they fit snugly against the masonry wall.

The sills of all windows should have sufficient pitch to drain water outward. Here is a place where decay may have occurred—probing with an icepick or small screwdriver will soon tell you.

AFTER A FINAL LOOK at the foundation walls to make sure the corners are even and walls are vertical, we can inspect the framed sidewalls.

They may be covered with wood or composition siding, shingles, brick, stucco, stone, or other types of enclosing materials. All are good if used properly.

Behind the covering is probably a frame of 2- by 4-inch studs to which is nailed a sheathing material such as wood, plywood, or fiberboard.

If the siding has been painted, examine the condition of the paint. See if the paint film is dense and opaque, or if the wood is showing through. Check for any gloss on the surface. Painted surfaces that are dull and chalky indicate that repainting is necessary.

The horizontal lap siding should be laid evenly with correct overlap and tight butt joints. At the corners, the siding may be mitered or fitted snugly against vertical corner boards. An end of the siding board should not be exposed to the weather because it will soak up moisture.

Make sure the nails are of the non-corroding type and that the space between the nailhead and the face of the siding has been filled in before painting or staining. Simply scratch to find out.

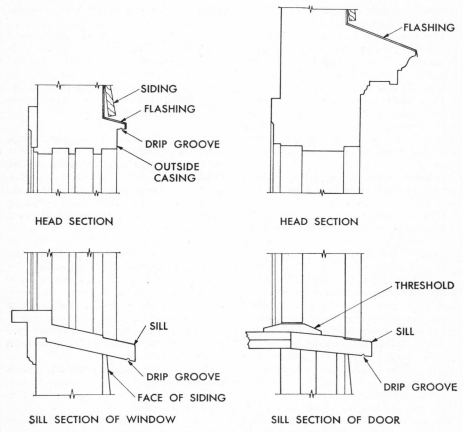

HEAD SECTION — SIDING, FLASHING, DRIP GROOVE, OUTSIDE CASING

HEAD SECTION — FLASHING

SILL SECTION OF WINDOW — SILL, DRIP GROOVE, FACE OF SIDING

SILL SECTION OF DOOR — THRESHOLD, SILL, DRIP GROOVE

Good construction in exterior windows and doors.

Windows and doors should have a protective flashing of noncorrosive metal above them. They should be checked for weatherstripping.

Check the sills for sufficient pitch for good drainage. A drip groove under the sill will permit the water to drip clear of the siding.

You have now had an opportunity to form an opinion on the quality of workmanship that has gone into the outside walls. Neat foundation walls, good metal gutters and downspouts, snug-fitting woodwork, and provision for surface drainage all indicate the builder has made a conscientious effort to erect a house that will endure.

Signs that the builder has skimped are chipped or honeycombed concrete, loose mortar in the brickwork, large cracks between the ends of the siding and window or other trim, rust stains from an inferior grade of outside hardware, and thin or flaked-off paint in a nearly new house.

Now GO INSIDE the house.

In the basement, look more carefully at the foundation walls, posts, and girders and at the floor joists if they are not concealed by the ceiling material.

The basement floor should be dry. Look for waterstains along the angle between floor and walls. Check to see that all holes where pipes come through the foundation wall and floor are properly cemented.

The basement floor should slope to the floor drain to permit quick runoff. A concrete floor should have a hard, smooth surface without spalling, cracking, or dusting.

The joists that support the floor above rest on the foundation walls and are intermediately supported by wood or steel girders. These girders in turn are supported by posts or by division walls.

If wood posts are used, they should be set on a concrete base block above the finish floor level.

When wood girders are built up by nailing several members side by side, make sure the members are well nailed together and that joints are over a post or a division wall.

Check to see that the ends of wood joists are not embedded in masonry or the concrete wall, as this practice may invite rot unless there is an airspace at the sides and end of the beam.

The wood joists should be spaced evenly, usually every 16 inches. Examine them for sagging, warping, or cross-breaks.

Look carefully at any joists that have been cut for heating ducts or piping. Notches or holes on the bottom edge or near midspan have the greatest weakening effect.

You may be able to see the grademark stamped on the joist, which will indicate the quality of lumber used.

Looking between the floor joists, you can probably see the subfloor. If it is of 1-inch boards, they should not be more than 8 inches wide and preferably laid diagonally to the joists.

Plywood often is used for subfloors. The 4- by 8-foot sheets should be laid with the face grain at right angles to the joists. Small knotholes on the undersurface of plywood subfloor are acceptable.

Check the area between the foundation wall and sill. Any openings should be filled with a cement mixture or a calking compound. The filling will lower the heat loss and prevent the entry of insects or mice into the basement.

MOST CONSTRUCTION in the living area will be hidden by various wall and ceiling finishes, but you can check the interior finish and such items as flooring, window or door trim, and other trim.

Examine the trim for any open joints, hammer marks, warped pieces, or rough nailing.

Over the door where the side casings meet the horizontal, the joint is often mitered. If this joint is tight, as all joints should be, you have a pretty good sign of careful workmanship.

Note, too, if the baseboard fits snugly against the flooring and the wall at all points.

Interior finishes are commonly of plaster or of such dry-wall construction as wood or composition materials.

You seldom see plaster cracks in a newly built home, because they develop slowly. In a house a year or more old, the absence of cracks indicates a well-built house. Of course, cracks can be concealed temporarily by wallpaper or a coat of paint.

Cracks extending diagonally from the corners of windows or doors may be signs of poor framing or that the house has settled.

If the nails that hold the dry-wall construction in place protrude (referred to as nail pops) from the face of the material, the framing lumber may have been at too high a moisture content at the time of installation. This problem can be corrected by redriving the nails, but you should take into account the cost of doing this renailing.

As you walk over the floors, notice if they squeak or seem too springy. If the floor joists are big enough and the subfloor has been laid correctly, neither fault should happen.

If you wish to check to see whether the floors are level, stretch a string across them.

If the flooring is exposed, hardwood flooring or the harder species of softwood are usually preferred. If carpeting is used, the underlayment may be

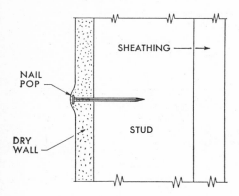

Nail popping in dry wall construction.

of any material that presents a smooth and firm surface.

Look carefully for signs of nailing. Flooring of a standard thickness is tongued and grooved and is blind nailed along the tongue so the nailing does not show. Small nailheads on the face or top of the flooring mean that a very thin flooring has been used.

Wood strip flooring normally becomes dry and cracks open between the strips in late winter in the colder States. These cracks, if they are not too wide, will close up the following summer.

Do not condemn floors in an old house simply because they are scratched and marred. Perhaps all they need is refinishing. If so, take this extra cost into account.

Perhaps the kitchen and the bathroom have tilework in the floor, on the wall, or wainscot. The tile floor should be smooth, without raised tile or depressed areas.

Wall tiles should fit snugly around all windows, door trim, and around the fixtures. Joints should be calked tightly to keep water out.

Check the doors to see if they swing freely and close tightly without sticking.

Is there a threshold under the exterior doors to keep out snow and cold winds? Some of these doors may have metal weatherstripping.

Are the interior doors hung so as to clear your rugs? Do they interfere with other doors? Do they latch readily and stay latched?

Check all doors to see that they are not excessively warped.

Windows usually are of the double-hung type—the lower sash slides up and the upper one slides down.

Open and shut all windows to be sure they work properly and there is not too much play in the sash. The weatherstripping, if there is any, should not interfere with the ease of operation.

It is a good idea to raise the window shades to assure yourself there are no cracked windowpanes.

Check window woodwork and plaster for waterstains and signs of decay.

Note the kind of glass in the window. Is it clear and flawless, or does it distort objects seen through it? Also see if the putty that holds the glass is in good condition and is painted.

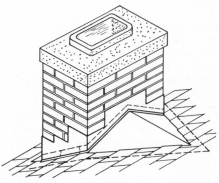

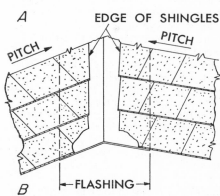

Correct flashing for A, chimney and shingles and B, valley.

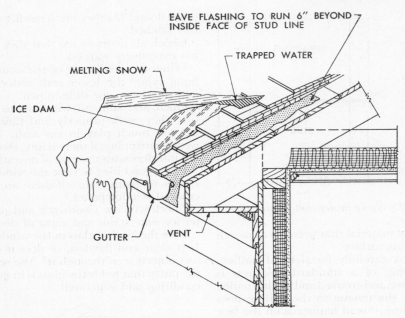

EAVE FLASHING TO RUN 6" BEYOND
INSIDE FACE OF STUD LINE

TRAPPED WATER

MELTING SNOW

ICE DAM

GUTTER   VENT

Proper eave flashings prevent snow and ice dams.

IT IS WELL to check the attic area for
the thickness of insulation between the
ceiling joists and to see if there is a
moisture barrier on the room side of
the insulation.

Check the attic ventilators. They
should be open summer and winter. In
summer, ventilation helps to lower the
attic temperature. In winter, ventilation removes moisture that may work
through the ceiling and condense in
the attic space.

Frost on the ends of nails in winter
indicates insufficient ventilation and
excess moisture.

Check the roof rafters or trusses to see
that they are unbroken and that framing joints are tight. Can you see daylight under the eaves?

Lumber grademarks on the rafters
will indicate the quality of lumber
used.

Waterstaining on the rafters or roof
sheathing is a sign of a roof leak.

INSPECT as much of the roof as you can.
For most types of shingles, the roof
slope should be at least 1 to 2; that

is, the roof should rise 6 inches in
every foot measured horizontally.

Among the numerous roofing materials you are likely to encounter are
wood shingles and composition shingles. If you can, find out for what
period the roof is guaranteed.

Check the flashing at the valleys and
around the chimney. They often are
the source of leaky roofs.

See if you can see roll roofing under
the shingles at the eaves. If it is there,
water held by ice dams above the
gutters will not work back into the
wall and cause damage.

YOU MAY BE UNCERTAIN if the joists
are big enough or if a crack in the wall
or a stain in the plaster means serious
trouble. Then maybe you should ask
for professional help.

First inquire whether the suspected
detail conforms with the local building code. If there is no local code, the
detail can be compared with the Minimum Property Standards of the Federal Housing Administration. They
may be examined at FHA offices in

most large cities. Perhaps all structural features comply with the local code or with the minimum standards, but that is not always so.

Questions that are more complex or that cannot be answered by comparison with a published standard may require the services of an architect or engineer. Find a man who has a good reputation and is well qualified. The cost of his services may be small compared to the troubles that can arise from a serious defect.

Specific technical questions can be referred to such organizations as the National Association of Home Builders in Washington or to its local chapters in the larger cities.

The Department of Agriculture Handbook No. 73, "Wood-Frame House Construction," shows good construction in detail. You can get it from the Superintendent of Documents at the Government Printing Office in Washington. (L. W. WOOD AND O. C. HEYER)

House Plans

NOTHING is more important than careful planning when you build a house.

The house plan is a key part of planning. It helps you visualize ideas and needs, shows the relationships of the various parts of the house to the entire building, and is the means of showing others your thoughts and desires. In its finished form, it becomes a basis for financial negotiations and building.

A plan can be developed by modifying an existing plan or by using a step-by-step process in which you consider the various elements and then fit them together by trial and error—on paper rather than in construction. You save money, time, and worry when

you are certain you have good plans.

Whichever your choice of procedure, your family's needs today and for several years must be considered first.

The family requirements are an expression of functional needs according to number, age, health, and occupations and include shelter from the elements, sleep, hygiene, food preparation, dining, recreation and entertainment, clothing care, study, business, and storage.

Resources and physical factors certainly will need to be considered before you make a final decision. Finances, building site, climate, utilities, experience of workmen, availability of materials, and local building codes are among the factors.

Features you will want to plan for include adequate size of rooms and closets; a good traffic pattern; adequate natural and artificial light; convenient kitchens and other workplaces; sound and economical construction practices and materials; pleasing views; good ventilation and an adequate and economical system of environmental control; an efficient and effective plumbing layout; and interiors and exteriors that are pleasing to the eye yet durable and economical to maintain.

The services of an architect to assist in making these decisions and to develop a plan are desirable but not always economically feasible. Thus, an individual usually turns to stock plans and selects one that most completely satisfies his needs.

Minor revisions are practically unescapable, but they should be made with care. Any change in one part of the plan may adversely affect other parts of the plan—and the result may be a disappointment. A discussion of the changes with experienced homebuilders can be helpful.

Stock plans are available through the State agricultural extension services and from various private sources, such as suppliers of building materials, magazines, and private plan services.

The Cooperative Farm Building

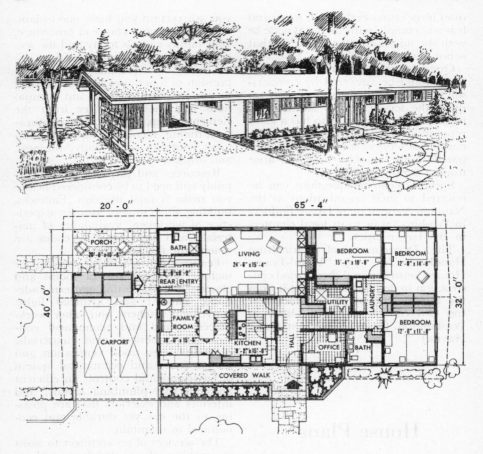

A perspective and floor plan of Plan 7140. This perspective and diagrammatic floor plan aid a prospective user in determining whether he should order the complete set of plans (working drawings). It features a convenient area for Dad and the kids to hang their clothes and wash up when coming in from the field and play. The living room is free from cross traffic. Another feature that is desirable is the proximity of the kitchen to both entrances. Any plan should be carefully studied for convenience in moving from one room to the other. This plan meets the desire of some homemakers to have the laundry area convenient to the bedrooms and bath. This plan also fills the need for an office in the house.

Plan Exchange of the Department of Agriculture and the States provides many of the plans that are distributed within the States.

It was established to determine needs and develop plans that were primarily for rural areas, but they have been useful also in cities.

Within it, State and Federal architects, home economists, and agricultural engineers—some as research scientists, others as extension special-

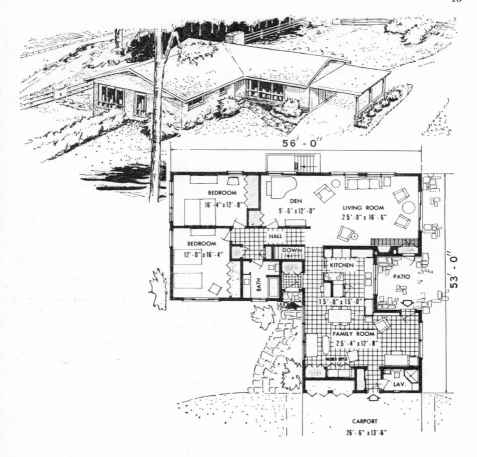

Plan 7149. This house was planned around the Beltsville energy-saving kitchen. The central location of this kitchen lends itself to convenient indoor-outdoor living by linking together living areas and affords spaciousness for entertaining large groups. Bedrooms are large and are isolated from the living area. A third bedroom could be provided by adding a partition between the den and living room. When bedrooms are added, the adequacy in size of the dining area and the number of baths should be checked against the family's needs. The dining space in this plan would be adequate for a three- or four-bedroom house.

ists—work together to incorporate research findings, space standards, sound structural practices, and convenient interior arrangements into plans that will fit a variety of climatic conditions, incomes, and practices.

Features of some of these plans are shown in the illustrations. The captions are written to assist the prospective homebuilder in understanding and evaluating a plan.

When you review the illustrations,

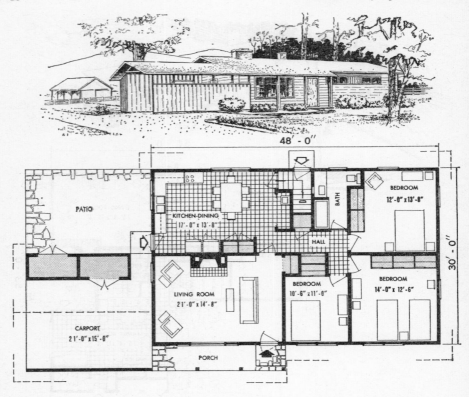

Plan 7143. The rectangular shape of the house is economical and permits good use of all interior space. The spaciousness of the kitchen-dining area allows this room to be used for family activities. Rooms and storage areas are large. A living-room width of more than 13 feet provides greater versatility in placement of furniture. Notice the value of spotting furniture on the floor plan. The beds can be placed under the window of the front bedrooms as these windows are well above the floor. Look for window placement in your plan. These high, front windows also aid in gaining privacy, although natural light will be reduced.

you should note that a complete set of working plans is more correctly called a set of working drawings and should include floor plans; foundation plan; elevations of various sides; elevations of kitchen and other interior details; the electrical outlet locations; a cross section of the entire house; and sections of critical details, such as framing and windows. It is usual also to have a set of supplementary specifications. (ROBERT G. YECK)

Materials

and Plans

When a house is being designed, it is well to consider first the lot, so that its slope, trees, and other features can be made part of the plan.

Local regulations in many communities control the type of house to be built to make sure it conforms generally with houses already constructed.

It is good practice to follow the general architectural style of existing houses. In a community of low ramblers, for example, a two-story house should be planned so that it does not detract from the general appearance of the neighborhood.

In planning a new house, consider also the future needs of the family. To get future bedrooms, you might select a one-and-one-half-story house rather than one of one story, but with the plumbing, heating, and electrical work only roughed in on the second floor. Thus, at small extra cost, space is at hand for extra rooms.

Accurate costs usually are not possible until the contractor submits his estimate, but you may use a figure of 10 to 16 dollars a square foot of living space as an initial guide.

Bear in mind, though, that cold winters, types of outside finish, a garage and porch, type of interior finish and flooring, the number of baths, a fireplace, the amount of millwork inside, and many other factors can change the basic costs a great deal.

You may get a better estimate of what your investment will be by asking about the cost of a nearby house of the general type and size you have in mind.

The wood frame house is easy to erect. It is adaptable to many types of exterior finishes. It can be insulated easily and is relatively low in cost.

All-masonry houses are common in some localities in the South because they resist termite damage. Builders of masonry houses in the North need to consider matters of moisture and insulation. You can take the general type of construction in your area as an index of which is the most practical.

Because the wood frame house has such general use, most of my descriptions apply to it.

First, the foundation.

If you select a slab foundation so as to have only one floor or because of a high water table, remember to include space for laundry, heating, and storage, which often are placed in the basement. Insulation is required in cold climates.

A crawl-space house has the comfort of a wood floor system, but it also requires additional area for laundry and storage and often for the heating plant. Floor insulation is required.

Often a ground cover, such as polyethylene or roll roofing, is needed to reduce problems caused by moisture in the soil.

A house with a basement can take advantage of a sloping lot that allows for full-size windows in basement rooms.

A full basement is a logical choice if ground water is not a problem and the house is in a cold climate where footings must be below frostline regardless of the type of house. Floor insulation is not normally required. A wood floor system and space for storage, a laundry, and the heating plant are a few of the advantages of a house with a basement.

A concrete slab is most adaptable to resilient-finish flooring, such as asphalt or vinyl tile. A woodblock floor can also be used. Strip flooring can be installed over anchored wood sleepers.

Wood flooring often is used for houses with crawl space or basements. Beams and posts at the center of the

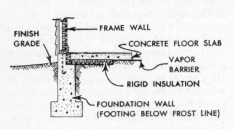

Section through wall of typical floor slab house.

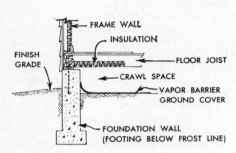

Section through wall of typical crawl space house.

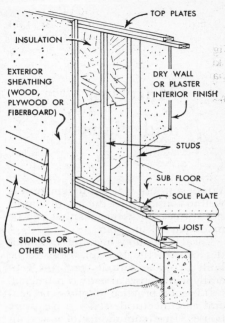

View of wood frame wall.

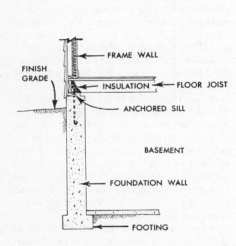

Section through wall of house with basement.

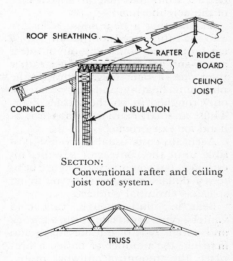

SECTION:
Conventional rafter and ceiling
joist roof system.

Wood frame ceiling joists and rafters.

house carry the joists. A subfloor gives a rigid platform for construction of the rest of the house. Sandwich or stressed-skin panels may be used for floors, but they are difficult to obtain in some localities. They are panels with thin facings, such as plywood, glued to a light inner wood framework (stressed skin) or to a core of foamed plastic or paper honeycomb (sandwich).

The wall in the conventional wood frame system consists of spaced studs, exterior sheathing, and a suitable interior and exterior finish. Bracing against wind is provided by diagonal wood sheathing, diagonal braces, or large sheets of plywood or fiberboard.

The post-and-beam system with light intermediate panels sometimes is used for contemporary designs.

Roof systems frequently consist of the conventional rafter and ceiling joist or the wood truss. A sheathing of plywood or boards supplies a base for wood or asphalt shingles or other types of roofing materials.

One advantage of a truss system is that it needs no interior supports and so gives freedom in the location of walls.

An adequate overhang at the eave and gable improves the appearance of most styles of houses and protects the walls from rain and sun.

Roof slopes are determined somewhat by the architectural style of the house. A Cape Cod house may have a steeply sloped roof and dormers that can be adapted to present or future development of the second floor. A ranch type or a rambler usually has a much lower pitch. A contemporary house may have a flat or low-pitch roof, a barrel vault, or a folded plate roof design.

A barrel vault design consists of a series of half-round forms supported by interior beams and posts. A folded plate design is a series of inverted V-forms supported in a manner similar to a barrel vault roof.

The slope of the roof usually governs the type of roofing used, whether of asphalt or wood shingles or of a built-up construction.

THE CHOICE OF MATERIALS for a house naturally affects the total cost.

We begin with the foundation and continue in the same general order that the materials are used.

A well-poured concrete wall is stronger and resists penetration of moisture better than a concrete block wall without treatment. A wall of concrete block has better insulation but must be waterproofed properly.

For a wood frame floor, tables are available to assure correct joist sizes by wood species for various spans and spacings.

Subfloors may consist of diagonally laid boards or of plywood. Either provides a good base for strip finish flooring, but a plywood base is normally required for resilient tile or other types of flooring that use adhesive for installation.

Where damp conditions prevail, as in bath and kitchen areas, it is good practice to use Exterior Grade (waterproof) plywood.

Required sizes of wood frame members to use for ceiling and roof are available in span tables.

Wall and roof sheathing is commonly wood boards, plywood, or fiberboard. Boards are used horizontally for walls and roofs, but diagonal corner braces are required for the walls to provide rigidity. No bracing is required when boards are used as diagonal wall sheathing.

Plywood is used also for wall and roof sheathing. When sheets 4 by 8 feet or longer are placed vertically on walls, with perimeter nailing, the house normally is rigid enough. If siding or shingles are to be nailed to this plywood, it should be one-half or five-eighths inch thick for the walls and three-eighths or one-half inch for the roof.

Fiberboard sheathing twenty-five thirty-seconds inch thick (or one-half-inch-thick medium-density fiberboard) commonly is used without bracing when placed vertically with perimeter nailing. When used horizontally or in 2- by 8-foot sheets, however, fiberboard and other similar materials need supplemental bracing.

In post-and-beam construction, filler wall panels usually are used between the posts. The roof can consist of 3- by 6-inch or 4- by 6-inch matched wood decking or laminated fiberboard, which also provide insulation and serve as interior finish.

Local codes sometimes specify which type of roofing materials are to be used. For moderate-to-steep roofs, wood shingles or shakes and asphalt shingles often are used, although slate and tile are popular in many places.

For flat or very low slopes, built-up roofs normally are used. They consist of several mopped-on layers of felt paper topped with a gravel finish. Some of the new plastic films, such as polyvinyl fluoride, are used as roof coverings over plywood.

In selecting the roofing, consider the initial cost and the probable life of each type. A built-up roof costs slightly more than an asphalt shingle roof. Wood shingles also cost more than asphalt shingles, but their life is considerably greater.

As to exterior finish and millwork:

A wood window and frame may be had in such styles as double hung, where two sash slide past each other vertically; the casement type, which opens as a door (usually outward because of better weather resistance); the awning type, which swings outward at the bottom; and fixed sash, as insulating glass in a stationary frame.

Windows and doors should be in keeping architecturally with the style of the house. A colonial design may require a double-hung or casement window cut into small lights. A rambler may take advantage of groups of the awning-type window in stacks and in double and triple widths.

Most wood sash and frames are dipped in a water-repellent preservative, which resists moisture penetration and decay and forms a good base for subsequent coats of paint.

Storm windows or combination storms and screens are good investments in cold climates. A storm window or insulated glass reduces heat loss and minimizes condensation on the inner glass surface during cold weather.

Exterior doors normally are of a panel type or a solid-core flush type. The use of a storm or combination door is recommended in cold climates.

Select the exterior siding or covering material to accentuate the architectural features of the house. Wood materials available vary from bevel siding to vertical boards and battens with smooth or rough-sawn surfaces. Plywood with paper facings provides a good paint base. Also available are the newer plastic-faced plywoods that are said to require no refinishing for 15 years or more. Grooved or face-treated plywoods are adaptable to stained finishes.

Exterior coverings also include wood shingles and shakes installed individually or as a prefabricated section, prestained or painted. Medium-density fiberboards, primed or plastic coated, are available in packaged units. Metal, cement-asbestos, or other nonwood covering materials can also be obtained in a variety of finishes, as can the many masonry veneers, such as brick and stone, which are adaptable to wood frame structures.

Other exterior millwork used for the house includes trim and molding for the cornice and gable ends, shutters, and similar items. Many are standard millwork items and should be used whenever possible, as variations requiring special machining increase the cost.

All exterior wood finish should be free of knots, sap streaks, or flat grain, which reduce the life of the paint film.

INTERIOR FINISHING includes wall finishes, millwork, and flooring.

Thermal insulation usually is installed in the walls after rough-in work for heating and wiring has been completed. Insulating blankets or batts are made of wood fibers, cotton, or mineral or glass fibers.

Because the difference in their insulating value per inch of thickness is small, selection may be based on cost or upon the efficiency of the vapor barrier.

Foamed plastics having good insulating qualities are available and often are used for perimeter insulation or as insulation and plaster base for a concrete block wall.

Interior walls and ceilings ordinarily are plastered or have a dry-wall finish. Plaster commonly is used on a gypsum lath base with a sand finish or a putty (smooth) finish for kitchen and bath.

Dry-wall finishes are available in sheet or other forms. They include gypsum board with taped and filled joints, wood or prefinished plywood paneling, plastic-coated hardboards, and fiberboards in a number of finishes and sizes.

Advantages of dry-wall construction are that installation time is reduced from the conventional plaster finish and no moisture has to be removed. The plaster wall is more resistant to impacts, and the surface can be leveled readily.

Interior finish and millwork includes door and window trim, baseboard and shoe, interior doors, stairway assemblies, and fireplace mantels.

Perhaps the most important factors in the selection of those materials are the species of wood and the correct architectural details. For example, the selection of a painted panel door for a traditional interior indicates the use of molding, mantels, and other millwork in keeping with this style.

Millwork that is to be painted often is white pine, sweetgum, or similar species. A natural or stained finish commonly is used on such species as oak and birch. The denser species, such as oak and birch, are more resistant to denting than the pines and other softwoods but usually cost more.

Floor coverings may consist of strip or woodblock flooring with an unfinished or prefinished surface in oak, maple, birch, beech, and other species.

Resilient flooring, such as vinyl, linoleum, cork, and rubber, also is available.

Ceramic tile, slate, and similar floors may be chosen for the bath and entryways where the presence of moisture would harm other materials.

IF YOU HAVE little or no knowledge of construction, seek the advice of a friend who has built a house and is somewhat more familiar with homebuilding.

Many lumber companies have planning services from whom you can get advice and details of costs.

Contractors are usually willing to give suggestions and allow examination of homes they have completed.

The time and care you spend on planning before construction begins will repay you in many ways. (L. O. ANDERSON)

Planning
for Safety

YOUR HOUSE should provide a safe environment for your family and for others who may occupy it later.

Give thought, then, to safety when you are remodeling or building new.

The elements of design that make a house safe generally make it livable, too.

Safety sometimes can be achieved by good management, but here we concentrate on details best handled when the house is planned. Often they involve simply inches and feet of space. Space is expensive, but so are accidents.

A porch, projecting roof, or recessed doorway that protects the entrance can add to comfort and safety. The shelter lets one remove wet footwear, set down packages, get the key, and open the door out of the weather. One can step out the door onto a dry area rather than directly onto the more dangerous ice, snow, or wet paving.

Make sure your plans call for a stoop large enough for the full swing of a screen or storm door and ample standing room for one or two persons. If the stoop is more than a step high, a safety rail in keeping with the architectural design should be provided.

Good arrangement of rooms and clear, free passageways between them allow safe traveling from one activity area of the house to another and can be a factor in preventing accidents.

Adequate, convenient, built-in storage places encourage family members to put things away where they do not clutter passageways.

Draw your furniture to scale on your house plan to be sure that there is space to place it and move around it. A room crowded with furniture is less safe than one with space in which to move about easily.

There is less chance of falls—a serious form of accidents in houses—in the one-level house.

If a one-level house requires a small change of grade, it is better to use a ramp than a step for less than a 3-inch change.

IF YOU CHOOSE A HOUSE on more than one level, good design of stairways will reduce the number and seriousness of falls.

Basement and attic stairways deserve the same careful planning one gives to the stairway between levels of a two-story or split-level house.

Since stairways usually receive little natural light, artificial lighting well placed and convenient to control at the top and the bottom of the staircase is necessary for safety.

A stairway should be at least 3 feet 4 inches wide so that furniture can be moved from one level to another.

Provide a smooth, easily gripped handrail on at least one side of the stairs, preferably on both, at a height reachable for toddlers and giving good support to adults—2 feet 8 inches above the nose of the tread.

On open stairways and around the stairwell, use balusters (upright supports), panels, or decorative screening between the railing and treads.

Space the balusters close enough together so a youngster cannot squeeze his head or body through, yet far enough apart so an exploring arm or leg cannot be caught between the spindles.

Short flights of stairs with intermediate landings are safer than long, straight flights, but they take more room. The landing should be at least as long as the stairway is wide.

Height of risers, size of treads, and width of stairs should be uniform throughout the flight.

For easy ascent in the average house with an 8-foot ceiling, 14 risers and 13 treads are generally preferred, with a total stair run of 124 to 130 inches.

When the run is less than 124 inches, the risers must be higher, and the angle of the stairs becomes steeper and more dangerous.

Stairs that turn without a landing are called winders; at the point where the staircase makes the turn, one end of each tread is narrower than the other. Plan not to use winders; they are a source of danger, particularly to children and elderly persons.

In remodeling work where winders of old stairs cannot be altered, a vertical handrail, 30 inches long and projecting 4 inches into the stairway, mounted on the existing newel post, will force users onto the wider portion of the treads where there is more footroom.

Headroom of less than 6 feet 8 inches over any point of the stairs is a hazard. Stairs with open risers are dangerous for small children, who may crawl or fall between any of the steps.

Sometimes a stairway opening must be placed between bedroom and bathroom doors, where in the dark it can be mistaken for the opening into a room. Have a constantly burning light in the hallway and put a gate across the stairway opening so that someone will not accidentally walk through this opening.

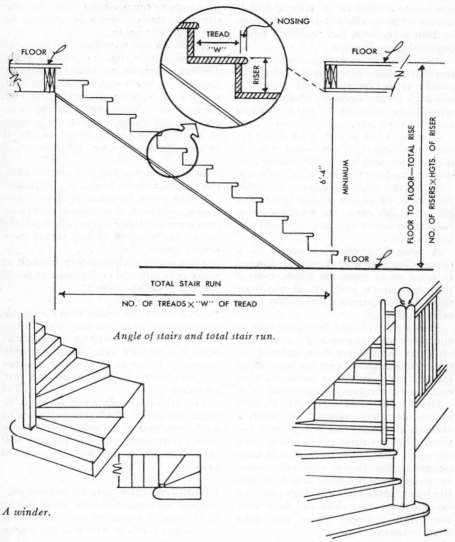

Angle of stairs and total stair run.

A winder.

Vertical handrail protection on a winder.

The top and bottom steps of a basement stairway are safer if they are painted a color different from that of the rest of the stairs.

Hallways at least 3 feet 4 inches wide allow room for passage of people and for moving furniture.

Room doors should swing into rooms, not into hallways, where they may interfere with walking.

Hinged doors on hall closets must open outward.

Bifold, sliding, or split doors hinged on both sides of the closet opening take up less hallway space and are less likely to be in the way than a full-width hinged door.

The main entrance door traditionally is 3 feet wide.

All other traffic doors throughout

the house should be at least 2 feet 8 inches wide to allow carrying persons or things through the openings without bumps or bruises.

Bathroom doors sometimes are narrower because placement of fixtures makes it necessary. Good planning allows a larger opening. Passage of a wheelchair without a tight squeeze can require 3 feet.

Draw the full swing of all doors on your floor plans. Then you will know if one door will bang into another or if an open door will block an opening. Substitute sliding, bifold, or folding doors in places where full-width hinged doors cause such problems or relocate a room opening to avoid the interference.

A door that provides access to a descending stairway should be hinged to open away from the stairs, even if it opens into a hallway. If the door must swing stairward, it should open onto a landing.

Doors that cannot be opened from the inside are dangerous for adults and children. Knobs on each side of the door or magnetic catches instead of latches can prevent a situation that could turn a room into a prison.

Doors on wall cabinets located above counters should be narrow enough that they do not project beyond the counter edge when they are open. One is apt to bump his head on projecting doors, especially when he straightens up from reaching into the base cupboard. Head bumping can be a problem over sinks and lavatories, too; sliding doors there are safer than swinging doors.

CASEMENT or awning sash windows project from the building when they are opened.

If you plan to use them on a side of the house that is directly adjacent to a walkway, porch, or driveway on the same level, use intervening plantings to route traffic away from the hazard.

Windows over a base cabinet, sink, or a bathtub should be of the types that slide or open with a crank to save strains or falls when you attempt to open or close them.

Glass doors or windows that come to the floor, unless they have safety glass, are hazardous for playing children or unwary or unsteady adults.

For each room without an exterior door, plan at least one window large enough, low enough, and easy to open to provide an exit in case of fire if other escape routes are blocked.

THE KITCHEN can be, but need not be, the most dangerous area of the house.

It has more equipment than other rooms, and family activities tend to be concentrated there, especially if people eat in the kitchen and it serves as a family room.

Time spent in designing a kitchen to make it as safe and convenient as possible is a good investment.

IN PLANNING the main bathroom, allow enough room not only for the fixtures but also for space for a mother to help a child or one adult to help another. There is always the danger of accidents when conditions are crowded.

The bathroom does not have to be large, however. An extra 6 inches in each direction in a "minimum" 5- by 7-foot bathroom in some layouts will give enough space for the second person.

CLOSETS carefully planned to store possessions conveniently are more likely to be used as intended than those that are simply shells in which to put things out of sight.

Rods installed at appropriate heights for the length of garments to be hung and convenient storage places for shoes and other items used every day help to reduce clutter and confusion that set the stage for falls in a bedroom.

Shelves properly spaced to allow independent and orderly placement of articles are safer for storage than stacked boxes and objects that may topple when you remove certain ones.

Some sort of movable step stool and storage bin right in the closet makes reaching a higher level simpler and safer than standing on a chair or other makeshift "ladder."

For safety and convenience, furnish a child's closet with a rod at the right height for his use now, with provisions for raising it as he grows taller. Storage for all possessions for which the child has some responsibility should be within his reach without climbing.

A light in the closet, especially a closet in a bedroom or an inner hall, saves dangerous groping in the dark. Sometimes in a bedroom, the closet light gives just the illumination needed for dressing or finding something in the night when a general light would be disturbing.

No matter how well we plan, we should ever be alert to ways to improve the safety of our surroundings and to correct any hazard that was not recognized in the planning stage. (W. RUSSELL PARKER AND R. KATHERINE TAUBE)

Painting the Outside

THE APPEARANCE of the surface of exterior woodwork, such as the siding of a house, will change slowly if it is allowed to weather without finish. Surface checks, roughening, and a gray color, which are characteristic of weathered wood, will develop.

You can apply finish on the exterior woodwork of your house to maintain the original natural color and grain pattern (stain, sealer, or varnish); preserve the original smoothness of freshly planed lumber (varnish or

paint); change the color (paint or stain); or improve the natural weathered appearance of wood (water-repellent preservative).

The first finishing job on your house is the most important one. It is the foundation for all subsequent finishing. If all goes well, it will remain there for the life of your house. Sacrificing quality of finish and finish application to reduce the initial costs very likely will lead to excessive maintenance over the years. Unfortunately, a standard grading system for finishes is not available.

There are three broad classes of finishes: Natural finishes, stains, and paints.

Your choice depends on personal preference, after considering the advantages and disadvantages of each.

Natural finishes penetrate the wood or form a film or coating on its surface.

The penetrating finishes may be clear or lightly pigmented.

The film-forming type (varnish) usually is clear. Varnish gives a smooth, glossy coat.

The penetrating natural finishes—oil finishes, wood sealer finishes, and water-repellent preservatives—leave little or no continuous coating on the surface.

The Forest Products Laboratory (FPL) natural finish is a recent development in penetrating natural finishes. It is described in U.S. Forest Service Research Note FPL–046, available from the United States Forest Products Laboratory, Madison, Wisconsin.

This finish has a linseed oil vehicle and ingredients that protect the oil from mildew and the wood from excessive water entry at joints.

It also has sufficient durable pigment to provide color but not enough to hide the grain of the wood. This type of finish is sometimes called a lightly pigmented (modified) stain.

One initial brush application of FPL natural finish normally will last about 3 years.

The clear finishes of the oil, wood

sealer, or varnish types generally require two or three brush applications at first and need refinishing after 1 or 2 years. In addition, varnishes may need complete removal after a few refinishings to restore a satisfactory finishing surface.

In most States, natural finishes must be resistant to mildew.

If you want to improve the natural weathered appearance of unfinished wood siding, brush or spray one application of an unpigmented water-repellent preservative solution on the siding at the start.

This should be followed by reapplication of the solution at intervals of 2 to 4 years or more, depending on the appearance of the siding.

GOOD SHINGLE STAINS (heavily pigmented) are inexpensive and more durable than natural finishes. They come mostly in dark brown, green, red, and yellow. Stains penetrate and color wood.

They usually are applied initially in two coats, which obscure the grain but leave little or no surface film. Rough-sawed or weathered wood surfaces are especially suitable for shingle stains and the modified stains.

Good stains should last at least 5 years on rough surfaces and may last as long as 9 or 10 years. Even on planed surfaces, they may last as long as paint.

Since stains form little or no coating on the surface of the wood, they do not crack, curl, flake, or blister.

Some stains, however, contain creosote, which may discolor light-colored paint applied over them later.

HOUSE PAINT is the most widely used finish for wood siding.

White house paint is the most popular. A good white house paint should last at least 5 years on vertical-grain lumber. Good dark-color paints should last 6 to 8 years.

House paint consists of two parts: A solid part (pigments) and a liquid part (the vehicle).

The vehicle of the commoner house paints consists essentially of a drying oil (usually linseed oil) or an alkyd resin modified with drying oils, and a thinner (usually mineral spirits or turpentine). Paints of this type are called oil paints or solvent-thinned paints.

A new type of exterior house paint has been developed. The vehicle in it consists of fine particles of resin dispersed or emulsified in water. This type of paint is known by a variety of names, such as emulsion, latex, water-thinned, or water-base paints, or by the type of resin it contains.

Acrylic resins and vinyl resins are best for exterior use on wood. Because emulsion paints are much newer, their properties are not so well known as are those of the oil paints.

Emulsion paints have some advantages over oil paints. There is less pull on the brush. They dry faster. They can be applied on a damp surface. Cleanup is easier. Tinted paints are more resistant to fading.

In repainting with emulsion paint over badly chalking oil paint, however, three coats are required, just as in painting new wood.

The first coat should be an oil primer (slow drying), followed with two coats of the emulsion paint.

For repainting chalky surfaces with oil paint, one coat may be enough if the old paint is in good condition (not peeling or worn too thin).

Emulsion paints are attacked more easily by mildew than oil paints if the paint does not contain an effective mildewcide.

In general, if you use paints and wood of good quality and follow good practices in building the structure and applying and maintaining the paint, you will have good overall service from both oil and emulsion paints.

THE GRADE of exterior woodwork will help you determine how long good-quality finish properly put on it will last.

The top grade will cost more initially, but it—and the finish—perform better, and the maintenance costs will be lower.

That is because the best grades of the more expensive woods are generally vertical grain rather than flat grain. They shrink and swell less than the lower grades and thus hold finish better. They also have fewer or no knots, pitch streaks, splits, and warp and have a more suitable moisture content for painting.

If you plan to put stain on lumber with rough-sawn surfaces or allow it to weather naturally, do not be too concerned about small, tight knots and other minor blemishes. Minor blemishes do not greatly affect stain performance or natural weathering. Furthermore, you may like their appearance.

The highest grades of the commercially important American woods have been classified for exterior painting into five groups (group 1 is best and group 5 is worst for painting):

(1) The cedars, baldcypress, and redwood, all softwoods.

(2) Eastern white pine, sugar pine, and western white pine, all softwoods.

(3) White fir, the hemlocks, ponderosa pine, and the spruces among softwoods; aspen, basswood, cottonwood, magnolia, and yellow-poplar among hardwoods.

(4) Douglas-fir, southern pine, and western larch among softwoods; beech, birch, the gums, and maple among hardwoods.

(5) Ash, chestnut, elm, hickory, oak, and walnut, all of which are hardwoods. These woods require wood filler in the pores before smooth coatings of paint or enamel can be applied.

Plywood does not hold coatings as well as lumber of the same species. Stains therefore usually are considered best for plywood.

Plywood will hold exterior coatings much better when a resin-impregnated kraft paper is glued on the surface of the plywood.

To reduce rain damage to paint, use exterior woodwork that has been treated with water-repellent preservative by the manufacturer. Brush the solution on all board ends that are cut by the carpenter. If you cannot buy treated wood, you can apply the solution by brushing or spraying after the wood is in place. Brush the solution well into joints and end grain. Allow the treatment to dry for 2 warm, sunny days before painting.

HERE ARE a few procedures to help you paint your house:

First, read carefully the instructions on the paint can.

New wood should be given three coats of paint. The first or prime coat should be applied soon after the woodwork is erected. Use a linseed oil primer free of zinc pigments.

Beginning painters tend to spread paint out too thinly. For best results, follow the spreading rates the manufacturer recommends.

The wood primer is not suitable for galvanized iron. Wipe such surfaces with paint thinner and then prime with an appropriate primer, such as a linseed oil vehicle pigmented with metallic zinc dust (about 85 percent) and zinc oxide (about 15 percent).

The following points you should keep in mind when you apply topcoats over the primer on new wood and galvanized iron:

Use two coats of a good-quality house paint.

To avoid future separation between coats of paints, called intercoat peeling, apply the first topcoat within 2 weeks after the primer and the second topcoat within 2 weeks of the first.

To avoid temperature blistering, do not apply oil-base paints on a cool surface that will be heated by the sun within a few hours.

Ideally, the north side of the building should be painted in the first part of the morning, the east side later in the morning, the south side in the first part of the afternoon, and the west side later in the afternoon.

Temperature blistering is commonest with paints of dark colors. The blisters are usually in the last coat of paint and occur within 1 or 2 days after painting. They do not contain water.

To avoid the wrinkling and loss of gloss of oil-base paint, do not paint in the evenings of cool spring and fall days. That is when heavy dews frequently form before the surface of the paint has dried.

Here are some general rules for repainting:

Repaint only when the old paint has worn thin and no longer protects the wood. The color of faded or dirty paint can often be restored by washing. Where wood surfaces are exposed, spot prime with a zinc-free linseed oil primer before repainting.

Too frequent repainting produces an excessively thick film that is more sensitive to the deteriorating effects of the weather. It is also likely to crack abnormally across the grain of the paint. The grain of the paint is in the direction of the last brush strokes.

Complete paint removal is the only cure for cross-grain cracking.

For the topcoat, use the same brand and type of paint originally applied, if it has given good service. A change is advisable only if a paint has given trouble.

To avoid intercoat peeling: Allow no more than 2 weeks between coats in two-coat repainting. Do not repaint oftener than at 4-year intervals. Do not repaint sheltered areas, such as eaves and porch ceilings, every time the weathered body of the house is painted. Repainting the sheltered areas every other time is suggested.

It is helpful to wash the sheltered areas with trisodium phosphate solution before repainting. Intercoat peeling indicates a weak bond between coats of paint. The condition usually gets worse with time, and complete paint removal is often the only cure.

TWO OTHER PROBLEMS, both related to water, are common. They are extractive staining and blistering and peeling of paint because of moisture. The same water often causes both difficulties.

When too much water gets into paint or wood, the paint may blister, crack, and peel. The moisture blisters normally appear first. Cracking and peeling follow. Sometimes the paint peels without blistering. Sometimes the blisters go unnoticed.

Moisture blisters usually contain water when they form or soon afterward. Eventually they dry out. Small blisters may disappear on drying. Fairly large ones may leave a rough spot on the surface. The paint may peel if the blistering is severe.

Young, thin coatings are more apt to blister before peeling because of too much moisture than old, thick coatings, which often crack and peel without blistering.

Construction features that reduce water damage to outside paint are: A wide roof overhang; wide flashing under shingles at roof edges; effective vapor barrier in ceilings and sidewalls, on top of the ground in crawl spaces, under floor slabs, and outside of the foundation walls below grade; adequate and properly hung eave troughs and downspouts; and adequate ventilation of the inside of the house, including the attic space.

If those features are lacking in a new house, persistent blistering and peeling may occur.

The first step in solving the problem is to determine the source of the water that does the damage.

The possible sources are: Outside water working in; inside water working out; and inside water vapor passing through the walls, condensing, and soaking into the exterior wood (cold-weather condensation).

Clues to moisture blistering and peeling caused by rain or dew going through joints and end grain are:

It occurs after rain or heavy dew.

Rain damage is worst on the sides of the building that face the prevailing wind and rain.

It occurs only on woodwork that can be wetted by rain or dew.

It may occur on unheated or heated buildings.

It will be centered around end grain and joints.

Rain leaking through the roof also causes damage. The damage often appears to be caused by condensation or inside water leaks.

Waterstains on the inner side of the roof boards are the best indication of roof leaks. Often the stains indicate where the water goes after getting in.

Ice dams at horizontal roof edges and in roof valleys dam the melting snow and permit the water to work in under the shingles and through the roof boards. Damage resulting from them will usually occur on the wall beneath their location. The inner surface of roof boards over the eaves and under the valleys will show waterstains if water is getting in because of ice dams.

Blistering or peeling of exterior paint also can be caused by plumbing leaks, overflow of sinks, leaky shower walls, and so forth.

Blistering and peeling caused by cold-weather condensation is recognized by the following clues:

It is usually most severe on the coldest (north) side of the building or on the outside of unheated rooms.

It is likely to be concentrated on the outside walls of rooms having high humidities, such as bathrooms, kitchens, or bedrooms in which water vaporizers are used.

The blisters appear in late winter or early spring.

The damage occurs on wood sheltered from wetting by outside water as well as on unprotected wood.

The damage occurs only on heated buildings.

These clues are not foolproof. Blistering and peeling caused by outside water, cold-weather condensation, or inside water may occur in the same place.

If the damage is caused by outside water that gets in, the following steps should be taken:

Apply water-repellent preservative to all joints before repainting.

Calk or putty open joints and cracks.

Check eave troughs for cleanliness, slope, and capacity.

Repair roof leaks.

Check downspouts to see if they are plugged.

Ice should not be allowed to form at roof edges and valleys. Removing the snow will prevent this.

Apply water-repellent preservative as follows:

Determine the need. Joints that show damage from rain or dew need treating before repainting.

Remove loose paint from wood.

Brush the water-repellent preservative into the joints and end grain. Brushing it on the paint will do no good and will waste solution.

Wipe off excess solution with a rag.

Allow 2 days of good drying weather before repainting.

If the moisture blistering and peeling is caused by cold-weather condensation, these steps should be taken:

Reduce vapor penetration by painting the interior surfaces of the outside walls and ceilings. Aluminum paint serves this purpose well. It can be painted over with decorative paints.

Lower the humidity in the house as follows: Shut off humidifiers. Vent clothes dryers and kitchen and bathroom exhaust fans to the outside. A dehumidifier will help. Ventilation in the attic and a ground cover in the crawl space will cut down on the moisture inside the building.

Apply a zinc-free oil primer where paint has peeled to the wood surface, and then one topcoat of paint overall.

Water-soluble color extractives occur naturally in western redcedar and redwood. The heartwood of these two species owes its attractive color, good stability, and natural decay resistance to extractives.

Discoloration occurs when the extractives are dissolved and leached from the wood by water. When the solution of extractives reaches the painted surface, the water evaporates, leaving a reddish-brown stain.

The water that gets behind the paint to cause moisture blisters also causes movement of extractives. Use the time of occurrence and distribution of the stains in the way indicated for moisture blisters to determine the source of the water. Follow the same procedures to eliminate it.

Emulsion paints and so-called "breather" oil paints are more porous than conventional oil paints. If these paints are used on new wood without a good oil primer, or if any paint is applied too thin on new wood (a skimpy two-coat paint job, for example), rain or even heavy dew can reach the wood easily by direct penetration of the paint coating. The extractives will come to the surface of the paint when the wood dries.

It is difficult to obtain an adequate thickness of coating on the high points of rough surfaces, such as machine-grooved shakes and rough-sawn lumber siding. Extractive staining is more likely to occur on such surfaces by penetration of water through the coating. The reddish-brown extractive will be less conspicuous if dark-colored paints are used. (VICTOR P. MINIUTTI)

Decay

of Wood

WOOD ROTS when minute plants— fungi—feed on it.

Fungi, like all plants, need the right conditions of moisture, food, and temperature to grow.

Wood absorbs or gives off water vapor when the relative humidity changes. Dry wood cannot absorb enough water vapor from the air to support active decay. Liquid water, as rain, tapwater, or condensate, must be added before any great amount of decay occurs.

Therefore, to control decay, build with fully dry lumber, and design buildings so that liquid water will not penetrate the surface.

When that is not feasible, any wood subject to wetting should be naturally decay resistant or treated with a wood preservative.

Redwood, cedars, and baldcypress have high resistance to decay. Douglas-fir, longleaf pine, and eastern white pine have moderate resistance. Only the dark heartwood of all of them is resistant; the light-colored sapwood of these, or any other wood, will decay if wet.

A decay-susceptible wood used under a high hazard must be impregnated under pressure by a commercial treating plant. Lumber that has been pressure treated with creosote, pentachlorophenol, or one of the inorganic salts is available in most cities.

Ask your lumber dealer about local sources and the preservative that is best for a particular need.

Water-repellent preservatives are particularly valuable for siding and other woodwork exposed on the surface of a building. They also restrict entry of rain into joints.

Sometimes finish items, like siding, are pressure treated with water-repellent preservatives, but usually only dip-treated material is available.

Water-repellent preservatives often must be applied on the job by dipping, brushing, or spraying. When you apply them after construction, brush or spray all joints thoroughly.

If you buy dip-treated lumber, retreat all surfaces exposed when the lumber is cut to size.

Remember that dipping, brushing, and spraying protect only the surface. Always supplement them with designs that limit wetting.

To prevent decay in houses, use dry lumber relatively free of stain and mold. The fungi that are responsible for stain and mold make wood porous, so it wets more easily.

Stained lumber often has the beginnings of decay that you cannot see. The infections remain alive, but dormant, for years in dry lumber. Decay again starts when the wood is rewetted. Bright, kiln-dried lumber is preferable. If you must use stained siding or trim, dip it in a water-repellent preservative. At the building site, store lumber off the ground and under cover.

Some parts of buildings should be made of naturally decay-resistant or treated wood. This need varies with design and climatic zone, as given in a map and tables on the next page.

Well-drained building sites are safest. Improve wet sites. Slope grades away from the house. Provide tile drains around basement foundations. Use splash block or other provisions to drain water from downspouts away from the foundation. Use a 4-inch layer of coarse gravel and a water-plus-vaporproof membrane under concrete slabs on ground. Waterproof the outside of basement foundation walls.

Condensation is likely in crawl spaces with wet soil in winter in places with average January temperatures below 35° F. and in summer in air-conditioned houses in hot climates.

The soil in crawl spaces should be dusty dry. If it is not so with normal drainage, cover the soil with 6-mil polyethylene sheeting or 55-pound roll roofing. The seams need not be overlapped. Soil covers are effective in keeping crawl spaces dry.

Well-spaced vents through the foundation also will keep wood dry. If vents are closed during the winter and the soil is moist, however, use a soil cover.

Except for poles and piling, no wood should be in contact with soil. Siding and trim should be at least 6 inches above grade. The amount of clearance in crawl spaces is not important so long as it is big enough to permit inspection.

Remove all wood forms and grade stakes used in pouring concrete steps, porches, slabs, and foundations.

Several practices besides the use of treated or decay-resistant woods will improve performance of steps and porches. Slope porch floors outward and provide drain holes under screen frames. Make the bottom step of concrete, brick, or stone. Provide good ventilation under porches. Avoid frilly rail and screen designs with many joints. Extend the step rail over the top of the newel rather than abutting it to the side of the post.

Self-supporting porch slabs are much safer than dirt fills. If dirt fills are used, enclose the fill completely in a separate foundation and leave a well-ventilated airspace of at least 3 inches between this foundation and the house sill. A noncorrosive metal flashing to separate the sill and fill also is effective.

The roof edge is particularly vulnerable to wetting by roof runoff that flows over the eave. Use an L-flashing on both eave and gable edges designed with a drip edge free of the fascia and rake board. Eave gutters also help.

Decay in siding, trim, windows, doors, and other parts of exterior walls results mainly from rain seepage into joints. Good roof overhang is the best prevention.

In zones 1 and 2 in the map, a one-story house with 2 feet or more overhang is safe from serious wall decay; elsewhere, less will do.

Except in the drier parts of the country (zone 3), eave gutters help prevent runoff from roofs from being blown or splashed against walls.

Other ways in which walls can be protected are: Place trim over the ends of drop siding and metal corner caps over bevel siding. Use only lightweight breathing papers under wood siding. In warm, high-rainfall areas, avoid sheathing if feasible, because it favors moisture accumulation; when sheathing is needed, a good roof overhang is important. Use water-repellent preservatives on all joints or prime the backs and ends of siding with a lead paint.

Some types of condensation lead to decay. In cold climates (average Jan-

Hazard zones for decay associated with rain seepage.

	Type of treatment needed [1]		
Building part	Zone 1	Zone 2	Zone 3
Posts set in ground..................................	A	A	A
Columns for porches, carports, etc..............	A	B	O
Porch flooring, joists, rails......................	A	B	O
Steps and step rails...............................	A	B	O
Roof edge (fascia, molding, exposed sheathing)..	A	B	O

	Type of treatment needed [1]			
	Zone 1		Zone 2	Zone 3
Building part	8″ or more above grade	Less than 8″ above grade	Less than 8″ above grade	Less than 8″ above grade
Sleepers in or on concrete on ground.	A	A	A	A
Sills or plates on concrete on ground..................	A	A	A	A
Sills or plates on foundation wall..	O	A	O	O
Framing and sheathing of shower walls and floors..............	A	A	A	A

	Type of treatment needed [1]			
	Zone 1		Zone 2	Zone 3
	Roof overhang		Roof overhang less than 2′	Any amount of roof overhang
Building part	Less than 2′	2′ or more		
Exposed load-bearing structures...	A	B	B	B
Siding and trim................	B	B	B	O
Window sash..................	B	B	B	O
Frames and trim (window, screen, door, etc.)..................	B	B	B	O

[1] A. Pressure treated according to Federal Specification TT–W–571 or standards of American Wood-Preservers' Association; or woods of high natural decay resistance.

B. Nonpressure treated according to standards of National Woodworking Manufacturing Association; or woods of high natural decay resistance. A 3-minute dip in a water-repellent preservative is adequate for most uses.

O. No treatment needed.

uary temperatures of 35° or below), install an effective vapor barrier on the warm side of walls and ceilings below unheated attics to prevent winter condensation.

Kitchens, laundries, and unheated attics should be well ventilated.

In hot climates, condensation may occur under floors over wet crawl spaces of air-conditioned houses. Dry out the crawl space and cool only to moderate temperatures.

WHAT SHOULD YOU DO when you find decay?

Periodically inspect attics, basements, crawl spaces, and exterior woodwork for signs of wetting. Make corrections before decay requires replacement.

On painted wood, look for paint peeling at joints, rusty nails, and stain coming through the paint as signs of rain seepage.

Keep gutters and downspouts clean and free of leaks.

Inspect attics and crawl spaces in early spring and crawl spaces again in late summer in air-conditioned buildings.

If you find damp wood, dry out the crawl space or attic as I suggested earlier.

When you find signs of rain seepage in siding and trim, brush or spray a water-repellent preservative into the joints. Replace the siding boards with horizontal splits. Calk joints of wood to the masonry. Reseal joints in gravel stops as often as necessary to prevent leakage.

If decay spots occur frequently in siding as a result of wetting by rain, the cheapest correction is to cover it with asbestos-cement or cedar shingles. Follow the manufacturer's recommendations.

In cold climates, winter condensation may be involved, however. In that event, covering the siding will increase the trouble unless it is corrected by applying a vapor seal on the inner wall.

Suspect condensation in winter if

a general paint failure is expressly troublesome on north walls and dark stains develop from moisture seeping out from under the siding.

Replace steps and porches, when decay occurs, with decay-resistant material—naturally decay-resistant or treated wood, concrete, brick, stone, and metal.

EXTENSIVE DECAY in sills, joists, and flooring, particularly if it extends into walls and interior trim, may mean that one of the rare but destructive water-conducting rotters is present.

These fungi can conduct water from a constant source, such as the soil, and wet normally dry wood many feet away.

They usually start at dirt-filled porches, forms left on concrete, or untreated wood in contact with moist concrete slabs. Rootlike conducting strands may develop, and thick white to yellowish felts usually form in protected places, as between finish and subfloors.

Use great care in treating this type of decay. Do not skimp—or replacements will be destroyed in a year or so.

First determine where the moisture source is—a dirt-filled porch, forms left on concrete, leaky plumbing, or wood in contact with soil.

The original soil contact may be gone, so that the only connections are gray to black water-conducting strands. Hunt for these on foundations. They may be hidden inside concrete blocks or in loose mortar.

Find them, remove them, and paint the foundations where they occurred with pentachlorophenol or other standard preservative. Replace loose brickwork.

If a dirt fill is present, open the foundation, remove the dirt from the sill area, paint the exposed foundation and slab with a preservative, replace the sill with pressure-treated wood, and ventilate the space from which the fill was removed.

When you are in doubt about the source of moisture, remove all decayed wood and sound wood within 2 feet and replace it with pressure-treated wood. Naturally decay-resistant wood is not suitable because water-conducting fungi will decay it.

If the source of moisture is removed, infected wood will dry out, and only the wood that is too weak for its load need be replaced. Unlike most decayers, water-conducting fungi die quickly in dry wood. (ARTHUR F. VERRALL)

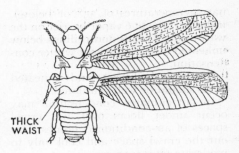

THICK WAIST

Winged reproductive termite.

Termites

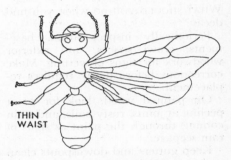

THIN WAIST

Winged reproductive ant.

GROUND-NESTING TERMITES occur throughout the United States. They flourish in the South Atlantic and Gulf Coast States and California.

Their chief food is cellulose obtained from wood, as in the woodwork of buildings.

One way to thwart the immense damage they do is to construct buildings properly.

Another way is to treat the soil near foundations and under concrete slabs with chemicals.

Action against them begins with knowing what they are.

Termites are social insects that live in colonies or nests in the soil from which they obtain moisture.

The adult workers and soldiers are wingless, grayish white, and similar in appearance. The soldiers have much larger heads and longer mandibles, or jaws, than the workers.

The workers are the ones that destroy wood and are usually seen when a piece of infested wood is examined.

The reproductives, or sexual adults, have yellow-brown to black bodies and two pairs of long, whitish, opaque wings of equal size.

They often are mistaken for ants, but the reproductive forms of true ants have two pairs of transparent wings of unequal size. Termites have thick waistlines. Ants have thin waistlines.

The first signs of an infestation may be the swarming of large numbers of winged reproductives from a building or their discarded wings on the floor beneath doors and windows or the presence of flattened, earthen, shelter tubes over the surface of foundations.

Often you cannot see the damage on the surface of the wood. You have to look inside.

The workers build galleries within the materials they attack. Occasionally they honeycomb timbers completely and leave little more than a thin shell. Grayish specks of excrement and earth cover the inside of the galleries.

Subterranean termites (ground nesting) do not reduce the wood to a powdery mass or push wood particles to the outside, as do some other wood-boring insects.

Termites enter buildings through

flat, earthen shelter tubes that the workers construct over the surface of foundations; through cracks and joints and around plumbing in concrete slabs; and through wood that connects the soil with the woodwork of the building.

SOME PREVENTIVE measures:

Remove all tree roots, stumps, and other wood debris from the building site before construction starts. Remove grade stakes, frame boards, and scraps of lumber. If no wood is left in or on the soil, the danger of an infestation is reduced.

Prevent moisture from accumulating in the soil under a building. Slope the soil surface so that moisture will drain away from the building.

Choose carefully the kind of foundation. Poured concrete foundations properly reinforced are best. If hollow blocks or brick foundations or piers are used, cap them with at least 4 inches of reinforced poured concrete or fill the top course of blocks and all joints completely with concrete to prevent attack through poor mortar and through hollows in blocks.

The beams and girders of buildings with crawl space under them should be at least 12 inches above the ground. The bottom of floor joists should be at least 18 inches above the ground. Make the outside gradeline at least 6 inches below all exterior woodwork.

In places where the termite hazard is extreme, the use of pressure-treated sills, joists, and headers is an additional safeguard.

Provide good ventilation underneath buildings with crawl space. In general, the net area of ventilation openings should be one-one hundred and sixtieth of the ground area beneath the building. Distribute the vents so that no dead-air pockets are formed.

Concrete slab-on-ground construction is susceptible to termite attack, and infestations are difficult to control. Slabs vary in susceptibility to penetration by termites.

The monolithic type is best, because

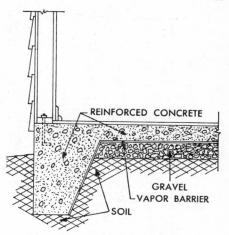

Monolithic concrete slab-on-ground construction.

the floor and the footings are poured in one operation, and there are no joints to permit entry.

The suspended slab is fair. The floor and the foundation are poured separately, but the floor extends across the top of the foundation. This prevents hidden termite entry.

The floating slab is the most hazardous. It may rest on a ledge of the foundation or be independent of it. Termites can enter at the joint between the slab and the foundation.

Because settlement cracks occur almost always in any type of slab, and termites can enter through them, you should treat the soil with chemicals before pouring the concrete of any slab.

Water emulsions of any of these formulations will give many years of protection:

Aldrin, 0.5 percent; chlordane, 1 percent; dieldrin, 0.5 percent; and heptachlor, 0.5 percent. These chemicals are sold as concentrated solutions, which can be diluted with water to the desired concentrations.

Apply 4 gallons of the water emulsion per 10 linear feet to the soil along the inside and outside of perimeter foundation, along interior foundation, and around the places where plumbing comes through the slab.

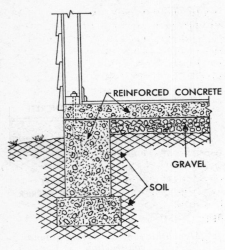

Suspended concrete slab-on-ground construction.

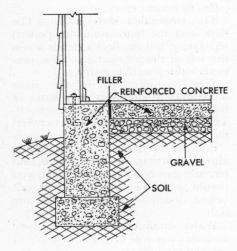

Floating concrete slab-on-ground construction.

Apply 1 gallon per 10 square feet as an overall treatment.

REMEDIAL MEASURES if your house is infested with termites:

Remove all scraps of wood, form-boards, and other debris containing cellulose from under and near the building.

Remove any wooden units, such as trellises, that connect the ground to the woodwork of the building, and replace them so as to break those contacts.

Replace structurally weakened sill, joists, flooring, and such with sound material.

Fill voids, cracks, or expansion joints in concrete or masonry with cement or roofing-grade coal tar pitch.

Provide drainage and ventilation.

THE CHEMICALS USED to prevent attack can be used also to control existing infestations. The buildings with crawl spaces very often can be treated easily and effectively in these ways:

Dig trenches 6 to 8 inches wide around all piers and pipes and along both the inside and outside of all foundation walls. For poured concrete foundations, the trench need be only 3 to 4 inches deep. For foundations of brick and of hollow block masonry, it should be at least 12 inches deep. Where the footing is more than 12 inches deep, use a crowbar, pipe, or rod to make holes about a foot apart and extend them from the bottom of the trench to the footing. This will prevent termites from gaining hidden entry to the building through voids in these types of foundations. Never dig the trench below the top of the footing.

Pour one of the chemicals into the trench at the rate of 4 gallons per 10 linear feet for each foot of depth. If the trench is deep, apply the chemical to alternate layers of about 6 inches of soil.

To treat basements, dig a trench 6 to 8 inches wide and about a foot deep along the outside wall and close to it. Then with a crowbar, pipe, or rod, make holes about a foot apart from the bottom of the trench to the footing. Pour the chemical into the trench at the rate of 4 gallons per 10 linear feet for each foot of depth from grade to footing; alternately replace and treat 6-inch layers of soil.

Infestations in houses built with a

slab on the ground are hard to control, because it is not easy to place chemicals in the soil under such floors where they will be effective.

One way to do it is to drill holes about one-half inch in diameter through the concrete slab close to the points where the termites are or where they may be entering. Space the holes about 6 inches away from the wall and about 12 inches apart to insure proper treatment of the soil underneath. Take care to avoid drilling into plumbing and electric conduits. Apply the chemical through the holes by any practical means available.

Another way is to drill through the outside foundation walls to the soil just under the slab and pour the chemical into the holes.

THESE METHODS are complicated and usually require special equipment. You may need to employ the services of a well-established, reliable pest control operator for such jobs.

Infestations often occur at porches, terraces, and entrance platforms.

The best way to control infestations there is to tunnel under the concrete slab next to the foundation wall, all the way from one side to the other, and apply a chemical in the bottom of the tunnel or trench. Remove all wood debris you encounter in digging the tunnel. Place an access panel over the opening to permit annual inspections and additional soil treatments, if needed.

Another way is to drill holes 12 inches apart, either through the adjacent foundation wall from within the crawl space or basement or through the entrance slab, and introduce the chemical through the holes.

DRYWOOD TERMITES and powder-post beetles also attack the woodwork of buildings. Their damage may be mistaken for that caused by subterranean termites.

Drywood termites occur most abundantly in southern Florida and along the coast of California. They do not require contact with the soil as do the subterranean forms.

Their damage can be recognized by the clean cavities cut across the grain in comparatively solid wood and the presence of slightly compressed pellets in the cavities. Some of the pellets are pushed outside through small openings and often form piles on surfaces below.

Localized infestations can be controlled by injecting 5 percent DDT, 2 percent chlordane, or 5 percent pentachlorophenol in No. 2 fuel oil into the cavities or by thoroughly brushing the surface with one or more applications.

POWDER-POST BEETLES occur throughout the United States. They attack both softwoods and hardwoods. The adult insects are seldom seen.

The whitish larvae, or grubs, work within the wood and reduce it to fine or to coarse powder, which is packed in the galleries or pushed to the exterior through small holes. The presence of this dust on the surface usually is the first sign of an infestation.

You can control local infestation by brushing or spraying the infested places thoroughly with 5 percent DDT, 2 percent chlordane, or 0.5 percent dieldrin in No. 2 fuel oil or deodorized kerosene. More than one application may be necessary if the infestation is deep seated.

If infestations of drywood termites or powder-post beetles are spread through a building, fumigation is the most practical method of control.

The service of a licensed pest control operator is required for fumigation.

All the chemicals I mentioned are poisonous to people and animals. Handle them carefully. If the chemicals accidentally come in contact with skin or eyes, wash the skin immediately with warm, soapy water and the eyes with plenty of water or with a solution containing a teaspoonful of boric acid per glassful of warm water. (HARMON R. JOHNSTON)

Disposal
of Wastes

BECAUSE THE PROPER handling and disposal of household wastes are essential to the health of any family and community, nearly all State, county, and local governments have regulations governing the disposal of wastes—particularly sewage—in built-up communities, suburban and resort areas, and at rural establishments that serve the public.

It is always advisable in such places to consult the local health authorities before you begin building a house or sewage disposal facility.

Some communities prohibit construction on certain building lots if the site will not absorb the expected sewage.

Household sewage consists of the water-carried wastes from the bathroom, kitchen, laundry, floor drains, and other plumbing fixtures. It includes human excreta, toilet paper, dishwater, food scraps, wash water, bits of soap, grease, hair, cloth fibers, bleach, bluing, cleaning compounds, sweepings, and the like. It may also include ground food wastes and backwash from regenerating water-conditioning equipment.

Paper cartons, wrappers, newspapers, sticks and stones, and discarded clothing are rubbish, not sewage, and should be kept out of sewage disposal systems.

Storm drainage from roofs and areaways also should be kept out of septic tank systems and other sewage disposal facilities.

The fecal excreta in sewage contain many kinds of bacteria—possibly including the disease-causing types that transmit such waterborne diseases as typhoid fever, dysentery, and various types of diarrhea.

You should therefore regard all sewage as potentially dangerous.

You should dispose of it in a way in which it cannot contaminate food and water, especially wells, springs, and other water sources.

THE SEPTIC TANK system, properly installed and maintained, generally is a satisfactory way to dispose of sewage from a household when connection to a public system is not possible, adequate land is available for absorption of the effluent, and the system is adequately separated from adjoining properties or sources of water supply. It should handle all the sewage from a normal household.

The system does not purify the sewage, eliminate odor, or destroy all solid matter. Rather, the septic tank conditions the sewage by partial settling and decomposition so that the soil can absorb the liquid effluent better.

A complete system consists of the house sewer, the septic tank, the effluent sewer, and the disposal or absorption area.

As a charge of sewage enters the tank from the house sewer, it displaces an equal volume of conditioned effluent, which is discharged through the effluent sewer to the absorption area.

It is wise to make a sketch of the locations, including depths, of all parts of the system and keep it handy for reference at times of inspection or repair.

In selecting a suitable site for the absorption area, the soil and ground water conditions are major considerations. They vary from place to place, and we cannot specify any one distance as a safe separation between the absorption area and a water source. Generally, though, an absorption area should be at a lower elevation and at least 100 feet from any water source, at

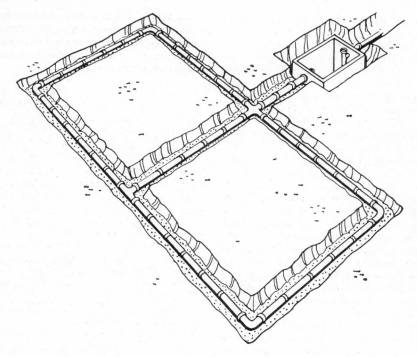

Closed or continuous tile system arrangement for level ground.

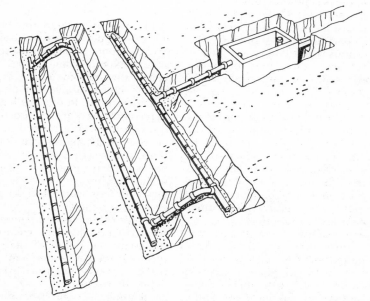

Serial distribution system arrangement for sloping ground.

least 50 feet from any stream or watercourse, and at least 10 feet from a dwelling or property line. A grassy, unshaded site sloping gently away from the house and water source is desirable.

The house sewer should be of sound and durable material, with watertight and rootproof joints. Generally, 4-inch pipe is recommended, laid at a minimum grade of one-eighth inch per foot (1 percent).

The septic tank should be designed to facilitate the separation and digestion of the sewage solids and provide for periodic inspection and occasional removal of sludge and scum.

Its capacity should be based on the largest regular occupancy to be expected in the house. If you have a food waste disposer, you should allow an extra 50 percent. Liquid capacities recommended for tanks to handle all the sewage from a normal household are given in a table.

Tanks may be of single- or multicompartment design. The single-compartment tank is satisfactory for many conditions and is simpler and less expensive to build and maintain.

Septic tanks should be of watertight, durable materials. Concrete, block, brick, tile, stone, and coated steel (that meets Department of Commerce Commercial Standard 177–51) are used.

The effluent sewer may be of the same material, size, and grade as the house sewer.

The success of the entire system depends on being able to dispose of the effluent in a sanitary manner for an extended period of time. Disposal by absorption in the upper layers of the soil is preferred. Soils differ in ability to absorb effluent. Not all are suitable. A percolation test is often used as a means of determining how much absorption area is required.

Effluent usually is discharged into the soil through a system of 4-inch, open-jointed agricultural tile or perforated drain pipe laid in absorption trenches or beds, 24–30 inches deep, and at a flat grade of not more than 6 inches per 100 feet.

ABSORPTION AREA REQUIREMENTS FOR HOUSEHOLD SEPTIC TANK SYSTEMS (PROVIDES FOR FOOD WASTE DISPOSER, AUTOMATIC WASHER, AND OTHER HOUSEHOLD APPLIANCES) [1]

Percolation rate (minutes per inch) [2]	Minimum effective absorption area required per bedroom [3] Square feet
1 or less	70
2	85
3	100
4	115
5	125
10	165
15	190
30	250
45	300
60 [4]	330

[1] Always provide for at least 2 bedrooms. If there is no likelihood of a food waste disposer, automatic washer, or other household appliance being added, these areas may be reduced by about one-fourth to one-third.

[2] Average time required for water level to fall 1 inch in percolation test.

[3] Square feet of standard trench bottom or seepage bed per bedroom.

[4] If more than 60 minutes, soil is unsuitable for use as subsurface absorption field. Select another site or use disposal methods for tight or wet soils.

The tile or pipe should be laid in a bed of clean gravel, crushed or broken stone, or similar material and should extend from at least 6 inches below the bottom of the pipe to at least 2 inches above the top.

Some sanitation officials have begun to recommend that the absorption area disposal lines be arranged in a closed or continuous pattern in level locations, where the surface slope does not exceed 6 inches in any direction within the limits of the field, and in a serial pattern where the surface slope exceeds 6 inches.

A septic tank system should be inspected annually and cleaned when the combined depth of the sludge at the bottom and scum at the top reaches about one-third the liquid depth of the tank.

Cleaning is done by pumping or bailing out the sludge and scum. A

RECOMMENDED LIQUID CAPACITIES FOR HOUSEHOLD SEPTIC TANKS (PROVIDES FOR FOOD WASTE DISPOSER, AUTOMATIC WASHER, AND OTHER HOUSEHOLD APPLIANCES) [1]

Maximum number served		Recommended minimum liquid capacity
Persons	Bedrooms	Gallons
4 or less.....	2 or less ...	750
6..........	3.........	900
8..........	4.........	1,050
10 [2].......	5 [3].......	1,250

[1] If there is no likelihood of a food waste disposer, automatic washer, or other household appliance being added, these capacities may be reduced by about one-fourth to one-third.

[2] For each additional person, add 125 gallons.

[3] For each additional bedroom, add 250 gallons.

small amount of sludge may be left in the tank as "seed," but the tank should not be washed or disinfected after cleaning.

Soap, detergents, bleaches, drain solvents, and other mild chemical preparations in the amounts used for normal household purposes have little or no adverse effect on the system.

The most common trouble with septic tank systems is the clogging of the absorption field. It may be due to improper design or construction, improper use, or neglect of servicing.

Clogged fields can sometimes be cleared by opening up and flushing the disposal lines with a hose, but usually it will be necessary to dig up, clean and re-lay them in new locations.

Sewer lines also clog, usually because of roots. Cleaning with a root cutter may remove the roots then in the sewer but will not prevent future entry. This requires making the joints root-tight.

Cesspools are seldom satisfactory for disposing of sewage, as they usually develop sooner or later into nuisances or health hazards. In some places they are prohibited by health codes.

THE EARTH PIT PRIVY, properly lo-

RECOMMENDED INSIDE DIMENSIONS FOR SINGLE-COMPARTMENT SEPTIC TANKS

Liquid capacity	Recommended inside dimensions			
Gallons	Width	Length	Total depth	Liquid depth
500.......	3'0''	6'0''	5'0''	4'0''
600.......	3'0''	7'0''	5'0''	4'0''
750......	3'6''	7'6''	5'0''	4'0''
900......	3'6''	8'6''	5'0''	4'0''
1,050.....	4'0''	7'9''	5'6''	4'6''
1,250.....	4'0''	9'3''	5'6''	4'6''

cated, constructed, and maintained, is a satisfactory facility for the house without indoor plumbing.

The privy should be at least 50 feet from the house and the well, preferably on the opposite side of the house from prevailing winds and downhill from the well.

Good, sound, tight construction, with screened ventilators, is essential to keep out insects and birds. The ground outside should be sloped to shed water away from the building. The roof should extend beyond the walls to shed water away from the pit. The pit should not extend to within 2 feet of the ground water or creviced rock.

A pit with capacity of 50 cubic feet should serve a family of 5 for 5 to 10 years. When the pit is filled to within 18 to 20 inches of the top, the privy should be moved and a strong disinfectant spread in the old pit, which then should be covered with earth.

Privies require periodic attention. Seats and covers should be washed weekly with a disinfectant, such as cresol or hypochlorite or chloride of lime.

The structure and screening should be carefully inspected before and during fly-breeding season to see that seat covers fit tightly, that screens are unbroken, and that floor, risers, and ventilators are intact.

Odors from privy pits can be reduced by adding commercial deodorants or covering the contents with dry earth, ashes, sawdust, or lime.

SANITARY HANDLING and disposal of waste materials will do much to improve conditions around the house and yard.

Garbage may include some items suitable for animal feed, and some not. Rubbish—bottles, cans, papers, rags, and the like—may be partly combustible, partly not. If garbage is to be fed, edible portions should be separated. Similarly, if rubbish is to be burned, combustible portions should be separated.

Garbage or rubbish held temporarily pending disposal or collection should be in watertight, rustproof containers with handles and tight covers. Outdoors, containers should be on a stand or rack elevated about 12 inches above the ground to allow space underneath for cleaning and to discourage rodents.

Containers and racks should be cleaned at least weekly.

Uncovered containers, or garbage scattered on the ground, will provide breeding places for flies and are undesirable. Garbage containers used in the kitchen should be small enough to require daily emptying.

Food waste disposers eliminate the need to handle these wastes as garbage—and may be used with septic tank systems that are designed to accommodate them.

FEEDING GARBAGE to animals is regulated by State laws, which should be checked before feeding.

Burning is a sanitary way to dispose of combustible materials. Combination incinerator-fireplaces are often built in backyards. Incinerators for building into the house or use in the yard are commercially available, as are trash burners suitable for burning small amounts of paper, rags, and the like.

If space and a suitable location are available, garbage and rubbish may be buried. Use trenches 3 or 4 feet wide, 4 or 5 feet deep, and 7 or 8 feet long. Place the material in the trench, compact or burn it, and then cover it with earth often enough to control odors, smoke, insects, and rodents. When filled to within 18 inches of the top, seal the trench permanently with a compacted earth cover and start another trench.

Garbage may be composted with leaves, peat, manure, and similar materials. Locate the pile in an inconspicuous place, build up to the desired height with materials that will rot, then cover with 2 or 3 inches of earth. Make the top level and the sides steep. Keep the pile moist to facilitate rotting. In time it will become a good material for use in gardens. (JOHN W. ROCKEY)

Water

YOUR HOUSE should have a water system that provides enough drinkable water under adequate pressure whenever and wherever it is wanted.

The water should be free of harmful organisms. Preferably it should also be clear, free of objectionable taste and odor, soft, and neither highly acid nor alkaline. It should not contain objectionable amounts of dissolved iron or manganese.

QUALITY is important.

Lack of sanitary quality is associated with the transmission of waterborne diseases.

Chemical quality affects the use characteristics. For example, certain minerals in water make it hard. Hard water may be less desirable for bathing, laundering, and cooking than soft water.

Physical quality relates mainly to appearance, taste, and odor. Suspended silt, for example, makes water look muddy or cloudy.

If you have your own well or spring, you should know something of how water occurs in Nature, because this has a bearing on its quality.

The earth's water goes through a natural cycle. It falls as precipitation—rain, snow, sleet, and hail. Part runs off on the surface, via streams, to the ocean. Part seeps downward through the porous formations of the earth, becomes ground water, and eventually reaches the sea. Part is evaporated back to the atmosphere from water surfaces and from vegetation.

Water can dissolve many other substances—solids, liquids, and gases. All natural waters contain materials dissolved from the air and soil. Precipitation dissolves gases from the air, sometimes causing it to become slightly acid.

After reaching the earth, the solution continues to dissolve organic matter and minerals with which it comes in contact on the surface and in the soil.

Since the earth's distribution of organic matter and minerals is not uniform, neither is the quality of the water in nature. Natural water in one place thus may contain materials quite different from those in another place.

As it flows over the earth, water picks up all sorts of organic, inorganic, dissolved, and suspended substances that pollute it. All surface sources of water supplies therefore should be regarded as polluted, and water from them should be disinfected before it is used in the house.

It is sometimes necessary or desirable to treat water to improve its quality.

Treatment to improve the sanitary or biological quality is known as disinfection. Public health authorities generally recommend chlorination, because it provides a ready means of checking to determine if disinfection is complete. The check, the chlorine residual test, is simple and easy to do with an inexpensive kit. It is wise to consult a health officer, sanitarian, or qualified agricultural extension or industry representative for advice on the selection and use of chlorinating equipment and procedures to suit your particular conditions.

Test kits, with instructions for use, can be had from dealers handling chlorinating equipment. A common type consists of a chemical reagent and a set of comparison colors. A small amount of the reagent is added to a sample of the chlorinated water and the resulting color compared with those in the kit. The matching color indicates the strength of the chlorine remaining. This strength indicates whether disinfection is satisfactory.

Vigorous boiling for one full minute will disinfect small amounts of water. The flat taste of boiled water can be improved by pouring it back and forth from one container to another or by adding a small pinch of salt for each quart boiled.

You also may use tablets containing chlorine or iodine. You can get them at drug and sporting goods stores. Follow the directions on the package. You can get information on other chemical treatments for emergency disinfection from city and county health officers.

Conditioning to improve chemical properties may include softening, removal of iron or manganese or both, neutralization of acidity to control corrosion, and removal of sulfur (hydrogen sulfide).

The methods and equipment need to be tailored to the particular water. A chemical analysis is needed as a basis for selecting the proper treatment. Do not try to do it yourself—consult a specialist.

Some heavily mineralized and alkali waters cannot yet be conditioned economically for household use. If you have that kind of water, you should seek a different source.

THE PHYSICAL CHARACTER of water can be improved by settling, filtration, and aeration.

Settling usually is done by allowing water to sit quiet in a pond, basin, or tank so that its suspended solids may settle to the bottom and leave the water above relatively clear.

Filtering is intended to remove the finer solids. You cannot rely on it to remove bacteria and other micro-organisms. Sand of filter grade is the usual filter medium. Filtering is chiefly in the upper few inches of the filter bed. When this upper layer begins to clog and choke off the flow, it is scraped off and washed for reuse. You can build effective filters according to instructions that you can get from your local or State health office, your State university, or the Department of Agriculture.

Aeration allows gases to escape and reduces the odors and tastes they carry. It also allows oxygen in the air to mix with the water.

Aeration may be done by forcing water through sprinklers or allowing it to flow over cascades. It is usually only partly effective.

You can buy equipment for treating water. Firms that sell such equipment are located in many places where water can be improved by their products. They normally analyze water samples for prospective customers in order to select appropriate equipment.

Chemical analyses can also be had from commercial water or chemical laboratories. They are listed in telephone directories under "water treating service" or "water treating equipment and supplies."

ONE SHOULD KNOW the average daily water use and the peak demand rate in order to determine the adequacy of a water source and to plan a satisfactory system of storage as well as distribution.

The average daily use of water in American homes ranges from less than 50 gallons a person a day to more than 100 because of differences in family living and activities. About 75 gallons is a fair average figure to use in planning.

Water is not used uniformly throughout the day. The peak demand rate (gallons per minute) is the maximum rate of usage that may occur. If the system cannot provide this peak demand, the flow at one or more of the faucets will be reduced, perhaps to an annoying trickle.

These rates of flow (in gallons per minute and based on a water pressure of 8 pounds per square inch at the fixture with full flow) for common household fixtures may be used for planning purposes: Kitchen sink faucet, 4.5 gallons; wash basin faucet, 2; bathtub, 6; shower, 5; watercloset, 3; laundry tub faucet, 5.

A 50-foot garden hose will take 3 to 5 gallons a minute, at a pressure two or three times that of the other fixtures.

THE COMMONEST SOURCE of water for the individual water system is the well. Others are springs, ponds, and rainwater catchments.

Wells should be located and constructed so they will be protected against entry of surface or shallow drainage.

Avoid locations close downhill from sewage or manure disposal areas.

Mound the surface at the well, set a watertight casing or lining that extends to above the surface mounding, provide a watertight platform that extends several feet in all directions from the well to shed surface wash away, and provide a watertight seal at the pump mounting.

Wells may be dug, bored, drilled, or driven.

Dug wells can be sunk to depths up to 40 to 50 feet in unconsolidated soils that permit digging. They are usually 3 or 4 feet in diameter, although they may be much larger.

Dug wells in good, permeable sand or gravel formations can yield ample water for a household. Because they normally extend only a short distance below the water table (surface of the ground water), they may go dry if the water table drops.

Bored wells are much like dug wells, except that they may be deeper and are usually smaller in diameter. The maximum practical diameter for boring is about 24 to 30 inches. Since they are smaller in diameter, their yield would be less than that of a well dug to the same depth in the formation.

Drilled wells may be sunk to great

depths through solid rock. The usual household size is 4 or 6 inches in diameter. The yield in good formations may well exceed the requirements of the largest household.

Drilling requires expensive drilling rigs, skill, and knowledge.

Driven wells, usually 1¼ or 2 inches in diameter, are driven not more than 40 to 50 feet into open sand or gravel formations. The small diameter limits the yield and the size of pump that may be used.

Wells yielding as little as 1 or 2 gallons a minute can be made to serve a sizable household if the pumping is almost continuous at the low yield rate into a storage tank of sufficient capacity to meet the peak demands of the family. One gallon a minute totals 1,440 gallons in a day; that is ample for most families.

Springs should be protected by a watertight enclosure. The enclosure usually is of concrete that extends down to rock, with openings in the inlet side for water to enter. It should have a removable cover to permit cleaning. Water should be withdrawn through a delivery pipe. An overflow pipe should be provided. The overflow outlet should have a screen.

Publications of the United States Department of Agriculture, Public Health Service, and State universities and health departments will give you more information on the construction and maintenance of wells, springs, and other sources of water.

THE TYPES OF PUMPS normally used with household water systems are the positive displacement, the centrifugal (including submersible), and the jet (ejector). They are available in shallow and deep well classes for suction lifts of less and more, respectively, than 22 to 25 feet.

The most common positive displacement pump is the reciprocating or piston pump, which has a pump cylinder. It is especially adapted to low capacities and high lifts and is best suited for pumping 5 to 25 gallons a minute against moderate to high heads. (Pressure expressed as difference in elevation—1 pound per square inch pressure equals 2.31 feet head of water, or 1 foot head of water equals 0.43 pound per square inch pressure.) It may vibrate and be noisy. It gives a pulsating discharge.

The jet pump has high capacity at low heads and does not have to be installed over the well. The capacity reduces as the head increases. At depths greater than 80 or 90 feet, the jet pump becomes uneconomical to operate because of the great increase in power requirement.

The submersible can be used at almost any depth. It is long and slim, to fit down in the well (4 inches and over in diameter). It can handle more water from a deep well at less operating cost than other pumps. It has a high efficiency over a wide range of discharge pressures and will deliver large amounts against high heads. It is quiet and requires no weather protection, but it may be damaged by sand or abrasives in the water.

Information and advice on pumps may be had from manufacturers or dealers. When you select a dealer, it is well to consider his facilities for servicing. That is more important than the make of the pump, as any pump is subject to occasional mechanical trouble.

IN A COMMUNITY that is served by a public water system, the municipality normally assumes responsibility for delivering a potable water to householders. The water must meet standards established by the local public health authority.

The water can be safe yet contain dissolved materials that give it annoying characteristics. For example, chlorine chemicals used in disinfecting the water may impart a slight taste or odor that some find objectionable. Other annoyances are hardness and dissolved iron or manganese, or both. To remove these minerals at the water plant would result in increased water bills. Should the householder so desire, he can obtain treatment equipment for his house from various dealers.

Occasionally a municipal supply may become depleted because of failure of a well, stream, or reservoir. The householder can do little about it except comply with whatever instructions are issued to conserve water for essential purposes.

States, counties, cities, and other governmental units have health or sanitary codes or regulations to regulate their water supplies.

Regulation is essential to the public health as a means of preventing spread of waterborne diseases, such as typhoid fever and dysentery. It is carried out by development of standards, inspections, and approvals for water systems, both public and individual, wherever the public health is a factor. (JOHN W. ROCKEY)

Good Lighting

GOOD LIGHTING adds to the beauty, cheer, comfort, convenience, safety, and value of your home.

It helps you move about and work rapidly and safely, do tasks when and where you wish, protect eyes from strain, and relax or concentrate.

To obtain those benefits, you need good task (or local) lighting and general background lighting—each helping the other—to attain proper levels and balance for usual activities.

For most tasks, soft, diffused light from a fairly large or long source helps avoid spotty or line reflections and harsh shadows, but fine handsewing or detailed hobby work may require some strong, direct, additional light to bring out details.

Choose and place local task lighting equipment in relation to eye levels— seated or standing. Average eye heights are 40 to 42 inches for women and men seated in lounge chairs and 61 to 64 inches when they are standing.

Workplaces must be well lighted, but when the general lighting is good, local light is needed only on the task you are doing.

The place where you do the work is important, too. For example, you can make good use of a task light (because of reflection) by placing a desk, sewing center, or workbench against a wall or in a corner.

Areas near the task should not be brighter than the task area and should not be less than one-third as bright if the task is to take long. If desk tops are dark, say, light-colored blotters, which reflect light, help get this relationship.

WHEN YOU choose lights, consider color effects as well as the amount of light.

Many bulb and tube finishes enhance cool or warm colors, but some affect the output of light considerably.

Choose white or warm white tubes and inside-frosted and white bulbs for the most efficient light, and deluxe warm or cool white tubes or tinted bulbs to bring out colors of furnishings.

Avoid daylight tubes or bulbs unflattering to skin, food, and furnishings.

Color is an important aid to light. For ceilings, choose white (for work areas), near-white, or pale tints.

Elsewhere, light-to-medium ranges reflect light fairly well and make rooms seem larger.

Dark colors absorb and waste light, as dust and dirt do. Dark-light contrasts, shiny finishes, and glare are annoying and can make even simple tasks more difficult.

Portable lamps or special-purpose fixtures that direct light over task areas provide light for close work. Well-designed types contribute to balanced lighting around tasks and add to the overall effectiveness of room lighting.

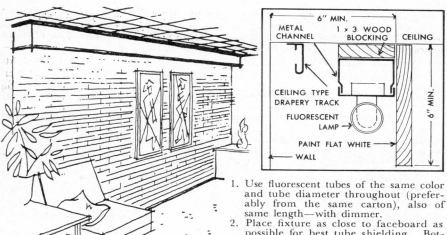

1. Use fluorescent tubes of the same color and tube diameter throughout (preferably from the same carton), also of same length—with dimmer.
2. Place fixture as close to faceboard as possible for best tube shielding. Bottom louver or diffuser desirable when cornice is viewed lengthwise.
3. For a smooth, uninterrupted line of light, paint inside of the faceboard a flat white, and use fixtures with white lampholders butted end-to-end.

Cornices direct all of their light downward to give dramatic interest to wall coverings, draperies, pictures. May also be used over windows where space above window does not permit using valance lighting. Good for low-ceilinged rooms.

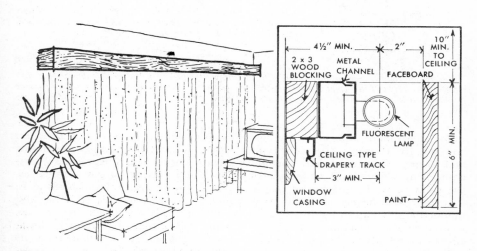

Valances are usually used at windows with draperies. The valances provide up-light, which reflects off ceiling for general lighting and down-light for drapery accent. When closer to ceiling than 10 inches, use closed top to eliminate annoying ceiling brightness.

High wall brackets provide both up and down light for general room lighting. Used on interior wall to balance window valance both architecturally and in lighting distribution. Mounting height may be determined by window or door height, should never be less than 65 inches unless used as low bracket over buffet, 60; sofa, 55-up; bed, 52; range, 58; also 15–18 inches above desk, centered over work.

CLM GLASS DIFFUSER "flared-top; crown"
Blown white glass—10% more light than best bowl
diffuser; most diffused light on reading surface. Shields
bulb at top.

Top	*Bulb Wattage*
8 in.	50–100–150, 50–200–250
10	100–200–300, 50–100–150

Shade: 9–10 inches up at center depth, 16–18 in diameter.

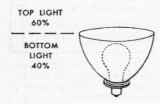

GLASS OR PLASTIC BOWL "open-bowl; bowl-shape"
Thin white glass best: 20% more light than thickest
pressed glass. Plastic bowl is cheaper but heat may discolor
it if bulb wattage is high.

Top	*Glass*	*Plastic*
6 in.	100w	75–100w
8	150w	100–150w
9¼	200w	150w
10	300w	200–300w
11½*		50/150w

*Shade-bowl, mesh disk.
Shade: 6–10 inches deep; 10–18, bottom diameter.

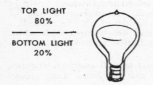

R–40 WHITE INDIRECT BULB IN WIDE HARP
Whiteness and large size (5-inch across) help diffuse
light and direct much up to ceiling, adding to general
lighting. Uses: Casual reading, short-time studying,
most types of sewing. Harp change is easy. Bulb comes
in 150, or 50–100–150 watt.
Shade: 8–10 inches up at center depth, 13–18 in diameter.

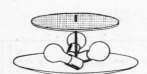

PLASTIC DISK DIFFUSER
May have metal disk or plastic disk over bulb. Plastic
or fiberglass disk is below bulb(s), 1 inch above bottom of
shade for most light. 1-socket (3-step type if 3-light
bulb used): 150 or 200 watt, 50–100–150 watt, 50–200–250
watt. Multi-socket (3-step): 3 bulbs, 60w each.
Shade: 6–8 inches deep; 14–18, bottom diameter.

*Undershade diffusers soften and spread light in portable lamps and in fixtures of open-bowl or disk
types. Better Light Better Sight study lamps, introduced in 1965, use inverted metal cone reflectors or
prismatic refractors to improve lighting further for close-seeing tasks.*

For long-range value, economy, and
comfort, give consideration to the types
and location of fixtures and portable
equipment. They should be fairly near
the ceilings, walls, objects, or people
that you are trying to light. Well
planned and balanced lighting in each
room creates a harmonious decorative
effect throughout the house.

Off-center and suspended equipment
bring light close to the task and add
decorative interest but may limit the
rearrangement of furnishings. Hanging
heights range from 30 to 36 inches
over a dining table to 48 inches above

laundry centers or workshop benches.

Just as daylight needs some window
treatments for full effectiveness, artificial light needs improving devices.
Some of these are bulb finishes, bowls,
globes, shades, shields, louvers, and
reflectors. They enlarge the source,
conceal it, soften or diffuse the light,
reflect and direct it, and increase its
amount where needed.

Dimmers and step switches let you
dim or brighten light. Adjustable posi-
tioning devices also are useful. These
include reels or pulleys with counter-
weights to raise or lower fixtures and

wall lamps; adjustable height shafts in floor and table lamp bases; and various swing-arm and other swivel devices or flexible shafts that bring light closer to work or help you to position it to decrease reflected glare or shadows on your work.

A number of materials make equipment attractive and efficient. Many light-diffusing plastics and white or milky glass, for example, are superior to etched or clear glassware. Also good are laminated combinations of fabric, plastic, fiber glass, or paper. Fabrics, stitched (not glued) for washability, are satisfactory for lampshades and fixture shields.

GOOD FIXTURES for all style periods are available. Large or long ones are good buys that should maintain their value, since they follow room proportions and couple low brightness with a wide light spread.

Recessed fixtures require thoughtful handling; near-white ceilings, lighted from below, and fairly light floors can dispel gloom. One such fixture should be used for each 40 to 50 square feet.

Especially good are inconspicuous fluorescent types. For local light, low brackets and built-in soffits—over sinks, buffets, sofas, and desks—bring the light close to the subject. For general lighting, window valances, ceiling cornices, coves, and other ceiling units produce an overall lighting effect to balance local lighting.

Small to medium rooms require 3 to 8 feet of shielded tubes when they are used with a ceiling fixture, or 6 to 16 feet without one. Large rooms with no ceiling fixture should average about 1 foot of tube for each 15 square feet of floorspace—roughly 16 to 20 feet of tubes for large living rooms. Use 1.5-inch (T–12) tubes unless space demands tubes 1 inch (T–8) in diameter.

Large panels and luminous ceilings with tubes installed between ceiling beams are practical in work areas and elsewhere if they have dimmers. Plastic diffusers in building dimensions, suspended on hangers below the tubes,

make a smooth, easily maintained installation. In building or remodeling, balance high initial costs against other costs of ceiling finishing, fixtures, and future maintenance.

The main problem with fluorescent lighting is choosing all fixtures of the right size and quality, because you cannot change the light output later, as you can with incandescent types. Ask about radio-interference suppressors, sound rating, starting speed, and dimming possibilities before you buy fluorescent fixtures.

WELL-STYLED LAMPS, all appropriately spaced, can add to the attractiveness of a room while meeting the requirements of task lighting.

The marks of good lamps are: Bulbs located low in the shade; undershade device to reflect, refract, or diffuse the light; broad, white-lined shades open at the top; harmonious shades; and good proportions that are neither squat nor gigantic.

Thin, long, portable lamps fit into tight places, under cabinets, and in, on, or behind furniture or room dividers. Average one lamp for each 40 to 50 square feet of floorspace.

COMMON incandescent bulbs are inexpensive, relatively hot, small, high-brightness sources. Their average life is 750 to 1 thousand hours. Ratings of 1,200–2,500 hours sacrifice some light output for longer life.

Bulb failures occur early when house voltage exceeds V-rating (115–130), as marked on the bulb, or the bulb overheats in a small or poorly ventilated fixture, or if it receives rough service or unusual vibration.

At extra cost, you can buy three-light or high-low bulbs to change light levels, and large bulbs with special finishes to lower brightness.

Comparatively, fluorescent sources—tubes, circles, or square panels—give greater light spread at lower brightness. They emit 3 to 4 times as much light and last 6 to 10 times as long as incandescent bulbs. They also feel

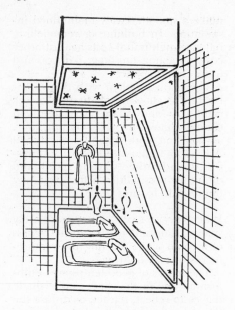

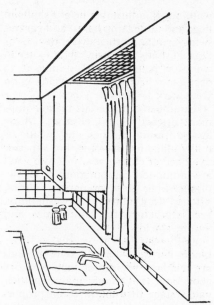

FOR PERSONAL GROOMING
Bathroom or dressing room soffits are designed to light user's face, hair. Therefore, cover bottom opening with highly diffusing material which will scatter light over face, top of head. Wide bottom opening (14–18 inches) helps also. Light-colored countertop or sink reflects light under chin.

HORIZONTAL TASK LIGHTING
Soffits over work areas are designed to provide high level of light directly below. Polished metal reflectors can double light output and increase seeing comfort when used with louvers or very lightly diffusing glass or plastic in the bottom opening. Bottom opening may be 12–18 inches wide. Paint cavity white.

cooler. Their average life of 7,500 hours balances against a higher initial cost. Frequent starting shortens the life of fluorescent tubes, however.

WHEN YOU BUY a new house or redecorate an older one, you often can offset the expense of adequate lighting equipment with a little ingenuity in modernizing or making equipment.

To obtain portable equipment inexpensively, consider buying assembly kits for study, wall, and vanity lamps or improving poor lamps.

Lamp improvers include large R–40 (5-inch diameter) white indirect bulbs and wide harps, threaded holders and bowls, or disk diffusers; shade risers, miscellaneous oil-lamp converters, and shade or disk materials.

Spray paint in color or metallic finishes gives old equipment a new look or new efficiency, as when you spray paper or metal lampshade liners white.

Fixture improvers include special fixture bulbs, candle shades, screw-in adapters, plastic converters, or diffusing lanterns (12 to 24 inches across), and other shielding material.

For help on how to improve, make, or choose equipment and where to put it, consult your power distributor, home extension agents, homemaking and shop teachers, and lighting dealers and distributors.

When buying equipment, rely on the labels of "UL" (Underwriters' Laboratories, Inc.) for safety testing, and "ETL" (Electrical Testing Laboratories, Inc.) for quality testing for certified equipment programs: BLBS (Better Light Better Sight Bureau)— study lamps with reflectors or prismatic refractors under shades; CBM

(Certified Ballast Manufacturers)—fluorescent ballasts; CLM (Certified Lamp Makers)—lamps, often special-order item; RLM (Reflector Lighting Equipment Manufacturers)—reflectors designed to specifications of the RLM Standards Institute, Inc., and used in workrooms with whitened-bowl or silvered-bowl bulbs and for outdoor equipment.

For further information on home lighting, booklets are available at a low cost from the American Home Lighting Institute and the Illuminating Engineering Society.

When you have met lighting needs for safety—outdoors, entries, stairs, halls, hazardous work—and for eyesight protection at main activity locations of all family members, you can concentrate on accent lighting, say, picture lighting, or decorative wall panels, garden lighting, and other delights of light for living. (LOUISAN MAMER)

Wiring

To ADEQUACY, convenience, and safety of electric wiring, you should add a fourth requirement when you buy or plan a house—expandability, to take care of future needs.

It is best to have a professional electrician install the wiring in your house, but some knowledge of the functions and capabilities of electric systems will help you when you contract for the installation and help you use electricity safely and economically.

To meet all your needs for electricity, you should have enough lighting and general-purpose outlets and circuits to spread the load evenly.

The National Electrical Code, a recognized authority, has given guide-lines as to needs and safe practices, although the code requirements in your own locality may differ in some details.

To be fully adequate, the minimum lighting in a house is 3 watts to the square foot of building area. The location of outlets is important.

Receptacle outlets on 15- or 20-ampere branch circuits must be spaced no more than 12 feet apart, so that no point on the wall measured along the floorline will be more than 6 feet from an outlet.

Outlets in the kitchen, laundry, pantry, dining room, and breakfast room should be equally divided between two or more 20-ampere branch circuits. This provision is required of kitchen outlets. Many homeowners have each kitchen outlet installed on an individual circuit. That increases costs of installation, but the extra convenience is worth the difference.

For safety, all outlets should be grounded. Grounding-type outlets permit the connection of parallel-blade, two-wire cords and plugs used on appliances, as well as three-wire plugs for cords that connect devices that must be grounded.

Ceiling outlets for lighting should be centered in bedrooms, dens, kitchens, dining and living rooms, halls, passageways, and stairways.

Lights in bathrooms are placed above mirrored cabinets and overhead in shower stalls. Work areas in kitchens, laundries, and home workshops need light directly over task areas.

Overhead lighting is recommended in basements and recreation rooms.

Outlets for lights are desirable over or alongside each outside entryway to the house and for floodlights around the dwelling.

Outlets for the switch control of lights are placed in the wall about 48 inches above the floor at the lock side of entrances.

Three-way and four-way switches are needed to control lights from two or more locations. These may be at entry points to the living room, dining room, kitchen, at the top and bottom of stairways, and at inside and outside entrances to the basement and recreation room. Switch control for outside floodlighting outlets may be desired in the master bedroom.

At least one receptacle outlet for floor or table lamps in the living room should be controlled by a switch, when ceiling outlets are not used. Here, silent-type or mercury switches may be desired.

Receptacle outlets should be installed in the wall, 18 inches above the floor in bedrooms, living room, den, and dining room. They should be no more than 12 feet apart. Additional outlets take care of varied arrangements of furniture.

One wall outlet in the dining room should be above table height to connect portable cooking or warming appliances at the table.

In kitchen and work areas, receptacle outlets should be 8 inches above the worktable level. Clock outlets in kitchen and workshop areas do not need a switch.

Weatherproof outlets are desirable on the driveway side of the house and on the opposite side about 4 feet above ground.

Additional weatherproof outlets may be needed in outside walls of the house for patios or porches.

Bathrooms may require an outlet for a heater. The frame of electric space heaters must be grounded for safety. Receptacles for electric shavers and the like may be incorporated in the lighting fixture over the mirror.

Switches and receptacles of specification grade work better and last longer at only a slight increase in cost.

Thought should be given to the proper selection of wire sizes in circuits throughout the home. General-purpose circuits and lighting circuits, for instance, require No. 12 (copper) wire or more. The wire sizes are increased wherever heavier loads for larger appliances and equipment are expected.

In the kitchen and workshop, indi-vidual circuits for each receptacle provide minimum interruption in the use of appliances. Circuits of 120 volts are a minimum requirement there. They include outlets for the iron, automatic washer, garbage disposer, dishwasher, roaster, waffle baker, food freezer, and the like.

Individual power circuits of 240 volts are needed for such major appliances as an electric range or tabletop cooking unit, wall oven, clothes drier, space heater, and large air-conditioning equipment.

Protective devices built into home electric systems for safety and convenience are of two approved types, circuit breakers and fuses.

Both provide acceptable protection. Only the procedure used to restore interrupted service varies. A blown fuse must be replaced with a new one of like capacity.

Circuit breakers require the operation of a toggle—a switchlike handle—to restore a circuit connection after the cause of the interruption has been removed.

Circuit breakers or fuses may be installed in cabinets whose trim and covers are flush with the finished surface of the wall in which they are placed.

The main service entrance of wires and load centers in most houses are of 100-ampere capacity and are located in the basement. When much of the heavy electric load is some distance from the main service entrance, a subfeeder is extended to a second distribution panel in order to shorten circuits.

In the choice and planning of main disconnect and load center equipment, branch circuits of 120 and 240 volts must be provided to care for the needs of installed circuits. In addition, at least two 120-volt and one 240-volt spare circuit spaces should be allowed for future circuits.

The cabinet door of each load center has a table of numbered circuits. Your wireman should list on this table exactly which area or individual appliance is served by each circuit.

Examples of methods used to calculate required circuits, feeders, and main services may be found in the *National Electrical Code*, a copy of which may be obtained at small cost from your State fire insurance rating bureau, which very likely is in your State capital.

Other helpful guides may be had from the Industry Committee on Interior Wiring and from the National Electrical Manufacturers Association, 155 East 44th Street, New York, N.Y., 10017. One of their pamphlets, "Residential Wiring Handbook," sells for 25 cents.

State universities generally have pamphlets to help you in planning. For instance, a pamphlet, "Electrical Wiring," is available for 15 cents from the Small Homes Council, University of Illinois, Urbana, Ill.

Finally, require your wireman to have his work checked and inspected for safety by an authorized inspector and furnish you with a copy of the certificate of approval. (THOMAS P. BRANCH)

Heating

THE METHODS you use to heat and cool your house depend largely on how comfortable you wish to be and how much you can afford to spend for them.

Central heating or complete house heating systems provide the comfort most Americans want. They are a good investment in all but the lowest cost houses and in warm climates. Thermostats make their operation almost automatic.

FORCED-WARM-AIR systems with blowers to circulate the air mechanically are the most popular. The type with ducts distributes filtered air to all rooms and provides uniform temperatures in a properly built house.

Furnaces for warm-air systems, using gas, oil, or electrical resistance heaters, heat quickly. This is a desirable feature for heating on chilly fall and spring mornings.

A basement is the best place for the furnace. If only crawl space is available, a horizontal type of furnace may be hung under the floor; there should be plenty of room to get to the furnace to service and repair it.

Stoker-fired furnaces often are used in places where coal is cheap. They should be in the basement because of dirt and because coal must be stored nearby. Some are made for floor mounting in a wide hall or another central location, but this type is less desirable.

Automatic oil and coal-fired central heating systems with ducts usually cost 800 to 1,500 dollars installed in the average three- or four-bedroom house. Gas-fired and electric furnaces may cost less.

Electric furnaces need no vents and require no maintenance other than servicing the fan, motor, and filters.

The installed costs of heating systems vary according to type of fuel, the duct system, climate, and labor rates.

When you compare installed costs, do not forget to include the cost of a larger capacity electrical system if one is needed for an electric furnace.

Do not buy too small a furnace because of a slightly lower price; you will not get the quick heat desired at times, you may use more fuel in the long run, and the heat exchanger may not last so long.

On the other hand, too large a furnace is inefficient and may not provide even temperatures.

Get a reputable dealer to figure the size you need.

In most central warm-air systems, the air is filtered through inexpensive replaceable or washable filters.

Electronic air cleaners remove pollen, fine dust, and other irritants that pass through ordinary filters and thus are especially desirable for persons with respiratory ailments. In the most efficient type, particles in the air are electrically charged before the air passes between closely spaced electrically charged plates. The cost installed with automatic washing and drying of the cleaner was about 600 dollars in 1965, or perhaps 25 percent less without the automatic feature.

Compact oil or gas forced-warm-air furnaces may be installed on the floor of the house in a closet or other recess at less cost than a central system with furnace in the basement.

Some have ducts running through the attic to discharge heated air through a diffuser in the ceiling of each room. The ducts should be tight and heavily insulated to save fuel.

Others have no ducts, but discharge the heat from a large register at the top of the furnace. This type is somewhat similar to a circulator heater with fan and heats best in an open-type plan where few partitions interfere with circulation throughout the house.

Without cold air return ducts, temperatures are less uniform. The cold air is drawn along the floor from the cooler outside walls, and floors may be cold. This applies also to circulator heaters even when equipped with electrically driven fans.

Furnaces mounted on the floor of the house may be noisier than basement installations, as the furnace is closer to the occupants.

If you plan to build a house with a concrete floor, you can use a downdraft furnace and form the ducts into the concrete floor. Provide openings for registers along outside walls. This system gives a warm floor and satisfactory heating.

HOT WATER SYSTEMS provide uniform heat, especially with baseboard convectors or a piping system in the floor.

They are compact and require little space for the piping. Two-pipe systems are best. In houses with basements, they eliminate ducts, which may interfere with headroom and any plans to finish the ceiling.

The baseboard convector is a hollow unit that looks like a baseboard and replaces the wood baseboard on outside walls. Cool air at the floor is warmed by passing over finned tubes in the unit.

Heating is fairly quick in the modern hot water systems, now often called hydronic systems. Boilers are small, and the hot water is circulated quickly by an electrically driven pump. The cost using baseboard convectors is slightly higher than a good forced-warm-air system.

Steam heating systems are sometimes used in very large residences in cold climates. Generally they are more expensive than other systems.

HEATING the entire house electrically is economical only in communities where rates are low.

Some power suppliers have rates as low as 1 to 1.3 cents per kilowatt-hour (kw.-hr.) above a specified minimum power usage. Seasonal costs of heating vary in different climates.

Your local power supplier can give you typical costs and may give you a guaranteed maximum cost per month or annually.

Baseboard heaters or cables in the ceiling are especially satisfactory for heating the entire house. They provide uniform temperatures and are noiseless. Usually these types are controlled by a wall thermostat in each room.

Some housewives object to the baseboard type because they interfere with floor-length draperies.

Baseboard and ceiling cable installations usually run from 50 to 75 dollars a room.

Electric wall heaters with or without fans and with self-contained thermostats sometimes are used, but may not provide uniform temperatures except in small rooms.

Heat pumps, which heat in winter

and cool in summer, are becoming more popular. They cost less to operate in winter than when heat is supplied entirely by electrical resistance heaters.

Consult your local power supplier before adding large electric heaters or installing a complete system. You may need larger service entrance wiring and distribution panel.

Portable electric and gas heaters are recommended mainly for supplemental heat.

You should inspect the flexible tubing connecting portable gas heaters to the gas supply line often to make sure there are no cracks developing which could cause leaks. Gas heaters are safer if vented to the outside.

Portable electric heaters should have an automatic switch to shut off the electricity if the heater is tipped over.

YOUR HOUSE must be properly insulated to get comfortable, uniform temperatures and comfortable heating bills.

Four inches of insulation in the ceiling and 3 inches in walls is the minimum recommended for most types of heating.

Electricity costs more per unit of heat (British thermal unit, or B.t.u.) than other fuels. If you use electrical heating, place at least 6 inches of insulation in the ceiling and 4 inches in walls and in floors with vented crawl space.

Some manufacturers stamp their insulation with an "R" value. A high "R" value means thicker, better insulation. For electrical heating, use an "R" value of 19 in ceilings, 11 in walls, and 13 in floors as a minimum.

In the colder climates, more insulation is desirable, particularly in ceilings. In new construction, be sure to insulate around the perimeter of concrete slab floors on grade.

Vapor barriers are essential in most areas of the country; otherwise, moisture passing through the construction from inside to outside may condense; that reduces insulative value and eventually causes the insulation and structure to deteriorate.

Some insulation batts and blankets are made with vapor barriers, but it is almost impossible to seal all joints. Place an additional barrier between the inside finish and the insulation. Use polyethylene film, metal foil, or duplex kraft paper with asphalt between laminations.

Seal all joints, even around light switches and electrical outlets, with special tape.

Some paints on interior surfaces are fairly effective. Two or three coats of alkyd gloss, semigloss primer-sealer plus enamel, or rubber-resin lacquer paint are needed.

Cover the ground of a crawl space with heavy plastic film, roll roofing, or other vaporproof material to reduce transfer of moisture from the ground to the wood floor above. Asphalt-saturated building felt is not effective.

You should also weatherstrip windows and doors and calk cracks between the frames and the siding or masonry walls to reduce air leakage.

Flexible weatherstripping of felt, rubber, or plastic may be easier to install on doors than interlocking metal or spring metal friction types but may need replacing oftener.

Storm windows and doors are essential in cold climates. For example, about 14 times as much heat goes through a single pane of glass per square foot as a wood frame wall with 3 inches of insulation.

Thus, if the house has large areas of glass, the total heat loss is high even with insulated walls unless the loss is reduced by use of storm windows or double-pane insulating glass.

You feel colder, too, with the single thickness of glass, because the body radiates heat to the cold glass surface.

Glass storm windows present problems of breakage and of storage in summer. Storm windows of plastic film are cheaper and light in weight, but the plastic has limited life. They must be handled carefully to avoid puncturing.

Storm windows must fit tightly. If they leak air, you lose the effectiveness of the dead-air space formed between the windows.

HUMIDITY CONTROL in the house is difficult.

The average person is comfortable if temperatures are within 73° to 77° F., and the relative humidity is between 25 and 60 percent.

Because high humidities may cause condensation on windows and sometimes cold walls in winter, humidity of less than 40 percent is desirable.

Exhaust fans operated occasionally in the bathroom, kitchen, and laundry room help remove moisture.

Condensation can be reduced if the heating system is designed so that warm air sweeps over window areas. Tight storm windows help solve the problem.

Electrically driven dehumidifiers are helpful in winter and summer if the humidity is too high. They reduce mildew and dampness during summer, especially in basements where moisture tends to condense on the cooler walls and floors.

Keep windows closed when dehumidifiers are operating.

If the humidity is not high enough in winter, use a humidifier in the furnace if you have a warm-air heating system.

Some humidifiers have absorptive plates that extend into the airstream from the humidifier water pan. The plates need replacing occasionally. The mechanical atomizing type of humidifer is better but is more expensive.

Vapor barriers in the construction and tight doors and windows will help retain moisture in the house. (JOSEPH W. SIMONS)

For further reading:
Benz, Raymond C., *Insulate for Comfort*. University of Arkansas, Circular No. 513, 1962.
U.S. Department of Agriculture, *Electric House Heating*. REA Bulletin 142–1, 1960.
———— *Your Farmhouse—Heating*. Miscellaneous Publication No. 689, 1962.
Witz, R. L., French, E. W., and Guest, R. W., *Comparison of Methods of House Heating*. North Dakota Agricultural Experiment Station, ASAE Paper No. 59–918, Fargo, 1959.

Cooling the House

SOME TIPS that will help you keep your house cooler in summer:

Orient the house (if you are building) with its long axis east and west if possible. If you do not plan to have mechanical air conditioning, make certain of good cross-ventilation and orient the house to take advantage of prevailing breezes. Arrange shrubs and hedges so they will not shut off the breezes.

Avoid large glass areas in east and west walls, where they are harder to protect against sun.

Shade the south windows with wide eaves or overhangs.

Shade the house with deciduous trees and shrubs (which lose their leaves) and let in sunshine during the winter.

Use awnings over the windows or louvered bar screens if it is not feasible to have trees or overhangs for shade.

Use light-colored roofing materials, light paint on exterior walls, and light-colored shades and draperies or curtains.

Insulate the house if it is not already insulated. Use the same thicknesses of insulation for cooling as for heating.

High-pitched roofs are cooler than low-pitched ones.

Avoid large paved areas next to the house because they may reflect the sunrays into the house.

WINDOW OR ATTIC FANS may be used where nighttime temperatures drop sufficiently to cool the house.

One air change in the house each minute is needed in most places. Use a 36-inch-diameter attic fan for a house with about 7,500 cubic feet of volume and a 42-inch fan for 11 thousand cubic feet of volume. In the Northern States and along the west coast, about two-thirds as much air is needed.

Operate the fan part or all of the night, depending on how cool you wish the house to be. Then close the windows early in the morning. If your house is well insulated and shaded, it will remain fairly comfortable most of the day.

Fans cost less than mechanical air conditioning, but may bring in dust, pollen, and dampness.

IF YOU HAVE a good supply of cold well water (60° F. or cooler), it can be pumped through coils and the cool air blown into the house. Commercial units are not available, but the equipment can be assembled from components. From 360 to 540 gallons of water per hour is required for cooling a house of ordinary size. The waste water can be used to irrigate the lawn or garden or for livestock.

Evaporative cooling is fairly successful most of the summer in hot, dry regions. Relatively inexpensive commercial packaged units draw air through wet excelsior or other good water-absorptive material and discharge the cooled air into the house. These units usually provide 20 to 40 air changes an hour. From 5 to 10 gallons of water per hour are used for a house of average size.

AIR CONDITIONING by mechanical refrigeration is the only certain method of obtaining uniformly comfortable conditions in summer in places.

The air is cooled and moisture is removed, so that the lower humidity provides greater comfort, especially in humid climates. A dehumidifier may be needed sometimes to help reduce the humidity. With the house closed, less dust and pollen enter.

The aged, those with heart ailments, babies, and persons affected by dust and pollen often are helped by this type of air conditioning. Less noise from the outside may be an additional benefit.

Houses should be insulated, relatively tight, and protected against the sun as much as possible to obtain effective, economical cooling.

ROOM AIR CONDITIONERS mounted in windows are generally less expensive than central systems but provide less uniform temperatures. They are noisier than well-designed central systems and shut out some light from the windows in which they are installed. Part of the house can be air conditioned initially and additional units added as funds permit.

Conditioners of small capacity operate on 115 volts, but larger ones require 208 or 230 volts; you therefore may need additional wiring.

Shade the units on the outside to protect from direct sun heat if possible.

The reverse-cycle or heat pump types of air conditioners, either room units or central systems, heat in winter and cool in summer. They are more expensive than conditioners that cool only. Auxiliary electrical resistance heating is needed in all but the warmer climates.

CENTRAL AIR-COOLING units can be installed in some hot air systems and thus utilize the same ducts for distributing cool air through the house. The ducts must be insulated.

Hot air systems with small delivery ducts, such as 3-inch diameter, are not fully satisfactory for air conditioning. The higher air velocities required for cooling need more power and create undesirable noise.

New forced-air-cooling systems may be installed in the basement, hung from the ceiling in central halls where the ceiling heights permit, or placed in the attic.

Existing hot water systems with upright forced-air convectors in the rooms may be adapted for cooling by adding a chiller to cool the water pumped through the system.

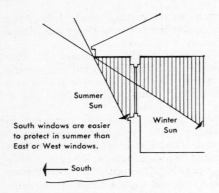

Roof overhang keeps out summer sun and lets in winter sun.

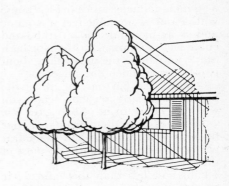

Shade from trees and large shrubs help keep house cool.   Use trees that lose leaves in winter to let sun in.

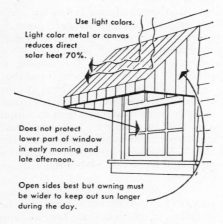

Awnings help keep house cool.

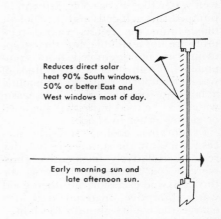

Louver or bar screens help keep out heat from sun.

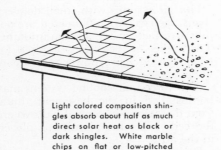

Light colors on roofs and walls reflect heat from the sun.

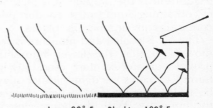

Large paved areas adjacent to house absorb and reflect sun's heat into house.

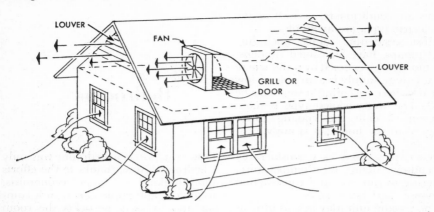

One method of installing an attic fan. Gable louvers or other openings must be large enough to let air escape from attic.

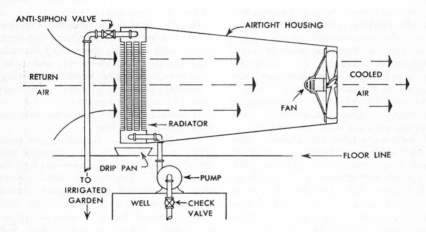

Coolers using well water may be built from commercially available parts. Some sheet metal duct-work may be necessary.

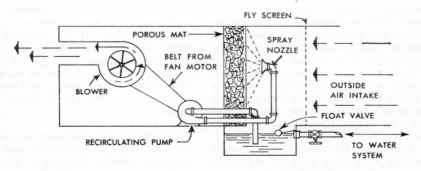

Evaporative coolers may be purchased for use in hot, dry climates.

Gas air conditioners, as well as the all-electric type, are available.

Most residential units, including heat pumps, have air-cooled condensers, but some are cooled by water where an adequate supply is available at low cost or where a cooling tower may be used. The water-cooled type is more efficient. Locate the cooling tower away from the house; it is noisy.

INSTALLATION COSTS vary considerably depending upon the temperature, exposure to sun, size and construction of house, and labor rates.

The cooling unit may add as little as 500 to 600 dollars to the cost of a new house if it is included in the heating system.

A central system installed separately from the heating system in an existing house may cost as much as 400 to 500 dollars per ton of refrigeration (a ton of refrigeration equals 12 thousand B.t.u.'s per hour—most units are now specified in B.t.u. capacity).

The cost should be less if installed in an existing heating system where ducts or piping can be used for cooling.

In sections where the outside temperature seldom exceeds 95°, a rule-of-thumb requirement is 1 ton for each 600 square feet of floor area in an insulated house and 400 square feet in an uninsulated house. If the temperature may exceed 100°, the capacity should be increased at least 15 percent.

Operating costs for mechanical air conditioning vary greatly because of many factors involved. With low electricity rates, a good average for warm climates might be 30 dollars per ton of refrigeration per season when uniform temperatures are maintained throughout the season.

Central air-conditioning equipment should meet standards established by the Air Conditioning & Refrigeration Institute. Consult your local power supplier about the wiring you may need.

The Better Business Bureau in your locality can refer you to reputable dealers. (JOSEPH W. SIMONS)

Bedrooms

TIME WAS WHEN a bedroom was only a bedroom. Now, thanks to the efforts and thinking of home economists, architects, and homemakers, it is coming into its own, as befits the room where we start and end each day, spend a third of our time, keep our personal possessions, and find a haven of rest and privacy.

In the bedroom, greater convenience comes from designing separate areas with enough space and furnishings for sleeping, dressing, and other activities—studying, reading, writing, lounging, sewing, hobbies—that may take place in the bedroom.

If space is limited, plans for sleeping and dressing are first.

For sleeping and napping you need a bed or beds that are comfortable and large enough; a surface or storage for articles near the bed; a light source over or near the bed for each person for reading or emergencies; some control of natural light, as with draperies or blinds; adequate ventilation; and quietness. The room should be away from noisy areas or insulated against noise.

For dressing and undressing you need space to stand, stretch, turn, bend; a mirror to see yourself full length; seating for putting on shoes and hose; clothes storage facilities grouped for each person; a dressing table with storage and a well-lighted mirror, and adequate artificial and natural lighting.

THE NUMBER of occupants, the number and types of activities, and the furniture needed determine the size of the bedroom.

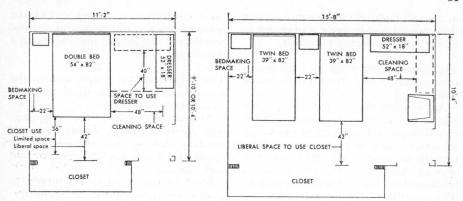

Two floor plans of bedrooms that show space recommendations for specific activities and the relationship of the space to items of bedroom furniture.

A guide to size: Very small, 80 to 110 square feet, one bed; small, 120 square feet, the minimum for twin beds; medium, 140 square feet; large, 190 square feet or more.

Some suggestions about arrangement:

Group the furniture by activities, as sleeping, dressing, and study.

Place the bed for good air circulation but away from drafts, street lights, and morning sunshine.

Locate the dressing area near the bedroom entrance or bathroom.

Keep traffic lanes open, short, and direct.

Place the dresser so that adequate light falls on the person dressing and not on the mirror.

Place the large pieces of furniture and rugs parallel to the walls of the room.

Place the writing unit to provide enough light, free from glare.

IF YOU LIVE to be 75 and sleep 8 hours a day, you will spend about 25 years of your life sleeping or resting. The foundation for restful sleep is a comfortable bed.

Each sleeper needs at least 38 inches of bed width and a bed length 9 inches longer than he is. A standard double bed is 54 inches wide by 74 inches long; that width, divided equally, allows each bedmate only 27 inches— the width of a baby's crib. A person more than 5 feet 5 inches tall finds the standard length too short for comfort.

Oversize beds and twin beds on swingaway frames attached to a king-size headboard are becoming popular. The larger bed does not necessitate a larger bedroom. A bed 70 by 80 inches

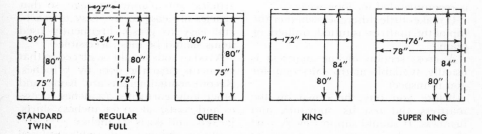

Mattress sizes.

in a small bedroom allows more space than separate twin beds. Coverings to fit the larger sizes are available.

THE THREE BASIC mattresses are innerspring, solid, and latex or urethane foam.

An innerspring mattress may have 180 to 850 or more coiled springs enclosed between two layers of insulating materials, such as sisal, and padding, usually of cotton. A large number of springs does not, however, insure a comfortable and durable mattress. The quality of steel and the shape and size of the coils used for the springs are more important than the number.

The borders of the mattress should be prebuilt or reinforced so that they will not sag or break down from sitting on the bed.

Solid filled mattresses may contain cotton, curled hair, kapok, or other material. These mattresses are not widely used in modern American bedrooms.

Foam mattresses are about half as heavy as innerspring mattresses. If they are of high density and 4 to 6 inches thick, they are equal to innersprings in comfort and durability.

A mattress of very soft foam or foam flakes should be avoided.

WHEN YOU SELECT a mattress, check for strong securely fastened handles; enough padding so that innersprings cannot be felt through the padding; ventilators on each side for air circulation; neat, firm stitching; and durable ticking.

Heavy 8-ounce ticking of twill weave is recommended for long wear.

It makes little difference whether the top of the mattress is tufted, quilted, or plain.

A cross section of the mattress is usually available at the salesroom for you to inspect.

Before you buy, lie down on the mattress and test its buoyancy and firmness. It should support every part of your body equally and not sag at points of greatest weight. If you prefer,

ask the salesman to stretch out on the mattress; then stand back and observe carefully if sagging occurs. Buy from a reputable dealer.

THE BEDSPRING, the foundation for the mattress, provides one-third or more of the total resilience.

At least 90 percent of the bedsprings sold are box springs. These consist of securely tied springs, mounted on a wood base frame, padded, and covered with ticking.

Most of the criteria that apply to mattresses apply also to bedsprings.

A headboard is not essential but has certain advantages. It protects the wall, holds the bed in place, and holds the mattress firm.

A CHEST of drawers provides space for folded articles and other personal possessions. Look for sturdy construction, dustproof drawers that are smoothly finished and slide easily, and handles that are easy to grasp.

Chests are available with special storage features, whose usefulness and flexibility you should evaluate in relation to their cost.

Most homemakers feel a need for more storage space in bedrooms than they have. A further need may be for making better use of available space.

Every closet should have enough space for the wardrobe of the person or persons occupying the room (3 to 5 linear feet for each person); a depth of 24 to 30 inches; doors that open almost the entire length and height of the closet for convenience in reaching articles; and planned storage, so that articles are easy to see, easy to reach, and easy to grasp. Frequently used items should be most accessible.

A rod or rods should be placed so that garments clear the floor by 6 inches. Recommended heights are: Robes and other long garments, 72 inches; dresses and coats, 58 to 63 inches; shirts, jackets, and skirts, 45 inches.

Shelves should be adjustable or placed to meet varying storage needs. Dis-

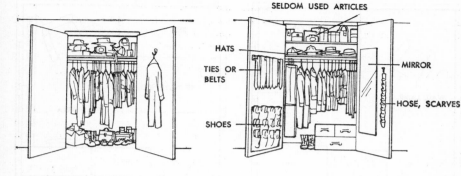

TYPICAL USE OF CLOSET   PLANNED USE OF CLOSET

tances recommended between shelves are 7 inches for shoes and 8 to 10 inches for hats.

Closets should have good light and the possibility of airing.

Of the two general types of closets, walk-in and reach-in, the reach-in closet is the more popular and economical use of space.

A single-hung door is economical and satisfactory for a walk-in closet. The back of it can be utilized for hooks, racks, mirrors, shelves. Such a door limits accessibility of a reach-in closet—a serious handicap if the closet is more than a foot longer than door width. Space must be allowed for the door to swing.

Double swinging doors permit good accessibility if they are the width of closet. Their backs can be utilized. Their disadvantages are that they need space to swing, and the storage of heavy items on them may cause the doors to sag.

Sliding doors require no floorspace for swing, but only half of the closet is accessible at one time. They may warp or stick. Their backs cannot be utilized.

Accordion-folding doors require no swing space, give good accessibility, and occupy a small part of door space when they are open. They occupy an inch or two of closet depth when they are open, however; the door back cannot be utilized; and a poor track mech-

anism may cause difficulty in opening and closing them.

Bifold doors give good accessibility and require little floorspace for doors to open. Their sliding mechanism may stick and require frequent adjustment. Door backs cannot be utilized.

GENERAL LIGHTING for the bedroom may be provided by ceiling fixtures or structural lighting, or both.

Ceiling fixtures should be large enough (15 to 17 inches in diameter for a small room or one of average size). The shielding material should diffuse light evenly so that "hot spots" are avoided. The low ceilings in to-day's houses suggest shallow fixtures with three to five lamp bulbs mounted horizontally. Fixtures mounted flush with the ceiling or inset do not collect dust and insects.

Structural lighting, in the form of valances, cornices, or wall brackets, may be used with ceiling fixtures or instead of ceiling fixtures. A cornice across a closet wall provides light within the closet and general light.

Wall switches controlling general lighting should be installed on the latch side of the door. Also desirable is an additional switch within reach of the bed or a master control switch near the bed to control selected lights inside and outside the house.

Light for reading in bed may be provided by table lamps, ceiling-

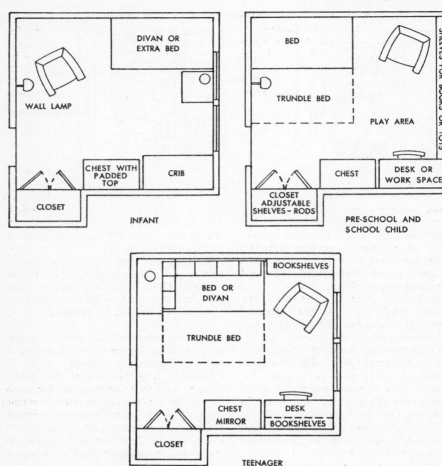

Three floor layouts show how a child's room 11 feet by 12 feet can be adapted to meet his needs at different ages—infant; preschool, and school-age child; teenager.

mounted adjustable fixtures, wall lamps, or wall brackets.

If a double bed is used, provide a light for each person.

For makeup, light is needed on both sides of the face at face height whether sitting or standing. Two lamps or two wall-mounted fixtures are good. Fixture shields or lampshades should be white or off-white and translucent, so that maximum light falls on the face.

If you read, write, study, or sew in the bedroom, you should have adequate lighting for each.

How to provide for all the bedroom activities of children and at the same time provide for their changing needs is quite a problem.

Some people maintain that children's bedrooms should be equipped with inexpensive child-size furniture, which will be replaced. Others believe the furnishings should be flexible enough in use and permanent enough to survive the growing and changing years.

Probably the best solution is a combination of the two, since the requirements for furnishings are different at each stage of a child's development.

The nursery should be near the master bedroom. A crib, chest, and dressing equipment are necessary. A chair for the mother is desirable. A work surface of convenient height for bathing and changing the baby may be improvised by padding the top of a chest.

Any surfaces accessible to chewing babies should be treated with lead-free paint. The furniture should be free from sharp edges and other safety hazards.

A night light is a convenience in checking on the child without disturbing him.

At the preschool age, the child outgrows the crib. The new bed may be one that will last him until adulthood. At this age, the child is exploring spaces and shapes. He needs free floor-space for play and open shelves so that he can reach his toys easily. A child-size table and chair provide space for games, puzzles, and crayons.

A rug protects the child from a cold floor.

Wall- or ceiling-mounted lights reduce the safety hazard of breakable lamps and trailing cords.

The rod in the closet should be low enough for the child to hang up his own clothes. Grooves should be provided for raising the rod as the child grows.

All surfaces should be of materials that can be cleaned easily.

The child of school age needs a table or desk with good light for study. Toy shelves continue to be useful and often become places to keep hobby materials and collections.

WHEN TWO CHILDREN share a room, each needs an area for his own interests and privacy. Children enjoy having friends visit them, and the school-age child's room needs some provision for overnight guests.

The teenager's room should allow for individual expression. Some teenagers want a bedroom that looks like a sitting room. At this age, grooming assumes greater importance, and a girl should have a dresser or dressing table with mirror, storage, and adequate lighting.

A teenage boy also needs a well-lighted mirror and places to store his clothing and books and to display or work on hobbies.

The bedroom has an important function. It is a private and rest area where you find a retreat for self-expression without infringing upon others. Its character may take any direction that suits you as long as it meets your needs. (SAVANNAH S. DAY AND REBECCA F. WAGONER)

Living Rooms

THE LIVING ROOMS of many families accommodate combinations of activities, like living-play, living-music, living-study, living-dining, and living-guest sleeping.

It is a family room, and it calls for well-chosen furnishings and backgrounds for them, easy-to-maintain surfaces, adequate size, provision for storage, utilities, and a convenient location.

As to location: The main entrance to the house should give easy access to the living room. It should have some parking space nearby. For guests, it should be the most easily reached entrance from the parking place. This main entrance should be separated when possible from the main living area, however.

DOORS LEADING to the living room should be placed so that the room does not become merely a passageway across furniture groupings. Doors placed on the short side or at corners

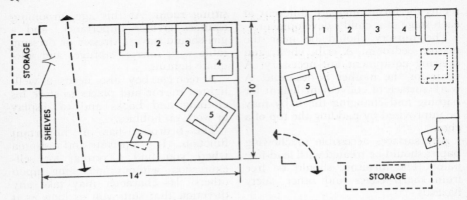

Placement of doors controls traffic through living area.

near such a sidewall help control the traffic through the living space.

Social routing into a residence usually is first to a reception room, the foyer; a cloakroom, the closet for wraps; the major social places for groups; to the minor social areas for hobbies or small group activities; to the dining or serving room; and sometimes to the bathroom or powder room for guests.

This movement of family and guests should be separated from sleeping and study rooms. In practical design, it seldom can be entirely separate, but hallways, rows of closets, different floor levels, and the like are features that achieve such separations.

AT LEAST 144 square feet is recommended for a living room. A square room, 12 feet by 12 feet, is more flexible than a room 10 feet by 14 feet 6 inches.

Any dimension less than 10 feet is not desirable, because furniture cannot be placed suitably for conversation and games.

Generally, however, a rectangular space has a more pleasing proportion than a square one. For a living room of liberal size with minimum furniture, 196 square feet is recommended. A dimension of 14 feet for the shorter room wall accommodates six persons in various group and individual leisure-time pursuits.

Liberal storage space for supplies used in the living area—card tables, folding chairs, records, books, games, cards, and the like—can be provided in a space about 8 feet long, 2 feet deep, and 6 feet 6 inches high.

Coat closets should be 2 feet 6 inches deep in the clear. Rods should be 2.5 inches below a shelf, if there is one, and high enough so that coats miss the floor by at least 6 inches. Dress wraps for a family of four require a rod 2 feet 2 inches long. Additional rod length of 2 to 3 feet should be added for hanging guests' wraps.

Space allowances need to be added to the floorspace I have mentioned for features such as fireplaces, built-in cabinets for television sets and record players, and pianos.

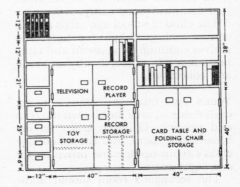

Suggested storage facility in living areas for leisure activities.

Regular and decorative fireplaces take 3 to 18 square feet of additional floor area.

Upright and grand pianos usually need 9 square feet (spinet) to 28 square feet (parlor grand), plus a seating allowance of 6 square feet.

FURNITURE ARRANGEMENTS should be planned with this in mind:

For television viewing: A distance of at least 1 foot from the screen for each inch of screen size over 7 inches; for example, for a 19-inch screen, allow a viewing distance of 12 feet. Provide seating within a 120-degree angle for screen viewing.

For four persons seated around a card table: 10 feet by 10 feet to walk past four persons seated in armless chairs, as in serving at a card table.

For viewing projected images (2 by 2 slides): At a 40-inch screen—11 feet minimum distance from the projector; at a 60-inch screen—17 feet minimum distance from the projector.

For conversational groups: Chairs for four to six persons, utilizing about 10 feet by 10 feet. Place chairs and tables close enough so that a seated person can reach a table.

For bookcases: Clearance of 36 inches in front of shelves at floor level.

It is good to make a floor plan to scale and try out various arrangements for furniture. Consider space requirements and location in relation to swing of doors, views, and such structural details as fireplaces and alcoves.

Enough space is needed so that every person who uses the living room is comfortable. A person seated in a chair uses 30 inches of free space in front of the chair. A person walking behind a chair or beside a piece of furniture will use 16 inches when he edges past and 24 inches when he walks past a seated person. You use only 22 inches seated at a desk, but 36 inches in the clear for space to use the desk, arise, and be seated.

ADEQUATE DAYLIGHT in the living room may be had by allowing space for windows equal to about one-fourth of the floor area.

The sun is the primary source of light for daytime. Its light is scattered in its passage through the atmosphere and thereby creates a secondary source, the sky.

The relative amount of outside illumination depends on the position of the sun as well as the atmospheric conditions.

The amount of daylight in living rooms also is affected by the placement of glass areas, the finishes of walls and ceilings, and the draperies, curtains, and shades at windows. In general, the upper half of a window admits diffused light from the sky; the lower half, from the ground and nearby shrubbery, which are much darker than the sky.

It is well to group windows in the living room so as to have a naturally lighted expanse, which reduces spotty interior effects, and to have an unbroken background for furniture. Concentrating the windows makes it simpler to use decorative fabrics on the walls.

FOR ARTIFICIAL LIGHT, indirect or semidirect light sources should be selected to provide general illumination. One light source in the living room should be operated by a wall switch on the latch side of the main entrance door.

Multiple switches are convenient if doors are more than 10 feet apart. An exterior light should be controlled by a switch inside the entrance.

Wall switches normally are mounted 48 inches above the floor.

Totally direct light might be chosen for decorative accent, as on a painting, a planter, or a piece of sculpture. A shield may be needed to keep direct glare from the viewer's eyes.

Lights in cornices, valances, and shielded wall brackets provide good general light in living rooms. They can be used to balance daylight in a large room.

Pleasing effects can be created by

Lighting for large wall areas using recessed ceiling fixtures.

using recessed down lights to wash entire walls. They are placed in the ceiling 1 foot from the wall and mounted 3 to 4 feet on center. The source of light needs to be correctly placed to eliminate glare and to produce a maximum amount of diffused brightness.

Furniture arrangements and installed utilities will determine where appliance outlets need to be placed.

Along continuous walls, duplex receptacles should be placed no farther apart than 12 feet, and wall space between doors should have a duplex receptacle if the wall length is 3 feet or more. Special outlets for television, room air conditioners, and clocks also may be needed. Dimmer switches give flexibility for decorative lighting. Floodlights in the ceiling may be installed to light music at the piano. Recessed light in ceiling cavities can be chosen above davenports or other furniture groups.

Portable lamps permit flexibility in the amount and the location of supplemental light. The light from lamps should be diffused for reading and study. White, eggshell, or ivory shades give the maximum light. All shades should have a white lining. All light sources should be shielded to avoid direct glare. The socket base should be 45 inches to 48 inches above the floor.

The Illuminating Engineering Society has recommended these levels of illumination: For general lighting, 10 foot-candles (entrances, hallways, stairways and landings, living room, family room, sunroom, and recreation room); for reading books, magazines, newspapers, 30 ft.-c.; for reading handwriting, 70 ft.-c.; for reading music scores, 30 to 70 ft.-c.; for study desks, 70 ft.-c.; for sewing, 30 to 50 ft.-c.; for table games, 30 ft.-c.

WOOD finishes, which emphasize the natural pattern and color of wood in walls, floors, and furniture have become popular. Smooth, dull surfaces usually are chosen for wall finishes.

Wood trim around doors, windows, and arches usually is finished in nearly the same value and hue as the walls. Ceilings are usually lighter—white, off-white, or a tint of the wall color.

Besides floors of wood, we have floors of resilient materials, such as linoleum and vinyl sheet goods or tiles. In addition, decorative floor treatments may be wall-to-wall carpets and rugs.

Large surfaces of one color in muted hues make small spaces appear larger. In general, we can say that pleasing effects in interior design can be achieved by repetition of a basic color.

Harmony in color can be had by adding two or more different colors in lesser amounts than the background color. In achieving color balance, bright colors are used in lesser amounts than the dominant background hue. Pictures or patterned textiles often can be used to tie together a color scheme for a living room.

THE PLACEMENT of hot-air registers and return ducts in the living room needs special attention.

Narrow openings in floors and baseboard and overhead openings for warm air are more desirable for living rooms than are large, nearly square floor openings.

Most of the specifications call for bathing the outside walls with warm air and maintaining a difference of not more than 4 degrees in the temperature at floor and ceiling. Cold-air returns need to be left free of low furniture to be satisfactory.

Curtain and drapery panels should not cover the outlets for air.

Windows and exterior doors should be weatherstripped. Ideally, fixed glass areas should be double glazed. An even temperature at sitting and floor level is especially desirable in the living area. (JESSIE J. MIZE)

Bathrooms

WHEN YOU PLAN the bathroom, it is wise to consider your present family needs and anticipate future needs.

The amount of money you can spend, whether you are building a new bathroom or remodeling an existing one, may determine the results.

Give attention to every detail of location, arrangement of fixtures, storage, lighting, and safety.

The bathroom, if there is only one in the house, should open into a hallway that makes it easily accessible to all rooms. Its entrance should not be visible from the front door or the living room. It should be placed so that children in daytime can reach it from the back door without going through other rooms.

If there are two bathrooms or an extra half-bath or lavatory, an economical plumbing layout is to have them back to back or, in a two-story plan, one bath may be directly over the first-floor bathroom.

A GOOD ARRANGEMENT within a bathroom also is important.

We usually think of bathrooms with three fixtures—lavatory, bathtub, and watercloset.

Compartmented or divided bathrooms can provide privacy for two or more persons at the same time and require less space than two rooms. The lavatory may be placed in one compartment with the tub and watercloset in the other.

When space is lacking for two baths, it may be possible to use one tub to serve two bathrooms, or the bathroom may be divided into a series of separate rooms—one for the watercloset, one for bathing facilities, and the remaining space for dressing and grooming.

The simplest and least expensive bathroom arrangement is one with all fixtures and plumbing pipes on one wall.

Greater convenience and better appearance may sometimes be achieved, however, by having fixtures on two or more walls and may sometimes offset the additional cost of piping. A washbowl placed near the window will have good light. It may be unwise to put the tub under a window because of drafts and because the window is difficult to open and close.

Leave enough floorspace around fixtures for comfortable use and accessibility. Space allowances around fixtures are shown in drawings on the next page.

The figures take into account the use and cleaning of bathrooms and provide slightly more space than the standards generally used.

Note that for a lavatory that is placed next to a wall, we allow 18 to 20 inches between the center of the lavatory and the wall to allow for the arm movements required for shaving and grooming.

The size, color, material, and style of bathroom fixtures affect their cost. It is wise planning to buy the best fixtures you can afford.

Vitreous china is used for waterclosets and many types of lavatories.

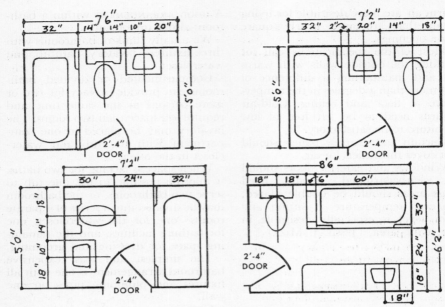

Minimum bathrooms.

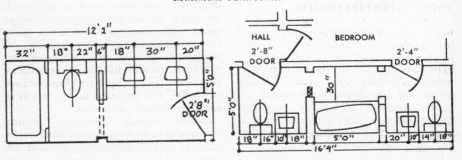

Compartmented bathrooms.

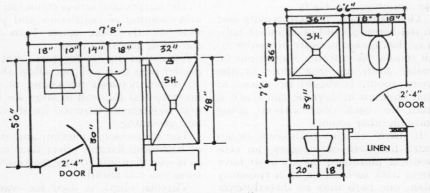

Bathrooms with shower stalls.

Porcelain-enameled cast iron and pressed steel are cheaper and can be used for tubs and lavatories. Stainless steel is used for washbasins designed for built-in installation. Reinforced plastic also is used for lavatories, tubs, and shower stalls.

Washbasins can be purchased with round, oval, square, triangular, rectangular, and D-shaped bowls. Some models are made to be hung on the wall with special brackets or hangers. Others are intended to be installed in a countertop. Legs of china or metal can be added to some designs for extra support. Corner basins are available for use in small rooms.

Install the basin at a height—say, 33 to 36 inches from floor to rim—that is convenient for adults.

THREE GENERAL TYPES of water-closets—toilets—are manufactured for home use—the siphon jet, reverse trap, and the washdown.

The siphon jet, the most efficient, has a quick and relatively quiet flushing action. The trapway is at the rear of the bowl, and the water surface is extra large.

Reverse trap bowls are like the siphon jet but have smaller water surface and trapway. Less water is required to operate them.

The washdown, the simplest in construction, is the noisiest. Its trapway is in the front of the bowl.

The standard waterclosets stand on the floor. Wall-mounted fixtures are neat, and it is easy to clean around and under them. They require special hangers or carriers.

RECTANGULAR BATHTUBS, for recessed or corner installation, usually are 4.5, 5, or 5.5 feet long and 29 to 32 inches wide. The 5-foot tub is the one most generally used.

Square bathtubs also are available. The smaller receptor type adapts well to a tub-shower combination where space is limited. The height of receptor tubs is about 12 inches. Other tubs are 13.5 to 16 inches high.

A shower head over the tub is the most economical way to add a shower. If the fittings are installed at the time the bathroom is built, the pipes for the shower can be concealed in the wall. Shower heads usually are made of chrome-plated brass with swivel joints for directing the spray. The shower head usually is 6 feet 2 inches from the floor.

The rod for a shower curtain should be at a height of 6 feet 6 inches.

Shower stalls can be built on the job or bought in prefabricated form. Factory-built units of porcelain-enameled steel or reinforced plastic are the easiest and quickest to install. They range in floor size from 30 by 30 inches to 36 by 36 inches to 34 by 48 inches.

PROVIDE FOR PLENTY of storage space for bathroom linens, toiletries, cosmetics, and other items.

Cabinets for medicines and toilet articles usually are mounted above the lavatory. They have sliding or hinged doors, may have built-in lighting fixtures and outlets, and come in different sizes.

For medicines and other items that should be kept away from children and half-asleep adults, it is wise to have a separate cabinet or a compartment within the cabinet that can be locked.

A convenient height for the cabinet is 69 to 74 inches from the top of the mirror to the floor.

Two shelves 12 inches deep and 18 inches wide, with between-shelf clearance of 12 inches, are adequate for storing 12 bath towels and 12 washcloths.

A hamper for soiled clothing is a convenience.

Space for storing linens and bathroom supplies can be had even in a small bathroom. Two likely places are under the lavatory and over the watercloset. Leave at least 12 inches between the top of the tank and a cabinet hung above it, to give access to the tank when it needs repairs.

Adequate light, properly placed, is essential. For shaving and makeup, light should shine on the face and not on the mirror. A ceiling fixture above the front edge of the lavatory and one light on each side of the mirror will illuminate the face without shadows. The side lights should be 30 inches apart.

Select light fixtures for bathrooms with white diffusers. Use white bulbs or shades, because tinted ones distort colors.

One fixture usually is adequate in a small bathroom. In large bathrooms, general illumination and area lights are needed.

One way to distribute light evenly is a luminous ceiling. These plastic-paneled ceilings can be installed in existing bathrooms.

Remember to install a grounded outlet at the lavatory, at a convenient height for electrical appliances that may be used there.

Ventilation must be provided for all bathrooms. Fans are often used. Most automatic bathroom fans operate at only one speed, but some have as many as five.

For small bathrooms, exhaust fans combined with heater and lights are a good choice. They can be installed with one switch, but separate switches are preferred if such an installation is permitted by codes and ordinances.

One may get a dangerous shock while operating an electric switch if he touches water and metal at the same time. Make certain that light and ventilating fan switches are out of reach of anyone in the bathtub or shower or anyone using a water faucet.

Lights with pull cords are dangerous and should not be used in bathrooms.

BATHROOMS used by the handicapped and the elderly need extra consideration. Safety, convenience, and ease of maintenance should not be forgotten.

Doorways may need to be wide enough to accommodate a wheelchair or crutches.

The door locks should be of the type that can be opened from either side.

Beware of slippery floors. Wall-to-wall carpeting with nonskid backing is preferable to scatter rugs.

Install grab bars in tubs and shower stalls in places easy to reach whether one is sitting or standing. They must be mounted securely to the studs—a grab bar that pulls away from the wall under a person's weight is worse than none at all.

Grab bars on each side of the water-closet make it easier for handicapped and elderly persons to sit down and rise safely.

Bathtub rubber mats, with suction cups, should be placed in the bottom of the tub to prevent slipping while sitting or standing.

Night lights add to safety. (GENEVIEVE K. TAYLOE)

The Kitchen

YOUR KITCHEN is your workshop, office, and studio. At times it is also a place for eating and recreation.

My advice is: Make the most of it; make it attractive and efficient and the way you want it to be.

As to efficiency, think of your kitchen as having four work centers—places to mix and serve and the range and sink—each of which has its equipment, appliances, counter, and storage space for the supplies and utensils.

The mix (or food preparation) center is most convenient if it is between two pieces of major equipment—sink and range, range and refrigerator, or refrigerator and sink. The counter, 24 inches deep, should be 36 to 42 inches wide unless it extends into a corner; then 24 to 36 inches of frontage is enough.

You may wish to provide under-counter knee space so you can sit comfortably to work. You can store an adjustable posture stool, if it has a folddown back, in this space.

A pullout cutting board that is adjustable to 26-, 30-, and 34-inch heights would provide a lower, more comfortable surface for certain mixing jobs and serve as a snack counter for children.

Stored at the mix center should be all the spices, flavorings, flour, sugar, measuring equipment, bowls, mixer, and baking pans you use there.

An efficient range center, convenient to sink and mix counter, includes a freestanding or built-in range or built-in surface cooking units and wall oven. Provide counters 12 to 24 inches wide on both sides of the surface cooking area and to one side of built-in ovens. These surfaces should withstand the heat of utensils taken directly off the range or out of the oven.

To insure enough elbowroom, avoid placing major cooking appliances in a cramped corner. Allow at least 16 inches between the center of the nearest front cooking unit and a wall or piece of high equipment, the same clearance as between the center front of a built-in oven and an adjoining wall. For space in which to stand, allow at least 14 inches between the center of a front cooking unit and a turn of the counter.

An electric wall oven should be installed so that the bottom of the interior is about 32 inches above the floor. The most frequently used rack positions are at about counter height, a comfortable lifting position for most women.

Likewise, place a gas oven so the broiler rack is about 28 inches from the floor and the lowest oven rack is at 37 inches.

Serving dishes, platters, trays, uncooked cereals, seasonings, pans, and small utensils used at the range should be stored at this center.

THE SINK probably is the most continuously busy work center of the kitchen.

A counter 24 to 36 inches wide to one side of the sink provides adequate space for stacking soiled dishes; 18 to 36 inches is needed to the other for draining clean ones.

Provide at least 14 inches of clearance between the center of the sink bowl and a turn of the counter for standing.

You may like a double-bowl sink, one side of which is a shallow bowl, about 3.5 inches deep, and has the drain and food waste disposer set back of center. This arrangement provides a convenient height and enough knee space so you can sit at the sink to work.

An undercounter dishwasher placed to the right or left of the sink or at right angles to it should be close to the dish storage cabinet as well as to the sink. A portable dishwasher may be stored elsewhere and rolled to the sink for use. A permanently installed dishwasher occupies 24 to 30 inches of valuable base-cabinet storage.

Soap, dishwashing supplies, and such foods as potatoes and onions should be stored here. Provide a place also for utensils for cleaning, cutting, and straining food, a can opener, paper towels, and clean and damp dish towels.

There should be a neat, convenient, and sanitary receptacle for trash at the sink center.

AT THE SERVE CENTER, close to both sink and dining areas, should be the items that go directly to the table, including dishes, glassware, tableware, linens, and accessories.

Ready-to-eat foods (like cookies, crackers, and dry cereals), and table appliances, including toaster, coffeemaker, and waffle iron, belong here.

A serving cart, especially if you have a place to store it, is a handy addition to any kitchen for serving and cleaning up.

THE AMOUNT of dining area you will need, whether it is in a dining room, dining L, family room, or the kitchen, is determined by the number of persons to be served; the size and pieces of furniture, including table, chairs, server, and cabinets; and clearances for passage and serving.

Allow 21 to 24 inches of table space for each adult. The smallest table at which eight adults can sit comfortably is 40 inches by 72 inches. The smallest for six adults is 36 inches by 60 inches. A round table 42 inches in diameter seats four, and one 48 inches in diameter accommodates six.

The space you need around the dining table depends somewhat on how you serve meals.

The minimum allowance between the edge of a freestanding table and a wall or piece of furniture is 32 inches. That much space is needed for a person to seat himself or rise from the table, but it does not give enough room for a person to pass behind occupied chairs to serve the meal or clear the table. Add 4 inches—making a total of 36—if you wish to allow for one person to edge past another seated at the table. Add 12 inches—a total of 44—for serving.

Built-in tables and benches in an alcove require less space than freestanding furniture but are less convenient for seating and serving. An arrangement with chairs on one side of the table and a built-in bench 22 inches deep on the other is preferable to one with two built-in benches.

A dining counter, 20 inches deep, may be considered for informal meals. The number you wish to serve should determine the length of your counter. To find the length, multiply 21 inches (the minimum width of each place setting) by the number to be seated.

A dining counter should be 30 inches high if chairs with seats 18 inches high are to be used. A depth of 20 inches should be allowed beneath this counter for legroom.

If stools 24 inches high will be used, your counter height must be 36 inches, with footrests 6 to 8 inches high. Knee space at least 14 inches deep should be allowed under this higher counter.

IN A LARGE kitchen you may wish to include a planning desk, food freezer, and laundry space.

Planning kitchen storage is worth while if it is done thoughtfully.

Tools, foods, supplies, and utensils used oftenest should be stored in drawers and bins and on adjustable sliding and revolving shelves and perforated hardboard at heights between 28 and 64 inches from the floor. Large, heavy, seldom-used items store best below this; small, lightweight pieces can go above.

The standard 12-inch deep wall cabinet holds all dinnerware except large serving pieces. They and small trays and baking pans may be stored neatly between vertical file partitions, which are slanted to accommodate their size or placed in a deeper cabinet—above a built-in oven, for example. Adjustable shelves are good.

Wall cabinets should be hung not more than 15 inches above the counter. Shallow cabinets that are 5 inches deep and have sliding doors may be installed under wall cabinets as convenient storage for small, often-used supplies and equipment.

Sliding shelves and pullout bins and drawers increase the usability of base cabinets and should be easy to pull, even when loaded. Bread, cake, and cookies may be stored in metal-lined drawers. Vegetables keep best in ventilated bins.

Special planning is necessary to utilize corner spaces in wall and base cabinets in the kitchen. One of the best ways is to install wall, base, or floor-to-ceiling cabinets with shelves that revolve individually or as a unit.

If base and wall cabinets are used as room dividers, the corner may be used from the adjoining dining area for linens, silver, and table appliances placed on sliding shelves and in drawers.

If you want a modern, built-in look, you will need to know the exact dimensions of appliances to be installed, so that the cabinets can be built or arranged to accommodate them.

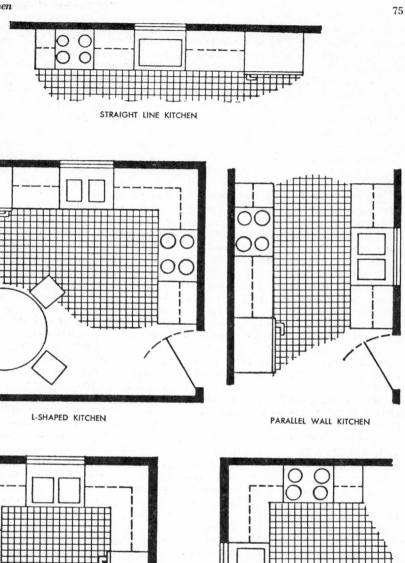

STRAIGHT LINE KITCHEN

L-SHAPED KITCHEN

PARALLEL WALL KITCHEN

U-SHAPED KITCHEN

BROKEN-U KITCHEN

Five basic kitchen arrangements.

If your cabinets are built by a cabinetmaker, they can be made to fit your space exactly without the use of filler strips.

Manufactured base cabinets in metal or wood come in widths from 9 to 48 inches on a 3-inch module. They are 36 inches high and 24 or 25 inches deep. The toe space at the bottom is 4 inches high.

Manufactured wall cabinets in widths and finishes to match the base cabinets are 12 or 13 inches deep and 15, 18, 25, 30, or 33 inches high. The doors should be no more than 12 inches wide, so they do not project dangerously beyond the front edge of the counter when they are opened.

The space between the top of the wall cabinets and ceiling may be enclosed so dust cannot accumulate there, or it can be used to store infrequently used items.

CERTAIN GENERALIZATIONS apply to almost all kitchens.

Allow 4 feet 6 inches to 5 feet 4 inches between facing counters and appliances—the space needed for two persons to work and pass each other.

Try to locate doors so that major traffic lanes do not go through the work area. A passageway at the end of an island or counter should be at least 3 feet 6 inches wide.

Refrigerators and wall ovens should be located at ends of a work counter, but preferably not so that their doors open into a doorway.

Provide 15 to 18 inches of counter space at the latch side of a refrigerator and at least 16 inches of clearance between the latch and a turn of the counter for standing.

The placement of doors, windows, and adjacent rooms puts most kitchens in one of five basic arrangements.

Straight-line arrangements fitted into alcoves or behind folding doors are suitable only for minimum kitchens. For work areas and storage to be adequate, these arrangements become too long to be efficient.

L-shaped kitchens tend to divert traffic out of the work area, provide a convenient location for dining or laundry, and have less walking distance between work centers than straight-line kitchens.

Although parallel-wall kitchens save steps between work areas, they often have doors at each end inviting traffic.

Well-planned U-shaped kitchens are compact, save steps, and are out of the way of traffic lanes. Special planning is needed, however, to make corner spaces in wall and base cabinets convenient for storage.

Broken-U kitchen arrangements frequently fit well into combination rooms such as kitchen-dining, kitchen-family, or kitchen-work rooms.

With these preliminary considerations in mind, put your plans on paper for your architect or builder.

If you are remodeling, you will need two plans, one showing your present kitchen and the other showing how it will be after doors, windows, and walls are moved, added, or eliminated and cabinets and appliances are installed.

Your plan should also indicate the locations of heating and air-conditioning units, lighting fixtures, electric outlets, and switches.

Measure your room accurately and draw its plan on squared paper. Use a scale in which one-fourth inch equals 1 foot. On your second plan, locate doors and windows and indicate the heights of window sills, the directions of door swings, and the height of the ceiling.

Work out the best arrangement of your kitchen, referring to the drawings of the basic arrangements for the correct way to show base and wall cabinets and appliances.

If you are planning a kitchen for a new home, all changes should be made on a tracing from the blueprint before construction begins. Detailed notes describing exactly what you desire in your kitchen will be of help to the architect or builder when he prepares the working drawings for the electrician, plumber, and carpenter.

Before a wiring contractor is consulted, sketch the locations of installed equipment and special-purpose outlets, lighting fixtures and wall switches, and convenience outlets for plug-in appliances.

One duplex convenience outlet for every 4 feet of counter is recommended, with a minimum of one outlet for each counter where portable appliances are likely to be used. Special-purpose outlets are located in places where appliances are permanently installed.

In addition to good, general, fluorescent or incandescent ceiling fixtures, area lighting is desirable at the sink and other work centers as well as at the dining table or counter. Fixtures beneath wall cabinets reduce annoying shadows on work surfaces.

This, the most expensive room in the home, is where the homemaker and family spend a considerable amount of time. Planning carefully for the kitchen you want takes time. It is time well spent. (CONSTANCE D. O'BRIEN)

A Place
To Play

CHILDREN NEED a place to play and to keep their playthings because play is vital to their development, it is an important part of their day, and a restful home atmosphere depends to some extent on orderliness.

Children who have an organized play area (with furnishings and materials grouped near free floorspace) tend to be attracted to it for most of their indoor play.

A room of his own for sleeping and playing is the ideal solution for any child and solves many management problems. It should provide a corner for play that is compact and well organized for toy storage, so that the rest of the room is relatively free for other activities.

The child should not be confined entirely to this space, but it will eliminate confusion in other parts of the house, develop his sense of ownership, and help him fit better into the household routine.

If the bedroom is small (9 by 11 feet) or if more than one child uses the room, play centers in other parts of the house are necessary.

The size of a house and the number and types of rooms determine the space available for play and for storage. It may be desirable to establish play places in an attic, basement, or a corner of the den, dining room, or living room.

Privacy is important. A child in his retreat does not interfere with the pursuits of others and needs fewer commands and warnings that tend to create a feeling of uncertainty and irritability and discourage creativity. Private and attractive playrooms help develop an ability to concentrate and encourage an appreciation of beauty.

Cross or through ventilation and abundant natural lighting should be provided by having two or more windows. For cloudy days and late afternoons, artificial lighting should be sufficient in height and indirectness to prevent eyestrain.

Since children play on the floor much of the time, floor surfaces should be durable, easy to clean, and not slippery. Floors overlaid with linoleum or cork are advisable.

Thirty-five square feet is adequate for one child; 50 square feet is needed for two or more in a major play center. Two or three feet here or there is not enough for a doll party or a fort made of blocks, and children naturally go to a room with more space.

THE PLAY EQUIPMENT—which should include some toys for physical activity, some to stimulate creativity, and some for imaginative play to foster a child's all-round development—should not be piled in a big box, stacked in a corner, or scattered through the house, lest a child become discouraged and frustrated when he tries to find a toy.

Open-shelf units are better for storing equipment than large boxes and chests.

The length of the shelves varies with the age, sex, and interests of children. For a preschooler, a shelf 12 inches deep will accommodate more kinds of toys, books, and games than a shelf 6 to 9 inches deep.

A shelf about 40 inches long, with a 15-inch clearance, is needed for trucks, dolls, and other long toys.

Shorter shelves (about 20 inches with a 10-inch clearance) are preferable for most items. On these may be placed shoe boxes, baskets, and bags for smaller items, such as dishes, small cars and trucks, toy animals and people, scissors, paste, crayons, and paper.

Other shelves may vary in length and height to accommodate things to be added later. Older children need deeper ones to accommodate scrapbooks, science kits, and various games.

The top of a low bookcase (about 28 inches high) provides a surface where airports, dollhouses, or farms can be left. A back on the bookcase keeps items from falling behind it, and an edge on the top shelf keeps balls and cars from rolling off.

If children of different ages use the same play area, the older child needs storage space inaccessible to younger children.

Staggered shelves from 25 to 70 inches form a pleasant, useful arrangement for children of different ages. Adjustable shelves are good, except when a small child may use them for climbing.

Thus, in planning for storage, you should consider the arm reach of the children who use the space. Suggested top heights are 38 inches for a 3-year-old, 51 inches for a 6-year-old, and 68 inches for a 12-year-old.

Out-of-season toys and less frequently used ones may be stored in a closet or in another part of the house.

Bookcases of brick and boards may be an inexpensive solution to your storage problem. Boards stained to match the brick, bricks and boards painted the same color, or large glass building blocks make effective, useful combinations.

For large picture books, shelves need to be 12 inches deep and 15 inches high. The second shelf, not so high, should have upright divisions 6 to 8 inches apart to serve as leaning posts. Later they can accommodate reference books.

Twenty-five linear feet per child is a liberal amount of shelf storage space for all of his possessions.

STURDY WOODEN boxes and crates can be used in a number of ways.

If they are strong and smooth, sandpapered, and lacquered, you can make interesting arrangements by placing them in various positions. When they are piled two or three high, a plywood shelf can be added to the top to hold flat books and small toys.

Three crates side by side, painted or covered with oilcloth on the outside and painted on the inside, can fit into any color scheme.

Two upright crates, 12 or 14 inches apart and topped with plywood, may serve as a desk.

Separate crates in a closet or corner or by the bed are handy.

When older children do not have a desk, a dropleaf attached to the wall or bookcase is satisfactory. The support legs should be sturdy. The height should be adjusted as the children grow. The top surface should be at least 25 inches square.

When space does not permit an easel for painting, a piece of plywood can be hung on a door or placed on the floor and a rack for holding paint placed nearby. Empty, sturdy milk or beverage cartons and empty cans can be used for holding paint.

A bulletin board of cork or plasterboard provides a place for displaying children's treasures and is a center of interest.

Small toys can be put in shoebags hung on the inside of closet doors. The divisions in the bags encourage neatness and make toys easy to find. You can buy them or make them by attaching rows of deep pockets to a piece of rather heavy material that measures about 20 by 48 inches. One row of pockets 8 by 12 inches can hold dolls, stuffed animals, toy cars, or trains; a row of 12- by 12-inch pockets holds larger toys or small blocks.

Bookcases that are headpieces of beds take care of some books, a radio, and frequently used items.

A trundle drawer under the bed adds extra storage. This big, shallow box can be made of plywood mounted on casters and covered to keep contents free of dust.

Trains are fun for older boys but are often in the way. A train track may be fastened to the inside door of a wall cabinet, which, when let down, becomes a surface supported by two legs; when closed, it is used for a bulletin board.

It is important for young children to spend part of their time with other family members.

In the living room or family room, a low, open shelf provides storage area for blocks, books, and a few toys for the times children spend leisure time with the family. One should not be embarrassed when unexpected guests arrive and find children's toys (while in use) in the middle of the floor. That is a part of normal, daily living.

A shelf in the bathroom for floating toys and a low shelf in the kitchen are useful. Very young children want to be near an adult much of the time, and if you are willing to make these shelves available, they will have hours of fun and will leave other things alone.

Regular kitchen equipment such as canned food, and miscellaneous unbreakable items (tin measuring cups, molds, funnels, old eggbeaters, old pans) have a great fascination. A child

will think of many ways to use them if they are put on a bottom shelf within his reach.

A place for play outdoors often is overlooked when parents consider an apartment or house, and yet it can be of great importance in children's emotional and physical well-being. Outdoor space, if possible, should have sunshine, shade, grass, sand, play equipment, and a place to dig.

Fortunate are those who have a yard—part of it for beauty and part for play. Any family who has a small yard should begin with the premise that it is a play area first and a beauty spot later.

Some simple equipment is needed in every yard where children play. It may include a swing, a jungle gym, or climbing bars; sandboxes and sand toys; boxes of assorted sizes; sawhorses, planks, and cleated boards. Many of these can be made inexpensively. Others may be had for the asking.

Outdoor apparatus should be firm and secure. Lumber that is well seasoned, preferably straight grained, and free from cracks or splits should be selected. The apparatus should be surfaced on four sides. The corners should be planed. Fir or pine are suitable woods for most outdoor equipment. Pipe is more durable than wood and needs less care.

To protect wooden equipment from the weather, one should coat it with linseed oil and paint it with waterproof paint. All parts that are placed underground should be treated with a preservative.

Galvanized iron pipe (2 or 3 inches in diameter) is best for play apparatus and may be bought from any hardware or plumbing company. Frames for swings and bars need not be braced if they are set at least 3 feet in concrete.

Playground equipment should be inspected often for loose bolts, frayed ropes, and rough planks.

Sandboxes are standard backyard equipment. A bottomless sandbox can be made by digging four shallow trenches, placing a log in each trench (the size depends on the room available), and filling the enclosed area with sand.

A sandpit 5 feet by 5 feet (larger for more than one child) and somewhat more than 1 foot deep is easy to make. To provide for drainage, cover the bottom of the pit with loosely placed bricks. A layer of gravel under the bricks is optional. Planks across each end provide a place to sit.

The sand must be clean. Animals can be kept out of it by a tarpaulin or other cover.

Basic equipment for the sandpile may include shovels, pails, scoops, plastic cups, sieves, toy cars, trucks and tractors, and rubber figures and animals.

Water is fun to use in sand play. Provide an old washtub, a large dishpan, large buckets, sprinkling cans, or some such container, from which water can be dipped or poured or on which toys can be floated.

Boxes of assorted sizes, from which nails have been removed, may be used for climbing and for boats, stores, trains, garages, and houses. A piano or refrigerator box with windows cut in the sides makes a good playhouse, boat, or fort.

Sawhorses 12 to 18 inches high and 12 to 24 inches wide can be combined in innumerable ways with boards and cleated planks. A few smooth boards of different widths, lengths, and thicknesses, not too heavy for a child to lift, can be used for building or climbing. A smooth plank 2 feet by 10 inches by 8 inches may be elevated at one end by a packing box or sawhorse and used as a slide.

Some boards 3 feet by 14 inches, 4 feet by 14 inches, and 5 feet by 14 inches with cleats on one end can be used for ladders.

The planks and boards should be made of clear-grain wood and have beveled edges and corners.

A balance board 12 feet long can be varied in height by placing bricks or hollow blocks under each end of the plank.

Nail kegs, with heads fastened securely, may be rolled, pushed, climbed upon, and used with other toys. Giant spools (like telephone wire spools) have many uses.

Very desirable, but not always possible, is a paved area to be used for skating, riding, shooting basketballs into a mounted goal, and other physical activities.

When not in use, much of the movable outdoor equipment could be stacked neatly in a corner of the yard (under shelter, if possible), in the garage or on the back porch, or in a storage shed or playhouse. If nothing else, a tarpaulin can be used to lengthen the period of usefulness. Such care of equipment helps children learn to respect their possessions.

On rainy and wintry days, more than ever, a child needs active play to release some of his energy.

Outdoor toys seem to be a novelty inside. Small wagons, scooters, tricycles, climbing bars, board ladders, and packing boxes can be used in the garage, basement, or family room.

You may have to shift some furniture, but the day will seem easier than if a child has nothing to do. There are limits, though, and children should understand these limits of their freedom just as they do at other times.

Inexpensive toys and amusements can please a child as much as costly ones and are good to have on hand to be pulled out on bad-weather days— empty egg cartons, old greeting cards, pots and pans, old clothes for dressup, pipe cleaners, and boxes of scrap materials, buttons, and ribbons. Doorway gyms and punching bags are especially good then, too.

When the weather is bad and children cannot play outdoors, one has to expect some romping and noise indoors. It is a natural part of childhood. When we listen to the noise, we find that it usually is simple, vocal, mostly harmless noise. (Nancy White)

FURNISHINGS

Basic Design

LOOK about you.

Look carefully at the things you take for granted—your house, its furnishings, and the yard. Possessions such as these—hundreds of them—create the backdrop of one's life.

If we select our possessions precisely, if they are carefully designed to meet the needs most important to us, if they are attractive and timely, they will ease the physical problems of living, stimulate our thinking, and lift our spirit.

On the other hand, possessions that enter our lives haphazardly may produce tensions that undermine family living.

A room crowded by frilly fabrics can smother its occupants. Jarring color combinations and obstacle-course furniture arrangements may evoke unpleasant responses without our realizing why.

How do we recognize high quality in design? The process of making sound choices concerning the things about us often is called having good taste. It is readily agreed that taste exists;

there are many disproportionate, grotesque things that can only detract from our homes.

At the same time, good taste should not imply a narrow process of selection. What is good for one individual or household at a given time is not necessarily good for another.

One family leads an active life, with an emphasis on what is happening at the moment. This concept expects energetic youngsters to damage and wear out the house and its contents. Things are considered expendable. It justifies buying for the short term.

A second family buys the best and expects its members to take great care to safeguard them for the future or even the next generation.

Yet another family has a middle-of-the-road outlook. Realistic life expectancies are attached to material possessions of moderately good quality, and respect for property is encouraged.

Taste, then, is the ability to recognize high quality or appropriate design.

As we begin to understand the importance of design, we may wish for some convenient rules whose application automatically would bring the positive effects of good design into our homes. Such rules do not exist in any true sense.

If we define "design" broadly, we may say with Joseph Albers that it is "to place and organize, to order, to relate and to control . . . in short, it embraces all means of opposing disorder and accident."

Design is comprised of certain definable elements—line, space-form, color-light, and texture.

It means consciously ordering these basic ingredients to bring the end product into line with our deepest needs.

It does not mean placidly accepting what already exists or seems most readily available.

LINE may be described as stretching a dot. It is essentially the boundary of form—the edge of things. Its length exceeds its width, and it has two dimensions.

Lines may be short or long, curved or straight, continuous or broken, horizontal, vertical, or diagonal. They may be tapered or blunt, sharply defined, or indistinct.

Which of these types of lines is present is important, for each expresses a unique quality.

The vertical lines of our churches were selected to convey strength and dignity.

Horizontal lines are quiet, like the landscape.

Broken lines express a sense of unrest and urgency.

SPACE-FORM must be considered together.

Space is the void within which we move.

Form is existing mass which interrupts space, creating its boundaries.

Shape usually denotes two dimensions, length and width.

Form indicates three items—length, breadth, and depth.

Form seems to be the strongest of the design elements.

If you want to paint a quiet landscape, you would not first cut your canvas into a jagged shape. To do so would misuse the element of form. To overcome the sense of chaos communicated by a jagged shape, you would have to use all the other elements most energetically. Even then, success would be limited. The square shape and the cube form are always more rest-suggesting than the pyramidal or triangular forms and shapes.

COLOR-LIGHT also must be treated as two sides of the same coin.

Color has been defined as the hue of light reflected from an object. We can have no color without light, but we know that light also plays an important part in our perception of form and texture.

Colors can influence our emotions. Large amounts of a strong red summon an aggressive response from us. Blue and green may make us feel at rest.

The hue is important. So are the amounts of darkness and brightness and the location of colors in relationship to each other.

TEXTURE is the way a thing feels or looks as it might feel.

Our appreciation of texture comes to us through both our eyes and our sense of touch.

Texture, of all the design elements, is the one we most seldom consider. Between the broad designations of rough and smooth lie soft, slippery, harsh, springy, limp, and so on.

Like color, texture may enrich or frustrate our lives. The look and feel of fine china—and the way its surface sheds food particles—represent texture at its best. To slide across a rough-woven upholstery fabric in a wool skirt is to know texture at its worst.

UNDERSTANDING each element of design takes time and experimentation. Once you are acquainted with them, though, you are ready to consider how the components fit together.

First you ask yourself, "What do I hope to accomplish?" When you have the goal in mind, the process of ordering the elements becomes manageable.

Suppose you have decided to buy a man's chair. What will be your major considerations? Comfort? Ease of maintenance? Durability? Appearance? Cost?

Such questions must be examined in turn. Is this chair one that will provide good support as well as squirm space? Will working or puttering clothes soil the fabric easily? Will it support considerable weight and give a sturdy appearance?

When you have decided on the most important qualities, you still have to decide how they may best be obtained and retained.

As the chair must meet the needs of its owner, so must it relate well to objects around it. Because it will be large, finding enough space for it may be a problem. The new purchase should not overwhelm other furnishings in the room.

If it is constructed of wood and fabric, the two should share some qualities to establish unity, yet vary enough to contribute vitality to the overall design of the chair. Lines probably should express solidarity and masculinity.

THE PRINCIPLES of design become useful tools in a concrete situation.

Proportion means that we are concerned with establishing a pleasing relationship between parts.

An item appears well proportioned when the size and shape of its parts are neither varied to the point of chaos nor repetitious to the point of boredom. Finally, does the chair help to make the room a unified whole?

Balance is a principle that urges us to study relative weight.

Is an otherwise heavy chair supported by spindly, fragile-appearing legs?

Will a massive piece disrupt the balance of a room by making it seem uncomfortably lopsided?

Broad lines, thick forms, and unbroken surfaces contribute a sense of weightiness.

Slender lines, shallow forms, and broken surfaces produce the opposite effect.

Balance is not entirely a matter of apparent weight. A colorful, active painting may be important enough to counter large areas of heaviness in other parts of a room. A sense of equilibrium is created through the careful combination of weight and the power of attraction.

Emphasis, a third principle, encourages us to give one element—color, texture, form, or line—dominance. It is the counterpart of harmony.

Emphasis stresses differences rather than similarities. The spirit of the principle is also served when we choose an article understated in every respect to help calm an overlively room.

Rhythm refers to the suggestion of movement produced intentionally by the use of design elements. Do strong vertical lines sweep our glance along? Do spindles in the back of a straight chair form a pleasant pattern of alternation?

The principles of design are concerned, in the end, with quantities of harmony and contrast.

We must often compromise as we struggle with their application. A long-felt wish for something red may bow to the fact that a bright color would overemphasize an already large piece.

We may like the maintenance features of a vinyl covering, but we may be unwilling to accept the textural attributes of hotness in summer and coldness in winter.

Other compromises often stem from the fact that most homes serve the needs and preferences of a number of people.

Our carefully selected chair should offer an experience in beauty as well as comfort, in interest as well as durability.

THREE ESTHETIC TESTS for good design—unity, intensity, and vitality—are offered by Victoria Ball in her book, *The Art of Interior Design*.

The test for unity is twofold.

First, the parts of the chair must be brought together in a way that expresses a sense of oneness. No single part of the chair should be uncomfortably conspicuous in relation to any other.

By the same token, the chair must be an integral part of the unity of the room. If this sense of unity exists, the chair seems to be unquestionably right.

If the first condition is met, we will experience intense, conscious satisfaction with the effect we have achieved.

Finally, because of its rightness, the chair will attract and hold our interest, generating in our relationship with it a vitality that will make it as enjoyable a decade hence as it is today.

Learning to furnish a home well is not easy. Like learning to swim or ride a bicycle, it takes practice and the determination to keep trying.

The main requirement is a willingness to observe what is about us and think about what we see—about things and about their relationship to each other.

If we find the decisions we have made were not, after all, the best of all possible ones, there is no cause for discouragement. Study and planning provide an important part of our education for living. (GERTRUDE NYGREN)

Selecting

Furniture

THIS IS THE DAY you will visit the furniture stores to make some of the most important purchases of your life.

You will spend considerable money for items that you must be friendly with for the next 20 years or more.

You must choose them with care to satisfy your taste, to fill the functional needs of your home, to select well-built, low-maintenance items, and to avoid high cost.

Here are a few suggestions.

First, consider the wood furniture to be used inside the house, where it is not expected to get wet.

Chairs, tables, chests of drawers or chiffoniers, beds, and similar common pieces should be strong, good looking, of proper size, and easy to take care of.

Preferences for different species of wood come and go, but the old standbys of walnut, cherry, pecan or hickory (you cannot tell them apart), maple, birch, and oak are the native hardwoods that will always be used in furniture of good taste.

Each of those woods can be finished in its natural color, darkened with stain, or made almost blond by bleaching. They are all strong and have distinct grain patterns.

Other native hardwoods, such as gum, poplar, and cottonwood, have little grain pattern but can be stained to resemble other hardwoods and often are used in combination with the more expensive hardwoods.

Mahogany, the major foreign hardwood, will maintain its popularity because it has a pleasing, warm grain, can take a dark or light finish, and shrinks and swells less than almost any other wood with changes in humidity.

Other foreign tropical hardwoods, such as luan, crabwood, and utile, resemble true mahogany in texture and properties and have been used more and more for fine furniture.

Yellow and white pines are used in early-American chairs, beds, tables, corner cupboards, and odd pieces of furniture. Pine is acceptable for such items, but it is not considered a fine furniture wood and is seldom used in contemporary items.

If an eager salesman assures you that a table is made of solid, genuine, virgin white oak from a mountaintop in eastern Kentucky, bear in mind that the geographic origin of the species (and even the species itself) is not the most important factor in selecting a piece of furniture.

If the wood is from one of the recognized and accepted furniture species and it pleases your fancy, then look

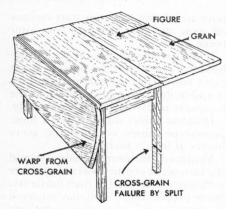

Avoid cross-grain; it can cause splits and warp.

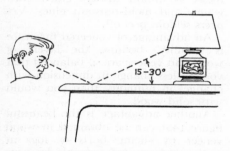

Inspection at low angle with light reveals defects in surface or finish.

closely at the grain of the wood, the construction of the piece, and the finish. That is really more important than the kind of wood.

The way a tree grows causes the grain of wood. It is the fiber direction and not the figure in the wood. If there is much cross-grain or slope of grain, beware.

Furniture parts that require strength, such as chair arms and legs, bedposts, and table legs, should have straight grain, or they may fail.

Drawer fronts, tabletops, and mirror frames should have straight grain, or they may warp with changes in humidity.

When you have satisfied yourself that the grain direction is all right, then look at the general construction of the piece.

First look for clean lines, properly smoothed edges and corners, and the absence of protruding annoyances.

Be sure that the piece rests firmly on the floor, with no leg or corner riding high.

Inspect the piece in a fairly strong light at an angle of 15 to 30 degrees to pick up irregularities in construction or finish. This angle of light will show you shadows of things that you may ordinarily overlook.

Now comes your most important and probably the most difficult inspection job. You should find out how the joints are made.

Because most joints are hidden, you may have to rely on the salesman. Ask him if he can furnish you with a factory drawing of the furniture construction. It is his responsibility to get this information for you, if he does not have it at hand.

Each of the joints shown in the drawing is suitable for some uses. None is suitable for all uses.

The weaker joints are the butt joint, the rabbeted joint, and the tongue-and-groove joint. They are not suitable for chair arms, table legs, bedposts, and similar items in which very high strength is required. These joints would be suitable for inserted panels in the sides and backs of dressers and for edge gluing furniture core material (center of plywood-type construction), and similar applications in which high strength is not demanded.

The dovetailed joint is used commonly and is highly satisfactory for fastening drawer corners or for practically any use where two boards or panels join at a right angle.

The properly made dovetail joint will not come apart without breaking the wood. The dovetail joint is used in dresser drawers of almost all fine furniture.

The doweled joint and the mortise-and-tenon joint are used to connect chair arms, posts, and rails; parts of beds that demand high strength; and in many other similar applications.

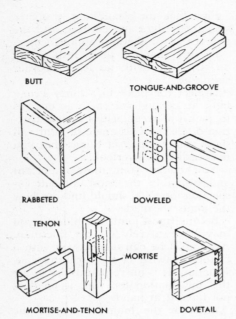

BUTT

TONGUE-AND-GROOVE

RABBETED

DOWELED

TENON

MORTISE

MORTISE-AND-TENON

DOVETAIL

Basic furniture joints.

When well made, one is about as good as the other.

Even the best made corner joints on chairs and tables must stand concentrated loads, and a good furniture manufacturer will often back up these joints with hidden metal braces or with triangular glue blocks of wood.

If glue blocks are used on the underside of tables and chairs, look closely to see that they fit tightly on all sides. If they are not snug and tight, they will do little good.

AFTER CHECKING on the furniture joints, look at all fastenings and hardware.

Good furniture is put together with glue and screws, not nails. See that all screws are drawn up tight and that all glue joints are tightly closed, with no telltale gaps that indicate poor workmanship.

Then check all drawer pulls and other hardware to see that they are properly fastened and tight. Nothing can be more disheartening than to have the drawer handles start coming off soon after the furniture is in your home.

If you are buying a table with drop-leaves or one that slides open to insert extra leaves, ask the salesman to turn it upside down so you can see that the hardware is fitted properly and tightly.

Dropleaf tables should have a long, piano-type hinge or three or more hinges at least 3 inches long.

Veneered furniture made around the turn of the century was put together with glues that failed in high humidity. Some people still believe that veneered furniture is not so good as solid furniture. That is not true. Furniture today is almost always glued with water- and mold-resistant glues. Veneers seldom peel off.

An advantage of veneered furniture is stability, because the layers of wood and veneer are so balanced that you get less change in dimension with changes in humidity than you would with solid wood.

Another advantage is the beautiful figure that can be obtained in wood veneer by slicing burls or logs at angles and arcs not possible by conventional sawing of lumber.

One caution, however: Veneered parts should have an odd number of plies or layers—three, five, seven, or nine—with the grain direction of adjacent plies at right angles so that they will be balanced around the central core. An even number of layers may result in warping.

One of the best ways to become an expert on what to look for in furniture is to visit a furniture repair shop and look at the failures that are being repaired and the parts that have stood up under long usage. You can learn more in an hour this way than by reading several books.

IF THE LINES suit your taste and the construction meets your standards, find out what kind of finish was used.

There are many good finishes of varnish, lacquer, and synthetic resins. All are good if properly applied.

Ask for a guarantee that the finish will not waterstain under sweating glasses or discolor under a warm dish. That is especially important in dining and coffee tables. Many finishes are resistant to water, alcohol, and other things that may be spilled.

The most important thing that I can recommend about finishes is that the furniture should have some type of finish on all exposed wood parts, whether they are on the underside, inside a drawer, or inside the case.

That is advisable because moisture from the air moves into wood—even through the best finish—and causes wood to swell. If more moisture moves in one side than the other, the wood will swell unevenly and cause warping and tight drawers and may cause glue joints to open up or the wood to split.

When furniture goes into a very dry place, the opposite happens, and the shrinking of wood parts in furniture can cause just as many problems as swelling.

An even application of a good finish on all surfaces will usually give long, trouble-free service.

JUST A WORD or two about outdoor furniture that must stand the ravages of the weather, even though your intentions are to bring it in out of the rain.

If your outdoor furniture is going to be primarily in one place, there is still no good substitute for well-made wood lawn furniture that is warm to the touch and sturdily comfortable.

Many manufacturers make outdoor wood furniture with treated wood or wood of durable species that will last for many years.

The durable woods are the heartwood or dark-colored part of redcedar, locust, redwood, and Osage-orange.

Less durable but still quite satisfactory are the heartwood portions of the oaks, pine, walnut, mulberry, cherry, and mahogany.

The woods to avoid (unless they are treated with a preservative) are the gums, poplars, cottonwood, hickories, soft pines, and many other lighter woods. When treated, however, these woods make fine outdoor furniture, and some are quite light in weight.

REGARDLESS of the type of furniture you buy, look for the manufacturer's name. It will be on the underside, on the back, or perhaps inside a drawer.

It will be there if he is proud of his product. He will back up his product if you should have any trouble. You may lose a drawer pull, or break a mirror, or have some part fail. Most good furniture manufacturers keep a supply of spare parts for several years for the furniture they make. They want your furniture to look its best—it's their best advertisement. (WALTON R. SMITH)

Refinishing Furniture

A GOOD JOB of refinishing furniture is well worth the invested time, patience, and effort if the piece is of good wood, sound construction, and good design.

For removing old finish you will need a good commercial remover; clean cans, wide-mouth jars, or old bowls for the remover; a pure bristle brush 3 to 4 inches wide (many removers dissolve synthetic bristles); a wide putty knife or spatula with filed-off corners to prevent scratching; medium (oo) steel wool; toothpicks, orangewood sticks, or match stems for carvings; heavy cord or a small, stiff bristle brush for grooves in turned legs; excelsior, old burlap, or other coarse material; soft, lintless rags; denatured alcohol or pure gum turpentine or both for the final cleaning (alcohol is most readily purchased under trade names for shellac thinners or solvent); old papers to protect floor and other surfaces; a box or can for wastepaper; and old clothes and rubber gloves.

It is essential that you work in a well-ventilated place. Some fumes are deadly in a closed room. Some of the materials are flammable. There should be no open flame, such as pilot lights no water heaters, near the workspace. All used rags and papers should be burned at the end of the work period—but not in the furnace.

COMMERCIAL REMOVERS are of three general types—nonflammable semiliquid, rinse-away-with-water, and liquid (with and without wax).

The nonflammable semiliquid removers are considered safe under normal conditions. They may be used on vertical surfaces when necessary. They do not raise the grain of the wood. They do not evaporate rapidly and may be left longer on hard, stubborn finishes without drying out. They do not burn the wood. They may be used on veneers.

The rinse-away removers as a group are the most expensive. They usually work quickly and easily, but they may burn the wood. The water used in rinsing may raise the grain, soften old glue in joints, and loosen veneer.

The liquid removers are the least expensive. They are effective on horizontal surfaces but too hard to control on vertical surfaces.

Most liquid removers are flammable. Some contain wax, which retards evaporation. All traces of the wax must be removed with a solvent before a new finish is applied.

Follow the directions on the container.

Use the remover generously. Allow plenty of time for it to work. Except when you are removing several thick coats, you will hope to remove most of the finish with the first application.

This means that the remover has been applied liberally enough and has had enough time to penetrate to the wood and lift the finish.

Do not disturb the finish until you are ready to scrape it off. Quite often stain from the old finish is rubbed into the wood by an impatient person who agitates the remover as it is working. It is better to scrape or wipe the entire surface and apply a fresh coat of remover.

Work on one surface at a time. Be careful not to let remover run down on an adjoining surface that has not been cleaned. Such runs often produce stains, which are hard to remove. It is a good idea therefore to begin at the bottom and work up.

Remove finish from carvings with a small, stiff brush, round toothpicks wrapped with oo steel wool, or other objects that will not scratch the wood.

Grooves on turned legs can be cleaned with ravelings from burlap or other heavy cord.

After all finish is removed, scrub the entire piece with denatured alcohol or turpentine and oo steel wool. Rub with the grain of the wood. Use alcohol and turpentine in a well-ventilated area and away from open flame. Both are flammable, and the fumes are unsafe.

Often an old, hard, thick finish is resistant to the remover. Light sanding with medium or coarse sandpaper will cut the surface of the finish so that the remover can get through. Nearly all quick-drying, easy-to-polish furniture waxes contain silicones. If silicone-bearing waxes have been used on the furniture, scrub it well with gum turpentine before and after removing the finish. Silicones retard the action of removers and also make the wood resistant to a new finish.

MATERIALS for gluing include glue (good-quality cabinetmaker's glue); clamps or strong cords; vinegar; and a small, stiff brush to apply the glue. Glued joints loosen because of

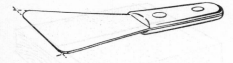

A wide putty knife or spatula with corners filed off to prevent scratching.

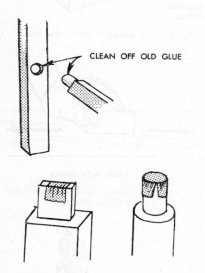

CLEAN OFF OLD GLUE

If some pieces are loose, glue strips of soft cotton cloth over the ends to make them fit.

excessive heat or moisture or poor fit.

Since new glue sticks better on clean wood, scrape off old glue. Be careful not to scrape off any of the wood.

Wash all glue out of the pores with warm vinegar. Wash away all vinegar with water. Dry thoroughly. Be sure joints fit tightly, or they will not hold.

Follow the directions on the container of glue.

Apply glue to both edges of wood to be joined. Clamp or tie together, using a tourniquet or clamps to hold them firmly. Wipe off excess glue with a damp cloth. Allow the furniture to dry the full time suggested on the container.

If the wood surfaces to be glued are very smooth, slashing with a knife will help the glue hold better.

Dampening with water will open the pores, but allow the wood to dry well before applying glue.

Both the glue and the wood should be warm (about 75° F.).

FOR REMOVING STAINS, the liquid household bleaches commonly used in laundering clothes often are effective. Apply them full strength or slightly diluted. Sponge off with clean water.

Or, for stains, you may use a saturated solution of oxalic acid (1 teaspoon of powdered oxalic acid or 2 teaspoons of crystals dissolved in a cup of hot water) or a solution of 2 ounces of oxalic acid crystals and 2 ounces of tartaric acid dissolved in a quart of hot water. Mix in a glass container.

These solutions should be marked *poison.* Avoid inhaling the fumes and the fine dust that comes from sanding.

Repeated applications may be necessary to remove some stubborn stains. Wipe the entire surface with the bleach to avoid light spots.

The action of these solutions should be stopped with a tablespoon of ammonia in a quart of water.

Commercial wood bleaches also are available.

Dents or bruises (not gouges) caused in solid wood by a heavy blow can be raised with steam. Do not use steam on veneer.

Steam may be applied with a steam iron used over several thicknesses of heavy, colorfast fabric, preferably wool. Or a dry iron may be used with damp cloth or four or five thicknesses of damp brown wrapping paper.

Several applications may be necessary before the steam swells the wood enough to bring it up to the surrounding level.

Because steam opens the pores of the wood, the surface must be sanded thoroughly to "repack" the grain; otherwise the area may absorb stain too rapidly; color will be uneven.

THE FINISH is no better than the smoothness of the surface on which it is applied.

The amount of sanding required to prepare the surface depends largely on how well the piece was sanded originally, the type of remover you use, and the thickness of veneer.

On an old piece, you will not want to sand through the patina—the mellow appearance that comes with age—but the surface must be smooth. If water was used in removing the finish, extra sanding is required.

Take care not to sand through thin veneer.

Garnet, silicon carbide, and aluminum oxide finishing papers are more expensive than the regular flint sandpaper, but they are sharper, last longer, and come in finer grits.

Regardless of the type you use, brush the sandpaper from time to time to prevent the sanding dust from clogging the surface. A lightweight metal brush or stiff utility brush may be used.

Use a fine-grit sandpaper on a fairly smooth surface. On a rougher surface, begin with medium grit and work to fine for the final sanding.

Wrap the sandpaper around a block of wood about 3 by 4 by 1 inches or a new, firm synthetic sponge, or use a hand sander.

Power sanders make the work easier, but orbital sanders should not be used except on wood with a pronounced grain running in different directions.

Sand with the grain—never across the grain—on flat surfaces. Sand across (around) the grain on round legs.

Keep the surface of the wood dusted as you work. If you have used bleach, wear a mask made of several thicknesses of cheesecloth to avoid inhaling dust.

After sanding until the wood is smooth to the touch, wipe it with a damp cloth. This will raise loose grain "whiskers." Allow it to dry for a few minutes and then rub with 3/0 (ooo) steel wool. Repeat this process if necessary. Brush the dust from crevices and carvings.

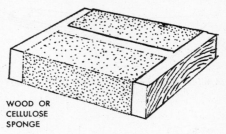

WOOD OR CELLULOSE SPONGE

Sandpaper wrapped around a block.

SAND WITH GRAIN

Sand with the grain—never across grain—on flat surfaces.

SANDPAPER

Sand across (around) grain on round legs.

Remove all traces of dust with a tack rag. Tack rags may be bought at automobile supply or paint shops, or you may make your own. Wash a lightweight, lintless fabric several times. (Closely woven cheesecloth is excellent.) Squeeze out most of the water. Wet with turpentine. Add enough varnish to make the surface of the cloth yellow. Squeeze out excess moisture, refold, and squeeze again.

Fold raw edges in to the center as the cloth is used. It should be damp enough to pick up dust but should leave no trace of moisture on the wood. Store in a closed jar or aluminum foil to prevent drying.

STAIN usually is not needed on woods that have natural beauty of grain and color, such as mahogany, walnut, cherry, pine, maple, and rosewood.

Immediately before any staining is done, be sure to sponge with water and remove "whiskers" with 3/0 steel wool or very fine finishing paper.

Water stains are especially good for hardwood, but are not recommended for veneer because of the danger of loosening the glue. These stains come in powdered form and are mixed with water to obtain any desired strength. They do not obscure the grain and produce clear, rich colors that do not fade or bleed. They are not generally available except in larger paintstores.

Oil stains colored with pigments are available ready mixed, or they may be mixed from tube colors in oil. You may also mix prepared stains of the same brand to vary the color.

These oil stains are easy to use. The greatest objections are that they do not work well on hardwood, the pigment may dim the grain a little, and they usually need to be sealed with a thin coat of shellac to prevent bleeding. This is particularly true with red mahogany stains.

To mix an oil stain, prepare a solution of 2 parts of boiled linseed oil (purchased boiled), 2 parts of gum turpentine, and one-half part of japan drier. To this mixture, add the desired colors blended thoroughly with a little turpentine.

Use about 2 ounces of color to 1½ cups of the oil and turpentine mixture. This will vary, of course, with the strength desired.

Some suggestions for mixing stains: Light cherry, 2 parts Italian raw sienna and 3 parts Italian burnt sienna; dark cherry, Italian burnt sienna; brown mahogany, 3 parts Italian burnt sienna, 1 part rose pink or maroon lake, and 1 part Vandyke brown; red mahogany, 3 parts Italian burnt sienna and 2 parts rose pink; dark oak, 1 part Turkey burnt umber and 4 parts Italian raw sienna; reddish honeytone maple, 1 part raw sienna and 1 part burnt umber; walnut, 3 parts burnt umber and 2 parts raw umber; brownish maple, burnt umber.

Test the stain on the same kind of wood as the furniture to be finished. Check the color in daylight after it is dry.

Brush the furniture with equal parts of oil and turpentine before applying the stain in order that the latter may be absorbed evenly. Be sure to coat the end grain with this mixture or with a mixture of 1 part shellac and 5 parts denatured alcohol. Rub shellacked surfaces with fine sandpaper or steel wool before applying stain.

Test a stain for color on a sample or inconspicuous spot of the wood on which it is to be used. It will be lighter when it is dry, so let it dry to see the true color.

If the color is too intense, follow the directions on the container for diluting and applying the stain, or dilute home-mixed stain with the original base mixture.

Apply the stain with a brush or cloth. Let it stand 2 or 3 minutes. Then rub it with a soft cloth. Use a circular motion to insure an even color. Let the stain dry at least 36 hours before sanding.

After staining a piece of furniture, be sure to protect the color against the operations that follow. Seal the stain with a commercial or home-mixed sealer.

New sealers now on the market greatly simplify the finishing process. Sealers have been developed to fit almost any type of finishing desired.

For best results when using two or more finishing coats on the sealer, use a medium-to-low solid sealer. If there is only one finish coat, a medium-to-high solid sealer is best.

For a homemade sealer, mix 1 part

shellac and 5 parts denatured alcohol. Apply with a brush to seal the color. Use this also to seal the filler on hardwoods.

USE A PASTE wood filler to obtain an extremely smooth surface on new, open-grain woods, such as oak, mahogany, and walnut.

Woods that are being refinished probably were filled previously.

Buy a filler of the desired color, or tint it to match the wood (or stain) by using colors ground in oil.

Follow the directions for application found on the container.

Be sure not to let filler harden on the surface of the wood.

FINISHES include penetrating wood seal, oiled finish, shellac and wax finish, varnish, paint, and enamel.

Penetrating wood seal is highly satisfactory for the amateur. It makes an excellent finish for furniture, floors, and woodwork. It is easily applied and maintained and is easy to retouch. Many seals may be had in various colors. Use a pigment stain if a clear seal is to be applied over the stain.

Penetrating seals vary in composition, penetrating characteristics, and durability. One kind has the characteristics of an oil finish. Another penetrates the pores of the wood and hardens level with the surface. A third forms a surface coating. The seals of the first and second kinds are the most practical.

For an oiled finish, have the furniture free from dust. Brush on a coat of 2 parts boiled linseed oil and 1 part turpentine. (Purchase boiled oil. Do not try to boil it at home.) Let stand 15 minutes. Let the wood absorb all the oil it can take. Wipe off the excess oil with a clean cloth. Be careful to clean all crevices; otherwise the oil will harden and will have to be removed with varnish remover.

Using a soft cloth, rub with the grain of the wood for 5 to 15 minutes or until a hard, lustrous surface results. Repeat the application of oil and the rubbing at intervals of not less than 2 days until all dull spots disappear and a uniform clear luster results.

Apply oil once or twice a year to keep the finish in good condition.

For shellac and wax finish, have the furniture free from dust.

Brush on a coat of pure shellac diluted to half strength with alcohol. Allow this to dry thoroughly. Then rub down to the surface of the wood with fine steel wool.

Repeat coats of shellac until all pores of the wood are filled.

Rub down each coat until only the shellac that penetrated into the wood remains. When rubbing down a finish, use care not to cut through the edges.

After the final coat has been rubbed down, place paste wax in several layers of cloth and apply with circular motion. After 20 minutes, polish with the grain of the wood.

Use a folded cloth for polishing.

Tabletops for hard wear may be finished with a coat of shellac thinned one-half with denatured alcohol, followed by two coats of furniture varnish.

Be sure the tabletop is perfectly clean and dry before you apply the first coat. Allow to dry thoroughly (at least 48 hours) before applying second coat. Several days would be better, especially if the weather is the least bit damp.

Rub each coat with 000 steel wool or fine sandpaper to remove glassy shine. Rubbing between coats is necessary to form a base for the next coat.

Rub the last coat with a pumice stone and oil or water, using a felt pad for rubbing. Or rub with very fine steel wool and linseed oil. Always work with the grain of the wood. Use a satin-finish varnish to eliminate some of the rubbing on the final finish.

These varnishes give a soft, rubbed effect but do not wear so well on tabletops as other varnishes do.

Varnishing should be done in a room as free from dust as possible. If a dining room table is varnished in the dining room, keep the doors closed and avoid sweeping in or near the room until the varnishing job is complete. Dust sticks readily to varnish and mars the attractive appearance of the surface. The temperature of room, furniture, and varnish should be the same and not less than 75°.

When paint or enamel is to be used as the finish, sometimes it is not necessary to remove all of the old finish. The surface must be smooth—free of dents and rough edges from chips in old finish—however.

A primer or undercoat is used before applying paint or enamel. This may be white or tinted to approximately the color of the finish. After the primer is dry, rub with steel wool or fine sandpaper. Wipe free of all dust. Two or three coats of the desired finish are applied over the primer. Sand between coats to make "tooth" for the paint to hold. Always dust carefully.

Alkyd-base enamel is the best paint for wood. It may be bought as high gloss, semigloss, or flat. The high gloss is the most durable, but it is less attractive and is used only if the furniture is to receive extremely hard use.

MANY PAINT companies sell "antiquing" kits. If only one piece of furniture is to be finished in this way, a kit may be cheaper than buying the needed supplies.

The general procedure is to paint the furniture, as outlined, with a flat enamel of a color lighter than the desired final finish. The glaze will make it darker.

You may either buy a glazing liquid from your paintstore or mix your own in either of the following proportions: 1 part clear varnish, 3 parts turpentine, and one-half part color ground in oil (more or less as desired); or 1 part boiled linseed oil (purchase boiled oil), 3 parts turpentine, and one-half part color ground in oil.

It is best to mix the color with a little turpentine before adding to the mixture.

If you have painted or enameled the surface in a light color, raw Turkey umber or burnt sienna will be a good choice for a brown glaze. On a surface that is painted in a dark color, such as green or red, thin lampblack oil paint is effective.

THE BASE PAINT SHOULD be lighter and brighter than the final finish you want. For instance, white enamel as a base under a glaze tinted with umber will be light tan or cream when it is finished, depending on the amount of color used. Any color, including gold, may be used. Make a sample before you begin work on your furniture. The base finish may be a transparent finish. The bare wood may be stained, sealed, and varnished before the glaze is applied.

Apply the glaze with a brush or folded cheesecloth. While it is still wet, wipe off with dry cheesecloth. Start wiping at the center and wipe toward the edges. Do not remove all of the glaze from grooves and carvings. A dry brush is helpful in completing the blending. If some areas are to be highlighted, wipe them lightly with some turpentine.

An unsuccessful glaze may be removed while it is still wet by wiping with turpentine.

Allow the glaze to dry 3 or 4 days. Apply two coats of satin-finish varnish. When the varnish is perfectly dry, rub with 000 steel wool; then wax. (ALICE PEAVY)

For further reading:
Grotz, George, *The Furniture Doctor.* Doubleday and Company, Inc., Garden City, N.Y., 1962.
How to Choose and Apply Wood Finishes. Iowa State University, HE–49, Ames, Iowa, 1962.
Johnson, Juanise S., *Refinishing Furniture.* University of Arkansas, Agricultural Extension Service, Circular 478, Little Rock, Ark., 1963.
Thames, Gena, *Furniture Restoration.* Rutgers University, New Jersey Extension Bulletin No. 355, New Brunswick, N.J., 1963.

Floors

THE SECRET of good floors lies in your understanding of the nature and limitations of the finish you select and how you take care of it.

Two kinds of wood are used for flooring. Softwoods include fir and pine. Among the more durable hardwoods are birch, ash, and oak.

Knowing the difference will help you decide on the finish.

The four main steps in finishing floors are smoothing the surface, applying a filler for certain woods, applying a stain to unify the color, and selecting and applying the finish.

A smooth surface is essential. First, make sure nails are sunk slightly below the surface of the floor. Then sand.

Use a heavy floor sander, an edger for sanding around baseboards, on the steps, and other hard-to-get-to places, and correct grit sizes of sandpaper to fit sander and edger.

A first and second roughing cut are made on old floors that have uneven boards or heavy coats of paint or varnish. These two steps are not necessary on new floors or floors in good condition.

Worn shellac on an otherwise smooth floor may be removed by mopping with a commercial cleaner, which must be used according to directions. The floor must be buffed with steel wool until smooth and allowed to dry thoroughly before applying the new finish.

During the cutting process in sanding floors that have an old coat of finish, the finish heats, and the large spaces between the abrasive grits fill up with melted material. When the sandpaper becomes filled, it will leave a dark line on the wood. At this point,

remove the paper and put a fresh sheet on the drum of the sander.

During the first roughing cut, guide the sander diagonally at an angle of about 45 degrees. Overlap each sanding path about 2 or 3 inches. Use a forward and backward motion to eliminate high spots and to remove paint and varnish accumulation. Use grit No. (coarse) 4 or 3½ open coat.

For the second roughing cut, guide the sander diagonally at an angle of about 45 degrees in a direction opposite to the one in the first roughing cut. Use grit No. (coarse) 4 or 3½ open coat.

Two smoothing cuts are necessary on all floors to remove scratches and produce the desired final condition.

For the first smoothing cut, use smooth lengthwise strokes in the direction of the boards or with the grain of wood. Use grit No. (medium) 2 or 1½.

For the second smoothing cut, use smooth lengthwise strokes in the direction of the boards or with the grain of wood. Use grit No. (fine) 2/0 or 1/0.

After sanding, remove all dust with a broom or a mop dampened lightly with turpentine. Turpentine is highly flammable. Use only in a well-ventilated room. Remove applicators and containers to a safe place when mopping is completed.

FILLERS are of two kinds.

Natural fillers are colorless and transparent.

Colored fillers are opaque and usually dark brown or black in color; they are commonly named for the wood on which they are to be used, as walnut or cherry wood fillers.

Fillers come in liquid and paste forms.

Open-grain woods have large pores, which must be filled to obtain maximum beauty and service. Close-grained woods do not necessarily require fillers when the finish to be used is varnish or shellac. Use a transparent filler if one is needed. You can omit the filler and use three coats of penetrating seal.

STAIN is used to change the color of the wood and to bring out its grain.

Staining is not necessary if the color of the wood in the floor is satisfactory.

A clear finish will darken a floor slightly—a point to remember when you decide on the use of a stain. If you use a stain, it should be an oil stain.

Stains penetrate somewhat deeper into softwood than into the hardwoods commonly used for flooring.

Instead of using stains, you may add color during the application of a wood sealer. Suitable oil stain may be mixed with the first coat of sealer, or you can buy wood sealers that already contain the color.

WOOD FINISHES are of three general kinds—penetrating (sealers); transparent (shellac and varnish are used most commonly); and opaque (paint or enamel).

Penetrating sealers, of the light-body, hard-drying oil type, sink into and seal the pores of the wood. They are recommended as being the most durable under heavy traffic when they are waxed regularly. They resist chipping, scratching, ordinary stains, and water spotting. They have a soft, satiny gloss, which wax increases and protects. They are easy to apply.

Paste fillers are optional for most brands. They dry quickly to a clear finish or stained effect. They may be patched without visible trace and can be maintained indefinitely without removing previous coats of seal. They can be used either as a complete finish or as an undercoat for a surface finish.

They have limitations, however. They can be applied only on well-sanded, bare wood or on previous sealer finish. Blemishes from poor sanding are not covered by the finish. They should be kept waxed. They need more than one coat to give a satin finish.

A floor sealer with a heavy body and resin content differs from the light-body oil type in that it is less durable, penetrates the wood partially but leaves some coating on the surface, gives a high gloss without waxing, buffing with steel wool produces a low gloss, and can also be used on concrete or terrazzo. It will scratch under heavy traffic.

Transparent film finishes (shellac and varnish) suit the needs of people who wish to let their floors go as long as possible without special attention. When the finish must be renewed, however, it usually is necessary to refinish the entire room.

Opaque finishes (paint or enamel) can be used to finish wood floors. Such a finish will hide the grain of the wood entirely. Hardwood floors inside buildings therefore are seldom painted.

An opaque finish provides colors that are not attainable in transparent finishes.

None of the transparent finishes resists weather well enough to last very long out of doors. Good floor paint or enamel are more durable for porches.

BEFORE YOU APPLY sealers, read the directions on the can.

Pour the seal into a shallow pan and apply with a long-handled lamb's-wool mop or lint-free rags, first across the grain, then smoothing out in the direction of the grain of the wood.

Let the seal penetrate until it becomes tacky (15 minutes to 2 hours, according to the characteristics of the sealer).

A correct interval between applying the sealer and buffing it is important. If you allow too little time, the sealer may still be too fluid to buff properly. Determine the interval you need by tests on samples of flooring.

Wipe off the excess with a clean, dry cloth. Buff with No. 2 steel wool and brush clean.

If you apply it carefully, one coat of sealer may be enough, but a second coat is generally recommended.

When the second coat is dry, use steel wool and buff as you did after the first coat. If you are not satisfied with the finish, apply a third coat. Wax and polish.

When the floor shows wear along paths of travel, remove the wax and patch with a floor seal. The patching does not show.

Conventional floor varnish has several advantages. Good varnishes give a durable protective coating if they are waxed and maintained properly. The finish will last if it is revarnished before it wears through. Varnish is tougher and more resistant to water and scratches than shellac and fairly resistant to stains and spots. Varnishes have several degrees of gloss.

The limitations of varnish are: The surface is scratched by heavy traffic. (Waxing increases scratch resistance.) It is difficult to patch worn areas without detection. Varnished floors are slippery, especially when waxed. The drying time varies by brands. Three coats usually are recommended. Varnished floors darken with age. Repeated coats form a buildup which must be removed for satisfactory refinishing.

When you apply varnish, use only floor varnish and apply with a clean, wide brush. The room should be at 70° F. or somewhat warmer, with plenty of fresh air.

First spread a brushful of varnish in a small space, with the grain of the wood. Then stroke it across the grain. Finally, brush it lightly with the grain again. Do not restroke areas that you have covered previously.

Allow at least 16 hours before you apply the second coat of varnish. Sand lightly, remove dust from the floor, and apply the second coat of varnish.

If filler was applied, two coats of varnish will be enough. Use three coats when the filler is omitted. Let dry 24 hours after the last coat of varnish. Then wax and polish.

Shellac dries rapidly and shows little change in color with age.

Limitations of shellac are: Water will turn it white. It scratches and wears off easily. It may be brittle when several coats have been used. Waxing is required for a lasting finish. It is slippery, especially when waxed. It is difficult to patch worn areas without detection. Repeated coats form a buildup that must be removed for satisfactory refinishing.

Use clear shellac (1 gallon of pure shellac thinned with 1 quart of No. 1 alcohol). Apply with a wide brush. The first coat on bare wood requires 15 to 20 minutes to dry. When dry, rub lightly with fine steel wool or sandpaper. Dust the floor to remove all particles. Apply the second coat and let dry for 2 to 3 hours. Again, rub the floor lightly with steel wool or sandpaper. Then dust the floor. Apply the third coat. Allow the floor to dry for 3 or 4 hours, wax and polish.

Floor paint and enamel come in a variety of colors and are easy to apply. They coat the surface of wood and cover discoloration and blemishes in the floor.

Paint wears off and scratches quickly. It is difficult to patch without detection. Repeated coats form a buildup that must be removed for a satisfactory refinish. Paint chips and peels when several coats have been used. It is slippery when waxed. One should use only types of paint made specially for floors.

On new floors or floor that has just been sanded, at least two coats of floor paint or enamel are necessary. The first coat should be thinned with paint thinner according to the manufacturer's directions. Subsequent coats usually should be applied unthinned. Each coat should be allowed to dry at least 16 hours before the next coat is applied or before the floor is open to traffic.

THE CARE of floor finishes depends on the amount and kind of traffic they receive. Finish wears off rapidly on floors near outside doors, where water may be tracked in, for instance.

The durability of floor finishes can be improved by keeping them waxed. An application of wax every 4 to 6 months may be enough in many homes, but more frequent applications may be necessary where traffic is heavier.

Well-waxed floors are easy to keep clean by dry mopping or an occasional polishing with an electric polisher.

Wax tends to make floors slippery unless the wax layer is kept very thin. Wax is usually less slippery on floors finished with sealers.

Wood floors with fine finishes should never be scrubbed with water or unnecessarily brought in contact with water, except in connection with removing old wax or when refinishing floors. Sweeping or dry mopping should be all that is necessary for routine cleaning.

A soft floor mop kept barely dampened with a mixture of 3 parts of kerosene and 1 part of paraffin oil is excellent for dry mopping. When the mop becomes dirty, it should be washed in hot, soapy water, dried, and again dampened with the mixture. Commercial preparations are available for this purpose also.

Rubber burns (from friction between rubber footwear and the floor) that cannot be removed with the mop may be removed by rubbing lightly with fine steel wool moistened with turpentine or paint thinner.

Stains on a floor finished with a sealer can be sanded by hand, patched with fresh sealer, and then buffed with fine steel wool. Patching on varnished or shellacked floors may not blend so well.

Wax prevents stains, scratches, and general deterioration. It also gives a luster that adds to the beauty of the floor. Many manufacturers have added information to labels about rebuffable water-base waxes that may be applied and polished by machine.

The label on the container will tell you which type you are buying.

A water-base wax (called self-polishing wax or polish) is a liquid that dries shiny without buffing. It is composed of fine wax particles in water, which serves as a carrier. It is recommended for use on asphalt, vinyl, and rubber tile. It may be used on enamel-surface felt-base linoleum and terrazzo. Do not use it on cork.

A solvent-base wax (called polishing wax) comes in liquid and paste forms and requires polishing after it dries. It is composed of wax particles dissolved in naphthalike solvent. It smells like drycleaning fluid. The liquid form is thinned with a cleaning ingredient. The paste form may be softened by placing the container in a pan of hot water. It is recommended for use on wood floors, linoleum, and cork tile. It may be used on enamel-surfaced felt base, vinyl-printed felt base, brick, stone, and terrazzo. Do not use it on asphalt and rubber.

Remove the old wax from the floor before you apply a new coat of floor wax. The kind of wax tells you the method to use in cleaning the floor, for it is the wax that determines the rest of the cleaning method.

For floors that can be washed with water, you may use:

(1) Mild household soap or syndet (synthetic detergent) for washing the floor. Rinse before waxing.

(2) Commercial floor cleaners, which are specially prepared for floor coverings on which water-base wax is used. When added to cool water, these cleaning mixtures are used for surface cleaning. A higher concentration in hot water gives a solution suitable for removing wax and discolorations.

(3) Commercial floor cleaners with a solvent base. These cleaners usually contain some wax, which helps to maintain the wax finish on the floor. They should not be confused with a solvent-base liquid wax.

Wax is not a hazard if you use it correctly. If there is too much wax, the result is a soft, smeary coat that may cause falls. Polish wax to a high gloss, because the more shine, the less slip.

Falls are apt to be caused by what comes between you and the floor, such as spilled liquids, loose rugs, foreign materials, or uneven floors. (STELLA L. MITCHELL)

Carpets
and Rugs

MOST OF US select carpets and rugs on the basis of their color, design, and durability.

Ideas of early weavers of what makes a beautiful and useful carpet continue to influence machine-made ones. Those weavers balanced esthetics and durability. Rugs centuries old are still in use.

The oriental carpet is a handwoven fabric, which has a pile knotted in during the process of making. The warp and pile generally are wool. The number of knots to the square inch (100 is a good average for an ordinary rug) indicates the fineness of the pile.

The leading types of orientals are named for the small villages and nomadic tribes of their origin. Often quality (luster, compactness of pile, and clarity of design) is associated with the names.

Rugs more than a century old are rare and expensive, but many 30 and 40 years old are available. Their colors have softened and the pile is polished. Often they are reasonably priced.

Used orientals sold in stores have been cleaned and carry a label stating their condition, such as excellent, good, fair, or poor.

Some American carpet manufacturers are making excellent reproductions of fine old orientals.

Early Spanish rugs, like the orientals, are knotted by hand. Spanish designs are used in machine-made rugs and in imported hand-knotted ones. A Spanish influence in furniture makes these rugs timely.

Aubusson and Savonniere are two famous types of French rugs. Machine-made rugs with designs based on them are made today.

The early Wilton, Axminster, and velvet rug looms were developed in England to reproduce handmade rugs. The power carpet loom was invented in America in 1839.

The first power looms produced narrow fabrics, 27 inches wide. These widths were sewn together for room-size rugs. Later looms were made to produce widths of 6, 12, 15, and 18 feet. These widths are known as broadloom. Broadloom is sold by the square yard.

Wilton carpet, regarded as a standard of high quality, is noted for sharply outlined patterns and textures.

The Axminster weaving is like the hand-knotted carpets in that each tuft of yarn is inserted independently into the warp. There is almost no limit to patterns and colors. The back is stiff and can be rolled only lengthwise, not crosswise.

The velvet weave is the simplest of all carpet weaves. The pile is woven over wire. Knife blades at the ends of the wires cut the pile yarn as they are withdrawn. When the pile is not cut, it is known as looped pile.

A major advance in carpet manufacture in 1951 was development of tufting, a high-speed method. It evolved from the hand tufting of bedspreads. With wide, multineedle machines, face yarns are sewn through the backing of woven jute or canvas. The finished carpet is passed over a latex roller, which coats the back to lock in the tufts. A secondary scrim backing sometimes is attached to the carpet.

WOOL has been the most widely used material for carpets for centuries. It is graded usually by the count system, which is based on fineness (40's, 50's, 60's, and so on) and designates the number of hanks of yarn 560 yards each that can be spun from a pound of wool top.

Carpet wools usually are coarse, wiry, harsh, and strong. They are imported duty free under the Tariff Act of 1930 and the amendment to the act in 1958. The 1930 act limited duty-free wool to the 40's. The amendment permits wools, not finer than 46's with a 10-percent tolerance to 48's, to be imported free of duty if used for carpets. Because of the amendment to the act, apparel weight wools are being used in carpets.

You have no way of knowing how much apparel wool is used in a carpet. If finer wools are blended in small amounts they may have little effect on durability, but if they are used in large amounts, naturally, less of the coarser carpet wool is used.

Three major characteristics desired in carpet wools are wearing quality (abrasion resistance), resilience (springiness), and luster (brightness). To get all of them in a yarn, manufacturers may blend wools from different countries.

COTTON was the first fiber to be used in tufted carpets. Cotton broadlooms were colorful and widely accepted for wall-to-wall carpeting, but there was a difference in quality. Rapid soiling and frequent cleaning caused loss of color. Cotton carpets resisted abrasion well. Cotton broadlooms of good quality were pleasing with bedroom furniture and furnishings.

Research on synthetic carpet fibers progressed rapidly. Rayon followed cotton in the tufting industry.

Today five groups of synthetics are used in broadlooms. They are classified by their general name and usually with the brand name and company. The classification, brand, and name of the company is one reason for so many different words used in advertising them.

The general names of synthetics are acrylic, modacrylic, nylon, polypropylene, and rayon.

The brand and company names, for example, for the acrylics include Acrilan by Chemstrand; Creslan by American Cyanamid; Orlon by E. I. du Pont de Nemours; and Zefran by Dow Chemical.

In the research on synthetic fibers, efforts are made to engineer a fiber to do virtually everything expected of a carpet fiber. No perfect fiber had been produced in 1965.

When a new fiber appears in a carpet, you find statements like the following: Can stand up under demanding wear conditions; good appearance retention; excellent resistance to abrasion; excellent resilience; excellent stain resistance; ease of spot removal; easily cleaned; essentially static free; resists mildew; high resistance to pilling; no attraction to moths or carpet beetles; good fire resistance; bright, clear colors; complete range of textures, styles, and patterns.

The fibers of the pile alone do not determine the quality of the carpet. The backing is of major importance. The face yarns are damaged if it gives way.

Jute, the most widely used fiber in backings, is a vegetable fiber imported largely from India. The quality varies.

Cotton can be a flexible and strong backing. Some of the finest woven carpets have cotton backings. Cotton is more expensive than jute.

Kraftcord, a "cellulose fiber yarn," often is used for filling or bulking for binding tufts in Axminster carpets.

Research has started on synthetic backings. Most of those mentioned in advertisements as a replacement for jute are polypropylene.

No large research project was underway in 1965 to determine the difference in the esthetic qualities and durability of all carpets on the market.

For the wear life of the pile of a carpet, exclusive of color, the amount of fiber on the face of the carpet is important. The dense pile fibers support each other. In high-pile carpets with tufts spaced far apart, the pile falls to the side. It takes longer to wear pile down from the tip than from the side.

Regardless of the fiber you are

buying, examine the carpet for denseness of pile. Bend back the face and look into the back. See how close the rows of tufts are placed. In a woven carpet, you can see the rows from the back. In a scrim-covered tufted carpet, you cannot see them from the back.

A CARPET is a background space in a room. It should recede in appearance and stay on the floor. If it is bright in color, it will appear to advance—come toward you.

A plain carpet, near the color of the walls, will make a room appear larger.

Carpets are usually designed to blend well with many styles of furniture. Plain carpet can be attractive with many.

Shading (dark or light spots) in plain carpets is caused by foot pressure and the lay of the pile pointed from the light. Shading appears in the best carpeting. If it disturbs you, avoid plain carpets.

Wear, spots, and foot tracks show less on patterned carpet than on plain. Pattern may become tiresome unless it is excellent in design and color.

The final choice of color for a carpet should be made in the room where it will be used.

The price of a carpet is based on the cost of production of the fibers of the pile and backing; styling, design, and color; construction; and sales promotion and distribution. Variation in one or more may mean wide price ranges and differences in the quality of carpet within the range.

THE CARE given a carpet in use may lengthen its years of service.

Wall-to-wall carpeting must withstand wear in traffic lanes. It cannot be removed to distribute the wear on different surfaces.

Establish a routine for care and follow it. Base the routine on the amount of wear the carpet receives.

For heavy wear, the carpet should have daily care. Remove the top surface dirt with a vacuum cleaner.

For weekly care, give it a thorough vacuuming, especially the dark surfaces under or around furniture. Remove spots immediately. Wipe up spilled water before it reaches the backing.

Every year, or at least every 2 years, have it cleaned professionally in a rug-cleaning plant where dusting equipment will remove dirt from the base of the tufts. Wool rugs may be mothproofed.

Precautions to be taken should include: Keep proper moisture in a room (40 percent to 50 percent relative humidity) to lengthen the life of the carpet and prevent the shedding of fibers; avoid walking on it with high-heel shoes to avoid cutting the pile and backing fibers; use small rugs at entrances in rainy or snowy weather; and do not shake or beat a carpet when you clean it. (MARTHA L. HENSLEY)

Window

Curtains

WHEN YOU GET new curtains, think of the likes and dislikes of the others in your family.

Each, for example, may like a particular color, all the favorite colors may go well together, and the whole family may like best a patterned fabric of those colors for the living room.

The dislikes are not to be ignored. One may have a distaste for blue curtains, because at one time he lived with poorly chosen, heavy-textured blue ones that shut out light and air.

Most windows are rectangular in shape. Without curtains, the frame creates harsh lines. But consider the purpose of the window before you consider the purpose of the curtains.

A window should let in light—controlled light. If too much sunlight pours in through a large window, you can diffuse the light with sheer curtains.

Rooms are spaces, usually walls of rectangles or squares, broken by windows and doors into spaces that not always are pleasing. These background spaces you can make into something that will be deeply satisfying for a long time.

Take radiators, which in older houses usually are under windows, where, framed with curtains of the window, they may stand out like sore thumbs. Conceal them with covers if you can, or paint them the color of the wall before you choose curtains.

A window, like a piece of furniture, may be a focal point, center of interest, or a nonfocal point.

The kind of window (whether double hung, casement, fixed, or picture), its location, and its curtain determine its full purpose as a window and its beauty as a background space. For example, a large window that frames a pleasant view, is protected from strong light by an overhang, and has textured curtains blending with the color of the walls is a satisfying background space.

Draw curtains have details for which you should plan before you buy rods or tracks. Corner windows can change the boxlike appearance of a room by a vista of the out of doors. The curtains therefore should draw away from the corner; otherwise, the design is destroyed by the stacking of the fabric in the corner when the curtains are open. You can get right and left draw traverse tracks for corner windows.

Good hardware—rods, poles, and tracks—will outwear many pairs of curtains and give much satisfaction. The general appearance of a curtain, when hanging, depends on the fixture that supports it. Proper hardware can be had for almost any type of window: Curved rods for bay windows, brass rods and wooden poles with rings, extension rods, and assembled or unassembled traverse sets.

Buy the sturdiest hardware you can afford. Your budget may dictate that you buy lightweight fixtures for windows where lighter and smaller curtains will be used in a stationary position—not drawn—and spend more for wider windows and spaces to be covered.

In a rented house or apartment, wooden poles with rings may serve us well. If you move, the poles can be cut to fit smaller windows, and the rings can be used if you have to buy longer poles. Poles with rings can be assembled for draw curtains.

CORNICES AND VALANCES are put at the top of a curtain to give a finished appearance to the window. They conceal curtain hardware. Those with a top protect the heading of curtains from dust. Cornices may be homemade or readymade.

Valances are made of fabric, usually the same material as the curtains. They hang from a wooden box or support screwed to the frame. Valances often are scalloped on the top or the bottom.

Badly proportioned cornices and valances may ruin the effect of the window. You can pretest the design, location, and dimensions of a cornice or valance by making one of wrapping paper, placing it in position, and looking at it from a distance.

Cornices are usually 4 to 10 inches high, according to the height of the window. The depth must be sufficient to cover the returns of the curtain rod—the part that extends from the curve of rod to window frame, plus the curtain.

Have accurate measurements when you buy or make curtains. Hardware should be installed before the measurements are taken. Use a yardstick, a folding rule, or a steel tape in good condition.

For draw draperies, measure the window or windows and all spaces the draperies will cover when closed. For a wall-to-wall and ceiling-to-floor draw drapery, the total area would include the window, space above, below, and on each side.

Curtains must be full enough to be pleasing when hung. Avoid skimpiness. A good standard for most curtains is 100 percent fullness. The heading of draw curtains should fit the track with ease, without taut appearance.

HARMONY OF COLOR in curtains and other furnishings in a room can be had in many ways, but there must be a starting point.

One place to start is with a color on which other colors are based—a color others can be related to, the dominant color, the one you come back to in building the color scheme.

All of us with normal color vision can use color harmoniously, if we learn to see color, not merely look at it. When we see color we can describe it.

To describe color accurately, we use three attributes: Hue, the name of the color, as yellow, red, or yellow-red; value, the lightness or darkness of the hue, as light, medium, or dark; and chroma, the brightness or dullness, as bright, medium, or dull.

Value and chroma have ranges. Yellow in a light value may be near-white, or it may be near-medium. Chroma may be nearer dull or nearer bright.

To illustrate a starting point for color harmony: In the background spaces of a room, the hue is yellow, the color from which other colors in the room may take their cue.

The walls are a yellow hue of light value, near-white. The chroma is dull, near-gray. The effect is neutral.

The rug is yellow-red in hue—the color departs from yellow because it is mixed with red, yet it is related as the name indicates. The value is light, slightly darker than the wall. The chroma is dull, the same as the walls. The color of the rug, in trade language, is beige.

The curtains are a yellow-red hue, more red than the rug. The value is the same as that in the rug. The chroma is medium, brighter than the walls and rug.

The room is cheerful because the dominant hue is yellow. All colors of the background are related and are not monotonous, because they differ in lightness and darkness and also in brightness and dullness.

It is a room of hues, values, and chromas often seen in the foliage of an autumn day.

BY TEXTURE I mean the effect of weave, fiber, and finish on the looks and feel of a fabric.

Textures may be described as harsh or soft, lustrous or dull, fine or coarse, fluffy or crisp.

Texture determines how well a fabric drapes—whether it falls in graceful folds or is stiff and awkward. A small contrast in texture may be pleasing. Too strong a contrast is distracting.

The motifs or repeats in patterned fabrics, measured lengthwise, vary from less than an inch to more than 36 inches in some fabrics. One has to plan carefully to match both lengthwise and crosswise repeats and be aware of how the motifs are arranged on one width of fabric. If they come to the edge of the selvage, fabric may be lost in matching them crosswise, because there must be a seam allowance when two or more widths are used in a panel of a curtain.

The selvage should not be used for a seam, because it may shrink when the curtains are cleaned and cause the seam to pucker.

Patterned fabrics require more yardage for the space to be covered than plain, because of matching the repeats.

The motifs in curtains at different windows in a room should match. The eye should follow the same line of motifs from window to window.

For complete satisfaction in a curtain fabric, it should be colorfast to light and laundering; not subject to shrinking or stretching; highly resistant to fire and soil; able to stand exposure to light and heat with little deterioration; excellent in draping qualities; and resistant to flexing—that is, the fibers will not break easily when bent as they are in the folds of curtains. (MARTHA L. HENSLEY)

Fireplaces

IF YOU WANT a fireplace in your new home, if you want to "sit by the fire and take hold of the ends of the earth" (as Ralph Waldo Emerson wrote), my first advice is that you plan its place, design, and size as you begin to plan the house itself.

Your architect, if you have one, will offer his experience and skill as to proportion, size, location, and design of the fireplace so that it is in harmony with the rest of the room and fulfills the functional requirements.

You will, of course, have many ideas from reading articles in magazines and other publications about styles and designs, but in selecting the most suitable type and design you are on surest ground if you choose a simple fireplace, use locally available materials, and install it according to tested principles.

You need not make it too fancy. The small house may have a fireplace, in keeping with its scale, that is as charming and comfortable as the pretentious rambler, which has a contemporary fireplace so built that the fire in it can be seen from two or three sides.

A fireplace should harmonize in detail and proportion with the room in which it is, but safety and utility should not be sacrificed for appearance.

Its position in the room should be coordinated with the location of the chimney, of course, so as not to spoil the exterior appearance of the house.

Also, there should be an area of comfort that is not affected by the toing-and-froing of other persons in the room.

Consider well the size of the opening, as heat radiated from a fireplace comes mostly from the heated brickwork that surrounds the fire.

For example, a fireplace 30 inches wide, well filled with fire, has greater heating efficiency than a 48-inch fireplace with the same fire. Openings usually are 2 to 6 feet wide.

The kind of fuel to be burned may suggest a practical width. For example, for cordwood (4 feet long) that is cut in half, an opening 30 inches wide is desirable. A narrower opening can be used for coal.

The height of the opening can range from 18 inches for an opening 2 feet wide to 40 inches for one that is 6 feet wide. The higher the opening, the more chance there is of a smoky fireplace.

In general, the wider the opening, the greater the depth. A shallow opening throws out relatively more heat than a deep one, but holds smaller pieces of wood.

In small fireplaces, a depth of 12 inches may permit good draft, but a minimum depth of 16 inches is recommended to lessen the danger that brands fall out on the floor.

Suitable screens in front of fireplaces minimize the danger of brands and sparks.

The chimney also must be soundly engineered. It should be designed and built so that it produces sufficient draft to supply enough fresh air to the fire and to expel smoke and gases of the fire.

ALL FIREPLACES are constructed in much the same way, regardless of design.

The construction of the foundation footing for chimneys with fireplaces is like that for chimneys without fireplaces. The footings must rest on firm soil below the frostline.

The fireplace hearth should be of brick, stone, terra cotta, or reinforced concrete at least 4 inches thick. It should project at least 20 inches from the chimney breast and should be 24 inches wider than the fireplace opening (12 inches on each side).

The hearth can be flush with the floor, so that sweepings can be brushed into the fireplace, or it can be raised.

A common practice, especially in contemporary design, is to raise the hearth to various levels and extend its length as desired.

If there is a basement, a convenient ash dump can be built under the back of the hearth.

In buildings with wooden floors, the hearth in front of the fireplace should be supported by masonry trimmer arches or other fire-resistant construction. Wood centering under the arches used during construction of the hearth and hearth extension should be removed when construction is completed.

Building codes generally require that the back and sides of fireplaces be constructed of solid masonry or reinforced concrete at least 8 inches thick and be lined with firebrick or other approved noncombustible material.

The jambs should be wide enough to provide stability and be pleasing.

For a fireplace opening 3 feet wide or less, the jambs can be 12 inches wide, if a wood mantel will be used, or 16 inches wide, if they will be of exposed masonry. For wider fireplace openings, or if the fireplace is in a large room, the jambs should be proportionately wider.

Fireplace jambs often are faced with ornamental brick or tile.

No woodwork should be placed within 6 inches of the fireplace opening. Woodwork above and projecting more than 1½ inches from the fireplace opening should be placed not less than 12 inches from the top of the fireplace opening.

A lintel must be installed across the top of the fireplace opening to support the masonry. For fireplace openings 4 feet wide or less, one-half by 3-inch flat steel bars, angle irons 3½ by 3½ by ¼ inch (or specially designed damper frames) may be used. Wider openings require heavier lintels.

If a masonry arch is used over the opening, the jambs must be heavy enough to resist the thrust of the arch.

The drawing shows the construction of a typical fireplace, and the table gives recommended dimensions for essential parts of fireplaces.

Proper construction of the throat area (*ff*, in the drawing) is essential.

The sides of the fireplace must be vertical up to the throat, which should be 6 to 8 inches or more above the bottom of the lintel.

The area of the throat must be not less than that of the flue. The length must be equal to the width of the fireplace opening and width will depend on the width of the damper frame (if a damper is installed).

Five inches above the throat (at *ee*, in the drawing), the sidewalls should start sloping inward to the flue (*tt*).

A damper consists of a cast-iron frame with a hinged lid that opens or closes to vary the throat opening.

Dampers are not always installed, but they are recommended, especially in cold climates.

With a well-designed, properly installed damper, you can regulate the draft; close the flue to prevent loss of heat from the room when there is no fire in the fireplace; and adjust the throat opening according to the type of fire to reduce loss of heat.

For example, a roaring pine fire may require a full throat opening, but a slow-burning hardwood log fire may require an opening of only 1 or 2 inches. Closing the damper to that opening will reduce loss of heat up the chimney.

A damper also permits you to close or partly close the flue to prevent loss of heat from the main heating system. When air heated by a furnace goes up a chimney, an excessive amount of fuel may be wasted.

Dampers of various types are on the

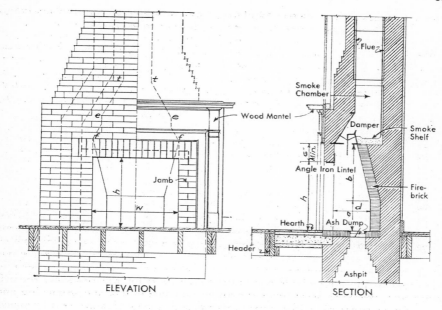

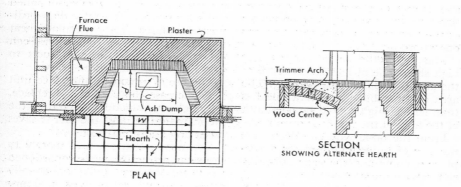

Construction details of a typical fireplace. (The letters indicate specific features discussed in the text.) The lower right-hand drawing shows an alternate method of supporting the hearth.

market. Some are designed to support the masonry over fireplace openings, thus replacing ordinary lintels.

Responsible manufacturers of fireplace equipment usually offer assistance in selecting a suitable damper. It is important that the full damper opening equal the area of the flue.

A smoke shelf prevents downdraft. It is made by setting the brickwork at the top of the throat back to the line of the flue wall for the full length of the throat. The depth of the shelf may be 6 to 12 inches or more, depending on the depth of the fireplace.

The smoke chamber is the area from the top of the throat (*ee*, in the drawing) to the bottom of the flue (*tt*). As I indicated, the sidewalls should slope inward to meet the flue.

The smoke shelf and the smoke-chamber walls should be plastered

RECOMMENDED DIMENSIONS FOR FIREPLACES AND SIZE OF FLUE LINING REQUIRED
(LETTERS AT HEADS OF COLUMNS REFER TO THE DRAWING)

Size of fireplace opening			Minimum width of back wall	Height of vertical back wall	Height of inclined back wall	Size of flue lining required	
						Standard rectangular (outside dimensions)	Standard round (inside diameter)
Width	Height	Depth					
w	h	d	c	a	b		
Inches	Inches	Inches	Inches	Inches	Inches	Inches	Inches
24	24	16–18	14	14	16	8½ x 8½	10
28	24	16–18	14	14	16	8½ x 8½	10
30	28–30	16–18	16	14	18	8½ x 13	10
36	28–30	16–18	22	14	18	8½ x 13	12
42	28–32	16–18	28	14	18	13 x 13	12
48	32	18–20	32	14	24	13 x 13	15
54	36	18–20	36	14	28	13 x 18	15
60	36	18–20	44	14	28	13 x 18	15
54	40	20–22	36	17	29	13 x 18	15
60	40	20–22	42	17	30	18 x 18	18
66	40	20–22	44	17	30	18 x 18	18
72	40	22–28	51	17	30	18 x 18	18

with cement mortar at least one-half inch thick.

A proper proportion between the size (area) of the fireplace opening, size (area) of the flue, and the height of the flue is essential for satisfactory operation.

The area of a lined flue 22 feet high should be at least one-twelfth of the area of the fireplace opening. The area of an unlined flue or a flue less than 22 feet high should be one-tenth of the area of the fireplace opening.

From the table, you can determine the size of lining required for a fireplace opening and the size of opening to use with an existing flue.

MODIFIED FIREPLACES are manufactured fireplace units.

They are made of heavy metal and designed to be set in place and concealed by the usual brickwork or other construction.

They contain all the essential fireplace parts—firebox, damper, throat, and smoke shelf and chamber. In the completed installation, only grilles show.

Modified fireplaces have two advantages.

Because the correctly designed and proportioned firebox provides a ready-made form for the masonry, there is less chance of faulty construction and more chance of a smokeless fireplace.

Properly installed, well-designed units heat more efficiently than ordinary fireplaces. They circulate heat into the corners of rooms and can deliver heated air through ducts to upper or adjoining rooms.

The use of a modified fireplace unit may increase the cost of a fireplace, although manufacturers say that the labor, materials, and the fuel it saves offset any additional cost.

You need not use a unit merely to insure an attractive, well-proportioned fireplace. You can build an equally attractive and satisfactory masonry fireplace if you plan carefully.

Even a well-designed modified fireplace unit will not operate properly if the chimney is inadequate.

ALONG with their beauty, pleasure, and comfort, fireplaces may have hazards and shortcomings.

Formation of creosote in the chimney is common and is likelier in cold than in mild climates. Green wood may contain as high as 40 percent water; dry wood, 15 to 20 percent. Wood burned slowly gives off acetic and pyroligneous acid, which in combination with water or moisture form the creosote.

Creosote is hard to remove. When it ignites, it makes a hot fire, which may crack the masonry and char adjacent timbers.

The safest method of removal is to chip it from the masonry with a blade or straightened-out hoe attached to a pipe or handle. A heavy chain drawn up and down the flue walls sometimes is effective.

When creosote is removed, care is necessary not to knock out mortar joints or to break the flue lining.

Large amounts of salt thrown on the fire in the grate or fireplace will extinguish a chimney fire.

A fire in a fireplace flue can be checked in its intensity and frequently extinguished by first quenching the fire on the hearth and then holding a wet rug or blanket over the opening so as to shut off the air.

A fireplace that smokes should be examined to make certain that the essential requirements of construction have been fulfilled. If the chimney is not stopped up with fallen brick, and the mortar joints are not loose, note whether nearby trees or tall structures cause eddies down the flue.

The flue area should be not less than one-twelfth of the area of the fireplace opening. To determine whether the fireplace opening is in correct proportion to the flue area, hold a piece of sheet metal across the top of the fireplace opening and then gradually lower it, making the opening smaller until smoke ceases to enter the room. Mark the lower edge on the sides of the fireplace. The opening may then be reduced by building in a metal shield or hood across the top so that its lower edge is at the marks made during the test.

Another way to reduce the opening is to raise the hearth by laying one or two courses of brick over the old hearth. The sides may be made narrower where further reductions are necessary.

Another cause for smokiness is lack of ventilation for the interior. New calking and weatherstripping techniques now can make a house so tight that there are few air inlets to provide air for draft such as fires need; the result is that the unlighted fireplace becomes an inlet for outdoor air necessary to fuel burning equipment needing oxygen. Then when the fireplace is lighted, the draft down the chimney is likely to drive smoke into the room. Opening a window an inch or two may let in enough oxygen so the fire will burn satisfactorily. (ARCHIE A. BIGGS)

Interior Paneling

PANELING of wood and other materials is versatile, easily applied, decorative, and utilitarian.

It is excellent for new construction, remodeling, and redecorating.

It can be had in hundreds of different combinations of materials, styles, textures, colors, and finishes that enhance the beauty, warmth, and usefulness of any room, whether a luxurious living room, a rustic recreation room, or a workshop.

Prices per square foot range from 10 cents to 3 dollars, according to the type of material and finish.

Panels are easy to handle, apply, and maintain. You need only a few tools. Many applications require only a few cuts and glue or nails to hold the paneling in place. An occasional wiping with a damp cloth (and mild soap or detergent) keeps it clean.

You can make use of the grain, figure, or parallel lines of the paneling to create effects you like.

Wood and other types of wall paneling serve many purposes and fit any style of architecture and decorative scheme. Here are examples of patterns for points of interest and decorative effects. At the bottom are examples of board-on-board paneling and paneling beveled with boards facing the center of the area.

Vertical grain and lines make a room look shorter or a wall look higher. Horizontal grain and lines give a longer and lower appearance.

Vertical or diagonal lines on the upper part and horizontal lines on the lower part of a wall, or a wainscot application will give variety to a room.

Paneling can be used to lead the eye to points of interest—the fireplace, a picture, or a built-in feature, such as a television set.

Use paneling to make room dividers, cabinet storage walls, and stub walls to hide or store equipment. Cover the wall above or around a fireplace, the back of bookcases, a sportsman's or musician's corner, between counter-top and kitchen cabinets, stair risers, or a dropped section of the ceiling with paneling of a contrasting or blending color.

Use smaller sections for emphasis points, decorative highlights, and special effects.

Perforated and shutter-wall types of paneling come in several designs suitable for utility and decoration.

The shutter-wall material is ply-wood routed on an angle at a close spacing to receive, like perforated panels, special types of hooks and fixtures for hanging items. These materials are excellent for a "working" wall or section in a utility or clothes closet, sewing room, bathroom, bedroom, kitchen, or anyplace where items are hung for useful, decorative, or display purposes. Use them also for covering a whole wall or part of a wall for hanging tools and equipment in the garage, toolroom, boathouse, and workshop.

Fire-retardant and incombustible paneling materials are available for meeting special requirements of building codes. Some types are waterproof or decay resistant.

Any of the several types of paneling can be used where excessive moisture is not a problem. Some are suitable for moist places, like a bathroom and shower stall.

SOLID-WOOD paneling comes in uniform or random-width boards made from hardwood and softwood species. Widths are 3 to 12 inches, but avoid using those wider than 8 inches in places where moisture may cause excessive swelling and shrinking of the wood. The boards may be three-eighths inch to nominal 1 inch thick and usually are nailed in place. They may be square-edged or have various machined patterns.

A new solid-wood paneling is cross-V-grooved, beveled edge, narrow strips and small thin pieces of wood with beveled edges (wood tile). They have a brick-and-mortar appearance when installed. The strips usually are nailed in place. The tile is applied with an adhesive.

Paneling boards may be clear wood or wood with knots, wormholes, and other defects of different size and number. The defects—"character marks"—add interest and highlights.

Clear wood generally is used for the more formal decorative scheme. Material of rough surface and character-marked wood are for informal and rustic effects.

Solid-wood paneling can be bought unfinished or prefinished and may be used anyplace that is not exposed to water or excessive moisture. It may be given a clear finish to preserve the natural color or stained to almost any color or intensity of tone to emphasize the wood grain and to match any decor.

PANELING that has a veneer surface of genuine wood is a popular wall material. The face veneer, a thin sheet of attractive wood, is made from hardwood or softwood species—from alder to zebrawood and of many colors, textures, and grain—and usually is laminated to a large panel of plywood, solid wood, hardboard, or particleboard.

The face veneer may be all clear wood or may contain character marks. The surface may be smooth or rough. It may be lightly grooved or scored parallel to the length of the sheet to give a uniform or a random-width board or plank effect.

Some are scored randomly across the board length and may have "pegs" added to simulate a random board length assembly. Deep U- and V-channel grooves and inlays of contrasting wood are used sometimes to emphasize the board pattern.

Some plywood without a thin face veneer is plastic coated, textured, sandblasted, steel brushed, or otherwise treated to produce attractive surfaces.

Flexible sheets of wood-veneer-covered hardboard, deeply grooved to form small squares and rectangles, are made with a cloth backing and are especially suitable for use on curved surfaces.

Plywood paneling usually comes in sheets that are 4 feet wide by 8 feet long. Other lengths are available. Some are narrower than 4 feet for greater ease of handling. Thicknesses range from one-eighth to one-half inch. The one-eighth inch material can be bent around moderate curves.

The paneling can be bought either unfinished or prefinished. It may be given a clear finish to retain the natural wood color or stained to suit decorative requirements and emphasize the grain and texture of the wood.

Some types that have a factory-applied plastic finish are suitable for use in bathrooms, except around the tub or shower stall.

HARDBOARD and particleboard are wood-base materials—wood fibers and wood particles, respectively, reassembled under heat and pressure into large, dense sheets.

Hardboard has been used for several years as the base for a wide variety of lacquer-, resin-, and plastic-coated panels.

The panel surfaces are finished with excellent reproductions of the grain and color of several species of wood. They usually are scored or grooved to simulate boards.

They also are finished with marble, mosaic, natural wood flake, and other patterns and in tinted or solid colors. Some are embossed to imitate burlap, basket weave, wicker, leather, and other designs.

They are suitable for any room where moisture is not a serious problem, but plastic-finished types are especially suitable for use in bathrooms, laundry rooms, and kitchens.

Hardboard panels are usually one-eighth to one-fourth inch thick, and particleboard panels are one-fourth to five-eighths inch thick, 16 inches or 4 feet wide, and 6 to 16 feet long. There are blocks 16 inches square and hollow-core panels. One can also get large murals on hardboard panels for bathrooms and other rooms.

Hardboard is the material used for perforated or punched panels. They are available in decorative designs, utility patterns, and combinations of the two. They are one-eighth or one-fourth inch thick, usually 4 feet wide, and 8 feet long or longer. They come in light tan or dark brown natural colors. Some are tinted or painted. They may have wood grain or other finishes and be smooth or grooved to indicate board widths.

GYPSUM PANELING is gypsum board or plasterboard covered with paper.

The paper surface may be printed with wood grain and board patterns, linen-textured finishes in an assortment of colors, or other attractive textures and patterns. Some have a vinyl film finish for extra protection and service.

It may be 16 inches, 32 inches, or 4 feet wide, three-eighths inch or one-half inch thick, and 6 to 12 feet long. The edges of the narrower panels may be beveled, tapered, or rounded. They may be left exposed for a board or plank effect or covered with matching wood strips for a more pronounced decorative effect.

Gypsum paneling may be used in any room where moisture is not a problem. Water-resistant types are suitable for use in bathrooms. The paneling can be nailed in place or applied with a wallboard adhesive.

LAMINATED PLASTIC paneling is used commonly for counter and table tops in kitchens and restaurants. It has gained in popularity as a wall material. It is a high-pressure laminate of plastics or resin-impregnated paper sheets. The surface patterns include a wide assortment of wood grains and colors, linen and marble effects in many colors, mosaic and solid colors, and symmetrical and custom designs.

It is available in several widths and lengths up to 4 feet wide and 12 feet long. Thin sheets can be applied to a smooth surface with an adhesive. Sheets already applied to a backing material, such as plywood, hardboard, or particleboard, can be nailed or glued in place.

Laminated plastic paneling can be used anywhere. The backing material should be of the waterproof type if it is to be used in a shower stall.

A wide assortment of unfinished and prefinished moldings and trim is available for use with all types of wall paneling. They make it even easier to apply the panels.

They are made from solid wood, hardboard, and metal. The factory-finished items match the color, texture, and finish of the prefinished paneling.

Nails with color-coated heads and colored putty, usually in sticks, are available to match almost any color of paneling.

Each of the paneling types is produced by several manufacturers. To find the type, pattern, texture, color, and finish that best fit your needs, visit the lumberyards and building supply and paneling dealers in your community and ask for descriptive leaflets. (E. GARTH CHAMPAGNE)

For further reading:
U.S. Department of Agriculture, *Wood Brick Strip Paneling—A New Way to Decorate.* Central States Forest Experiment Station, Research Note CS–10, Columbus, Ohio, 1963.
——— *Wood: Colors and Kinds.* Agriculture Handbook 101, 1956.

Applying Paneling

SEVERAL ITEMS should be considered when you select and apply interior wall paneling in order to achieve an attractive, serviceable result.

Occasionally city building codes require fire-retardant or fireproof materials and finishes and establish approved methods of application for specific wall areas. Determine the requirements for your location.

The decorative scheme and purpose of the paneling—formal or informal, utilitarian, and full or partial wall coverage—influence the type of paneling you select and your preparations for applying it.

A family recreation room or playroom for children will require more rigid and durable paneling than a library. Areas subject to frequent soiling should have a durable, easily cleaned finish.

The width of the jambs around windows and doors, the method for handling the trim around them, and your plans for using furring strips and insulation, as I discuss later, may determine the type and the thickness of the paneling you can use most conveniently.

Humidity and other moisture conditions in the room should be recognized also.

PLANNING the job and preparing the walls for paneling will vary according to the condition of the wall and the exterior or partition walls, location above or below exterior ground line, and type and thickness of paneling.

Many of the jobs are similar for all walls. Some, such as foundation walls, because of possible moisture problems, however, require special wall preparations for satisfactory service of the paneling.

The development of specific plans for any of the following items that relate to your job will aid you in scheduling it in an orderly way.

Plan the location of electrical switches and outlets. For walls with exposed studs, use an approved in-the-wall method for wiring and installation of the outlet boxes.

By using furring strips that are a nominal 1 inch thick (about three-fourths inch) and shallow boxes, you can put the wiring behind paneling that is to be applied over a surfaced wall. It may be necessary to chisel away some of the wall surface to accommodate the boxes.

If local electrical codes permit, you may be able to route or chisel channels and holes in the plaster so you can hide the wiring and boxes behind paneling that will be nailed or cemented directly to old walls.

Or, you may want to consider using exposed electrical conduit and outlets on the surface of the paneling.

If the walls are not already insulated, thermal insulation probably is desirable for the exterior walls, both above and below ground level, to assure protection against changes in temperature or to prevent moisture condensation on the surface of the paneling. Follow the practice recommended for your community.

Flexible blanket or batt-type insulation can be placed between exposed studs or furring strips.

Rigid sheets or panels of insulation fiberboard or plastic foam material are suitable for insulating all types of walls. The sheets may be applied to studs, furring, or surfaced walls. The rigid insulation also may serve as the backing material for thin paneling.

A vapor barrier should be used on stud-type exterior walls of new construction that will have a wood siding and painted exterior surface. A barrier can be placed also over the inside surface of old walls where exterior paint problems exist or may develop. This will reduce the possibility of exterior paint problems in the future due to the moving of moisture through the wall from inside to outside.

The vapor barrier can be on the inside surface of the thermal insulation or backing material, or it can be film or sheet material, such as 6-mil polyethylene film, paperbacked aluminum foil, or asphalt or plastic laminated or coated paper.

Film or sheet barriers can be tacked to the wall surface, studs, or furring strips above grade. If used on foundation walls below grade (below the exterior ground line), the barrier should be behind the furring.

Sound insulation may be needed in new or over old partitions to reduce sound transmission between rooms. The thermal insulating materials I discussed will serve satisfactorily for this purpose.

The thickness and toughness of the finish wall paneling you plan to use will determine the need for a backing material behind paneling that is to be applied to exposed studs or furring.

Thin or easily punctured paneling should be strengthened with a backing of plywood, particleboard, hardboard, fiberboard, or gypsum board, applied as shown in the drawing.

The backing should be of the type and thickness to give the rigidity and strength required for the intended use of the area. The less-expensive materials, such as sheathing or underlayment grades, are suitable. A mastic between the backing material and finish paneling will provide additional rigidity and strength.

An exterior-type plywood or other stable material should be used on walls below grade where moisture may be a problem.

Backing is not required to strengthen thick paneling materials or thin paneling that will be nailed or cemented to a rigid surface.

Most paneling comes with an attractive joint, but occasionally it is desirable to cover the joints or to emphasize them for special effects. Panel sections can be spaced one-fourth inch or more apart for a shadow line effect. Or, the joints can be filled with an insert or covered with flat or molded wood strips or with special metal strips of matching or contrasting color.

The rough or exposed edges and ends of paneling should be sanded, filled, and stained to match the surface, or covered. Usually it is better to cover them. Suitable covering materials include veneer, thin or molded strips of wood such as lattice, one-fourth round, one-half round, shoe, cove, or outside corner mold, and the metal edge bandings.

Two types of corners—inside and outside—may be represented in the area you plan to panel.

Plans for the trim around openings in walls and at floor and ceiling are important. For old walls, they may affect the use and thickness of the furring and insulation or backing material and the thickness of the finish paneling. In new construction, the use of furring or other materials under the paneling will determine the width of door and window jambs.

The trim can be removed and replaced after the paneling is installed, or you can fit the paneling around it and cover the joints. Usually it is best to remove and replace the baseboard and the ceiling trim. You may want to use new trim materials to match the paneling.

THE EASIEST preparation for applying sheets of thin wall paneling over exposed studs or furring on unsurfaced walls above grade is to cover the area with a backing material, as I discussed earlier. Then the paneling can be nailed or cemented in place.

Thicker sheets of paneling, which do not require a backing, can be nailed or cemented to exposed studs or furring. If the faces of the studs or furring have been covered with insulation tabs or a vapor barrier, it will be necessary to nail the paneling in place.

Horizontal furring strips or blocking between studs should be used behind boards of solid wood paneling that are applied vertically. The same is true for the vertically applied sheets or "planks" of other paneling that do not fit the spacing between studs.

PANELING can be nailed or cemented directly to an existing, above-grade wall surface if it is plumb and your plans for adding insulation, a vapor barrier, or electrical fixtures will permit it. Just chip away all bumps and trowel on a patching plaster or cement, spackling compound, or rock-hard putty to fill any depressions.

Furring should be used to aline non-plumb wall surfaces and where necessary to fit your plans for adding items behind the paneling.

The studs or furring strips in a surfaced wall can be located easily by drilling or driving a nail through the wall surface at intervals of one and one-fourth inches. Sometimes you can locate them by checking the nail spacing in the baseboard or by marks on the wall or sill under the baseboard. The furring may have been placed horizontally on a masonry or concrete wall.

After you locate the first stud or strip, you usually will find others every 16 or 24 inches apart, center to center. A chalkline, square, or straightedge can be used to mark their locations for convenience when nailing furring strips or paneling in place.

MASONRY or poured concrete walls entirely or even partly below the ground level may require special preparation to assure satisfactory service from wall paneling. There are three locations to consider: Exterior walls; retaining or interior walls, as in partial basements between the excavated area and a crawl space or unexcavated area; and freestanding partition walls.

The first is the most critical because of the possibility of water seepage

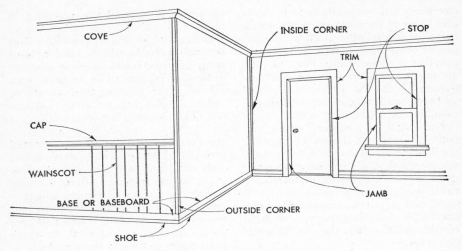

A description of some wall components.

through the wall and of moisture condensation on the surface.

Exterior walls with a dirt fill on the outside should be given waterproofing and special treatments if there is even a remote possibility of a moisture problem.

Remove the rough spots, especially loose cement at the mortar joints, and coat the wall to at least 12 inches above the exterior ground line with a cement, asphaltic, or epoxy sealer, according to the manufacturer's instructions.

The use of a solid sheet of 6-mil polyethylene film over the entire wall surface is also recommended for added protection from moisture. The film may be tacked to the sill or floor joists, or possibly embedded in the sealer, to hold it in place.

Then furring strips should be applied. They will further protect the paneling from any moisture that may come through the wall and provide an air or insulation space behind the paneling to reduce the possibility of moisture condensation on the face of the paneling.

Additional insulation can be used between or over the furring strips for further protection against condensation. The use of furring gives another

advantage; you can run electrical wiring behind the paneling.

If the wall has a history of moisture seepage, or if seepage seems probable, it would be desirable to use preservative-treated wood for the furring strips at least at the base of the wall. You can purchase treated furring strips or treat your own by giving them a 3-minute soak in a 5 percent pentachlorophenol solution. A 10- or 12-foot length of eave trough, with sealed ends, makes a convenient and inexpensive vat for treating a few strips at a time. Use weights to keep the strips submerged.

The furring strip at the base of the wall and any insulating or backing material that is used should be at least one-fourth inch above the floor surface to keep them dry.

An alternate method of preparation for paneling a masonry or poured concrete wall may be satisfactory under conditions where seepage moisture, high humidity, and moisture condensation on the wall surface are not problems or a likely possibility.

It could be considered also for rooms serviced by an air conditioner or where a dehumidifier will be used; they reduce the possibility of condensation problems. The method consists of a heavy application of an asphaltic or other mastic-type waterproofing sealer troweled onto the wall; a sheet of 6-mil polyethylene film embedded on the sealer before it dries; and sheathing grade, exterior type plywood, one-fourth or three-eighths inch thick, well nailed to the wall. This will provide a good surface for adhesive application of paneling, but it generally requires surface conduits and fixtures for electricity.

Partition walls of masonry or poured concrete do not require special prep- arations, because there should be no moisture or condensation problem associated with them.

Furring strips can be used if needed to plumb the wall or for convenience in installing electrical wiring and nail application of the paneling. Or, if the wall is plumb and you are satisfied with using surface-type electrical serv- ice units, just chip away all rough spots, especially at the mortar joints, and use a mastic for applying the paneling.

Retaining walls or interior founda-

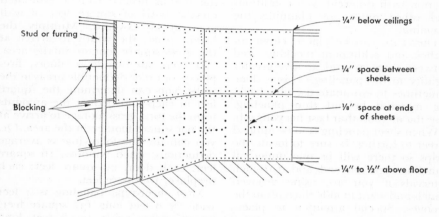

A. Horizontal application

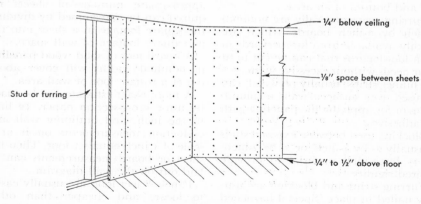

B. Vertical application

Sheets or panels of rigid backing material or thermal or soundproofing insulation can be installed in a horizontal or vertical position. The methods shown are suitable for use over surfaced walls or over exposed studs or furring strips.

tion walls with dirt behind them either full or partial depth, as found adjacent to a crawl space or in a partial basement, should be prepared the same as an exterior foundation wall if there is any possibility of moisture seepage or condensation problems. Otherwise, they can be prepared as suggested for a partition wall.

Sometimes it may be practical to use the exterior wall method on the bottom part and the partition wall method on the top part of a retaining wall.

The need for furring strips and blocking has been discussed in connection with different wall conditions and other phases of planning the paneling.

The strips can be placed closer together and additional blocking used between strips or studs to give greater rigidity to the paneling. This is done sometimes to eliminate use of a backing material behind thin paneling. Use the method that best fits your job.

When sheet paneling is to be applied direct to furring, be sure to locate the strips so there will be one under all paneling edges and ends and at 16-inch intervals if you are using grooved panels and want to hide the nails in the grooves. Special attention to placement of strips is also necessary for a balanced panel pattern at the ends and top and bottom of an area.

Furring strips generally are nominal 1-inch by 3-inch boards, which are readily available from lumberyards in even-foot lengths that can be cut to fit your needs without excessive waste.

Thinner strips, usually plywood, can be used over surfaced walls to plumb them or for applying the paneling with an adhesive.

Blocking used between exposed studs is usually 2- by 4-inch, or 2- by 2-inch, or 1- by 3-inch material to provide desired rigidity.

Furring strips and blocking are usually nailed in place. Special hardened nails are available for driving into masonry and poured concrete walls. Nails used to apply 1-inch-or-thinner furring to masonry or concrete walls

should penetrate about three-fourths inch. Use a heavy hand sledge or hammer and hard blows to sink the nails. A better job can be done by using more nails rather than longer or larger ones.

Other methods for fastening furring to concrete or masonry walls include toggle bolts, anchor nails cemented to the wall, wood plugs and lead or plastic expansion anchors for screws or nails, and mastic-type adhesives.

Toggle bolts, wood plugs, and expansion anchors require the drilling of holes in the walls.

The approximate amount of paneling that is needed can be estimated on the basis of square feet of wall area to be covered. Multiply the height times the width to arrive at the gross square footage in the area.

If there are windows, doors, fireplaces, or other deductible areas in the walls, you can determine the square feet in each and deduct the amounts from the total gross footage to arrive at the net square footage in the area. Or, you can use the following as average deductions: Each window, 16 square feet; each door, 22 square feet; each fireplace, 16 square feet.

Most sheet-type paneling is 4 feet wide by 8 feet long (32 square feet) or 16 inches wide by 8 feet long (about 10.6 square feet). Thus the approximate number of sheets required can be determined by dividing the square footage in a sheet into the net square footage of wall space.

A board foot of solid wood paneling in nominal widths will cover about 0.9 of a square foot of wall area.

A more exact estimate can be made by using cross-section paper, 12 lines to the inch, and outlining wall and deduction measurements on it at a scale of 1 inch equals 1 foot. Then the sheet or board measurements can be laid out on the wall diagram.

Panels 8 feet long are usually easier to locate and cheaper than other lengths. However, the 8-foot length may create a problem for vertical application in rooms with ceilings over 8 feet high. The problem can be

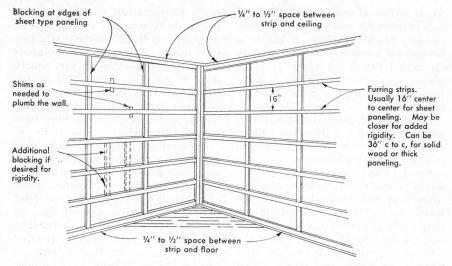

Horizontal furring strips for vertical application of board or sheet types of paneling can be nailed to exposed studs of a new wall, to studs or furring in an old wall, or to a masonry or concrete wall.

solved by placing horizontal strips of the paneling at the bottom or at the bottom and top of the wall.

Have the paneling delivered a few days before it will be used.

Do not store or install it in a room or building that has been freshly plastered or where the humidity is high.

Be sure that room humidity is about normal before applying the paneling.

Unpack it at least 48 hours before it will be used and flat-stack it with narrow strips of wood between the sheets, or distribute it around the room, so air can reach all sides of it. This will permit balancing of the moisture content of the paneling with that of the air in the room.

If moisture or excessive humidity may be a problem during some seasons of the year, back-treat wood and wood base paneling, as recommended by the manufacturer.

A good practice is to brush-coat a water repellent preservative containing 5 percent pentachlorophenol followed 24 hours later with a coat of sealer—aluminum paint for wood, shellac, varnish, or similar material.

If there are differences in grain and color of the paneling, distribute it along the wall and rearrange the boards or sheets to get the most attractive combinations of grain and color. Use numbers to identify the sequence for applying the paneling.

Nail a temporary, level strip of wood at the bottom of the area that is to be paneled. The bottom end or edge of the paneling can be set on it, and you will be sure that the lines in the paneling are plumb.

Application of paneling is usually started at a corner or an end of an area. However, paneling that contains squares or repeated patterns should be balanced on the ends of the area. Balancing at top and bottom of the area may be desirable also if it does not cause excessive waste of paneling.

Sometimes it may be easier to get the desired balance if you start applying the paneling at the exact center of the area and work outward.

Accurate marking, measuring, sawing, and fitting are necessary for a satisfactory job. Use a keyhole, saber, or coping saw to cut irregular lines on wood and wood base paneling. A knife can be used for scoring and breaking gypsum board paneling. A router is needed for putting a smooth edge on laminated plastic paneling. A block plane, rasp, and sandpaper will be helpful for fitting and smoothing the edges.

Plastic wood, colored stick putty, and other patching materials can be used to repair or fill mistakes that will not be covered by the trim.

Panels grooved to represent random-width boards generally have a groove at each 16-inch interval, which is the usual spacing for studs and furring strips. Thus, nailing can be done in the grooves to hide the nailheads.

Some paneling has tongue-and-grooved or overlapped edges, which make it possible to hide the nails in the joint.

COLOR-COATED NAILS that match the paneling can be used without countersinking to hide the heads. Otherwise, use finish nails, preferably of the spiral or annular grooved type; countersink them; and fill the holes with a matching color of stick putty.

Stick putty, a waxy material, should not be used on wood before it is stained and finished. Otherwise, the stain and finish will not enter the wood.

The panels should be well nailed around all edges and to intermediate supports.

Two gluing systems often are used for applying sheets of paneling.

One uses a contact cement, which must be applied to both surfaces at points of joining together. The cement can be applied with a brush or a serrated or sawtoothed spreader. The cement should dry to a nontacky condition before the panels are set in place. Position the panels accurately before joining the coated surfaces— the panels cannot be moved after the coated surfaces make contact.

The second system uses a mastic-type adhesive that is applied to the studs, furring strips, or rigid backing material. A serrated spreader, with deep grooves that form the mastic into high ridges, is generally used to apply the mastic, but a calking gun can be used to put it on studs and furring strips. Generally, it is necessary to use a few nails along with the mastic adhesive to hold the paneling snug until the adhesive dries.

Use a hammer and block of wood or a rubber or padded mallet to tap the panel face and embed it in the glue.

Boards of solid wood paneling are usually nailed in place. If they are hard to nail, or split easily, predrill holes for the nails. Use a bit slightly smaller than the nail. Spiral or annular grooved nails are recommended. The nailheads can be hidden in tongue-and-groove joints and other types of overlapping joints. Avoid surface nailing except where nails will be covered with trim.

Fit all joints snugly but not too tightly. If paneling must be forced into place, put a scrap of paneling or board over the edges and tap with a hammer. For stubborn pieces, clamp a piece of 2 by 4 to a furring strip or stud and use a wrecking bar to force the paneling into place.

Now that the paneling is all in place, you are ready to remove the leveling strip (and replace it, if necessary, with a strip of the paneling to fill the space) and to replace the old or install new trim.

IF YOU USED an unfinished type of paneling and trim, sand them lightly to remove all rough spots. Then brush off the dust and apply a clear penetrating wood sealer if you wish to retain the natural color of the wood.

If you want to change the color of the wood, use a stain, followed by a sealer and a good coat of paste wax.

Plastic surfaced and prefinished types of paneling and trim should be wiped clean and waxed.

Fill all nail holes with a matching color of stick putty before you wax the paneling and trim. (E. GARTH CHAMPAGNE)

Finishing Walls

ADD GLAMOUR to your walls by re-decorating them with one of the spectacular new materials or one of the old familiar items in a new color or pattern. The choice today is so great there is no longer the excuse that you cannot find a material that you like or that is easy to apply.

Visit department, hardware, variety, building-supply, and wallpaper stores. Look through the mail-order catalogs, the advertisement and home sections of the newspapers, and the house-and-home magazines.

In them you will find ideas and materials to fit any use and decorating scheme—in solid colors, stripes, floral designs, marble and textured patterns, and even materials made to look like brick, stone, and wood.

Paint and wallpaper are the familiar items, but they have been improved, and they are easier to apply.

The water-thinnable, emulsion-type paints—sometimes called latex, vinyl, or other names—are easy to apply with a brush or roller. Being water soluble, the cleanup job is simplified.

Semi- or full-gloss enamel should be used for the woodwork and for walls in the bathroom, kitchen, and laundry. The enamels do not show fingermarks and stains as quickly as flat paints. Enamels withstand frequent washing and scrubbing very well.

There are spackling compounds and other thick coatings that can be brushed or troweled over a wall. Interesting textures and patterns can be worked into them with a stiff brush or crumpled paper.

Wallpaper is available with the paste already applied. All you need do is dip the strips in water or moisten the back with a sponge and put the strips on the wall. There are leathers, fabrics, plastics, and plastic-coated papers and fabrics for use where you need a durable surface.

One of the newer wall coverings is a self-adhesive plastic material. It comes in rolls like wallpaper. You cut it into strips of desired length, remove the paper that is covering the adhesive, and put the strips in place—somewhat like applying a wide width of masking tape.

Wall tiles of ceramic, metal, plastic, and wood are easy to apply with the new mastic- or cement-type adhesives.

You trowel the adhesive on the wall or "butter" it on the back of the tile and press the tile in place. Some manufacturers furnish a strip of plastic material with an adhesive on each side for applying their tile.

Wall tile comes in assorted sizes. The heavier ceramic tile is usually 4 inches square. The lighter weight materials come in 4-, 9-, and 12-inch squares and in rectangles.

Mosaic patterns—small squares and triangles—laid on a paper or woven backing material, come in 12-inch squares and larger panels. The new grouting or joint-filling materials have simplified filling the spaces between the tile.

Linoleum and hardboard types of partial wall coverings are available, too. They usually come in 4- to 5-foot widths for application as a wainscoting with matching color-coated nails, contact cement, or a mastic adhesive.

WALLS that are to be painted or covered with a material that is applied with a paste, contact cement, or other type of adhesive should be brushed to remove all dust.

Greasy and soiled areas should be washed with an ammonia solution or strong detergent, followed by a rinse with clear water, and allowed to dry.

Loose and excessive layers of wallpaper should be removed by steaming and scraping.

Old paint, if it is in good condition, may be left in place, but glossy painted or varnished surfaces should be washed with a paint-dulling liquid or rubbed with steel wool or sandpaper.

All cracks, large and small, should be filled with patching plaster, rock-hard putty, spackling compound, or other suitable material. Sand it smooth and wipe off the dust. Do not depend on paint, wallpaper, or other thin wall coverings to hide the cracks—they will show through every time.

You will need a plumbline or level starting strip for everything, except paint or spackling compound, that you may use.

The floor, top of the baseboard, a countertop, or edge of a bathtub, if level, can serve as the starting point for applying the tile. If it is not level, you should nail a narrow strip of wood or other material at the bottom of the area for a starting line. Use a hand level to make certain that the strip is level. The strip should be removed later and the space filled with tile or covered with a baseboard or other trim material.

A plumbline—a straight and true up-and-down line—is needed for placing the first strip of wallpaper, fabric, or similar material. That first strip is the most important one. If it is straight and true, all the others will line up properly.

Start at a door or window if there is one in the wall—otherwise at a corner. Check the door or window casing or corner for plumbness. Measure out a distance equal to the width of the strip of wallpaper or other material. If the casing or corner is not plumb, make allowance to correct it. Mark the width on the wall. Hang a weighted string from a nail near the ceiling. The string should reach nearly to the floor. The weight can be any item—even a bolt or a fork—that will draw the string straight. Shift the nail at the ceiling so the string, when hanging plumb, will pass directly over the mark you put on the wall. Rub chalk, powder, or flour along the full length of the string, draw it taut when hanging plumb, and snap it to transfer a chalkline onto the wall. Remove the nail and string.

Cut enough strips to cover the wall area. Be sure to match the pattern or design for all strips by rolling them out alongside each other. Cut all strips a few inches longer than the wall height so you can trim a little off at the top and bottom as you put each strip in place.

Paste the strip, wet the paste, or remove the paper covering from self-adhesive materials and put the first strip on the wall. Let it overlap a little at the ceiling and line up the edge exactly with the chalkline that you made on the wall. Brush it in place, working from top to bottom and center to edges. Crease the end of the strip into the ceiling joint with the scissors or by tapping it with the brush. Pull it away from the wall just far enough so you can scissor cut along the creased line. Brush it back in place.

Repeat the procedure around the door or window frame and at the top of the baseboard and for succeeding strips. Wipe off any paste that may be on the window or door casing, ceiling, or baseboard.

Match the pattern perfectly and butt the edge of each succeeding strip to the edge of the previously applied strip. Open joints may be closed by pushing the strip with your hands.

When you apply linoleum or other wainscot-type wall coverings, make a level chalkline at the top of the area that is to be covered. Use a taut string, as I explained for a plumbline. The covering will have to be cut to fit around window and door casings and other fixtures.

Exact measurements at top and bottom are necessary because the casings and other items may not be plumb. The bottom of the covering material may have to be trimmed also for a good joint at the floor or at top of the baseboard. Usually it is easier to remove and replace the baseboard. (E. Garth Champagne)

EQUIPMENT

To Save Energy

MOST HOMEMAKERS want to know how to save—or to make better use of—the time and energy they need to care for their families and homes.

Organizing their work and improving their skills can help, but the arrangement of work areas, the design of the house, and the selection of tools also are important in reducing the time and the energy required for homemaking.

The homemaker (like everybody else) expends energy when she works. Even when she rests or sleeps, her body is performing work to keep the heart beating and other organs functioning to maintain life.

Much work is done by the muscles in maintaining their own tension, for there is tension in every muscle even when it is completely relaxed. The total energy the homemaker expends varies with the amount of internal and external work the body does.

Measurement of the energy she expends at housework allows us to make comparisons of ways of doing tasks and indicates why she may become tired.

We all know what it is to be tired. Fatigue is hard to define, but it is known that body changes result with overwork and that certain changes can be measured.

When a muscle works hard, energy is expended, but there also are changes throughout the body: The heart beats faster, breathing is faster, the body temperature rises, certain chemical changes take place in the bloodstream, and new excretion products appear in the urine.

How then can the design, arrangement, and equipment of a home help minimize fatigue and save energy?

WHEN WORK SURFACES, such as counters, sinks, baby bathtubs, and ironing boards are too low for the worker, proper posture cannot be maintained.

Good posture helps to assure the proper use of the muscles. When posture is correct, the bony framework supports the weight of the body without strain on the muscles and ligaments.

In correct standing, the body should be alined so that the center of the hips, of the trunk at the shoulders, and of the head are in a direct line over the center of the arches, the weight-bearing parts of the feet.

In sitting, where the base of support is the chair rather than the floor, the head and trunk should also be alined with no flex or bend at the waistline.

Fatigue can result from poor posture or continued stooping over an improperly adjusted work surface level.

121

What, then, is the most convenient and comfortable height for work surfaces for homemakers?

In performing certain hand-arm motions associated with food preparation and cleaning, homemakers 5 feet 2 inches to 5 feet 5 inches tall expend least energy when working at counters placed 32 to 40 inches from the floor.

For ironing while standing, least energy is expended when the board is adjusted to a height of 36 inches.

For loading and unloading a mechanical clothes dryer, these same homemakers expend least energy when the center of the opening of the dryer is installed at 38 inches from the floor and the clothes are transferred to or from a basket on a table 29 inches high.

Heights for built-in ovens also have been determined according to the energy expended by women using them.

For certain tasks performed over short periods of a few minutes, the homemaker expends less energy to work while standing than sitting.

For longer tasks performed while seated, the work area should be designed for comfortable sitting with the feet of the operator supported and with ample room for the knees. The work surface and chair should be arranged so that it is possible to work with elbows near waist level.

In the kitchen, the design should allow for free space under the counter or a pullout lapboard deep enough to give the necessary knee space.

A sink with a shallow bowl not more than 3.5 inches deep allows the worker to sit comfortably at the sink.

For tasks performed while sitting on a chair, the height of the work surface should be 24 to 30 inches. For sitting to work at higher surfaces, such as a counter or sink 36 inches high, a stool with a seat and footrest that can be adjusted for comfort is recommended.

Important in lowering the expenditure of energy and minimizing fatigue is a design of facilities that allows for change of body position. Changes from sitting work to standing work and changes of tempo and type of work, together with interspersed rest pauses, help to improve working efficiency.

USING THE CORRECT TOOL can also help to maintain good posture and efficient methods of work.

Long-handled equipment can be chosen to avoid bending one's back. Some house-cleaning tools have the controls high on the handles so that the homemaker does not have to stoop to start and stop the equipment.

Human dimensions help to determine the form and size of equipment, the location of controls, and the space requirements in a work center.

Tools should be as simple as possible and of proper size and have handles that meet the normal grasp limitations of the human hand.

Control levers of equipment should be placed conveniently between elbow and shoulder height.

Efficient design in storage facilities can reduce the amount of reaching and bending the homemaker must do. It takes about 19 times as much energy to get something 3 inches from the floor as to get it at elbow level.

The limits of comfortable reach have been established for wall cabinets hung over work counters that are 36 inches high and 25 inches deep.

The top shelf in a wall cabinet should not be higher than 52 inches from the floor for the homemaker 5 feet 2 inches to 5 feet 5 inches tall, if the item to be stored requires two hands to place it on the shelf.

For lightweight items that can be placed or removed with one hand, the top shelf should not be more than 68 inches from the floor.

In base cabinets, the space below 28 inches—about fingertip height—should be reserved for storing pots and pans that are seldom used.

If seated work is planned at the mix counter, the top shelf of the wall cabinet should be only 64 inches from the floor.

The space between the counter and the bottom of the wall cabinet is the space easiest to reach, but also the one frequently neglected for storage in the conventionally designed kitchen.

This space can be used to hang utensils used often. It takes less energy to hang a pan on a wall than it does to store it in base cabinets that require opening and closing of cabinet doors.

Space often overlooked on wall and door surfaces can be utilized in food preparation, sewing, and laundry areas for easy-to-reach storage.

A homemaker can determine how convenient work and storage facilities are for her if she stands about a foot away from the wall and moves her arm freely from the shoulder so that the hand makes a large circle. Another person can record the high and the low points of the circle.

A smaller imaginary circle made by moving the arm only from the elbow should define the work and storage areas for things used oftenest.

Storing articles within these imaginary circles can help the homemaker to eliminate bending in laundry, sewing, and kitchen work centers.

Walking, like bending, takes considerable energy. Walking requires two to three times as much energy as standing quietly.

Many extra steps are taken in a year by walking through the living room in order to get from the kitchen to a bedroom or a poorly located bathroom.

If an American woman weighing 125 pounds walks 7.5 miles a day or takes roughly 19 thousand steps, her feet take a daily load of more than 2 million pounds. Some women may walk as much as 500 feet in preparing a simple meal. Good design of work centers can considerably cut down on the energy expended in needless walking.

The relationship of rooms and the arrangement of work and storage facilities should be considered if walking is to be reduced.

Storing things near the place they are used should eliminate many steps. For example, bath linen should be stored near the bathroom; bed linen, near the bedrooms; sewing supplies, wherever sewing or mending is done;

dishes, near the dining table and sink or dishwasher; all mixing supplies and utensils, at the mix center; and other foods and utensils, where they are first used.

Walking upstairs requires three to five times as much energy as walking on the level. Getting work done in a house in which the work and living centers are on different floors requires more energy than does similar work in rooms on one floor.

PREPLANNING of work should help to eliminate unnecessary stair climbing.

An analysis of ways of working—including body movements in relation to design of the house and its facilities—should also be helpful: Can the effort put into washing dishes, cleaning, sewing, ironing, and caring for the children be reduced?

Are work centers planned to allow free body movement, which for greatest ease should be rhythmical and, if possible, circular? It saves effort to learn literally "to swing" the job.

Are counters free of clutter and big enough to allow you to work with both hands?

Are storage and work surfaces designed so that tools and materials can be stored in readiness for use? ("A place for everything, and everything in its place.")

Are tasks planned to minimize controlled movements and are working-space designs adequate to allow the use of the pull of gravity whenever it can aid the operation?

Is there counter space enough to allow the left hand to carry its share of the workload or alternate with the right hand? Time spent by the homemaker in the critical appraisal of the arrangement and equipment of the work facilities of the house—the one being planned, the one already occupied, or the one considered for purchase—will be time well spent.

The returns will be in energy and time saved and less fatigue in the years ahead. (MARTHA RICHARDSON AND MILDRED HOWARD)

Only if the positive considerations outweigh the negative ones are you concerned with selection. If they do not, you do not need to make a choice now.

Selecting

Equipment

I OFFER some general guidelines that may help you when you buy household appliances.

An appliance bought chiefly because it is on sale at so many dollars less than the "regular price" may be satisfactory, but you are more likely to select equipment appropriate for you if you evaluate your needs and all the facts you can get about it.

Do you need the appliance?

Will it make your homemaking tasks easier?

Will it contribute to more effective performance of homemaking tasks?

Will it make your home safer? More livable? More enjoyable?

Will it make extra space in your home by replacing items that take more space?

Will it save energy for members of the household and permit more creative activities than they now undertake?

Consider possible negative factors.

Will the appliance add excessive heat or noise in your home?

Is it better to save the money or use it for another purpose?

Will the appliance occupy space that you prefer not to give up?

Will it complicate your way of doing things? For example, if your laundry has been done out of the home, what changes are likely to take place in your work habits if you acquire laundry equipment? If you buy a separate freezer or a large refrigerator-freezer, will you feel you should do home-freezing that you do not now do?

NEW HOUSES sometimes have equipment that the contractors supply. Many contractors are willing that the home buyer specify the models. In some instances, you will pay more than you would if you accepted the contractor's choices—but that means you are making a selection according to your estimate of your needs rather than on price alone.

Consider the kitchen sink, for example. How wide it should be and whether it should have one, two, or three wells depend on the layout of the kitchen and on plans for a built-in dishwasher next to the sink.

You know your work habits better than the contractor does, and you know whether you want more counter and storage space or a sink with two wells rather than one.

Also, you may want a sink of better quality than the contractor plans to supply. You will be wise, then, to consult retailers of plumbing supplies, visit the showrooms of a large manufacturer, or compare prices and details given in mail-order catalogs.

Stainless steels vary in composition. Two sinks of the same type of steel may have different thicknesses. Different types of fittings are available at different costs.

Somewhat similar considerations apply to a waste disposer to be installed in one well of a kitchen sink. If you inform yourself about what is available, you may want a more expensive model than the contractor has planned. If the model you choose is cheaper, you may expect a cash allowance for some other part of the kitchen or house. An informed consumer will ask that the disposer have its own trap to insure better operation. That means two traps for a double-well sink.

YOU GET and evaluate information in

this way: Check printed sources—books on household equipment, bulletins, advertisements, articles in magazines, catalogs of mail-order firms.

Check recent issues of Consumer Bulletin and Consumer Reports for articles on the type of appliance in which you are interested. These magazines are available in public libraries. Current issues may not have the information you want, but for many appliances, issues that are 2 or more years old may supply useful tips on construction and operating characteristics. For example, in purchase of a gas water heater, the recovery rate (gallons of water that will be heated through a 100° temperature rise in an hour) is as important as the size or gallon capacity of the water heater. A Consumer Bulletin or a Consumer Reports article that alerted you to recovery rate would do you a service regardless of whether the article was new or old.

Reading the entire article is as important or more important than the ratings assigned to different models—you should then be better able to evaluate the ratings relative to your needs.

Chat with friends who own the type of appliance you are interested in to learn what they like and do not like about a particular model. Find out why. A woman may say she does not like a dishwasher because it does not get dishes clean. You may learn in chatting with her that she uses water that is not hot enough, or the water is excessively hard, or she expects too much—for example, she puts unscraped, heavily soiled breakfast dishes into the appliance and operates it after the evening meal.

When you visit stores that sell the appliance, have in mind the main points in which you are interested. Look at the appliances on display. Try to visualize different ones in your home. Request a sales presentation on features and ask for printed specifications and the user's folder or booklet. If a manufacturer's representative is in the store, chat with him.

Ask questions: When a salesperson speaks of automatic defrosting in a refrigerator-freezer, is only the refrigerator section automatically defrosted or are both sections automatically defrosted?

Ask the salesman about local codes. He may be able to tell you, for example, whether the type of chimney you have is suitable according to local codes for venting a gas incinerator.

He may say a particular clothes dryer will receive a washer load—meaning a load from a washer that is the companion model to the dryer. But will it handle the load of the washer you already have?—or will you have to divide the load?

Ask particularly about features that are new to you. Some new features may be useful; some you may not care for.

Ask about safety seals; warranties (which parts are covered and who pays for labor); arrangements for servicing; trade-in values and installation cost; the approximate operating cost per month, day, cycle of operation.

Servicing arrangements may include the purchase of a service policy. Most household appliances are not designed for servicing by the user, and do-it-yourself work within a warranty period invalidates the warranty.

CONSIDER costs. The most deluxe models of small electrical appliances—mixers, coffeemakers, saucepans, frypans—are not inexpensive. Indeed, the total cost of three or four most deluxe (top-of-the-line) models may equal or exceed the cost of a stripped-model range.

Consider also where you will store such appliances. You may not use often a stand mixer if you have to keep it in a cabinet near the ceiling. Perhaps you can store a smaller one in the storage space in the mix area or on a countertop.

A point to remember is the size of an appliance in relation to the way in which you are most likely to use it.

If, for example, you usually make only 2 cups of coffee at a time, a 10-cup model that is to be used for 2 cups regularly and 10 cups once in a while is a poor choice.

IT IS UNREALISTIC to buy an attractive and expensive frypan that can be used at the dining table if, like most persons, you do not take an electric pan to the table. On the other hand, if you plan to use a waffle iron for informal entertainment, a large size may be best, for you can serve several persons at one time.

Some knowledge of the automatic features helps. A light that indicates an appliance is on is different from a control that turns the appliance on and off automatically. It is not reasonable to expect complete accuracy in the thermostats of some small electric appliances.

Some knowledge of materials also is helpful. A nonporous material, like stainless steel, ceramic, or glass, for the inside of a coffeemaker is easy to keep clean.

FINALLY, these points should be checked:

The warranty or seal of a recognized agency—Underwriters' Laboratories, Inc., for electric devices and nonelectric household wares such as pressure saucepans and American Gas Association seal for gas appliances.

Effectiveness of the appliance for the primary purpose you have in mind.

Ease of use.

The space it takes in your kitchen.

Ease of cleaning and maintaining. (It may be easy to clean the surfaces of a nonvented range hood; is it easy also to clean or replace the filter or filters and to oil the motor?)

The design of the appliance.

Durability.

Availability of servicing.

The reputations of the manufacturer and dealer for standing behind the articles they sell.

Price.

(FLORENCE EHRENKRANZ)

Kitchen Tools

THE TOOLS you use to cut, mix, beat, strain, roll, sift, and measure food may each be small and inexpensive, but a collection of them can be large and costly.

A bride does well to buy a carefully selected minimum set of good utensils. Friends are likely to add pieces as shower gifts, and other items will be bought impulsively from display counters.

ALL TOO SOON A kitchen becomes cluttered with tools that are less useful than expected or do not work so well at home as in the skilled hands of the demonstrator at the fair.

Tools that seldom are used may not be worth the space they take and may well be discarded.

The clues to tools that actually are needed are in recipes. Tools can be considered in groups according to use. Within each group there is choice of tools, materials, and designs.

Comfortable handles and water- and stain-resistant materials are important. Insulated handles on much-used equipment should be attached by rivets.

FOR ACCURACY, choose measures that are labeled "U.S. Standard."

A minimum measuring kit consists of a set of spoons, one-fourth teaspoon to 1 tablespoon; a nested set of metal cups, one-fourth cup to 1 cup; and a glass cup with a pouring lip.

The metal cups are packed with firm fat or heaped with dry material and then leveled with a straight-edged spatula.

Transparency of the glass cup enables you to match the level of liquid to markings on the side, a rim prevents spillage, and the lip aids in pouring. A 2- or 4-cup liquid measure is good for larger amounts.

MOVING FOOD calls for spoons, tongs, forks, and turners.

For hot food, tools should have long, insulated handles and should be large and strong enough to hold food securely.

Take your choice of long- or short-blade turners and straight or offset handles.

Offset handles are somewhat easier to use in pans with sides. Straight handles are fine for use on griddles or cooky sheets.

A STRAINER, frequently used with moist foods, should be of rust-resisting metal and of medium mesh and diameter. Other sizes may be added for special needs.

A colander is useful for draining some foods. A metal frame, from which the strainer can be removed, facilitates cleaning and gives support to the wire mesh.

A large flour sifter is needed only if you frequently handle several cups of flour at a time. Otherwise a small one is adequate and takes less storage space. The strainer may serve the purpose if you use packaged mixes and rarely sift flour. Most sifters are difficult to clean thoroughly.

TOOLS TO beat, blend, mix, stir, and whip range from large electric mixers to a dime-store whip.

An electric mixer reduces the work in many tasks. The mixer with its own stand leaves your hands at least partly free.

The hand electric mixer is not designed for heavy doughs. It may give less volume to egg whites or whipped cream, and you have to hold it. It requires little storage space, is relatively light in weight, and costs much less than its big brother.

Stainless-steel blades, large plastic handles, and smooth gears that give high speed with little effort are essentials for a good rotary beater.

Many women like to have a sturdy rotary beater even if they have an electric mixer. The rotary beater is handy and sometimes quicker and easier to use than either of the electric mixers for some tasks.

The electric blender does jobs different from those done by the mixers. Its sharp blades and high speed reduce solids to liquids in moments. Directions need to be followed to avoid overblending. The blender is a boon for preparing special diets and children's food. An imaginative cook finds many other uses for it.

For blending fat and flour or other dry ingredients, there is a choice of fork-type or cradle-shaped blender. Either works well. For light beating of small amounts of food or for blending of liquids or sauces, handy wire whips or the blending fork will serve. The blending fork can be cleaned somewhat more easily.

Large, strong mixing spoons are essential. The shape of the bowl is a matter of choice. Whether the spoon is slotted or solid is immaterial. The wooden spoon may be preferred for some purposes, such as stirring in metal pans. Wood is less durable than stainless steel and harder to keep clean, but it is inexpensive. Hardwood spoons are more desirable than spoons of softwood.

TOOLS THAT mash, grate, shred, and puree reduce soft solids to a smooth state and firm ones to small pieces.

An ordinary potato masher or blending fork will do the first job.

The grater or shredder should be of steel to provide a firm, sharp cutting edge at each hole. It may be of stainless steel or tinned steel to resist rust. Sharp, round, or oval holes produce shreds of a definite form. Punched holes tear food, releasing juice and flavor but producing a mushy product (grated lemon rind, for example).

Some shredders are box shaped and have different kinds or sizes of holes

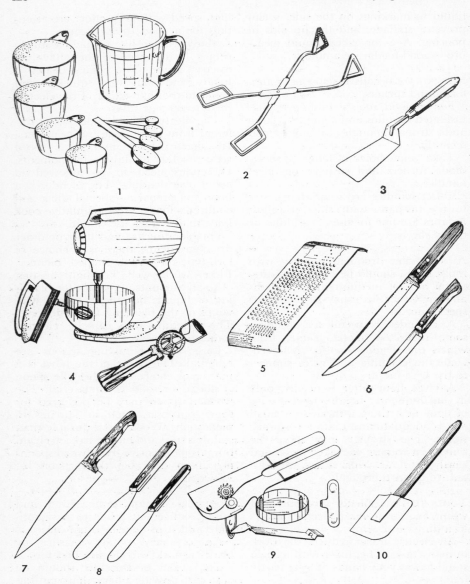

1. A minimum measuring kit.
2. Tongs have many uses—handling broiled steaks and hot ears of sweet corn.
3. Turner with an offset handle.
4. Rotary beater, portable hand mixer, and standard mixer perform similar tasks.
5. This grater has holes with smooth edges.
6. A paring knife and slicer are basic cutlery needs.
7. French cook knife—the offset handle makes chopping easy.
8. Two sizes of spatulas.
9. Openers: Essential for modern-day food preparation.
10. Less food is wasted and dishwashing is easier when you use a rubber spatula.

on the four sides. Others are flat shredders and saladmakers, operated with cranks.

There are several types of utensils that puree and can be used to separate skins and seeds. One type has a perforated metal pan with a crank-operated blade. Another type uses a lever arrangement to force a flat disk against the food, which is riced as it goes through a perforated cylinder. A third type has a tapered wooden pusher by which food is pressed through openings in a conical utensil.

Still another is the crank food chopper, which has plates that vary the fineness of the product. It is indispensable to some homemakers but of little use to others. Some of these grinders or shredders have to be firmly (although temporarily) mounted to a table or cabinet top. Some have suction feet, which hold the tool in place.

THE CUTLERY GROUP—tools that cut, dice, chop, pare, peel, mince, slice, and spread—is one of the most important in the kitchen.

As an absolute minimum, everyone needs a good paring knife and a general-purpose slicer or carver with a 7- or 8-inch blade.

Besides these, you have a wide choice as to type and size to be selected according to preference and need: The utility knife (a king-sized parer); the French cook's knife, with a heavy, straight-edged blade for mincing on a cutting board or cutting large, solid vegetables; the roast slicer, with a long, slender blade and blunt end; the bread or cake knife; and many special ones.

To take and hold an edge, the blade must be of high-carbon steel. Stain resistance is also desired. High-carbon stainless steel, vanadium steel, and chromium-plated high-carbon steel are all satisfactory.

A flat-ground blade (tapering evenly from back of blade to the ground edge) is durable, but hollow-ground blades cut thinner slices, are easier to use in

paring, and often are recommended for general household use. They are more easily damaged.

Some knives with scalloped-edge blades stay sharp a long time, because the point of the scallop gets most of the wear from cutting surfaces.

Keeping a knife blade in good condition through reasonable care is better than frequent sharpening. That means cutting on a board, protecting the blade in storage, not storing a knife with other tools, and never using it to pry off lids, open packages, or sharpen pencils.

Keep an old, cheap knife for the rough jobs. Never, never use a knife to open cans. It is unsafe.

One way to sharpen a knife is to stroke the cutting edge on an oilstone. Hold the blade at a slight angle to the stone. If you use a hand-operated or electric rotary sharpener, let the knife rest lightly in the groove.

If you invest in high-quality knives, follow the recommendation of the manufacturer as to sharpening.

Cutlery handles, whether of plastic, hard rubber, hardwood, or plastic-impregnated wood, should be attached with medium-sized rivets and should fit your hand comfortably.

Dull-bladed spatulas have many uses, from leveling flour in a measuring cup to spreading frosting on a cake. The blade should be flexible.

Other members of the cutting family are the kitchen shears and plain and fancy biscuit and cooky cutters.

ONE WORD—open—means a variety of operations.

For tinned cans, the opener may be a hand model, a wall-mounted one, or an electric opener, either wall mounted or with its own stand.

A properly designed high-carbon steel blade cuts clean and leaves no sharp edge on cans.

It is a convenience to have the can lid tilted up for easy grasping or held up out of the food by a magnet. The blade and magnet that hold the lid should be easy to remove for cleaning.

Often they are not. For cans of liquid, the simple, inexpensive punch is most useful.

Screw caps call for an opener that is adjustable to grip any size. A variety of tools are available for pry-off lids. If you have several located strategically, you will have less temptation to use a good knife for the purpose.

SEVERAL ACCESSORY tools and utensils are useful.

Several bowls of various sizes are needed. For use with a small electric mixer or a rotary beater, a bowl should be deep and narrow. A 4-cup measure may double for the purpose. Weight helps to hold the bowl in place when beating is done.

A cutting board is necessary if you care about keeping knives sharp and protecting your countertops. You have your choice of sizes and shapes.

A large board is needed for rolling dough. You may prefer a plastic board or a pastry cloth to a wooden board.

The rolling pin, too, can be of plastic or wood. Hardwood, such as birch or maple, is desirable for cutting boards and rolling pins. Hardwood, cut across the grain, makes the best chopping board.

If you do not own a rubber spatula, you have no idea how handy it is. The rubber should be flexible. Buy a new one when the rubber becomes stiff.

Some homemakers consider the pastry brush an indispensable aid in oiling baking pans, buttering crusts of hot breads, basting meats for broiling, and similar operations. Nylon brushes are easy to clean but should not be used on extremely hot surfaces.

Cakes, cookies, and pies placed on a cooling rack after removal from the oven cool quickly because air can circulate underneath as well as around and over the pan or the food. For the homemaker who bakes layer cakes, two cooling racks are desirable. Store the racks carefully so they do not become misshapen.

Many recipes state the temperature to which a food should be cooked.

Correct use of thermometers gives assurance that food will be cooked to the right stage. Meat, candy, and deep-fat thermometers differ slightly. Select one for the intended use. The numbers on the thermometer should be easy to read.

The list of available gadgets could be pages long. It includes garnish cutters, cake decorators, and devices of many kinds for special purposes. To the homemaker who makes good use of it, any gadget is worth having. Seasonal ones, like Santa Claus cooky cutters, can be kept in a back corner or on a high shelf most of the year.

To earn a priority position in a top kitchen drawer, any tool should prove its worth through frequent, satisfactory service. (ELIZABETH BEVERIDGE AND LYDIA INMAN)

For Cooking

RANGES for homes are of four types: Freestanding, built-in, drop-in, and slide-in. They are 19 to 42 inches in front dimension and may have one or two ovens. Ovens may be at eye level, below the range surface, or both.

Most electric and gas (LP, natural, or manufactured) ranges have four surface units. Usually one unit (or two) is larger and has greater heat output than the others and so can heat larger containers of food more quickly.

Electric surface units may have five or seven switch positions. Some have graduated cooking positions over the entire dial. Some have pushbuttons for 4-, 6-, or 8-inch heating coils to suit the size of pan.

Many gas ranges are equipped with burners with four click positions and may be used at any number of positions.

The gas and electric ranges may be equipped with thermostatically controlled surface units. The unit operates on full heat until the food reaches a selected temperature. Then the heat lowers or cuts off automatically and continues to cut on and off to maintain the temperature.

Some ovens have a clock mechanism that turns the oven on and off at a time set in advance. The clock also may control an outlet, to which a small appliance, such as a coffeemaker, may be connected.

The heat controls on some ovens have a range of 140° to 550° F. Low settings may be used for thawing frozen food, warming plates, or keeping food at serving temperatures.

The controls on some gas ovens automatically change from one oven temperature to another, usually from a cooking to a keep-warm temperature.

An automatic meat thermometer eliminates the worry about undercooking beef or a turkey. When the meat reaches the preset internal temperature, the heat is reduced, and the oven keeps the meat serving hot without further cooking.

You may like to have a rotisserie in the oven or on the top of the range if you enjoy barbecued foods. Thermometers built into the spit assure properly done fowl or heavier cuts of meat.

Ceramic burners, higher wattage units, and reflectors provide concentrated heat for broiling. Multiheat broilers eliminate raising and lowering the grill. Grills on some constant-heat types can be raised or lowered from the range control panel. Vertical broilers that cook both sides at once are also available. To keep down spattering on the oven walls, some ranges have a high-walled pan, which is cooled by a water pan below.

Thermostatically controlled griddles are built into the surface of some models of gas and electric ranges. In one gas range, the griddle may be substituted for a large grate and converted to a fifth surface burner.

In one electric range, the oven can be cleaned automatically by setting the proper controls. A high temperature in a closed oven burns off the soil.

A plastic coating, easily cleaned with a damp cloth, on slideout oven sides is a feature of another range.

On other models, oven doors that lift off, an oven lining that rolls out, and sides and backs of ovens that are covered with replaceable aluminum foil contribute to easier cleaning.

Knobs, burners, trim rings, surface units, and drip pans are easy to remove for washing in many ranges. Several ranges have built-in ventilating or exhaust systems.

No one model has all the convenience features I have outlined. As models increase from the low end of the line to the top of the line, convenience features generally increase, with corresponding increases in price.

WHEN YOU SELECT a range, check for sturdy construction and a well-insulated oven.

Look for well-spaced surface units.

Check the clearance between the surface units and the oven on high-oven ranges.

Check for easy-to-read controls so placed that you do not have to reach over steaming pans to make adjustments, shelf stops that prevent oven and broiler racks from being pulled out accidentally, and parts that are easy to clean.

Pass up features that duplicate the jobs of small cooking appliances you already own. Choose the features that will make cooking easier and more pleasurable.

Look for the approval seal of the American Gas Association on gas ranges and the Underwriters' Laboratories seal on electric ranges.

Check the availability of adequate and prompt service.

THE PROPER SELECTION and use of utensils for the top of the range and for the oven are important.

The material used in top-of-the-

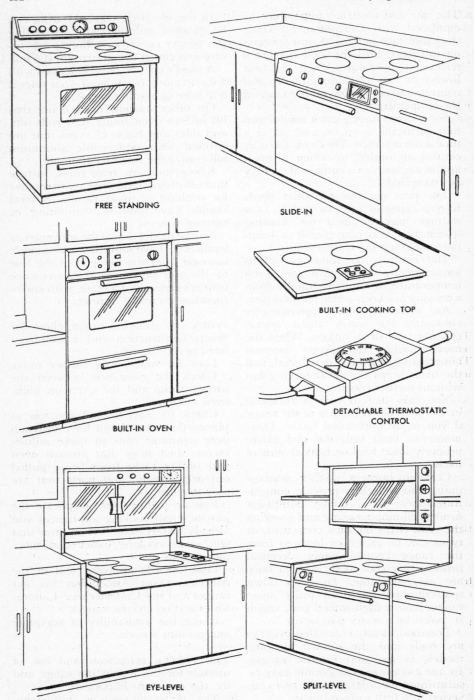

FREE STANDING

SLIDE-IN

BUILT-IN COOKING TOP

BUILT-IN OVEN

DETACHABLE THERMOSTATIC
CONTROL

EYE-LEVEL

SPLIT-LEVEL

range utensils should be a good conductor of heat so that the bottom of the utensil will heat quickly and evenly, with no hot spots on which food can stick and burn.

The bottoms of utensils should be flat and remain flat after heating to make good contact with the heating unit. The sides should be straight to conserve heat.

Covers should fit closely to hold steam within the pan and reduce cooking time. Covers, knobs, and handle grips should be of heatproof material and be easy to grasp without burning the fingers.

The handle should be firmly attached so that it cannot come loose and turn in the hand.

Pans are easier to clean if they have a pronounced curvature between the sides and bottom and no ledges or rivets on the inside where food can collect.

THE SIZE OF THE PAN should be matched to the size of the burner. Thermostatically controlled surface units are calibrated to operate with medium-weight aluminum utensils. If skillets of other materials are used, you will have to modify the temperature settings.

Utensils to be used in the oven should be selected to produce the product desired.

For double-crust pies, glass, Pyroceram, anodized aluminum, or porcelain enamel will give crisper crusts.

For cakes, pans with dull, rough bottoms and shiny sides will give the largest volume and tenderest crumb.

For cookies, use a moderately shiny sheet of a size that allows 2 inches of free space in the oven on all sides for circulation of heat.

Casseroles of glass, Pyroceram, and porcelain enamel are good selections.

When you use several pans in the oven at the same time, you should stagger them to allow for proper circulation of heat and place them so they do not touch each other or the sides of the oven.

IN ELECTRONIC RANGES, cooking times are one-third to one-tenth those of conventional ranges.

High-frequency microwaves penetrate the food to a depth of about 2.5 inches from all sides. The air in the oven is not heated.

Glass, china, and paper transmit microwaves, but metals reflect them. Cooking in a microwave oven, therefore, must be done in glass, china, or paper containers.

Because food does not brown in an electronic oven, some electronic ranges have incorporated a high-speed, conventional broiler in the top of the oven for browning. Ovens available in 1965 are about the size of a separate built-in oven and operate on a standard 240-volt range outlet.

MANY PORTABLE ELECTRIC cooking appliances supplement or substitute for the kitchen range. Most of them provide fast, controlled heat. Most have relatively high wattages. To use them efficiently, the home wiring system must be adequate to carry the wattages that are indicated on the nameplate of the appliance.

Some portable appliances have permanently attached heat controls. Others have detachable controls.

Those with detached controls have a water-sealed heat unit, so that you can immerse them completely when you wash them. The same heat control is interchangeable among appliances of one manufacturer but not with other brands.

Select portable cooking appliances that have easy-to-grip handles and heat-resistant, nonmar feet, with adequate airspace beneath the appliance to prevent damage to tabletops.

Frypans are of several sizes and may be round or square. Covers are sometimes sold separately and may have a domed or a shallow cover. A domed cover will make the pan usable for pot roasts, fowl, and stews.

Some lids are vented to allow steam to escape and permit browning. Some skillet covers have broiling units that make the skillet a broiler as well. Large skillets are easier to handle if they have an auxiliary handle opposite the long handle, or have two side handles, as on a casserole.

An electric griddle should be large enough to eliminate frequent refills but not so large that it is awkward to handle or heats unevenly at the corners and around the outer edge. A grease-drip container that holds 6 ounces and is large enough at the top to insert a spoon for basting, and with provision for emptying hot fat from the container is desirable.

On a rotisserie, foods are cooked as they turn on a motor-driven spit. A rotisserie may also be used for broiling. Some, which have a second heating unit in the bottom and a means of closing the spit opening, may also be used for baking. Some of the models have a thermometer on the end of the spit to indicate the interior temperature of the meat, a timer, and a switch that turns off the motor when the rotisserie is being used for other cooking. Some are large enough to handle a large fowl or roast.

Portable ovens and broilers come in a variety of sizes and wattages. Many are equipped with thermostats. Some have a unit for baking and one for broiling. One has a single unit that serves for baking and broiling; the oven itself is turned upside down to broil. Most controlled-temperature ovens are satisfactory for baking a single pie, a cake, or casserole, biscuits, and potatoes and so may make unnecessary a second oven in a range.

Electric coffeemakers are of the percolator or vacuum types. Most cut to a keep-warm temperature after brewing. Some have signal lights, flavor selectors, and reheat settings.

Coffeemakers make the best brew when they are used to capacity. The size you buy, therefore, should provide the number of servings you need frequently. Most deliver fewer servings than the rating indicates and disregard the ratio of coffee to water for top-quality brew.

To determine the number of servings a coffeemaker delivers, measure the number of ounces of cold water required to reach the full mark, divide by 6 to determine the number of servings, then use two tablespoons of coffee for each serving.

Points to check on percolators: Securely fitting lids, glass perk top, and tight-fitting basket tube; a basket large enough to hold the required amount of coffee when the grounds are wet; and a tight-fitting spreader plate to prevent the grounds from floating off into the brew.

Vacuum types should have filters that are easy to clean. (MILDRED G. ARNOLD)

Refrigeration

REFRIGERATORS are cooled by the absorption of heat required to change a solid to a liquid (as in a refrigerator that uses ice) or a liquid to a gas (as in the mechanical refrigerator). The heat is disposed of outside the refrigerator.

The mechanical refrigerator uses electricity, gas, or kerosene as its source of energy.

The electric type has moving parts, which become worn and may be slightly noisy in operation.

Gas or kerosene refrigerators have additional flame heat to dispose of.

THE COST OF ENERGY and the cost of the refrigerator itself are factors to consider. The initial cost of the electric refrigerator is less than that of the other mechanical types.

The types of mechanical refrigerators are all-refrigerator, conventional, and combination refrigerator-freezer.

In the all-refrigerator, most of the interior space is above freezing, 32° F.

The conventional type usually has a single outside door and an inner door enclosing a freezing section at the top.

In the combination, the refrigerator and freezer spaces are two separate compartments, each with a separate door. The freezer may be above or below or at the side of the refrigerator space.

THE SIZE you should buy depends on your marketing habits; the size, age, and health of your family; and the amount of entertaining you do.

A family of two should have a refrigerator of at least 6 (preferably 8) cubic feet. Add an extra cubic foot for each additional family member, plus 2 cubic feet if you have guests often.

If a separate freezer is not available, the freezer space in the refrigerator should contain 2 cubic feet per family member.

Next, you should consider where the refrigerator is to be placed, because the wall space available determines its height, width, and depth.

The three sizes of refrigerators—compact, standard, and combination—vary in total capacity from 0.37 to 27.5 cubic feet. The freezer spaces are 0.2 to 16.11 cubic feet, depending on total size and style. If the freezer space is given in pounds, divide by 35 to determine the relative size in cubic feet.

These refrigerators come in free-standing and built-in styles. The standard size is a smaller, less expensive conventional type and has fewer features than the combination one.

Dimensions do not necessarily determine food storage capacity. Thin-wall refrigerators with storage to the floor give more interior space without increasing the exterior dimensions.

Most refrigerators have right-hinged doors, but left-hinged ones usually are available at additional cost. Choose a refrigerator whose door opens on the side nearest the counter workspace. Door hinges are usually flush, and the door opens within the dimensions of the cabinet.

MOISTURE from warm air within the refrigerator condenses when it comes in contact with the evaporator coils and freezes.

The frost acts as insulation and increases the operating cost if it becomes more than one-fourth inch thick.

Defrosting, to remove this crystalline ice, is done in one of three ways—manual, semiautomatic, and automatic.

In the manually defrosted refrigerator, you set the control to "defrost" and reset to normal temperature after defrosting.

The semiautomatic defrost cycle is started by pushing a button, which causes the refrigerator to defrost, but it resets itself automatically.

In the automatic, the refrigerator defrosts at predetermined times. A clock timer, a compressor cycling, or a door counter are the control devices.

Freezer and refrigerator spaces may be defrosted in the same way or by a combination of ways. A few less expensive refrigerators do not provide a mechanical or electrical means of defrosting.

The defrosting period is reduced by having an electric heater come on during defrost cycle, or a hot gas flows through the evaporator coils or a separate set of coils.

In the frost-free combination, the evaporator coils are located outside the refrigerated spaces. A fan is used to blow cold air into these spaces. Forced-air circulation makes it important to protect foods from moisture evaporation. Frost on the evaporator coils melts during the automatic defrost cycle, and the moisture flows into a pan located at the base of the refrigerator. Here heat from the condenser evaporates it.

The frost-free refrigerator maintains a more uniform interior coldness and a lower door-shelf temperature, but it may take longer to freeze ice cubes than a conventional model.

The initial cost of the frost-free refrigerator is higher than the conventional type. Operating cost may be 40

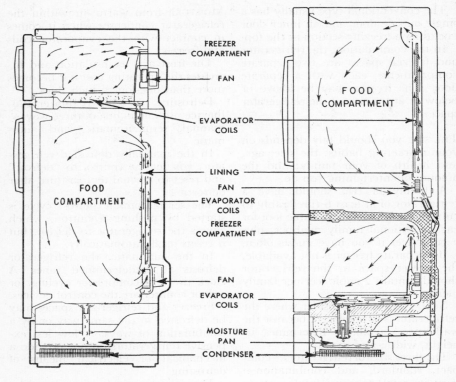

Airflow and Water Disposal Diagram—   Airflow and Water Disposal Diagram—
         Top Freezer Models   Bottom Freezer Models

Schematic drawing showing the operation of a frost-free refrigerator-freezer.

to 100 percent more because of the fan used for circulating air and the heater used in defrosting.

The freezer temperature of the conventional refrigerator is above 0°. That of the combination is 0° or below. If you wish to maintain frozen food at top quality for more than a few days or at most 2 weeks, the freezer space must maintain 0°.

Most refrigerators have a single temperature control for the refrigerator and freezer compartment. Avoid setting this temperature too low, because foods may freeze in the refrigerator space. The operating instructions give the normal setting, which should maintain a refrigerator temperature of 37° to 40° and a freezer temperature of 0°.

THE EXTERIOR FINISH usually is a bonderized steel with an acrylic or a baked-on enamel in white or color. A few are of porcelain-enameled steel. Porcelain is more expensive and more durable than baked enamel. Vinyl-coated steel is another durable finish. Brushed chrome and chromium are used as a trim.

The interior may be acid-resistant porcelain, baked-on enamel, aluminum, plastic, or combinations of them. The door liner and its shelves are made of high-impact plastic. The gasket of the door is of plastic or rubber—which grease causes to soften.

The construction should be sturdy and without cracks and crevices. Since you cannot see all construction features, you should buy from a reliable manufacturer. Door construction may be checked by putting weight on it to see if it sags.

Features built into refrigerators include slide-out shelves with stop lock and stop rail at the back; revolving or swing-out shelves; half or divided shelves; adjustable shelves; full- or half-width crispers; meatkeeper; removable egg and cheese containers; butter compartment; removable shelf front on the door; interior lights; a separate drawer for vegetables; a foot pedal for opening the door; a can dispenser on the freezer door; ice-tray ejector; automatic icemaker, which needs a water connection; pull- or swing-out baskets or trays in the freezer space; and levelers.

Each raises the cost of the refrigerator, and may or may not be of value to you.

You can reduce the operating cost by keeping the evaporator coils defrosted; cleaning the condenser; providing air circulation to remove heat given off by the condenser; placing the refrigerator in a cool, dry area; and cooling foods to room temperature before storing them.

To maintain sanitary, relatively odor-free storage conditions, all refrigerators need to be cleaned frequently and thoroughly.

Use a clean, nontipping container of proper size to prevent drippage and spilling. Wipe up spillovers immediately. Wash and drain vegetables and fruits (except berries). Wipe off meats, using vinegar, not water.

When cleaning, wash the interiors with water in which you have dissolved baking soda; then rinse and dry. Use detergent and water on the exterior finish, plastic door liner, gasket, and shelves.

Since the refrigerator has an applied finish, do not use an abrasive, which may scratch or dull it. Cover most foods to prevent loss of moisture and intermingling of flavors.

You can adjust the refrigerator to an uneven floor with levelers. The level refrigerator has little vibration, produces less noise, and makes the door easier to open and shut.

The newest type is a small, portable thermoelectric type, which has no moving parts.

A home freezer is a convenience, but it saves money only if turnover is rapid and you use it at full capacity.

The details of selecting a freezer are like those I mentioned for refrigerators.

Its size is important because it is a 15-year investment. Freezer sizes range from 3.2 to 30.1 cubic feet. Selections tend to be 13 cubic feet or more.

The freezer space you need depends on whether you use it in addition to a locker in a freezer plant; how much freezing you do at home at one time; how much and what kind of frozen food you plan to store; how long the growing season is; how much frozen food is available in your market; how large your family is; and how much space is available for the freezer.

A farm family may need at least 5 or 6 cubic feet per person—unless a locker can be rented to store part of the homegrown food; then 3 cubic feet may be enough.

The urban or rural family that shops once a week probably will need to allow 3 to 4 cubic feet a person.

Two medium-sized freezers may be better than one large one, for you can disconnect one when you have little food in it, store only the food from one during mechanical failure, or use one as a freezing space and the other one for storage, thereby reducing fluctuations in temperature.

Types of freezers are the upright (vertical or front opening) and the chest (horizontal or top opening).

The upright occupies less floorspace and usually provides more convenient storage, but it costs more to purchase than the chest type.

The vertical type is no more expensive to operate than the horizontal one.

The flat top of the chest freezer can be used for workspace. It does not need to be defrosted so often, but defrosting is more difficult than in the upright model. A freezer scoop or plastic dustpan helps you remove ice before it melts.

The upright freezer may be frost free the same as the combination refrigerator. In a no-frost freezer, storage space is not reduced because of frost, packages of food are easily separated, and labels are not frosted over. This type is more expensive to buy and to operate than a comparable conventional type. The operating cost is about twice as much.

Freezers need to have better insulation than refrigerators.

The cost of buying a freezer will vary with its size, finish, and construction. The cost per cubic foot drops as the size increases.

The best place for a freezer is one that is convenient, cool (usually not below 40°), dry, and well ventilated. The floor should be well braced to carry the weight.

Before you decide on the freezer and its location, be sure that it will fit the space and go through the passageways.

The upright freezer may have drawers or dropdown door shelves, which increase accessibility but add to the cost of manufacturing.

The chest freezer may have baskets or space dividers to make food more accessible. They reduce storage space. Loaded baskets may be hard to lift.

Freezer features include locks; warning devices to indicate that the temperature has risen or the electricity is off; built-in defrost drain; interior lights; a thermometer; toe space; and rollers for moving the freezer.

I recommend that you buy a freezer made by a well-established company and from a reliable dealer who will install and service it.

To learn the manufacturer's responsibility, read the warranty carefully. With the warranty there usually is a card that you must fill out and return to the manufacturer to make the warranty valid.

A gas refrigerator should carry a star of approval from the American Gas Association (AGA), which means it meets requirements for good construction and performance.

All refrigerators and freezers should carry the seal of approval of Underwriters' Laboratories, Inc. (UL), which indicates that the refrigerating system and electrical connections are safe. (LYLE M. MAMER)

Dishwashers

YOU DO NOT really need a mechanical dishwasher. Dishes can be handwashed in the dishpan or sink, as they have been these many years. A dishwasher, though, saves time, adds to cleanliness, and eliminates much of the work many homemakers dislike.

Two main types are available.

Portable models can be moved around, even to another house, if you move. Others are permanently installed. The convertible is a combination of the two types.

The portable costs little to install but is not always convenient to use. It must be rolled to the sink, where it blocks easy access. Connections are made to the sink faucet. Some models are so made that you cannot use water for other purposes while the portable dishwasher is operating. It needs a parking space in or near the kitchen.

Permanently installed dishwashers come in freestanding, countertop, and undercounter models. All require plumbing and electrical connections.

The undercounter models, generally bought without tops or sides, must be built in. Installation therefore requires a carpenter, a plumber, and an electrician.

Installed dishwashers do not interfere with use of the sink, but usually they are a permanent part of a house and cannot be moved to another.

The convertible is a freestanding dishwasher on wheels. It can be used first as a portable and later converted to an undercounter model by removing the wheels and top and connecting it to the plumbing lines.

Portable and installed dishwashers are available in top- or front-loading models. In some top-loading dishwashers, the lid lifts up. In others, the tub pulls out—drawer style. In front-loading machines, the door drops down and the racks pull forward.

The choice between the two types of loading is mostly a matter of individual preference and perhaps the user's ability to reach into a deep tub.

Models with dropdown doors and pullout drawers require 42 inches of floorspace in front of the dishwasher to allow for opening and loading.

An important detail is the cycle for washing a regular load—the complete sequence of an operation from start to finish.

Only one cycle is provided on some machines. It may be minimum—a wash and two rinses, followed by drying. It may be a more complex sequence on some washers—a rinse, a wash, a second wash, two rinses, and drying.

Some top-of-the-line models have several different cycles, such as "regular wash," "china and crystal," "pots and pans," and "rinse and hold."

The way a dishwasher is to be used will determine whether the extra cycles are worth the extra cost within a brand.

The cost of a dishwasher usually is not related to the basic cycle, for the more complex sequences are available on a number of low-priced models. If you plan to scrape and rinse dishes before putting them in the dishwasher, one with a minimum cycle probably will be satisfactory.

If dishes are to be washed without rinsing and with only enough scraping to remove bones and other large pieces of food, a cycle providing two separate washes and at least three rinses is important.

The detergent holder generally indicates the kind of cycle. A dishwasher with two containers for detergent, both covered, gives a prerinse with clear water and two separate washes with detergent.

In a machine with a double holder but with only one covered container, the washing compound in the open holder is dispersed in the first fill. Later in the cycle, there will be a second wash.

Machines with a single holder, with a cover, give only one wash unless the user puts detergent on the tub floor to be dissolved in the first fill.

Other dishwashers have only a single uncovered holder—or none at all. With these, the first fill provides the only wash.

Water temperature boosters and rinse injectors are special features on some models. Many washers have heaters that operate during the cycle, but they help to maintain—not increase—the temperature of the water. A booster provides water at a specified temperature in the wash or in the final rinse, or in both.

A gas burner in some dishwashers heats water before it is circulated. In others, the cycle is delayed until the electrical unit in the bottom of the tub heats the circulating solution to a specified temperature. A booster may increase the time required to complete the cycle.

The rinse injector automatically adds a solution in the final rinse to help the water slide off the dishes and keep them from spotting. This may be important in places where the water is hard.

Some racks are designed for random loading. Some are arranged in such a way that certain kinds of dishes go in certain places.

Personal preference should be the basis for choice, because either kind is satisfactory if it is loaded so that the dirty side of each article faces the washing mechanism and if dishes in one rack do not block the cleaning solution from the other rack of dishes.

WASHING MECHANISMS are of two major types, each of which has adaptations.

The hydraulic mechanism employs a perforated hollow tube, which turns on a shaft as the recirculating water is pumped through it.

Some dishwashers bring in cleaning solution from more than one area; for instance, from hydraulic mechanisms under both racks or on both sides of the dishwasher.

The impeller mechanism is a type of rotor. It is in the lowest part of the tub, and so is in the water when the tub has filled. The turning rotor throws the water with considerable force over the dishes.

Both types of washing action give good results, but the trend has been toward the use of more hydraulic systems and fewer impellers.

Drying methods vary. Some dishwashers use only natural evaporation from hot dishes, but most use an electrical heating element in the bottom of the tub to heat the air.

Some designs employ a heating element and fan outside the tub to blow hot air into the tub and over the dishes.

Another utilizes a gas burner to heat the final rinse water to 180° F. before circulating it. Then the door pops open and water evaporates from the hot dishes.

The drying method may not be so important as the rack design, or the way dishes are loaded, or the shape of the cups, glasses, or other objects to be dried. Some water will remain in a deeply indented surface flat on a rack regardless of the drying method. The same dish properly tilted on the same rack, or on a rack designed so the dish must be tilted, probably will dry.

THE DISHWASHER can do a good job if it is properly used.

If the cycle provides two separate washes and several rinses, it generally is not necessary to scrape and rinse dishes, glasses, and flatware before putting them into a machine.

If a dishwasher has only a minimum cycle, a wash and two or three rinses, dishes should be scraped and rinsed.

This extra handwork can be eliminated, however, if (after the wash and first rinse) you stop the machine, add a second measure of detergent, and reset the control for the complete cycle.

Whether pots and pans can be satisfactorily washed depends on your willingness to accept discoloration in aluminum and copper and to pretreat utensils in order to loosen cooked-on food.

Good management can make the difference between delight and disgust with a dishwasher. It makes good sense for the small family to accumulate dishes from several meals before operating the dishwasher. Time, energy, water, and cleaning compound are saved.

If used dishes are put in the dishwasher for later washing, they should be rinsed by hand, by using the rinse-and-hold cycle, or in a single-cycle machine by manually supplying one of the rinses and then turning the machine off.

If platters and other large dishes and the tableware from a meal will fill the dishwasher, you can wash the utensils you used in preparing the meal while you are eating. Then they will be ready to put away when the dishes go in.

At company time, one particularly likes to be with guests, and a dishwasher frees one for that. Therefore, if your company dishes must be washed by hand because their decorations may be damaged by the washing compound and the high temperature in the machine, good management suggests consideration of the purchase of new dishes guaranteed to be washable in the dishwasher.

Sometimes a simple rearrangement may provide a convenient place closer to the sink for a portable and thus encourage more frequent use than if it must be stored in a back hall or other out-of-the-way location.

To get the maximum satisfaction from a dishwasher and to operate it effectively, you should:

Read the instruction booklet carefully and get acquainted with the various visible parts of the dishwasher and with the directions for use, care, and cleaning.

See that the machine is properly grounded. If a dishwasher is installed, the electrician should connect the ground. With portables, this responsibility rests with the user. Most portables are equipped with three-pronged plugs, including a ground connection, while outlets are generally designed for the older, two-pronged plugs. The safe way to ground these dishwashers is to have a proper outlet installed. Manufacturers generally supply adapters, but unless the outlet itself is grounded, the adapter is useless. If one must be used, see that the outlet is grounded and always be sure that the grounding wire is connected to the center screw on the cover plate. Never leave it hanging loose.

Try several of the special dishwashing compounds for mechanical dishwashers to find the one best suited to local water. Never use a detergent formulated for hand dishwashing or laundering; the heavy sudsing may cause flooding.

Store the dishwashing compound in a tightly closed container, once the box is opened. The ingredients are especially susceptible to moisture and will deteriorate rapidly if the container is not airtight.

Load the dishwasher so that the cleaning solution can reach all pieces in a load.

Be sure the water temperature is at least 140° at the source. If the water heater tank is small, operate the dishwasher at a time when demand for hot water is light.

Whether care by the user is related to length of service is a question difficult to answer. Most of the internal mechanisms—the pumps, motors, and hoses—are not accessible to the user and probably do not require much special care. But precautions should be taken that such things as small bones that may damage a pump do not get into the drain.

Special care should be taken that children do not tamper with the controls and that the washing mechanism and heater are not damaged by carelessly loaded articles. Gaskets should be replaced if there is leakage.

In general, a dishwasher is more likely to be replaced because newer models are superior than because it is worn out. (NADA D. POOLE)

Waste Disposers

TWO TYPES of appliances are available for disposing of food wastes—the grinder and the incinerator.

The electrically operated grinder, which utilizes water to carry food wastes down the sink drain, is probably the most familiar type.

The incinerator, which burns wastes, is fired by a number of fuels, but since gas-fired appliances are commoner, I limit this discussion to that type.

The grinder, in the sink, is essentially a small metal cylinder, or hopper, and a motor that operates some type of pulverizing mechanism in the cylinder bottom. It cuts food wastes into tiny bits and flushes them into the drain as water flows through the hopper.

In a batch-feed disposer (which is one of two types), you put the wastes into the hopper (capacity 1 to 2 quarts) and then lock the cover in place. Water and the electric switch are turned on, and the food is ground up.

Some grinders have a double switch arrangement. One is turned on by locking the lid in position. The other is turned on automatically as the water reaches an adequate flow. Neither starts the mechanism without the other. Thus the ground food usually cannot go into the drain without enough water to wash it away. In a double-bowl sink, however, the grinder will operate when the water is running into the wrong sink.

The continuous feed disposer can be fed as it operates. It disposes of large amounts of waste more conveniently than does the batch feed because it is not necessary to load and lock the hopper before grinding.

Since one can operate the continuous disposer without the cover, households with small, adventuresome youngsters may feel it safer to use the other type. The possibility that a piece of bone will be ejected or a stray spoon will slip into the hopper is less if the cover is placed loosely over the opening of the continuous disposer.

A grinder is less expensive to purchase, install, and operate than an incinerator. It is small and out of sight, and so are food wastes that accumulate during the preparation of meals.

A grinder will not dispose of nongrindable but burnable waste, metal, glass, and ceramic materials; these must still be handled by other means.

Materials such as soft dough, liquid fat, and fibrous vegetable wastes may require special handling to be properly disposed of.

In other words, everything cannot be dumped into a grinder and made to disappear like magic. There are limitations on size of waste. For instance, watermelon rinds must be cut into small pieces.

The sink drain may become clogged if something is put in that should not be, if a particular kind of waste is loaded improperly, or if too little water is used. In that case, the advantage of location at the sink becomes a disadvantage, because the sink is unusable.

If a dishwasher drains through the disposer, manufacturers generally recommend that the grinder be emptied first so that the dishwasher can drain properly.

Grinders are relatively noisy, and in some installations may cause nearby items to vibrate.

Wastes from a grinder will increase the load on a septic tank by as much as one-third. Therefore, the size of the tank must be adequate, or it will have to be cleaned oftener. Ordinances in some localities prohibit grinders.

In some places where water is limited, too much may be needed (even though it may be only a few gallons each day) to permit the use of the grinder type.

To USE a disposer efficiently, you should:

Read the instruction booklet and be familiar with types of wastes that the grinder will handle. Many give suggestions for special ways to handle fibrous or doughy wastes.

Locate the overload switch and find out how to reset it. Learn how to use the wrench (if one is provided) or to follow directions for unjamming the grinder. Knowledge of the minor problems and how to deal with them may save service calls.

Be sure that there is always a good flow of water when the grinder is operating. It is the water that carries away the wastes.

Use cold water in flushing away wastes. This is especially important with fats. When hot water is used, melted fat is flushed into the drain pipes, where it cools and can coat and clog the pipes.

Be sure the split rubber disk at the opening to the hopper on continuous-feed disposers is in good condition. The disk helps to protect the user from bits of bone or fruit pits that otherwise might be forcibly ejected.

Never use drain-cleaning chemicals

in the grinder. They may corrode the shredding mechanism.

THE GAS-FIRED INCINERATOR consists of a heavy metal container with a grate, a gas burner, and an ash drawer built into the bottom.

Wherever it is placed, it requires a connection to the fuel and to a chimney with a tiled flue of proper capacity.

The gas-fired incinerator is available with a low-input or high-input burner. The latter consumes wastes much faster. Some models provide special settings for extra wet or for dry loads. Capacities range from 1.5 to 2 bushels.

Models that carry the American Gas Association Seal for Smokeless and Odorless Operation have a special afterburner that consumes smoke, fly ash, and odors. This is a desirable feature, especially if the burning of wastes may be annoying.

City ordinances in some places prohibit incinerators.

The incinerator will dispose of anything that will burn, including wet food wastes, old shoes, and newspapers. It will not handle metals, glass, or ceramic materials. It is relatively quiet and will take large pieces of waste. Its purchase price and cost of installation and operation may be higher than for the grinder.

The location of the incinerator, even in the kitchen or nearby utility room, is probably less convenient than the grinder in the sink.

Heat generated by the burning may or may not be a disadvantage, depending on where the incinerator is placed and the season of the year.

Although the accumulation is small, ashes must be emptied every few weeks.

The user of an incinerator should:

Read the instruction booklet and be familiar with the types of wastes it will handle. Follow the directions for use. Load the incinerator properly.

Learn how to relight the pilot. If the unit fails to operate properly, check with the local gas company to be sure that the burner is adjusted correctly.

Remove ashes as often as necessary. The pilot may be extinguished and the burner may not operate properly if ashes build up.

Remove nonburnable material from the grate to prevent clogging.

Consider the convenience of a grinder or an incinerator installed in a home. Is it worth the investment? Spilled-over garbage cans and smoky trash burners may provide an affirmative answer. In communities where garbage is disposed of by the householder, they are almost necessities.

The ideal situation may be to have both types—the grinder-disposer in the sink and the incinerator-disposer in the utility room. (NADA D. POOLE)

Your Laundry

FOR WASHING at home, you need an ample supply of good water, a heater or other convenient way to heat it, disposal facilities, and a way to dry the clothes.

Being able to wash at home anytime and to care for emergency needs are conveniences. But washers and dryers are almost certain to need repair sometime during the 10 years and 14 years, respectively, that they are estimated to last when they are bought new and have only one owner.

On the other hand, if you have transportation—or can walk to one— you may prefer to take your washing to a coin-operated laundry, which supplies hot and cold water and has enough machines so that you can wash several loads at one time.

Some of these laundries provide hotter water for washing than home water heaters usually do. Others may not provide water hot enough—at least 140° F.—to assure good soil removal and sanitizing. (Take along a thermometer to check the water temperature, if you are in doubt.)

Large dryers often are available in these establishments to dry several washer loads at once. Public laundry activities may transfer germs from family to family. A later chapter deals with laundry sanitation.

WHEN YOU BUY a washer, you can choose between nonautomatic and automatic types.

In a nonautomatic washer, an electric motor provides for agitation and runs the mechanism for extraction of water. The user controls the filling of the tub, temperature of the water, washing time, water extraction, and emptying of the tub.

An automatic washer fills itself with water of a preselected temperature, washes, rinses, extracts water, and stops—all at one setting of the controls and without further attention from the user.

Unless an automatic has a suds-saver attachment (the wash water is drained into a stoppered tub, then pumped back later for reuse), it will fill with fresh water for each of its processing steps and automatically empty used water down the drain.

If water is scarce or expensive or if fuel to heat it is expensive, a nonautomatic washer may be a better choice.

Nonautomatics use agitators to create movement in the tub. Some have wringers to extract water. From wringer washers, it is customary to rinse by hand in two or more tubs of water, since this can be done while another load is washing, either in fresh water or in the water that has been used. Less human energy but more total time is used if rinsing is done in the washer tub with mechanical agitation.

One manufacturer makes a double-tub wringer machine. The second tub can be used for either washing or rinsing. For safe operation, wringers should have a simply operated mechanism for instant emergency stopping and release of pressure.

Another nonautomatic washer type extracts water with a spinner, located in a second tub next to the washer tub. Some spinners are designed to rinse by injection of water into the spinner basket after the wash water has been spun out. This rinse water generally is discarded.

Rinsing could be done by hand from the spinner, too. Galvanized or fiberglass tubs on stands with casters are convenient for hand rinsing. If water is reused in nonautomatic washers, fewer gallons are needed per laundry than with automatics.

Several small nonautomatic washers are available. From some of them the clothes must be wrung by hand. They are suitable for washing personal laundry or small loads of family laundry, but generally are neither large enough nor sturdy enough to be the only washer for a household.

Automatics range from the simplest (with a single speed and cycle) to the multiple-speed washer that has automatic dispensers for cleaning agents and programed cycles activated by pushbuttons to suit almost any combination of laundering needs.

Automatics are generally more expensive than nonautomatic washers.

Since laundry needs no handling from the time it goes into the automatic washer until it is ready to dry, the user has more free time than with a nonautomatic. Cycles may include such variations as a soak; choice of washing time, water temperature, and washing and spinning speeds; and choice of rinsing without spinning.

But even the simpler automatic models are versatile and with ingenuity can be made to achieve some actions that are automatic on higher priced models.

For instance, for wash-and-wear articles, the user can shorten the washing cycle, cool the rinse, and interrupt the spin to minimize wrinkling.

Agitator automatics and those with adaptations of the agitation principle open at the top. For most users, they are more convenient to load and unload than the tumbler type, which opens at the front and requires stooping and bending.

There is also a washer that dries the clothes. Combination washer-dryers are all front-opening tumblers. They automatically complete both washing and drying or do either job separately. Electric and gas models are available.

The washer-dryer needs less floorspace than two separate appliances, and the clothes need no handling between washing and drying. Since one mechanism does both jobs, it may need repair or replacement earlier than a separate washer and dryer would. The washer-dryer and other tumbler automatics generally use less water for each load than top-loading washers.

For safety, the equipment should be so designed that all operation ceases when the lid or door of a washer or dryer is opened.

GAS AND ELECTRIC DRYERS heat air and blow it through fabrics tumbling in a metal drum to accomplish drying at any time, in any weather.

Because warm air and the moisture from the clothes are expelled into the air surrounding the dryer, venting to the outdoors may be advisable.

In some electric dryers, the moisture is condensed in constantly running cold water, which then goes down the drain. Such a dryer requires permanent connections with the cold water and the drain.

Consider the features of a dryer in relation to convenience. Some sense the moisture in the drying load and stop the process at a preselected moisture level. Such a feature saves tumbling time and fuel and eliminates underdrying and overdrying.

On other dryers, there are timers that can be set for the drying time of your choice. Some have settings that

allow a selection of controlled temperatures within the dryer drum. Others provide a single temperature.

Those and other features are available on both electric and gas models. The choice between the two probably will depend on the relative local cost of electricity and gas.

Tumble drying makes some fabrics soft and fluffy and minimizes the need for ironing in many. Items such as table linens retain more crispness if hung to dry.

To many homemakers, the most desirable place for drying clothes is outdoors. On breezy days in clean air with low humidity and warm temperatures, fabrics dry quickly and have a pleasant odor.

Because fabrics dried outdoors lose strength faster than dryer-dried fabrics or those hung indoors, they should be brought indoors as soon as dry.

Storms, birds, insects, soot, pollen, broken lines, unpredictable weather, and the work of carrying wet clothes to the line and hanging them take some of the joy from drying clothes outdoors.

Drying by hanging indoors is often slow. Hanging single thicknesses and supplying extra heat and air circulation (with a heater and a fan, for instance) speed the drying.

Although hanging indoors means fewer problems than outdoors, fabrics may pick up odors from the atmosphere and add humidity to the room.

WHETHER YOU LAUNDER at home or at the coin-op, proper sorting is imperative.

First separate according to color of fabrics. Separate further according to washer size—articles should move briskly about in the washer.

The size of load that washes best in a washer may be several pounds less than its capacity rating.

A load made up of small and large pieces seems to wash better than a load of articles all of one size, but articles as bulky as bedspreads should be washed singly.

Very dirty articles should be washed separately from those with less soil.

If some articles are to be line dried, put them into separate loads so you can transfer other loads to the dryer without further sorting.

How much separating you do, of course, depends partly on the total amount of laundry.

UNDERSTANDING an appliance is basic to its use and care.

The instruction book is the text. Read it and underline things you may want to refer back to.

If the appliance requires a sequence of attention, make a step-by-step outline to follow until you are completely familiar with its operation.

Stay near the equipment when it is operating.

Be alert to sounds or odors that indicate trouble.

A misplaced drain hose or stopped drain may cause flooding.

An unbalanced load may trip the release that stops extraction, so you will need to redistribute the load and reset the safety button to finish the cycle.

A motor that is burning out has a characteristic odor. A slipping belt may smell like burning rubber. A dryer may continue to heat and tumble past the "off" and need to be stopped manually.

Fit the cycle to the job.

Extra-dirty clothes need a soak, 10 to 15 minutes of washing time at fastest speed (if there is a choice), and water as hot as color and fabric permit.

Lightly soiled fabrics of manmade fibers may wash clean in a short cycle at low speed with warm water; use the "wash-and-wear" cycle for both washer and dryer if the machine has one.

To cool manmade fabrics at the end of drying, tumble them without heat. Use the right amount of detergent.

Articles in contact with the skin for long (underwear, shirts, sheets, pillowcases) are heavily soiled whether they show it or not. Insufficient detergent leaves soil in fabrics.

On the other hand, too much suds can create spin problems in automatics and overflow in tumbler washers and add to the rinsing job.

Incorrect bleaching causes damage to fabrics that sometimes is blamed on the equipment. If you use a bleach, measure it carefully and dilute it properly before adding it to the wash.

Make full use of your equipment. You can use the washer to remove water from hand-washed articles. You can also use the washer for dyeing and starching clothes. Dry starched loads in the dryer, but clean the dryer drum with a damp cloth afterward. Use the dryer for partly drying wool blankets and to fluff and air (without heat) draperies and stored or dusty fabrics.

Learn which articles need no ironing when dryer dried.

When the laundry is finished, turn off the water to automatic washers to relieve the pressure on valves and hoses. Empty and clean lint filters on washer and dryer; clogged filters interfere with operation. Remove and clean the agitator, as the instructions direct. Wipe away any spilled laundry agents. Leave washer and dryer openings ajar until the interiors are cool and dry. (R. KATHERINE TAUBE)

Handy Tools

THE JOBS you plan to do, the money you wish to spend, and storage space are matters to consider when you buy tools.

Buy tools of good quality. Premium-quality tools are not necessary, but very cheap tools, especially edge tools, such as saws and chisels, often are unsatisfactory.

Usually it is wise to rent costly tools that you use only occasionally.

Keep your tools in good condition. The teeth of a crosscut saw should be nearly as sharp as a needle. Keep chisel and plane irons nearly razor sharp. If you lack the ability or equipment to sharpen tools, have a skilled craftsman do it for you.

Keep your tools clean. Dry metal tools to prevent rust. Put a light coat of oil on sharp-edged tools, such as saws and planes, before storing—especially if they are kept in a place that may be damp.

Our table on the next pages lists items we recommend for common tasks around the house. The least expensive tools and supplies to perform the job we list in the column headed "Minimum equipment." Other practical equipment that may aid or replace items in that column we list as desirable equipment. Additional equipment that may make the job easier or faster is mentioned as supplementary equipment.

Tools and equipment should be stored as close as possible to the site of frequent use. The crate opener, jar and can openers, scissors, ruler or yardstick, screwdriver, and pliers, for example, may be kept in a drawer or closet in the kitchen, workroom, or utility room.

A carrier for cleaning supplies may be used to carry cleaning supplies or tools needed for jobs of household maintenance. When not in use, it may be stored with the other cleaning supplies, polishes, waxes, or tools.

Store other larger and less frequently used tools in one common area. Duplicate items of the more frequently used tools, such as screwdrivers and pliers, also are stored there. Storage in one specific place makes it easier to find the desired tool.

Well-planned storage also provides protection for the sharp edges of cutting tools and protects the user from accidentally cutting himself on one tool while reaching for the other.

Cutting edges of saws, auger bits, planes, chisels, and rasps should be protected so they will not bump or

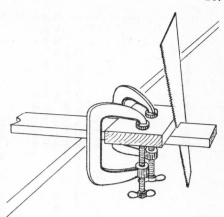

Saw guide clamped in position. You may clamp a 1- or 2-inch piece beside your mark to serve as a saw guide for an accurate cut.

come in contact with other metal. They should be stored so that other tools will not fall on them and they will not fall on anything else.

The storage area may be simple or elaborate, as determined by space, interest, and finances.

Providing ample storage space should be the first step. Pegboard or shelves installed in an existing area or closet may be the simplest arrangement. A specially built tool cabinet could very well be an improvement.

A workbench is a practical means to provide both a work area and storage facilities. Hip height is a comfortable and practical height for the workbench top unless you plan to do a great deal of hand planing. In that event, it may be well to build it a little lower.

Light the workbench with fluorescent fixtures placed over the front of the bench and 48 inches above the work, or use an incandescent 150-watt silvered-bowl bulb in a 12- to 14-inch-diameter metal reflector.

Keep all instruction books and warranties with your important household records and papers. However, some people may wish to keep some instruction books in the workshop. In that event, protect them from dust, oil, and damage. (GLENN D. BARQUEST AND MARION W. LONGBOTHAM)

TOOLS FOR HANDYMAN AND HANDYWOMAN
FOR HOUSEHOLD OPERATION, MAINTENANCE, AND REPAIR

If you plan to do—	Minimum equipment	Desirable equipment	Supplementary equipment
Household or kitchen activities:			
open crates and boxes	crate opener or pry bar or 8″ screwdriver.	12 or 13 oz. claw hammer.	
open jars, can, etc.	jar and can openers.	combination opener.	
cut cardboard	scissors and paring knife.	utility knife.	
lubricate appliances, locks, hinges, etc.	high-grade oil suitable for small appliances.	powdered graphite. graphite in oil.	
measure and space items	ruler or yardstick or good-quality measuring tape.	6′–10′ steel tape or folding rule.	25′ or 50′ tape.
attach items to walls	paste-on tabs for light items. hangers with nails or screws for heavier items: 12 or 13 oz. curved claw hammer. hand drill and bits. screwdrivers.	Hollow-wall screw anchors and toggle bolts; hand or electric drill and twist drills ¼″ and up. stud locator.	For masonry or concrete: screw anchors and screws. proper size star drill or electric drill and tungsten carbide masonry drill.
level items	pan of water to level appliances. string with attached weight.	level as part of combination square.	9″–12″ level.
Small repair jobs:			
tighten or loosen screws	4″ and 6″ screwdrivers. Nos. 1 and 2 Phillips screwdrivers.	hex wrenches. special screwdrivers and wrenches.	ratchet screwdriver.
tighten nuts or hold small items	6″–7″ slip joint pliers. adjustable wrench.	locking-type wrench pliers. needle-nose pliers.	open-end and box-end wrenches.
drive or pull nails, etc.	12 or 13 oz. curved claw hammer. 6″ screwdriver.	hand stapler. pry bar.	staple gun. tack puller.
repair plastic items	plastic mending tape.	liquid mender for type of plastic.	plastic repair kit with strips and adhesive.
seal openings and joints	special sealants and tapes.	calking gun.	
replace ordinary faucet washers.	adjustable wrench. screwdrivers.	tape or cloth to place between wrench and polished fitting.	flexible drain auger.
open drains and pipes	force cup.	small wire. putty knife.	glass cutter.
other minor jobs	packaging material and string. polishes and waxes. cleaning supplies and equipment. step stool.	vacuum cleaner. stepladder.	fabric mending and fastening kits.
Small jobs with wood:			
measure and mark	sharp pointed No. 2½ or 3 common pencil.	8″ by 12″ utility, steel combination, or try square.	dividers. rafter or framing square.

(NOTE.—Operations are listed in their usual sequence.)

Operation			
cut wood	ruler or yardstick. tablet back or drawing triangle may serve as a square. pencil compass. coping saw. friction vise or bench hook to hold wood.	6' to 10' steel tape or folding rule. 20''–22'', 10–11 point hand saw. two 4'' C-clamps.	hand ripsaw. miter box. electric hand and sabre saws. jack or smoothing plane. electric sander.
smoothen wood (may be repeated after assembly)	fine, medium, and coarse sandpaper. sandpaper block.	block plane, or multiblade wood smoothing tool. rasps and scraper.	
assemble pieces into unit	assorted sizes of wire nails and brads. 12 to 13 oz. curved claw hammer. 1/16'' nail set. 6d nails. white glue (not moisture resistant).	wood screws. countersink. 4'' and 6'' screwdrivers. hand drill with drills and bit brace with bits or light duty electric drill with bits. nails with heads cut off may be used as small drills. urea or plastic resin glue (moisture resistant).	gluing clamps. 8'' or stub screwdriver. assorted sizes of common, finish, and special nails. set of combination drill and countersink bits for use with screws. resorcinol glue (waterproof).
fill holes in wood: nail holes	colored putty.		
larger holes	wood dough, plastic wood, or surfacing putty.	spackling compound for surfaces to be painted.	
finish wood	see other chapters.		
Work with metals: measure and mark	see measure and mark wood.	see measure and mark wood.	metal scribe.
cut	utility saw or keyhole-type hacksaw.	tin snips. 3/8'' cold chisel. vise. hacksaw with set of blades.	power grinder and safety goggles.
drill holes	hand drill with twist drills.	light-duty electric drill with a set of twist drills.	high-speed drill bits desirable for frequent heavy use.
smoothen or sharpen	8'' mill file. sharpening stone.	8'' half round file. 8'' round file.	emery cloth.
assemble	4'' and 6'' screwdrivers. Nos. 1 and 2 Phillips screwdrivers. 6''–7'' slip-joint pliers.	locking-type wrench pliers. adjustable wrench.	grinder and safety goggles. small sets of open-end and box-end wrenches.
polishing		emery and crocus cloths.	
repairing	epoxy resin.	epoxy resin and fiber glass.	soldering equipment.

FINANCES

To Own

or To Rent

FOR SOME FAMILIES, ownership of a home savors of a love affair. They find exactly the right place in the right location. Homeownership has always been their goal. It will make them independent and respected.

For others, ownership has an economic value. A house is an inflation-resistant investment and a tangible incentive to save. Rents are too high and ownership is cheaper. Ownership improves their credit rating, or suitable rental properties are not to be had.

Others are less enchanted by ownership. They have neither time nor inclination to manage the upkeep of a house. They may find available rental properties best suited to their needs. They fear hidden or unexpected expenses sometimes connected with ownership and shrinkage of capital if property value goes down.

Others do not have or may never have the capital to buy a house. Renting makes adapting to changing family needs easier than owning. Because real estate transactions take so much time, the mobile one-in-five family wants no house to lessen its bargaining power for a new position or to lose mobility for other than occupational reasons.

But homeownership is not necessarily a white little cottage or a farm. Apartment ownership has developed through cooperatives (a share of an apartment complex) and condominiums (title to a specific apartment). Also, although not counted in the statistics, are owned mobile homes, usually sitting on a tract of rented land.

The decision to own or rent is related to stages in the life cycle that begins at marriage and extends some time after the dissolution of the family by death of one of the mates.

A typical sequence of changes upgrades shelter with increases in assets, age, and family needs. Net worth is highest after age 35. Homeownership is greatest after age 45, but does not begin extensively before age 25.

The residential cycle may begin in a small, furnished, rented apartment, perhaps after a couple has lived for a time with the parents of one.

The next step may be a larger unfurnished apartment or the purchase of a mobile home. After age 25— following the arrival of children—the family may buy a small new or used house and build up an equity. The family may sell this after about age 35 in favor of a larger, new (perhaps a project-built) house.

150

Later demands of children call for expansion by remodeling it or buying another and larger house. If finances permit, a custom-planned house may be built.

It may be the last house until old age and retirement indicate a smaller house; a condominium apartment to which specific title is held; a mobile home; or a rented apartment. The spouse remaining after the death of the partner may remain a while, but later may seek quarters with children or other relatives or in homes or projects for the aged.

Families move through the life cycle at varying rates and with varying numbers of moves. When changed residential status is not caused by migration for a new position or upgrading accommodations, turning points usually come during the expanding and contracting phases.

Changes in residence, rented or owned, entail changes, often abrupt and substantial, in allocation of family resources. Whether as rent, mortgage installments, taxes, or repairs, the residence claim is regular, and it is inexorable.

Homeownership is achieved oftenest by means of mortgages. Three-fifths of the owner-occupied nonfarm homes were mortgaged in 1960.

The average time required to pay off a mortgage on a house is about 20 years, about the same as it takes to rear a child from infancy to maturity and slightly longer than the couple has together after the children have left.

If a family moves several times during this period, the feat of finally owning a home free and clear of debt is accomplished by enlarging the equity on succeeding houses.

LENDING INSTITUTIONS and homeowners alike have worked out several principles in regard to financing.

The attitude toward mortgages on homes has changed from something feared and liquidated quickly to "open-end" mortgages. These may be extended (without renewal expense) for additions to the house, education for the children, health maintenance, or other new financial needs.

In general, annual cash outlay may be burdensome if the ratio of the purchase price to income is more than two and one-half times the income.

The ratio of the downpayment to the purchase price is determined by available family financial resources and by lending policies of financing institutions. The lower the ratio, the more limited the choice of lenders.

A young family buying its first home often has little money. The only choice may be a loan insured or guaranteed by a Government agency but lent by a conventional lending institution, like commercial banks, savings banks, insurance companies, trusts, and savings and loan associations. Their houses must be new and built to certain standards. Their credit rating and prospects must be good.

For a house valued at 15 thousand dollars, they need only 450 dollars for a downpayment, as they can borrow 97 percent of the property value as appraised by the Federal Housing Administration. If they want a house of higher value, they must have a larger downpayment until at the maximum value, 30 thousand dollars, they need 3,500 dollars.

Other avenues are open to those who can make only a small downpayment.

The second mortgage, formerly used to close the gap between a low downpayment and lender's requirements, has been largely replaced by the installment land contract. In this contract, a deed held in trust is a safeguard, but if the seller retains title, he may mortgage it.

Other lenders, whose policies permit loans of only 50 to 60 percent of appraised valuation, insure loans above this amount (up to 15 to 20 percent) with private mortgage insurance corporations. This relieves them of risk for amounts above their regular lending policy.

Besides the downpayment, buyers need closing costs for a lender's initial service charge; costs of title search and title insurance; charges for preparing, recording, and notarizing the deed and mortgage; and perhaps a fee for the FHA application. Other costs prepaid at purchase are taxes and premiums for hazard and other insurance.

Although closing costs are low in some localities, they usually vary from 100 to more than 600 dollars.

WHETHER RENTING or buying, the annual cash-outlay-to-income ratio is important.

It generally ranges from one-eighth to one-third net family income, depending on the age of the family, income, and value placed in housing. Cash outlay may be rent alone. For homeownership free of debt, it includes taxes, maintenance, and hazard insurance. With a loan, it includes payments and interest in addition. The ratio is determined when renting by the amount the family is willing to forgo and when buying by the policy of the financing institution also.

The institutions base their decision on use made of buyer's income for food, clothing, shelter, recreation, and any debt obligations.

Considered also are stability of job, chances for promotions, credit record, and other financial data. Some refuse loans when the cash outlay for housing is more than one-fifth of net income. Others feel that if approximately one-sixth has been paid for rent, one-fourth or a little more could be devoted to purchase, since both rent and savings are included.

When a squeeze from reduced income and increased housing expenses occurs, homeowners who use 30 percent or more of their income for housing expenses are likelier than others to have mortgages foreclosed.

There are, of course, exceptions to any of those ratios. Demands made on the net income differ from family to family and are affected by the size, age, and health of the family; stability of job and income outlook; amount of savings accumulated; and the importance of housing in the family scale of preferences.

Terms of home mortgages have lengthened substantially. Conventional institutions lend for 20 years or more. FHA insures mortgages on new homes for 35 years or 40 years for families displaced by urban renewal, Government purchase for water conservation, military, or other public purposes.

Long-term mortgages allow some families with relatively low incomes to become homeowners. They enable some to buy more expensive houses than would otherwise be possible. They may make it easier to sell a house when necessary, because buyers may be attracted by a long-term mortgage and a small cash downpayment. Also, income tax deductions from interest paid can be made so long as such interest is paid.

The chief disadvantages of long-term mortgages are higher total costs and slow buildup of equity, as interest may exceed the principal payment for much of the life of the loan.

The rate of interest and length of term are determinants in keeping payments low. Lengthening the loan period is more potent than reducing interest rate but is more costly in the long run.

For example, total interest cost on a loan of 15 thousand dollars at 5.25 percent is 17,823 dollars for 35 years, but only 9,264 dollars for 20 years, a difference of 8,559 dollars.

With the rate at 6 percent, total interest is 20,623 dollars for 35 years and 10,793 dollars for 20 years, thus increasing the total interest by 2,800 and 1,529 dollars, respectively.

At the same time, it takes 22 years on the 35-year loan for more than half of the monthly payment to be applied to principal rather than interest and 7 years on the 20-year loan.

Should one, then, own or rent a home?

Given the desire to own, compare

the costs. A loan of 15 thousand dollars at 6 percent costs 85.65 dollars a month—in all, 20,623 dollars in interest for 35 years. At the end there is an owned house, perhaps somewhat depreciated, but continuing with some rental value. Rent at 75 dollars a month totals 31,500 dollars—without homeownership. Nothing is left except the savings on 10.65 dollars, the difference between monthly payments and rent.

The decision is yours, but there are costs either way, and they must be fitted into the budget. (TESSIE AGAN)

Mortgages

HAVING DECIDED to become a homeowner, you very likely will need a loan to finance the purchase of the house.

Of prime importance at the outset to you and the prospective lender is how much you can afford to pay for a home—whether your family pocketbook is large enough to meet the payments on the loan.

Three basic estimates are involved.

One is a realistic estimate of the income the family can reasonably expect to receive.

The second is the family's living costs and payments on other debts.

The third is the total housing expense, including taxes, insurance, maintenance, and loan payments.

In estimating future income, a family should consider income received during the past 4 or 5 years and the income prospects in the years ahead. Take into account the age of the family wage earners, their skills, the stability of employment, and the job opportunities in the area. Be realistic, not overoptimistic.

The largest expense of most families is living costs. Usually it is a rather rigid one. If your family includes growing children, living costs—food, education, clothing, entertainment, and other expenses—also will grow.

Other expenses may have to be provided for. If you own a farm or a business, you need to allow for the cost of operation. The house itself will add costs you may not have had before, such as taxes, insurance, fuel for heating and cooking, utilities, maintenance, and repairs. Payments on existing debts must be met. You will have to allow for savings for education and retirement.

How much is left after deducting all these expenses from the hard-core income is the beginning point in determining how much you can pay on a home loan.

Various ratios have been suggested between a family's income and the highest price it can prudently afford to pay for a home. Rules of thumb used by some lenders range from two to two and one-half times the family's annual income, but these are only general guides.

You and your family must decide on the basis of the budgetary facts of your personal situation and the relative value you place on homeownership in comparison with other possible uses of your income.

WHEN YOU SHOP for housing credit, you may encounter various terms to describe different types of loans, such as conventional, FHA-insured, and GI or direct VA loans. In rural areas, there may be Farmers Home Administration and Federal land bank loans.

The rates, terms, and conditions depend on the local policies and practices of the lenders and, in the case of Government or Government-assisted loans, the statutory authorizations under which the loans are made or insured.

Shopping for the best available mortgage credit may save you money. The rates and terms at which you will be able to finance a home will depend on the house itself and on the family's financial position, income prospects, and credit rating.

The ability to make a substantial downpayment may be an important factor in obtaining credit at a reasonable rate.

The extent to which the rate of interest and length of repayment affect monthly payments and the total amount of interest paid during the life of the loan for each 1 thousand dollars borrowed are:

Repayment period (years):	Monthly Payments of Principal and Interest	
	at 5%	at 6%
10............	$10.61	$11.11
20............	6.60	7.17
30............	5.37	6.00

Repayment period (years):	Total Interest Paid During Period of Loan	
	at 5%	at 6%
10............	$273.20	$320.00
20............	584.00	820.80
30............	923.20	1,160.00

Conventional loans are the commonest type of credit extended to buy and build homes. They are made by savings and loan associations, commercial banks, mutual savings banks, insurance companies and mortgage companies, individuals, and other lending agencies without the benefit of Government insurance or guarantees.

The terms vary with local policies and practices of the lenders. You can get information about conventional loans from the lender or from the real estate firm selling the home if the firm has made prior arrangements with a lender to finance the home.

FHA-INSURED HOME LOANS are made by private lending institutions and insured by the Federal Housing Administration.

FHA insurance protects the private lender against loss if the borrower cannot repay the loan. To cover possible losses, the FHA charges a mortgage insurance premium of one-half of 1 percent a year on the average scheduled mortgage loan balance outstanding during the year. The premium is included in the monthly payments.

FHA-insured home loans are available only for the purchase of new or existing dwellings or the refinancing of the completed home if the home is built by the owner. They are not available to finance the construction of a home. Anyone interested in building his own home must arrange for interim financing during the construction period.

The seller or agent usually will be able to suggest a lender if the house meets FHA specifications. The lender will supply the necessary forms, help the applicant complete them, and, if he is willing to make the loan, submit the application to the Federal Housing Administration office serving the area to obtain a commitment to insure the loan.

The Federal Housing Administration will review the application, appraise the property, and analyze the applicant's ability to pay.

The interest rate on FHA-insured home loans is 5.25 percent. An additional one-half of 1 percent is added as a mortgage insurance premium. The total monthly charge for such a loan to be repaid in 30 years is 5.95 dollars per 1 thousand dollars.

A first lien is required. The FHA-insured loan must be secured by a mortgage that will give the lender first claim on the property if liquidation becomes necessary.

Besides the downpayment, the borrower pays the settlement costs and other initial charges, including the FHA application fee and loan closing costs, such as recording fees and title examination. The charges may vary from one locality to another.

FARMERS HOME ADMINISTRATION rural housing loans are available to farmowners and to residents in the open country and small country towns and villages of 2,500 population or less that are not associated with urban areas.

These loans are made only to families who are unable to qualify for credit from other sources. This gives families in the lower income levels an opportunity to own a home of their own.

Another characteristic is that the loans may be secured by either a first or junior lien. This may permit an applicant to obtain a Farmers Home Administration loan even though the property is mortgaged to another creditor.

A third feature is that these long-term loans are used to finance construction. Since Farmers Home Administration loans are closed before the family starts construction, funds may be disbursed either as construction progresses or upon completion of the construction. The interest rate on these loans is 4 percent. The maximum period for repayment is 33 years.

Applications for rural housing loans may be made at the local county offices of the Farmers Home Administration. The agency's local county supervisor will obtain information regarding the applicant's assets, debts, obligations, income, and building plans, and submit the information to a committee of three local residents for review.

If the family is found to be eligible, the county supervisor will inform them regarding final plans and specifications, title clearance, appraisal, and loan closing requirements.

VA (GI) GUARANTEED home loans are made to eligible veterans by private lending institutions.

The Veterans' Administration enters into an agreement with the lender to guarantee only part of the loan but in such a way that the lender has little likelihood of loss. The interest rate is 5.25 percent. The repayment period may be as long as 30 years. A first lien is required.

The veteran who has selected a house and expects to finance it with a GI loan will need to get a certificate of eligibility from the Veterans' Administration. A lender will want to see that certificate, the house plans or

sales contract, a financial statement, and an appraisal report of the property before committing himself to make the loan.

If a veteran wants to build his own home, he usually will need to arrange for interim financing during the construction period.

VA (GI) DIRECT home loans also are made by the Veterans' Administration to eligible veterans in areas where a shortage of credit for housing exists. Generally they are rural areas and small cities or towns where housing credit is not readily available.

Veterans who are interested in finding out whether their area is eligible should get in touch with the Veterans' Administration regional office or the local Veterans' Administration center.

The procedures are similar to those in getting a GI-guaranteed loan. The main difference is that the funds are furnished by the Veterans' Administration rather than by a private lender.

BUYING OR BUILDING a home and obtaining a loan to do so involves the execution of a series of documents to formalize and complete the purchase.

When a family has selected the home it wants to buy, the seller usually requires the buyer to sign a sales contract. Between execution of the contract and closing of the loan, usually the property will have to be appraised, evidence of title obtained, and a survey made if establishment of the property lines is necessary.

At the time the loan is closed, the note and mortgage will need to be signed, and the deed conveying title to the buyer will be executed and then recorded.

If the sale is on the basis of a long-term sales contract, the seller may retain title to the property until a specified amount of the debt has been paid.

A SALES CONTRACT usually is the first document you sign after you have selected the home you want to buy.

Such a contract customarily requires a cash deposit as evidence of good faith.

When signed, a sales contract obligates the buyer to buy and the seller to sell, subject to any special conditions that may be specified.

A sales contract often provides that the contract is effective only if the seller can show satisfactory evidence of title and the buyer can qualify for a loan.

Sometimes a potential buyer may be able to obtain an option from the seller. The main difference between an option and a sales contract is that an option gives the buyer a specified period during which he can decide whether or not to buy the property.

Before signing a sales contract, you should read it carefully. The contract should be specific in its terms and state clearly the conditions of the sale and the responsibilities of the buyer and the seller. It should state that you, the buyer, will get a refund in case you are unable to get a loan or if the seller does not comply with the terms of the agreement.

If you do not go through with your part of the agreement, the contract may provide that you will forfeit your downpayment.

EVIDENCE OF GOOD TITLE is necessary to assure that the applicant actually owns or will own the property and that there are no claims against it that would restrict its marketability.

Lenders usually require a title certificate or title opinion or title insurance.

A title certificate or title opinion usually is prepared on the basis of a search of the public records or the examination of an abstract by an attorney. The lender may require title insurance to protect his interest. The home-buyer may also want to purchase an owner's title insurance policy for his protection in case a defect in the title should develop.

A PROMISSORY NOTE is a personal promise of the borrower to repay the loan. The note usually states the amount of the loan, the interest rate, and the repayment schedule. It also may include other provisions, such as penalties, prepayment privileges, and any special conditions the lender may wish to insert if the borrower agrees to them.

The note ordinarily is signed by both husband and wife. The original note is held by the lender. In the event the property is foreclosed, the lender may be able to hold the signers of the note personally liable for any deficit.

A bond is used instead of a note in some States.

THE MORTGAGE describes the note and, in case of default by the borrower, gives the lender the right to have the property sold and the sale proceeds applied on the debt.

The mortgage usually includes special conditions that apply should the borrower fail to comply with any of his agreements, such as making payments on the note and maintaining insurance and paying taxes on the property.

If the borrower defaults, the lender can declare the entire debt due immediately and foreclose on the property in order to collect the debt.

The mortgage is signed by the owners of the property. Most lenders prefer that the property be in the name of both the husband and the wife. The mortgage must be recorded in the public records. This is notice to other parties that there is a lien on the property.

When the loan is repaid in full and the note and mortgage are satisfied, either the lender or borrower should have the mortgage satisfied or released on the public records. Other forms of lien are used instead of mortgages in some States.

The home the buyer wishes to purchase may have a mortgage on it that is satisfactory to him. If so, he may be able to make arrangements with the lender to assume the indebtedness.

The buyer should, however, have the title as well as the loan papers examined by a competent person to be sure that he knows exactly when he will become the owner and understands all of the other terms and conditions of the mortgage.

A deed is the document issued by the seller transferring ownership of the property to the buyer. The deed should be recorded in the public records.

Shop carefully for your home, select the neighborhood you want, and be sure the house is one that you can afford and will meet your needs.

Shop for credit to obtain the best terms available.

If you plan to build, construction should not be started until you have arranged for financing. Once a lender has agreed to make a loan, you should proceed in accordance with the lender's requirements.

Obtain from the lender a complete, itemized list of all the costs you will need to pay at the time of closing the loan. The list should be dated and signed by the lender.

Read your contract carefully before you sign it. Check to see that it is specific on all important points. When you and the seller sign the contract, it becomes a legally binding agreement. (Louis D. Malotky)

Installment
Credit

Installment credit can be a help or a hindrance, depending on how you use it.

It has helped many families to furnish a home, buy a car, and meet all kinds of financial emergencies.

It also has caused many families worry, hardship, and loss.

You are urged to use installment credit by merchants who want to sell their goods and by banks and loan companies that want to lend their money. You are encouraged with promises of "loans on your signature," "no money down," and "very easy payments."

You easily can be carried away by such promises, as was the family that recently wrote us to ask for help with budget problems. The real problem came out in the last sentence, which said, "I think that banks and loan companies should stop using the term 'easy payment' because there is no such thing as an easy payment."

You will be wise to learn the facts about installment credit, so you can make sensible decisions about it.

Consumers can get installment credit in a number of places. Retail merchants offer credit in the form of deferred payments for goods you take and use while you are paying for them. Banks, credit unions, finance companies, and small loan companies lend money, which you repay bit by bit.

When you buy goods on the installment plan, you have to pay out more than when you buy for cash. When you get an installment loan, you pay back more than you receive.

The installment seller or lender adds a charge to cover such costs as investigating to find out if you are a good credit risk; the work of making out the contract, collecting the installments, and keeping the records; and interest on his money while you have the use of it.

He may also add the cost of filing fees, insurance to protect him from loss should you die before the debt is paid, and other charges.

Some merchants and lenders charge more for credit than others. Charges for different kinds of loans differ, too. The credit rate is usually higher for small than large loans and for unsecured than for secured loans.

For example, the rate is higher when the lender has only your signature or promise to assure him of getting his money back (this is an "unsecured" loan) than when you put up a car, refrigerator, bonds, or some other security he can take if you do not pay.

LENDERS USE different methods of figuring credit charges on installment purchases and loans.

There are two common methods.

One is to calculate the amount you owe for credit each time you pay an installment. It is figured as a percentage of the debt you owe at that time (the "unpaid balance"), so it gets smaller as the debt decreases.

The lender quotes the charge as a certain percentage of the unpaid balance per month. Notice that this is *per month* and not *per year*. If you want to know the rate per year, multiply the monthly rate by 12.

Here are some typical monthly rates and corresponding yearly rates:

If the monthly rate is—	The rate per year (the true annual rate) is—
¾ of 1%	9%
1%	12%
1½%	18%
2%	24%
2½%	30%
3%	36%

This method of calculating credit charges is generally used by credit unions and small loan companies. Retail merchants use it for revolving or budget charge accounts.

Another way of figuring credit charges is to calculate the credit charge all at one time—when you get the loan or make the installment purchase. It is figured as a percentage of the total amount you borrow or the price of the item you buy.

The charge for the entire loan period is added to the loan by some lenders and subtracted from it by others. Then the total is divided into installments.

The lender may quote the charge as a certain number of dollars per 100 dollars per year—as 4, 5, or 6 dollars per 100 dollars.

Take a loan at 4 dollars per 100

dollars as an example. If the lender adds the charge ("add-on" method) you receive 100 dollars and pay back 104 dollars. If he subtracts it ("discount" method), you receive 96 dollars and pay back 100 dollars.

A credit charge of 4, 5, or 6 dollars per 100 dollars per year on these loans appears to be 4, 5, or 6 percent a year, and the lender sometimes quotes it that way.

Actually, however, since you do not have the use of the entire 100 dollars for a whole year, the true annual rate is much higher than that. In fact, it turns out to be about double.

Figures in a table on the next page show the true annual rates on loans repaid in 12 monthly installments. (The rates would be slightly higher than these if you took longer to pay.)

Usually banks and sales finance companies use either the "add-on" or the "discount" method of calculating credit charges when they make loans for buying cars and other consumer durable goods.

The retail dealer usually figures your debt by the "add-on" method when you buy equipment or furniture on time. He is likely to quote you the total credit charge in dollars rather than the credit rate.

One more thing to note here: Lenders sometimes add more charges on top of the add-on or discount rates they quote. These may include charges for investigation of your credit rating, credit insurance, filing fees, and such. Watch for these extras, for they make the true annual credit rate higher.

Some of these look like very high rates to pay for credit. They look especially high when you compare them with the rate of interest you get on your savings. Think of this if you have savings you could use instead of credit.

PERHAPS YOU WILL find credit costs easier to understand if you see them in dollars rather than percentages.

Here is how the dollar cost of a loan on a new car worked out for one

TRUE ANNUAL RATES ON LOANS REPAID IN 12 MONTHLY INSTALLMENTS

	The quoted rate	*The true rate per year is—*	
If the credit charge per year is—	*per year is—*	*For "add-on"*	*For "discount"*
$4 per $100................	4%	7.4%	7.7%
$6 per $100................	6%	11.1%	11.8%
$8 per $100................	8%	14.8%	16.1%
$10 per $100..............	10%	18.5%	20.5%
$12 per $100..............	12%	22.2%	25.2%

CREDIT RATES COMMONLY CHARGED BY DIFFERENT LENDERS

Lender	*True annual rate*	*Quoted rate*
Retail dealers (including mail-order companies) on—		
Revolving or budget charge accounts.	12% to 18%...	1% to 1½% per month on the unpaid balance.
Installment purchase of appliances, furniture.	12% to 20% (or more).	Usually quote dollar charge only.
Banks.....................	6% to 16%....	3% to 8% per year (or $3 to $8 per $100 per year).
Credit unions..............	9% to 12%....	¾ of 1% to 1% per month on the unpaid balance.
Small loan companies........	18% to 42%...	1½% to 3½% per month on the unpaid balance.
Auto finance companies......	12% to 24%...	6% to 12% per year (or $6 to $12 per $100 per year).

buyer—a fairly typical case. He bought a car priced at 3,075 dollars, received 375 dollars for his old car as a trade-in, and made a cash downpayment of 700 dollars. He financed the rest of the cost through the dealer (who probably turned it over to a sales finance company), who added 149 dollars to cover insurance for the car. The buyer agreed to pay 24 monthly installments of 111 dollars.

Calculations to find out the dollar cost were:

(1)	Price of the car.............	$3,075
(2)	Value of trade-in...	$375
(3)	Cash downpayment..	$700
(4)	Total downpayment [(2)+(3)].......	1,075
(5)	To be financed on car cost [(1)−(4)]............	2,000
(6)	Car insurance...............	149
(7)	Total to be financed [(5)+(6)]......	2,149
(8)	24 payments of $111 each.....................	2,664
(9)	Dollar cost of credit [(8)−(7)]............	515

This buyer paid 515 dollars more for his car than if he had bought it for cash. This is not an unusually large amount to pay for credit on a major purchase like an automobile.

Here is an example of how dollar costs can add up on smaller purchases. Many families equip their homes (or replace household equipment) by buying pieces one by one on the installment plan.

Let's say a family plans to buy a washing machine, dryer, refrigerator, electric range, and vacuum cleaner. Buying them from a mail-order company, one after the other, the family would pay about 200 dollars more for them on the company's installment purchase plan than by paying cash. The credit price would be about 1,260 dollars; the cash price, 1,060 dollars. By planning and saving ahead, the family could pay cash and save enough to buy another convenience—perhaps an air conditioner, a TV set, or a piece of furniture.

A table on the next page gives the dollar cost of credit charges on a debt of 1 thousand dollars, at different credit rates. It shows how the cost mounts when you take longer to pay off a debt. Take a loan of 1 thousand

DOLLAR COST OF CREDIT CHARGES ON A $1,000 LOAN AT DIFFERENT CREDIT
RATES, REPAID IN DIFFERENT NUMBERS OF INSTALLMENTS

	Dollar cost of credit charges when number of monthly installments is—					
Credit rate	12	18	24	30	36	42
"Add-on" rate (added to beginning amount of debt):						
$4 per $100 per year.....................	$40	$60	$80	$100	$120	$140
$6 per $100 per year.....................	60	90	120	150	180	210
$8 per $100 per year.....................	80	120	160	200	240	280
$10 per $100 per year	100	150	200	250	300	350
$12 per $100 per year....................	120	180	240	300	360	420
Percent of unpaid balance:						
¾ of 1% per month......................	49	73	96	120	145	169
1% per month..........................	66	98	130	162	196	230
1½% per month........................	100	149	198	249	301	355
2% per month..........................	135	201	269	340	412	488
2½% per month........................	170	254	342	433	528	627

dollars at an add-on rate of 6 dollars per 100 dollars per year as an example. The credit charge would cost you 60 dollars if you repaid the debt in 12 monthly payments, but 180 dollars if you took 36 months to pay it.

It will be to your advantage to choose as short a repayment period as you can manage the payments for.

Now you have some information about where you can get installment credit and how much it costs.

The next problem is whether you want to get into this sort of thing at all. If you have in mind some particular thing to buy, you might think about such questions as: Could we pay cash for it without using too much of our savings? Is having it now worth the extra cost of buying it "on time"? Can we handle this much debt?

Perhaps you have read the rule of thumb that a family should not commit itself for installment payments amounting to more than 20 percent of its income.

The truth is that many families would be unwise to commit as much as 15, 10, or even 5 percent of their income to installment payments.

Some, on the other hand, might pay installments amounting to more than 20 percent of their income—for a time, at least—without hardship.

Each family has different financial resources, as well as different needs, wants, goals, future prospects, and management skills. These are the things that will determine how much installment debt they can handle.

Instead of searching for a rule to tell you how much installment debt you can safely assume, take stock of your own financial situation.

Have a family budget session to review your spending plan, your accounts, assets, and liabilities.

Considering these questions will help you to make a decision:

How much do we have left from our income each month now, after we have paid all our living expenses, made the payments on our present debts, put the planned amount into our savings account, and taken care of other obligations? (It makes sense not to take on another installment payment larger than this amount.)

Is it always easy to make the payments on our present debt? (If it sometimes means scraping and squeezing or skipping a payment, better think twice before taking on another debt.)

How much do we have in savings accounts, bonds, or other funds we can easily draw on? (Unless it is enough to pay living expenses and keep up debt payments for at least a month or so in case of illness or layoff from work, go slow.)

Will some debt be paid off soon, so

we can use the money we now pay on that for installments on a new debt? (A "yes" here may be a go-ahead indicator.)

Will another installment debt mean we have to postpone or give up some goal we have planned for? (If the answer is "yes," weigh the pros and cons carefully.)

Taking time to think things through like this may save you from the kind of impulse installment buying that gets families into trouble.

Every installment payment you promise to make has to fit into the budget somewhere. The time to make sure it does is before you sign on the dotted line.

ONCE YOU HAVE made up your mind to buy or borrow on the installment plan, keep the price you pay for credit as low as possible.

First, shop around for a good credit deal. If you are considering credit from a retailer, compare prices on the item you are buying as well as the credit charges. Sometimes merchants who sell on time charge more for the goods they sell.

Also, look into the possibility of getting a loan from a bank or credit union instead. Either way, be sure you are doing business with an established dealer or lending agency—one with a good reputation.

Do not be taken in by the unknown door-to-door salesman who offers to sell on the installment plan.

Make as large a downpayment as you can without reducing your savings to the danger point.

Finally, make monthly payments as large as your budget will allow. This way, you can pay the debt in the shortest possible time and save dollars.

When you buy things on time or get an installment loan, you have to sign a contract. Be sure you get a copy. Keep it in a safe place so you can refer to it if you need to.

Before you sign the contract:

Read and understand everything in it, including the fine print.

See that there are no blank spaces left when you sign.

Be sure the contract tells exactly what you are buying; the purchase price, or the amount of cash you will receive from the loan; all the credit charges; the downpayment and trade-in allowance, if any; the total amount you have to pay; the amount you have to pay for each installment; the number of installments to be made, and the dates due.

Find out to whom you are to make the payments.

Know what will happen if you cannot pay, and if you want to pay ahead.

Know what the seller's responsibility is for maintenance, service, or replacement of the goods purchased.

ONCE YOU HAVE MADE a credit deal, it's up to you to see that the installments are paid regularly.

If you fail to make the payments, the creditor can take the washing machine, car, or whatever it is you owe for. This means you lose the money you have already paid on it. In some States, you can be required to pay more, too, if the creditor cannot sell the washer or car for as much as you owe.

Your rating as a credit risk depends on how prompt you are in paying your debts. Because you may want credit again, it will pay you to keep this rating good. (EMMA G. HOLMES AND MINNIE BELLE MCINTOSH)

For further reading:
Consumer Bulletin. Monthly, Consumers' Research, Inc., Washington, N.J. Subscription, $5 a year.
Consumer Reports. Monthly, Consumers Union, 256 Washington Street, Mt. Vernon, N.Y. Subscription, $6 a year, including annual Buying Guide.
Margolius, Sydney, *A Guide to Consumer Credit.* Pamphlet No. 348, Public Affairs Pamphlets, 22 E. 38th Street, New York.
U.S. Department of Agriculture, *A Guide to Budgeting for the Young Couple.* Home and Garden Bulletin No. 98, 1964.
—*Consumer's Quick Credit Guide*, 1964.
—*What Young Farm Families Should Know About Credit.* Farmers' Bulletin No. 2135, 1965.
—*When You Use Credit . . . for the Family.* U.S. Government Printing Office, Washington, D.C., 1965.

The Family Budget

A BUDGET is something you make and remake until it works for you and you are satisfied with the results.

There is no magic formula.

Budgeting does not mean pinching pennies and recording every cent spent.

It is a way to get what your family wants most, whatever that may be.

If you do not have money to pay bills when they are due or cannot accumulate enough for a vacation trip, a budget can ease worry about money and start you on a savings program.

Making and following a budget help all members of your family to understand how and where to use money. That, we believe, is a cornerstone of education for modern living.

THE FIRST STEP in making a budget is to set goals. Some goals are for the distant future. Some are for next year. Some are for right now.

Decide what your family's needs and wants are. List them in order of importance.

Add to the list—and also subtract from it the items that time makes unimportant.

Do not let long-term goals get lost in day-to-day demands. Too many porterhouse steaks this month may crowd out a new dishwasher next year.

Define your goals clearly. Then they will be easier to reach. An example: Long-term goals may be paying off the mortgage, establishing a fund to cover the children's schooling, or saving for retirement. Your goal for the next year may be a new car, a living room rug, an encyclopedia, a fine phonograph and records.

THE NEXT STEP is to estimate how much money you will have available to spend for the planning period.

The planning period may be a month, a year, or any period. A year is a usual time for which to plan, but you may wish to set up a trial budget for a shorter period to see how it works out.

Start by considering your income in two ways—before taxes and after taxes. Income after taxes is the true amount available to spend and save. Thinking only of the amount before taxes may lead you to buy more than you can afford.

Write down all income you expect to receive. Include wages or salary, net money earned from a farm or business, interest from a savings account, dividends, and any extra money that may be earned from odd jobs.

Then estimate your income taxes and subtract them from your total money income. Write the answer down. That is the figure to keep in mind in making the budget.

Now estimate your expenses. You can recall some expenses well enough to make an estimate. Checkbook stubs, receipts, and old bills are good reminders for some items.

For other items (food, clothing, household operation, recreation), a record of present spending to see where your money is going is more helpful.

You might buy a form for keeping records or draw up your own. Rule off a form on a sheet of paper or in a looseleaf notebook. Allow a separate column for each category of expense that you want to keep track of. Leave enough space to enter the items you bought and their cost. Add up the amounts at the end of a week or a month.

Keep the record for a month or two. Use it as a guide in estimating expenses in your plan for future spending. In the estimate, make any changes you think are needed in order to get the things your family needs and wants most.

AT THIS POINT you are ready to set up your plan. The plan needs to be based on your goals, income, and expenses.

On the next page we give a sample of a form you may wish to use.

Start by planning to save something for a purpose or toward a goal. Decide on an amount and treat it as you do any other bill that must be paid.

We strongly recommend that you build up an emergency fund for illnesses, repairs that unexpectedly become necessary, accidents, and such.

After you have an emergency fund, start saving for your other goals.

If saving for retirement is a long-time goal and a certain percentage of your salary is being withheld to be applied toward retirement, count it as part of your savings goal. Or if the social security tax is deducted from your paycheck, consider it as savings, too.

Some of your expenses occur once or twice a year or every month. Some of them have to be paid in definite amounts at definite times.

In setting up your plan for future spending, list the expenses that come up only once or twice a year, such as real estate taxes, insurance premiums, vacation, fuel, and perhaps certain debt payments. Divide these expenses by 12 and set aside the required amount every month. Thus you spread the cost and have money to meet them when due.

Next list the expenses you expect to be the same from month to month. Your rent likely will be the same. If you are buying a house, or a car, or furniture on the installment plan, your payments will be the same. You may have other obligations, such as contributions to church and relatives.

After you have estimated your savings and regular expenses, you are ready for the day-to-day expenses.

Estimate how much to spend for food and beverages, clothing, transportation, and all the other budget groups. Go back over the records you kept and see what you spent for each of the budget groups. You may decide you need to spend more on some and less on other groups.

Remember to allow some leeway for unexpected or forgotten items.

A personal allowance for each person that need not be accounted for is a good thing, we believe, even if it has to be small.

Now work in the items you and others in the family have listed as your immediate goals.

WITH THE INFORMATION you have now, you are ready to add the totals and compare your planned outgo with your estimated income for the planning period.

If your income covers your savings and expenses, you have no problem. Any surplus you can add to savings for future goals or use to satisfy some immediate wants and desires.

If, as more likely will be the case, you have planned for more than your income will cover, you will need to take a new look at all parts of your plan.

You will need to decide which of your wants are less important, important, and very important. Look at the day-to-day expenses. Try to trim them.

For example, you may be able to defer some of them, or substitute a cheaper item, or paint your house yourself instead of hiring someone to do it, or take advantage of free community services (like your library and a free recital instead of going to the theater), or patch John's pants instead of buying a new pair.

Scan your regular expenses, too. Maybe you can reduce some of them. It may be better to move to a less costly house, get a cheaper car, or convert an endowment insurance policy to a cheaper form of life insurance.

A BUDGET PLAN

Item	Amount
Money income after taxes...	$_____
Savings:	
Future goals and emergencies..	$_____
Seasonal and large irregular expenses...............................	_____
Regular monthly expenses:	
Rent or mortgage payment..	$_____
Utilities...	_____
Installment payments...	_____
Other..	_____
Total..	_____
Day-to-day expenses:	
Food and beverages...	$_____
Household operation and maintenance................................	_____
Housefurnishings and equipment....................................	_____
Clothing...	_____
Transportation...	_____
Medical care...	_____
Education and reading...	_____
Recreation...	_____
Personal and miscellaneous...	_____
Gifts and contributions..	_____
Total..	_____
Total..	$_____

ESTIMATES OF SPENDING BY CERTAIN FAMILIES

	Income after taxes	
	$4,000 to $5,000	$6,000 to $7,500
	Percent	Percent
Total...	100	100
Savings..	2	4
Personal insurance...	5	5
Gifts and contributions..	4	4
Total for current living.......................................	89	87
Food and beverages...	24	21
Shelter (rent or mortgage interest payments and upkeep, insurance and taxes)......................................	12	11
Fuel and utilities...	5	4
Household operation..	5	5
Housefurnishings and equipment.............................	4	5
Clothing...	8	9
Transportation...	15	14
Medical care...	6	6
Education and reading......................................	1	2
Recreation...	3	4
Personal and miscellaneous.................................	6	6

Look at these things realistically—are they nearly as important as the really big things you want, such as security, education, and the means whereby you attain your ambitions?

After trimming here and cutting there, if your budget still does not balance, you may want to consider ways of adding to your income.

IF THIS is your first budget, it may help to have some idea of how other families divide their income. We give in a table some estimates based on studies of spending by families at two income levels with three or four members.

The estimates show that a budget based on one set of percentages would not fit both income groups. Neither would one set of percentages fit all families in the same income group. Families have different needs and different desires.

For example, if your family prefers to live in a house with plenty of space, your plan may allow more of your income for shelter, fuel and utilities, and household operation, and less for some other items.

ONCE YOUR BUDGET is made, try it out. It helps to keep records to see how the budget works. (Records are also helpful when it comes time to make out your income tax report.)

An easy way is to have a spindle on which to stick receipts and other notations of amounts you spend. At the end of the week or month, add up the amounts and record them. Or you may wish to continue using the same form you set up earlier to record your expenses.

Keep records simple—the simpler the better. Once you know where your money goes, you may not need a detailed account.

At the end of the budget period, compare what you actually spent with what you planned to spend. Were you fairly close? Were you satisfied with the results? Did you spend more than you planned? If so, why? Did you buy on impulse?

Your first try at budgeting may not be completely successful, but each time you try means improvement.

Even if your first budget is "perfect," it will need adjusting from time to time. For example, if you have a change in income, children are added to the family, or you move to a different community, you will find you need to adjust your budget.

Through a budget, however, you can plan to get your day-to-day needs and future dreams. (LUCILE F. MORK AND MINNIE BELLE MCINTOSH)

Insurance

THE LANGUAGE of insurance may be puzzling, but your decisions about insurance will be easier if you keep a few fundamentals in mind.

You should first know what insurance is supposed to do. Basically, it is to help protect you and your family against financial hardship due to hazard, accident, death, and so on. To rebuild your home after a fire, pay a large court judgment, or provide for your family if you die early may require more money than you have. Damage to your car or theft of property, however, may be less serious financially.

Knowing your risks, then, is important to selecting the right insurance.

Start by looking at your property and your family responsibilities. Think about the chance of various mishaps or events, which could cause major trouble and expense. It is wise to insure against them.

Do not insure against the little losses that will not hurt.

Few families can afford all the protection they need and should insure the greater risks first.

A little study before you see an insurance agent will help your money go as far as it can in fitting you with proper insurance. He will answer questions and advise you on details, but the final decision is yours. The kinds of insurance from which to choose seem limitless.

THE FOUR BASIC policies of life insurance are term, whole-life or straight, limited-payment, and endowment.

They differ mainly in whether the insurance is permanent or temporary and the extent to which savings, as well as insurance, are involved.

Your family responsibilities and goals and your pocketbook will guide you in your selection. The best insurance for you may be a combination of two or more types.

Term insurance is protection bought for a limited period or term, usually 5 or 10 years. Protection ends at the end of the term, and the policy has no savings or cash value. Because it is strictly for protection, the cost (premium) for young people is relatively low, but the cost increases with each renewal and becomes prohibitive at older ages. Some term policies do not permit renewal without a medical examination.

If you are younger than middle age and need every dollar's worth of protection you can buy, term insurance is good. It can provide stopgap protection for young couples, for example, until they are able to afford insurance to cover permanent responsibilities. Usually, however, it should supplement regular permanent life insurance. It is best used as additional protection for temporary periods of extra risk, such as when children are growing up or when debts are heavy.

Straight life insurance is commonest. Sometimes called whole-life or ordinary insurance, it runs for your lifetime. The premium depends on your age when you first take the insurance and stays the same each year. Part of the premium goes into savings, and the cash value of the policy increases as the years go by. After the need for insurance is past, the cash value can be obtained for retirement or other purposes.

Straight life insurance is the least costly lifetime protection you can get. Usually it is the most suitable for young families. Taken out early, it will be the foundation of a permanent insurance program.

Limited-payment life insurance is similar to straight life insurance, except that you pay premiums only for a stated period, say 20 or 30 years or up to age 65. At the end of the period, the insurance continues as a paid-up policy and no more premium payments are required. It is designed mainly for people who do not want to pay premiums as they get older. The cash value increases faster than with a straight life policy, but it is more expensive for the protection received.

Endowment insurance is important for its savings features. Money accumulates faster than with other types of policies and at a certain date it is paid as income or in lump sum to the insured, and the insurance protection ends. Should the insured person die before that date, the insurance is paid to his beneficiary. Because savings are emphasized, endowments are the most costly way to buy insurance protection.

Each of the four kinds of life insurance has many variations and special features, and two or more kinds can be combined.

The so-called family income plan offered by most life insurance companies combines one of the permanent policies, usually straight life, with gradually decreasing term insurance.

For example, a young family covered by a 20-year family income policy of 10 thousand dollars would have that amount of permanent insurance. If the father dies within 20 years after he took out the policy, his family would also receive a stipulated monthly income during the remainder of the 20-year period—a period when income would be most needed.

How MUCH life insurance you should buy may depend largely on what you can afford. Young families seldom can buy all they need.

As an amount to aim at, however, figure the money you need to live on and pay sickness and funeral expenses. Then buy what you can, keeping in mind other sources of income you can fall back on, such as savings and social security benefits.

Figuring out how much insurance you need and how much you can spend for it will also help you decide the kind to buy. If income is extremely short, you might consider term insurance as a temporary measure. Transfer it to permanent, straight life insurance as soon as possible, however. Until your needs for basic protection are met, it is best to postpone taking out endowment or limited-payment life insurance.

Also, keep in mind that to protect dependents in a family, the income earner's life is the one to be insured. Hold off insuring the lives of children until you can afford to do so.

KNOWING HOW TO BUY insurance also can help get most for your money.

Usually it is best to buy policies of at least 1 thousand dollars and pay premiums quarterly, semiannually, or annually.

Premiums paid annually are less than those paid semiannually, and the semiannual payments are less than quarterly payments.

Policies for smaller amounts, for which the insurance agent collects premiums weekly or monthly, are costly relative to protection received because of the extra expense to the company.

On the other hand, if group life insurance is available where you work, probably you should take it, as it is good, low-cost insurance. But consider it mainly as supplementing your regular insurance because it may not protect you if you change jobs.

If you have Government life insurance you took out while you were in the Armed Forces, keep as much of it as you can. It is low in cost. Consult your nearest Veterans' Administration office before making any changes in it.

If savings banks, credit unions, fraternal organizations, or others sell life insurance in your area, check the features and cost of their policies.

When you take out life insurance, you may choose a settlement option, which specifies how the money will be paid to your dependents when you die.

The choice can be a lump-sum payment, monthly income payments, or only payments of interest until the full amount is needed.

If you do not specify an option, your beneficiary usually can decide the method of payment at the time of your death. You may have to change settlement options and beneficiaries as time changes the financial requirements of your family.

That underscores the importance of reviewing your life insurance program every year or two to bring it up to date, for example, to include additional children.

If, after your policy is in force, you are unable to pay your premium within the grace period (1 month after the due date) your policy will ordinarily lapse. Some policies, however, include an automatic premium loan provision, under which the company will automatically pay the premium and charge it as a loan against your policy.

Your policy, unless it is a term policy, probably will also have nonforfeiture value if payments have been made for 1 to 3 years. You can turn in the policy and get its cash value or use the built-up values to obtain reduced paid-up insurance or obtain extended term insurance for as long as the cash value permits.

MANY FAMILIES protect themselves against the rising costs of sickness and hospitalization through health insurance. Policies generally cover three types of expenses—hospital, surgical, and medical. Insurance against loss of income because of illness or accident also is available. Further details are given in the chapter that follows.

If you cannot afford health insurance for the entire family, consider it at least for the breadwinner. His sickness would mean loss of income as well as medical expenses.

It is important to read the health contract to know what benefits it includes, particularly if you are not in a group. Find out what operations and illnesses are covered and what hospital services are offered. Some families may want to be sure of maternity benefits. Older persons should check whether the policy can be canceled or benefits reduced at a particular age. Ask for one that is guaranteed renewable.

To learn more about health insurance, talk to your employer or to your insurance agent.

FIRE INSURANCE is needed for both the house and furnishings.

In most States, a so-called "standard fire insurance policy" contains terms that comply with State laws and regulations. This policy protects you against fire and lightning losses.

It is customary also to add extended coverage to protect against some other hazards, such as windstorms, hail, explosion, smoke, riots, and damage by aircraft and vehicles.

Many homeowners carry personal liability insurance as well as regular fire insurance. Under a liability policy, the insurance company agrees to defend you in court and pay damage claims in the event someone is injured on your property. Injuries or damage resulting from activities of anyone in your family also are covered. Some liability policies provide medical payments up to 250 dollars or more, regardless of your liability.

Most insurance companies sell a package, or homeowners', policy, which covers personal liability and fire and extended coverage insurance. Policies for tenants also are available. The cost of the package will probably be less than if coverages were bought separately. Some package policies, however, may include more protection than you want. Consult your agent about the policy that best meets your need. Companies usually have three basic homeowners' policies that differ in the extent of coverage.

SOME FAMILIES spend more for insurance on their automobiles than for coverage on all other property they own. An automobile may be stolen, wrecked, and burned, cause damage to other automobiles, and injure persons.

Liability insurance is most important. Some States require it. It protects you against financial loss that may result from property or bodily injury damage suits. As the number of automobiles on the highways increases, the chance of accident and injury rises. Court judgments of thousands of dollars are not unusual. Few automobile owners can afford not to insure against this big risk.

Automobile liability insurance is spoken of as 10–20–5, 50–100–5, and so on. The meaning of 50–100–5, for example, is maximum coverage in the policy of 50 thousand dollars for each injury, 100 thousand dollars for each accident, and 5 thousand dollars for property damage. The larger policies do not cost much more than the minimum coverages and usually are well worth the difference.

Insurance to cover medical expenses of passengers who may be injured in your car is also desirable. It is relatively inexpensive to buy. The maximum medical care insurance offered is customarily 2 thousand dollars per person.

Collision insurance protects the automobile owner from expense of damage to his own automobile in an accident. This type of insurance is relatively expensive, and many persons reduce the premium cost by agreeing to pay the expense of repairs up to, say, 50 dollars. It is called deductible insurance.

Comprehensive insurance covers damage to your car by a variety of causes, such as fire, lightning, flood, theft, and breakage of glass.

If you are buying the automobile on credit, the lender undoubtedly will require you to carry collision and comprehensive insurance. Damage to your own car, however, would not be so great a financial loss to you as would be a liability loss resulting from injury or death to someone.

CHOOSING the amounts and kinds of insurance that fit your needs will take study. Insurance problems will always be with you as your situation and responsibilities change.

That usually means choosing an insurance agent in whom you have confidence and with whom you can work out a sensible insurance program. The agents recommended by your friends, your banker, or your lawyer are likely to be the best for you. (LAWRENCE A. JONES)

Medical Bills

STATISTICIANS can tell you how much medical care will cost in a year for the country as a whole, but they cannot predict which families will need to spend little and which will need to spend much.

Since most families will not know ahead of time what to expect in the way of medical bills, a twofold approach to fitting medical care into the family budget is best.

Plan to pay for run-of-the-mill and small expenses directly out of income.

Carry insurance to take care of unexpected and costly emergencies.

You may find also that occasionally you will need to draw on your emergency fund to backstop both your budgetary allowance for health care and your health insurance.

Most health insurance available today does not cover expenses for minor illnesses, preventive medical care, or dental care. These costs must then be taken care of directly out of your budget allowance for health care or out of your emergency fund.

In any case, you generally will save money by planning to pay directly for constantly recurring items.

It does not pay to insure against expenses that are a virtual certainty. If you do, you must pay not only these expenses but a share of the cost of running the insuring organization.

An exception to the principle that the expected, day-to-day expenses will cost you less if you pay them directly will be found in some organizations offering comprehensive prepaid care through their own staffs of physicians and supporting personnel. In such organizations, the savings possible through group practice may outweigh the bookkeeping and related costs involved in insuring.

While you may be ahead financially by paying directly for the run-of-the-mill health expenses, the charge you must pay for the protection against the unexpected that insurance provides is a worthwhile expenditure.

Through insurance you can reduce the costs of major illnesses and accidents to manageable proportions by spreading them over the years. Depending on the level of your insurance program, you can safeguard both your family's health and your savings.

Considerable diversity exists in the health insurance on the market today. To do a good job in providing for your family's health, you should find out what is available to you and then choose the type that gives the most protection for the amount you can afford to pay.

Health insurance can be divided into three broad categories: Hospitalization with or without medical-surgical insurance; major medical insurance; and comprehensive service programs.

HOSPITALIZATION insurance provides stated amounts of protection against hospital charges. Medical-surgical insurance does the same against doctors' bills arising from illness requiring hospitalization and accidents.

Neither hospitalization nor medical-surgical insurance offers blanket protection. Both carry limits on the amounts of care covered (the number of days of hospital care or the number of doctor's visits, for example) and the types of care covered (the type of hospital room, laboratory and other services in hospital, and perhaps limitations on treatments for some diseases).

Both may also carry limitations on the total payment for covered services. If your insurance reimburses you for bills you have paid, the reimbursement will be in line with a schedule of allowances included with your policy.

Blue Cross and other service policies assure you of full payment for the hospital services specified, but Blue Shield guarantees full payment of doctors' bills only if your income is below specified limits.

MAJOR MEDICAL INSURANCE is more inclusive in coverage than hospitalization and medical-surgical insurance.

In addition to the coverage they provide, it includes physician's care for other illnesses, private nursing care, drugs, X-ray and laboratory examinations, physical therapy, prosthetic devices such as artificial limbs, and ambulance service.

But major medical insurance usually does not cover preventive health examinations, dental care, and eye examinations and glasses. It also provides limited coverage only for the treatment of tuberculosis and psychiatric disease.

Major medical insurance, a later entry to the insurance field, was designed to cover the upper level of risks left uncovered by hospitalization and medical-surgical insurance. Consequently it is written with a "deductible" clause requiring the subscriber to pay a specified amount before benefits begin. The deductible may range from 50 to 500 dollars per person covered.

Benefits are stated in terms of total cash indemnity to pay covered expenses and may range from 2,500 to 10 thousand dollars.

To encourage the subscriber to hold down expenditures, major medical insurance also includes a coinsurance provision that requires the subscriber to pay a stated proportion of all expenses above the deductible—usually 20 to 25 percent.

You may combine hospitalization and medical-surgical insurance with major medical insurance to get more coverage than either provides alone.

Hospitalization and medical-surgical will usually meet the deductible for major medical if illness requires hospitalization.

If hospitalization is not required, you will quite possibly have to meet the deductible directly before benefits begin.

COMPREHENSIVE SERVICE programs differ from other health insurance in the range of benefits offered and in the form in which benefits are provided.

These programs may fall short of being completely comprehensive (all have limitations on the total amounts of service and most have specific limitations on treatment of psychiatric diseases and tuberculosis), but they have a broader scope in that they generally provide all the benefits offered by the other two types of insurance, plus preventive care and care of illnesses not requiring hospitalization.

Comprehensive group practice programs are organized on a clinic basis and provide care through their own staffs and to varying extents through their own facilities.

In contrast to the other types of insurance that permit the subscriber almost unlimited choice of hospitals and doctors (Blue Cross and Blue Shield subscribers must use member hospitals and doctors, but this requirement is not restrictive, since many hospitals and most doctors are members), comprehensive service programs limit the subscriber's choice to members of their own staffs and selected facilities.

This can work to the subscriber's advantage, since the administrators of the program, whose responsibility it is to select staff, are usually better judges of qualifications than the public.

Since a group policy always costs less than an individual policy providing the same benefits, you will want to give serious consideration to getting your health insurance as a member of an insured group.

The group forming the basis for this kind of insurance is most frequently the employees of a business concern, but any group not organized for the purpose of obtaining insurance and of sufficient size can be the basis for such a policy.

Depending on the size of the group, the insurer may require a specified proportion of the whole number to subscribe.

If you or members of your family are not "good risks"—that is, if you have conditions that make it likely you will need medical care—group insurance has an additional advantage. You may be rejected if you apply for an individual policy, or the policy may restrict benefits for these conditions. A group policy, however, is available to all members of the group.

To avoid an overload of unfavorable risks, your opportunities to enroll under a group policy are usually limited to the time the policy is negotiated or you join the group, and to occasional "open seasons." So, do not wait until you need the protection of insurance to apply for it. If you wait, you may find you cannot get it or that the cost is much higher.

SOME OTHER considerations in buying health insurance:

Make sure that your hospitalization or medical-surgical policy gives you the right to continue it as long as you keep the premiums paid. Such a policy will cost somewhat more than if the insurer has the right to cancel the policy for reasons other than nonpayment of premiums, but it is worth the additional cost. The reason for cancellation by the insurer would be your becoming a bad risk, and you then would find yourself without protection when you need protection most.

If age 65 is in sight, look for a policy that does not terminate on the anniversary following that birthday. Many do, and insurance taken out after 65 is likely to be more limited in the amount and kind of protection offered and much more expensive.

Of course, a policy you can carry after 65 will be somewhat more expensive than one that expires when you reach that age, but it will be worth the difference.

If, on the other hand, you are a long way from 65, do not pay extra for the privilege of carrying your insurance beyond that age. New developments in health insurance are still so frequent that there is little likelihood that youngsters will carry their present policy to age 65.

If you are 65 or older and without health insurance, look into the new policies developed by Blue Cross-Blue Shield and commercial insurers especially for your age group. These policies are offered without regard to health status at premiums roughly comparable to those offered good risks.

To make this possible, processing expenses are held to a minimum by offering only limited choices and subsidizing this type of business by absorbing its overhead costs and in other ways.

SO FAR, my emphasis has been on the protection available to you and little consideration has been given to its cost.

The fact remains, however, that we all must consider costs, and most of us cannot afford as much insurance (health and other kinds) as we might like.

In deciding how much to carry, consider whether the cost of the insurance is reasonable for the protection offered; what the chances are that you will need the various elements of protection offered; and whether you can fit the premium into your budget without too great a strain on other important elements of family living.

Once you have decided on your insurance, you can decide how much to budget for those run-of-the-mill expenses I discussed earlier.

Set the amount to cover what you might have to spend before your insurance begins to pick up the tab. Be sure that you have provision one place or the other for routine examinations and preventive services and dental and eye care.

If you are drawing up a budget for the first time and have not kept records of your expenditures in the past, you may be at a loss to know what your health care should cost you.

Here are some generalizations that will give you an idea what other families spend, but remember, when you use them, that averages always hide variations.

The average family in the United States (single persons count as families in these figures) in 1961 spent about 350 dollars for medical care in direct payment for care received and as insurance premiums. That amounted to 7 percent of all expenditures for family living.

Some of the known factors that influence the amount spent are income level, family size, and the age of the head of the family. What you spend will not be affected much by where you live—city, small town, or farm—but will reflect your income level.

Up to a point, the larger your family,

the more you can expect to spend on medical care. In large families, however, other demands on income force some reduction in spending for medical care.

You can expect to spend most for your family's medical care when you are between the ages of 45 and 54, which is also when your family will probably be largest. Your medical expenses will drop off somewhat thereafter, but not in proportion to the decrease in the size of your family.

Not all of your health needs must be met out of your own budget. Even though you are not indigent, you can expect some services from your local or State health department and from voluntary societies organized to combat the various chronic diseases.

If you have reached age 65 and can provide for your other needs but cannot meet more than routine medical expenses, you may be able to qualify for State assistance under the federally sponsored Kerr-Mills program. Ask at your public assistance office.

To get the most from your health

AVERAGE MEDICAL CARE EXPENDITURES OF FAMILIES IN SELECTED CLASSES, 1961

Family class	All families	Urban	Rural nonfarm	Farm
			Place of residence	
All families..............................	$345	$362	$297	$310
Income class (income after taxes):				
$2,000–$2,999......................	230	237	208	245
$3,000–$3,999......................	272	280	241	296
$4,000–$4,999......................	298	291	311	334
$5,000–$5,999......................	346	347	345	338
$6,000–$7,499......................	399	404	370	424
$7,500–$9,999......................	475	486	427	434
$10,000–$14,999...................	589	585	641	493
Family size:				
1-person............................	168	173	151	126
2-person............................	351	371	303	282
4-person............................	409	428	357	353
6-person............................	349	379	284	349
Age of family head (years):				
25–34..............................	331	340	306	280
35–44..............................	365	385	309	324
45–54..............................	373	393	317	340
55–64..............................	364	381	336	290
65–74..............................	326	352	261	285

Source: Survey of Consumer Expenditures, United States Departments of Labor and Agriculture.

budget, once you have set one up, have a "family doctor"—one or more. You may have a general practitioner who will care for all members of your family, or you may have an internist for the adult members and a pediatrician for the children. Just be sure that someone knows the health status of your family.

If illness strikes and specialist care seems indicated, let your family doctor direct and advise you.

Do not hesitate to discuss costs with your doctors.

Providing for your family's health does not begin and end in the allowance for medical care in your budget. Nutritious meals, healthful living conditions, good habits of work, exercise, recreation, and rest in balanced amounts—all will help safeguard your family's health. (JEAN L. PENNOCK)

Saving on Cars

A CAR is the most expensive item, next to a house, a family is likely to buy, what with the original cost, the upkeep, and the operating expenses.

There are ways, though, to save quite a few dollars every year.

Some facts:

The average family with a car (or cars) spends about 900 dollars a year for car expenses. That is more than is spent on shelter, clothing, medical care, or any other item, except food.

The average price paid is about 3 thousand dollars for a new car and 900 dollars for a used car.

New cars are kept an average of 6 years; used cars, 4 years.

Every few years a family has to

decide whether it is time to buy another car. The most economical time to buy generally is when your present car costs you more for depreciation, repairs, gasoline, and oil than a new one would.

A car depreciates—goes down in value—at a slower rate each succeeding year. The cost of upkeep and operation, on the other hand, goes up as the car ages. The best time to trade varies according to the use the car has had and the type of driver.

WHEN IT COMES to buying a car, the choice among sizes, models, and extras may not be easy to make.

The car you choose should fit your own needs and purse. At the same time, the selection of a car that buyers of used cars will want when you are ready to trade is one way to cut the high cost of depreciation and protect your investment.

If your family is small or you need a second car to drive to work, a low-priced compact may be the one for you. If you have several children, a standard-sized car may be better for you and worth the higher cost. If you cannot decide between these two sizes, consider one in the intermediate size—between compact and standard models in size, price, and operating costs.

As for body styles, the four-door sedan is a good investment because it is the most popular. If you prefer a two door, the hardtop generally is considered a better buy than the regular sedan. You will get back most, if not all, of the extra cost when you trade in the hardtop. Station wagons (the four-door models) are always in demand among big suburban families.

The extras can add several hundred dollars to the cost of a new car without adding much to trade-in value later. Judge them on their worth to you.

Radio, heater, automatic transmission, and power steering are among the accessories most likely to offer a fair return. An automatic transmission will add to the cost of running the car, because it takes more gasoline than a standard transmission. All-vinyl upholstery looks good and is easy to care for.

Some accessories are nice to have but do not add much to the usefulness of the car. In general, you get back only a small part of their original cost. Among them are whitewall tires, tilt-type steering wheels, and power seats and windows.

Pick the right time to buy. Some of the best times are toward the end of the month, when salesmen and dealers are anxious to meet their quota; during slow winter months (February and March); and during contests.

Liberal discounts generally are given just before the new models come out, but you may have a limited choice. Remember, too, you will have an old model within a very short time, but that is less important if you keep your automobile a long time.

Pay cash if you can. No additional charge is made then for interest, investigation, recording, and so on.

If you must borrow money, make as big a downpayment as possible and keep the financing period short. The appraised value of your trade-in car becomes part of your downpayment.

If you are planning to finance, shop for the lowest terms. To do so you need to have certain information: The cost of the new car; the trade-in allowance for your old car; any additional downpayment; the amount of your loan; the amount of the monthly payment; and the number of payments required.

Multiply the monthly payment by the number of months you are to pay. Subtract the amount of your loan from this total. The remainder is the amount you will pay for the use of credit on your dealer's plan.

With that information, you can shop for the lowest financing terms. Go to lending agencies and compare costs. You may find it costs less to borrow directly from a bank or credit union.

MOST OWNERS have some form of insurance. When you buy auto insurance, you usually are buying several kinds of coverage in one package.

You can shop for the best insurance buy if you know the kind and extent of coverage you want.

Liability insurance gives you financial protection for bodily injury or property damage to others. State laws tell you how much to buy to fulfill the legal requirements. It is a good idea to buy more than the minimum amount required, if you can possibly squeeze out the extra cost. The additional cost is relatively small compared with the greater protection. Jury awards can be very high; judgments of 50 thousand dollars are not uncommon.

Comprehensive insurance provides for loss or damage to your car from a number of hazards—fire, theft, windstorm, glass breakage, and vandalism. Comprehensive insurance becomes less important as a car grows older, if you can absorb the loss.

Collision insurance covers damage to your car from collision or upset, if you or someone else is at fault. This kind of coverage is expensive. To reduce the cost, it usually is written with an amount—50, 100, or 250 dollars—deductible. You pay for the deductible amount of the damages on your car, and the insurance company pays the rest. The higher the deductible limit, the lower the premium.

If you consider yourself a reasonably safe driver or feel you can pay the first 100 or 250 dollars in case of an accident, you can cut the cost of your insurance with one of the higher deductibles. It may not pay you to carry this kind of coverage on an older car.

If you finance the purchase of a car, you will be required to carry comprehensive fire and theft and collision insurance to cover the full value of the car. Be sure you also have liability coverage.

You can also buy medical-payment insurance that pays medical and hospital bills should you or anyone riding in your car be injured. This kind of coverage may not be necessary if you have an adequate medical coverage through other insurance plans.

On other kinds of insurance, such as towing and uninsured-motorist coverage, you will need to decide how important they are to you in relation to the risk involved and the cost.

Car insurance rates vary from company to company. Some companies offer lower rates because they specialize in auto insurance, sell directly to the customer, or sell only to good risks.

GASOLINE is a big item in the operation of a car. A change from premium to regular or regular to economy gasoline can save you money on your car.

Unless the manufacturer specifies it, most cars do not need a premium grade. Some cars do just as well on one of the economy fuels.

Buy the lowest grade of gas that will give satisfactory operation in your car.

Develop good driving habits to get as much mileage as possible from the gasoline you buy: Avoid jackrabbit starts and sudden stops. Accelerate smoothly and with a light touch. Look ahead and slow down gradually. Maintain a steady speed. Travel at moderate speeds.

Another way to save on gasoline is to keep your car in proper running order: Have a tuneup periodically. Clean the spark plugs and make replacements when necessary. Check the carburetor occasionally. Keep the air filter clean.

When it comes to oil changes and chassis lubrications, it is best to follow the recommendations in the owner's manual. The new, longer periods between oil changes for new cars are a convenience and save money. To insure safe and reliable operation, though, it is still necessary to give your car the attention called for.

Do not overbuy on tires. You may need premium-grade tires if you do a lot of driving on rough roads, but the cheaper first-line grade should be adequate for most ordinary driving. Keep the tires inflated to the pressure the manufacturer recommends. Check the alinement of the front wheels. Make the necessary corrections. Good driving habits mean the most wear out of your tires and hold the cost down.

KEEPING YOUR CAR in good condition helps to cut depreciation to a reasonable minimum. The new paints used on cars may need less polishing and waxing than the old paints, but regular washing is necessary. Paint that is protected from the sun, sleet, and snow lasts longer and looks better. If you have a garage or carport, make a point of running your car under cover.

Some of these savings may seem small. When you add them up, you will be surprised at how much you can save. (LUCILE F. MORK)

The Employed Wife

COMES A TIME, as it does to many wives, when you think you would like a paying job.

You believe, of course, that a woman's place is in the home, but before the children come or when they are well along in school, you think of putting your skills to work, adding variety to your life, and contributing to the family income.

Then the first order of business is to talk it over with the family, whose care is your first responsibility. A job will not work out unless you have family approval and cooperation.

They need to be in on the decisions to be made—how and when housekeeping chores are to be done; what help they will give; what provisions are to be made for caring for the young children; and how your earnings are to be used.

Do not spend your income before you get it, though. You will not have all you earn to use as you wish. You will have expenses that you do not have as a housewife. Take them into account before you start.

They may make a sizable list. They may include Federal, State, and local income taxes; social security tax (old age, survivors, and disability insurance); contributions to retirement plans (other than social security); transportation to and from work; meals and snacks at work; dues to work-connected organizations (labor or trade unions, professional and business organizations, employee clubs); flowers and gifts for and social occasions with fellow employees; tools and licenses required for work; special work clothing; professional and business meetings and publications; educational expenses connected with the job; and extra expense for general-wear clothing, personal care, and paid service for household tasks.

It is unlikely you would have all of those expenses, because not all apply to every kind of job or to every family situation. Go down the list. Decide which items you will probably have expense for. Then make estimates.

If you think of something else you are going to have to pay for, add it to the list. Do not skimp; you want a true picture.

You may as well estimate your expenses for a year, if you expect to be working that long, or for the duration of a short-time job.

WILL YOUR EARNINGS put the family income into a higher tax bracket and boost your income taxes? Consider any additional tax as a job expense.

Get Federal income tax forms and figure what the tax will be on the combined income you and your husband would have if you were employed, and on the income you and your husband have had.

If you like, try it as if you were making a joint return and then as separate returns. You can use the one that gives the lower tax. Then subtract, like this:

Tax on combined income........ $———
Tax on husband's income........   ———
Wife's job-related expense........   ———

If your State, city, or county has an income tax, get the proper forms and figure in a similar manner.

The social security law applies to workers in most kinds of jobs. It requires them to pay a certain part of their earnings toward old age, survivors, and disability insurance.

Find out if your job will be covered by social security. If so, find out what the tax rate is and figure how much you will have to pay. (The rate in 1965 was 3.625 percent of the earnings from salaries or wages, or 5.4 percent of your net income from a business you own. In either case, the maximum amount taxed is 4,800 dollars a year. The social security tax rate is expected to increase after 1965.)

Some jobs are covered by other retirement plans instead of (or in addition to) social security. Most Federal Government workers, for example, come under a civil service retirement plan. They pay 6.5 percent of their salary into the retirement fund.

Get the facts from your prospective employer. You will want to know what benefits you can expect to receive as well as what you will have to pay.

Figure what the deductions will amount to in the year, and add the total to your list of expenses.

YOU CAN SKIP the cost of transportation to and from work if you live close enough to walk to work or if your husband drives to work and can drop you off without going out of his way.

If you will be riding a bus, train, taxi, or some other conveyance where you pay a set fare per ride, you can calculate the cost for the year easily.

If you will be driving the family car, it is more complicated and probably more costly. Charge yourself with a fair share of the expense of the car.

For example, if you expect your trips to and from work to add up to 10 miles a day, or 2,500 miles a year (fifty 5-day weeks), and family travel adds up to 5 thousand miles a year, estimate the total cost for the 7,500 miles. Count car depreciation, license fees, insurance, repairs, washing, gas, oil, lubrication, personal property tax (if you have to pay one), and whatever other expenses apply. Charge one-third of this total to your job, since the 2,500 miles you drive is one-third of 7,500 miles. Or you may charge somewhat less if you prefer to think of such costs as license fees and insurance as expenses you would have even if you did not work. Add an allowance for parking fees at work and road and bridge tolls, if they apply.

If you are going to have to buy another car in order to get to your work, your car expenses will mount. You will have the entire expense of the second car if you use it for work only. Be realistic in calculating this expense.

UNLESS YOU PLAN to go home at noon or carry a lunch from home, add an allowance for meals at work. This may have to be a pure guess for the time being. Make your best estimate of what the kind of lunch you usually eat will cost in a cafeteria or restaurant. Remember to put something in for coffee breaks, too.

To find out about other job expenses you are likely to have, you might talk with your future employer or fellow employees. They can tell you the cost of uniforms and other special work clothing and of licenses and tools, if the job requires them. They will know what dues you will be expected to pay, the usual expenses for flower funds, gifts, parties, and meetings. Your employer will let you know if you will be expected to take (and pay for) a refresher course or special training to qualify for the job.

Then there are items that we labeled "extra" expense. Even as a full-time homemaker you have some expense for clothing and personal care and perhaps

for help with household tasks. But you may pay out more when you are employed. Estimate how much more you will spend for each of these items.

Your spending for clothing is likely to go up even if you do not have to buy special types of work clothing. The wardrobe that serves very well for wear at home, to the shopping center, to church, and for social gatherings may not offer much that is suitable for work.

You may need more changes of clothing, too. And you will find it hard not to treat yourself to a dress or coat a bit more expensive than usual when there is more money to spend.

More visits to the beauty parlor and more generous use of beauty preparations mean additional expense for many a wife with a job away from home.

Some wives seem to handle their homemaking tasks with one hand while they earn a paycheck with the other. How about you? Will you be sending more laundry out, having a woman come in to do the housework, sending children to nursery school or hiring a sitter to look after them while you are away? If the answer is yes, put it into your estimate. Look into the going rate for these types of services in your community, if you have not been using them.

NOW CHECK over your estimates for the expenses you have listed.

Add them all up and subtract the total from what you expect to earn.

The result is the net income you can expect to have. It is the amount you can plan to put into the family purse.

If your estimated net income is smaller than you expected, this need not necessarily keep you from taking the job. You may still decide the job is worth while if it promises to close the gap in the family budget or bring you personal satisfaction.

Now that you know about what your net income will be, you can set up a plan for using it. Let your husband in on this, for planning for any family income—yours and his— needs to be a family affair. Not that your income has to be combined with his and divided among budget items.

The decision may be to use a good share of it this way and give you the rest for some special project you have your heart set on. Or it may be to put all or most of what you make into a fund for educating the children, building a house, buying a car, or reaching some other family goal.

The important thing is that the decision be satisfactory to both you and your husband, because you both had a part in making it.

ACTUAL EXPENSES on the job could turn out to be more or less than you estimated. You will want to check on them as you go along.

Home economists in the Department of Agriculture made some surveys to find out what employed wives actually spent on job expenses. They interviewed groups of wives in Georgia, Ohio, and North Carolina. They got information about their expenses for the items in our list.

They learned that the working wives with no preschool children at home netted about 6o percent of their total wages or salaries, on the average. Those with preschool children (under 6 years) netted less— an average of about 50 percent of their earnings. It was mainly their expense for the care of their children that made their net income lower. Some in each type of family did much better than the average; some, not so well.

You may come out better than these wives. You almost certainly will if you have no expense for transportation and can manage your work at home without hiring extra help.

You may find you had some expenses besides those on our list, too. Your food bill may be higher than before because your family eats out more or you buy more expensive foods for meals at home because they take less time to prepare. Clothing for the family may cost more because you do not have time to sew and mend. You

may make larger money contributions to community projects because you cannot donate time as you used to.

On the plus side, however, is that not all of what we counted as job expense is lost to the family. Payments made for social security and other retirement plans build toward a retirement income. The social security tax also provides protection against other economic hazards. Extra amounts spent for clothing and personal care usually give a woman the personal satisfaction of being better dressed and better groomed. The cost of a wife's meals at work is not all an added expense, since it would cost her something to eat at home. (EMMA G. HOLMES)

Children
and Money

THE KNOWLEDGE, attitudes, and skill that children acquire concerning money come from a variety of sources. The most important is the family.

What is learned at home is reinforced, weakened, or changed by the influence of friends, other adults outside the home, and pressures in the social world at large.

Those pressures are strong. Children themselves have become important consumers. They have control over more money at earlier ages than ever before. A rise in family incomes has meant that more parents can give their children more money for their own use. Business knows this full well. Modern advertising regards children and teenagers as major targets. All that emphasizes the urgency of teaching children how to manage money.

You probably want your children to learn several important principles:

To spend wisely in such a way as to get full enjoyment and satisfaction.

To save for future purchases.

To understand credit and how to use it well.

To have experience in earning money for their own use.

To be able and willing to share within the family, with friends, and with others who are less fortunate.

In other words, you want your children to learn that money is valuable as a tool in reaching goals rather than as a goal in itself. This implies that as adults, we need to examine our own attitudes toward money and to resist the temptation to look upon money only as a restricting rather than also as a facilitating element in our lives.

If adults overemphasize the importance of money, we need not be surprised when children also do so.

On the other hand, when adults in the company of children can enjoy some of the many fine things in the world that require no spending of money and can consistently meet children's needs for affection and companionship, they are well on the way toward teaching the proper place that material possessions should have.

FOR THE VERY YOUNG child, not yet in school, the most important contribution adults can make is in providing a basic sense of trust and security.

Children at this early stage are not able to understand and deal with numbers and the complexities of money as a medium of exchange.

Often the preschooler's first idea about money is that it is just something that makes other things happen. We push buttons, and lights go on. We turn keys, and cars start. We put coins in machines, and candy or soft drinks come out. Preschoolers in playing store do go through the motions of "buying and selling," but they are merely imitating an adult process without really understanding the function that money performs.

Very young children do pick up from adults around them important attitudes that form the basis of their later values and choices. They absorb feelings about money even before they know how money operates.

When parents show by their actions that they understand each other's needs and are willing to share in fair ways without feelings of jealousy, children will arrive easily and comfortably at the idea that money is a valuable tool but not the all-important one. In times of family financial crisis, such children are likely to be realistic and relatively free of worry.

Most adults face money problems more or less constantly. America is a consumer-oriented society. Families make daily choices about how much of their money they will spend for which things.

Parents do well when they avoid showing anxiety and worry about money in the presence of small children. Anxious arguments about bills are quite likely to give children an impression that money is an insurmountable and depressing problem.

Obviously there will always be gradations in wealth. It is honest and surely the part of discretion to teach children early the meaning of the statement, "We cannot afford this."

When such teaching is combined with enjoyable family activities, children will readily accept differences in material possessions between their own and other families.

The earliest experiences children have with money probably should center around spending rather than saving. A child has to learn what money is used for before he can understand reasons for saving.

For the preschool child, it is both a source of fun and also instructive to go with his mother when she shops in the supermarket. He will enjoy putting coins in the parking meter and perhaps making a small purchase himself with a few pennies jingling in his pocket. He will feel important when he hands the service station attendant the money for gas or pays the paperboy when he comes to the door.

When the preschooler is spending his own money, he should have some freedom of choice. He will learn in time that his dime will buy either one ice cream cone or a candy bar. He can then gradually proceed to more difficult decisions regarding a larger amount, like a quarter, which can be used to make either several small purchases or one larger one.

When his money is all gone, it is probably unwise to allow him to cajole you into giving him more, simply because he has changed his mind after the decision was made. Otherwise, you permit him to postpone learning to accept the consequences of his choices.

Preschoolers are generally not ready for allowances. It is better to give them small amounts of money two or three times a week to help them gain experience in spending. This practice will be of value to them when they learn to handle timespans and numbers.

The small child can learn to enjoy sharing through spending when he is encouraged to share something he has bought with other members of the family. He also gains pleasure in using money to buy birthday or Christmas gifts for friends and other members of the family.

Especially when the child is the youngest of several children, he should be helped to see that as he gains more experience with money, he will be given more and allowed more freedom in deciding how to spend it.

Until he is of school age, it is probably best to concentrate on finding as many kinds of experiences in spending and sharing as possible.

By ABOUT AGE SIX, when a child starts school, he may be ready for an allowance.

Children's needs vary, even at this age. You may find that somewhere around 50 cents a week is enough spending money for 6- to 9-year-olds.

When your child receives his first allowance, it may be wise to have a small ceremony, to recognize that he is growing up. You and he together can talk about his needs and decide with him how much money he will require to meet a reasonable number of them.

Special occasions will call for supplementary contributions on your part. If he has a fixed expense, such as buying his school lunch, you will have to take it into account.

Increases should be based on expanding needs and duties, together with growing skill in managing.

It is a good idea to schedule increases to coincide with some regular interval, such as a birthday or New Year's. Especially if there are several children, each learns in this way that advancing age brings both increased privileges and responsibilities.

MANY ADULTS believe that the best way for children to learn the value of money is to work for it.

Some parents, consistent with this viewpoint, tie a youngster's allowance to household chores and withhold all or part of it if the tasks are not done. Most child guidance workers agree, however, that allowances and household jobs should not be connected in this way.

Giving children money for help with routine family chores suggests that a normal share of responsibility in the family deserves to be paid. Children have the right to share in family pleasures and privileges, and they should be encouraged to take on their share of the chores without bribery.

There will be times when children will want to earn some extra money by doing jobs that otherwise the family would have to pay for. An allowance, on the other hand, should be given to the child as his rightful share of the family income. Once agreed upon, it should be his with no strings attached.

Just as assuming responsibility for household jobs is part of a child's duty to himself and his family, so also is his obligation to do his best in school. Payment for good grades puts undue emphasis on the grades themselves and also may deprive the child of an important chance to prove himself to his own inner satisfaction.

WITH READINESS for school, come also, for most children, the desire and the ability to start saving for special purposes. Between ages 6 and 10, it is wise to stress saving for some tangible goal that can be achieved within a short period of time. Saving for a small toy or a birthday present helps a youngster to learn to save for using, not just for having.

Before about age 10 it probably is best not to insist that a child put aside part of his allowance in savings. To encourage a habit of thrift in a child of this age, try supplementing his allowance with a special amount which he understands is for this purpose alone. His allowance then becomes his to manage.

After about age 10, he is probably becoming experienced enough in managing his money to set aside part of his allowance in a savings program directed toward a not-too-distant goal.

At this age and later, he can supplement his savings by additional earnings beyond his allowance. This is a good time to acquaint him with your bank by having him open a savings account.

Helpful beginning lessons in the use of credit can be part of a child's learning during the school years. There is nothing wrong in letting a child borrow small sums once in a while against his allowance as long as he follows through with repayment.

But it is not fair to let him assume a debt of such size that it keeps him broke seemingly forever. Later on, when he can understand the reasons for interest payments, you can help him explore different ways of borrowing for some major purpose, choosing with him a reasonable plan.

Children need an atmosphere of "protected risk taking" while they are learning the important lessons of money management. A child's natural tend-ency is to mortgage his entire future for some immediate pleasure. If adults do not help him to see the lack of wisdom in such a policy, the youngster will be poorly equipped to handle his responsibilities when he matures.

Children are likely to lose or misplace money just as they do toys, gloves, and overshoes. They need to learn to wait until the next payday, just as you would have to do if you lost money of your own. If the money is needed for some fixed expense, such as buying lunch, you may have to replace it. If a child loses money often and seems to be forming habits of carelessness, it may help if you encourage him to carry only part of his money with him at any one time.

We can and should sympathize with children when they lose objects, knowing our own failings.

Possibilities for children in grade school to earn money will vary. Farm children have unique opportunities to share in the farm enterprise beyond their routine chores. City children can earn from paper routes, from doing errands, and from a variety of after-school jobs, including babysitting.

Through the school years, children can be helped to see that their funds need to be divided to take care of various obligations and pleasures. A system of envelopes, jars, or cans labeled for different purposes can aid in teaching how to plan income and outgo.

Many parents, as children grow older, increase allowances to include major purchases of clothing, bicycles, room furnishings, record albums, insurance, and the like.

Here again, give children as much freedom as possible in making choices. While this may mean for you and them seemingly endless discussions of alternatives and many long hours of shopping around for the best buys, these are, after all, the facts of life for consumers, big and little. Such practice in making choices, as children, forms a sound basis for spending their own paychecks in the years ahead. (EDWARD V. POPE)

SAFEGUARDS

Motor

Accidents

THE 87 MILLION motor vehicles in the United States in 1964 were operated by 96 million licensed drivers and traveled 838 billion miles.

They were involved in 12 million traffic accidents, which caused 48 thousand deaths, 1.7 million disabling injuries, and a huge junk pile. The costs of accidents exceeded 8.2 billion dollars.

Deaths, injuries, and costs, however, are not the traffic problem. They are the symptoms or proofs that a problem exists. They indicate that we may not know what the problem is or that it has not been solved.

The problem is how to transport people and property via automotive transportation safely, efficiently, and rapidly.

Air, rail, and sea transportation systems can provide safe, efficient, and rapid transportation through their selection and maintenance of equipment and their controls over profes-

sional pilots, engineers, or navigators.

It is not that simple in the case of automotive transportation. Each of the 96 million drivers selects, maintains, and operates the equipment of his choice.

Traffic officers, highway engineers, and manufacturers of vehicles sometimes are blamed for the accidents.

The person actually responsible for your safety in traffic is you.

Passing a driving test and having a driver's permit do not qualify you as a proficient driver in today's traffic. Proficiency requires skill, knowledge, and a desire to avoid accident-building situations. Because most accidents are caused by people, people must prevent them.

One way to do that is to take part in activities that will help eliminate accidents—in the educational programs by which a community seeks to improve the skill, knowledge, and attitude of its drivers and thereby make driving safer.

Such educational programs exist in many communities. They usually are sponsored by the local traffic police or safety council. Their effectiveness is limited because people feel the programs are for somebody else.

If you and a group of your friends join to encourage the development and conduct of such traffic safety educational activities in your community, you and they can do much.

My 30 years of experience as a motor vehicle safety officer leads me to suggest, therefore, that each service, civic, school, business, and church organization in a community set up a safety committee—

to encourage its members to study the cause and prevention of accidents and the principles of safe driving;

to make known the importance of courtesy on the road;

to remove road and street hazards;

and to acquaint drivers with the rights and problems of pedestrians.

That was done in one community I know well. Through such group efforts, its 500 thousand residents cut in half the number of accidents in their city. (THURLOW J. BIDDLE)

Accidents
at Home

WHEN WE DRIVE along a highway, signal lights tell us, "Slow down, there's danger ahead"—an accident, road construction, a detour, a slippery pavement. We proceed with caution.

But home, man's sanctum of peace and security, is the place of more injuries each year than any other place. Accidental death here is second only to death on the highway.

The home and its premises are the scene of almost two-thirds of all accidental deaths of children under 5 and almost half of the accidental deaths of persons 65 and over.

Accidents in the home are responsible for more than three-fourths of all deaths from fire and explosion and for almost two-thirds of those from poisonous gases and vapors, solid and liquid poisons, and firearms.

Danger spots exist all through a house, but we install no warning lights for the young and old. We light our houses for convenience, comfort, beauty, and pleasure. Why not install signal lights in places where caution is necessary and where we need reminders to slow down, look, and walk, not run?

For example, when the light is switched on in the bathroom, a blinker by the glass shower door or tub enclosure warns one to be careful. A light at the top of stairways or at the bottom step will reduce the number of falls.

More than 12,700 persons died in 1964 (according to preliminary estimates) from falls from one level to another (stairs, ladder, roof) and on the same level (floor, sidewalk).

Falls happen for many reasons.

The condition of the floor may be to blame, whether it is old, new, or sloped, or has cracks, splinters, and broken tiles.

Floors may be dangerous because of spilled liquids, children's toys, and other things that should have been removed. The floor may be too slippery. The rugs may be unanchored. Lighting in a room, stairway, and hall may be inadequate.

Glass doors and panels are attractive but risky. People have been hurt when they walked into them.

A person may slip and fall against a glass shower door or tub enclosure. The use of skidproof mats on the bathroom floor, suction-type bathmats, nonslip adhesive strips for solid footing, and wall-mounted grab bars or handrails help prevent slipping.

Scatter rugs, toys, and other articles that may cause one to slip, trip, or fall should be cleared from glass-door areas.

About 30 children, most of them under 6, each year get trapped in refrigerators and suffocate.

A refrigerator that is temporarily out of use should be encircled with strong filament tape or a chain with a padlock. The doors of a refrigerator that is to be junked, discarded, or abandoned should be removed. Better yet, the box should be carted away immediately and destroyed.

Accidental poisoning has become common.

Many children have been poisoned by swallowing large amounts of aspirin, which usually is considered a standard, reasonably safe medicine. Aspirin tablets should not be left on night tables or anywhere within easy reach of children.

Young children are apt to chew woodwork, stair railings, and window sills, especially when they are cutting teeth. If the wood is painted, the child may become ill from lead poisoning.

Small children are apt to eat anything, regardless of fumes, tastes, or smell. Medicines, cleaning supplies, paint, waxes, rat poisons, garden chemicals, disinfectants, bleaches, and all such materials should be labeled plainly and put beyond the reach of children. The outright poisons should be kept in a locked cabinet.

Half of all home fires start in kitchens and living rooms. Good construction and good equipment and maintenance reduce the risk, but no house is firesafe unless the people in it are careful.

Fires in clothing are commonest among children (particularly little girls), who play with matches and cigarette lighters, around stoves and heaters, and too close to outdoor fires. Elderly people may set their clothes on fire while using stoves carelessly, warming themselves at fireplaces, or falling asleep while smoking.

ONE OF THE SADDEST things about an accident: It need not have happened.

Plan to eliminate hazards throughout the home by a little forethought and planning.

Clear the stairways of toys and other objects.

Add lights on stairways or in dark areas and halls.

Install grab bars or handrails in the bathroom. Use skidproof mats in tubs. Do not leave cakes of soap in the tub or shower.

Anchor down rugs.

Keep flammable articles away from fires.

Check gas burners often for leaks.

Wipe up liquids immediately to avoid falls.

Label medicines and store them out of reach of children.

Some safety tips: Watch where you are going. Walk, do not run, on steps. Light the way into a room and put lights on steps and stairs.

Store sharp objects separately from blunt ones.

Check to be sure matches are out.

Avoid smoking in bed.

Read the label before you take any medicine.

Keep household cleaning aids out of reach of children.

Teach children especially to be careful in the shower and in swimming pools. (BEATRICE A. JUDKINS)

Fire

Protection

THE AVERAGE NUMBER of unwanted fires in American homes each year is 550 thousand. They cause 6,300 deaths, 250 thousand other injuries, and property damage of 329 million dollars.

Thirty-seven percent of the home fires occur in living rooms; 22 in kitchens; 13 in bedrooms; and the others in attics and basements.

The main causes are faulty heating equipment, 24 percent; smoking materials, 18; electricity, 14; children with matches, 10; mishandling flammable liquids, 9; cooking equipment, 5; and miscellaneous, 20.

For a fire, fuel, oxygen (or air), and a source of heat are necessary. If you heat a combustible fuel in the presence of oxygen, you have an ordinary fire.

FIRE EXTINGUISHERS

TYPE OF EXTINGUISHER	FOR WHAT KINDS OF FIRE	CONTENTS	HOW TO START	RANGE AND DURATION
SODA-ACID	CLASS A (Wood, paper, textiles, etc.)	Water solution of bicarbonate of soda and sulfuric acid.	Turn over	30 to 40 feet 50 to 55 seconds (2½ gallon size)
PUMP TANK		Plain water	Pump by hand	●
GAS CARTRIDGE	CLASS A ("Loaded stream" model is also good on Class B)	Water and cartridge of carbon dioxide	Turn over and bump	●
FOAM	CLASS A and CLASS B (Oil, gasoline, paint, grease, etc.)	Water solution of aluminum sulfate and bicarbonate of soda	Turn over	DANGER: Do not use these water base extinguishers on electrical fires.
CARBON DIOXIDE	CLASS B and CLASS C (Live electrical equipment) ● NOTE: If nothing else is available, these extinguishers may have some effect on small Class A fires.	Carbon dioxide	Pull pin and open valve	6 to 8 feet about 42 seconds (15 lb. size)
VAPORIZING LIQUID		Carbon tetra-chloride and other chemicals. CAUTION: Avoid breathing vapors from extinguisher, especially in small, closed places.	Turn handle, then pump by hand	20 to 30 feet 40 to 45 seconds (1 quart size)
DRY CHEMICAL		Bicarbonate of soda with other dry chemicals and cartridge of carbon dioxide	Pull pin and open valve (or press lever), then squeeze nozzle valve	About 14 feet 22 to 25 seconds (30 lb. size)

Remove one of the elements, and fire cannot occur. An explosion is a rapidly burning fire.

To prevent fires:

Dispose of trash regularly.

Get rid of accumulations of old clothing, mattresses, curtains, drapes, lampshades, furniture, paper, magazines, and rags.

Hang up oily mops and keep oily rags in closed metal containers.

Replace all worn or frayed electric cords.

Have enough electrical circuits to take care of appliances without overloading the wiring.

Keep home tools, machinery, motors, and appliances serviced and clean.

Have your heating system and chimney cleaned at least once a year.

Cover the roof with a fire-retardant material.

Keep the grounds around your house free of dead grass, weeds, trash, and dried brush.

Keep matches in a safe place, out of the reach of children. Have plenty of ashtrays.

Invite your fire department to inspect your home periodically to help you spot fire hazards.

If a fire should occur in your home, these procedures are recommended:

Clear the building of all persons.

Call the fire department. Give the switchboard operator your name, address, location of the fire, and the type of fire—whether trash, flammable liquids, wood, and so on.

Attempt to put out the fire if it is a small one.

If you try to put out a small fire before the fire department arrives, concentrate on smothering out or controlling the oxygen supply, because you may not be able to remove the fuel or source of heat, the other two essentials of fire.

Water may be the handiest and most effective extinguishing agent. A spray or fog of water that blankets the fire smothers out more oxygen than a heavy stream.

Do not use water on electric, gasoline, and oil fires. Electricity may travel up a stream of water to injure you. Gasoline and oil, being lighter than water, will float and continue to burn.

Every house should have one or more fire extinguishers of approved types. (THURLOW J. BIDDLE)

Safety With Tools

POWER TOOLS make work faster, easier, and more accurate—but also more dangerous. So fast are they that you can get caught by one of them and lose a finger, toe, or eye faster than you can release your finger from a power switch.

Here is some advice about the safe use of any power tool, whether a saw, drill, grinder, sander, solder iron, mower, trimmer, cutter, sewing machine, cleaner, washer, or mixer.

The speed at which a power tool operates is the first point to bear in mind. A centrifugal clothes wringer can injure an arm in less time than it takes to make a quarter turn with a hand-operated wringer.

Training in the use of power tools is a serious responsibility. Read and understand the literature the manufacturer provides.

Buy tools that have guards. A bandsaw blade that can jump off the track and whip out at you, a mower blade that can throw stones, a grinder that can throw particles into your face, or a meat slicer or grinder that you can get your hands into is hardly the tool to use.

Some tools or parts of tools cannot

be guarded. Sometimes the work you are doing makes the guards useless. The bit of a drill, for example, or the needle of a sewing machine cannot be guarded always.

Therefore, wear face shields, goggles, or glasses when working with grinders, drills, needles that might snap, and so on.

Do not wear loose-fitting clothing, gloves, or neckties around tools that rotate.

Wear shoes that will grip the sod when mowing your lawn with a power mower.

Plan your work and take the precautions needed for safety.

Ground every electric tool. Ungrounded tools can cause burns and shock capable of killing. Even a slight shock can lead to loss of control of the tool and injury. Moisture, such as perspiration or standing on a wet surface, can lower your resistance to voltage and invite even a low-voltage current to pass through your body.

Inspect your power tools often. Grinding wheels do crack; electric cords do wear and fray; mower blades do loosen; metal, plastics, and fibers do wear out.

A poorly maintained power tool wears out faster and is more hazardous.

If you repair a power tool, disconnect the source of the power. For example, unplug the electric cord or disconnect the spark plug on a gasoline motor.

Store power tools so as to protect them and also to protect you and other members of your family from sharp cutting edges. (THURLOW J. BIDDLE)

Can You Answer Yes to All These Questions?

Have you a definite place for every tool when not in use?

Do you have electric cords repaired or discarded when they become frayed or worn?

Do you use a safe stepladder instead of a chair?

Are all poisons separately stored and clearly identified?

Have you a first-aid kit?

Do you know the motor vehicle laws of your State?

Do you walk facing the oncoming traffic on roads?

Household

Insects

THERE ARE MANY insects that may invade your home. These invaders may endanger your health, damage household goods, or become a general nuisance. However, the use of good sanitary practices and modern insecticides will enable you to control these pests.

An accompanying table will help you select the proper concentration of pesticide for use against the common insects and pests that we discuss in this chapter.

ANTS are silent thieves that may steal into a house unnoticed until their trails become heavily populated.

The quickest way to eradicate them is to follow their trail to their nests, which may be treated with an insecticide—chlordane, diazinon, dieldrin, lindane, or malathion.

Many species of ants nest indoors. Others prefer to nest outdoors.

The application of a surface (or residual) spray over the area of their trail will hasten their elimination, but their line of march may change, and you may have to spray more than once.

BED BUGS feed on blood—often blood of people. They are not so common in the United States as in past years but still may be carried into a house from theaters, hotels, roominghouses, or public conveyances.

The names "red coats," "chinches," or "mahogany flats" may be heard in reference to this pest that feeds on people mostly at night.

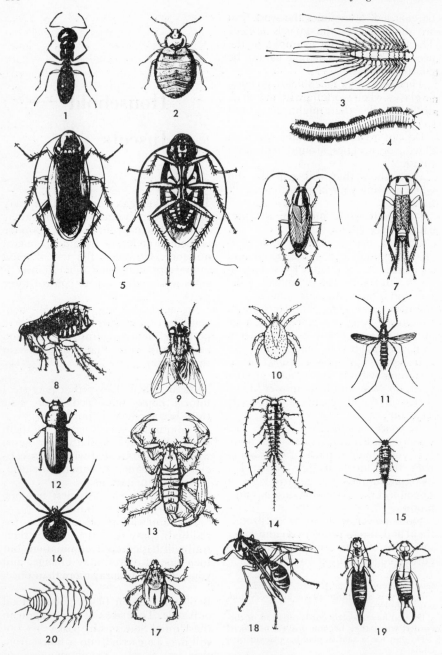

1. Ant
2. Bed bug
3. Centipede
4. Millipede
5. American cockroach
6. German cockroach
7. Cricket
8. Flea
9. Housefly
10. Mite
11. Mosquito
12. Flour beetle
13. Scorpion
14. Silverfish
15. Firebrat
16. Black widow spider
17. Brown dog tick
18. Wasp
19. Earwig
20. Sowbug

If a small infestation is established in a house, the bed bugs may be found along the tufts, seams, and folds of mattresses and sofas. Later they spread to crevices in the bedsteads.

As the infestation increases, they may become established in furniture and cracks or crevices of each room.

Household sprays containing DDT, lindane, malathion, or pyrethrins plus a synergist (a chemical that increases its efficiency) usually are effective against bed bugs. The bugs may be resistant to DDT or lindane in some localities.

The slats, springs, and frames of beds should be thoroughly wet with the spray. The mattresses should be covered lightly with spray, with particular attention to seams and tufts.

Do not treat mattresses with a spray containing more than 0.1 percent of lindane or 1 percent of malathion. Allow a drying period of 2 hours before you use the bed.

Baseboards and cracks or crevices in walls and the floorboards should be sprayed.

A second application of spray may be necessary in 2 weeks if some bed bugs are present at that time.

THE COCKROACH is one of the most exasperating of all household insects.

The major house-invading species are the American, Australian, brown-banded, German, and oriental cockroaches. Other species, such as the brown and smoky-brown cockroaches, may be less frequent invaders.

Cockroaches carry filth on their legs and bodies and may spread disease by polluting food. They destroy food and damage fabrics, garments, books, papers, and other materials.

Cockroaches in the home can be controlled by several methods.

Cracks and crevices around doors, windows, and pipes should be tightly sealed with proper weather stripping, calking compound, or other materials to prevent their entry.

Good housekeeping and the proper use of insecticides also are helpful.

In many sections, German cockroaches have developed resistance to such insecticides as chlordane, dieldrin, and lindane; therefore, diazinon, malathion, or ronnel should be used for efficient control.

DDT is not satisfactory against German cockroaches, but it and others we mentioned previously may be used for the control of other species of cockroaches.

The insecticide of choice may be used as a surface spray or dust. A combination of spray and dust is effective where severe infestations are encountered.

If you use the combination treatment, apply the surface spray first. Allow it to dry. Then apply the dust into cracks and openings difficult to reach with a spray and areas where the dust will not be unsightly.

A space spray or aerosol mist containing pyrethrum may be used to penetrate deep cracks and crevices and so drive the cockroaches onto surfaces treated with the surface spray or dust.

Surface sprays or dusts may be applied with an ordinary household spray gun or dust gun.

Cockroaches hide under the kitchen sink and drainboard; inside, around, and under cupboards and cabinets; near pipes or conduits that pass along or through walls; behind window or door frames; behind loose baseboards or molding strips; on undersides of tables and chairs; behind and under refrigerators and ranges; and on closet and bookcase shelves.

Food and utensils should be removed from cupboards and pantries before they are treated.

If the infestation should persist after 3 or 4 weeks, it will be necessary to apply insecticides again, particularly if the house is reinfested from outside.

CRICKETS occasionally invade a house, where they may chew and damage clothing, but it is not their normal habit to live in such an environment, as their breeding sites are outdoors.

HOUSEHOLD PEST CONTROL CHART

Insects or pests	|	Surface sprays [1]												|	Aerosols or space sprays					|	Dusts [1]				
		Chlordane, 2–3%	DDT, 5%	Diazinon, 0.5%	Dieldrin, 0.5%	Fenthion, 3%	Lindane, 0.1%	Lindane, 0.5%	Malathion, 1%	Malathion, 2–3%	Methoxychlor, 5%	Naled, 1%	Pyrethrins, 0.2% + synergist	Ronnel, 2%	DDT, 3–5%	Dichlorvos, 0.5%	Malathion, 2–3%	Methoxychlor, 3%	Pyrethrins, 0.1–0.25% + synergist	Ronnel, 0.4%	Chlordane, 5–6%	DDT, 5–10%	Dieldrin, 1%	Lindane, 1%	Malathion, 4–5%	Methoxychlor, 10%
Ants		X		X	X			X		X											X		X	X	X	
Bed bugs			X		X		X	X	X				X													
Centipedes		X	X		X			X		X											X	X				
Cockroaches		X	X	X	X			X		X											X	X	X	X	X	
Crickets		X	X	X	X			X		X											X	X	X	X	X	
Earwigs		X	X	X																	X	X				
Firebrats		X	X		X			X		X											X	X	X	X		
Fleas		X	X							X			X									X			X	X
House flies											X	X	X	X	X	X	X	X	X	X						
Millipedes					X																X					
Mites			X							X				X											X	
Mosquitoes						X										X	X		X							
Pantry pests			X							X															X	
Pillbugs		X																			X					
Scorpions		X		X	X			X													X					
Silverfish		X	X		X			X		X											X	X	X	X		
Sowbugs		X			X			X		X											X		X			
Spiders		X	X	X	X			X		X											X					
Ticks		X	X					X		X											X	X		X	X	
Wasps		X	X		X					X						X					X		X			

[1] Limited areas only, such as baseboards, except DDT, methoxychlor, or pyrethrins + synergist.

If you should be bothered by crickets in your house, make a close inspection of all windows, screens, and doors to make sure that they fit tightly enough to keep crickets out.

A surface spray containing chlordane, DDT, dieldrin, lindane, or malathion may be applied along baseboards, in closets, and in cracks where the crickets may hide. Dust formulations also may be used in places where they will not be unsightly.

EARWIGS live outdoors mainly, but they often crawl into houses or are brought in with flowers, vegetables, or fruit.

Earwigs are reddish brown and about three-fourths inch long. They have six legs and a pair of strong forceps on the rear part of the body.

Their presence is annoying. They emit a foul odor when crushed.

Control is by the application of surface sprays along baseboards and across the thresholds of outside doorways. Use chlordane or DDT.

The application of emulsion sprays or dusts to the soil near outside steps also helps control their entry.

FLEAS are likely if a dog or cat is allowed inside the house.

If you do not inspect the animal regularly, fleas may become so numerous they attack you and the animal.

The female flea lays her eggs on the pet. The eggs fall off and hatch indoors in chairs, sofas, rugs, carpets, and the pet's bed.

The larval fleas that hatch from the eggs soon develop to maturity, and a new crop of adult fleas will be seeking blood meals from human beings and household pets.

Good housekeeping and the proper use of insecticides are the means of controlling fleas in the house.

Carpets, rugs, upholstered furniture, and other items in infested rooms should be thoroughly cleaned with a vacuum cleaner. Then destroy the contents of the vacuum bag.

Then apply a surface spray containing DDT, diazinon, malathion, methoxychlor, or pyrethrins plus a synergist to limited areas, such as baseboards and cracks in the floor.

Rugs, carpets, furniture, and places in the house where the pet habitually sleeps may be treated with DDT, methoxychlor, or pyrethrum sprays or with DDT, methoxychlor, or malathion dusts. Follow the instructions on the label.

It may be necessary to repeat the treatment in 7 to 10 days.

A dust containing 4 or 5 percent of malathion or 10 percent of methoxychlor is safe and effective when it is applied directly on dogs or cats. The dust should be rubbed into the fur to the skin.

A dust containing 5 percent of DDT or 1 percent of lindane also may be used on dogs, but do not use DDT or lindane on cats of any age or on puppies under 2 months old.

HOUSE FLIES breed outdoors in decaying organic matter but are persistent about invading the home and using your food as choice landing fields. They thereby spread filth from their legs and bodies.

Good sanitation outdoors and proper screening of all doors and windows of your house help to eliminate flies.

If it is necessary to use an insecticide inside your house to control the flies, use a space or aerosol spray containing dichlorvos, malathion, pyrethrins plus a synergist, or ronnel.

Be certain the product you buy specifies its use for the control of flying insects. Be careful to avoid contamination of food or cooking and eating utensils.

Additional control of flies inside can be had by applying surface, or residual, sprays to outdoor objects or places, such as garbage cans, door or window frames, screens, and other sites flies frequent. Malathion, naled, or ronnel are suitable for this purpose.

MOSQUITOES pester people at inconvenient times, such as bedtime.

If these six-legged pests arouse you, you may reach for a fly swatter, rolled newspaper, or insecticide aerosol.

If you use an aerosol or space spray, be certain the product is specifically intended for flying insects.

Aerosols or space sprays containing DDT, dichlorvos, malathion, or pyrethrins plus a synergist are suitable.

The application of surface sprays (DDT, fenthion, or malathion) to dark and secluded spots under chairs, tables, and beds, in closets, and behind furniture will be helpful, as the residue of the insecticide may be effective for several weeks.

Inspect and change the water in flower vases or in saucers under potted plants frequently, as mosquito larvae (wigglers) may develop in them.

PANTRY PESTS include several kinds of insects that infest dry-food products kept in pantry or kitchen cupboards.

Many people call them "weevils." Actually they are small beetles, moth larvae, or true weevils.

Infestations may be controlled by keeping food shelves clean; inspecting food packages for infestations; sterilizing suspected infested dry foods in your oven at about 140° F. for 30 minutes; storing uninfested or heat-sterilized dry foods in clean containers with tight-fitting lids; and applying a surface spray of chlordane, DDT, lindane, or malathion to the shelves.

Remove all items from the shelves before spraying. Allow the spray to dry thoroughly before you replace any items.

SILVERFISH and firebrats are slender, gray, wingless insects about one-half inch long. They have three slender "tails."

They feed on cereal, flour, paper that has paste or glue on it (wallpaper, bookbindings), and starch in cloth.

They can be controlled by treating with chlordane, DDT, diazinon, dieldrin, lindane, or malathion.

THE TERM "WASP" applies to hornets, yellow jackets, mud daubers, and other slender-waisted, flying insects.

They build nests in trees, under eaves, and in the ground. Some wasps enter buildings in the fall to hibernate.

Wasps can inflict serious and sometimes fatal stings. A fly swatter can be used to kill one or two wasps in the house. If a nest is located on or near the house, it should be treated with chlordane, DDT, dichlorvos, or dieldrin. Nests should be treated at night. A dust can be used to treat ground nests.

OTHER ARTHROPODS besides insects may invade your house. There are many different kinds.

Centipedes and millipedes are worm-like creatures with many legs. Except for the house centipede, they normally live outdoors. They may be driven into a house by heavy rain, extreme dryness, or cold weather.

You most likely will find these creatures in your basement or other damp areas of the house.

Millipedes are harmless, but centipedes have a pair of powerful poison claws just behind the mouth that can pierce the skin and cause severe pain and swelling. Therefore, some centipedes, especially the large ones, are dangerous, and you should avoid contact with them.

To kill them, apply chlordane, DDT, dieldrin, or lindane to all the places where you find them.

Mites are tiny creatures. The commonest one, the clover mite, infests houses in the fall as cold weather approaches. Some mites also come from rats, mice, and birds and their nests. Some mites occur in foods, such as cheese and grain.

To control mites, try to find where they are coming into the house and prevent their entry. If the mites are coming from rats, birds, or their nests, remove these sources of infestation. A residual spray containing malathion can be used to treat infested areas.

Scorpions normally live outdoors under lumber piles, rocks, or loose bark on trees. They sometimes enter the house, where they hide during the day in closets, attics, folded blankets, shoes, and papers. Their sting is painful and sometimes fatal, but usually they will not sting unless molested. If one should sting you, call your physician at once.

To control scorpions, use chlordane or lindane inside as well as outside the house in the places where they may be hiding.

Sowbugs and pillbugs are slaty gray and about one-half inch long. The pillbug can roll up into a spherical ball. At times they invade damp basements or first-floor rooms. They do not cause any damage but are annoying when they occur in large numbers. To kill them, apply chlordane, DDT, lindane, or dieldrin to the places inside and outside the house where they crawl or congregate.

Only three species of spiders (the black widow, its close relative, and a brown spider found in the Midwest) are known to be dangerous in the United States. Others cause annoyance by building webs in houses. Basements, eaves, porches, and under steps are places most likely to be infested. The elimination of breeding places outside the house is important in control.

Spiders may be killed by chlordane, dieldrin, lindane, or malathion. Do not spray a spider directly overhead, as it may drop on you and bite.

Any ticks in your house are probably brown dog ticks that entered on your dog. This tick rarely bites people, but its presence is annoying. Other species frequently attack human beings. These ticks must feed on your dog three times to complete their life cycle. After each feeding, the ticks drop off and hide while they change to the next stage. Sometimes large numbers appear around baseboards, window and door casings, curtains, under the edge of rugs, and furniture.

Control of ticks requires treatment of your dog and the infested areas of the house.

A veterinarian can treat your dog, or you can do the job yourself by washing the animal with a 0.5 percent water emulsion of malathion.

In many areas, brown dog ticks have developed resistance to DDT, but malathion or diazinon usually give good control in such situations. When resistance is not a problem, DDT or chlordane are suggested as surface treatments in houses.

TO SUMMARIZE: You can rid your house of practically all pests, and keep it free of them, by a combination of continuous good housekeeping and the proper use of the right pesticide at the right time.

The first rule in using any pesticide is to read and follow the directions and precautions on the container label.

Note that some insecticides are for use on limited areas only, such as baseboards.

Store pesticides away from food and in places where children or pets cannot reach them.

Oil sprays may damage asphalt-tile or other composition-type floors.

When sprays are to be used outdoors, use water-emulsion sprays only, as oil sprays will damage plants.

Because some pesticides may cause staining of fabrics, check the label before you use them.

If necessary, wash cabinet shelves before you spray them. Do not scrub the shelves after treatment. Instead, place shelf paper on the shelves after they dry.

The control of household pests usually requires a small amount of pesticide—do not use excessive amounts. (G. S. BURDEN AND B. J. SMITTLE)

For further reading, consult the following Department of Agriculture publications:
Ants in the Home and Garden: How to Control Them, Home and Garden Bulletin 28; *Cockroaches: How to Control Them*, Leaflet 430; *Controlling Household Pests*, Home and Garden Bulletin 96; *Controlling Mosquitoes in Your Home and on Your Premises*, Home and Garden Bulletin 84; *Fleas: How to Control Them*, Leaflet 392; *The House Fly: How to Control It*, Leaflet 390; *How to Control Bed Bugs*, Leaflet 453; *Silverfish and Firebrats: How to Control Them*, Leaflet 412; *Wasps: How to Control Them*, Leaflet 365.

Health Care

GOOD HEALTH comes from the day-to-day practice of habits that promote health.

Health is more than the absence of disease. Health is a "state of complete physical, mental, and social well-being."

Some habits that promote health: Personal hygiene and cleanliness.

A well-balanced diet.

Good body posture.

Adequate rest and relaxation and sensible exercise.

Good mental attitudes.

Observance of safety measures.

Regular medical and dental supervision and care, correction of remedial defects, and immunization against preventable diseases.

SIMPLE nursing procedures can be carried out in the home. Care of an ailing family member at home may be more desirable than care in the hospital or nursing home.

Those who give such care must understand the physical and emotional needs of the patient and must learn and practice the skills that are basic to the comfort, safety, efficiency, and appearance of the patient and the nurse.

It is difficult to carry out strict isolation techniques in the home, but exposure to others should be as limited as possible.

Some of the safety measures to be followed, subject to doctor's orders:

Keep the patient in his own room and explain to other family members why they should stay away from the sick person.

Dispose of waste material from a sickroom safely, because it may carry infection. Paper sacks can be used for the disposal of soiled materials in the sickroom. You can easily make a bag for the same purpose by following these steps:

Place two sheets of newspaper so that the center fold is toward you.

Bring the top edges of the top half of the paper down to the fold at the bottom. This makes a cuff.

Turn the paper over, smooth side up, keeping the fold toward you.

Fold it in thirds from the side. Crease it well to hold the fold.

Lock it by tucking one whole side under the cuff of the other side.

Fold the flap over the locked cuff.

Place a hand in the opening at the top. Stand the bag up and shape.

Use the flap as a cover for the bag or as a means of fastening the bag to the side of the bed.

HANDS should be washed often and always before and after caring for the patient. Clean hands reduce the possibility of transferring infection to the patient or from the patient.

All children should be taught when, how, and why to wash their hands.

Some older persons may tend to be careless about their personal habits, and it may be necessary to urge them to wash their hands after going to the toilet, before meals, and before handling food.

Make sure to wash the entire surface of the hands, especially between the fingers and around the nails. Rinse the soap so that it will be clean when next used.

Dry the hands well to avoid chapping. Older people tend to have dry skin and may need to apply skin lotion after washing. Used towels should be put in a paper bag and removed.

THE HOME NURSE should select an apron that covers as much of the clothing as possible.

It should be put on when entering the sickroom if direct care is to be given to the patient. When finished,

| WORK UP A LATHER | RINSE WITH THE HANDS DOWN | DRY WELL TO PREVENT CHAPPING |

For protection, wash the hands thoroughly.

the home nurse should wash her hands, remove the apron, and hang it in the sickroom or just outside the door, with the soiled side out.

Consider the apron soiled after its outer surface has come in contact with the patient or his bed, but it may be used again for the same patient.

Resistance to disease and rapidity of recovery from many illnesses depend on a well-balanced regular diet. Modify such a diet only on the doctor's orders to suit the diagnosis and needs of the body during illness.

All the basic food groups should be included in the daily meals unless the physician orders otherwise. These include milk and milk products, meat, vegetables, fruit, bread, and cereal.

PROTECTION against communicable diseases requires that all family members, from the youngest to the oldest, should be encouraged to—

Avoid contact with people who are suffering from communicable diseases.

Use disposable handkerchiefs that can be destroyed after use, especially when you have a cold or a cough.

Cover the nose and the mouth when coughing or sneezing.

Keep the hands away from the face, especially the mouth and the nose.

Turn the head to avoid droplets if someone coughs or sneezes nearby.

Always wash the hands before eating and before preparing or handling food, after handling soiled articles, and after going to the toilet.

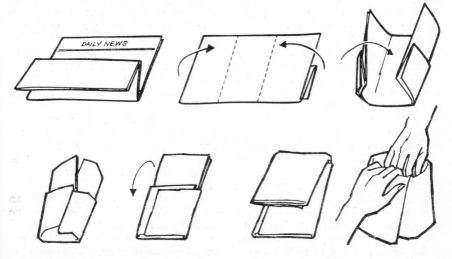

Steps in making a newspaper bag for waste disposal.

Wash the hands before and after giving care to a sick person to avoid carrying disease to or from the patient.

Keep personal articles, such as toothbrushes, hairbrushes, and combs, clean and reserved for one person's use.

Use safe water, milk, and other foods.

Keep milk and perishable foods refrigerated. Cover unrefrigerated foods to keep them clean.

Use clean glasses, dishes, and eating utensils. Do not touch the parts that come in contact with the mouth, such as the rims of cups and glasses, the bowls of spoons, and the tines of forks.

Eat the right kind and amount of food.

Get an adequate amount of sleep, rest, sunshine, fresh air, and exercise.

Obtain protection against the diseases for which there are known immunizing agents.

Treat with suspicion any illness that starts with such symptoms as headache, fever, nausea, sore throat, discharging eyes or nose, stiff neck, sneezing, aching, and a feeling of being "all in."

Prevent accidents by making every family member mindful of his responsibility to all other family members and seeing that each room has no unsafe and hazardous conditions.

Information, understanding, and caution must be the basis for living with possible hazards such as machines, poisons, and medicines.

Many recommendations in this chapter are the techniques and procedures taught in the home nursing courses of the American National Red Cross.

I recommend a close reading of the American National Red Cross Home Nursing Textbook (seventh edition, 1963, Doubleday & Co., New York).

At least one person in every family should prepare herself to care for the sick at home by taking a Red Cross home nursing course. Your local Red Cross chapter will give you information about it. (HELEN L. BECKER)

Health
Services

SICK OR WELL, we all need and use a battery of health and medical resources.

Some of them we may be only vaguely aware of, since, like an iceberg, they are largely unseen. They include a community's provisions to insure safe milk and water and proper disposal of garbage and the statistical programs that enable us to measure the impact of illness and disability.

Others are more conspicuous. Everyone is aware of the physician, the dentist, and the hospital. Most people hear about a community immunization program. Many know there is a visiting nurse service, for they have seen visiting nurses on rounds.

Some of the services have been with us for generations. Others are recent developments, the result of the growing importance in public health of chronic diseases, new knowledge produced by research, and growing public demand for health and medical services.

Some are free. A county may offer free rabies shots for every dog—all you have to do is get your dog to the appointed place at the appointed time. Some are available at a nominal cost and free to those who cannot pay—a community may ask a contribution of 25 cents for a dose of oral polio vaccine but give it without charge if you are unable to pay.

Some are expensive. A hospital stay, corrective treatment for a child's eyes, or a long series of rehabilitation procedures may run into hundreds or thousands of dollars. Help to pay for some services, however, is available in many communities, perhaps through the local chapter of a national voluntary organization, the welfare department, a public clinic, or a civic group.

In short, an array of health and medical resources exists in cities, towns, and rural areas across the country. The number and quality of services vary from one locality to another, as do the specific arrangements for using them. But what you need may well be available, either right at home or in a nearby city.

ALTHOUGH HEALTH and medical resources find their application in specific communities, where the people are, they normally come about through cooperative arrangements and involve other than local agencies.

The cooperation may be horizontal, as when a civic organization in a big city extends a particular health service beyond the boundaries of the metropolis into nearby rural counties, or a medical center provides specialist help to neighboring hospitals.

Or, it may be vertical—up through the State headquarters of professional societies to the national offices of the American Medical Association, the American Dental Association, or the American Hospital Association, for example.

The cooperative arrangements may stem from the voluntary organizations, such as the American Cancer Society, the Society for Crippled Children & Adults, and the American Diabetes Association.

They may result from joint actions of the official agencies—the local and State health department and the Public Health Service of the United States Department of Health, Education, and Welfare.

A case in point is the network of poison control centers.

Half a million children under 5 years of age accidentally consume potentially poisonous substances each year. About 500 of them die. But the number

of deaths can be reduced and the nonlethal aftereffects mitigated when doctors know at once the properties of whatever the child swallowed and the antidotes and treatments.

The value of immediate access to this information was proved by a handful of poison control centers set up in the Midwest in the fifties. The American Public Health Association recommended and the Public Health Service undertook the establishment of a poison control clearinghouse, which would help the centers keep their information up to date and encourage the establishment of additional centers.

The idea was accepted with alacrity by States and communities. More than 500 poison control centers were operating in 1965 on an around-the-clock basis in strategically located hospitals and health departments.

The centers are controlled and supported locally. The Public Health Service makes available to them, in the form of poison-index filecards, detailed information on potentially hazardous substances; keeps the cards current and adds new ones when new toxic substances come on the market; recommends to them other appropriate items, such as books and scientific papers having to do with the business of the centers; and publishes a bulletin carrying supplementary information on toxic substances.

Another example is the fluoridation of public water supplies. Communities decide for themselves to fluoridate their water—more than 2,600 of them with a combined population of 47 million had done so by 1965. But to help a locality arrive at a decision, many State and local health departments provide consultation and educational materials. The Public Health Service maintains a file of the studies of fluoridation and its results and provides technical assistance, on request, to interested State and local government officials.

TYPICALLY, the situation is this. The national headquarters of health-related interests—the Public Health Service, the national offices of the voluntary agencies, and of the medical professional organizations—may conduct or support programs of scientific research; may set national standards for institutions, preventive practices, qualifications of health workers, and other matters in which many localities have a common interest; may furnish technical aid or financial assistance; and may develop guidelines for their State and local counterparts.

The State offices of these same interests may use or adapt these aids. Some operate statewide programs and services, such as the laboratories and special hospitals for victims of tuberculosis or mental illness, which are standard State health department activities. They may conduct case-finding projects, statewide studies, and demonstration projects. They may provide financial help for one or another type of local program.

The primary target of these activities is the community, where health and medical services actually take place. The aim is to help hospitals that may want technical consultation on architectural design or new kinds of equipment; and local agencies planning new programs and wanting to find out about the experience of other localities in setting up such projects.

The aim is to help the individual who seeks any of the scores of specific health and medical aids that people need: A physician, dentist, nurse, speech therapist, physical therapist, nursing home, mental health clinic, for example, or advice on nutrition, insect and rodent control, immunizations, care of the sick at home, prevention of accidents, ways to keep a septic tank in order.

In the face of the myriad variations in community organization, the person with a health problem new to him may be at a loss. Where does one start?

The place to start is usually your own family physician (and if you do not have one, the local medical society

will help you find one) or the local health officer. These two persons are at the nucleus of what, ideally, is an effective complex of health and medical resources. They have the answers to most health and medical questions, and they will know where to go for replies to the rest.

The doctor will know whether specialist consultation is indicated and where to turn for it. He will be knowledgeable about local nursing homes and outpatient and rehabilitation services. If a local hospital has an organized home-care program that will obviate the need for keeping a person in the hospital, he can find out about it. If there is a local agency that loans wheelchairs, crutches, and hospital beds, he can help arrange for them.

The health department also is a prime source of much information and, in some jurisdictions, of services. It may operate a homemaker project, which will send a trained woman to keep a household running while the mother is incapacitated, and it will know if such help is available from the welfare department or some other local agency.

Is there any place to get help in paying for treatment for cancer, a crippling condition, or mental illness? How do you get the well water tested? Can transportation be arranged for a person who cannot get himself to a clinic? Whom do you talk to about polluted streams? Is there a place to get a free test for glaucoma? Where can we get a speaker and a film on prevention of home accidents? The health department usually has the answers or can get them.

IT WOULD BE UNREALISTIC to hope that all the services here suggested, and more, can be obtained quickly and easily for the asking, everywhere.

It is safe to say there is no community in the country that has enough of everything of an acceptable quality. The situation has improved in recent years, however, and this improvement is accelerating.

There are two main reasons for this improvement.

The first is the realization that the only satisfactory arrangement is a coordinated community organization of health services to provide comprehensive care for everybody, when and where the care is needed. To this end, many communities are making good headway in eliminating duplications, filling gaps in service, and improving the quality of health resources.

Secondly, recent Federal (and in some instances State) legislation has provided new avenues for communities trying to improve their health situations.

For example, legislation in 1961 authorized the Public Health Service to support studies, experiments, and demonstrations that will lead to new or improved community health services outside the hospital, particularly for the chronically ill and aged. Under this authorization, more than 88 communities are working on such diverse projects as rehabilitating Selective Service rejectees, providing dental care for the chronically ill and aged, venereal disease case finding, and improving followup care for tuberculosis patients.

Migrant health legislation in 1962 permitted the Public Health Service to pay part of the cost of programs to improve health conditions and services for domestic migratory farmworkers and their families.

The 1963 Vaccination Assistance Act permits the Public Health Service to extend financial aid to community-wide campaigns for vaccination of preschool children against diphtheria, poliomyelitis, tetanus, and whooping cough. In the first year of the program, 34 States and 27 local health departments took advantage of this opportunity.

Other legislation in 1963 aims to replace custodial care in large mental institutions with comprehensive mental health services in the patient's own community. It authorizes Federal funds to help build community mental health centers and community centers for the care of the mentally retarded and to help train teachers of the mentally retarded.

Another Federal move toward augmenting the supply of scarce health workers is the Nurse Training Act, which was signed into law in 1964. It authorizes funds for rehabilitating outworn buildings of nursing schools and building new ones. It established a loan fund for student nurses and extended the traineeship program for professional nurses.

The agencies that share the responsibility for health and medical services need the support of the people. In the localities that lead in provision of the services, they get it. Only with public support can clean air, clean water and a host of other important programs succeed. The help that is available from outside sources must be sought and put to use by the communities themselves. Communities take these actions when an interested citizenry demands and supports them. (LUTHER L. TERRY)

Welfare Services

WE HAVE DEVELOPED in this country a great variety of welfare services under the auspices of government and voluntary agencies, sectarian as well as nonsectarian.

Some, like the American Red Cross and Public Welfare, are available in every county. Some are in only a few communities. Others, such as voluntary family counseling agencies, are primarily in urban communities.

Some agencies, among them Boys'

Clubs of America, offer service to one group of persons only. Others, such as the Salvation Army, offer a variety of services, for example, to homeless men, unwed parents, families, children, and the ill.

VARIOUS KINDS of child welfare services are offered by public and voluntary, sectarian and nonsectarian agencies. Some agencies offer several services; others, only one, such as day care or institutional care.

Child welfare services include counseling children and adolescents who have problems of adjustment and parents who have problems of parent-child relationships; protective service for children suffering from neglect, cruelty, or deprivation; homemaker services, which I discuss later; day care (through group care or in qualified family day-care homes) for children of working mothers or of parents whose children need such care; care of children outside their own homes in foster families, group homes, or in institutions; services to unmarried parents; and adoption services.

NEARLY 2,000 local public employment offices throughout the Nation are operated by State employment services affiliated with the United States Employment Service.

A local office charges no fee to workers or employers. It helps workers to find jobs, aids employers in recruiting employees, and provides job counseling and testing services to help applicants enter the right fields of work and employers to obtain qualified workers.

It provides special employment services for farmworkers, older workers, youths, veterans, and the handicapped.

Each office collects and distributes information on current labor demand and supply conditions.

In many cities are commercial agencies that match job applicants with needs of employers. Frequently they specialize, as for secretarial or clerical workers, or engineers. They charge the employee a fee for placement; the

amount in some States is set by the State licensing agency.

SERVICES TO HELP families and individuals with their personal or social problems are given by different kinds of voluntary and governmental agencies.

Voluntary family service agencies, which are under sectarian or nonsectarian auspices and primarily in cities, offer counsel and service on problems of family interrelations concerning children, adolescents, parents and grandparents, unwed parents, and problems of social adjustment.

Some offer service to one group of persons only. For example, the American Red Cross Service to Military Families is primarily for members of the Armed Forces and veterans and their families; the travelers aid service is to help moving, uprooted, or rootless individuals and newcomers to a community to establish themselves in a community.

The public assistance programs, besides giving financial assistance, help needy and low-income families with services designed to prevent or reduce personal and economic dependency and to strengthen family life.

Family life education programs have been developed under many auspices, such as churches, mental health agencies, State extension services, parent-teachers' associations, Young Women's Christian Associations, and family casework agencies.

These group programs may be a single lecture or a series. Because of the lower average age of engagement, more programs are designed for preparation for marriage of teenagers, who want specific information on such matters as budgeting, buying on credit, and family planning.

Courses for parents may center on parent-child relationships. Public welfare departments are devoting increased attention to training to upgrade family living for low-income families.

TWO FEDERAL insurance programs are designed to help individuals and their families maintain income and purchasing power. One is related to unemployment; the other, to old age, death, or permanent and total disability of the family wage earner.

Unemployment insurance, a Federal-State program, provides for partial replacement of wages lost during periods of involuntary unemployment. Most jobs in industry and commerce, but few in agriculture, are covered.

If you lose your job and cannot find another one immediately, you should register at the local public employment office for employment and for unemployment insurance. A railroad worker files his claim for unemployment insurance through the railroad.

Old-age, survivors and disability insurance, commonly called social security, is a federally administered program that offers protection against loss of income in the form of benefit payments to qualified wage earners and self-employed persons and their families when old age, death, or permanent and total disability cuts off earning capacity. Monthly payments are based on a record of the insured worker's earnings covered by the program. Applications for benefits can be made at the nearest district office of the Social Security Administration.

THROUGH Federal and State and, in some instances, county financing, all States provide public assistance and services to the aged, the blind, and families with dependent children. Most States also include the permanently and totally disabled.

These public assistance programs are available in every county, usually through a county welfare department.

Some States provide financial assistance to single persons and families who do not meet the qualifications established for the special programs. Such assistance may be administered by the county welfare department or by a special county or local community department or agency.

Some voluntary counseling agencies, such as the Salvation Army and Travelers Aid Society, may provide temporary financial assistance to families who are receiving their help on personal problems.

ADOPTION of a child should be effected through a recognized, licensed child welfare agency, which in consultation with lawyers will safeguard the well-being and legal rights of the child, the natural parents, and the adoptive parents.

Competent legal advice should be obtained when you prepare a will, buy property, and need to protect other legal rights.

An individual who needs an attorney may ask the local bar association to refer him to one.

In almost all urban and some rural communities, a Legal Aid Society or Defender Office provides without charge, or for a nominal fee, the services of lawyers in civil or criminal cases to persons financially unable to engage private counsel.

MANY KINDS of informal education-recreation programs are offered by many kinds of public and voluntary organizations, such as public schools, departments of parks and recreation, Extension Service (4–H Clubs), settlement houses and community centers, Girl Scouts, Y's, and church groups.

Some programs are for boys or girls in specific age groups. Some are for the handicapped and some are for the elderly. Others are family centered. All have the common objective of providing under responsible leadership a group experience that contributes to the personal and social development of individuals.

Adult education programs under a variety of auspices offer organized activities to adults to accomplish specific educational objectives.

Informal educational recreation programs for children and youth provide fun and constructive use of leisure time through which an individual may achieve self-expression and better physical and mental health and maturity.

Some aim to develop certain ideals and values and to so contribute to the member's personality and social development that he will become a well adjusted adult. Programs under religious auspices also include spiritual growth as an objective.

An increasing number of organized cultural, social, and recreational activities are available for the elderly through centers and clubs under the auspices of churches and public and voluntary welfare agencies.

CONSIDERABLE emphasis has been placed on the value of services that enable persons to remain in their own homes, rather than having to enter or remain in a hospital or institution. This applies to children when the mother is hospitalized or convalescent and to the elderly, the acutely or chronically ill, and disabled persons.

Increasingly, although still in limited geographical areas, public and voluntary health and welfare agencies are providing a homemaker service free or for a fee in accordance with ability to pay. This community service is sponsored and supervised by a health or welfare agency, which employs specially selected and trained women with skills in child care, work with aged and ill, and in homemaking to help maintain, create, or preserve wholesome family life in times of crisis.

The need for such service and the length of time it will be given are determined by a social worker, nurse, or another professional person connected with the sponsoring agency.

A new service is the delivery to their homes of meals to the aged, handicapped, or ill who are unable to obtain or prepare adequate meals for themselves. These nonprofit programs—Portable Meals or Meals-on-Wheels—which may charge a fee according to ability to pay, provide one hot and one cold meal and sometimes breakfast 5 to 7 days a week. Current standards call for the meals (and special diets) to be prepared under supervision of a dietitian, and

the appropriateness of this service to a specific individual is determined by a public health nurse or qualified social worker. About 30 such programs were in operation in 1965.

Visiting Nurse Service—available through the local department of health, a voluntary Visiting Nurse Association, or both—provides a variety of services for the sick of all ages at home. These services are related to the physician's orders for his patient and the patient's need for nursing. A fee is charged for those who can afford to pay.

The visiting nurse may give or teach a member of the family how to give nursing care and treatments to someone who is sick at home; change dressings and give hypodermic injections, as prescribed by a physician; advise in planning nutritious meals and help carry out the doctor's orders for special diets; give instruction on how to prevent the spread of communicable disease; and instruct expectant parents in infant care.

The board of education in many communities provides a special teacher, called a homebound teacher, to tutor, in his own home, a child under prolonged or convalescent care. Such tutoring is given only when the attending physician specifies the child is ready.

The homebound teacher confers regularly with the child's classroom teacher so that she can relate the child's studies to the classroom, in anticipation of his rejoining his class.

PUBLIC WELFARE and voluntary sectarian and nonsectarian agencies offer confidential service to unmarried mothers and fathers and to their parents, especially if the mother is a minor, in sound planning for the mother, the father, and the child. Early requests for help are advisable, as multiple services, such as planning medical or shelter care and financial assistance, may be involved. Many of the family service agencies provide counseling.

Some agencies, such as Florence Crittenton, the Salvation Army, and Catholic Charities, provide care for the unmarried expectant mother in residences or in other supervised living arrangements.

THERE ARE TIMES of personal crisis not related to a community disaster when an individual or a family finds itself without a place to live. The public welfare department usually will provide or arrange for such shelter while helping the individual or family plan for the future.

In some communities the Salvation Army may provide shelter for the transient individual or family. The Travelers Aid Society may provide temporary shelter for those who do not have legal residence or are in transit through the community.

VOCATIONAL COUNSELING services are available through local boards of education, college guidance counselors, local offices of State employment services, unions, and nonprofit organizations, such as the Urban League.

Vocational training is offered by public and commercial vocational schools, public and private organizations, employers and labor unions. It also may be available under the Area Redevelopment Act and the Manpower Development and Training Act through local offices of State employment services.

Because of a relatively high rate of unemployment and fewer jobs for the unskilled in recent years, the Federal Government has accelerated programs for training the unemployed and underemployed.

The Area Redevelopment Act provides short-term training in communities of high unemployment.

Under the Manpower Development and Training Act, training is not limited to distressed areas; it may be for longer periods and may include a combination of basic education and vocational training. Training allowances may be paid under each act.

The Economic Opportunity Act of 1964 emphasizes the training of jobless youths, especially the school dropout.

The Job Corps programs offer work experience in conservation camps or residential training centers for young men and women 16–21 years old.

The Neighborhood Youth Corps program offers full or part-time employment in the home community to young men and women 16–21 years old to continue or resume their education or to increase their employment capacity. A work-study program with colleges and universities for young persons from low-income families permits them to begin or continue their college education.

You can get information about these programs through the local public employment service office and through public schools, public welfare offices, or other community organizations.

Vocational rehabilitation of disabled persons with employment handicaps includes counseling, physical restoration and related services, training, and job placement. Most of these programs are under State auspices (often the State board of education), although some rehabilitation workshop programs are under private auspices, such as Goodwill Industries.

MOST OF US take for granted our public services, such as the fire, police, and public health departments, whose major responsibilities we see as to protect us from fire, theft, and communicable disease.

Each offers some service of an emergency nature to individuals or families. Here are a few:

Dog bite: When a person has been bitten by a dog, the department of health will observe the dog for rabies and give the person anti-rabies vaccine, if indicated.

Food poisoning: The department of health will investigate an outbreak of purported food poisoning.

Lost child: If a child has disappeared, the police department will institute a search.

Guarding property: The police department on request will make a daily reconnaissance of your house when the family is away on vacation.

Rescue of animals: The fire department will help to rescue a cat from a tree or a dog from a ditch.

Lock out or lock in: The fire department will help an individual or family gain entry to his house if he has lost or forgotten his keys or the lock is faulty. Conversely, it will help to rescue a child or adult who has locked himself in a room.

WHETHER A COMMUNITY has many or few social welfare agencies, whether we are supporting them through taxation for the public services or through annual contributions to United Funds or Community Chest drives, most of us, when we are faced with a problem on which we want help, are not sure that we know where to go for that help.

Several central sources of information can help you get to the appropriate agency:

Information and Referral Services: In about 500 cities, generally those with a population of 50 thousand or more, there is a community welfare council, which is a coordinating and planning organization for the health and welfare services in the area.

This central body may be known by other names, such as Social Planning Council, Community Services Council, and Council of Social Agencies. Each has information about all community welfare agencies in the area and can steer you to the appropriate social agency.

Practically all community welfare councils publish a directory of social welfare and health agencies. Depending on the number, it may be a one-page mimeographed list or, as in New York City, a bound book of 700 pages that lists approximately 1,200 agencies that give service.

Even in smaller communities where there is no formally organized community welfare council, the United Fund or Community Chest, which raises money for the support of the social services under voluntary auspices, will be able to tell you whether there is an agency that can help you with your problem.

Public Housing Authority: If you live in a public housing project, tell the project manager about your problem and ask his help in referring you to the right agency. Handbooks on neighborhood services may be available in your management office. Residents may also turn to the tenant council which often is responsible for publishing a newsletter that may mention community resources.

Union Counselors: If you or someone in your family is a member of a union, ask the union counselor where you should go for help. Most AFL–CIO unions have at least one counselor who knows all the resources in the community and will be glad to guide you to the right social agency.

When asking anyone of the above resources for information, give them enough information about your situation so that they can select the agency best suited to help you. None of the above will help you solve your problem; they will direct you to an agency that can help you.

Other Sources: Local public welfare departments are a readily available resource for information and referral. Your clergyman or your doctor may be able to advise you as to the suitable agency. In rural areas, the American Red Cross chapter or the county agent also may be able to help you find the proper service. (LOUISE N. MUMM)

National agencies in the following list are among those that can provide further information about programs.

CHILDREN'S SERVICES

Children's Bureau
Welfare Administration
Dept. of Health, Education, and Welfare
Washington, D.C. 20201

Child Welfare League of America
44 East 23d Street
New York, N.Y. 10010

National Committee for the Day Care of
 Children
44 East 23d Street
New York, N.Y. 10010

The Salvation Army
120 West 14th Street
New York, N.Y. 10011

EMPLOYMENT

Bureau of Employment Security
U.S. Department of Labor
Washington, D.C. 20210

National Committee On Employment of
 Youth
419 Park Avenue South
New York, N.Y. 10016

National Urban League
14 East 48th Street
New York, N.Y. 10017

FAMILY COUNSELING

American National Red Cross
Service to Military Families
Washington, D.C. 20006

American Social Health Association
1790 Broadway
New York, N.Y. 10019

Bureau of Family Services
Welfare Administration
Dept. of Health, Education, and Welfare
Washington, D.C. 20201

Child Study Association of America
9 East 89th Street
New York, N.Y. 10028

Executive Council of the Episcopal
 Church
815 Second Avenue
New York, N.Y. 10017

Family Service Association of America
44 East 23d Street
New York, N.Y. 10010

Lutheran Church—Missouri Synod
210 North Broadway
St. Louis, Mo. 63102

National Conference of Catholic Charities
1346 Connecticut Avenue NW.
Washington, D.C. 20006

National Lutheran Council
50 Madison Avenue
New York, N.Y. 10010

National Travelers Aid Association
44 East 23d Street
New York, N.Y. 10010

Planned Parenthood Federation of America
551 Madison Avenue
New York, N.Y. 10022

The Salvation Army
120 West 14th Street
New York, N.Y. 10011

Young Women's Christian Associations of the
 U.S.A.
600 Lexington Avenue
New York, N.Y. 10022

FEDERAL INSURANCE PROGRAMS

Bureau of Employment Security
U.S. Department of Labor
Washington, D.C. 20210

Social Security Administration
Department of Health, Education, and
 Welfare
Washington, D.C. 20201

FINANCIAL ASSISTANCE

Bureau of Family Services
Welfare Administration
Department of Health, Education, and
 Welfare
Washington, D.C. 20201

National Travelers Aid Association
44 East 23d Street
New York, N.Y. 10010

The Salvation Army
120 West 14th Street
New York, N.Y. 10011

LEGAL ADVICE

Child Welfare League of America
44 East 23d Street
New York, N.Y. 10010
 (re: adoption)

National Legal Aid and Defender Association
American Bar Center
1155 East 60th Street
Chicago, Ill. 60637

ORGANIZED   LEISURE-TIME,   IN-
FORMAL EDUCATION PROGRAMS

American Camping Association
Bradford Woods
Martinsville, Ind. 46151

Boy Scouts of America
New Brunswick, N.J. 08903

Boys' Clubs of America
771 First Avenue
New York, N.Y. 10017

Camp Fire Girls
65 Worth Street
New York, N.Y. 10013

Federal Extension Service
U.S. Department of Agriculture
Washington, D.C. 20250

Girl Scouts of the U.S.A.
830 Third Avenue
New York, N.Y. 10022

Girls Clubs of America
101 Park Avenue
New York, N.Y. 10016

National Council on the Aging
49 West 45th Street
New York, N.Y. 10036

National Federation of Settlements and
Neighborhood Centers
232 Madison Avenue
New York, N.Y. 10016

National Jewish Welfare Board
145 East 32d Street
New York, N.Y. 10016

National Recreation Association
8 West Eighth Street
New York, N.Y. 10011

Young Men's Christian Associations of the
U.S.A.
291 Broadway
New York, N.Y. 10007

Young Women's Christian Associations of the
U.S.A.
600 Lexington Avenue
New York, N.Y. 10022

Youth Department, National Catholic Welfare Conference
1312 Massachusetts Avenue NW.
Washington, D.C. 20005

SERVICES TO THE AGED, HANDI-
CAPPED, AND ILL IN THEIR OWN
HOMES

Children's Bureau
Welfare Administration
Department of Health, Education, and
Welfare
Washington, D.C. 20201

National Council for Homemaker Services
1790 Broadway
New York, N.Y. 10019

National Council on the Aging
49 West 45th Street
New York, N.Y. 10036

National League for Nursing
10 Columbus Circle
New York, N.Y. 10019

Office of Education
Department of Health, Education, and
Welfare
Washington, D.C. 20201

Public Health Service
Division of Chronic Diseases
Department of Health, Education, and
Welfare
Washington, D.C. 20201

SERVICES TO UNMARRIED PARENTS

Bureau of Family Services
Welfare Administration
Department of Health, Education, and
Welfare
Washington, D.C. 20201

Children's Bureau
Welfare Administration
Department of Health, Education, and
Welfare
Washington, D.C. 20201

Child Welfare League of America
44 East 23d Street
New York, N.Y. 10010

Family Service Association of America
44 East 23d Street
New York, N.Y. 10010

Florence Crittenton Association of America
608 South Dearborn Street
Chicago, Ill. 60605

National Association for Services to Unmarried Parents
44 East 23d Street
New York, N.Y. 10010

National Conference of Catholic Charities
1346 Connecticut Avenue NW.
Washington, D.C. 20006

The Salvation Army
120 West 14th Street
New York, N.Y. 10011

The Volunteers of America
340 West 85th Street
New York, N.Y. 10024

TEMPORARY SHELTER

Bureau of Family Services
Welfare Administration
Department of Health, Education, and
 Welfare
Washington, D.C. 20201

National Travelers Aid Association
44 East 23d Street
New York, N.Y. 10010

The Salvation Army
120 West 14th Street
New York, N.Y. 10011

VOCATIONAL COUNSELING AND TRAINING

Bureau of Employment Security
U.S. Department of Labor
Washington, D.C. 20210

Goodwill Industries of America, Inc.
1913 N Street NW.
Washington, D.C. 20006

National Committee on Employment of
 Youth
145 East 32d Street
New York, N.Y. 10016

National Urban League
14 East 48th Street
New York, N.Y. 10017

Office of Economic Opportunity
Washington, D.C. 20506

Office of Education
Department of Health, Education, and
 Welfare
Washington, D.C. 20201

The Salvation Army
120 West 14th Street
New York, N.Y. 10011

Vocational Rehabilitation Administration
Department of Health, Education, and
 Welfare
Washington, D.C. 20201

The Volunteers of America
340 West 85th Street
New York, N.Y. 10024

HELP IN FINDING THE PROPER SERVICES

AFL–CIO Community Service Activities
815 16th Street NW.
Washington, D.C. 20006

American National Red Cross
Washington, D.C. 20006

Department of Health, Education, and
 Welfare
Washington, D.C. 20201

Federal Extension Service
U.S. Department of Agriculture
Washington, D.C. 20250

Public Housing Administration
Housing and Home Finance Agency
1741 Rhode Island Avenue NW.
Washington, D.C. 20413

United Community Funds and Councils of
 America, Inc.
345 East 46th Street
New York, N.Y. 10017

The following directories give information about agency programs:

Service Directory of National Organizations
 Affiliated and Associated with the As-
 sembly
National Social Welfare Assembly, Inc.
345 East 46th Street
New York, N.Y. 10017

Public Welfare Directory
American Public Welfare Association
1313 East 60th Street
Chicago, Ill. 60637

The National Health Council
Member Organizations
1790 Broadway
New York, N.Y. 10019

A comprehensive resource on social welfare pro-grams is the Encyclopedia of Social Work, Pub-lished by the National Association of Social Workers, 2 Park Avenue, New York, N.Y. 10016.

The following publications issued by the Department of Health, Education, and Welfare are available from the Government Printing Office, Washington, D.C., 20402.

Casework Services in Public Assistance
 Medical Care. 1962. 50 cents.
Child Welfare Services. 1963. 25 cents.
Day Care Services. 1960. 25 cents.
Directory of Local Health Units. 1964.
 30 cents.
Directory of State and Territorial Health
 Authorities. 1964. 35 cents.
Group Services in Public Welfare. 1964.
 30 cents.
Homemaker Services in Public Welfare.
 1964. 10 cents.
Where to Write for Birth and Death Records.
 1964. 15 cents.

Help in

Disaster

IT IS SENSIBLE to know beforehand where to turn for help should a natural disaster—storm, fire, flood, drought, earthquake, tidal wave, avalanche—strike your community.

One of the agencies that can help—the only one discussed in this chapter—is the United States Department of Agriculture, which generally makes assistance available to victims of disaster on a request from the Governor, rather than as a result of requests of individuals.

Emergency responsibilities include control of forest fires, food for hungry people, and aid to farmers whose property has been damaged or destroyed.

Assistance available to assuage the effects of natural disasters include crop insurance, emergency loans, cost-sharing help to restore and conserve disaster-stricken land, emergency livestock feed programs, and advice on the best ways to avoid or alleviate effects of disaster.

FOOD BOUGHT by the Department of Agriculture in surplus removal programs can be made available for use in an emergency. Such food normally is supplied for school lunch programs and for distribution to needy families.

The State agencies that normally handle the distribution of this food are authorized to make them available for emergency feeding, as when Alaska suffered an earthquake, hurricanes hit Florida and Georgia, and floods damaged parts of Montana and the Northwest.

In Florida in 1964, some schools were used to house people whom floods had driven from their homes and who received food the Department of Agriculture had donated to the schools. The food stocks later were replaced from Department stocks. The stocks usually include canned meat, dry milk, dried eggs, rice, other cereals, cheese, butter, and peanut butter.

If additional supplies of those foods are needed, the Department can arrange to divert other eligible food supplies to meet the emergency needs.

Such agencies as the local civil defense organization, the Red Cross, and the Salvation Army may obtain foods donated by the Department of Agriculture for use in emergency group feeding centers. Field officials of the Department generally go to the major disaster areas to determine what additional food is needed and arrange for shipments of those types available from the Department's supplies. Food donated by the Department also may be supplied directly to families by the appropriate welfare agencies.

THE DEPARTMENT helps farmers whose lands have been flooded by making emergency loans, arranging for feed for livestock, or helping to rehabilitate damaged land.

Credit and rights to graze or harvest hay on diverted acres—land that was taken out of crop production—may be made available to victims of hail and windstorms and unseasonable freezes.

Farmers may be reimbursed up to 50 percent of the costs of approved conservation practices. If any large amounts of assistance are needed as a result of a disaster, the U.S. Department of Agriculture State disaster committee recommends the kinds and amounts of aid it believes are needed.

The flood-repair practices eligible for cost-sharing assistance are recommended by the local office with approval from State and national Agricultural Stabilization and Conservation Service offices.

After a program is authorized, the local office of the Agricultural Stabilization and Conservation Service approves individual requests from farmers for assistance for land rehabilitation. Payment of up to 80 percent of the cost is made when the approved disaster practices are completed. Included are such practices as removal of debris from farmland, shaping and grading eroded farmland, and restoring flood-damaged drainage and irrigation systems.

A farmer may request technical help of the Soil Conservation Service. It is primarily in the form of advice on how to restore and conserve flood-damaged land.

The Farmers Home Administration can make loans to farmers to finance expenditures necessary as a result of flood or storm damage that cannot be met by local lending institutions.

Government-owned grain can be donated to flood-stranded livestock or can be sold at reduced prices to farmers who have lost their crop or feed supply. These are grains that farmers stored under price-support loan programs and were turned over to the Government in lieu of repayment of the loan.

In small watersheds in farming districts where there are dangers of flooding or other water problems, the Soil Conservation Service can assist local organizations in planning and carrying out measures for flood prevention, erosion control, and drainage. In forested areas, the Forest Service and its cooperators provide similar assistance. Similar assistance for larger projects is provided by the Corps of Engineers.

SHOULD SMALL FIRES in forests spread, help from outside the area may be needed. The Forest Service trains firefighters and at all National Forests has firefighting equipment, which can be rushed to help control such fires.

To fight a fire near Santa Barbara, Calif., in 1964, the Forest Service brought in firefighters, aerial tankers, and helicopters from adjoining States to bring under control a fire that endangered the city and burned about 80,000 acres before it was brought under control.

The Forest Service also arranged for seeding quick-growing grass on the burned area to prevent flash floods that might endanger Santa Barbara.

The Forest Service has standby arrangements for exchange of help with other local and Federal agencies that have firefighting equipment.

The Forest Service conducts such disaster services as the removal of avalanche debris, rescue operations, insect control, and flood relief assistance on National Forest land.

NEARLY EVERY SUMMER some part of the country may have water shortages, which stunt crops, dry pastures, lower yields of crops and forage, and may cause cattle to suffer. Drought conditions usually develop gradually.

When a Governor feels that a drought situation in his State has become sufficiently serious to warrant a request for help, he calls on the Department of Agriculture for assistance. The request may be for emergency credit, permission for farmers to harvest hay or graze cattle on diverted acres, cost-sharing to reestablish the drought-damaged pastures, or provide livestock feed.

The type of assistance follows the recommendations of the Department's disaster committees, which comprise Department employees and Cooperative Extension Service people in the area.

An emergency credit declaration can make loan funds available to farmers whose needs cannot be met by local sources.

Under a hay and grazing declaration, farmers in a drought district may be authorized by the Secretary of Agriculture to harvest hay or graze livestock on land diverted from crops. Such permission is usually conditional on their forgoing or returning a part of the diversion payment.

The assistance under the Emergency

Agricultural Conservation Program in drought areas usually is in the form of the sharing of costs of farmers. Practices eligible for cost-sharing include seeding grass and other practices necessary to replace vegetative cover lost because of drought and to conserve the land.

Crop insurance is offered on one or more crops in more than 1,000 counties. When insured crops are destroyed or damaged by drought or other causes beyond a farmer's control, the farmer receives indemnity payments for them.

To benefit from crop insurance, farmers must purchase such insurance about the time the crop is planted.

Government-owned grain can be made available to farmers in drought areas. Such feed-grain programs usually are authorized only after drought conditions have become extremely serious. Farmers can be authorized to buy Government-owned feed grains, in areas designated for such drought assistance, at 75 percent of the feed-grain support price for the preservation and maintenance of herds, including producing dairy cattle, sheep, and goats, and other livestock, at 100 percent of the support price.

When an area is hit by extreme drought conditions and the President has declared it a disaster area, feed grain owned by Commodity Credit Corporation may be donated to eligible farmers to preserve foundation stock.

The county office of the Agricultural Stabilization and Conservation Service determines eligibility for livestock feed assistance. It also determines the amount of feed each farmer may buy.

The Commodity Credit Corporation is the agency of the Department that takes title to and manages stocks of grain acquired by the Government under price-support programs.

AN OUTBREAK of plant and animal diseases may require extensive action to keep it from becoming an economic disaster.

The Department employs many vet-erinarians, plant pathologists, and entomologists who are skilled in crop and livestock protection methods. Pest and disease control programs usually are carried out in cooperation with State officials. Any unusual plant or animal disease should be reported to the county agent or veterinarian.

When a blizzard, flood, or drought threatens the existence of migratory birds and other wildlife, the Commodity Credit Corporation can donate bulk grain to State agencies and regional officials of the Department of the Interior for use as feed. Help is provided through the appropriate agencies, which ask the Grain Division of Agricultural Stabilization and Conservation Service in Washington for grain for such purposes.

County, State, and Federal Cooperative Extension Services are ready to give advice to farmers and other rural residents in times of emergency and disaster. Information on how to cope with the problem or where to get assistance is a most valuable aid and is available in every county in the country.

In every county and State, the Department of Agriculture has defense boards, which include Department employees and cooperative Federal-State extension workers, who have special assignments to perform under defense emergency conditions. They meet periodically to discuss how they would handle such problems and to coordinate Federal plans with those of State and civil defense organizations in the localities.

Many Department employees are trained to do radiological monitoring and to be ready to measure radiation and advise people on the measures they should take. (GEORGE H. WALTER)

For further reading, consult the following Department of Agriculture publications:
Family Food Stockpile for Survival, Home and Garden Bulletin 77; *First Aid for Flooded Homes and Farms*, Agriculture Handbook 38; *The U.S. Department of Agriculture: How it Serves You*, Program Aid 394; *What the U.S. Department of Agriculture Can Do When Disaster Strikes*, Program Aid 533.

Help in Nutrition

IF YOU FEEL overwhelmed by the deluge of stuff about what to eat and why, where to buy it, and how to store, prepare, and serve it, you can turn to qualified persons in your own community for answers to your questions on food, nutrition, and diet.

They have had professional training and experience in nutrition. They belong to one of two groups—the nutrition experts and members of other professions whose training and experience include some work in nutrition.

The nutrition experts are dietitians and nutritionists, medical and nonmedical.

Most qualified dietitians have had a dietetic internship in addition to basic college training.

Community nutritionists usually have also a master's degree in public health nutrition or in nutrition education. Others, most of whom are staff members of colleges and universities, have doctoral degrees in nutrition, biochemistry, or food technology.

Medical nutritionists are physicians with a special interest in nutrition.

Membership in professional organizations is another mark of a qualified person. Dietitians and nutritionists, unlike nurses, are not registered, but membership in the American Dietetic Association is open only to individuals who have satisfied stringent requirements as to education and experience.

Among physicians and scientists with doctorates in a basic science, members in the American Society for Clinical Nutrition, a section of the American Institute of Nutrition, are specialists in human nutrition.

The second group, the professional workers who have had some training in nutrition, are the coworkers of the nutritionist. Among them are doctors, nurses, home economists, teachers, and others whose work may concern food.

You may ask, as many do, about the difference between a home economist and a nutritionist.

The training of a home economist is more general in nature and, as far as food is concerned, has more to do with the use of food in the home than with the science of nutrition.

Generally speaking, you would not go to people in this group with technical questions on nutrition unless the question related also to their specific professions. For example, you could expect a doctor (M.D.) or a nurse to give assistance in the interpretation of a sodium-restricted diet, but you would not expect it of a teacher or a home economist.

Every community has some nutrition workers whose focus of attention is on the community at large and some who focus on one segment of the community. The first group includes persons working in public health, welfare agencies, agricultural extension programs, voluntary associations, and industry. Their positions were created to provide service to the community; they therefore are the first to turn to for help.

THE PUBLIC HEALTH nutritionist is a key source in the community for information on nutrition.

One of her main responsibilities is to know the community. If she does not have the answers to your questions, she will find them or refer you to another source of information.

Her specialty is nutrition as related to health. She promotes health through activities designed to teach people what to eat and why, and she does it with an understanding of the racial, religious, and psychological factors involved in food habits.

Among her special interests are nutrition in maternal and child health, in rehabilitation, and in the control of disease, particularly such conditions as diabetes and diseases of the heart and circulatory system.

Almost any questions on nutrition could be brought to her—questions on the selection, preparation, and serving of food; food costs and budgeting; food service in nursing homes, hospitals, schools, camps, and other group-care facilities. She knows also about food fads, emergency rations, and current research in nutrition.

She gives service to individuals and groups by providing leaflets, reference lists, and exhibits; assisting in planning programs; and participating in community activities.

All local health departments do not have nutritionists on their staffs, but all have professional workers with some training in nutrition. Among those available to assist you are physicians, nurses, and health educators.

SOME LOCAL and most State welfare agencies employ home economists to assist in the development of public assistance standards to meet individual needs and the development of services related to home management on limited budgets.

These home economists gather information as needed to justify recommendations for food allowances, give consultation to the social caseworkers who work directly with families, and sometimes give assistance directly to welfare recipients.

Departmental policies determine how much service is available to persons other than clients, but we could expect that some time would be given to community service, such as answering individual questions, participating in meetings, furnishing informational materials and referrals, and working with other community agencies on related problems.

As specialists in food economics, they know food costs, food budgets at various levels of cost, the makeup and cost of adequate diets, normal or therapeutic for persons of all ages, and practical aspects of food money management, such as menu plans for limited budgets.

THE EXTENSION SERVICE provides through its home advisers one of the Nation's most accessible sources of information related to food.

The program itself is part of a cooperative Federal, State, and county system of education in agriculture and home economics. It is administered through the land-grant colleges and universities and is brought to people through field personnel assigned to the counties. Almost every county has at least one home adviser.

The home advisers usually are home economists. Many have had specialized training in areas related to nutrition. All have available the assistance of nutrition specialists on the staff of their central office.

The home adviser's primary function is to work in the community to improve family living. She does her work in a number of ways—giving individual consultation, conducting short courses, acting as resource person for other community workers, preparing newsletters, and providing visual materials, such as posters, slides, and pamphlets and leaflets.

Home advisers are specialists in family feeding—menu planning to meet normal nutritional needs and the costs, budgeting, selection, storage, preservation, preparation, and service of food. They also help in planning and equipping home kitchens, equipment maintenance, and work simplification. Consultation on diet in disease usually is not available.

VOLUNTARY AGENCIES, such as the Visiting Nurse Association (VNA), Homemaker and Home Care Services, Family Service agencies, local chapters of organizations, such as the American Red Cross, American Heart Association, and American Diabetes Association, are organized to give service to the community. Some have nutrition specialists on their staffs. All have other professional persons with some training in nutrition.

The type of questions they can answer reflects the scope of their agencies. A nutritionist in a heart program, for example, would be a specialist on diets in many types of heart disease, food composition as related to those diets, and research on nutrition in heart disease. Those in home-care programs and service agencies offer general consultation.

Professional organizations are another source of information. Dial-A-Dietitian programs, sponsored by local dietetic associations, are an example. Through a telephone answering service, they answer questions on foods and nutrition except those related to diet therapy.

MANY nutrition workers work in the many branches of the food industry and in public-service agencies, such as newspapers and public utilities.

Food manufacturers and trade associations—for example, the National Dairy Council, Cereal Institute, and Western Fruit and Vegetable Growers—maintain consumer-service divisions to promote the use of their products. Their home economists sell sound nutrition as a part of their promotional programs. They reach the public through leaflets, newsletters, posters, and other visual aids, which contain recipes and information.

Public utilities employ home economists in their consumer-service programs. They visit homes to help people who have problems related to use of equipment, conduct cooking schools and food demonstrations, and prepare informational materials.

Some of the utility companies employ dietitians to give consultation on group feeding, particularly in nursing homes and boarding homes.

THE SECOND GROUP of nutrition workers in a community, those whose focus of attention is one segment of the community, includes dietitians and nutritionists working in hospitals and teachers of home economics and nutritional science in all kinds of schools.

They serve their community indirectly. Their first responsibility is to the group served by the institution for which they work.

Most of the dietitians in the country work in hospitals. Usually their responsibilities are limited to hospital patients and staff, but as hospitals are taking an increasingly active role in the community, we can expect that the dietitians' services will be broadened.

Meanwhile, hospital dietitians are willing to answer individual questions, serve as resource persons for community groups, and give consultation to other professional persons.

Therapeutic dietitians are experts in modified diets. They interpret diets ordered by doctors. They do not prescribe diets. As a patient referred by a doctor or as a member of the patient's family, you could expect a dietitian to help you adapt your diet to your usual food practices, explain why some foods may not be allowed, provide information on composition of food, tell you about special dietary products on the market—in short, help you to understand the diet and how to plan meals within its framework.

Administrative dietitians have information on questions related to group feeding—quantity recipes, menu planning, purchasing, personnel requirements, and the like.

Teachers of home economics and nutritional sciences in secondary schools, colleges and universities, research centers, and departments of adult education are a convenient source of information. Almost any kind of question related to nutrition could be asked of them.

They do have direct responsibility for their teaching programs, but most of them are available also to answer a person's questions, make referrals, act as consultants in community programs, and participate in special programs. (DOLORES L. NYHUS)

PLANTS

How To

Grow Plants

CITY AND SUBURBAN householders who are beginners in gardening should first size up the gardening possibilities of their own places and find out how to grow the plants that can be grown in those places.

Gardening is an art.

To be successful in it, the gardener must learn what conditions different kinds of plants require.

Then he can choose plants that will grow well under his conditions as he finds them. Or he can try to change conditions so he can grow other plants that he wants to grow. Most gardeners do both.

The beginner should get to know successful gardeners in his locality. He should learn all they can teach him about local problems and practices.

He should join a garden club, know his local county agricultural agent or garden adviser, and get the publications of his State agricultural extension service for gardeners in his area.

Publications of the Department of Agriculture will be of great help.

Many good books and magazines on gardening are available in bookstores and libraries.

NO ONE KIND of plant grows well everywhere, even within one locality. Climate and soil largely determine what can grow where. Other factors also enter.

Most common garden plants can grow reasonably well on many kinds of soil, ranging from sands to clays.

Sandy and clay soils are generally less desirable than sandy loam, loam, and clay loam or silt loam soils.

Sandy soils are poor in plant nutrients and dry out quickly. On the other hand, they are easy to work and can be improved with peat, sawdust, manures, composts, and fertilizers.

Clay and other "heavy" soils are hard to work, may form troublesome clods, and generally take up water very slowly.

It is difficult for small seedlings to emerge through heavy soils, and these soils become badly compacted when repeatedly walked upon. It is possible, however, to improve gradually the physical properties of these heavy soils by repeatedly working manures, composts, and other organic matter into them.

Peat and sawdust improve the physical properties of both very light (sandy) and very heavy soils. The use of sawdust, however, creates a problem of nitrogen fertilization. (See Circular No. 891, "Use of Sawdust for Mulches and Soil Improvement," of the Department of Agriculture.)

Many soils in humid sections are so acid that they must be limed before one tries to grow acid-sensitive plants on them. In the arid and less humid regions, many soils are salty or so alkaline that they must be treated before salt- or alkali-sensitive plants can be grown.

Soil must be well drained naturally or drained by effective tiling or ditching. Garden plants will not tolerate waterlogged soil.

Irrigated soils also must be well drained, although there may never be too much water in them—they must be drained so that excess salts from irrigation water and fertilizers can be leached from the root zone.

Agricultural agencies in most States operate soil-testing services and make specific recommendations for fertilizing or otherwise treating the soils tested. Take advantage of this service if you need it. Your county agent can give you instructions and addresses.

Growing one kind of plant year after year in the same spot favors the buildup of disease agents and insects that affect that plant and persist in the soil. When it is feasible, change the location of planting each season, so that one kind of plant is grown in any one spot only once in 3 or 4 years.

ALMOST ALL lawns and gardens need some irrigation water, even in the so-called humid parts of this country. No section is always free of dry spells.

Supplemental water may be needed for valuable perennial specimens as well as annual plants. Shallow-rooted shrubs, such as azaleas, may be lost in a short time for lack of water.

A relatively small amount of water may be of great value in establishing a stand of seedlings or transplants and (applied at the proper time) keeping them in good growth.

One or two moderate irrigations later may spell the difference between success and failure with an important part of the lawn and garden.

Sprinkling is generally the easiest way for the householder to apply water, but it is not always the best. Frequent wetting may increase damage from leaf diseases of many garden plants or impair the quality of flowers or edible products.

Running the water through furrows near the plants is preferable when the contours and properties of the soil permit.

Perforated or porous hose helps to place water precisely where it is desired on small plots without waste and without wetting the aboveground parts of the plants.

It is better to water plants thoroughly and wet the soil down to a depth of several inches, at intervals of about a week, than to sprinkle or dribble a little water on the soil every day.

Mulching the soil with straw, leaves, peat, wood chips, or similar materials helps to conserve moisture and to control some weeds. Black polyethylene film is also used as a "mulch." Such mulches also prevent crusting of the soil and reduce the bad effects of walking on it when it is wet.

Do not work the soil when it is wet. Do not walk on it when it is wet unless you must do so.

To determine when a soil is dry enough to spade or cultivate in any way, squeeze a handful tightly into a lump. Then try to break the lump between your thumb and one finger. If the lump crumbles, the soil is dry enough. If the lump does not break or if it breaks without noticeable crumbling, it is too wet.

TOO LITTLE LIGHT causes trouble in home gardening oftener than you may suppose.

For most vegetables and many flowers, it is necessary that unobstructed sunshine reach them more than half of each day. Such plants may not develop as desired when grown close to the east, north, or west sides of buildings or trees although the sky above them is unobstructed. Leafy salad vegetables and greens will tolerate some shade, but tomatoes, for example, are highly intolerant.

Later chapters deal further with this subject.

When you grow seedlings in the house for transplanting, set the container of young plants close to the glass of a window that receives unobstructed sunshine. You should turn the plant container every day to keep the plants from growing crooked.

A spot near a window that receives 25 to 30 foot-candles of light may appear bright enough. One can read and work well in such light. But it takes 50 to 75 times that much light for most of the popular garden plants to develop normally. So-called house plants require much less.

If your prospective garden spot is at all shady any part of the day, choose carefully the plants you want to grow. Shade seriously reduces the fruitfulness of tomatoes, peppers, cucumbers, and other fruit-bearing vegetables.

EACH KIND OF PLANT has its characteristic temperature requirements and tolerances to heat and cold.

Do not expect all plants to grow equally well at any one temperature or season of the year—plants differ greatly in this respect.

In sections where the temperature changes markedly from season to season, one must learn when to plant and when not to plant each species. The aim is to plant each at such times that its temperature requirements will be met by the naturally occurring temperatures of the season.

The maps on pages 218 and 219 show the average dates of the last killing frost in the spring and the first in the fall for the 48 adjoining States.

Directions on some seed packets and in many publications tell when to plant different species, with respect to frost dates.

YOU NEED only a few simple tools for home gardening—but the tools should be good ones. Cheap, light materials and shoddy construction will be unsatisfactory and expensive in the long run.

Minimum needs, even for small and simple garden activities, are:

A spade or a long-handled, round-pointed shovel; a steel bow rake; a common steel hoe of the socket type; garden hose of large-enough bore to deliver ample water; a sprinkler, mainly for the lawn, and porous or perforated hose; a trowel; a sturdy, all-purpose bucket; a jackknife; a strong cord for marking rows; a small sprayer; hand shears for trimming shrubs; hand shears for trimming grass edges; and, of course, a lawnmower—the hand-pushed, reel type is adequate for small-to medium-sized lawns.

Those items, including 100 feet of good rubber hose but not the lawnmower, cost about 70 to 90 dollars in 1965.

For larger operations, the list of tools can grow almost endlessly. Gardeners are fascinated by gadgets as well as by plants, but even for fair-sized and varied operations you need relatively few additional tools.

The most important are heavy, long-handled shears for pruning cuts too heavy for hand shears; a pruning saw for cuts too heavy for shears; hedge shears for hedges and related pruning; a hand sickle; a mattock for heavy digging or grubbing roots; a wheel hoe for working between rows of plants; and a good wheelbarrow. These added items cost about 50 to 60 dollars.

Try to have an obscure or hidden spot for composting leaves, grass clippings, and all manner of plant residues. If space is limited, a simple pen or crib of wire or stakes will contain these materials neatly.

A WIDE RANGE of vegetable and ornamental plants for transplanting can be bought at garden supply and other retail stores and by mail.

If you need only a few plants, you may prefer to buy them rather than produce them.

SEEDS AND SPACE REQUIRED FOR VEGETABLES WHEN GROWN INTENSIVELY FOR HAND CULTURE

	Approximate distance between—			*Seeds or plants required for—*		
Crop	Rows	Plants or hills in rows	Depth to cover seeds or roots	1 foot of row or per hill	100 feet of row	1 acre
	In.	In.	In.	No.		Lbs.
Asparagus [1]	30	18	8	.....	70 plants....	3
Beans, lima (bush)	28	4	1½	4	¾ pound....	100
Beans, lima (pole) [2]	36	24	1½	2 4	½ pound....	60
Beans, snap (bush)	28	3	1½	5	¾ pound....	100
Beans, snap (pole) [2]	36	24	1½	2 4	¼ pound....	40
Beets	16	3	¾	6	1 ounce.....	12
Broccoli, sprouting [3]	30	18	½	3	1 packet.....	¼
Brussells sprouts [3]	30	18	½	3	1 packet.....	¼
Cabbage [1]	30	18	.....	.....	70 plants....	¼
Carrots	16	1½	½	20	¼ ounce.....	4
Cauliflower [1]	30	18	.....	.....	70 plants....	¼
Celery and celeriac [1]	24	6	.....	2	200 plants...	¼
Chard	24	6	¾	4	1 ounce.....	12
Chives	16	2	½	15	.....	.....
Chicory, witloof	20	4	½	10	1 packet.....	2
Collards [3]	30	18	½	3	1 packet.....	¼
Corn, sweet	36	12	1½	2	¼ pound....	15
Cress, upland	16	3	¼	20	1 packet.....	2
Cucumbers [2]	72	72	1	2 12	½ ounce.....	2
Eggplant [1]	36	30	.....	.....	40 plants....	¼
Endive	20	10	½	10	1 packet.....	2
Garlic [1]	16	3	1½	4	1 pound.....	325
Horseradish [1]	30	18	2	.....	70 roots.....	.....
Kale [3]	24	10	½	4	1 packet.....	4
Kohlrabi	16	4	½	10	¼ ounce.....	4
Leeks	16	3	½	20	¼ ounce.....	4
Lettuce, head [1]	16	12	.....	.....	100 plants...	¼
Lettuce, leaf	16	6	½	10	1 packet.....	2
Mustard	16	6	½	10	1 packet.....	2
Okra	36	18	1	3	1 ounce.....	8
Onions, seed	16	3	½	20	¼ ounce.....	4
Onions [1]	16	3	.....	4	{ 1 qt. sets.... { 400 plants...	600 3
Parsley	16	4	¼	20	¼ ounce.....	2
Parsnips	16	3	½	15	½ ounce.....	3
Peas, garden (dwarf)	18	1	1½	12	1 pound.....	120
Peas, garden (tall)	24	1	1½	12	1 pound.....	120
Peas, black-eye	28	3	1½	5	½ pound....	60
Peppers [1]	30	18	.....	.....	70 plants....	¼
Potatoes	30	12	4	1	7 pounds....	1,200
Radishes, spring	12	1	½	15	1 ounce.....	12
Radishes, summer or winter...	20	3	½	10	½ ounce.....	6
Rhubarb [1]	42	42	4	.....	30 roots.....	.....
Rutabagas	20	4	¼	20	¼ ounce.....	2
Salsify	20	2	½	15	1 ounce.....	12
Spinach	12	4	½	12	½ ounce.....	10
Spinach, New Zealand	30	12	1	3	1 ounce.....	4
Squash, bush [2]	48	48	1	10	½ ounce.....	3
Squash, trailing [2]	96	48	1	10	½ ounce.....	2
Sweetpotatoes [1]	36	12	.....	.....	100 plants...	.....
Tomatoes, [1] not staked	48	48	.....	.....	26 plants....	⅛
Tomatoes, [1] staked	36	24	.....	.....	51 plants....	¼
Turnips	16	3	½	20	¼ ounce.....	2

[1] Plants or sets.   [2] Hills of about 4 plants each.   [3] 4 or 5 seeds planted in 1 spot where plants are to stand; later thinned to 1 plant.

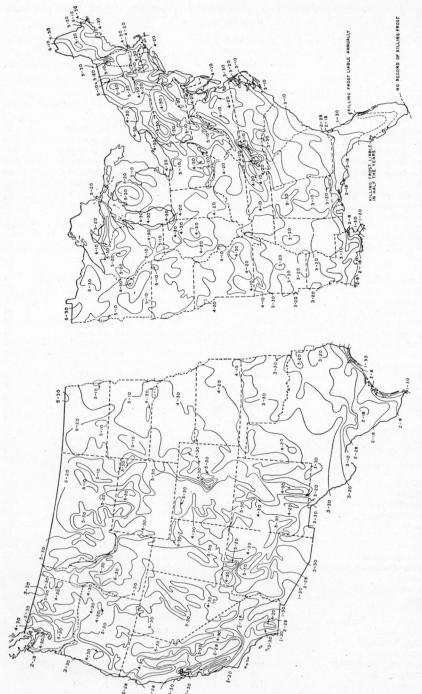

Map showing average dates of last killing spring frosts in the Western and Eastern United States.

Map showing average dates of first killing fall frosts in the Western and Eastern United States.

Often, however, varieties you want may not be available at convenient commercial sources, and you will have to start them at home.

Few residences have enough indoor light, a suitable temperature range, and convenient space for growing good seedlings ready for transplanting to the garden. The job can be rather messy unless you take care to protect against spillage of soil (or another planting medium) and leakage of moisture from the containers. The plant-growing containers should all be set in a larger shallow pan or tray that is leakproof.

If you grow more than a few plants, you need a small hotbed or coldframe on the sunny side of the house in which to start them and later acclimate them gradually to outdoor conditions before planting them in the garden. Home and Garden Bulletin No. 9, "Suburban and Farm Vegetable Gardens," Farmers' Bulletin No. 1171, "Growing Annual Flowering Plants," and Leaflet No. 243, "Sphagnum Moss for Seed Germination," give details.

IT IS BETTER to plant seeds in a moist soil than to plant in a dry soil and sprinkle it to get the seedlings up.

Seeds should be pressed into contact with the moist soil and covered immediately with moist soil. The soil over the seeds should then be pressed down firmly but not packed. If the seed is not in intimate contact with the soil, it may be unable to absorb moisture rapidly enough for prompt and vigorous germination. Light pressure can be applied to the uncovered seeds with the straight edge of a board, or a light, narrow wheel can be run over the seeds. After covering, the flat side of a hoe or a conventional pressure wheel of a planter can be used.

An accompanying table shows planting distance and planting depths for seeds of vegetables. The depths given are for a moist sandy loam soil. In heavy soils, plant less deeply. On sandy soils, plant more deeply to reach more moisture.

In general, plant seeds only deeply enough to insure they are in moist soil and that they will not be splashed out by an ordinary rain.

FOR MOST SOILS in good workable condition, a general garden fertilizer containing 5 percent nitrogen, 10 percent phosphoric acid, and 5 percent potash (5–10–5) will be useful. Amounts to use depend on the original fertility of the soil and its past treatment. If it is rich enough to produce a rapid and rank growth of weeds, it may need little, if any.

New ground, especially ground that is disturbed by construction work, generally will need up to 4 to 5 pounds per 100 square feet (about a ton per acre) of 5–10–5 fertilizer. It should be mixed thoroughly into the surface 6 to 8 inches.

If the plot has been heavily manured, superphosphate alone may be all that is needed, at about 2 to 3 pounds per 100 square feet.

Keep the weeds down by cultivating, hoeing, or mulching. Kill them when they are small.

After planting, work the soil no more than necessary to control weeds. Avoid trampling the soil, especially if it is wet.

Watch for evidence of insects and diseases, and apply control measures promptly. (See Home and Garden Bulletin No. 46, "Insects and Diseases of Vegetables in the Home Garden," and Agriculture Information Bulletin No. 237, "Controlling Insects on Flowers.")

Examine the soil and the plants to see if they lack water. Do not let the plants wilt. Dig into the soil a few inches to see if it is losing its moist appearance. If so, water thoroughly about once a week unless a rain has moistened the soil well down into the root zone.

Harvest products at prime quality.

Remove spent annual plants promptly when they are no longer useful for harvest or beauty. Trample them into the compost pile or work them into the soil.

Then plant another crop in the vacated space if there is time for it to develop before frost. If there is not time for that, cultivate or mulch the space to control weeds.

Protect the garden spots against winter erosion by mulching with plant residues or compost. (VICTOR R. BOSWELL)

Organic

Matter

THE WONDERFUL STUFF we call organic material is rotting leaves, stems, and other parts of plants. It is a soil amendment; it adds life to soil.

With it and some planning and effort and lime and chemical fertilizer, which also are called soil amendments, you can modify almost any soil to meet the needs of a wide range of vegetables, flowers, shrubs, and trees.

Decomposing organic matter mellows stiff, compacted clay soils and adds body to loose sands.

On the surface of the soil, where it serves as a mulch, it provides protection from beating rains, prevents soil crusting, reduces runoff and erosion, conserves moisture in the soil, helps to control dust, and reduces weeds.

The improved soil condition that results increases plant growth and root development. Each plant, therefore, has a larger volume of soil from which to obtain water and nutrients.

Organic matter also increases the ability of soils to release nutrients gradually to plants during the growing season.

It is not a substitute for commercial fertilizers, but it increases the efficiency of fertilizer applied.

Many forms of organic materials are available. Leaves come to mind first.

A new housing development may be barren at first, but in many localities homeowners can get all the leaves they want by calling their municipal street cleaning department in the fall. Often the leaves are delivered free or for a small delivery charge.

Several purposes are served thereby. A valuable but often wasted resource is conserved. The city authorities are relieved of the work of disposing of them.

A good idea is to shred the leaves with a rotary lawnmower or, even better, a leaf shredder, which can be bought for not very much money—no more, very likely, than the cost of two or three first-class shrubs or trees.

Since, though, a shredder may be used only a few days a year, neighbors may buy one jointly.

The boys and groups that earn money in summer by mowing lawns can extend their operations by buying a shredder and perform a leaf raking-shredding-composting-conservation service in the fall.

ORGANIC MATERIALS differ in nitrogen content and in rate of decomposition.

Certain types release nitrogen to the soil during decomposition.

Other types require additional nitrogen during decomposition, and nitrogen fertilizer must be added. Materials that decompose readily if enough nitrogen is supplied for them to rot include leaves, sawdust and bark from some trees, small woodchips, straw, cornstalks, ground corncobs, cotton burrs, cane bagasse, and peanut hulls.

When you mix them with the soil, you should add nitrogen fertilizer. Otherwise, the material, as it breaks down, will take up nitrogen from the soil, and plants will grow poorly because the available nitrogen is tied up.

Ammonium nitrate applied at the rate of 4 or 5 pounds per 100 pounds of dry organic matter or 12 to 15 pounds of lawn fertilizer, such as 10–6–4, will correct this deficiency.

Materials that contain enough nitrogen to decompose include grass clippings, legume hay, well-rotted manure, sewage sludge, tobacco stems and stalks, spent hops, and coffee grounds.

Materials that decompose so slowly that very little tie-up of nitrogen takes place include peat, buckwheat hulls, and sawdust and bark from redwood and cypress trees.

Cottonseed, soybean, and cocoa meals, castor pomace, activated sewage sludge, dried blood, meat and fish meals, process tankage, hoof and horn meal, guanos, and manipulated sheep, cattle, and poultry manures contain enough nitrogen for use as fertilizers.

Some people advocate that only organic fertilizers be used. The fact is, though, that the nutrients in organic fertilizers are available for plant growth only as the organic matter decomposes and the nutrients are changed to the same forms present in chemical fertilizers. Fertilizer elements are far more concentrated in chemical fertilizer than in organic matter. They therefore are cheaper and less bulky.

Organic fertilizers do have the advantage of releasing nutrients more slowly over a longer period, and an overdose of organic fertilizer is far less likely to burn the plant than an overdose of chemical fertilizers.

A few organic materials are toxic to plants or should not be used for other reasons.

Sawdust from California incense cedar and bark from white pine are poisonous to plants. Rare instances of toxicity following the use of sawdust that rotted without adequate oxygen have been reported. Such sawdust is easily recognized by its sharp acid odor or irritating fumes.

Peanut hulls with brown or dark discolorations are likely to contain nematodes or fungi harmful to many plants.

Cocoa hull mulches more than 2 inches deep have been reported to injure azaleas and rhododendrons.

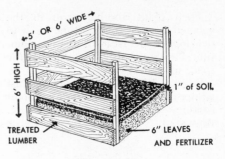

Compost pile.

Lawn clippings, fresh manures, leaf mold, and similar materials often contain weed seeds.

Heavy mulches of dry organic materials, such as peat, leaves, hay, and wood shavings, are a potential fire hazard. Mulches of finely divided materials, such as sawdust and coffee grounds, occasionally crust over and shed water. They should be stirred occasionally.

Coarse materials, such as woodchips, applied on the soil surface, make an excellent mulch. They do not blow away or crust.

COMPOSTING is a biological process that encourages the activity of microorganisms, which break down organic materials.

An adequate and balanced supply of nutrients, air, and water and warmth are needed.

Smaller particles decompose faster than large ones, although particles that are too small may pack together and shut out air.

Soft organic materials, such as grass clippings, compost better if they are mixed with coarse material, such as leaves and straw. Never put meat scraps in a compost pile.

The compost pile should be moist but not excessively wet. It should be large enough to maintain favorable temperatures. The best size is 6 feet high and 5 to 6 feet wide. It may be of any length.

A compost pile has alternate layers of organic materials and soil. Make each organic layer about 6 inches thick and put a few shovelfuls of soil between each layer. Add plant nutrients to each layer of organic material.

For the nutrients, as a general guide, we recommend that you add a cup of ammonium sulfate, one-half cup of superphosphate, and a level tablespoon of epsom salt to each packed bushel of leaves or organic material. If you do not plan to use the compost for acid-loving shrubs, add two-thirds cup of ground limestone or wood ashes.

Other recipes for compost piles may be just as good—for example, one and one-half cups of 10–6–4 lawn fertilizer or two and one-half cups of a 5–10–5 garden fertilizer to each packed bushel of leaves or organic material. Two-thirds cup of ground limestone or wood ashes are added when the compost is for general use rather than for acid-loving plants.

It is advantageous to build the pile with a flat top that slants toward the center to catch rainfall or hold water when watered with a hose.

If you use dry materials in building the pile, composting can be speeded by adding water as the pile is built.

Composting will not kill all disease-carrying organisms, insect eggs and larva, and weed seeds. Therefore, you should avoid using obviously infested materials.

Ordinances in some cities prohibit composting, perhaps because some compost piles are no more than heaps of garbage. Some persons in closely built communities may object to their neighbors' compost piles, but properly made and cared for piles need not be objectionable.

ORGANIC MATTER is particularly good for flowerbeds, which need a loose, friable soil that is easily cultivated and planted. Organic materials are added to develop such a soil.

Compost, peat, sawdust, shredded leaves, and ground corncobs are suited for flowerbeds. If the soil is extremely hard and cloddy, you should spread a layer of organic matter 2 or 3 inches

deep over the bed and work it into the soil to a depth of 6 or 8 inches. Remember to add ammonium nitrate or a lawn fertilizer to balance organic materials, such as sawdust, shredded leaves, and ground corncobs.

Lime, if needed, and phosphorous fertilizer should be worked into the soil at the same time. If the soil below 8 inches is extremely compact, pile the top layer of soil to one side, loosen the subsoil, and replace the topsoil. Mix a little organic matter with the subsoil. Do all this when the soil is moist but not wet.

After spading in the organic material, spread a complete fertilizer, such as 5–10–5, on the surface at the rate of 50 pounds per 1,000 square feet. Rake to mix in the fertilizer and level the bed. Break up any large clods.

If the soil has a tendency to crust after a heavy rain, spread a thin layer of organic material on the surface. You may have to buy some topsoil. Allow time for rain to settle the soil or add water to firm it before planting.

Additional organic matter should be incorporated each year or as needed to keep the soil in good condition. A mulch will further protect the soil and aid in the control of weeds. Mulches are particularly desirable for perennials.

In preparing the flowerbed, provide for drainage. Once in a while, tile drainage may be needed, but usually all that is needed is to build the bed up a little so that surface water drains away.

BECAUSE SHRUBS are a long-term investment, a little extra time in preparing the soil for them will be rewarded.

Work organic matter, lime, and phosphorous fertilizer into the soil as we recommended for flowerbeds.

Remember, though, that lime should not be applied if azaleas, rhododendrons, or other acid-loving plants are to be grown. Peat is especially recommended as a source of organic matter for azaleas and rhododendrons. Pine needles are effective as a mulch. They do not dry out and blow away in win-

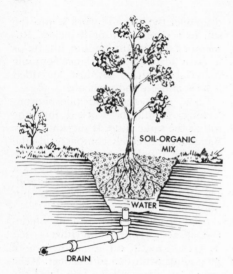

SOIL-ORGANIC MIX

WATER

DRAIN

This drawing emphasizes two points. The roots are well spread out in a mixture of soil and organic matter. Good drainage—not necessarily by pipes—is important.

ter. In places where acid-loving plants are to be grown, remove any building debris containing liming materials, such as plaster and cement.

Allow time for rain to settle the soil or add water to firm it before you set out the shrubs.

When you transplant in beds the shrubs you bought bare rooted, dig a hole large enough so you can spread the roots as they were before they were dug at the nursery. Place the plants in the hole with the original ground line of the plant at ground level. Arrange the roots and half fill the hole with the granulated soil-organic mixture carefully placed around the roots. Add water to settle the soil around the roots. Then finish filling the hole.

Balled-and-burlapped or container-grown plants are planted in holes larger than the packaged roots, so that the soil-organic mixture can be filled in around the package. If the container is a clay pot or metal pot it must be removed. Peat pots or pots of other decomposable materials are not removed before setting out the plant.

Set the ball of roots in the hole with the top of the ball at ground level. Add enough soil to half fill the hole. Then add water to saturate the soil. This aids in eliminating air pockets between the ball of roots and the side of the hole. After the water soaks into the soil, fill the hole with soil. Then mulch and water the entire bed.

Except in special situations, the mulch should be maintained at all times, particularly for evergreens, which must have water available to the roots throughout the year.

INDIVIDUAL SITES are prepared for planting trees and isolated shrubs. If the subsurface drainage is not good, water will collect in the hole, and the roots will rot.

Trees and large shrubs usually are moved with their roots in a ball of soil, which has been wrapped in burlap.

Sites for them are dug one and one-half to twice the diameter of the ball and about one-third deeper, especially if the subsoil is hard or poorly drained. An equal volume of organic matter (such as peat, compost, and sewage sludge) is mixed thoroughly with the soil that is removed from the hole. While mixing, add a quarter of a cup of a mixed fertilizer, such as a 5–10–5, to each bushel of the soil-organic matter mix to be returned to the hole. Put enough of this mix in the hole so the ground line of the ball will be 1 or 2 inches above the ground line of the soil. This allows for some settling.

Hold the tree erect and fill the hole halfway up with the soil-organic mixture. Thoroughly wet the hole to settle the mixture and fill any air pockets before filling the hole.

When the planting is complete, build a ridge around the root area to hold water. Keep the site mulched until the tree is well established.

Watering the trees during dry weather is especially important the first year. (R. S. DYAL AND R. R. ROBINSON)

Ground
Covers

GRASS is the best of all the ground covers. It can be walked on, played on, and trampled on frequently, yet it remains an excellent cover for the ground if it is fertilized, watered, cut regularly, and weeded occasionally.

Some other plants withstand a certain amount of pedestrian traffic, but grass still is the most serviceable of all.

Many gardeners look for other ground-covering plants that require little or no care. Trees and shrubs that grow with branches touching the ground do well in certain situations. Annual and perennial flowering plants will suffice in other places.

If you want other plants in order to make a planting more interesting or to avoid the care that grass needs, you should consider certain factors before you choose a specific plant:

Is the site in the sun or the shade?

Is the soil poor and dry or medium to good?

Do you want evergreen plants?

How high is the ground cover to be—a few inches or a foot or more?

Need the ground cover be serviceable all year, or can it be an herbaceous one, which dies to the ground in the late fall, leaving the ground bare and ostensibly lacking in plant material during the winter?

Those questions are important. Once you have made your decisions respecting them, it is much easier to select the proper plant as a ground cover for the area.

Careful preparations should be taken in the planting. The ground should

contain organic matter, such as well-rotted manure, compost, or peat moss. Work it in well before you plant.

Water should be available in order to get the plants off to a good start and to prevent them from suffering during dry periods.

The planting can be done in the spring or the fall, according to the general practice in your area. Fall planting often is satisfactory if it is done early enough to allow the young plants to become established thoroughly before the ground freezes. Spring planting may be better in many sections.

To space the individual plants properly at planting time, you should know the growth rate of the plants you select and decide whether you want a complete ground cover the first season or whether you can wait a few years until the plants eventually grow together.

For instance, the honeysuckles and the memorial rose grow rapidly, and individual plants may be expected to cover several square feet during the first year.

Other plants, like the European wildginger, grow slowly, and it may be several years before plants spaced a foot apart will grow together.

Evergreens, such as some of the creeping junipers, are expensive compared to small herbaceous plants, yet an individual evergreen may cover 4 square feet when you buy it.

Large clumps of herbaceous plants may be bought and pulled apart at the time of planting to cover as much space as possible. With certain exceptions, it is well to allow about 2 square feet of space for each of the herbaceous plants generally used as ground covers.

One of the purposes of ground-cover plants is to help prevent soil erosion. All plants prevent erosion to some extent, but fast-growing vines and shrubs that root readily along the branches that touch the soil are better to use in such situations than are herbaceous perennials, which die to the ground in winter and give little protection to the soil in early spring, when melting snows cause the worst erosion.

Give careful thought to ways to prevent erosion at planting time. One method is to terrace the bank and planting slightly in such a way that the runners of the vines go at right angles to the slope. Also, you can sink boards at right angles to the slope; let them protrude a few inches above the soil, and keep them in place for the first year or two until the plants become established.

Mulching with hay or straw helps prevent runoff for the first year or two. Placing large wire hairpins over the stems of the plants to keep them in place on the soil surface may encourage rapid rooting, especially if you put a shovelful of soil over the stem to keep the branch moist.

In any event, select healthy, vigorous-growing woody plants for this type of planting.

Among such plants are the dwarf bush honeysuckle (*Diervilla lonicera*), Arnold Dwarf Forsythia, English ivy (*Hedera helix*), varieties of creeping juniper (*Juniperus horizontalis*), Henry honeysuckle (*Lonicera henryi*), Hall's honeysuckle (*Lonicera japonica halliana*), dwarf Japanese fleeceflower (*Polygonum cuspidatum* 'Compactum'), fragrant sumac (*Rhus aromatica*), and memorial rose (*Rosa wichuraiana*).

Some of these rapid-growing ground covers, like the Hall's honeysuckle and the dwarf Japanese fleeceflower, can become pests in good soil, unless they are rigidly restrained.

If you select the right plant for the situation, maintenance will be reduced to a minimum. It is always well, when possible, to add mulch just after the plants have been set in the ground. The mulch keeps the soil moist about the young plants and aids in their rooting. It helps control weeds.

An application of fertilizer can help after the plants are started, but of the two things, the mulching is the more important.

Peat moss, wood chips, pine needles, ground sugarcane stalks, ground bark of almost any kind, ground corncobs—any such material aids in conserving the moisture in the soil and reducing weed growth, but none of them should be applied more than 2 inches deep.

In northern regions, one must watch for the heaving of small plants in the early spring. Heaving is brought about during the late winter and early spring by warm, sunny weather alternating with freezing temperatures. Covering a young planting with evergreen boughs, burlap, or hay the first winter helps to prevent the heaving of small plants. Replanting of heaved plants should be done immediately.

Pruning a planting of ground cover sometimes is necessary to aid the plants in becoming bushy and dense. Sometimes a shrub may grow too vigorously and need to be reduced to conform with the rest of the planting. We do this occasionally with the fragrant sumac or Arnold Dwarf Forsythia merely to make the planting more uniform in appearance.

Certain plants, like the yarrow, can even be mowed if necessary with a reel-type or rotary-blade mower. You could also use a brush scythe on some of the woody ground covers if its use will improve the general appearance of the planting.

A few bulbs here and there in a low ground cover create a color contrast during the early spring.

To SELECT the best possible plant as a ground cover for a specific situation, one must consider the extremes of winter and summer temperatures, the amount of rainfall, and the vagaries of the site itself.

A few suggestions of some of the better ground covers for specific situations are noted in the following lists. An asterisk in front of the name indicates hardiness in the colder parts of northern New England and the northern Great Plains States. Specific notes on hardiness of the other plants should be noted in standard reference books, but all are grown as ground covers in gardens throughout the United States. (DONALD WYMAN)

Ground Covers That Increase Rapidly

Aegopodium podograria (goutweed), *Ajuga reptans* (bugleweed), *Convallaria majalis* (lily-of-the-valley), *Forsythia* 'Arnold Dwarf,' *Lonicera japonica halliana* (Hall's honeysuckle), *Phalaris arundinacea picta* (ribbongrass), *Polygonum cuspidatum* 'Compactum' (dwarf Japanese fleeceflower), *Rosa wichuraiana* (memorial rose), *Sasa* species (hardy bamboos), *Vinca minor* (periwinkle).

Evergreen Ground Covers

Arctostaphylos uva-ursi (bearberry), *Euonymus fortunei* varieties (wintercreeper), *Galax aphylla* (galax), *Gaylussacia brachycera* (box huckleberry), *Hedera helix* (English ivy), *Juniperus* species (junipers), *Mahonia* species (hollygrape), *Pachysandra terminalis* (Japanese pachysandra), *Thymus serpyllum* (mother-of-thyme), *Vinca minor* (periwinkle).

Flowering Ground Covers

Ajuga reptans (bugleweed), *Calluna vulgaris* (Scotch heather), *Cytisus* species (brooms), *Erica* species (spring heaths), *Helianthemum nummularium* (sunrose), *Hosta* species (plantainlilies), *Hypericum* species (St. Johnsworts), *Lonicera* species (honeysuckles), *Phlox* species (phlox), *Rosa* species (roses).

Ground Covers for Shade

Ajuga reptans (bugleweed), *Aegopodium podograria* (goutweed), *Asarum* species (wildgingers), *Epimedium* species (epimediums), *Hedera helix* (English ivy), *Hosta* species (plantain-lilies), *Pachysandra terminalis* (Japanese pachysandra), *Sasa* species (hardy bamboos),

Tiarella cordifolia (Alleghany foamflower), *Vinca minor* (periwinkle).

Ground Covers for Dry Soils

Aegopodium podograria (goutweed), *Coronilla varia* (crownvetch), *Genista pilosa* (silky-leaf woadwaxen), *Hosta* species (plantain-lilies), *Hypericum calycinum* (Aarons-beard St. Johnswort), *Juniperus* species (junipers), *Phalaris arundinacea picta* (ribbongrass), *Polygonum* species (fleeceflowers), *Rhus aromatica* (fragrant sumac), *Vaccinium angustifolium laevifolium* (lowbush blueberry).

Ground Covers for Wet Soil

Asarum caudatum (British Columbia wildginger), *Asperula odorata* (sweet woodruff), *Galax aphylla* (galax), *Geranium sanguineum prostratum* (dwarf blood red geranium), *Hosta* species (plantain-lilies), *Lysimachia nummularia* (moneywort), *Myosotis scorpioides* (true forget-me-not), *Phlox divaricata* (wild sweet-william), *Veronica repens* (creeping speedwell), *Xanthorhiza simplicissima* (yellowroot).

Ground Covers for Seashore

Arctostaphylos uva-ursi (bearberry), *Artemesia stelleriana* (beach wormwood), *Calluna vulgaris* (Scotch heather), *Campanula* species (bellflowers), *Cerastium tomentosum* (snow-in-summer), *Comptonia peregrina* (sweetfern), *Cytisus* species (brooms), *Juniperus conferta* (shore juniper), *Rosa wichuraiana* (memorial rose), *Vaccinium vitis-idaea minus* (mountain cranberry).

Ground Covers That May Be Cut With a Lawnmower

Aegopodium podograria (goutweed), *Hypericum repens* (creeping St. Johnswort), *Lysimachia nummularia* (moneywort), *Mazus reptans* (mazus), *Nepeta hederacea* (ground-ivy), *Potentilla tridentata* (wineleaf cinquefoil), *Prunella vulgaris* (selfheal). *Thymus* species (thyme), *Veronica* species (speedwells), *Viola* species (violets).

Ground Covers for Warm Areas of Gulf Coast and Pacific Coast

Gazania species (South African daisy), *Hypericum calycinum* (Aarons-beard St. Johnswort), *Mesembryanthemum* species (ice plants), *Lippia canescens repens* (creeping lippia), *Ophiopogon japonicum* (mondograss), *Pelargonium peltatum* (ivy-vine pelargonium), *Santolina chamaecyparissus* (cypress lavender-cotton), *Saxifraga sarmentosum* (strawberry saxifrage), *Sedum* species (sedums), *Verbena peruviana* varieties (Peruvian verbena).

Lawns

You DO NOT have to be an expert to make and maintain a good lawn. Follow a few general principles. Avoid hit-or-miss methods.

Some common causes of poor lawns are: The use of grasses not suited to the locality, too little or too much fertilizer, improper mowing and watering, too much shade, too much traffic, and poorly drained or droughty soils.

Choose a grass that is adapted to your locality and to the maintenance program you plan to follow. For example, bentgrass lawns require frequent mowing, watering, fertilizing, and treatment with chemicals to kill fungi. If you do not want to expend labor and money for this kind of lawn, you should choose a grass that requires less care.

Three broad groups of lawn grasses are:

Cool-season grasses for cool, humid areas (Kentucky bluegrass, red fescue, tall fescue, and bentgrasses);

warm-season grasses for warm, humid areas (carpet, zoysia, centipede St. Augustine, and bermudagrasses);

and grasses for the dryland area of the Great Plains (crested wheat, blue grama, and buffalograsses).

Temperature and moisture largely determine the adaptation of grass.

In general, the best time to seed or plant cool-season grasses is in the fall or early spring.

Warm-season grasses are planted in the spring or early summer.

A POORLY COLORED, thin, or weedy lawn is a hungry lawn.

Nutrients that grass plants need in large amounts are nitrogen, phosphorus, and potassium. They are listed as N, P, and K on all fertilizer bags, in that order, with the percentage of each.

Many kinds and ratios of fertilizers are suitable for lawns. Choose one whose first—nitrogen (N)—number is as large or larger than the amounts of P and K. For example, a 10–6–4 fertilizer contains 10 percent nitrogen, 6 percent phosphorus, and 4 percent potassium.

The amount of fertilizer to apply to lawns we calculate on the percentage of nitrogen in the fertilizer. It is generally recommended that not more than 1 pound of actual nitrogen per 1 thousand square feet be applied at any one time. That would amount to 10 pounds of 10–6–4, 5 pounds of 20–10–5, 20 pounds of 5–10–5, and so on per thousand square feet of lawn.

Grasses vary in their need for nitrogen. A rough guide to the annual requirements is given in the table.

Too much fertilizer applied at any one time may burn the grass and will overstimulate top growth and weaken the plant. You can reduce the danger of burning by applying fertilizer when there is no moisture on the leaves and by watering immediately after you apply the fertilizer.

Organic types of fertilizer may be used in greater amounts than chemical types without burning the grass.

Lawn grasses grow poorly in acid soils. Test your soil and apply ground

Climatic regions, in which the following grasses are suitable for lawns:

1. *Kentucky bluegrass, red fescue, and Colonial bentgrass. Tall fescue, bermuda and zoysia grasses in the southern part.*

2. *Bermuda and zoysia grasses. Centipede, carpet, and St. Augustine grasses in the southern part; tall fescue and Kentucky bluegrass in some northern areas.*

3. *St. Augustine, bermuda, zoysia, carpet, and bahia grasses.*

4. *Nonirrigated areas: Crested wheat, buffalo, and blue grama grasses. Irrigated areas: Kentucky bluegrass and red fescue.*

5. *Nonirrigated areas: Crested wheat grass. Irrigated areas: Kentucky bluegrass and red fescue.*

6. *Colonial bent and Kentucky bluegrass.*

limestone if the tests show a need for it.

Soils in the Eastern States generally require lime.

If you do not make a test and if you have not used lime in the past 4 to 6 years, apply 50 to 80 pounds of ground limestone per 1 thousand square feet of lawn area.

Lime may be put on at any time of the year, but fall is the best time. Rain and snow will wash it into the soil.

How HIGH you should mow the grass depends on the kind of grass that predominates in your lawn.

Upright-growing grasses (Kentucky bluegrass, bahia, tall fescue, and red fescue) are mowed at 1½ to 2½ inches.

Grasses that spread by runners (zoysia, bermuda, centipede, and bentgrasses) will withstand close mowing, one-half to 1 inch.

The lawn should be mowed with a sharp mower often enough so as not to remove more than one-half of the top growth at any one time.

In the spring, mow the lawn as soon as growth reaches cutting height. Continue throughout the season until the growth stops in the fall. Excess growth remaining over the winter may smother and kill the grass.

MOST GRASSES show remarkable tolerance to drought. Grasses may become brown and dormant if not watered, but generally they recover when the fall rains come.

Established lawns should not be watered until they show signs of wilting or going offcolor.

Footprinting and the appearance of a bluish cast in parts of the lawn indicate that the lawn needs water. Then water the soil to a depth of 6 inches or more. Frequent, light watering encourages shallow rooting and increases the chance of plant diseases.

Sandy soils, because of their low moisture-holding capacity, require more frequent watering.

Clay soils require less frequent watering, but more water should be applied at any one time.

STEPS IN MAKING a new lawn:

Shape the soil to provide the desired contours and landscape features. The most satisfactory grade generally is one that slopes gently away from buildings in all directions.

Dark-colored loam soils are ideal surface soils for lawns. Organic matter is an important part of the surface soil. It can be supplied by mixing sawdust, peat, muck, sewage sludge, or green plant material into the soil. Organic matter may be omitted if 4 to 6 inches of good-quality top soil is present, but it should be added to heavy clay and sandy soils.

Have your soil tested by your county agent or State agricultural experiment station. Apply fertilizer and lime as they recommend.

If you did not have the soil tested

LAWN GRASSES: PLANTING TIME, PROPAGATION, FERTILIZATION, AND MOWING HEIGHT

Grass	Best planting time	Method of propagation		Fertilizer (lbs. per 1,000 sq. ft.)	Height of mowing (in.)
		Seed (lbs. per 1,000 sq. ft.)	Sod (sq. ft.)[2]		
Bahia	Spring	2–3	....	4	2
Bentgrass, Colonial	Fall	1–2	....	4–6	½–1
Bermuda (hulled)	Spring	1–1½	5–10	5–10	¾–1
Blue grama	....do	1–1½	....	(1)	1–2
Buffalo (treated)	....do	½–1½	25–30	(1)	1–2
Carpet	....do	3–4	8–10	2–3	2–2½
Centipede	....do	2–3	8–10	2–3	1–1½
Crested wheat	Fall	1–2	....	0–1	2
Ky. bluegrass	....do	1½–2	....	3–6	1½–2
Red fescue	....do	3–4	....	2–3	1½–2
St. Augustine	Spring	None	8–10	4–5	2–2½
Tall fescue	Fall	5–6	....	3–5	2
Zoysia	Spring	None	8–10	4–6	¾–1½

[1] Seldom required on most soils.   [2] Needed to sprig 1,000 sq. ft.

and if you live east of the Mississippi River, apply 50 to 80 pounds of lime per 1 thousand square feet. The addition of 30 to 40 pounds of superphosphate per 1 thousand square feet is desirable in many sections. After liming, you should spread a complete fertilizer uniformly at the rate of 20 pounds of 10–6–4, 10–10–10, or similar analysis per 1 thousand square feet.

Work the organic matter, ground limestone, and superphosphate (0–20–0) thoroughly into the soil to a depth of several inches. If 4 to 6 inches of good grade top soil has been added, omit the organic matter.

Prepare a fine, firm seedbed by raking several times. Loose, fluffy seedbeds should be rolled in order to firm the soil. Before final raking, apply the recommended amount of fertilizer.

Seed, sprig, or sod with adapted lawn grasses. Most southern grasses are established from sprigs (individual plants and runners) or pieces of sod. The sprigs or sod may be planted in the soil at intervals of 1 foot or more. The closer the sprigs or sod pieces are planted, the more rapidly will your lawn become established.

An even distribution of seed may be had by adding a quantity of dry soil or fertilizer to the seed for bulk. Sow one-half of the seed in one direction and the remainder of the seed at right angles.

Rake the soil lightly to cover the seed to a depth of one-fourth inch or less.

After planting a new lawn, you can reduce erosion and seed washing by a light application of straw, pine needles, bark, or other mulch material. Approximately 50 percent of the soil surface should be visible after applying a mulch. Mulch also creates a more favorable medium for germination of seeds.

Water the seeded area lightly two or three times daily until the seedlings become established.

Mulching materials need not be removed if you use them in moderate amounts and distribute them well.

Mow the lawn as soon as the grass reaches the recommended mowing height.

OFTEN it is more economical to improve an old lawn than to make a new one. If 40 to 50 percent of perennial grasses remain, it is possible to improve the lawn a great deal.

Steps to renovate a lawn are:

Apply herbicides according to manufacturers' directions to eradicate the weeds. Weed control should precede seeding by 2 or 3 weeks. Mow closely.

Rake up the clippings and other debris.

Apply 50 to 75 pounds per 1 thousand square feet of ground agricultural limestone if none was applied in the past 4 to 6 years.

Apply fertilizer of 10–6–4, 10–10–10, or similar analysis at the rate of 10 to 15 pounds per 1 thousand square feet.

Rake the bare areas to loosen the soil.

Seed, sprig, or sod perennial grasses in bare areas.

Water the seeded or sprigged areas lightly. Keep the soil moist until the grass is well established.

Continue mowing the lawn. (F. V. JUSKA AND A. A. HANSON)

Diseases

in Lawns

HEALTHY, vigorously growing, adapted lawn grasses that are properly managed can best survive attacks of diseases.

You should select grasses that are adapted to the soil, climate, and light conditions under which they will be grown.

Proper care does not prevent or cure diseases entirely, but it helps to curb them so that treatment with fungicides can be more effective.

Fungi cause most of the serious and widespread diseases of lawn grasses.

THE RELATED GROUP of fungi responsible for Helminthosporium leaf and crown disease attack most grasses except St. Augustine and centipede. Kentucky bluegrass may be severely damaged.

Symptoms of the disease are most conspicuous on leaves, but the pathogen, the disease-inciting organism, also attacks the sheath and crown and kills the plant. Leaf and stem spots usually are tan to reddish-brown or purplish-black and often have a brown to light-tan center.

Affected areas containing dead grass may be several inches to several feet in diameter and resemble drought injury.

Merion Kentucky bluegrass, Pennlawn red fescue, and the Tifton bermudagrass hybrids are moderately resistant to Helminthosporium diseases.

Mow upright-growing grasses to a height of 1½ to 2½ inches. Apply enough fertilizer to keep the grass thriving. Avoid overstimulation with nitrogen, especially in the spring. Remove clippings if growth is excessive.

Fungicide treatments help control Helminthosporium diseases. Do not use phenyl mercury formulations on Merion Kentucky bluegrass, because it is injured by the fungicide.

BROWN PATCH is prevalent in warm, humid regions. Practically all grasses are attacked by the causal fungus. The disease occurs during periods of warm, humid weather and is most damaging on heavily fertilized, succulent turf.

Brown patch develops in roughly circular areas, a few inches to several feet in diameter. The fungus threads (mycelium) frequently are observed as filmy, white tufts, while grass is wet with dew. As the leaves dry, the mycelium shrivels and becomes less conspicuous.

The fungus attacks so rapidly that grass leaves become infected and severely damaged almost overnight. Affected areas first appear darker gray-green; then they turn brown. If weather favorable for the development of brown patch lasts only a few days, just the leaves are infected, and the turf recovers in 2 or 3 weeks.

If the disease is severe and weather conditions remain favorable for disease development, the fungus attacks the crown and kills the plant. Dead grass blades generally remain erect and do not lie flat, as does grass killed by Pythium fungi.

To combat the disease, avoid excessive applications of nitrogen fertilizers. When watering is needed, water the turf early in the day to give grass leaves time to dry before evening. Remove excess clippings.

Apply recommended fungicides when symptoms of disease are first observed. Fungicides containing mercury should not be applied at rates higher than recommended because the turf may be injured. Apply fungicides during the coolest parts of the day.

THE DOLLAR SPOT fungus attacks most lawn grasses in the United States. It is particularly severe and conspicuous on bent, Kentucky blue, bermuda, and zoysia grasses.

Dollar spot is most prevalent and damaging in lawns of low fertility and during droughts.

The disease occurs as small, brown spots a few inches in diameter. The spots bleach to a light straw color and often merge to form large, irregular damaged areas. The affected grass dies, and the turf becomes pitted. Whitish lesions develop on individual grass blades at the margins of diseased areas.

Dollar spot can be controlled by treatment with fungicides and by applications of additional nitrogen.

OF THE LAWN GRASSES commonly grown, only ryegrass, bermuda, and Merion Kentucky blue are damaged seriously by attacks of rust fungi.

Symptoms are presence of yellow-orange or reddish-brown powdery pustules on leaf blades. When a white handkerchief is brushed across diseased leaves, the spores adhere and leave a yellow or orange stain.

Pure stands of susceptible grasses are especially prone to attack by rust fungi. Damage is reduced if mixtures of grass are seeded.

Merion Kentucky bluegrass should be seeded with common Kentucky bluegrass or with red fescue. Rust-resistant varieties of turf bermudas and annual ryegrass are available in the South. Common annual ryegrass used for winter lawns in the South is usually heavily infected and damaged by rust.

Maintain an adequate fertility level so that new leaf growth can be mowed often to remove developing rust pustules.

Treatment with fungicides reduces the incidence of rust but does not prevent infection on new leaf growth.

PYTHIUM DISEASES (grease spot, cottony blight) occur during periods of wet weather, especially on poorly drained areas, when temperatures exceed 70° F.

Young grass seedlings are most susceptible to attack by Pythium fungi, but older grass stands can be killed or damaged severely.

Affected areas may be a few inches to several feet in diameter. Damage sometimes occurs in streaks as though the fungus had spread from mowing or from waterflow following heavy rain. Diseased leaves appear water soaked, tend to mat together, and feel slimy. Cottony tufts of fungus mycelium develop on leaves if humidity is high.

The darkly discolored grass blades wither and rapidly turn reddish brown as they dry. Diseased grass usually dies within 24 to 48 hours. It lies flat on the ground rather than remaining upright.

Provide adequate drainage for low-lying places. Avoid excessive watering during hot weather. Avoid keeping the foliage and ground wet for long periods. Delay seeding until the weather is cooler and dryer.

Treatment with fungicides at the earliest sign of disease is helpful.

SNOW MOLD or winter scald is caused

by several different fungi. It is most severe in places where snow accumulates and covers grass for long periods. Grass that is growing actively when covered by lasting snow is especially susceptible to injury. Diseased grass is particularly noticeable at the thawing edge of a snowbank.

Snow mold also occurs in the absence of snow if the turf is excessively wet and the temperature is above freezing.

Patches of diseased grass, usually 1 to 12 inches or more in diameter, are a discolored dirty white, gray, or slightly pink. Diseased leaves bleach grayish tan and mat together.

One of the fungi that cause snow mold forms tiny, hard, brown to black fruiting bodies (sclerotia), which are embedded in diseased leaves and crowns.

Do not apply high nitrogen fertilizers late in the fall. Keep grass cut to prevent it from matting. Apply fungicides before lasting snow covers the grass.

MUSHROOMS that grow individually or in clumps in lawns usually develop from buried organic matter, such as pieces of construction lumber, logs, or tree stumps. Such mushrooms are harmless to grass. They usually develop following long periods of wet weather.

Most mushroom fruiting bodies disappear when the soil dries or after the grass has been mowed several times. Mushrooms that grow from buried lumber, logs, or stumps can be eliminated by digging up the buried wood. If this is impractical, drench the soil with a fungicide or treat the affected area as we recommend for the control of fairy rings.

FAIRY RINGS are distinct circles or arcs of stimulated grass surrounding areas of unthrifty or dead grass. The bands or arcs may be 1 or 2 feet to more than 100 feet in diameter.

The fungi that cause fairy rings grow outward from 5 to 24 inches annually, depending on growing conditions. During wet periods, usually in spring and fall, mushroomlike fruiting bodies of the causal fungi outline the circle or arc.

Fairy rings seldom occur in lawns that are adequately fertilized and treated with fungicides to control other diseases.

The simplest control measure is to punch holes 6 inches apart and about 12 inches deep in the ground within the affected area and about 2 feet beyond the visible outer edge. Fill each hole with a double-strength fungicide solution to which some detergent has been added.

FUNGI known as slime molds often cover grass blades with a dusty, bluish-gray, or yellow mass.

Slime molds do not parasitize the grass. They discolor grass blades and are unsightly when they occur in spots several feet in diameter.

Slime molds occur during wet weather. They disappear rapidly as soon as it becomes dry.

The slime mold masses can be destroyed by sweeping them with a broom or by spraying them with a strong stream of water.

Masses that persist can be eliminated by treating the affected areas with any good garden or turf fungicide.

NEMATODES are microscopic eelworms that feed on roots of lawn grass and other plants.

Most nematode injury occurs in the southern half of the United States. It is a serious problem.

The affected turf is generally unthrifty and has the appearance of suffering from drought or fertilizer deficiency. Plants are frequently off-color, and the turf thins out.

Affected turf may respond temporarily to increased applications of water or fertilizer, but the symptoms soon return.

The only effective control is treatment with a nematocide. (K. W. KREITLOW AND B. A. APP)

Insects

in Lawns

ALL OF THE LAWN GRASSES grown in the United States are susceptible to attack and damage by one or more of some 50 species of insects that we regard as important lawn pests.

Some of the insects live in the soil and feed on the roots. Some feed on the leaves or stems. Some suck juices from the plants.

Damage by most of these pests is not consistent enough to justify annual preventive treatment. It is important therefore to obtain early identification of any pest causing injury so that you can apply the proper insecticide before injury becomes extensive.

The most destructive soil-inhabiting insects that attack lawn grasses are the grubs that are the larvae of several species of beetles.

The grubs of different species generally look much alike. They are soft bodied, whitish, or grayish. They have brownish heads and brownish or blackish hind parts and usually lie in a curled position.

The grubs hatch from eggs deposited in the ground by the female beetles. Most of them spend about 10 months in the ground, although a few species may stay in the soil for 2 or 3 years. They feed on the roots about 1 inch below the surface of the soil.

Moles, birds, and skunks feed on grubs and often damage a lawn as they search for them.

Larvae of May beetles (or June beetles) are known as white grubs, of which there are more than 200 species in the United States.

The blackish or brownish adult beetles are common from May to mid-July. They feed on the foliage of plants and trees.

Grubs of the Japanese beetle cause extensive turf damage from North Carolina to New England. The adult is about one-half inch long. It has a shiny, metallic-green body with coppery-brown wings and six small patches of white hairs along each side and back of the body just under the edges of the wings.

Other important grubs that infest lawns are the larvae of the Asiatic garden beetle, the oriental beetle, and the European and masked chafers.

Several species of ants damage lawns mostly as a result of their nesting habits. Some ants form hills around the openings of their nests. Others, like the fire ants, build large mounds, which smother the grass. When ants build their nests near grass roots, they often destroy them.

Some species, such as fire ants and harvester ants, attack people. Their bite is painful.

Several other soil-infesting insects damage lawns. Mole crickets feed on the grass roots and may uproot seedlings. They are about 1.5 inches long and velvety brown. They have large, shovellike front legs.

Wireworms, certain bees and wasps, desert termites, and the larvae of billbugs frequently damage lawns.

THE WORST chewing insects that feed on leaves and stems of grass are the sod webworms, armyworms, and cutworms.

Sod webworms are the larvae of small, whitish or grayish moths or millers. Often they are called lawn moths. The moths fold their wings closely about their bodies when at rest. They fly over the grass in the evening and the females scatter their eggs over the lawns.

The larvae, on hatching, feed on the grass leaves. As they become larger they build silk-lined tunnels close to the soil surface, cut off blades of grass,

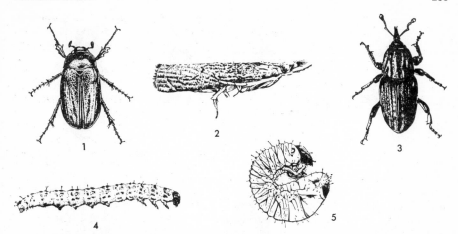

1. *Adult May beetle.*   2. *Adult sod webworm.*   3. *Adult billbug.*   4. *Larva of sod webworm.*
5. *A white grub, the larva of a May beetle.*

and drag them into the tunnels for food. The larvae attack many kinds of grasses, and damage is apt to be especially severe in new lawns.

Larvae of armyworms and fall armyworms are about 1.5 inches long when full grown. Their color is greenish to nearly black. The adults are brownish-gray moths that measure about 1.5 inches across the wings.

The fall armyworm overwinters only in extreme southern parts of the United States and migrates north each season. During heavy infestations, the larvae may devour the foliage down to the ground.

Cutworms are occasional pests that feed on the grass, cutting it off near the soil surface. They may damage new seedings severely.

INSECTS THAT SUCK the juices from lawn grasses include chinch bugs, scale insects, and leafhoppers.

Two species of chinch bug are major lawn pests. The adults are similar and are about one-sixth inch long and black with white markings. Newly hatched nymphs are bright red and have a white band across the back. They become darker as they mature.

The hairy chinch bug, *Blissus hirtus*, is important in the East from Virginia

into New England. Another species, *B. insularis*, is destructive in the South from Florida west to Texas, where it severely damages St. Augustine grass, occasionally injures centipedegrass, and rarely attacks bermudagrass and pasture grasses.

Plants infested by chinch bugs turn brown. The damage is usually seen in patches. In severe infestations, the grass is killed.

The rhodesgrass scale occurs in Texas, the Gulf States, and in Arizona, New Mexico, California, and Hawaii. These white, cottony-covered scale insects, about one-eighth inch long, attack the plant crowns and cause the plants to turn brown and die. This scale attacks bermudagrass and St. Augustine grass.

Other scales that may cause damage to lawns are the bermudagrass scale and ground pearls. Both cause irregular brown or dead spots and are especially important pests on lawn grasses in the South.

Leafhoppers of several species are sometimes numerous on lawns. They suck the sap from the grass leaves and stems and produce whitish looking patches. New lawns may be so extensively damaged that reseeding is sometimes necessary.

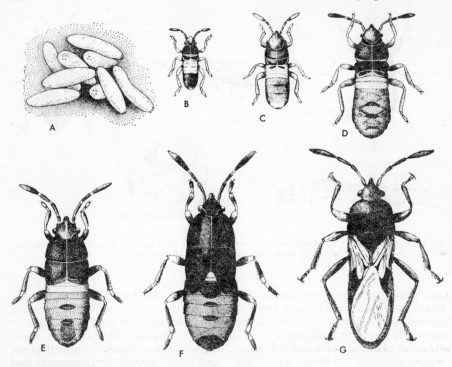

Chinch bug.   A. Eggs; B–F. Nymphs in different stages; G. Adult.

MOST LAWN INSECT PESTS can be controlled with insecticides.

An accompanying tabulation gives current recommendations for some of the important lawn pests. There are at present no satisfactory control methods for scale insects in lawns.

Insecticides are available in different formulations that contain varying amounts of the insecticide. The recommendations we give specify the amount of actual insecticide needed for control.

Most pesticides are poisonous. Be sure that pesticides are clearly labeled. Keep them away from children and pets.

Follow the directions on the container label and heed all precautions. Wear clean, dry clothing when you apply them. Avoid inhalation and skin contact. Keep pesticides away from the eyes, nose, and mouth. Wash thoroughly with soap and water immediately after you apply the pesticides.

Do not apply pesticides to a lawn when people or animals are on it. Do not allow pesticides to drift to an area where they might injure people and animals and contaminate food, feed, or water.

After a pesticide has been applied, do not permit children and pets on the lawn until the pesticide has been washed off by sprinkling and the grass has dried completely. To protect fish and wildlife, do not contaminate streams and lakes with pesticides.

The pesticides listed are solely for the purpose of providing specific information. Mention of a trade name does not constitute a warranty of the product named and does not signify that this product is approved to the exclusion of other comparable products. (K. W. KREITLOW AND B. A. APP)

PESTICIDES FOR CONTROLLING LAWN DISEASES AND INSECTS

Disease	Chemical	Ounces recommended per 1,000 sq. ft.	Where and when to apply
Helminthosporium leaf and crown disease.	Acti-dione-thiram.....	4..............	Spray lawn with fungicide when
	Captan..............	5–7.............	disease symptoms
	Dyrene..............	4–6.............	first appear and
	Ortho lawn and turf fungicide.	4–6.............	repeat at 7–14-day intervals as needed.
	PMA...............	1–2 of 10% soln.	
Brown patch.......	Mercury-containing fungicides.	Manufacturer's directions.	Do.
	Dyrene..............	4–6.............	Do.
	Ortho lawn and turf fungicide.	4–6.............	Do.
	Tersan OM..........	5..............	Do.
Dollar spot........	Cadmium-containing fungicides.	Manufacturer's directions.	Do.
	Dyrene..............	4–6.............	Do.
	Ortho lawn and turf fungicide.	4...............	Do.
	Tersan OM..........	5..............	Do.
Rusts.............	Acti-dione-thiram.....	4..............	Do.
	Zineb..............	2–4.............	Do.
Pythium diseases....	Dexon..............	2..............	Do.
	Zineb..............	2–4.............	Do.
Snow mold........	Dyrene..............	4–6.............	Treat before lasting snow.
	Mercury-containing fungicides.	Manufacturer's directions.	
	Ortho lawn and turf fungicide.	4..............	Do.
Mushrooms and fairy rings.	Mercury-containing fungicides.	Manufacturer's directions.	Treat affected areas only.
Slime molds........	Any good garden or turf fungicide.	....do..........	Do.
Nematode injury....	Nemagon............	....do..........	Drench with
	Fumazone...........	....do..........	nematocide when
	V–C 13.............	....do..........	soil temperature is at least 65° F.
Ants.............	Aldrin.............	1...............	To entire area or to
	Chlordane..........	4...............	individual nests.
	Dieldrin............	1...............	Sprinkle thoroughly
	Heptachlor.........	1...............	after application so insecticide reaches nests.
Armyworms........	Chlordane...........	2...............	As soon as infestation appears.
	Dieldrin............	1...............	
	Heptachlor.........	1...............	While worms are small.
Chinch bugs........	Chlordane...........	4...............	As soon as damage
	DDT...............	4...............	occurs. A second
	Diazinon...........	3...............	application may
	Dieldrin............	1...............	be needed in 7–10
	V–C 13.............	9...............	days.
Cutworms..........	Chlordane...........	2...............	In late afternoon.
	Dieldrin............	1...............	Do.
	Heptachlor.........	1...............	Do.
Grubs.............	Aldrin.............	1...............	When examination
	Chlordane..........	4...............	shows grubs are
	Dieldrin............	1...............	present. Usually
	Heptachlor.........	1...............	in early fall.
Sod webworms......	Aldrin.............	1...............	In late afternoon or
	Chlordane..........	2...............	evening. A second
	DDT...............	2...............	application may
	Dieldrin............	1...............	be necessary.
	Heptachlor.........	1...............	Do.
	Toxaphene..........	2...............	Do.

When You
Buy Seed

FEW PEOPLE buy a car solely on the basis of its appearance and price, but many buy lawn seed because its package is attractive and it seems cheap. Value in a car and value in seed are in performance.

All agricultural seed (farm, field, and lawn seed) if it moves in interstate commerce or is offered for sale within a State is required under Federal or State laws to be labeled with certain specific information for the purchaser's benefit.

In interstate commerce, the information includes the name of the kind or kind and variety; the percentages of pure seed, weed seed, inert matter, other crop seed, and germination; the date of the germination test; and the name and number of noxious-weed seeds.

A kind name, such as Kentucky bluegrass, is a general classification. A variety name, such as the Merion variety of Kentucky bluegrass as distinguished from the Park variety, is a subdivision of a kind that has one or more specific characteristics differing from other varieties within that kind.

Insofar as possible, you should buy seed by variety name.

Because different varieties may be better adapted for certain localities or may produce crops or lawns having certain desirable characteristics, the recommendations of county or State extension agents, colleges, or qualified seedsmen should be sought.

Once you have decided on the variety you want for a particular purpose, you have narrowed your choice considerably.

MANY OTHER important factors are given on a container of seed.

The percentage of pure seed is the percentage of weight of seed of the kind or the kind and variety named, exclusive of other kinds of crop seeds, inert matter (such as chaff, sticks, and dirt), and weed seeds. The percentages of these useless or contaminating materials in the seed also are stated.

Seldom is agricultural seed, particularly lawn seed, 100 percent pure. Most kinds cannot be produced economically with high percentages of pure seed. For example, Kentucky bluegrass can be produced under certain refined cultural conditions and processed to be 98 percent pure seed, but the seed that is harvested from natural growing fields and processed is usually sold as 80 or 85 percent pure seed.

The percentage of pure seed therefore must be related directly to price, or price has no meaning.

Besides the percentage of pure seed (which goes down as the percentage of other factors goes up), you must consider the percentage of weed seeds and the names and rates of occurrence of seed of noxious weeds. These may be present in such high percentages or rates that planting would require expensive chemical treatment to remove the weed infestation. Seeds of noxious weeds that are harmful and difficult to control may create weed problems in fields or lawns for years.

Related directly to the percentage of pure seed is the percentage of germination. This is the percentage of seeds that under favorable conditions can be expected to produce normal plants. If you buy seed that is 100 percent pure seed but germinates only 50 percent, you may just as well purchase seed with 50 percent pure seed and 100 percent germination. The same number of plants could be expected in each case.

This gives us a clue for determining

which package of the same kind of lawn seed is the best buy. If you plan to buy seed for your lawn, here is how to figure out the true value of two packages of the same kinds of seed.

Multiply the percentage of pure seed by the percentage of germination; then divide this result into the actual cost per pound, and compare.

Say your local store has one package of Kentucky bluegrass seed at 90 cents a pound, and the label indicates it has 85 percent pure seed and has a germination of 80 percent. Another package is a dollar a pound but has 98 percent pure seed and 85 percent germination.

	No. 1 Lowest quality 90¢ a pound	No. 2 Highest quality $1 a pound
Germination	80%	85%
Purity	85%	98%
Germination × purity	80×85	85×98
Pure-live seed . . .	68%	83%
Price divided by pure-live seed .	90¢ ÷ 0.68	$1 ÷ 0.83
Actual cost per pound of pure-live seed .	$1.32	$1.19

You find thus that the seed priced at 90 cents a pound has an actual cost of 1.32 dollars a pound of pure-live seed. The seed priced at a dollar a pound has an actual cost of 1.19 dollars a pound of pure-live seed. The percentage of weed seeds may be an overriding factor in deciding which package to purchase.

YOU SHOULD NOTICE the date of the germination test.

It is not absolute assurance that seed that once was high germinating seed is still high germinating. That depends on the kind of seed, the maturity and moisture content when the seed was harvested, and the temperature and relative humidity during storage of the seed.

Other conditions being equal, the seed most recently tested and truthfully labeled should be in the best condition.

State seed laws vary in their requirements for retesting seed offered for sale. The length of time seed may be

sold on the basis of a test may vary from 5 months in one of the Gulf States, where humidity and temperatures are high, to 18 months in a State in the cool Pacific Northwest.

Under most State laws, seed offered for sale must have a germination test date less than 9 months old.

Under Federal law, seed cannot legally be shipped interstate if the seed has not been tested for germination within 6 months.

Seed carried over on a dealer's shelf from one planting season to another in cloth or ordinary paper containers is suspect, even though in regions of low humidity or low temperatures the seed may retain relatively high viability for several years.

One State permits seed of low moisture content, when placed in approved containers, such as cans or specially constructed bags, to be sold for 3 years without retesting.

WHEN YOU BUY vegetable seeds in small amounts for the home garden, you are apt to find no helpful information as to quality on the packet except the name of the kind and variety of seed.

That is because under Federal law and under most State laws the seed need not be labeled to show germination quality if it meets a certain minimum standard of germination. If it is below that standard, it must be labeled to show the percentage of germination, the date of the germination test, and the words "Below Standard."

In purchasing above-standard vegetable seed, the purchaser must rely on the efficiency of seed enforcement officials who sample and test garden seed offered for sale to see if it is above standard. Some States have requirements for labeling such packets with the year for which the seed was packed to insure that the seed will not inadvertently remain on sale year after year and deteriorate in germination.

Vegetable seed generally consists of 100 percent pure seed and rarely contains weed seeds, inert matter, other crop seeds, or noxious-weed seed. Therefore, no requirements for labeling vegetable seed with these factors are considered necessary, and none is given on packets of the vegetable seed you buy.

Flower seeds are not regulated by Federal seed laws. Some States have laws regulating labeling of flower seed. In those cases, the requirements for labeling are similar to the requirements for labeling vegetable seed.

YOU MAY ASK, "Where is the best place to buy my seed when I plant a lawn or garden?"

The best guide is to buy from a reputable local firm, preferably a firm that specializes in selling seed. That is not always possible, however. You will have to assume that every container, regardless of who is selling it, is truthfully labeled in compliance with the seed laws.

When you suspect the seed does not comply with the seed laws, you should notify your State seed law enforcement agency. Through agreements between State and Federal seed enforcement agencies, violations of the Federal Seed Act are referred to the United States Department of Agriculture for investigation and action.

Federal and State seed laws protect the consumer from false statements in advertising and labeling. More than 400 State seed inspectors all over the United States obtain samples of seed on sale for testing to determine if it is correctly labeled. Seed firms are notified of violations, the seed is taken off sale and relabeled or destroyed, and the firms are subject to prosecution in Federal courts for interstate shipments found to be in violation of the Federal Seed Act.

The vast bulk of seed on the market is of high quality and is truthfully labeled. At the price, it is probably the best buy of any product purchased by the consumer on today's market, considering the wealth it produces in food and enjoyment. (S. F. ROLLIN)

Vegetable Gardens

I CAN GIVE four good reasons why a householder may want to devote some of his garden space and energy to growing vegetables.

The reasons: To save some money; to have a pleasant hobby; to enjoy the perfection of quality that is possible from one's own garden, without reference to cost; to get the satisfaction of digging and sweating and producing one of life's essentials for himself and his family.

Few gardeners would wish to devote all their space to vegetables at the expense of ornamentals, however, nor should they. Except in time of emergency, I believe, a generous share of garden space and effort should be devoted to ornamentals.

If soil, light, and climate are favorable, a few salad vegetables and greens may well be included in the general garden plan, and sometimes utilitarian plants, including vegetables, can be grown as "ornamentals." Runnerless strawberries, the French fraisiers de Bois, for example, make an attractive border. Small-fruited peppers, thyme and tarragon and other herbs, frilly lettuce or mustard, endive, carrots, red-leaved Swiss chard, and a few plants of parsley are at home among flowers.

ASSUME THAT, like most urban and suburban householders, you have but a very small plot (say, up to 400 or 500 square feet) that is suitable or that you wish to grow vegetables on. What should you grow?

First, choose a few kinds that require little space for growing the amounts you may want. Generally, under such conditions, you would not grow such things as pumpkins, melons, sweet corn, and potatoes.

Next, among the kinds that require little space, choose those you and your family enjoy most, especially those that produce a high dollar value per unit of land or that on the market may have disappointing quality.

Among the vegetables for use fresh, tomatoes probably are foremost. Other good fresh salad vegetables and greens are sweet peppers, tender varieties of lettuce, endive, green onions, radishes, spinach, turnip greens, mustard, collards or kale, and parsley and chives (a few plants of each). You may want a few plants of other herbs for flavoring soup and salads.

You may have no place available for vegetables but strips around boundaries or along walks in the backyard. You can grow tomatoes on stakes in the back of such narrow beds and have low-growing flowers on the sunny side of the rows, if you wish. Or low-growing vegetables can be grown on the sunny side, or very quick-growing early vegetables (such as green onions, radishes, and leaf lettuce) on either side of the row.

Cucumbers and pole beans can be trained up on the sunny side of a high wire fence. Low-growing vegetables or flowers can be planted to the sunny side of them. The few plants of parsley and flavoring herbs you need can be put at some inconspicuous place in a flower border or mass.

You can transplant a few parsley plants into big flower pots in the fall, trim them back close to the crown, and keep them in sunny windows in the house for continuing harvests of leaves during the winter.

Now SUPPOSE you have space for a small garden in a compact plot, say 1,200 to 1,500 square feet.

You could still use some of the devices I mentioned, if you wish, to save

space in this larger plot, in which you profitably could grow larger amounts of the several items.

Also, you would be justified in growing additional kinds, including some that require more space to produce significant amounts, or that have lower money value. Examples are cabbage, broccoli, bush squash, and snap beans.

In this larger plot, if you like them, grow bush snap beans; such root crops as beets, carrots, and turnips; and cabbage, broccoli, cucumbers, eggplant, leeks, onions, bush squash, and others described in Home and Garden Bulletin No. 9, "Suburban and Farm Vegetable Gardens."

The principles are the same for growing on the very small scale mentioned in preceding paragraphs as for growing on a larger scale. On very small areas you grow only a few plants, usually of small-growing kinds.

I do not recommend growing sweet corn, melons, potatoes, and sweet-potatoes in a garden of 1,500 square feet. If, however, you prefer to use the space for such items, and sacrifice something else, go ahead and do it. After all, tastes and desires differ. Keep in mind, however, that the items I just named take a lot of space and may crowd you out of growing small amounts of many other desirable things.

If you have a garden area approaching one-fourth acre (say, 10 thousand square feet) with ample water, you can grow all the fresh vegetables an average family needs during the growing season and probably more.

A half acre of good soil in a good climate can produce all the fresh vegetables a large family needs with considerable quantities for canning and freezing. Do not, however, grow such quantities for your own use unless you have ample help and facilities for processing and for proper storage of root and tuber crops. See Home and Garden Bulletin No. 9, "Suburban and Farm Vegetable Gardens." It contains tables for planting according to season and information on seed requirements, spacing, and the planting depths.

Do NOT PLANT more of one thing at one time than you can enjoy using before it is past the proper harvest stage. Planting too much at once is a common error of the beginner. You learn by experience how much is enough for your needs.

Remember that a single planting of many vegetables is "good" for harvest for very few days. You can use but little from some plantings before the product becomes poor in quality or useless.

For example, radishes are ready to harvest in 3 to 4 weeks from planting and are "good" hardly a week. Sow only 3 or 4 feet of row per person who will eat them, every 5 to 7 days up to early summer.

Many new varieties of snap beans tend to bear for only a short season, but they produce an abundance of pods of high quality. At first, plant 5 to 10 feet of row per person about every 2 weeks for as long as you want fresh beans and there is time to grow them before frost. If you want a big yield at one time for canning or freezing, plant more, but do not overdo it. A good crop of Tendercrop, for example, will yield a bushel (32 pounds) or more per 100 feet of row, of which about half can be obtained at the first harvest.

A half-dozen plants of one variety of cabbage is enough for the average family to plant at one time if it is to be used fresh. Plant a half-dozen plants of each of three or four varieties that will reach harvest over a period of weeks, if you want cabbage over a period of weeks.

If you grow spinach and peas, do not try to get a spread of harvests by successive plantings in the spring. These plants are very sensitive to hot weather. They must be planted very early. Delayed planting causes serious reduction in yield and quality. Get some spread of harvest by planting varieties that have different times of maturity.

Many other vegetables are sensitive to hot weather. Study the planting timetables and get your local recommendations.

If you have a large enough garden for supplying sweet corn from successive harvests, plant 3 or 4 short sections of rows side by side at intervals of 5 to 7 days. When plants of one planting date stand close together in short multiple rows, pollination often is better than if the plants are in a single long row. Plant at one time no more than you will use in 3 or 4 days. One planting of a single kind yields ears of good quality for only 2 or 3 days. Mixed seed of two hybrids that mature 2 days apart gives a better spread of harvest from a single planting date than does seed of a single hybrid.

Six tomato plants of indeterminate habit (not "self-topping") and medium or later maturity can supply enough fresh tomatoes for one person. Plant a few plants of one of the very early small-vined varieties to harvest before the later varieties start ripening. A half dozen to a dozen sweet pepper plants can supply enough peppers for salads and an occasional cooked dish, for the average family, for the season.

Here is a rough and conservative estimate of the yield to be expected from 50 feet of row—not that 50 feet is the amount you necessarily should plant:

Asparagus, 13 pounds; shelled lima beans, 7; snap bush beans, 12; beets, 40; sprouting broccoli, 17; cabbage, 62; cantaloups, 76; carrots, 38; sweet corn, 22; slicing cucumbers, 55; eggplant, 47; escarole, 30; kale, 17; lettuce, 29; mature onions, 40; green shelled peas, 4; green peppers, 50; potatoes, 67; spinach, 13; sweetpotatoes, 25; tomatoes, 79; watermelons, 83.

You may want more, or less, or none of these. The figures are based in part on the average yields per acre of the several crops as grown commercially in this country. Good yields by good gardeners may be two to three times as much. Some may be less.

Again, you will have to learn from your neighbors and from experience what yields you can expect from your various crops; assuming you have enough space, how much you need to plant at one time and in one season to satisfy your requirements; or, conversely, what you can expect to produce on a small space available to you.

HERE ARE SOME TIPS on management.

Protect your soil. Loose, dry, bare soil can blow away in a high wind. Newly planted seeds and very small plants can be blown out of such soil, and small plants can be damaged by blowing particles or covered by them.

Try to keep the soil moist, covered with plants or mulch, or protected by windbreaks to keep it from blowing. Leaving the surface between the rows a bit rough and trashy with organic matter will help.

Sloping soil can be washed away easily by rainstorms or runoff from rapidly melting snow. Do not let that happen. Keep the surface covered with plants or mulch to retard runoff.

Work organic matter into the soil to increase penetration of water. Run the rows on the level instead of up and down the slope, even if you have to curve the rows to do so.

Do not let water from higher ground flood across your garden. Divert it into drainways where it will do no harm.

Keep your garden space at work for you throughout the season.

Plan your plantings, if possible, so that as soon as one crop is all harvested you can plant another in its place. Quick-growing crops should be planted together so that after harvest, convenient space for others is available.

It is often feasible to plant small, quick-maturing things between the rows of large, slow-growing ones (or close to one side) and harvest the quick-maturing things before there is any serious interference.

Sometimes, after a rather long-growing, spring-planted crop you will have

time to plant a quick-growing crop for autumn harvest.

Do not overlook possibilities of late summer or early fall plantings for harvest in autumn, and (in the South) during the winter.

Study the planting tables in Home and Garden Bulletin No. 9 to see what you can develop for your garden.

Remember to watch for the first signs of plant diseases and insect infestation. Home and Garden Bulletin No. 46, "Insects and Diseases of Vegetables in the Home Garden," will tell you how to guard against them and to fight them if they appear.

The Department of Agriculture does not have vegetable or flower seeds for distribution free or for sale.

Thousands of retail seed, hardware, and general stores all over the country sell seeds, plants, tools, fertilizers, pesticides, and other garden supplies.

For local sources, consult your neighbors, the classified section of your telephone directory, or your agricultural adviser.

Hundreds of firms also sell all these items by mail. They may be located through advertisements in garden magazines and the garden pages of newspapers and through neighbors or agricultural advisers.

Some free publications of the United States Department of Agriculture of interest to home gardeners are:

"Electric Heating of Hotbeds." Leaflet No. 445

"Insects and Diseases of Vegetables in the Home Garden." Home and Garden Bulletin No. 46

"Salt Tolerance of Vegetables in the West." Agriculture Information Bulletin No. 205

"Storage of Vegetable Seeds." Leaflet No. 220

"Suburban and Farm Vegetable Gardens." Home and Garden Bulletin No. 9.

Most States issue publications on home vegetable gardening that are designed for the prevailing soil and climatic conditions of the respective States. (VICTOR R. BOSWELL)

Flowerbeds

PUT A FLOWERBED in the right place, choose plants of good colors, and give it and them the care they deserve, and you have a thing of beauty and a joy forever, wherever you are and however small the space you can use for flowers.

First, choose a site where the garden will complement the general landscape effect.

It may be a border along the side or across the back of a property line, along a driveway or in a triangle at a corner of the property, in an ell between house and garage, along a walk or path, or just a spot directly opposite a picture window, terrace, or patio.

It may even be confined to large planters, strategically placed and massed with cascading petunias.

A circular bed in the middle of a lawn panel is rarely, if ever, good.

Your time and energy for maintenance should dictate its size. Better to have a small, neat, well-cared-for garden than a long, rambling border that you must always apologize for.

THE SECOND STEP is to select the plants that are appropriate for the place.

The amount of sun or shade, the nature of the soil (heavy clay, loam, or light sandy soil), drainage, and existing windbreaks or shrub borders are some of the determining factors.

If the spot is next to a terrace or patio, you may choose low-growing plants, many in the white-yellow range to pick up the highlights of early evening hours.

If the garden is in front of a high hedge at the back of a property, taller plants, bolder in their effect, would predominate.

Problems of steep changes in grade sometimes are solved by making a rock garden on the slope or by constructing a dry rock wall, in which low-growing, rock-garden types of plants are set in the spaces between the rocks.

For the average flower garden, a border about 6 feet wide permits a variety of plants. The tallest plants are put in the background, the intermediate ones go in the middle area, and the lowest plants grow in the foreground.

FLOWERBEDS may contain only annuals (which live only one season) or only perennials (which live over more than one winter), but it may be well to have some of each.

If you have a newly built home, you may wish to concentrate on annuals for immediate effect the first year and gradually add perennials for more permanent plantings.

Regardless of the type of plant material, the best effect is usually created by massing. Avoid a single row of zinnias spaced 18 inches apart. Instead, plant them 12 inches apart in groups. A thin line of dwarf marigolds is pathetic, but the same number of plants grouped together is effective.

For most perennials, a clump of three is a minimum. If space permits, five or six may be better.

Large specimen plants, such as peonies, hostas, and oriental poppies, need not be set in groups but are better spaced throughout the planting.

Solid plantings of a single genus of perennials, such as peonies or iris or oriental poppies, usually are to be avoided because before and after their burst of bloom there is nothing but foliage, but you can relieve the monotony of such a planting by adding annuals for all-season color.

Roses should be segregated in an area by themselves. They lose much of their effectiveness if they are planted among annuals and perennials.

The smaller the garden, the greater is the need to choose plants that are in flower for a long time in order to have continuous color.

Among the perennials in this classification are golden marguerite (Anthemis), coreopsis, gaillardia, coralbells (Heuchera), *Campanula carpatica*, Shasta daisies, summer flowering phlox, and the tufted pansy (*Viola cornuta*).

As you enlarge the bed, you can add plants with a shorter period of bloom.

If you are away all summer, perhaps a combination of spring flowering bulbs and chrysanthemums or hardy asters that bloom in the fall may suffice. Otherwise, select the plants that will give you the most color throughout the growing season.

To insure a succession of bloom from early spring to late fall, the backbone of many gardens over much of this country, in order of bloom, consists of spring flowering bulbs, such as narcissus and tulips, and these perennials: Iris, peonies, summer flowering phlox, and chrysanthemums or hardy asters. To this skeleton, annuals, biennials, additional spring and summer flowering bulbs, and other perennials could be added.

The chief purpose of the spring-flowering bulbs, such as crocus, narcissus, hyacinths, and tulips, is to extend the period of bloom of a garden, as most of them provide a striking mass of early color.

They are a versatile group and are satisfactory in borders, along walks, around pools, and in front of foundation plantings or shrub borders. They may be spotted in groups throughout perennial beds. Many, except hyacinths and tulips, can be naturalized.

Many of the dwarf and miniature bulbs also are appropriate for rock gardens.

If you plant solid beds of bulbs for mass effect in the spring, you can use annuals in the same bed for color during the rest of the season without disturbing the bulbs.

Summer flowering bulbs, such as lilies, are specimen plants that enhance any planting. The common species

combined with new hybrids make it possible to have one lily or another in flower from early summer until late frosts. Their many colors, heights, flower forms, and season of bloom can improve every garden.

Tender bulbous material, such as tigridias, acidantheras, and gladiolus, and tuberous material, such as dahlias and tuberous begonias, require more care, because they must be dug and stored yearly. Gladioli often are lined out in rows in a separate area, as they do not usually blend in with a miscellaneous planting. The others can be included in a general flowerbed.

ANNUALS, which are grown each year from seed or cuttings to produce a good show of color during the current season, provide the quickest results, are relatively inexpensive, and present few cultural difficulties.

They can be planted directly over beds of spring flowering bulbs. Many are useful in planters or window boxes.

Annual vines offer many possibilities for screen plantings.

Because of their transient nature, annuals provide versatility for temporary gardens. They enable you to correct any mistakes in design, color combination, or placement because of habit or height the following year.

SEEDS of most annuals can be sown directly in the garden, but quicker and better results are achieved if you set out plants started by amateur or professional growers in frames or greenhouses. The plants often are in bud or in flower when they are set out after danger of frosts and give an immediate effect.

Petunias, zinnias, dwarf marigolds, and ageratum are among the annuals that provide colorful plants all season.

Lobelia, impatiens, and bedding begonias are excellent choices for shaded areas. Portulaca requires full sun.

If you are interested in color but not flowers, many plants, which are treated as annuals, have variegated or multicolored foliage. Among them are coleus, variegated geraniums, purple leaf basil, alternantheras, bloodleaf, and (in the tender bulbous group) caladiums.

Taller annuals, such as cleome, cosmos, some sunflowers, and gloriosa daisies, add interest as background.

PERENNIALS provide the greatest range of material. For any given location, very likely you will find some perennials that are appropriate.

They range in height from creeping bugleweed (Ajuga) and the six-inch crested iris to towering monkshood (Aconitum) and foxtail lilies (Eremurus). Some, like the vertical foxgloves and delphiniums, are erect. Some are an airy mass, like babysbreath (Gypsophila) and sea-lavender (Limonium). Candytuft (Iberis) is low, compact, and moundlike.

Gardeners interested in texture may choose among the coarse-leaved hostas, the delicate foliage of blue flax (Linum), the huge, coarse flowers of hibiscus, and delicate columbines.

Adaptability to various locations recommends primulas, monardas, bleedingheart, and hostas for the shade; rudbeckias, helianthus, and heliopsis for the sun; cardinal flower (Lobelia), for the wet area; artemisias where it is dry; and german iris and dianthus where the soil is somewhat alkaline.

Lythrums, hemerocallis, and spiderworts seemingly do well anyplace.

The Christmas rose (Helleborus) flowers under the snow. Leopardsbane (Doronicum) blooms before the tulips fade, and the last chrysanthemum flowers will be finished off by late frosts.

Because most species of perennials are in bloom about a month, you should have a variety of material to obtain a sequence of bloom if you use only perennials. Some species have early- and late-flowering varieties that can be combined to extend the flower interest of any one type.

Some genera, such as the hostas and veronicas, contain some species that flower early in the season, others at midseason, and still others that are late flowering.

Hemerocallis (daylilies) comprise an almost foolproof group. They do well in almost any situation and require practically no maintenance. A selection of varieties makes it possible to have one or another in bloom at any time of the season. Their colors range through the various shades and tints of cream, yellow, orange, and red and maroon.

BIENNIALS are grown from seed, produce a rosette of leaves the first year, flower the second year, and are then discarded. Among the commoner ones are sweet-william, hollyhock, foxglove, and Canterbury-bells. They may selfsow in the garden, but the seedlings that result often revert to ordinary or undesirable colors. It is recommended therefore that you buy new seed regularly.

As TO COLOR in the garden, the important point is that you have what you enjoy.

You may prefer a riot of color and find bright, clashing colors stimulating. Or you may want only pale pastels in your garden. Again, you may like, as many do, a garden with all flowers of one color—white, for example, or blue. Have what you like. If you tire of it, change.

Temperature, humidity, amount of rainfall, soils, and length of growing season vary so greatly over the United States that no blanket recommendations can be given for the selection of plants. It is not hard for you to get lists and suggestions applicable to your locality, though—from your neighbors who garden, nearby nurserymen, county extension workers, and books.

Remember this: A flower garden is a dynamic project. It is never static. Over the years, you change what you do not like, eliminate some, add new types or varieties, and try different combinations. That is one reason that gardening is a continually engrossing hobby, a joy for all. (R. E. LEE)

Pests Among Flowers

PREVENTION is a watchword for the flower garden. Keep the plants growing vigorously, and you will have fewer troubles with pests and diseases.

Too much fertilization, which seems commoner than underfertilization, often kills or injures plants and makes them more susceptible to diseases and pests.

Too much of one fertilizer element can cause an imbalance of another element and produce a yellowing of leaves and other symptoms.

Too little fertilizer may produce stunted, unhealthy plants.

Deep cultivation and too much mulch (leaves, compost, peat moss) can be detrimental, particularly to such shallow-rooted plants as azaleas. Injury caused by careless cultivation to roots, the crown, and stem offers points for disease organisms to enter the plant.

When you select plants, consider their needs for moisture, temperature, shade, soil acidity, and other environmental factors.

Leaf spot organisms, crown-attacking fungi, and flower-blighting organisms may attack plants spaced so closely that air circulation around them is poor. You can reduce the chances of pests and diseases if you keep weeds in check, for weeds may cause crowding, harbor disease organisms and pests, and compete with other plants for water and nutrients.

Another way to keep disease organisms and pests out is to select healthy plants, seeds, and bulbs or treat them to eliminate the disease organism or pest before you plant. Preventing entry into a garden often is easier than other control measures.

Buy plant materials from reputable dealers.

Avoid plants that show root-knot nematode galls or root decay.

Propagators control geranium bacterial stem rot by establishing disease-free mother blocks to obtain healthy stock.

Dusting seeds lightly before planting with a fungicide, such as thiram, ferbam, or captan, eliminates many seed-rotting or damping-off organisms.

Lily bulbs are dipped with ferbam plus pentachloronitrobenzene to reduce bulb and root rots.

Many disease organisms and nematodes enter the garden in infested soils. The camellia flower blight fungus may be brought into a blight-free garden in the soil ball, which harbors the resting stage of the fungus, or on flowers.

DISEASE ORGANISMS and pests that do become established despite your careful management should be eradicated.

Often it is advisable to remove and destroy the plants or plant parts that are affected by such diseases as root-knot, lily fleck, aster wilt, and southern blight.

The spread of aster wilt and southern blight and other diseases involving damping off, crown and root rots, and stem cankers can be reduced by removing the affected plants and drenching the place they grew. A general-purpose drench consists of captan plus either thiram or pentachloronitrobenzene (1 tablespoonful of each per gallon of water). Apply it at the rate of one-half gallon per square foot.

The removal of cankers on trees or shrubs also may be advisable to prevent infection in the other parts. Make the cut into healthy wood and, as in normal pruning, make it flush against a larger limb or just above a leafbud to induce faster healing. On larger cuts, use a wound dressing, which you can buy at seedstores.

Destroy the diseased plants or plant parts you remove and weeds that can harbor pests. Camellia flower blight often is reduced in severity by destroying old flowers. Powdery mildews and a few other diseases can be eradicated by spraying or dusting with recommended fungicides.

Rotation is another aspect of prevention. Move your planting area after 3 or 4 years. Thereby you can aid in control of some soilborne diseases and pests, as wilts, crown rots, and root rots. Some rotation can be practiced even in a small flower garden.

The soil in which plants are to be grown can be treated to reduce or eliminate soilborne organisms.

You can do this in the seed flat by baking moist (but not wet) soil in an oven until a potato placed in the soil is cooked.

For a larger area, methyl bromide (1 to 3 pounds per 100 square feet) may be released under a plastic covering. The soil should be loose, with enough moisture for seed germination and above 50° F.

Other general-purpose fumigants you can use without a plastic covering are formulations of dichloropropene-dichloropropane mixture plus methyl isothiocyanate (DD+MENCS) or sodium methyl dithiocarbamate.

To control nematodes, products containing ethylene dibromide (EDB), dichloropropene-dichloropropane (DD), dibromochloropropane (DBCP), or other recommended materials can be used as preplanting treatments.

The manufacturers' directions should be followed carefully. Be careful lest these poisons harm or kill people, pets, trees, shrubs, and other plants that have roots in or near the treated area.

Allow ample time for the fumigant to dissipate from the soil before you plant it.

Another nematocide that can be used directly around many plants is dibromochloropropane (DBCP).

PROTECTIVE BARRIERS placed between the susceptible plant part and the attacking disease organism or pest are helpful. Usually they are chemical sprays or dusts. To be effective for disease control, the sprays and dusts must be applied before the disease appears or before it becomes well established.

Insect pests can be killed by an insecticide after the pests attack the plant, but by then they may have disfigured the plant.

Insecticides, which kill by contact or upon being eaten, should be applied when they will be on the plant for at least several hours.

Sprays or dusts for control of disease are more effective when applied before rains, heavy dews, fogs, or watering because infection occurs when moisture is present or the humidity is high. Thus a spray or dust applied after a rainy period to control black spot of roses may be too late to prevent some infection.

For black spot and many other diseases for which sprays or dusts are used, repeated applications are necessary. The interval depends on the life cycle of the organism, the weather, and sometimes the plant. Applications of zineb or thiram, for example, to control azalea petal blight should be made two or three times a week (rather than once a week), while new flowers are opening and developing to the susceptible stage.

Some systemic insecticides, as demeton, schradan, and phorate, which plants absorb, kill many sucking insects when the insects suck the toxic agent from the plant. Liquid forms for foliage application and granular forms for soil application are available. Growers of Easter lily bulbs have used systemic insecticides to control aphids capable of carrying viruses that cause fleck disease by soaking the bulbs before planting, spraying the plant, or applying to the soil. These insecticides can be absorbed through the skin of humans, so all precautions must be taken when you handle them.

Apply sprays uniformly as a fine mist from the top of the plant down and from the bottom up until the spray just begins to run off the foliage. Keep the spray nozzle moving. The sprayer, unless it has a mechanical agitator, should be shaken often to prevent settling of the chemical.

Dusts should be forced through the foliage to give an even, light coating to both leaf surfaces. Apply them when the air is still, preferably early in the morning or at dusk.

Either dusts or sprays can be used satisfactorily in the flower garden.

Dusts are usually more expensive, but the dusters cost less than comparable sprayers and are more convenient and easier to use.

Sprays are less difficult to handle in windy weather.

Plunger-type dusters are the smallest kind and can do a fair job for a few plants. A small bellows or rotary fan duster will give better coverage for a small garden. Larger rotary dusters and power dusters can be used on larger gardens for better distribution.

Household sprayers that hold up to 4 quarts can do a reasonably good job of spraying if they deliver a continuous fine spray or mist.

Compressed-air sprayers that hold 1 to 5 gallons are satisfactory for garden use. Larger sprayers with a continuously operated hand or motor pump are needed in larger gardens.

Clean sprayers thoroughly after use and allow them to dry.

Ready-to-use sprays in pressurized cans are useful on house plants or a few plants in a garden. They may be expensive.

You may like the hose-proportioner sprayers, in which the chemical is placed in a jar and mixed with the water at the hose nozzle. They are convenient, but more chemical is used than with a conventional sprayer, and the proportioners vary in distribution of spray material.

AVAILABLE general-purpose sprays or dusts will eliminate the need for mixing several control materials. Better, cheaper results can usually be had by using a material specifically recommended for a particular disease or pest. Recommendations should be followed closely in all cases.

CHOOSE, whenever possible, varieties that withstand a disease. Examples are rust-resistant snapdragons, wilt-resistant asters, and wilt-resistant mimosas.

Resistance does not always mean that the disease will not develop. Sometimes it does develop, frequently because the disease organisms also have many varieties or strains, and a plant resistant to one disease strain may fall prey to another. (D. L. GILL)

For Shade;
for Sun

GARDENS may be sunny or shady, but even the sunniest will have a few places where taller plants or the house cast shade for part of the day. The shadiest usually has some sunny corners or clearings.

Showy and attractive gardens can be developed in either situation, but the more interesting gardens are likely to be those in which shade and shade-loving plants are used as a restful foil to the heat and brilliance of the sun-drenched places.

The attainable balance between sun and shade is regulated by the garden site and the owner's needs and wishes: He can cut trees and shrubbery when they are overly crowded. He also can plant them. Seldom does an owner have a situation (for example, where land slopes are such that shade cannot be avoided or where planting soil is lacking) in which he cannot achieve a balance.

The adaptability of plants in their many kinds to conditions of full sun, full shade, or part shade, is remarkable. In their wild state they have come from the high light conditions of the desert, from the prairie and open meadows, from the partial shade of the ravine or open woodland, and from the denser shade of the thick-canopy forest.

Moreover, their liking for the conditions of their wild state to a large extent are inherited and persistent.

Most trees and shrubs of the garden are sunlovers. So are most vegetables and most of the showier annuals and herbaceous perennials, such as marigolds, zinnias, herbaceous peonies, and daylilies. Although a lesser number require or tolerate shade for at least part of the day, fewer still may require or tolerate conditions of relatively constant shade. Few indeed will succeed under the difficult conditions of constant, dense shade.

Conditions of partial or light shade may be found near the house, beneath such sparsely leaved trees as the honeylocust, or in woodlands where the trees are scattered and high branched. Many shade-tolerant shrubs and smaller plants can be grown in such places.

A denser tree pattern and lower branching excludes more sunlight and permits the growth of fewer kinds of plants.

An extreme situation is the constant, dense shade of low-branching evergreen trees. There, plantings have to be limited to the most shade-tolerant kinds of all—the delicate woodsorrel, wintergreen, English ivy, Canada mayflower, partridge-berry, and a few of the ferns.

Remember, however, that shade usually is not constant throughout the year. The angle of the sun varies, and many wildflowers and such bulbs as scillas, grape hyacinths, and daffodils will grow in deciduous woodland and virtually complete their flowering cycle before the overhead shade canopy becomes dense.

Each plant has its particular preference for full sun or for part or denser shade and will remain true to this preference. In too dense shade, sun-loving plants fail to grow normally. Their foliage becomes thin and susceptible to disease. Their branches become spindly. Their flowers are sparse or offcolor.

Set in full sun, a shade-loving plant may become poor and stunted, if indeed it succeeds at all.

A second factor, soil moisture, bears close relationship to the shady and sunny situation. Certain soils or sites may be inherently dry. Dryness in shade usually is the result of the root competition of the trees.

A shady, root-infested soil may be difficult to cope with unless the plants used are drought-tolerant as well as shade-tolerant (pachysandra and periwinkle are among the best) or unless the worst of the surface tree roots are removed with a spade and ax before planting. Under oaks and tulip poplars, such efforts may provide root freedom for some time, but under maples and elms the roots will return within a few months.

By the nature of their origins, most shade-tolerant plants thrive on an abundance of soil organic matter. The incorporation of peat moss, decayed leaves, pine needles, and the like fills this need and also provides a desirable increase in both the air- and water-holding capacity of the soil.

Just as root competition and soil moisture are complicating factors in shady gardening, so may the driest situations in full sun be the most difficult.

In climates of normal rainfall, soil dryness in open areas may be a product either of the soil or the site. Shallow coverings over rock and open, sandy soils tend to warm and dry rapidly, but a clay bank facing full south or west can also suffer from summer drought.

Because so many plants either need sun or tolerate it, we concentrate our attention on plants that are especially useful for covering and decorating dry banks, shallow soils, and other tough, dry, sunny situations.

IN LIGHT or partial shade, in the shade of scattered, high-branched trees, against buildings where the sun penetrates for at least part of the day, or in similar situations, a comparatively wide variety of plants can be grown satisfactorily.

Among evergreen trees, the hemlock is perhaps the best. Arborvitae can be satisfactory with fair sunlight if the soil is not too dry. Suitable smaller trees include dogwood, both eastern and western, shadbush, sorrel tree, sweetbay magnolia, American and English hollies, and the Florida *Illicium anisatum* and the species of *Podocarpus* in warmer areas.

Adaptable shrubs for shade include such natives as spicebush, the maple-leaved and arrow-wood viburnums, sweet pepper bush, oak-leaved hydrangea, inkberry (*Ilex glabra*), and native andromeda (*Pieris floribunda*). Good also are Japanese andromeda, Japanese holly, the boxwoods, the Oregon grapes (*Mahonia aquifolium, repens,* and *nervosa*), kerria, Morrow honeysuckle, and many of the privets, the deciduous ones in the North, and the more evergreen forms in the Southern States. For the milder sections, the Indian hawthorn (*Raphiolepis*), banana-shrub, pittosporum, and the Turks-cap (*Malvaviscus*) can be added.

Where soils are acid, as in the coastal States of the East and the Pacific Northwest, some of the showiest of all shrubs—the azaleas, rhododendrons, mountain laurel, and camellias—are admirably adapted to conditions of light or high shade. Such plants will grow in relatively heavy shade.

We like them for their flowers, however, and for flower production, an hour or two of sunlight a day is essential for most kinds.

Many varieties of leaf-shedding azaleas are adapted to northern cultivation, both in native species and in garden hybrids. Evergreen Kurume,

Kaempferi, and Glenn Dale forms do well south of Philadelphia. The Indian hybrids are suited to the Gulf States and California.

Hybrid rhododendrons will need to be selected for recommended climatic performance, as also will camellias. Some varieties of both the Japanese and sasanqua camellias perform well in Washington, D.C., and the State of Washington, but others need the milder climates of the South.

Some of the most famous display gardens of this country are the shady azalea-camellia gardens of the Southeastern States and California.

Shrubs and trees may form the upper story, but no part-shady garden can be complete without an interesting ground pattern.

To provide that pattern of flower and foliage, a long list of plants can be suggested. The following are perhaps among the best:

For taller effect, the white spikes of snakeroot (*Cimicifuga*), the multi-colored lilies and columbine;

For lower flowering, bleedingheart, wild hepatica, blue phlox (*Phlox divaricata*), trillium, violets, Virginia bluebell, foamflower, wild cranesbill (*Geranium maculatum*), beebalm, lily-of-the-valley, Aarons-beard (*Hypericum calycinum*), forget-me-nots, and bugleweed (*Ajuga*);

For foliage effects, meadowrue (*Thaltcirum*), wintergreen, wildginger, barrenwort (*Epimedium*), wintercreeper (*Euonymus fortunei radicans*), mayapple, many ferns, and, in warmer areas, lily turf, *Begonia evansiana*, selaginella, and aspidistra.

But bulbs, besides lilies, should not be forgotten. Many daffodils and narcissi will do well with sufficient early-season sunlight, as also the Spanish and Scotch bluebells, the small chionodoxas, grape hyacinths, crocus, snowdrops, and snowflakes, which are so well adapted for quantity planting in drifts and clusters.

Should vines be needed as wall cover or for smothering old stumps or trees, English ivy, climbing euonymus, Dutchmans-pipe, Virginia-creeper, and several of the clematis are all shade tolerant.

Clematis jackmani and other large-flowered hybrids are capable of good performance on a north-facing wall. The heavier shade of closely spaced buildings or of a lower or denser tree canopy quite rapidly reduces the inventory of potentially useful plants. Many of those I mentioned will still grow, but not quite so thriftily, and the flowering kinds will not be so showy. Among woody plants, mountain laurel will still provide good foliage, whether or not its flowers become rather sparse. Rosebay rhododendron (*Rhododendron maximum*) must substitute for the showier hybrids. Ground hemlock (*Taxus canadensis*) is good for dense, deep green cover, as well as *Leucothoe catesbaei*, which is actually tolerant of a broad range of sunlight and deep shade conditions.

Japanese spurge (*Pachysandra*), periwinkle (*Vinca*), and English ivy will continue to perform as ground covers.

Ferns come very much into their own, especially the maidenhair, sensitive, ostrich, cinnamon, New York, and beech ferns for moister situations, and Christmas, hayscented, polypody, and the spleenworts where the soil may be relatively dry.

More conspicuous for their flowers or berries are a number of small plants that come largely from our own woodlands. Trillium should still give returns, and the wood anemones, as well as dwarf iris (*Iris cristata*), goldthread (*Coptis*), Solomons-seal, galax, bunchberry (*Cornus canadensis*), Canada mayflower, herb Robert (*Geranium robertianum*), partridge-berry, pipsissewa, and wintergreen.

ON SOUTH-FACING banks or in any situation conspicuously hot or well drained and dry, the depth and kind of soil will serve as part determiner of the adaptable plant cover.

Sedums and ground phlox can grow in shallow soils on rocks, but most woody plants will need a deeper root run. Whatever plants are chosen, the soil should be predug and improved as much as possible. Poor and untreated soil adds to the drought problem.

Where a shrubby effect is desirable, coralberry is a hardy plant for tough situations. For midsouthern to southern climatic areas, the firethorns are useful for plantings of 2 to 8 feet in height, according to variety.

In similar regions the brooms (*Cytisus*) succeed in sandier soils, and in California the species of sun roses or *Cistus*. Hardy dwarf rockspray (*Cotoneaster horizontalis*) withstands much drought when established, as also does yellow-flowered, shrubby cinquefoil (*Potentilla fruticosa*).

For lower and different effect, yuccas and many kinds of cacti and other succulents may be suitable in the warmer States. However, *Yucca filamentosa* (=*Y. smalliana*) and *Opuntia compressa* and *polyacantha* are hardy in all but the coldest parts of the country. Surrounded by stone chips or sand, and with a scattered undercover of stonecrops (*Sedum*) and houseleeks (*Sempervivum*), such plants as these will add interesting accentuation to the feeling of desert dryness.

An orderly evergreen bank cover may be obtained with periwinkle (*Vinca minor*) in cooler areas, if moisture conditions are not too extreme, or with the several excellent, low-growing junipers. The trailing, gray-leaved, disease-resistant Waukegan juniper (*Juniperus horizontalis douglasi*) is one of the best. Both the glossy green bearberry (*Arctostaphylos*) and feathery green or gray lavender-cotton (*Santolina*) are effective in sandy or other well-drained soils.

Where flower color is important, some suitable choices may be found among the color forms of moss pink (*Phlox subulata*), the rockroses (*Helianthemum*), evening primroses, butterfly-weed (*Asclepias tuberosa*), snow-in-summer (*Cerastium tomentosum*), or the dwarf catmint (*Nepeta mussini*). All these are persistent.

If a showy but temporary effect is needed, some of the most sun-loving and drought-tolerant annuals include the mesembryanthemum (*Cryophytum, Dorotheanthus*), portulaca, California-poppy, Cape-marigold (*Dimorphotheca*), annual phlox, and snow-on-the-mountain (*Euphorbia marginata*).

Such plants as these should all be available from specializing commercial sources.

In learning their habits and in discovering their particular niches in relation to plant neighbors and to the terrain, lie the pleasures of gardening. (HENRY T. SKINNER)

Fruit Trees

GROWERS OF FRUIT on small properties should realize that they must face most of the problems that confront large commercial growers, plus a few more.

Among them are choice of varieties, planting, fertilizing, control of pests, pruning, pollination, and irrigation. The small growers do not have problems of labor, storage, and marketing, but they must get along with less efficient sprayers. Often they have to cope with unsuitable soils and sites. They may have to find means to prevent pillage by birds and rodents.

Furthermore, because the small grower may be a weekend grower, he cannot always time properly the application of sprays to control pests.

His trees also may have to be adapted to yard and garden culture rather than standard orchard practices. He may tend to overwater, overfertilize, and sometimes underdo.

All this is negative, I know. Purposely so; I raise the question whether gardeners should undertake to grow tree fruits on small properties.

For those, however, who believe the end is worth the effort, I give some do's and don'ts with the hope they will succeed.

CLIMATE, especially temperature and rainfall, limits the kind of fruits that can be grown anyplace.

We can classify fruit trees on the basis of their temperature requirements, particularly the lowest temperatures they can stand.

The truly tropical fruits that require long, warm seasons with minimums of 50° F. include bananas, mangos, papayas, coconuts, cocoa, durians, sugar apples, and mangosteens.

The subtropical fruits like long, warm growing seasons but will stand short, cold seasons. Some will even stand small amounts of frost. They include oranges, grapefruit, lemons, limes, guava, avocados, litchi, dates, and macadamia nuts.

Hardier subtropicals, including olives, figs, pomegranates, and Oriental persimmons, stand down to 10° to 15°.

The temperate or hardy fruits include apples, pears, sweet and sour cherries, plums, peaches, nectarines, apricots, almonds, pecans, walnuts, and some other tree nuts.

Growers should not try to grow fruit trees in climates not suited to them. The pecan, for example, endures winter temperatures of the Northern States, but the growing season is too short for it to set and mature nuts.

Figs prefer long growing seasons; they may survive zero temperatures in the Coastal States, but often they are killed back. New growth is erratic in production there and does not mature crops some years.

Apples and pears are hardy and when fully dormant will stand temperatures far below zero, but they cannot be grown in the far South, where temperatures may not be low enough to break their dormancy.

Peaches and sweet cherries are moderately hardy when fully dormant, but their fruit buds generally are killed at −10° and wood injury occurs at −20°.

Apricots are slightly more winter hardy but tend to bloom too early in the spring, and frosts kill the young fruit.

There is considerable variation in hardiness among varieties of the various fruits. Plant breeders try to develop new varieties with greater winter hardiness for the colder areas or less chilling requirement for southern sections with short winters.

WHAT TO PLANT, a frequent question, depends on climatic limitations, the gardener's likes, the space he has, and the amount of time and care he can give his plants. Some types of fruit trees are more subject to pests than others. In general, fruit plants in the dryer western sections require less care than in the Eastern States, where control of pests often spells the difference between success and failure.

The following lists are intended as a general guide.

The culture of truly tropical fruits, such as mango, papaya, banana, and coconut, should be limited to small areas along the Florida coast.

The hardier subtropicals (oranges, lemons, limes, grapefruit, avocado, macadamia nuts, guavas, dates) can be grown farther north and in the Southwest in places that may occasionally have light frosts.

Dates require long, hot, dry summers and are suited only to the desert areas of the Southwest. Macadamia and litchi can be grown in a few warm areas of California and Florida but stand little frost.

Citrus can be grown in the warmer parts of Florida, California, Arizona, Texas, and the Gulf coast. Limes are the most sensitive to frost. Some of the mandarin oranges are the most hardy.

In citrus areas where fruit of the ordinary kinds are easily obtainable from commercial markets, the mandarins make more attractive garden plants. The Robinson tangerine and Nova tangelo, recent introductions of the Department of Agriculture, ripen in October in Florida. Fairchild, Fortune, and Fremont, new tangerines, ripen in succession from November to May in California. The Owari satsuma is the hardiest and has been planted along the Gulf coast. Kumquats also are hardy, require little space, and provide novelty.

THE GUATEMALAN or Central American type of avocados do well in southern Florida and in the warmer parts of Texas. The most important varieties are Lulu, Booth 7 and 8, Waldin, and Pollock. In California, the Mexican hybrids, including Fuerte, Puebla, Anaheim, and Haas, do best.

In southern California, where nights are cold, some of the deciduous fruits can be grown alongside of citrus. The Persian walnut, notably the Payne variety, apricots, figs, plums, pomegranates, Japanese persimmons, olives, jujube, and certain peaches that have a low chilling requirement can be grown together. Pears and apples generally require more chilling.

In the valley areas of central and northern California, any of the stone fruits, pears, olives, almonds, and walnuts are well suited. Apples are grown at higher elevations or along the coast.

In the Pacific Northwest, at lower elevations, the stone fruits, apples, pears, the more hardy walnuts, and filberts do well.

In the Great Plains of the Midwest, gardeners have to be satisfied with fruits that stand low temperatures—the winter-hardy apples, like Duchess, Wealthy, Yellow Transparent, and Heralson; sour cherry; American-type plums; and cherry-plum hybrids.

In the Ohio Valley and warmer parts of the Great Lakes States, most apple varieties, the hardier peaches, sour cherries, blight-resistant pears (such as Seckel, Magness, and Moonglow), Manregian walnuts, and sweet cherries can be grown.

In the coastal and Atlantic States, apples, blight-resistant pears, cherries, damson and domestica plums, peaches, Manregian walnuts, Chinese chestnuts, and figs are common in gardens.

One should remember that great variations in climate occur with variations in elevation and proximity to large bodies of water. Some varieties grow well in sheltered places, but in other locations they will be winter injured.

More specific varietal recommendations as to varieties can be obtained from State agencies and the bulletins on home fruit gardens of the Department of Agriculture.

GOOD CULTURAL CARE is essential if fruit trees are to be productive.

Trees planted and forgotten or planted in unsuitable places are a waste of time and money. Proper fertilization and pest control are vital.

Almost no varieties of fruits come true from seed. Nursery stock therefore must be home propagated or obtained from nursery companies. You can get the names of reputable nursery companies and lists of varieties suitable to your locality from your State extension service.

Trees should be well grown (as shown by good current season's growth) and plump. They should show no sign of having dried out during handling. Many nursery trees are ruined by rough handling.

Fruit trees, like most other plants, prosper in good, well-drained soils.

They should not be in the shade of other trees or have to compete with roots of other trees. They should be given enough space for eventual development to the size desired.

Low areas are inclined to be frosty or too wet after heavy rains.

Deciduous trees usually are planted bare root when fully dormant in the fall or spring, depending on locality. The hole should be large enough for the roots to be spread out. The topsoil removed from the hole should be spread over the roots; 3 to 4 gallons of water should be added and the remainder of the hole filled. Planting depth should leave the crown of the tree at the same level as it grew in the nursery.

Apply no fertilizer until growth has started and the tree is well established.

The purpose of pruning is to develop the tree so that it will have maximum strength to carry a load of fruit and to keep it to the desired size. Only crossed branches, suckers, and dying limbs should be removed from young trees. Excessive pruning tends to make trees vegetative but may be necessary when space is limited. Pruning is usually done during the dormant season, but summer pruning may be necessary to maintain the desired size.

The ground under the drip should be kept clean cultivated from April to September.

The amount and kind of fertilizer varies with age, kind of tree, and soil type. Nitrogen is the commonest element needed. In western alkaline soils, nitrogen usually is applied as ammonium sulfate. In acid soils of the East, calcium nitrate or sodium nitrate is preferred.

Approximately one-fourth pound, spread on the soil surface around the tree, 3 feet from the trunk after the tree is well started, is enough during the first year. The amount should be increased by one-third pound per year of age up to 10 years and applied in early spring before growth starts.

Mixed fertilizers, such as 5-10-5, can be used but are more expensive. The first digit indicates the percentage of nitrogen.

Acid soils should be limed to bring them up to pH 6. Deficiencies of some minor elements may exist in some locations; advice about them should be obtained from the county agent.

Most fruit trees set too much fruit after they reach fruiting maturity. To get good size and quality, you must remove the excess fruit early in the season. Apples and peaches should be hand thinned to a spacing of 8 to 10 inches or more, depending on the vigor of the tree.

Dwarf trees are available for some kinds of fruit. They are liked by gardeners whose space is limited. Besides being smaller in size, dwarf trees usu-

ally fruit earlier in the life of the tree.
Dwarfing in apples is accomplished
by using one of the series of English
interstocks or rootstocks. These produce a range in dwarfing, of which
Malling IX is the most extreme and
VII and II are progressively larger.
Apples on Malling IX will reach a
spread of 8 to 10 feet in good soil. They
are very unsatisfactory when planted
in poor soils.

Pears are dwarfed when grown on
Angers quince.

No satisfactory dwarfing rootstocks
have been found for peaches, plums,
and apricots.

Spur-type trees are available in several varieties of apples. Such trees are
semidwarf on conventional rootstocks.
They tend to earlier production of fruit
spurs than conventional trees. They are
even more dwarfed when grown on
dwarfing rootstocks.

Dwarfing also can be accomplished
by severe pruning in the dormant season and by pinching out growing ter-
minals during the growing season.

Birds sometimes take the whole crop
of fruit even before it is mature. Many
types of repelling apparatus have been
designed and tried, but covering of the
whole tree with net is the only satisfactory method of protection. Several
companies make netting for this purpose, and used nylon fish netting can
be purchased relatively reasonably.
(L. C. COCHRAN)

COMMON AND TRADEMARK NAMES

Common designation	Trademark name
dalapon	Dowpon.
DCPA	Dacthal.
dicamba	Banvel–D
DMPA	Zytron.
DMTT	Mylone.
DSMA	(Many companies.)
R–4461	Betasan.
silvex	(Many companies.)
SMDC	Vapam.
trifluralin	Treflan.
2,4-D	(Many companies.)
2,4,5-T	(Many companies.)
Stoddard solvent	(Many companies.)

Protecting Trees

MOST SHRUBS and ornamental and
fruit trees are attacked by relatively
few insects and diseases, which leave
only minor troubles if they are controlled.

The insects are of two general
types—those that chew the plant parts
and leave holes or some other evidence
of their presence and those that suck
plant juices.

Beetles and caterpillars are examples
of chewing insects.

Aphids (plant lice), leafhoppers, and
scale insects are among the sucking
insects.

Plant disease—which may be considered as any deviation from normal—may be caused by fungi,
bacteria, virus, mineral deficiency, or
even some abnormal physiological
condition brought about by drought.

All of them may be of major importance, and your ability to recognize
the cause of the trouble is the basis of
your campaign against them.

Most of the time you will be dealing
with fungi, bacteria, or some environmental condition as the cause of your
trouble.

Fungi are low forms of plantlife that
lack the green color (chlorophyll) of
higher plants. Because they lack
chlorophyll, they cannot make their
own food and have to live on dead
organic matter (saprophytes) or on
living organisms (parasites).

We are concerned primarily with the
parasites because they often cause
disease in living plants.

The fungi include mildews, rusts,

smuts, molds, mushrooms, puffballs, and allied forms.

Bacteria are one-celled microscopic organisms, which also lack chlorophyll and mostly are saprophytic or parasitic. The parasitic types cause blights, cankers, leaf spots, and galls on their host plants.

If you do not recognize an insect or disease, place a specimen in a polyethylene bag and send it immediately to your county agricultural agent or State experiment station for diagnosis. Include a description of the conditions under which the trouble occurred.

IT IS IMPORTANT to keep your shrubs and trees healthy, because often the weak ones are most susceptible to attack.

Trees and shrubs may be weakened by malnutrition, drought, whipping by wind, sunscald, mechanical injury, poor drainage, and transplanting at the wrong time of year.

Your plants will suffer from malnutrition when they cannot get the major elements (nitrogen, phosphorus, potassium), and sometimes some of the minor elements (sulfur, calcium, magnesium, iron, and several others).

It is best to apply a complete commercial fertilizer in the spring before the buds break. Drill holes in the ground 8 to 10 inches deep and fill with fertilizer. The holes should be about 2 or 3 feet apart and distributed out as far as the branches extend.

The amount of fertilizer (10–6–4) to use for a tree you can calculate quickly. Use 2 pounds per inch of trunk diameter, measured 3 feet above the soil surface.

Never let your plants suffer from lack of water. If you are away from home for long periods during the dry season, arrange with your neighbor to water your plants, because extensive damage can occur during this time.

Wind whipping can be corrected by a few guy wires.

Wrapping a tree trunk with heavy paper or burlap will prevent sunscald. The paper or burlap should be sprayed or treated with a DDT suspension (2 tablespoons of 50 percent DDT wettable powder per gallon of water) to prevent borers from getting into the trunk.

Mechanical injury can be prevented if you are careful while working with mower or tools around the tree trunk.

Poor drainage can be corrected by tiling the wet spots.

WHEN YOU PLANT shrubs and trees, inquire of your State agricultural experiment station if disease- or insect-resistant varieties or species are available. Even though they are more costly, you may save yourself many troubles by planting them.

A few varieties of trees have been bred that show some degree of resistance to certain diseases. Among these are mimosa (wilt), chestnut (blight), apple or flowering crabapple (scab and powdery mildew), pear (fire blight), and American elm (phloem necrosis).

Do not plant trees or shrubs with galls on the roots or stems.

CLEANLINESS is the first commandment in a control program.

Prune out diseased or dead branches and destroy them and all trash, because they may harbor insects and disease-causing organisms. If you do not do so, no matter how good a spray program you follow, the plants may be reinfested with insects or reinfected with disease organisms.

Paint pruning wounds with an asphaltum base tree-wound dressing to prevent invasion by secondary wood-rot organisms.

If you follow those practices, you have solved many problems. The remaining problems very likely are those caused by insects and diseases and usually can be corrected by applying fungicides and insecticides.

Most chemical control programs for fruit trees are based mainly on protective sprays or dusts.

Sprays are more effective and last longer. Sprays protect the plant by

CHERRY LEAF SPOT

BROWN ROT ON PEACH

FRUIT SPOT OF PEAR

PEACH SCAB

POWDERY MILDEW

APPLE SCAB ON FRUIT AND LEAF

a thin layer of chemical. In time, the layer loses its effectiveness and must be replenished or renewed. As the plant grows, the new growth must be covered with chemical.

A thorough and complete spray schedule is needed for fruit trees. It is important to cover both surfaces of all leaves completely, as well as the fruit, with a fine, mist-type spray.

In most parts of the country one simply cannot get effective control with two or three applications. The reason for failure usually is that the gardener sprays only once or twice during the growing season.

The climate and other environmental conditions in your part of the country usually determine the number of applications needed for effective control. Some sections require 10 or more applications, although 7 or 8 may be the average.

Applications on fruit trees should begin when a small amount of color (pre-pink) is visible in the blossoms.

Make the second application just before the blossoms open (the pink stage).

Make a third application when most of the petals have fallen.

Subsequent applications (fruit-cover sprays) should be applied at intervals of 10 to 20 days, depending on the weather.

Because the chemical barrier is worn away rapidly during rainy periods, the shorter interval should be maintained, but the spray interval can be lengthened when the weather is hot and dry.

Besides the sprays during the growing season, about every 2 to 3 years during the dormant season you should apply an oil spray to control scale insects. This spray may also kill some eggs of aphids and mites.

I suggest that backyard gardeners use mixtures of the fungicides and insecticides that are needed to control the main diseases and insects of fruit trees. We call such formulations all-purpose fruit sprays.

They usually contain captan, dodine, or ferbam as the fungicide or a combination of those chemicals. Ap-plied according to directions, those fungicides control organisms that cause scab (apple, pear), leaf spot (cherry), and brown rot (peach, cherry, plum).

Fungicides, such as wettable sulfur or Karathane, sometimes are included in all-purpose formulations to control powdery mildew. Sulfur also is included usually in peach sprays to control scab.

Insecticides usually included with the fungicides are DDT, methoxychlor, carbaryl (Sevin), and malathion. They control one or more insects, such as plum curculio, apple maggot, codling moth, and aphids. Malathion sometimes is also included to control small spiderlike animals (Arachnids), called mites or spider mites.

Do not use copper in any form on peaches during the growing season. Copper compounds often cause peaches to lose their leaves.

Copper-containing compounds, however, sometimes can be applied to other fruit trees without serious damage. In fact, although various copper formulations under certain conditions may produce some degree of russeting on apple and pear fruit, fixed coppers or bordeaux (copper sulfate plus lime) mixtures are the only effective materials that can be recommended to backyard gardeners for control of the bacterial disease fire blight. The antibiotic streptomycin sometimes is used commercially to control this disease, but in most parts of the country its use is limited to the prebloom or bloom period.

Usually it is not necessary to keep a protective deposit of insecticide and fungicide on shrubs and ornamental trees as it is on fruit trees.

The chemical is applied during the season when a certain disease or insect usually makes its appearance or when a small amount of damage is observed.

After one lives in a locality for a few years, he learns when to expect a certain disease or insect and applies the proper materials at that time. In this way he keeps damage to a minimum. The Japanese beetle is an example of an insect that usually makes its appearance in the northeastern part of the country about the same time each year.

Some insects that cause trouble on certain plants are Japanese beetles, cankerworms, bagworms, leaf miners, aphids, bark beetles, lacebugs, borers, pine shoot moth, juniper webworm, and scale insects. Spider mites also may be serious on some trees and shrubs.

In general, malathion is a good allround insecticide, which controls many chewing and sucking insects as well as some of the spider mites.

Malathion, however, tends to have a short residual life and sometimes requires frequent applications.

Methoxychlor, DDT, and carbaryl (Sevin) normally give much better control of chewing insects than sucking insects and usually last 2 to 3 weeks.

Mildew, leaf spot, blight, rust, and other diseases attack certain shrubs and ornamental trees. A variety of fungicides, such as sulfur, dodine, zineb, maneb, captan, thiram, and copper, may be suggested as controls. Before you buy and use them, read and follow the directions on the package. (HARRY L. KEIL)

Weeds

WE HAVE COME a long way in our struggles with weeds.

We know that we will have fewer weeds in lawns and gardens if we plant weed-free seeds.

We know the value of controlling weeds in fence rows, roadways, and other marginal places.

Good cultural practices, such as control of insects and the plant diseases, balanced and regular fertilization, routine mowing, pruning, and irrigation provide good conditions so that vigorously growing plants will crowd out weeds.

We have new chemicals to eradicate weeds.

We give some suggestions for the use of new methods for the control of weeds around the home. Which of the alternative methods you choose will depend on your individual problem and situation.

Herbicides must be used and stored with care.

CONTROL crabgrass, chickweed, lambsquarters, pigweed, and many other broad-leaved weeds and weed grasses in patios and along the margins of walks, roads, and flowerbeds with carefully directed sprays of Stoddard solvent drycleaning fluid.

Use full strength in a hand sprayer. Thoroughly wet the foliage with the solvent. It kills foliage on contact.

Repeat the treatment as new weeds appear. Three to four treatments usually control the weeds for the growing season.

Do not let the solvent touch the foliage or stalks of wanted plants, which it also will kill. Carefully direct the spray, therefore, and use a low pressure that reduces drift of the spray.

Weeds die the day of treatment in hot weather. The solvent evaporates quickly and does not leave a chemical residue.

AGAINST WEEDS in woody ornamental and tree plantings, use Stoddard solvent as a carefully directed spray.

Keep the solvent away from the bark and foliage of valuable plants.

Repeat the treatments as new weeds appear.

Black polyethylene film may be placed in strips, squares, or circles when you make new plantings to control many germinating annual weeds and conserve moisture.

To protect established plantings,

place the film carefully around the bases of plants after cultivation or spraying to remove growing weeds.

DCPA, used in spray or granular form, controls germinating grasses and some broad-leaved weeds without injuring many woody ornamentals and trees.

WEEDS in annual vegetable gardens can be controlled most effectively by a treatment with SMDC, DMTT, or methyl bromide before planting.

These herbicides are called soil fumigants. They control most annual and perennial weeds. They dissipate rapidly.

A short time after treatment, vegetables or ornamentals may be planted without injurious effects.

Apply SMDC and DMTT on newly worked soil followed by sprinkling to form a soil-crust seal to hold the vapors in the soil. Wait 2 to 3 weeks between treatment and planting.

Methyl bromide is applied under a polyethylene film on newly worked soil. Planting may be done 48 hours after removal of the cover.

Methyl bromide is a deadly poison. Prevent children and pets from being exposed to it. Never release it in a closed room.

Many germinating weeds, including annual grasses in flowerbeds, can be controlled with DCPA.

In general, the soil fumigants should not be used in flowerbeds in lawn areas, although they may be used effectively when the plantings are isolated from lawns or woody ornamentals.

SPECIAL TREATMENTS are needed for some weeds, including dodder, mugwort, and poison-ivy.

Dodder has become increasingly bad among herbaceous annual and perennial ornamentals, apparently because of the wider use of animal manures that contain dodder seed.

Dodder is controlled by soil treatments with DCPA. Apply in the early spring immediately after transplant-

ing the ornamentals and before the weeds come up. Most established ornamentals are tolerant of DCPA.

Mugwort, a perennial weed, sometimes mistakenly is called wild chrysanthemum because of resemblance of its foliage to cultivated chrysanthemums. It is spread by seed, the transport of roots in soil accompanying ornamental plants, and creeping root stocks. It is difficult to control. You may have to sacrifice some ornamental plantings in order to control mugwort with herbicides, although the loss can be minimized by carefully localized treatments.

Directed spot treatments with amitrole are effective if you repeat them two or three times at monthly intervals during the growing season. Wet the foliage thoroughly with the spray.

Brush plants, such as oak, elm, cherry, sassafras seedlings, honeysuckle, Virginia-creeper, poison-ivy, and others in wooded areas also can be killed with amitrole.

If ornamental plantings are not near, 2,4,5-T may be used for the woody weeds.

The resprouting of trees after cutting can be stopped by the use of ammate herbicide applied in liquid or crystalline form to the stump.

Bamboo may be a problem in places where the climate is warm. It can be controlled with repeated treatments with dalapon, beginning when the plants are 18 inches to 2 feet tall.

Ragweed and goldenrod often grow in fence rows and other marginal areas. Spraying with 2,4-D controls them and minimizes the allergic reactions they may cause in some persons.

WEEDS occur in lawns where the grass is thinned by heavy use, diseases, and insects; in disturbed areas; and along borders.

Most weeds are a minor problem if the lawn grass is dense and vigorous.

Lawn management practices recommended in another chapter should accompany the weed control methods we recommend.

Broadleaf weeds—dandelion, buckhorn, other plantains, moneywort, pennywort, and others—are controlled by a single spraying of 2,4-D in the spring or fall and when the plants are making rapid growth. The rates of application are given on the label.

Nutsedge is hard to control. 2,4-D at about double the normal rate for broadleaf weeds every 6 weeks for two or three growing seasons will greatly thin stands of nutsedge.

Control wild garlic with repeated annual treatments in the early spring with 2,4-D. Use the rate suggested for nutsedge. Add a teaspoon of liquid household detergent to each gallon of spray.

Silvex is more effective than 2,4-D for control of chickweed, ground-ivy, yellow woodsorrel, knotweed, and mat spurge. For greatest effectiveness, spray in spring while the plants are small and growing actively. Many of these weeds can be controlled at any season as long as they are growing well.

Red sorrel is not well controlled by sprays of 2,4-D or silvex. Dicamba is effective, but it must be used only at the rate of one-half pound per acre, because it may be absorbed by roots of trees and shrubs if it is used at higher rates.

Red sorrel likes acid soils. Therefore apply lime if your soil needs lime.

Many organic herbicides control such annual grasses as crabgrass, foxtail, goosegrass, barnyard grass, and annual bluegrass if the chemicals are applied before their seeds germinate. Trifluralin, DMPA, DCPA, and R-4461 prevent infestations of crabgrass and foxtail.

DMPA and R-4461 are moderately effective on goosegrass when it is applied in the spring and on annual bluegrass if it is applied early in the fall before it germinates.

Lawn grasses should not be seeded for several months after you use these herbicides.

Dallisgrass and related *Paspalum* species are perennial plants that can be controlled by spraying the foliage with DSMA. Repeatedly spraying the foliage with DSMA every 7 to 10 days for two or three treatments effectively controls crabgrass, foxtail, goosegrass, and sandbur.

Occasional plants of coarse perennial grasses, such as orchardgrass, tall fescue, timothy, redtop, velvetgrass, and broomsedge, are unsightly in lawns. They may be spot-treated with Stoddard solvent. Repeated treatment will be necessary.

Nimblewill and bentgrass often are undesirable and difficult to eliminate from lawns.

Silvex applied repeatedly at about double the usual rate of treatment will reduce the stand of bentgrass. Spraying should start early in the spring.

Nimblewill stands are reduced by spraying DMPA at heavy rates in May or June. A second treatment should be applied about a month later.

Such aggressive perennials as bermudagrass and quackgrass cannot be killed in lawns without hurting other plants. Effective herbicides kill all the grasses, and reseeding the area is necessary.

Only methyl bromide, a fumigant released under an airtight cover that is kept in place 24 to 48 hours, will kill all these weeds in a single treatment. Special application equipment is required.

Treated areas may be reseeded within 48 hours after removal of the cover.

Repeated treatments of dalapon, SMDC, and DMTT control bermudagrass and quackgrass. Start the treatments in July on actively growing grass; irrigate the lawn about a week before treatment if necessary to encourage growth. Water the area after treatment if necessary to encourage the growth of dormant, unkilled buds. Make a second treatment 4 to 6 weeks later to kill any regrowth.

If it does not rain, irrigate every 7 to 10 days after the second treatment for 3 to 5 weeks to help dissipate the herbicide from the soil. Seed lawn grasses late in September. (L. L. DANIELSON AND D. L. KLINGMAN)

HERBICIDE SUMMARY CHART FOR WEED CONTROL AROUND THE HOME [1]

Weed	Lawns General	Lawns Spot treatments	Woody ornamentals and shade trees	Herbaceous perennial ornamentals	Wooded and marginal areas
Nutsedge	2,4-D, repeated heavy rates.	2,4-D, methyl bromide, SMDC, DMTT.	....	....	....
Bermudagrass	dalapon	dalapon, methyl bromide.	dalapon	....	dalapon.
Crabgrass	DCPA, DMPA, R-4461, trifluralin.	....	DCPA, DMPA	....	....
Goosegrass	DMPA, R-4461.	....	DCPA, DMPA.	....	....
Dallisgrass	DSMA.	Stoddard solvent, DSMA.	Stoddard solvent spot treatment.	....	....
Nimblewill	DMPA, repeated heavy rates.	DMPA.	....	....	....
Plantain	2,4-D	2,4-D	....	....	....
Dandelion	2,4-D	2,4-D	....	....	....
Ground-ivy, Chickweed, Henbit, and Knotweed.	silvex	silvex.	....	....	silvex.
Pigweed	2,4-D	2,4-D	DCPA, sesone, DNBP.	DCPA, sesone.	....
Lambsquarters	2,4-D	2,4-D	do.	do.	....
Dodder	....	....	....	DCPA, CIPC.	....
Wild garlic	2,4-D	2,4-D	....	....	....
Purslane	....	....	DNBP, CIPC.	DNBP, CIPC.	....
Red sorrel	dicamba	dicamba.	....	....	dicamba.
Spotted spurge	silvex	silvex.	....	....	....
Mugwort	....	....	amitrole.	amitrole.	....
Poison-ivy	2,4,5-T	amitrole.	amitrole, ammate.	....	2,4,5-T, amitrole, ammate.
Virginia-creeper	....	....	do.	....	Do.
Honeysuckle	2,4-D	2,4-D	do.	....	amitrole, ammate, 2,4-D.
Hardwood seedlings	2,4,5-T	2,4,5-T. Stoddard solvent.	amitrole	....	amitrole, 2,4,5-T.
Orchardgrass, Tall fescue, Timothy, and Broomsedge.	....	....	....	....	....
Woodsorrel	silvex	silvex.	....	....	silvex.
Ragweed	2,4-D	2,4-D.	....	....	2,4-D.

[1] Home vegetable gardens: Preplanting treatments with SMDC, DMTT, methyl bromide control most annual and perennial weeds. Black polyethylene plastic may be used. Annual ornamental plantings: Preplanting as for vegetable gardens.

Bermudagrass.

Large crabgrass.

Nimblewill.

Nutsedge.

Red sorrel.

Common purslane.

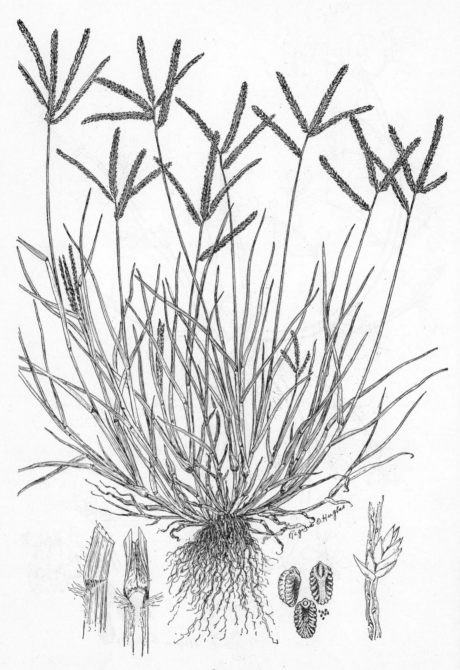

Goosegrass.

Lambsquarters.

Common chickweed.

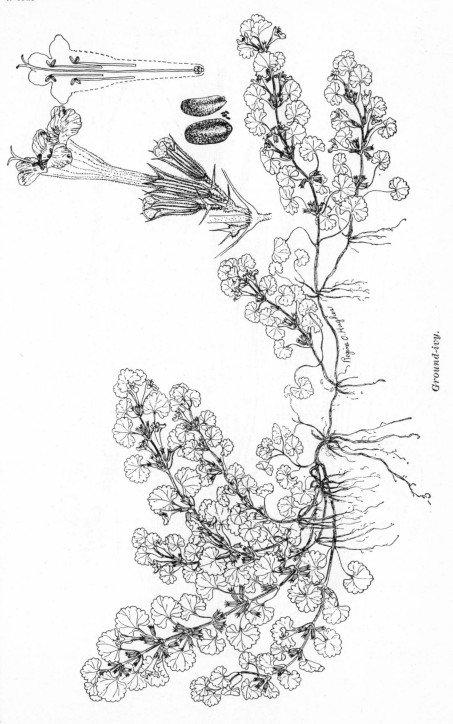

Ground-ivy.

Plantains.

House Plants

Two GROUND RULES for selecting and maintaining house plants are:

Select the right plant for the conditions in your house.

Water the plants to maintain them rather than to grow them.

Many types of plants may be used as house plants. Some of them are:

Iron-clad plants, which are useful under many conditions: Aglaonema, aspidistra, ciccus rhombifolia, crassula (Jade), dieffenbachia, ficus, philodendron, sansevieria, schefflera, scindapsus, and syngonium.

Tough plants, which are useful for extremely dry conditions: Bromeliads, cacti, peperomia, sansevieria, scindapsus, and zebrina.

Plants for large tubs: Dieffenbachia, dracaena, fatshedera, ficus elastica, ficus pandurata, palms, pandanus, philodendron, and schefflera.

Plants for low temperature (50° to 60° at night): Bromeliads, cineraria, citrus, cyclamen, English ivy, German ivy, Jerusalem cherry, kalanchoe, and primrose.

Plants for medium temperature (60° to 65° at night): Christmas cactus, chrysanthemum, gardenia, grape ivy, palms, pilea, peperomia, ti plant (*Cordyline terminalis*), tuberous begonia, wax begonia.

Plants for high temperature (65° to 70° at night): African violet, aglaonema, croton, dracaena, ficus, gloxinia, philodendron, scindapsus, schefflera, cacti and succulents, caladium, and syngonium.

Many other plants are grown in the home, but they require much more attention than the ones I have listed.

Most flowering plants do not grow and flower well in the home unless supplemental fluorescent light is used. African violets, gloxinias, begonias, geraniums, primulas, and bulbs require this special care.

Grow your plants in individual pots or in a planter.

Here are some tips that make it easy to maintain plants in individual pots in a window garden.

Plastic pots are good because water is not evaporated through them. Their use means you need not water the plants so often.

Glass wicks inserted in the bottom of the pot conduct water from a reservoir.

Put a sheet of vinyl film, matching or contrasting with the plants, under the pots to protect the window sill from water.

Turn the plants every week toward the sun to encourage symmetrical development.

Fluorescent lamps, controlled by a timeclock, supplement sunlight for a 16-hour day (6 a.m. to 10 p.m.). The plants thus are lighted for evening display. A combination of cool white and lavender (Gro-Lux) lamps enhance the color of plants and furnishings.

Night temperatures that are comfortable for people are good for plants—65° to 75° F.

Trays containing gravel and water increase the humidity around the plants.

A planter that is easy to care for has an outer shell of plywood, painted to match walls, or of wood veneer, stained or oiled to match the furniture. The planters may be put on platforms or rollers to make handling easier.

The inner shell is a watertight, galvanized tin liner, painted with asphalt to retard rusting. Heavy polyethylene film stapled into the outer shell may serve as a temporary liner.

A layer of gravel in the bottom of the planter provides airspaces.

To have all plants and pots at the

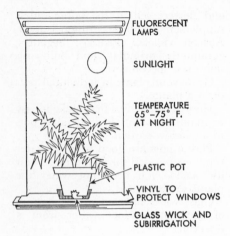

Easy maintenance of individual pots in a window garden.

A cross section of an easy maintenance planter.

same level, put small pots on top of larger ones; use unmilled sphagnum moss or pea-size marbles or granite chips to fill the space between pots.

You may wish to use fluorescent lamps to supplement sunlight for the planters.

Plants should be grown in individual clay pots, never planted directly.

START TO ADJUST the plants to the new conditions of the home as soon as you get them.

The soil ball, clay pots (if that is the kind you use), and the material you use in big pots should be watered to saturation, but not to excess.

Allow the whole area of the soil ball and the planter to dry until the plant is near wilting. Detect wilting by a change in leaf color from green to gray-green, a drooping of the foliage, and wrinkling of the stem.

Water again thoroughly to saturation. Allow the excess water to moisten the soil ball and the surrounding moss or stone chips in the planter.

Some of the oldest leaves may turn yellow at this time. Wash the foliage with warm, soapy water; remove the yellow foliage; and stake the plants.

Water thoroughly each time, but lengthen the number of days between waterings to the maximum.

Each time you water, try to increase the number of days over the previous number of days for watering. Watering on a regular schedule often kills house plants because no judgment is involved.

A successful watering procedure is based on constant observation—to observe that the soil ball is dry and the first signs of wilting are evident. One then waters to saturation. Again, the time of observing—waiting until the first signs of wilting are evident again.

The number of days between watering should gradually increase, and so you have the plant trained to maintain itself without extensive growth, the whole root system continues to function, and care is at a minimum, but you continue to observe it.

If you do not water enough each time, part of the roots will die from lack of water, and eventually the whole plant will die. Thorough watering keeps the entire root system functioning.

If you have many sizes of pots in the planter, you may have to water different plants at different times.

A planter should not be static—the same plants in the same place.

Introduce new plants, even potted flowering plants, to give a seasonal look to the planter—chrysanthemums in the fall, poinsettias at Christmas, azaleas and hydrangeas in the spring, and gloxinias and tuberous rooted begonias in the summer.

Plan to replace them; do not try to carry them over to the next season.

The planter in the home is a poor place to grow flowering plants. The many sizes of pots will require special watering consideration—flowering plants will require much more water than foliage plants. Avoid overwatering the planter so that the foliage plants will not receive too much water.

A plastic funnel may be used as an aid in watering to saturation. The size of the funnel depends on the size of the pot. The diameter of the funnel should be at least half the diameter of the clay pot. Insert the neck of the funnel into the soil in the pot and fill the funnel with water. The soil will hold only a fixed amount—never an excess. Continue to add water to the funnel until saturation, then remove the funnel. Avoid spilling excess water from the funnel. Push your index finger into the soil and cap the neck of the funnel before you remove it.

The soil should be watered thoroughly but never to excess. The poor aeration that results from overwatering will kill the roots. Watering to saturation at longer intervals keeps the roots active and lengthens the life of plants.

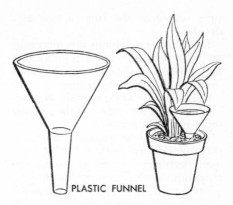

PLASTIC FUNNEL

Plastic funnel may be used as aid in watering to saturation.

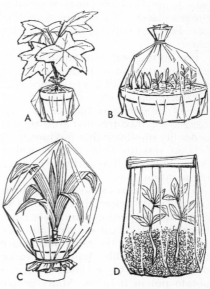

Use of polyethylene films. A. Cover clay pot of well-watered plant with polyethylene film. B. Cover propagation pan to keep humidity high around rooting cutting. C. Cover recently rooted, air-layered plant to retard water loss from foliage. D. Wrap unrooted cuttings in sphagnum moss and cover with perforated polyethylene film.

APPLY water-soluble fertilizers through the top of the pots every 4 weeks while the plants are in active growth. Use the concentration the manufacturer prescribes, but use one-fourth strength when you add water to the subirrigation pans or funnels.

Fertilize only when the plants are in active growth. Withhold fertilizers from resting plants.

Sparing but continuous feeding is desirable for most house plants. It helps keep all foliage green.

A good rule is to feed by adding a water-soluble fertilizer each time a new leaf emerges on a large-leaved house plant. Unless the fertilizer is added, the oldest leaf on the plant will turn yellow at the time a new leaf develops.

Dry fertilizers seldom are successful for house plants, because a great part may remain in the soil, and repeated use may kill the roots in time.

Remove any white deposit that accumulates on the surface of the soil and replace it with new soil.

When clay pots turn white or crusty, they are loaded with insoluble, unused fertilizers—primarily phosphorous compounds (calcium phosphates), which are toxic to root development.

You should replace old pots as they become useless. Many people feel that they can wash or soak the fertilizer out, but that is impossible. Throw the pots away. They are not even useful as broken pieces in the bottom of another pot. For best culture, use a new clay pot.

For potting soil, mix equal parts of garden soil, sand or perlite, and peat moss. To each gallon of mixture, add a tablespoon of rock phosphate and one of limestone if the soil is acid. Bagged soil mixtures that are available generally duplicate that mixture.

If the mixture holds a great deal of water, add one-third perlite to increase the aeration.

These soil mixes should be sterilized (pasteurized) before they are used as a medium for potting plants. The commercial soil mixtures generally are pasteurized. For the home mix, place the soil in a shallow pan; set it in an oven held at 250° F. Hold it until a potato put in it bakes. Many people lose house plants from rot organisms found in home-prepared mixes.

YOU CAN MAKE good use of polyethylene film in several ways.

Use it to cover the clay pot after you have watered the plant well. Thus some plants can be left unattended for many weeks before they require additional water.

Cover a propagation pan to keep a high humidity around rooting cuttings. Place the pan in indirect light to avoid overheating by the sun. Remove

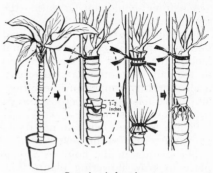

Steps in air layering.

the film as the cuttings start to root.

Cover recently rooted, air-layered plants to retard water loss from the foliage. Open the film gradually to establish the plant in air.

Wrap unrooted cuttings in sphagnum moss and cover them with perforated polyethylene film. The cuttings may be shipped or held several days before they are inserted in the rooting media.

TO PROPAGATE PLANTS, you may wish to try air layering, which is the only way for plants that have stiff or woody stems and eventually grow too tall to be attractive.

Do it this way: Attach the stem securely to a stake. Make an upward cut into the stem, separating the bark with a small stick. Cover the cut area with a ball of moist (but not soggy) sphagnum moss. Reduce the water loss by covering the area with polyethylene film. Continue to grow the mother plant in the usual way. When you can see the roots in the moss, cut the rooted top off the mother plant and plant it in a pot. Continue to grow the mother plant; new lateral branches often develop down the stem. You can air-layer the same mother plant many times.

You may wish to send to the Office of Information, United States Department of Agriculture, Washington, D.C., 20250, for a copy of Home and Garden Bulletin No. 82, "Selecting and Growing House Plants." (HENRY M. CATHEY)

OUTDOORS

Basic Points
of Landscaping

WE KEEP several basic details in mind when we undertake landscaping—the overall plan, balance, orientation, scale, soils, ecology, plant material, texture, three dimensions, restraint, and repetition. Patience, too.

Ideally, the overall plan should be drawn when the building is being designed, so the building and grounds may be planned as a single, interrelated unit by a qualified landscape architect and architect.

We say this over and over, but still many owners are left with a building on bare ground. They still have the task of forming a happy relationship between ground and architecture.

In Japan, where I lived and studied, I observed a more desirable method of planning. The Japanese design and build the structure and garden at one time, because they consider the garden as important as the structure. The result is a complete harmony.

Balance is essential in landscape de-

signing. Balance may be symmetrical (or formal) or asymmetrical (or informal).

Formal—symmetrical—balance is the easier for most Americans, because we have lived more with it than with informal balance. Many of the European gardens with which we are familiar typify formal balance. The garden of Versailles is an outstanding example. Some of the American gardens in Williamsburg are noteworthy.

In this type of balance, an axis extends down the center. Whatever is placed on one side is duplicated exactly on the other. Frequently plants are clipped, lines are straight, and edges are clearly defined. Sometimes there are retaining walls and different levels.

Informal—asymmetrical—balance is a little more difficult for most persons of European ancestry and experience to express. Many often photographed Japanese gardens exemplify this subtle form, but it is more easily observed in Ikebana—flower arranging.

Although both sides of an imaginary axis are in balance with each other, informal balance is accomplished by deliberately leaving some elements unequal in form, color, size, or position.

The natural look of the unclipped plants, curved lines, obscure and merging edges, and natural contours identify asymmetry in the garden.

Some pleasing effects are achieved in modern gardens by the combination of formal and informal balance.

ORIENTATION also is highly important.

If you have a voice in the placing of your house, you probably will consider the orientation of the planting as well.

The placing of the structure depends on the site, the neighborhood, the existing zoning laws, the climate, and the need for privacy.

Planting is determined more by climate and a desire for privacy.

If you build in a section where the afternoon sun is intense in summer, you must think of some shade for the western exposure by choosing sun-loving plants. Some plants thrive in a sunny southern exposure. Others prefer shade. Since most plants like at least a little sun each day, however, a place north of the structure will not do for a colorful, varied garden.

Keep in mind that the plants you select ought to be in character and in scale with the building and with each other for interest.

The ultimate use of the area is decisive in the selection of plants. Is the area to be used by babies, or teenagers, or young adults, or elderly persons? If, for example, babies and old people will visit the area, you would hesitate to use plants with thorns, but such plants may be useful for restricting or confining purposes in another situation.

BY SCALE of the plant we do not necessarily mean its size at the time of purchase, but the ultimate height and spread it will attain in the future.

In the small garden, plants as a rule should be kept to a minimum number. Their leaf texture should be medium to fine. Their growth habits should be compact.

Let me illustrate the use of scale by assuming that you live in a small, one-story house. The most natural solution would be for you to plant a medium-sized tree that grows to about 30 feet as the main accent to the house. That would be in scale.

If you were to choose a tree that grows to about 15 feet, your house would appear much larger than it

really is. If you chose a tall shade tree, one that grows to about 120 feet, your house would look like a dollhouse.

By your choice of scale you can create various illusions or effects. You must decide which one you wish to achieve, for, especially if it is distorted, the effect should be planned and not the result of a mistake.

YOU SHOULD CONSIDER the type of soil with which you must work before you choose your plants.

The soil may be acid, sweet (alkaline), sandy (well drained), clay (poorly drained), or swampy. A bit of reading in garden books will tell you that most plants have preferences for a certain type of soil and show inclinations to grow with wet or dry feet. Usually, however, you need not reproduce exactly the original conditions under which they grew.

Ecology is concerned with plants as neighbors in Nature. You can see their relationship when you drive in the country. If you keep this natural association in mind and try to combine plants that originated under the same conditions of light, shade, moisture, soil, and so on, you will achieve unity more easily and your garden will be more successful. I do not mean, however, that the observance of ecology is mandatory for success.

Although the type of soil (or the ecology) sometimes limits the use of certain plants, there are some plants for almost every kind of situation. Choose them carefully.

DECIDUOUS PLANTS, which lose their leaves in winter, offer much beauty in the way of flowers, fruit, and color, which change with the seasons. They are lovely and interesting not only when they are in leaf, but, if you choose carefully for their structure, they can contribute beauty of shape and outline in winter.

The conifers, the needled evergreens, usually are dark green, but at times their shade of green is more on the blue or yellow side. Perhaps because of their silhouette or because the needles absorb rather than reflect light, they strongly accent the garden, and should be selected wisely. For a more dramatic effect, they usually should be used with deciduous material and broad-leaved evergreens.

The broad-leaved evergreens appear to be lighter green than the conifers, perhaps because they reflect light and often have shiny leaves. Rhododendrons, azaleas, and hollies are examples.

Again, for best results, try to combine the three types of woody plants—deciduous plants, conifers, and broad-leaved evergreens.

REMEMBER texture also.

Texture may be fine, medium, and coarse, with gradations in each. The texture of a plant may vary at different times of year.

For example, in winter, when you see only its structure of thick and heavy branches and twigs, a deciduous plant may appear coarse. It may appear medium in summer, when it is covered with medium-sized leaves, and fine when it is in bloom if its blossoms are small.

You get the best results when you combine different textures of leaves and branches. Otherwise, you achieve only monotony.

ANOTHER WAY to avoid monotony is to work in three dimensions. Consider the plant material from the top of the tallest shade tree down to the ground material. Sound selections insure an interesting, attractive, and natural-looking planting.

First, decide on the large tree to complement your building. Suppose you choose a tulip tree, *Liriodendron tulipifera;* a sweetgum, *Liquidambar styraciflua;* or a plane tree, *Platanus occidentalis,* which would tend to join your garden and the sky sympathetically.

Next you will want to plant an understory tree or large shrub, one that has horizontal, rather than upright or drooping, branching habits, and grows naturally under other trees. It may be the flowering dogwood, *Cornus florida;* doublefile viburnum, *Viburnum tomentosum;* or western dogwood, *Cornus nuttali.*

Near and under the understory tree, you can plant evergreen or broad-leaved evergreen shrubs, perhaps rhododendrons, azaleas, or leucothoe.

Finally a layer of ground cover, such as ivy, *Hedera helix,* or myrtle, *Vinca minor,* will give the finishing touch to your garden and also tie it to the ground.

According to this system, you will have at least four different levels to attract the eye.

If you build in a locality where you must forgo the tall shade tree and the understory tree, by all means consider constructing an overhead arbor or trellis as a substitute. It also will achieve the desired three-dimensional effect.

RESTRAINT is a good principle. If you plan to construct supplementary buildings, the materials you choose for them should be well coordinated with your original building. Use as few different types of materials as possible.

The same principle applies to the use of plant materials. One reason for restraint is that you are dealing with living, growing, ever-changing materials, all of which must have room to develop. The saying, "If one is good, two are twice as good," does not apply to landscape gardening.

It is better to use too few materials than too many, and it is wise to repeat some of the same plants, the same texture, the same color, or various tones of the same color in different parts of the garden.

Restraint will help unify your garden by making it rhythmic and harmonious.

Your application of restraint, like the use of repetition, however, should never be carried so far as to make all your plants a uniform size, texture, and color. Try to vary the height of the plants. Try to use at least three of the textures and either two complementary or two contrasting colors and their tones.

Do not forget that living things require food, water, and maintenance (some more than others). Plants have their likes and dislikes, just as they have their own characteristics and lifespan. It takes time to make a garden. The finest gardens have taken years to develop. The most fundamental precept of all, therefore, is patience. (MARILYN H. JOHNSON)

Fences

THE GOLDEN RULE applies to fences, too, and you will do well to talk over your plans for them with your neighbors. They will see and like or dislike the fences you build, as you do theirs.

Neighborly consultation will help you have a fence that is functional and attractive (the main points in selecting its style and appearance) and suited to the neighborhood and your landscaping.

Fences of straight, prim, formal lines go with formal landscaping or must be softened with shrubs or shadow lines in the design to make them blend better into an informal setting.

Wood, masonry, and steel fences may be used informally in many ways to increase the attractiveness of the landscape.

YOU CAN BE imaginative as well as practical when you fence your residential lot.

Solid fences for screening usually are 5 feet 6 inches to 6 feet 6 inches high. Because the lengths are short, cost is not a major factor. An attractive fence that hides trash, provides privacy for outdoor living, or adds living space to your property may add to the value of your house.

If a wall needs to be ventilated so as not to shut off breezes, yet must be screened solidly, wood in basketweave, alternate side covered or of a louvered design, serves its purpose and is attractive. Masonry can be designed for this purpose by alternating airholes 2 to 4 inches wide.

Enameled-steel strips woven into steel chain link fences produce decorative patterns and give solid visual screening.

Fences with straight lines may be too formal to suit the landscaping around houses set in a natural landscape—woods, rock gardens, and ungraded sites. Screening fences to fit such sites may be built of rustic timber, cobblestone, or rubble masonry.

Open fences for boundary lines usually are 2 feet 6 inches to 3 feet 6 inches high. Materials of construction and design should fit into the landscape plan. Cost is also a factor in the lengths required for large lots.

Some people like the old rail-type fences. Few city lots are big enough to let land use be taken up by a zigzag rail fence, but mortise and tenoned split-rail fences may give a pleasing antique look.

If fence boards are to be painted, they should be treated with pentachlorophenol or an equivalent preservative that will not bleed through the paint. Apply two liberal brush coats of pentachlorophenol to the ends of all boards and to all parts where wood touches wood and may leave a crack that may retain moisture.

Posts and wood in contact with the ground should be impregnated with a preservative like creosote or pentachlorophenol applied at the rate of 6 pounds per cubic foot of wood.

Forcing the preservative into the wood under pressure is the usual way to get this level of impregnation.

Ordinary mild steel corrodes quickly in the open air. Steel fences therefore must be treated to resist corrosion.

They may be made of corrosion-resisting alloys, but the best of the alloys, stainless steel, is too high priced for consideration as fencing.

Manufacturers therefore coat the wire with a corrosion-resistant material—zinc, aluminum, or plastic resins. The durability of zinc or aluminum coating is greater for greater thickness of coating.

A steel wire coated with 2.7 ounces of zinc per square foot of surface may be expected to be uncorroded after 16 years in an industrial atmosphere. Comparable life for a wire with 0.4 ounce or no coating of zinc would be 9 years and 5 years.

A steel wire with 0.24 ounce per square foot of aluminum on the surface of the wire has a life of 35 years under the same conditions.

Vinyl resin jacketing of 6 to 10 mils thickness produces a colorful chain link fence. The mechanical wear resistance of the coating has not been evaluated. Vinyl resins melt at temperatures above 180° F.

Permanent fencing on productive farmland often is made with a combination of woven wire and barbed wire. Woven wire is packaged in 20-rod (330 feet) rolls. The size of woven wire is designated by two numbers—the number of horizontal wires (line wires) and the height of the fence in inches. For example, fence 939 has 9 line wires and is 39 inches high. The vertical wires (stay wires) may be 12 or 6 inches apart.

Bracing of corners, ends, and long runs of fences is important. Suspension-type fences should be braced every 80 rods (one-fourth mile) by placing posts 8 feet apart with a horizontal compression strut between them and an X-bracing of 9-gage galvanized wire twisted to tension the brace assembly.

Double-corner braces are serviceable when they are properly alined and set firmly. Firmly tamped corner posts set with the bottom 3 feet below the ground surface will be rigid enough in most soils. (NORMAN C. TETER)

Backyard—
or Garden?

THE AMERICAN BACKYARD usually is just that and no more.

In new housing developments it may be a bit of lawn next to another bit of lawn: Monotony.

In older neighborhoods, there may be a few trees, a flowerbed, a vegetable patch, play equipment, a bench: Hodgepodge.

We Americans do not appreciate the true meaning and importance of *garden*. A garden to most of us is a patch of worked earth, a gesture of petunias in front, and a rose or two in back.

But *garden* is a larger, more important concept. A garden, said Garrett Eckbo, an American landscape architect, is outdoor space around private homes, enclosed for the use and pleasure of the family. A garden is an extension of indoor living space into the out of doors.

We create a garden in the full sense if we apply some of the principles of organizing indoor living space to organizing outdoor space. We also make use of otherwise wasted or misused space.

Backyards need only to be planned to become gardens.

Gardens need some sort of walls, just as houses do.

Indoors, walls are solid and have openings for doors and windows. Draperies, paintings, bookshelves, light brackets, tapestries, and decorative panels are hung on them for variation. Even when wall is treated as wall, it usually is painted, papered, paneled, or otherwise altered to create background for objects.

To create an outdoor living space— a garden—we use shrub borders (a single line of one kind of shrub is better than a conglomeration of different kinds), hedges, fences, and building walls to create an enclosure for garden space and provide some privacy. Unlike indoor walls, however, the outdoor walls need not be continuous, nor need they be completely limiting.

If you wish to create an outdoor living space in a corner lot, for example, it is necessary to use a fairly solid fence or hedge to cut out the view of passers-by on the side street. It becomes a restricting wall.

But if you live at the edge of an open meadow or field or by the edge of a woodland or park, the view would contribute so much to your enjoyment that you would not want to block it off. If there is no public intrusion, there would be no reason to do so. The pleasant view in itself, then, becomes a part of your garden wall, unrestricting and indefinite though it may be.

Just as indoor walls serve as background for paintings and furniture, so the outdoor walls can serve as background for a handsome shrub, bright flowers, a specimen evergreen.

NEW HOMEOWNERS often start landscaping with flowers, but they do not succeed because most flowers, beautiful as they are, are so fragile as an element in design that they need background structure.

To clarify the point: Try to visualize the difference between a handsome desk or chest standing in the middle of the living room (as when you are in the process of moving into a house) and how much more effective it is against a wall that complements its color and shape. The wall provides the strong structural background the chest needs.

If you keep that vision in mind when you plant roses, tulips, or zinnias,

you will find that organizing a garden is not so difficult, either.

Indoor floors may be wood, stone, carpeting, or composition of some sort. Garden floors are made of many materials, some of which we walk on and some of which we do not. Paving stones, concrete, brick, wooden decks, gravel, smoothly mowed lawn are practical and durable garden floors comparable to the ones indoors. All provide good footing.

On the other hand, in gardens we also have flooring materials that provide only variation in texture, color, and pattern and are not meant to be walked on.

Evergreen ground cover and beds of low-growing plants provide rich texture or color and are used much as a brightly colored small rug is used indoors to focus attention in a certain place and provide additional interest. With these special carpets outdoors, however, seasonal change enters the picture and adds much to the challenge of planning outdoor space for year-round enjoyment.

Garden ceilings are even less confining than garden walls, but they exist. The sky itself, the most important ceiling, is the source of sunlight, which plants need, as do we for psychological and physical health.

But because we also need protection from sunshine at times, we plant trees, whose overhanging limbs become a garden ceiling, too.

Arbors, trellises, awnings, and other overhead enclosures are other ceilings. A porch is a part of garden space (it is more outdoor living space than indoor), so its solid roof becomes a part of the garden ceiling, too.

Once the relationship of floor, walls, and ceiling in outdoor space is understood, organizing your property for the use, pleasure, and comfort of your family becomes relatively easy.

FIRST, get a plan or a map of your property down on paper.

No matter how poorly you draw or how limited your understanding of

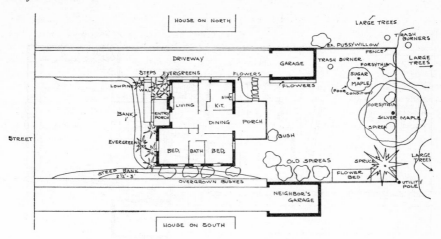

1. *The first step in improving your property is to plot all its elements.*

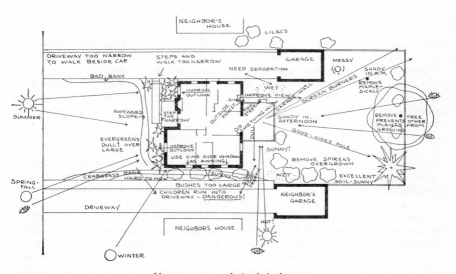

2. *Next comes an analysis of the features.*

mechanics, you ought to be able to make an understandable plan of your property as it exists now.

Note in the first drawing how simply various elements are plotted. A fairly accurate plan of the house floor plan is important, because in planning your outdoor living room you will want to consider views through windows from various rooms, too.

Notice, for example, that the plan shows the location of the kitchen sink under the window. If your sink has a window over it, why not plan something lovely to look at when you stand there? The hours spent at the kitchen sink will be easier if a flowering tree (maybe one that has bright leaves in autumn and a bird feeder in winter) or a handsome evergreen with a bird-

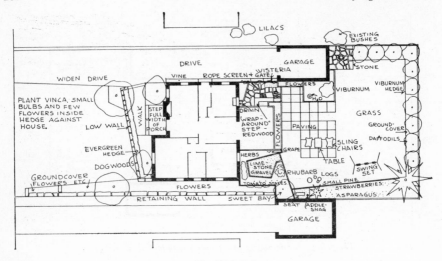

3. *The finished plan.*

house and a spring family of wrens is
seen through the window—these things
add pleasure to everyday activities.

Notice that the second step in the
second drawing is the analysis of the
property on the plan you have already
drawn. If you use a red pencil for the
undesirable features and a green for
the desirable ones (which you will
want to keep), it will be easier to separate each when you come to the planning stage.

I GUARANTEE that once you start ana-
lyzing your lot, you will find several
features that you will wonder how you
have put up with, but you will also
find some that are really on the plus
side of your landscaping ledger and
that maybe you have not even noticed
before. This is an eye-opening experience.

In your analysis, use symbols to de-
note features or problems or make
notes. You are the only one who needs
to understand the final plan; use whatever notation comes to mind.

In the second drawing, for example,
the "eyes" represent invasion of privacy. The sun with wiggly rays is hot in
summer and undesirable. The one

without rays (spring and winter) is
desirable and needed. Notice, too, that
many windows have an arrow and a
note, "improve outlook." Even such
an ordinary object as the garage wall
is taken into consideration, because, in
this particular backyard, the garage
wall is part of the garden wall.

Once you have proceeded this far, it
is simply a matter of doing something
about the problem spots and making
the best use of the good features.

If you follow through, reading back
and forth between the analysis of the
sample background and the third illus-
tration, the finished plan (an actual
one, by the way—I lived in this house),
you will note that a hedge was installed
to block out the "eye" at the rear of
the property. A rope screen, gate, and
wisteria vine were installed where the
note on the analysis reads "needs
separation" between garden and driveway. You can see this screen, gate, and
vine and the manner in which it connects garage and house in the upper
section of the fourth drawing.

Where the garage wall stood, naked,
the raised flowerbeds were installed
and also a small birdbath (shown in
the fourth drawing). Note in the plan

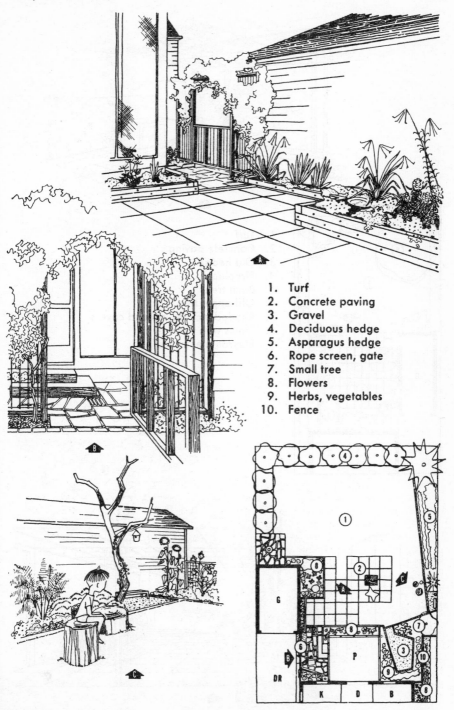

1. Turf
2. Concrete paving
3. Gravel
4. Deciduous hedge
5. Asparagus hedge
6. Rope screen, gate
7. Small tree
8. Flowers
9. Herbs, vegetables
10. Fence

4. *Suggestions for handling trouble spots.*

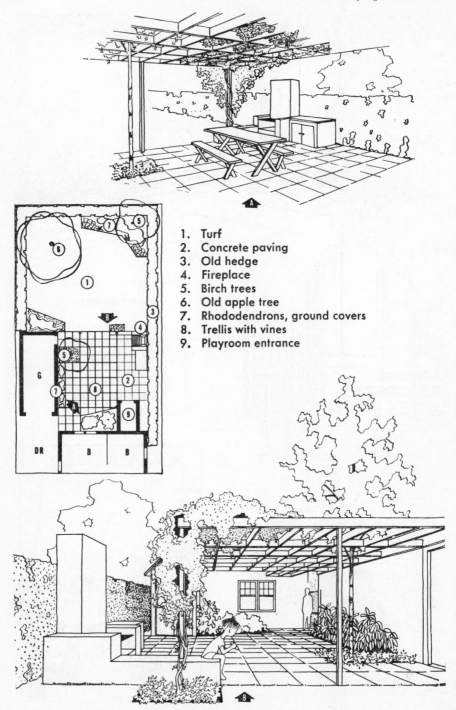

1. Turf
2. Concrete paving
3. Old hedge
4. Fireplace
5. Birch trees
6. Old apple tree
7. Rhododendrons, ground covers
8. Trellis with vines
9. Playroom entrance

5. *A backyard has been made into an easy-to-care-for garden.*

that these also contribute to that important kitchen-sink window view.

Also in the fourth drawing, you can see a sketch of the neighbor's garage wall. An old, cut apple tree trunk was fastened to the wall, with rustproof screw eyes and wire, and a vine was trained to grow up on it. The little boy, in the sketch, sits on a slice from a tree trunk. Children use these for games and for seats and tables. In winter, when they are capped with snow, they look like elegantly frosted cupcakes.

IN DRAWINGS 5, 6, and 7 are examples of other small gardens, which have been created out of what were once backyards.

The first was designed almost entirely for outdoor cooking and dining. The space is tiny. The owners are at business during the day, and their need was for a compact, convenient, low-maintenance garden that would be cool and quiet at the end of the day. The owners did all planting and construction. The concrete paving squares were precast in the basement one winter and placed on a sand and gravel bed, when installed, to insure perfect drainage. The egg-crate trellis ("egg-crate" for design, not source of wood) is covered with vines for air conditioning and fragrant flowers.

The sixth drawing shows how owners of a ranchhouse, newly built on a woodland lot, achieved a large and extremely pleasant outdoor living space, by projecting a natural stone terrace outward from the small dining room.

The seat wall, in the lower part of the sketch, serves to keep people from stepping off the elevated edge of the terrace and is a comfortable bench for sitting, for picnic trays, and children's games. From this terrace, one descends to the free-form lawn panel, which was literally carved out of the woods, the tree positions dictating the shape of the lawn.

The rest of the property, all shady woods, is devoted to ground covers of various sorts, to spring flowering bulbs, naturalized, and to wildflowers. It offers the opportunity to collect a great many kinds of native plants and, like most woodsy places, is attractive to small birds—here is a miniature bird and wildflower sanctuary, easy to maintain, comfortable, useful, and certainly productive of pleasure to the everyday activities of the family.

The seventh drawing illustrates a garden entirely different from the others. It is more formal. It was designed for a family who like lots of roses, flowering plants, perennials, annuals, and spring bulbs.

Because a porch already existed next to the actual garden space, the paved area beyond is small. It ties garden to house, provides strong ground pattern (notice in lower sketch that the lawn panel becomes almost ruglike), and eliminates the worn patches of grass that otherwise would exist in the high traffic area near porch door.

The low hedges are a background for flowering plants and provide design structure during the winter, when the flowering plants are covered with light mulch. The whole garden achieves a sense of spaciousness, although it is quite small. (Compare the entire area with the size of ordinary two-car garage on the plan.)

HOW TO ACHIEVE the most pleasurable results from a small space?

In one word: *Planning.*

Planned backyards become gardens.

Well-planned gardens add to the richness of your environment, extend indoor living space outside, use what often is wasted space, and give you a place for dining, reading, entertaining, and taking a Sunday afternoon nap.

A garden is essential to good living. (CARLTON B. LEES)

The seven drawings in this chapter are from *Budget Landscaping*, by Carlton B. Lees, and are reproduced by permission of Holt, Rinehart and Winston, Inc., the publishers. Copyright 1960 by Carlton B. Lees.

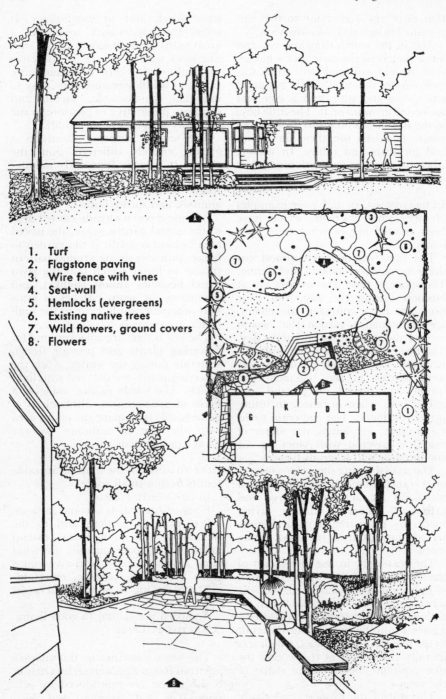

1. Turf
2. Flagstone paving
3. Wire fence with vines
4. Seat-wall
5. Hemlocks (evergreens)
6. Existing native trees
7. Wild flowers, ground covers
8. Flowers

6. *The extension of a natural stone terrace achieves a pleasant living space.*

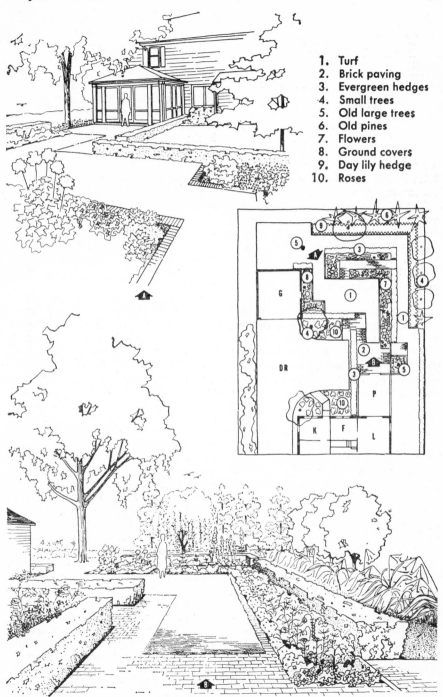

1. Turf
2. Brick paving
3. Evergreen hedges
4. Small trees
5. Old large trees
6. Old pines
7. Flowers
8. Ground covers
9. Day lily hedge
10. Roses

7. A more formal garden.

Patios

A GOOD IDEA is to plan your outdoor living spaces as though they were roofless rooms.

Plan them so members of your family can use them now and later, when they will need space for new activities. Undeveloped space in the beginning will be useful in the future.

One large patio may be as inappropriate for a family as a one-room house. This is what I mean: Maybe you should have several, for which you provide the space and items needed for the things you plan to do in each.

Use is the key. People plan rooms for use, not just as backgrounds for furnishings. By the same token, it is a mistake to place too much emphasis on landscaping an outdoor room and not enough on its present and future use. The consequence is that more time is spent maintaining the outdoor areas than enjoying them.

Another error is to use too many plants and too many of the kind that spread into space intended for people. Tall, dense plants are good sound barriers; they belong in the background.

Neither a room nor a patio, furthermore, should be so cluttered or indefinite in purpose and function that getting it ready for use becomes a discouraging chore.

Your climate determines more or less what you do outdoors and how often you use your outdoor areas. Let me suggest some uses, based on the relation between indoor and outdoor "rooms."

IF YOU LIVE in a contemporary house without an entry hall, an entrance patio will shield your front door from the street.

It is smaller and less elaborate than the front patios of the Spanish-style houses. A masonry wall, structural panels or vertical louvers to head height, and paving are essential.

Potted plants are attractive during the growing season. Evergreens do well in the shade and give this patio an all-season look.

THE LIVING PATIO, a quiet place for relaxation, extends the living room for informal hospitality.

It may be one to three times the size of a living room. An irregular shape can be interesting and useful. Small patios, 300 to 400 square feet, generally are more useful if the surface is paved.

If the living patio is twice the size of a living room, or larger, it may have a plot of grass, but a generous amount of paving is desirable. Paving makes it usable when the ground is damp. In larger patios, a shelter with screening for privacy and a windbreak is pleasant and useful.

Select plants that mature to an appropriate size for the space that is allotted to them. Specimen plants add interest because of their form, foliage, or color. Evergreens and nonplant materials, such as rocks, give an all-season appearance. Annuals and potted plants add color. Outdoor furniture and built-in seats are ready to use. Additional chairs should be stored nearby. If there is a tree, put a square or circular seat around its trunk.

For a swimming pool in a living patio, allow at least 800 square feet. Concrete decking, in a color that reduces glare, adds to the appearance of the patio. Grass in front of the pool and evergreen shrubbery or trees back of it make a good setting. Short walls that form sheltered corners on the patio side are useful and attractive.

If you include a pool, design the living patio so that it is not accessible to uninvited persons. Remember that a pool may entail legal responsibilities and liabilities, about which you should find out.

A living patio convenient to the kitchen may be used for dining. If it is on the opposite side of the house, you may want to reserve a terrace near the kitchen and equip it for outdoor cooking and eating.

Portable charcoal braziers provide amply for most patio cooking and have replaced outdoor fireplaces in many new homes. Food that is prepared in the kitchen may be served from a buffet table indoors.

Be forewarned that outdoor eating is not all beer and skittles.

Flying and crawling insects or drift and residue from insecticides may make outdoor meals unpleasant. Air-conditioned indoors may be pleasanter than torrid outdoors. There are problems of logistics and management, although good managers can overcome them by preparing much of the food indoors.

ANOTHER KIND of patio is the master-bedroom patio.

It may take any shape that is left on the site. Half the area of the bedroom is large enough—room for two persons. A paved surface is desirable. Use slender growing plants and a planter with annuals for color. If a swimming pool is not a part of the plan, a plunge pool may be included in this patio. If so, add the width and length of such a pool. Repeat the bedroom colors in this patio to give a related feeling.

THE MULTIPURPOSE PATIO may change its name during the family cycles. It may begin as an unassigned plot on the back of your lot. It should be accessible to an alley or side driveway. A double carport size is minimum space.

Without grass, it is a good place for children to dig ditches and heap dirt into hills. If so, enclose it with a high wall or permanent fence that cannot be climbed and a drive-through gate.

Later, this patio is a safe place for novice campers to pitch a tent and cook out. It meets the requirements of a puppy yard, rabbit hutches, or a pigeon loft. When an interest in animals has passed, it can be a place to remodel an old car or drydock the family boat. Sometime it may become a garden. Vines on the fence will provide some privacy. Put a bench in the shade for adults.

A UTILITY PATIO is a workshop.

It is a good place for a shelter for garden tools and supplies, a portable brazier, fireplace wood, the stepladder, outdoor furniture, and sports and camping equipment. It should be convenient to the kitchen entrance, the carport, and, if possible, to the outdoor living area. An area 20 feet by 24 feet is ample for it.

The craftsman in the family has a place here for a workbench and lumber. The gardener may like a potting bench.

An 8-foot extension of the carport roof gives protection. Vertical board or plastic siding on the ends keeps out the sun and rain. It costs less to protect an area with the long side open than it costs to build storage cabinets. A concrete slab raised a few inches above ground level is desirable under the roof.

The open area is a good place for a drying line.

If a homesite is selected because there is a wooded area, distant hills, or a stream, the view should be featured in the development of a terrace. It is especially nice when patios are active and noisy. Trees and shrubbery can hide an unattractive foreground. Such a terrace may be a few steps higher or lower than other patios.

LIKE THE ROOMS in a house, patios should be connected with passageways that are direct and avoid crossing conversational, work, or recreational areas.

If walkways are used frequently, paving is desirable. When they are used infrequently, steppingstones are adequate and attractive.

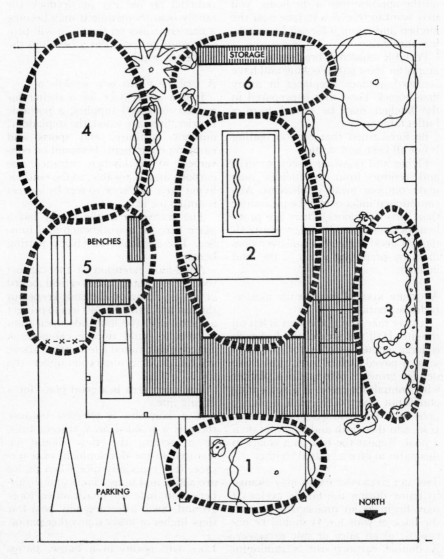

1. ENTRANCE PATIO   4. MULTI-PURPOSE PATIO
2. LIVING PATIO   5. UTILITY PATIO
3. BEDROOM PATIO   6. VIEW TERRACE—ROOFED

Layouts for different kinds of patios.

If your family's interest in gardening exceeds the space in the patios, make the passageways wide enough for planting along the walks.

You need dividers to define the different patios, reduce noise, give privacy, and provide background. You can avoid the "rat in a maze" feeling by planning short dividers. Structures or plants may be used.

When dividers serve as windbreaks, solid masonry blocks, wood louvers, and slender evergreens should be considered. Vary the kind of dividers, but do not use so many kinds that your patio will look like a display room.

Finish two different materials in the same color to avoid the impression of too many materials.

Seldom is a housesite so level that grading is not necessary. One or more steps may be required between patios.

Keep the utility and living patios near the floor level of the house for convenience but low enough to prevent water from flowing into the house or through covered areas. Establish grade levels beyond the living and utility patios.

When grading requires one or more steps between patios, plan wide treads and low risers. They look better and they are easier to climb. Make the steps wider than the openings that connect the patios for safety.

A sunny day is a good time to plan a patio, but a poor time to remember that good drainage is needed. It is difficult to change a natural drainage feature and seldom advisable. Make ditches a part of your plan and use bridges where they are needed.

Lighting may be functional or decorative. Steps in the dark are a hazard, but low lights can make them safe. Decorative lights are pleasanter than a strong floodlight in conversational centers.

Swimming pools and work areas especially need adequate light. Floodlights, controlled within the house, are a protection and convenience.

Eating areas should be lighted if you plan to eat outdoors in the evening.

Electrical outlets for power tools, work lights, and kitchen appliances should be placed in appropriate places.

Investigate the tax rates (and building codes) on the various kinds of structures, paving, and fencing before you build. The rates may vary according to the kinds and heights of walls and the kinds of paving and fencing.

In some localities, everything is taxable except noncommercial trees and shrubbery. The taxes may influence your choices, but the higher taxes you may pay on some materials and structures may be offset by maintenance and replacement costs on less durable materials.

Decide if the use of a patio will justify the cost and labor.

Avoid conflicting uses in the same patio.

Do not overplan. Plan before you build. Plan before you plant. (FAYE C. JONES)

You Can Do It

THERE REALLY is no need for the apathy and thoughtlessness that let many American cities become dreary, dirty, dull warrens.

Consider Philadelphia, which is redeeming itself from squalor that some persons thought was almost as bad as the pitiful mediocrity of a Calcutta.

A group of Philadelphians—ordinary citizens in all respects except their active wish to improve the place they live—in 1953 began a project that has become known as the garden-block program. Seven pilot garden blocks were sponsored the first year. There were more than 400 garden blocks in 1965.

The activity has been carried on in

blighted areas under the sponsorship of the surburban garden clubs and other groups connected with the Neighborhood Garden Association of Philadelphia.

It is a down-to-earth program, in which all the people in the blocks participate actively. It has improved the lives and environment of hundreds of thousands of people in congested sections.

In a typical garden block, flower boxes at all the windows along the street are filled with bright geraniums and cascading petunias. In small flower bays, built of bricks or cement blocks between the windows, a climbing rose is planted.

Any trash-filled vacant lots in the block are cleared and made into community gardens. Streets are kept tidy and free of litter.

Residents of a block become participants in the program by applying to the Neighborhood Garden Association and giving assurance that certain requirements will be met.

They must have an interested leader, who usually is the man or woman who presents the application. At least 80 percent of the residents on the block must agree to participate. (Participation usually is 100 percent.) The people on the block agree to make their flower boxes or to buy boxes approved by the association and to have them prepared and ready for planting on a date specified in the instructions.

After a block has been accepted, a sponsoring suburban garden club is assigned to the block. On a designated day, the members bring in the flowers, show the residents of the blocks how to plant their boxes, and leave with them instructions for their care and membership seals to be placed in windows.

All garden blocks are judged by a special committee during the late summer. Blocks that have maintained a high standard receive an award of merit at an annual award dinner in November.

The garden blocks are sponsored for 2 years. During that time, the rose bays are built, and the vacant lots become gardens or play areas for children. After 2 years, the blocks become independent blocks and are responsible for buying their own flowers (which they can obtain at wholesale rates through the association).

All independent blocks remain members of the Neighborhood Garden Association, and many continue to be blue-ribbon award-of-merit winners year after year.

In depressed areas where people were indifferent to their surroundings, the garden-block program has instilled new spirit and pride. It has taught neighbors to work cooperatively together to improve their communities. It has developed leaders in areas where there had been little opportunity for leadership. It has fostered friendship and understanding among persons of diverse nationalities and races. It has helped people in underprivileged areas grow in awareness of their responsibilities as concerned citizens.

People in other cities have adopted the garden-block program, so successful has it been in Philadelphia.

For these forward-looking residents of Philadelphia and the other cities, I am certain several paragraphs of President Johnson's state of the Union message on January 4, 1965, had special significance:

"In our urban areas the central problem today is to protect and restore man's satisfaction in belonging to a community where he can find security and significance. . . .

"For over three centuries the beauty of America has sustained our spirit and enlarged our vision. We must act now to protect this heritage. . . .

"Within our cities imaginative programs are needed to landscape streets and transform open areas into places of beauty and recreation."

As Lewis Mumford, who has written a number of books on cities and the American scene, has said, "Any city planning worthy to be called organic must bring some measure of beauty and order into the poorest neighborhoods."

City planning commissions have been formed in many communities. Many exciting advances have come in urban redevelopment programs. Zoning ordinances in many cities and towns guide expansion and protect the stability of business and residential communities. Among more and more citizens, awareness grows of their civic responsibilities.

But countless towns and cities remain untouched by this upsurge of civic pride—communities where apathy prevails.

Perhaps they do not see how nondescript their communities are, so accustomed are they to it. People from Europe who visit the United States see it from an undulled viewpoint; they remark the drabness and the dreary aspect of our cities and towns. They find it hard to understand why so much apathy exists and why no effort is made to make communities attractive. In their own towns and cities, no richer or better endowed than ours, flowers are cherished everywhere.

In the cities of Denmark, Norway, and Sweden, large, well-designed containers filled with a great variety of flowers grace the main shopping streets, every plaza, and many stores, office buildings, houses.

In the great city of Paris, all but a few people live within walking distance of a park.

Compare the French capital with our National Capital: A few tubs here and there of artificial plants; uncaredfor trees; litter everywhere, including the Capitol grounds; a few expensive but abortive attempts to grow grass on the Mall, over which thoughtless residents and tourists soon make paths; a citizenry that values a dusty, sordid parking lot (like the shameful disgrace in what was planned as a magnificent plaza in the center of the city) to a block of grass and trees.

Every village, town, city in this country needs citizens who feel a deep,

personal sense of civic responsibility. Maybe there are such, but maybe they feel that any effort toward civic improvement that they might make as individuals would not count for much.

My answer to that is the observation of an English philosopher, Herbert Spencer: "I am constantly impressed with how infinitesimal is anything that I can do; yet I am ever more impressed with how important it is that I do it."

One person working alone may be able to accomplish little. If he adds his effort to a community of effort, each person finds his own efforts enlarged and strengthened.

Thus it is in the constructive projects for civic betterment initiated by garden clubs, women's clubs, neighborhood groups, service clubs, junior chambers of commerce, and other civic organizations. Their efforts have changed the face of some cities and towns and have put to shame the communities whose citizens have not cared enough or who have been too afraid, shy, lazy, indifferent to take action.

ONE OF THE FIRST cities to undertake a comprehensive program of beautification was Portland, Oreg., which is noted for its flowers. In many parts of the city are borders of magnificent roses between the street and the sidewalk. Attractive plantings set off public buildings. Citizens take great pride in the beauty of their city.

In many towns and villages in New Hampshire, the women's clubs, the 4-H Clubs, and the Scouts are active. Flower boxes are planted at post offices, town halls, the Grange hall, libraries, and other buildings. The approaches to the towns often are planted with flowers, which are tended with loving care.

In Allentown, Pa., beautiful baskets of flowers adorn the poles along the shopping streets and add to the charm of the city.

In Woodstock, Vt., and Wolfeboro, N.H., shopowners have long, attractive boxes in front of their shops filled with a variety of flowers.

Charleston, S.C., Savannah, Ga., and other southern cities have active garden clubs whose projects have done much for their communities.

In places like Baltimore, Philadelphia, and Brooklyn, where many streets have houses that open directly on the sidewalk, one would think there is little possibility of dressing them up. Not so; much has been done to bring bloom and beauty to such communities. Where people have vision, much can be done.

I have merely skimmed the surface in this rapid survey, but my examples indicate what can be achieved by citizens working together.

WHEN AN ORGANIZATION or group wishes to undertake a civic project, it is wise to survey the needs of the community.

You may list scores of possibilities—planting trees along some of the main streets; setting out shrubs around a public building; developing an open plaza with benches and tubs of flowers; making an ill-kept lot into a park; preserving trees that are jeopardized in an unnecessary street-widening proposal; installing containers for litter on corners; sharing surplus shrubs and seeds with neighbors; encouraging all homeowners to improve (or at least keep clean) the public sidewalks and curbs in front of their property; enlisting children in a continuing clean-up, pretty-up drive.

There could be many more. The list made after a survey should not be overly long. All should be considered on a basis of urgency and desirability before a decision is made. Do not bite off more than you can chew.

One of the first projects most community groups consider is the planting of trees—certainly nothing enhances appearance more than beautiful, tree-lined streets.

A word of caution, however. Before a group embarks on such a project, several points must be considered. Some trees are not well adapted to city conditions because they are sus-

ceptible to fumes, soot, and grime. Few evergreens can tolerate such hazards.

An example: The merchants along a street in a large city got together and with eager enthusiasm bought large, handsome redwood tubs, in which young evergreens had been planted. Unfortunately, the trees were unsuited to city conditions. By the end of the first season, they began to show the effects of their uncongenial environment. Before the end of the next, most of them were dying and had to be removed. It was a disheartening and costly endeavor.

Such pitfalls can be avoided by first consulting a local nurseryman, city park official, a consulting forester, the State department of forestry, the division of horticulture or forestry of the State university, or a book, like *Trees*, the 1949 Yearbook of Agriculture. (I recommend also *A Place To Live*, the 1963 Yearbook of Agriculture, which is of value to all who want to improve their communities.)

The eventual size of a tree must also be considered. Where streets and avenues are broad, that is not so important a consideration as it is in many of the older cities where streets are narrow.

But in narrow streets, if trees are planted at all, they should be slender and pyramidal in shape and moderate in height.

THE LARGE-SCALE planning of cities can be left to city planners, who are trained professionals, but much can be accomplished by community-minded, dedicated citizens.

They can add the touches of beauty that give a lift to an otherwise drab neighborhood. They can enhance the beauty of a newly built mall with an allée of magnolias. They can take a neglected corner in a park and make it a spectacular point of interest with a planting of brilliant azaleas.

Then our villages, towns, and cities will become places of dignity, beauty, and pride. (LOUISE BUSH-BROWN)

ACTIVITIES

Country

Vacations

A VACATION in the country is a quiet, joyful, broadening—but usually not expensive—experience for a growing number of American city families.

Many farmers and ranchers with large homes, fully modernized for comfort comparable to city living, welcome paying guests.

Some make vacation farming or dude ranching a major source of income, but most prefer to continue their operations as working farms or ranches, with the addition of recreation and vacation services to city people as an extra source of income.

They offer good food served family style, comfortable lodgings, and a low-key sort of fun different from anything Coney Island, Miami Beach, and Disneyland can offer.

The things that farmers take for granted are the main attractions—friendliness, peace, the life of farm animals and plants, space, good air, sun, country smells, simplicity.

Some provide much more, depending on location and size of enterprise—picnicking, camping, fishing, hunting, swimming, boating, water skiing, tobogganing, sledding, skating, other winter sports, guided trail rides, canoeing, horseback and pony riding, hayrides and wagon trains, nature trails, cave and cavern exploration, playing fields, and maybe even golf.

You can get information about certain of these enterprises from commercial listings.

Farm Vacation Guide to Recommended Farms, Ranches, Lodges and Inns, published by Farm Vacations and Holidays, Inc., 36 East 57th Street, New York City, is one. The guide has listings in all States and Canada and sells for a dollar.

Most of the State vacation and travel bureaus in the State capitals offer brochures and other helpful information regarding these and other rural recreation facilities. These materials are usually free.

The county agricultural agents in the county-seat towns can give details about rural recreation enterprises.

THE FOOD AND AGRICULTURE Act of 1962 gave the Department of Agriculture new authority and responsibility pertaining to the recreational use of private land, water, and related natural resources. Help is given farmers, ranchers, and other private landowners to plan and install outdoor recreation enterprises.

Vacation farms are one of several categories of outdoor recreation enterprises being developed under this program. For most of them, recreation management is a new phase of their farming enterprise, in which the whole family must enjoy working with people as well as land, water, livestock, wildlife, plants, and trees to form the desirable outdoor recreation setting.

We give a few examples of the enterprises that offer a wide variety of opportunities to urban people to enjoy a few hours, a day, a week, or longer in wholesome outdoor activity.

A Vacation Farm: A farm-reared man retired to a small farm in the Northeast after being employed in the construction business for many years. Shortly thereafter he and his wife began accepting summer guests to supplement their income. Most of their guests are elderly couples with good incomes from eastern cities. The main farmhouse and two housekeeping cottages can lodge about 15 persons. Most of the guests come between May and September. Many couples return year after year. Entertainment includes cards, TV, a library, croquet, and other simple activities.

Weekly rates for the cottages, without meals or linens, start at 65 dollars for two persons. Rates per person in the home, including meals, are 9 dollars daily for a single room, 8 dollars daily for a double room, or 45 dollars for a week.

Weekly rates at other vacation farms, including lodging, meals, and recreation facilities, may be 26 to 35 dollars for a child and 30 to 50 for an adult.

A modest family-owned working ranch of 1,200 acres in the Southwest has a ranchhouse and small cottages large enough to accommodate as many as 30 guests. Livestock consists of a small herd of beef cattle and some 40 pack and saddle horses. Guests are mainly family groups. The mother, two daughters, and a son-in-law and extra help run the ranch and associated recreation activities.

The activities include horseback riding, pack trail trips, barbecues, trout fishing, and hunting grouse, turkey, deer, and elk.

Most of the guests, who generally return year after year, are doctors, lawyers, and other professional people. Rates for lodging and meals and most activities are 15 dollars a day. Riding horses for those who desire them are an extra 3.50 dollars a day.

Picnicking and Sports Center: A dairy farmer near a midwestern city started his outdoor recreation business by developing picnic sites on 4 acres around a nice pond. Interest in his enterprise has grown. He now has a new clubhouse and 25 acres developed for various outdoor sports and activities. He leases the site to organized groups, such as civic clubs, school classes, churches, and athletic clubs. He has facilities for picnicking, softball, fishing, volleyball, horseshoe pitching, and swimming. The farmer and his wife provide a catering service in the clubhouse for parties and banquets.

His recreation enterprise has grown from a few picnic sites to a fairly large private park for public use. As many as 100 persons can be accommodated in the clubhouse and much larger groups in outside activities. A charge of 40 dollars a day is made to a group for exclusive use of the park and 3 to 4 dollars a person for banquets. The farmer has an investment of more than 60 thousand dollars in the 70-cow, 114-acre dairy farm and about 12 thousand dollars in the park and associated recreation facilities.

He received technical help from the Department of Agriculture in laying out his farm pond and in developing a management plan for his woodlands, including recreation use features. The State wildlife agency provided specifications for stocking his pond with suitable species of fish and prepared a fish-pond management plan.

Recreation in a Small Watershed Project Area: In a small pilot watershed project, 24 floodwater-retarding structures were built to help protect farms and cities downstream. Seven of the landowners who had given permanent easements on the parts of their farms that held the impounded water charge 50 cents to 1 dollar a day per person for fishing privileges.

A supervisor of the local soil conservation district operates a farm on which one of the lakes is located. He has made the area around it available to church groups, Boy Scout troops, a fox hunters' association, and friends.

Fishing Waters: A farmer in a north-central State stocked a pond on his 85-acre farm with bass and other warm-water species. The fee for good fishing in it is 1 dollar a day per pole. The farmer later developed a trout-fishing facility. By keeping it well stocked, he now has all the customers he can handle most of the season at the rate of 3 dollars a day with a limit of five trout.

He added a snackbar and bait and tackle shop. Many of his customers are family groups who come from more than 100 miles away.

A Campground: A beef and general-crop farmer in the Northeast also worked in town because his farm operation was not large enough to return an adequate income for his family. The farm was in a scenic area, so he set out to develop a campsite. Ten sites were established the first year. The second year he added 20 more.

His facilities include a camp pantry, campfire area, a pond, and fields for playgrounds. Camper fees are 1.50 dollars a night. Camp use averages 80 percent of capacity for the season.

Hunting Areas: Through the efforts of the county agent, 50 farmers in a midwestern county arranged for deer hunting on their property. Through this association, 26 thousand acres of privately owned land were opened to hunting. The hunter is charged 10 dollars a day for the right to hunt on the private land. Of course he must have a hunting license and abide by State hunting regulations. This cooperative effort made available the first year 1,600 man-days of hunting, much of it on land that had previously been posted. Some of the farm families also provide rooms and meals.

Shooting Preserves: Most outdoor recreation enterprises on farms and ranches are of the type requiring relatively low costs to the recreationist. Many farm pond owners permit the fisherman to enter on an honor system. In a metal box at a farm gate, for example, he drops 50 cents for the privilege of fishing an hour or all day.

Other farmers have made large investments to provide luxury recreation. A livestock and crop farmer in the South converted his 640-acre farm largely to a high-quality shooting preserve. He provides the birds, dogs, guides, and motor service to and from the shooting courses. He has built a center with lockers and lounge.

For these services, plus a gun if the hunter does not bring his own, the farmer charges 20 dollars per person per day, for which he guarantees three pheasants, five quail, or four chukars. He has four shooting courses. Each one can take only four hunters and a guide at a given time. In addition, he has two small lakes for flighting mallards. The charge for duck hunting is 15 dollars a day, plus 4 dollars per duck in excess of three.

All the assistance to develop recreation facilities that is made available by technical agencies of the Department of Agriculture is for the consideration of the landowner or operator in making his own decisions. His final plan covers a complete land use and conservation program for his entire land unit. It becomes a cooperative agreement between the landowner and his local soil and water conservation district.

In all this work, full attention is also given to quality of outdoor recreation enterprises and facilities for the good of both the land and the people. City people who want wholesome outdoor recreation and relaxation for themselves and their families may find it on the farms and ranches of rural America. It is being made available on more and more acres in great variety. (LLOYD E. PARTAIN)

Camp
and Carry

A backpacking family.

BACKPACKING opens new horizons. It offers solitude and adventure, quiet without silence, serenity in wildness, and satisfaction in the discomforts of primitive living.

With comfortable shoes and an easy-riding pack, anyone in reasonably good health can backpack. The step from the charcoal grills of the backyard to the cook fires of the back country is short.

Opportunities for backpacking are many. You can follow the trail of the Indian, the prospector, the mountainman. You can penetrate deep wilderness or explore the narrow trails that beckon from the paved highway.

In the 154 National Forests administered by the Forest Service, more than 100,000 miles of trails lead backpackers to tiny, unnamed lakes fed by permanent snowfields; boulder-strewn canyons; alpine meadows; cool, cathedrallike stands of pine, and granite peaks high above timberline.

Of the 181 million acres of National Forests open to the backpacker, 9.1 million are in the national wilderness preservation system. The 22 million acres of national parks and national monuments, 5 million acres of State parks, and 17.5 million acres of State forests offer opportunities for weekend or weeklong trips.

Trails also traverse many miles of lands owned by the timber industry. They also are open for your enjoyment.

THE SECRET of happy backpacking is a light load.

Men can carry up to 50 pounds but prefer weights under 40. Women should keep their packs to about 30 pounds. When weighing your load, include camera and the items you carry on your belt.

That means careful selection of clothing, food, and equipment.

The following items are essential: Tent or tarp for shelter; sleeping bags; cooking utensils; plates, cups, and cutlery; food, 1.5 pounds per person per day; slacks or jeans, long-sleeved cotton shirt, wool shirt or sweater, parka or windbreaker, wool socks, underwear, camp shoes, rain gear; flashlight with extra batteries and bulb; first-aid kit (make your own, but include bandages, 4-inch elastic bandage, triangular bandage, antiseptic, aspirin, eyewash, and adhesive tape); bug dope; maps and map case; hatchet or lightweight saw; small pliers; matches; soap and towel; needle and thread; safety pins.

MENUS you should work out in advance to get a balanced diet on dehydrated foods and to enable you to use only one or two pots for cooking.

All grocers carry many food items for backpacking: Dried soup, rice, dehydrated potato, macaroni and noodles with dried sauces; cereals, dried fruit, cheese, and hard salami that needs no refrigeration.

Take the food out of cardboard containers and put in plastic bags.

Dehydrated vegetables, salads, applesauce, fish patties, beef, chicken, and bacon are available from sporting goods stores or mail-order houses. More expensive but more natural in taste and quicker cooking are the freeze-dried foods, which offer a variety—such as swiss steak, pork chops, and chicken stew. These, too, are available at sporting goods stores.

Depending on how economical you want to be, the cost of food for one person a day may be 2 dollars or somewhat less. Leave nothing to chance in your menu planning. Do not count on living off the land—you may lose more pounds than you should.

Large tin cans that you can get for nothing from almost any restaurant make fine cook pots, either by themselves or as a supplement to a nesting set of pots and frypans. You may want to attach a bail at the top of the can. You will need a holder for it.

COOK FIRES should be small. For safety's sake, scrape pine needles and dry leaves away from the fire area. Build your fireplace of stone if one is not provided.

When you break camp, dismantle your fireplace, leaving no sign of your stay.

When you are traveling in country where wood is scarce or wet, take along a lightweight single-burner stove that uses gasoline or other liquid fuel. One quart will be enough for 14 meals. It will provide quick, intense heat.

Check with rangers regarding campfire permits on public lands and with the landowner if you are on private land.

Burn, flatten, and carry out any tin cans.

SHELTER AGAINST bad weather also is a prime matter in backpacking. In only a few parts of the country can a backpacker be almost sure of no rain during certain seasons. It is advisable therefore to carry some type of tent. Nothing can dampen the spirits more than rain in the face in the dark of night, and

A pause on the trail.

nothing adds more weight to the pack than a soggy sleeping bag.

For tents, the plastic tube is most popular. It is similar to the tube used by drycleaners to cover clothing, but it is heavier. A rope stretched through the tube with each end tied to trees or brush forms the ridge pole. Stones at each corner anchor the tube to the ground and give it a triangular shape. It costs about 75 cents a yard.

A nylon ground cloth or a painter's plastic drop cloth, 9 by 12 feet and with grommets, can be used for a shelter. It may be fixed in many ways. Plastic material and grommet kits are inexpensive, if you wish to make your own.

In places where there may be insects, use a tent that has a floor and netting at the openings. There are many types; some with aluminum telescopic poles weigh 4 to 5 pounds. Two-pound tents also can be bought.

One of the joys of backpacking is that you can stop when and where you will—with the setting sun, a good view, or tired feet. But a good campsite must be level and near drinking water and should have wood for a fire.

After those three basics, look for shelter from the wind that blows off the lake and down a canyon at night—

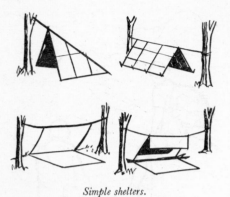

Simple shelters.

and in reverse during the day. Try to catch the morning sun, which will dispel moisture from night dews or showers.

FOR A GOOD night's sleep do not count on fatigue alone. Warmth and comfort are essential.

A sleeping bag is practical and warm. Your choice among the many kinds should be based on how much money you want to spend and the temperature of the country you intend to hike in most. Kapok bags are warm but bulky and heavy. Down is light but expensive and too warm for some climates. Down and feather mixtures are less expensive but heavy. Wool bat bags are fine for summer. Dacron is popular though bulky. Some campers make sleeping bags from a comforter. Costs are 10 to 100 dollars.

There comes a time, usually just after a person's 29th birthday, when an air mattress makes all the difference between a good and a poor night's sleep.

Young folk can awake from sleeping on the ground with all the zip needed to face a new day. The older backpacker sleeping without a mattress wakens early and gets up tired. Sporting goods manufacturers these days cater to his needs with nylon air mattresses in short lengths. A 4-foot mattress is long enough to get shoulders and hips off the ground and saves many ounces of weight. If the ground

is cold, put gear under knees and feet and use a sweater for a pillow.

The pack into which food and equipment is stuffed must be light and roomy. Least expensive of the suitable packs is the rucksack, a bag with a drawstring at the top and with straps for the shoulders. The weight of the load in this pack, however, rests heavy on the back, cuts your wind, and pulls on the shoulders.

The army designed a frame pack that places the weight largely on the hips. If you can find an army frame pack that fits you, it is an excellent buy. There are many commercial variations, which are lighter in weight and better in fit but more expensive than the army pack.

Most experienced backpacking enthusiasts like a lightweight aluminum packframe, which is angled at shoulders and waist to fit the contours of the body with only nylon bands resting against the back. These frames come in sizes to fit different weights and heights. Straps from the lower part of the frame fasten just below the waist, and the weight of the pack is on the hips. The frame may be bought with or without a pack attached.

Without a pack, the frame is like the old packboard used by hunters and trappers, but it is more comfortable. Items of all sizes and shapes can be lashed to it with rope. The main disadvantage of the frame without a pack is that it is not easy to get out little items needed during the day, such as lunch and rain gear.

BEFORE YOU TAKE OFF on a backpacking vacation, take 1-day hikes to loosen muscles and break in boots.

Test the equipment in the backyard. Put up the tent. Light the stove. Build a fire with damp wood.

Make a trial run. Hike 3 or 4 miles to a favorite lake or mountain. Set up camp and stay the weekend. For that short time, it will not matter that your checklist of items was incomplete or you left the salt at home.

Get maps of the area in which you

want to hike. Regional offices of the Forest Service can provide maps of the National Forests and usually have special maps for National Forest wildernesses.

Write to the State recreation departments. Maybe you will want the Geological Survey's topographic maps, which can give details of the height of the land and steepness of climbs, as well as streams, lakes, and trails. Plot your course.

And now, with pack on back, take with confidence that first step that leads from backyard to backwoods, to the marvelous country that you cannot see from a jeep, a bike, or even a horse. (DOROTHY M. MARTIN)

Comfort
Outdoors

YOU CAN DO a great deal to protect yourself when you are outdoors from the attacks of most insects by using safe and inexpensive repellents, which can prevent biting; properly applied insecticides, which can reduce the abundance of insects; and protective clothing, screened tents, and bed nets, which can keep pests and disease carriers away without the use of repellents or insecticidal sprays.

Repellents are effective against mosquitoes, biting flies, gnats, chiggers, ticks, and fleas. They are not effective against yellow jackets, other wasps, and spiders or scorpions.

Insect repellents you can buy contain such active ingredients as deet, dimethyl carbate, dimethyl phthalate, ethyl hexanediol, and Indalone.

Each of these repellents is outstanding against certain kinds of insects but varies in its effectiveness with different insects and on different persons.

Each brand must specify the ingredients on its label. All are safe to use and may be applied to the outer clothing or to the exposed skin. Any of them may cause some smarting if it is applied to the mucous membranes or to places where the skin is especially tender, such as the eyelids.

All these repellents affect paints, varnishes, and many of the plastics to some degree. Ethyl hexanediol and deet are much less injurious to painted surfaces than the other repellents and usually do little damage to plastics.

Methods of applying repellents differ with the kinds of insects involved.

To ward off mosquitoes and biting flies and gnats, spread the repellent uniformly over the exposed skin and clothing. Treat especially well shoulders and thighs where the clothing is tight.

Shake a few drops from the bottle or spray from the pressurized can into the palms, smear evenly, and then apply with the hand to the skin or clothing. Skin and clothing may be sprayed directly from a pressurized can if you are careful so the repellent will not get into the eyes.

For protection against chiggers, ticks, and fleas, rub or spray the repellent on the socks and other clothing. Apply liberally along all openings of the clothing, such as inside the neckband, the fly and cuffs of trousers, and the tops of socks.

THE NUMBERS of biting, stinging, and other annoying insects can be reduced through the use of insecticides.

Space sprays and aerosols are designed to treat the air to kill flying insects. Aerosols are sold in pushbutton cans. Space sprays require a sprayer that emits fine droplets.

Their small particles are not satisfactory for treating surfaces on which insects crawl. As their effectiveness is fleeting, they do not offer hazards to the user, to other persons, or to wildlife when they are properly used.

Sprayed into the air around a picnic site, in a tent, or other small areas, they will kill flies, mosquitoes, and gnats. They clear the area of flying insects for at least 30 minutes. Control may last much longer if the insects are not actively migrating.

Space sprays usually contain pyrethrins or allethrin and may also contain DDT, methoxychlor, lindane, malathion, or dichlorvos in low concentration. They will be clearly labeled for flying insects, such as flies and mosquitoes. They will not be labeled for control of crawling insects, such as ants and roaches. Only a few seconds of spraying is necessary in a tent or closed automobile or trailer. Follow the instructions on the product label.

When you spray a small place, such as a picnic site or backyard, hold the can upright as close to the ground as possible and walk back and forth upwind of the area to be protected. If you use a hand sprayer, hold it about 3 feet above the ground while you spray. Do not allow the spray to contaminate food, water, and utensils. Do not spray trees, shrubs, and other vegetation from close up; spray burn may result.

MECHANICAL MEANS of insect control should not be overlooked. For example, windows and doors on tents should be screened. If you sleep outside a tent, use a bed net.

A hat will help prevent the bites of deer flies. Some persons find that a tasseled brim aids in keeping gnats out of the eyes.

In tick country, wear slacks or long trousers and tuck the bottoms of the legs into the tops of boots or socks.

A fly swatter is the most efficient way to kill one or two flies. In an automobile and trailer, a folded map or newspaper makes a good improvised swatter for killing a wasp or yellow jacket.

In tents, floors properly fastened to the sides will keep out scorpions and spiders.

Deer fly.

Mosquito in act of biting.

Small nets should be used to cover food in open dishes.

Always place garbage in the containers provided for the purpose. In wilderness areas where containers are not supplied, bury the garbage at least 2 feet deep or burn it. In a semipermanent camp, your cleanliness and sanitation are the best means of preventing insect buildups. Body wastes should be buried, if there are no toilets.

MOST KINDS of spiders and most scorpions are not particularly dangerous, although bites and stings may be painful.

A clean campsite is not likely to be infested with black widow spiders. Before pitching your tent, clear the area of dead leaves, twigs, and loose stones—scorpions and spiders may be hiding there.

If you are in scorpion territory, check your shoes in the morning before putting them on; scorpions may be hiding in them. Scorpions and many kinds of spiders are active at night and hide during the day. Their hiding places include fallen leaves, underneath loose bark of logs and trees, under rocks, between layers of shalelike rocks, and animal burrows. Do not camp nearer than necessary to rockpiles and fallen trees.

Yellow jackets nest in holes in the ground. Various other kinds of wasps nest in trees and bushes, under rock ledges, in hollow trees, and under some open shelter, such as the eaves of a building. Stay away from the nests when you see them.

Sometimes the various wasps visit picnic areas where they feed on watermelon rind, bits of hamburger, and other garbage. If yellow jackets are numerous in a picnic site, it may be almost impossible to eat even a simple meal, as the wasps will even alight on a sandwich on its way to the mouth.

Except in a backyard, little can be done about yellow jackets and other annoying wasps. At home, the nests can be sprayed with insecticide, but in a public park, wilderness area, or other location away from home, the nests quite likely cannot even be found and should not be sprayed by anyone but the park ranger. You may simply have to move to another location where the wasps are less numerous.

Since spilled food and garbage may attract yellow jackets, see that your picnic or camp site is well cleaned up when you leave. For those who are camping, a tent-size mosquito bar or well-screened tent fly will keep these pests at a distance. There are many outdoor recreation areas where wasps are not a problem.

You cannot, need not, and must not feel that all insects are bad or bothersome.

There are at least 120,000 different kinds of insects in North America north of Mexico, but only a few kinds are inclined or even capable of interfering with your fun.

Many kinds are beneficial. All are worth learning about. Some are even beautiful to look at.

Take along an inexpensive book on insects and read about those you see. Insects are an important part of Nature. Without them, many plants could not be pollinated and would have no fruit. They have helped make the world around you what it is.

By all means get outdoors and enjoy Nature. You should realize, though, that you may encounter insect problems. Go prepared. Take along some insect repellent and an aerosol bomb. You will expect to wear outdoor clothes. Shorts are cool but let too much skin be exposed to mosquitoes and are no barrier at all to ticks and chiggers. Even one mosquito when you are falling asleep can be annoying. You may find dozens or even hundreds, so take a screened tent if you plan to camp out.

Above all, keep your camp or picnic site clean; properly dispose of garbage and other wastes. You are about to meet Nature, and insects are a part of outdoor living. (JOHN A. FLUNO AND D. E. WEIDHAAS)

You and Wildlife

MOST WILD CREATURES fear man instinctively and avoid him whenever possible. But remember, when you are on vacation in the country or mountains, or woods, that you are invading their home territories, and it is only natural that they resent your intrusion. If they mistake your intentions, they may stand up for their rights, occasionally in aggressive fashion.

To the uninitiated, nothing seems to inspire more dread than the possibility of encountering poisonous reptiles. This deep-seated fear is understandable, but also it may be unreasonably exaggerated.

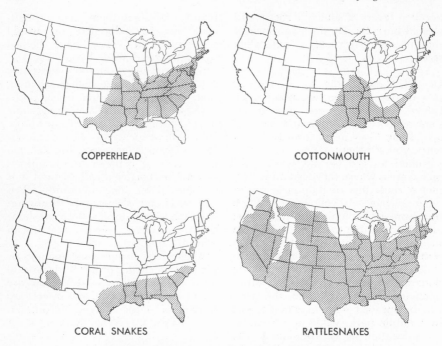

COPPERHEAD   COTTONMOUTH

CORAL SNAKES   RATTLESNAKES

Distribution of poisonous snakes in the United States.

In the United States there are four types of poisonous snakes. Their stronghold is in the Southern States. Rattlesnakes (of some 20 species) are by far the most widespread. They should, of course, be treated with respect, but there is no need to panic at the sight of a snake, for its instinctive reaction is to remain motionless or retreat except when it is suddenly alarmed or stepped on.

Good rules are: Keep always alert, particularly on steep, rocky slopes or in brushy areas. Wear protective clothing, such as heavy trousers, high boots, or leather leggings, on the feet and legs. Hang up bedding and clothing during the day. Never tease or handle any strange snake. Avoid camping in swampy sites or near rocky ledges.

Most of our poisonous snakes are pit-vipers, a name derived from the presence of a pit on the face between the eye and the nostril. Their eyes have vertical pupils, but you had best not approach a living snake closely enough to observe these features. They are typically thick-bodied, long-fanged snakes with flattened heads.

The rattlesnakes are distinguished by a terminal structure that, when rapidly vibrated, produces a buzzing sound that warns of the snake's presence.

The cottonmouth or water moccasin, black or gray in color, frequents sluggish waters and the margins of swamps and bayous.

The copperhead of the uplands, inclined to activity at night, has a striking pattern of dark hourglass bands on a paler, brownish background.

Beware of all of these.

The coral snakes are smaller, short-fanged, brilliantly colored poisonous species that are somewhat slow to bite and very secretive in habits. They may be identified by their pattern of red and black rings *separated by* rings of yellow or whitish (black and red rings never adjoin), and by their black snouts. They lack facial pits and have round pupils.

The Gila monster, a large beaded lizard of our southwestern deserts, is also poisonous, but is so sluggish in habits as to be no great menace.

IF A POISONOUS SNAKE should bite you, try to kill it or at least determine its identity.

Apply a tourniquet between the wound and your heart, loosening it briefly every 20 minutes.

Above all, try to keep quiet, avoid exercise, and take no stimulants, including alcohol.

If a doctor is close by, see him *at once* without further treatment. If not, with a razor blade make an incision as deep as the bite through each fang puncture, then stimulate bleeding by squeezing or sucking (if your mouth and lips are free of cuts).

Cooling the wound with ice or a damp cloth will retard the absorption of the venom.

In any event, consult a doctor as soon as possible. He can provide the necessary serum or other treatment.

All snakes have teeth and can bite, but remember that relatively few are poisonous and that many are beneficial because of the pests they destroy.

Still, there are occasions when they cannot be tolerated. Nuisance snakes may be killed with a gun or club or captured alive and safely transported in a sack for release at a distance.

No repellents are really effective against them, but they may be discouraged about buildings by clearing out brush and tall grass and removing trash heaps, loose boards, and stone piles. Such spots provide cover for snakes and homes for mice and other creatures on which snakes prey.

Snakeproof fences are costly but may be desirable for a children's play space. They should be made of galvanized screen at least 36 inches high, sloping outward at a 30-degree angle. The base should be buried a few inches in the ground. Gates should be tightly fitted.

Snakes may be prevented from entering houses by well-constructed base-

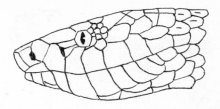

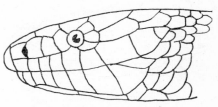

Heads of poisonous cottonmouth (top) and nonpoisonous black racer (bottom). Note the differences in facial structures.

ment walls, preferably sealed with cement. In extreme cases, fumigation may be necessary, but this is a laborious and expensive business.

OTHER potentially dangerous reptiles, none of them poisonous, include the southern alligators and crocodiles of sluggish waters. They are normally timid and attack only when blocked from retreat to water. A blow from the flailing tail can be as destructive as the powerful jaws.

In fresh-water lakes, be on the alert for snapping turtles or softshell turtles lurking in the shallows. Both can inflict severe wounds with the jaws. Softshell turtles also have dangerous claws.

Troublesome turtles may be disposed of by shooting or by capture in a trap baited with a dead fish or other bait.

Aside from gnats, flies, midges, and other vexing insects, no flying creatures are really a problem.

Hawks, eagles, and owls, despite their size, are not dangerous unless one molests their nests.

Bats are harmless, contrary to many lurid tales about them, except for the rare case of a rabid individual. They do not get into a person's hair, nor do they carry bed bugs.

American alligator.

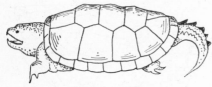

Snapping turtle.

Bat in flight.

bats depart in the evening, board up or screen off all openings where they might gain access—louvers, vents, broken windows, loose shingles. Bats can find and utilize amazingly small crevices. Should this fail, fumigation may be used as a last resort. It is expensive, and has the disadvantage of killing the bats in inaccessible spots, where the odor of their decaying bodies may be unpleasant.

FOR THOSE who make excursions to the ocean, there is the possibility of meeting up with harmful aquatic creatures. Most of the dangerous forms are confined to tropical waters, but a few occur along our shores.

Sharks and barracudas can easily maim a swimmer; guards usually warn of this danger at public beaches. Although inquisitive, these fishes generally are timid and wary. They prefer to attack lone victims, especially if the quarry is wounded or bleeding. So swim in groups. The use of dark clothing affords some protection.

The electric ray, met rarely on sandy or muddy bottoms, gives a paralyzing shock when touched.

The flesh of some fish, such as the puffer and porcupine fish, contains a toxin not destroyed by cooking; eating them can cause severe poisoning.

The Portuguese man-o'-war, some sea anemones, and some jellyfish have stinging tentacles, which can produce severe pain and swelling for several hours. The application of a dilute ammonia solution helps to relieve the pain.

Among snails of tropical and subtropical shores are the uncommon cones and terebras, which possess poisonous teeth. Their bites can be fatal.

The spines of sea urchins are sharp and sometimes poisonous. Avoid walking barefoot when exploring rocky ocean shores at low tide.

The blood-sucking vampire bat lives in South America. It attacks only sleeping animals and may be avoided by use of mosquito netting.

Our bats are insect-eaters and actually do us a great service. Occasionally they gain entrance to a building, where they sleep by day, emerging to forage after dusk. Their chirping sounds and the objectionable odor of their droppings may necessitate control. Use of a repellent may serve to exclude them; 3 to 5 pounds of paradichlorobenzene (PDB) or of naphthalene flakes, scattered about the attic floor, should suffice.

A more permanent solution is batproofing the building. After the

CAMPERS in forested areas sometimes have unexpected visits from their new neighbors.

White shark.

A jellyfish.

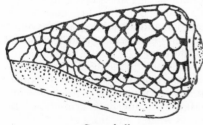

Cone shell.

Sea urchin.

Chipmunks and native mice may appear at your cabin, a wandering skunk or porcupine on your doorstep, a raccoon or deer in the yard. They are motivated by curiosity or the quest of food. They are mostly innocuous but, if they are objectionable, the practice of eliminating brush piles, burying garbage deeply, and carefully covering stored foods will keep them at a safe distance.

Skunks are well behaved if not antagonized. Should you fall victim to their gas warfare, you and your clothing may be deodorized by a dilute solution of sodium hypochlorite (a common bleach) or by prolonged immersion in flowing water. Caught in the eye, the skunk's fluid causes intense irritation and temporary blindness. Washing with plenty of fresh water gives some relief.

The porcupine's fondness for salt leads it to gnaw doors, oars, tool handles, and other wooden items. The creature cannot throw its quills, but they are sharp and barbed, and a flick of the tail may lodge them in your flesh if you stand too close.

Troublesome small creatures may be excluded by an electric fence about a foot above the ground. They may be taken in a No. 1 or No. 1½ steel trap or, better, in a box trap, then covered with a burlap sack and released across the lake.

Trapped animals may be dispatched painlessly with a few tablespoonfuls of carbon disulphide or chloroform poured into the trap. But check first with local officials, for many animals are protected by State laws.

Do not kill them without reason. God made them, too.

If unwelcome guests are denning beneath the garage or under the porch, carefully seal off all openings but one. Sprinkle the ground by this opening with flour, and when tracks indicate that the animal has left (probably at night), seal it off completely.

Deer that are robbing your garden or orchard may be discouraged by chemical repellents sprayed on the

Striped skunk.

Porcupine.

Black bear.

crop. One formula contains pine tar and anthracene oil. Another contains chlorinated coal-tar oils and nicotine sulfate. An organic chemical sold under the trade name Goodrite Z.I.P. may be sprayed in concentrations from 1 to 5 percent at a cost of about 7.50 dollars an acre.

A VEXATION in some recreation areas is bears that break into camps for stored foods.

More serious is the problem of "panhandling" bears whom foolhardy tourists, contrary to regulations, persist in feeding by hand. The mauling that sometimes results is only to be expected, for these are still essentially wild beasts. They are not ordinarily dangerous if unmolested, unless they consider themselves or their young to be threatened.

Normal precautions are to keep at a safe distance, never to get between a she-bear and her cubs, to store all foods in bearproof containers (preferably suspended out of reach), to incinerate all garbage, and not to feed the bears.

Other animals accused of attacking human beings are wolves and mountain lions, but they are now so uncommon and secretive that the average camper never sees a wild one during his lifetime.

Tales of "maneaters" are grossly exaggerated. The occasional "killer" usually is driven by extreme hunger, perhaps because he is crippled or too old to secure his normal prey, or is rabid. Cases involving persons are extremely rare.

Any unprovoked attack by a wild animal is suspect, however, and one bitten should consult a physician for vaccine treatment, especially if the animal was vicious or noticeably sick or paralyzed.

Actually, in this country, far more people are injured each year by domestic dogs and bulls than by all our wildlife species, poisonous and otherwise.

At about the turn of the century, Theodore Roosevelt wrote that the five most dangerous African mammals were the buffalo, elephant, lion, leopard, and rhinoceros.

We have their counterparts in this country, but they have been so reduced in numbers or subdued as to pose no real threat. Like most wild animals, they avoid man if possible.

Herds of large ungulates, such as bison and elk, may be dangerous if suddenly frightened into stampeding. But many of them are now on fenced lands, in a semidomesticated condition. Old females may attack if their young are in jeopardy or when wounded or cornered. Old males, exiled from the herd, may become cantankerous and charge if provoked.

Reindeer, moose, and others may become vicious during the breeding season. Most will fight in self-defense. So watch them from a distance and try not to arouse their suspicion as to your motives.

One final tip: To avoid provoking incidents, and to permit you to enjoy more fully the wildlife during your outing, leave your own pet dogs and cats at home. (RICHARD H. MANVILLE)

Safety
in Forests

BE SURE, and safe, when you go to the forests for vacation and recreation.

S—Size up your hazards.
U—Use all signs and follow instructions.
R—Remember the safety of everybody.
E—Establish a margin of safety.

Hazards are in forests and every place else. Many visitors to forests, in holiday mood, become careless. They come up against hazards they never saw before, do not recognize, and do not understand. Accidents therefore are bound to happen, unless precautions are taken.

The first hazard is roads. Roads in forests are not superhighways. Drive slowly always, and even more slowly on curves and gravel.

Practice the buddy system. Whether swimming or hiking or whatever, always travel and play in pairs. Even better to have three along in case somebody gets hurt. Then the two can carry him out, or one can hike out for help.

Get in good condition before you start, especially if you are over 40. Practice pushups and stoopfalls and other exercises two or three times a day for a month. Daily walks will put you in good trim beforehand, too.

There is the hazard of being lost. When you get lost, or think you are, use your head and not your feet. The person who keeps his head and does not panic has the best chance to come through all right. Sit down and try to figure out where you are. If it's stormy or cold, build a fire. Try to rest at night. In the morning, start walking downhill and downstream. Above all, do not quit. Then you will eventually reach civilization. A thinking person is never lost for long.

Have a first aid kit handy wherever you go and know how to use it.

Know what to do in case of emergency. Learn first aid.

Know what hazards you may run into, such as poison-ivy, snakes, and dangerous animals, and keep away from them.

Animals and snakes will not strike unless you provoke them, but the chances are that each local situation has new hazards you never saw or heard of before. If you are safety-minded, in most cases you will know what to do—accidents are caused mostly by people who do not think.

Be cautious when you walk on roots and rocks and uneven ground. One sprained ankle can spoil a whole family's fun.

I strongly recommend that you take one or more of the free courses in safety as a preparation for a vacation and for life.

Examples are the Red Cross First Aid and Life Saving course; the National Safety Council's Operation Waterproof Fourth Grade, to teach everybody over 10 years old to swim; courses in the use of firearms, offered by the National Rifle Association and some States; instruction in boating, offered by the Coast Guard auxiliary; and courses in safe driving, given in many schools. (SETH JACKSON)

Nature Study

YOU DO NOT HAVE to become a scientist or have a laboratory to enjoy Nature.

You can observe or study one or another of its fascinating aspects—birds, butterflies, animals, flowers, plants, rocks, weather—at your window sill, in gardens and parks, on your way to work or school, any place.

Nature study can be as intense or as casual as you want to make it. You can do it alone or as a member of a group. You can stay in your own backyard, hike through nearby countryside, or travel a thousand miles from home.

It can involve special equipment or none. If you wish, you can study Nature without spending a cent.

You are the one to decide what you want to study. Many persons, many organizations, and many books are ready to help you in your new hobby.

YOU MAY WISH to study birds, which have a wider appeal for many Americans than any other wild creatures. Their songs, colors, and spirit have endeared them to people for centuries. Birds are accessible. Most of them are abroad during daylight. They are reasonably easy to approach. Some you can attract with food and water. Their numbers and kinds change with the seasons.

Bird study is so popular that we consider it the prime example of nature study, and we deal mostly with it here. Many of the points we mention in connection with the study of birds can be related to other kinds of Nature study.

The first step in any kind of Nature study is to learn to recognize the objects of your study. In bird watching, that means learning to distinguish one species from another and to give each its correct name. It will be simpler if you have at hand one of the several modern bird guides, which have colored illustrations and shortcuts to identification and sell for less than 5 dollars.

With diligence and a good book on identification, you will soon know most of the common kinds of birds that visit your feeder or occur in your neighborhood.

With somewhat more effort, you can learn to identify the less common birds and the migrants—the birds that in springtime stop briefly with you on their way to their northern nesting grounds and stop again in autumn when they return to their winter homes.

The pleasures and the successes of bird watching can be greater if you have a pair of binoculars, which reduce the distance between you and the object of your interest and so make identification easier and enlarge your appreciation of color and action.

For most bird watchers, the binoculars should not be less than 6 power nor more than 9 power.

You can buy binoculars of acceptable quality for about 40 dollars at optical shops, sporting goods stores, and local bird clubs. Do not buy one simply because it is cheap.

As they learn to recognize more and

more kinds of birds, most bird students start a life list—a record of the species they have seen and identified.

You can compile a sizable list without leaving your community, but the desire to add more species soon leads most watchers farther afield. Sooner or later you will want to visit marshes, prairies, forests, or mountains to find the birds that can be seen only in such places. A trip to the seashore or even to another country will acquaint you with still more new birds.

Bird watching is an exciting game and like other kinds of recreation has a strong element of competition in it.

Regardless of whether you start a life list, you should keep a record of your observations. You can do that by writing in the margins of your bird guide, on 3 by 5 cards (one for each species), or in a small notebook. Such a record will help you recall the sighting of especially unusual birds and will enable you to accumulate information on the occurrence and the life history of the birds in your region.

One of the activities that attracts many bird watchers is the Christmas Bird Count. It is a bird census that the National Audubon Society has sponsored for more than 67 years. It is an annual event that a bird student can do alone or share with others. If it is continued year after year in the same location, the accumulated records can be valuable in showing the increase or decline of midwinter birds in the community.

ONE NICE THING about bird study is that you can attract many kinds of birds to your backyard and even to your window sill. If you provide food, water, and housing, you can increase the numbers and even the kinds of birds normally found in your area.

Feeding trays, birdhouses, and watering devices are easily made, or you can buy them in a variety of sizes and designs at pet stores, which also sell birdseed mixtures, sunflower seeds, nut meats, suet cakes, and other kinds of bird food. You can also buy bird-seed at your grocery, as well as peanut butter, raisins, and suet, which birds also relish.

The seed-, insect-, and nectar-eating birds are the ones most likely to be attracted by your efforts.

If you wish and have a site that permits development, a more natural method of attracting birds may be used. Trees, shrubs and vines and grasses and flowers may be planted to serve the dual purpose of landscaping and attracting birds.

Birds like variety. With this in mind and some knowledge of the needs and habits of different birds, you can select plants that provide food, nesting and shelter cover, and perching and singing sites. A variety of plants intermingled and planted in varied patterns, consistent with plant-growth habits and good landscape design, will attract ground-feeding birds as well as those that live in the crowns of tall trees.

Plantings of annuals, such as millet, buckwheat, sunflowers, and corn, help to meet the fall and winter food requirements of many kinds of birds.

The seeds and berries of conifers provide fall and winter food that some birds prefer. The crossbills and siskins like the seed of spruce. More than 68 species of birds are known to eat the berries of redcedar.

The fruits of the autumn olive, Russian-olive, hawthorns, chokecherry, and Virginia-creeper are favored by many birds, including Bohemian and cedar waxwings, evening grosbeaks, robins, and some of the game birds.

Many other fruit-bearing plants may be selected to meet local soils and climatic conditions and the habitat requirements of many birds in most parts of the country.

Space and interest are about the only limitations in developing an all-season habitat for birds and other wildlife in many sections.

Since water is important, a pond, lake, stream, or spring, especially if it makes water available all year, can enlarge the resident wildlife population of a community.

An interest in birds, their songs, plumage, habits, and requirements, often leads to associated recreational hobbies.

Among them are photography and painting, recording of bird songs, bird-banding, study of migration, life cycles, food and nesting habits. Proficiency in these have developed into professional, technical skills for many.

THE STUDY of plants, particularly flowers, trees, and ferns, is an interesting Nature hobby for thousands of persons. Insects—primarily butterflies and moths, because of their beauty—interest many of us.

Mammals, fish, reptiles, and amphibians are studied by large numbers of people, young and old. The seashores and tidal pools, where live a multitude of fascinating sea animals and plants, attract many hobbyists.

Others turn to the study of fossils, rocks, and minerals, which, in turn, may lead to lapidary, the art of cutting and polishing stone.

All these Nature study hobbies are within easy reach of anyone. You may wish to limit your interest to one of them or to reading about Nature for pure enjoyment.

But, more likely, you will want to combine interest and knowledge with active physical exertion in the out of doors—hiking, mountain climbing, cave explorations, or guiding and teaching others to enjoy Nature.

With a good handbook or field guide, a few items of equipment and a notebook, you are prepared to explore the fascinating world.

You can extend your enjoyment, whatever your interest, by reading about it. Your school and public libraries have a number of books you will enjoy. We list some of them.

Two series of pocket-size nature manuals are available at bookstores and libraries. One is the "Peterson Field Guide Series" and the other is the "Putnam Nature Field Books." Each series includes 15 or more books on as many different Nature subjects.

The Peterson Field Guide Series, Houghton Mifflin Co., Boston:

A Field Guide to the Birds (Eastern and Central North America).
A Field Guide to Western Birds.
A Field Guide to the Birds of Britain and Europe.
A Field Guide to the Birds of Texas and Adjacent States.
A Field Guide to the Mammals.
A Field Guide to Animal Tracks.
A Field Guide to Reptiles and Amphibians.
A Field Guide to the Butterflies.
A Field Guide to the Shells of Our Atlantic and Gulf Coasts.
A Field Guide to Shells of the Pacific Coast and Hawaii.
A Field Guide to Rocks and Minerals.
A Field Guide to the Ferns (and their related families of Northeastern and Central North America).
A Field Guide to Rocky Mountain Wildflowers (from Northern Arizona and New Mexico to British Columbia).
A Field Guide to Trees and Shrubs.
A Field Guide to the Stars and Planets.

Putnam Nature Field Books, G. P. Putnam's Sons, New York:

Birds of the Ocean.
Field Book of Fresh Water Fishes of North America.
North American Mammals.
Western Wild Flowers.
Marine Fishes of the Atlantic Coast.
Field Book of Common Ferns.
Field Book of Eastern Birds.
Field Book of Nature Activities.
Common Rocks and Minerals.
Field Book of Insects.
American Wild Flowers.
American Trees and Shrubs.
Field Book of Seashore Life.
Field Book of Ponds and Streams.
Field Book of Animals in Winter.
Field Book of the Stars.
Field Book of the Skies.
Shell Collector's Handbook.
Field Book of Snakes.
Common Mushrooms.
Streamside Guide to Naturals and their Imitations.
New Field Book of American Wild Flowers.

Audubon Bird Guides, Doubleday & Co., Garden City, N.Y.:

Audubon Land Bird Guide (Eastern and Central North America).
Audubon Water Bird Guide (Eastern and Central North America).
Audubon Western Bird Guide.

All are reliable sources of information and guidance. (LAWRENCE V. COMPTON AND ADRIAN C. FOX)

Handcrafts

NEARLY EVERYBODY seems to feel a need at some time or other for an absorbing hobby that gives a sense of accomplishment—an engrossing outlet on which one is willing to spend effort for no reward other than a personal satisfaction.

There are many types of satisfying, creative outlets. A craft is one, an excellent one, especially for a person who must or prefers to pursue the interest at home.

To study and follow a handcraft, you need not be an artist. The idea that art is for the gifted only was abandoned long ago.

More important are personal qualities of flexibility, alertness to new ideas and ways of doing things, and awareness of color, texture, and patterns.

Before you take up a craft, learn what it involves in time, effort, materials, and cost. To avoid disappointment, find out by reading or asking.

Explore a bit.

If you are after a meaningful leisure-time pursuit, do not dabble. Concentrate on one thing and give it all you have. The first experiences can be fun and productive, but sooner or later, if you are really serious, you will discover that learning is not quick and easy. You probably will not want it any other way. Things that come too easily may be boring, as all the challenge is taken away.

At first, try only small things and be content to experiment. These experiments will take little time and be less precious than a large project. Try out various techniques with little bits of material just to see what they will do.

You also will be storing up ideas and skills for the future. This is like adding words to your vocabulary so you can eventually describe things more vividly or trying out various seasonings or combinations of food to see if the results can be more interesting.

Do not be afraid of failures. If you are experimenting (not just playing it safe), you will have failures, and they will teach you much.

Designing and making any article is often like solving a problem. The idea you visualize in your head or on paper begins to look different as you work it out in the real material. It may not please you, so you begin to try different shapes, colors, or lines. That is, you must redesign it. Many new ideas may be tried before you are satisfied.

IF YOU HAVE DONE little in crafts, and especially if you are unsure of your interests, it is wise to build on a skill you already have.

If you have worked with metal and wood and know the feel of these materials, the step toward designing and making furniture, toys, and jewelry or to wood carving would be logical. Sewing, knitting, applique, and other forms of needlework are all related.

If handwork takes more patience than you have, try speed hooking, machine stitchery, or knitting on big needles. Printed fabrics could be your specialty if you like to sew, or designing stuffed toys and puppets may interest you.

Some people can begin with a stamped pattern or kit and branch out. The danger is that you will not branch out. Insecurity makes you start with the kit, and using it probably will not add to your confidence. All you need to do with a kit is read the directions, and the limited materials do not allow you to vary the colors or modify the pattern. You will be inclined to feel that other people's ideas will always be better than your own. Although there are exceptions, most kit designs are bad, and exposure to them can influence your future work.

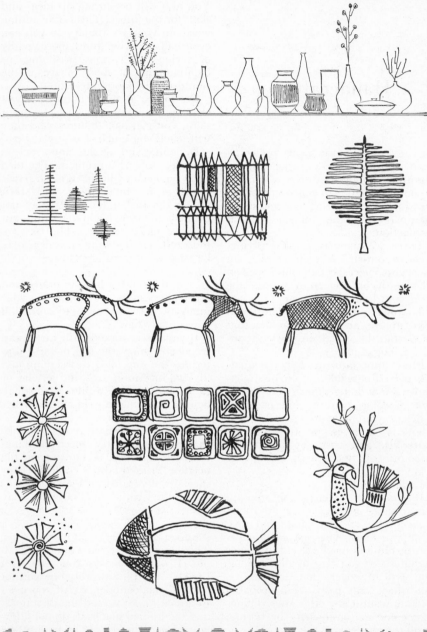

Craftsmen draw inspiration from many designs and objects.

Following patterns does have therapeutic value for those who do not have the energy or ability to do otherwise. They can give an ill person a sense of accomplishment or help regain strength in the hands or the mind. Many of those people should not be required to create designs. The skills themselves will be difficult enough. However, most of us owe our minds and talents a lot more challenge than this.

For a good beginning, study books on the crafts of your choice and equip yourself with a supply catalog. Many books do not give much help on design to beginners. You may need to read several. I list some of them at the end of this chapter.

The best way to learn may be to join a class. Even if the facilities are not the best, you have advantages. Skills can be learned from books, but being taught is quicker and less frustrating. A class also will commit you to spending a certain amount of time, and you cannot help but learn from the successes and failures of others in the group. A teacher often can help most by introducing you to sources of ideas and how to use them.

For instance, Nature is an excellent source. How would you go about capturing the spirit of a flower for use as a repeat pattern, for a silver pin, or a mosaic tray? Exact copying is never the answer. A natural form will never seem the same in wood or metal or cloth as it does in its natural environment.

A teacher can also help you plan useful, workable projects and advise you when you are stuck.

Above all, go into a class with an open mind, a willingness to try suggested ideas, and a willingness to work. If you lack confidence and are afraid to try, remember many others feel the same way.

PERHAPS you are not sure what you would like to do, but wish to explore a variety of things. And even if your main interests lie elsewhere, you may still enjoy an evening or so exploring crafts with family or friends.

Papier mache sculpture, mobiles, finger painting, plaster carving, seed mosaics, party decorations, and paper-bag puppets are some of the short-time projects that can be imaginative and fun. These, too, have great potential. With further exploration, your specialty may become ornaments for Christmas trees; or your family could be topnotch puppeteers. These activities take inexpensive materials, many of which you have at home.

For you, I would recommend *Art for the Family* by Victor D'Amico, and *Meaning in Crafts* by Edward Mattil.

CRAFT ACTIVITIES can benefit a child greatly if he is allowed to think for himself and decide what he wants to make and how.

In other words, the activity must allow him to be creative. Kits and precut pieces do not permit this. Provide the materials and show him how to use them.

If it is papier mache, for instance, you may suggest that he could make a menagerie—a roaring lion, giraffe, or something—and then let him do it in his own way.

Do not criticize him for doing something in a way that is different from what you would have done. He has his own world of experiences. For that matter, no two adults are alike. So, to tell the child his dog does not look like a dog or that cats are not pink may stifle his imagination and take the joy out of his work. He may lose confidence and stop working altogether.

WHAT HE LEARNS BY DOING—manipulating the material, deciding on shape and color—helps develop his creative potential. This is far more important than the appearance of the product.

Creative people are needed in all walks of life—not just in the arts. A child who learns to think for himself has a far better chance of developing into this type of individual than the child who is ever dependent on others to tell him what to do and how to do it. A creative person tends to have ideas which he can express in his own way. He tends to be flexible and easily adjusts to new situations, ideas, and things.

You may not have been taught this way. Perhaps you were told to copy a picture of a dog, or the teacher may have helped you draw a tree the way she thought it should look. If so, you may have trouble freeing yourself. Ideas may not come easily, and you may yearn to copy.

The books I list should help you. And, as you become more creative, you will develop more sensitivity to what you see and do. More ideas for your work will come from these experiences. The quality of your work will improve. Your enjoyment will increase. (JANE GRAFF)

BASIC REFERENCES FOR ALL CRAFTSMEN

Basic Design; Principles and Practice, Kenneth Bates, World Publishing Co., Cleveland, 1960, $4.95.

Designs for Craftsmen, Walter Miles, Doubleday & Co., Inc., New York, 1962, $5.95.

Handbook for Craftsmen, Society of Connecticut Craftsmen, 17 South Main Street, West Hartford, Conn., $1. (Craft standards, marketing, professional practices, and lists of books and periodicals for all crafts.)

Craft Horizons, American Craftsmen's Council, 44 West 53d Street, New York, N.Y., 10019, bimonthly magazine, $8 a year. (Work of professional artist-craftsmen, folk art, historical and contemporary. Lists schools and workshops, national calendar of events, book reviews, sources of supplies.)

BASKETRY

Basketry, F. J. Christopher, Dover Publications, Inc., 180 Varick Street, New York, N.Y., $0.75.

American Reedcraft Corp., 417 Lafayette Avenue, Box 154, Hawthorne, N.J. (Ask for free folders of supplies and directions for chair seat weaving, basketry.)

LEATHER

General Leathercraft, Raymond Cherry, Sax Arts and Crafts, 1103 North Third Street, Milwaukee, Wis., $1.50.

The Sunset Leather Craft Book, Doris Aller, Lane Publishing Co., Menlo Park, Calif., 1952.

JEWELRY AND ENAMELING

How to Make Modern Jewelry, Charles Martin and Victor D'Amico, Museum of Modern Art, 11 West 53d Street, New York, N.Y., 10019, $1.50.

Enameling: Principles and Practice, Kenneth Bates, World Publishing Co., Cleveland, 1951, $3.95.

MOSAICS

Sunset Mosaics, Doris and Diane Lee Aller, Lane Publishing Co., Menlo Park, Calif., 1962, $1.95.

Mosaics; Principles and Practice, Joseph Young, Reinhold Book Division, 430 Park Avenue, New York, N.Y., $6.50.

NEEDLEWORK

Adventures in Stitches, Mariska Karasz, Funk & Wagnalls Co., Inc., 360 Lexington Avenue, New York, N.Y., 10017, 1959, $7.50.

Machine Embroidery, Jennifer Gray, B. T. Batsford, Ltd., London, 1963.

Create With Yarn, Ethel Jane Beitler, International Textbook Co., Scranton, Pa., 1964, $7.50.

Woman's Day Magazine, 67 West 44th Street, New York, N.Y., 10036. (Write for current list of reprints of articles on a variety of needlework techniques.)

POTTERY AND CERAMIC SCULPTURE

How to Make Pottery and Ceramic Sculpture, Julia H. Duncan and Victor D'Amico, Museum of Modern Art, 11 West 53d Street, New York, N.Y., 10019, $1.50.

Creative Clay Design, Ernst Röttger, Reinhold Book Division, 430 Park Avenue, New York, N.Y., 1963, $4.95.

RUGMAKING

Hooked Rugs, Catherine Eichelberger, New York State College of Home Economics, Ithaca, N.Y., Cornell Misc. Bulletin No. 43, $0.50.

Handmade Rugs, Doris Aller, Lane Publishing Co., Menlo Park, Calif., 1953, $1.95.

TEXTILE PRINTING AND DYEING

Block Printing, Jane Graff and Gertrude Hoffmann, University of Wisconsin, Cooperative Extension Service, Madison, Wis., Circular 414.

Block Printing on Textiles, Janet Doub Erickson, Watson Guptill Publications, Inc., New York, N.Y., 1962.

Fabric Printing, Lotti Lauterburg, Reinhold Book Division, 430 Park Avenue, New York, N.Y., 1962, $6. (Information on silk screen and stenciling processes.)

Batik: Art and Craft, Nik Krevitsky, Reinhold Book Division, New York, N.Y., 1963, $5.50.

American Crayon Co., Sandusky, Ohio. (Information on silk screen and stenciling processes.)

WEAVING

New Key to Weaving, Mary E. Black, The Bruce Publishing Co., Milwaukee, 1957, $12.

Swedish Handweaving, Malin Selander, Wegäta Förlag A.B. Göteberg, Sweden, 1961, $6.95. (Available from Craft and Hobby Book Service, Big Sur, Calif., 93920.)

Handweavers and Craftsmen, 546 Fifth Avenue, New York, N.Y., 10001, 4 issues, $5 a year.

WOOD

How To Make Objects of Wood, Bassett, Thurman, and Victor D'Amico, Museum of Modern Art, 11 West 53d Street, New York, N.Y., 10019, $2.50.

Creative Wood Design, Ernst Röttger, Reinhold Book Division, 430 Park Avenue, New York, N.Y., 1963, $4.95.

MISCELLANEOUS

Crafts for Retirement, American Craftsmen's Council, 29 West 53d Street, New York, N.Y., 1962, $2.95. (Emphasis on teaching crafts to older people. Brief reviews on working with different media; also lists of supplies and references.)

Meaning in Crafts, Edward Mattil, Prentice-Hall, Inc., Englewood Cliffs, N.J., 1959.

Art for the Family, Victor D'Amico, Museum of Modern Art, 11 West 53d Street, New York, N.Y., 10019, 1954, $2.95.

Creative Paper Design, Ernst Röttger, Reinhold Book Division, New York, N.Y., 1961, $4.95.

Craft and Hobby Book Service, Big Sur, Calif. (Write for a catalog of books on the craft of your choice.)

Curiosity; Learning

A CHILD'S INTEREST in every new experience in the world about him is the beginning of learning.

To a child, nothing is too small or too ordinary to be examined, explored, and asked about.

Everything he touches will be something more added to his experience. The richer the experience, the more eagerly will he face the mysterious world. His unending curiosity will lead him on and into, let us hope, manhood in which he is still curious, interested, and eager to learn.

A personal experience may illustrate my point. One day I missed my young son and after a search found him sitting under a grapevine. Clamped tightly into the end of one of his fingers were the pincers and head of a large bug. He said he could not get it to let loose and so had cut its head from its body. He was afraid to come to me, because I had told him not to hurt living things. I used pointed scissors to pry open the pincers. The boy became interested in bugs and why the severing of the head had locked the pincers.

LET CHILDREN draw on their own ideas. Personal discovery gives them deep satisfactions.

We should encourage children to learn to appreciate things they see, feel, hear, smell, or touch—the rustle of leaves, the wet leaves, the feel of cat's fur, the chime of bells, the feel and the color of stones.

If Jane had not been stung with a

bee one day, she would not have been too interested in why it hurt. What happened? Do all bees sting? Why? Why don't we kill all bees?

Jane became interested in watching bees on flowers. Why are the honeysuckle bushes full of bees? Why did they go down into the flower? Her mother had her pick a blossom and suck on the end to find the sweetness. Jane began to learn how honey is made and how pollen is carried from one plant to another. She carefully looked to find the pollen on the bee's body.

We were raking leaves in the backyard when John gave a shout, "Come and see what a funny thing I've found!" He was holding in his hand a thin, struggling plant, white from its burial under the leaves.

He learned this plant had been in the dark. Did plants need light to be green? Why does sunlight help plants to grow?

Only a plot is needed to help children to learn to experiment with seeds and plants. Seeds may be started in the house, and the child can see how the sprout begins and the roots start. He can learn that a seed will not develop into a plant if the sprout is broken off. Covering a plant indoors will help him to learn it needs sunlight to be green. If he puts a plant in a glass jar and covers it tightly, he learns that plants need air.

With guidance from others, the child can learn that growing tips of many plants, cut off and put into water or moist sand, will grow a new root system.

This new growth is not confined to plants. Many living creatures will regrow or regenerate body parts. A crab, for instance, will regrow a missing claw. Little flatworms found under rocks (where moisture is), if broken or cut in two parts, will regrow head end or tail end.

Children at different ages are curious as to what becomes of food when eaten. To show something of the process, one can buy a whole, undressed

chicken, dress it, and explain to him the functions of the different organs.

One can help children understand animal life better by means of a pair of hamsters. Children are curious about the birth of the little hamsters; if lucky, they may observe the birth of the little hairless creatures. Watching from day to day for the opening of eyes and the growth of hair can be a wonderful experience. The little animals need proper care—warmth, food, and shelter. It will interest the child to know that if the male is left in the cage, the female will not have her young unless first she kills the male or she will kill her young.

NOT ONLY can curiosity be fostered if a child has a chance to explore Nature. Love and affection also can be developed.

A child seeks affection, and learning to care for pets helps to satisfy this need. Pets show affection.

My neighbor's little boy wanted a dog. Yes, he would be glad to take care of it; feed it, water it, and see that its house was cleaned. It was not long until Mother was caring for the pet, and David gave little thought for the dog's care. Finally, he either had to care for it or the dog would be given away. It took much reminding, but soon the responsibility became a habit. The romping boy and dog became strong pals. Rover knew when David was in need of extra affection. David knew Rover understood and he could put confidence in him.

The love growing between the pet and his master was a way of learning to show love to others, but David learned real love meant keeping his dog happy by considering his needs for food, warmth, and shelter. David learned, too, that he himself was happier when he had given his dog good care. Indirectly David was learning to consider the needs of others whom he loved. The love attachment to the dog was helping David to live a more secure and productive life, because he was learning consideration for others.

As ERIC FROMM said in his book, *The Creative Attitude*, children have the capacity to be puzzled; their whole effort is one of attempting to orient themselves in a new world, to grasp the ever-new things which they learn to experience; they are puzzled, surprised, capable of wondering, and that is what makes their reaction a creative one.

Almost from the moment of birth, a child has within him not only the drive of curiosity but the drive to manipulate or manage. Through exploring he also learns new ideas and puts these ideas to work.

Why does a boy take a clock apart? Can he put it together again? Why does the little girl "dress up" in mother's clothes? Why do youngsters play doctor and nurse and father and mother?

Everyday experiences for the child help him to grow into the adult years. The kinds of experiences he has help him to look at himself as a certain kind of person. He molds himself by his experiences and how he feels adults "see" him as an individual. Too many times adults belittle the efforts of children and youth.

A mother once confided in me about her 9-year-old son. She was concerned because his father wanted him to make model airplanes and enjoy doing it. The father was a perfectionist and expected the same result from the unskilled 9-year-old hands that the more skilled hands could do. The boy would finish a model plane to a certain stage and quit, feeling that he was not capable of doing a good job. The father forgot the boy's interest and experience had not been of many years standing but only 9 years.

THE FIRST THING that brings about creativeness is coming face to face with a situation.

I believe we try to keep children and youth too busy with things we think they should do, thereby causing them to depend on entertainment in all of their leisure hours. We do not give the small child a chance to make his own play. We shower him with toys until he does not know how to learn to wonder.

Creativity develops best when children have little or no thought of making a usable product or of pleasing others. In teaching and learning, it is important to let a child explore on his own.

In the sandbox, for example, children use imagination in preparing foods or building with mud. Imagination is given a chance.

Educators recognize that imagination is a foundation of progress, and that imagination that leads to constructive action is good.

Action may be telling an imaginary story or writing an imaginary play or creating an invention, however useless.

CHILDREN go through rather specific stages of development in music and rhythm activities, in clay modeling and sculpturing, and other art activities. The first efforts of a very young child may only be scribbling; then he soon learns to give his scribbling a name.

For example: Rhythm is present in the physical body, but the child in reproducing or being able to beat a rhythm will have to start with perhaps the beating of two sticks together. To the older child or adult, this is not rhythm, but to the small child it is.

The modeling of a clay rabbit to the adult may look like a gob of clay with only a few knobs on it, but not to the child. It's a rabbit. The drawing of an airplane may only be a few lines, but he sees an airplane.

As years are added to his life, these same experiences become more nearly like the real thing, and his music, modeling, and drawing take on more realistic life.

I BELIEVE THE HOME to be the first and the main place for children to begin to strengthen their curiosity about things around them and to begin to incorporate into their lives a way of living that will encourage them to probe further into reality with a wholesome attitude toward things and people.

I believe that parents can encourage or discourage the creative ability children may have. Parents can make it possible for their children to look further into and, as time goes on, study more about their environment.

A parent can spend a few minutes out on the lawn with a youngster hunting for new objects in Nature and talking about them. Take him on a trip into a natural park where exploring can be done. What different trees do you find? What kind of stones do you find along the creekbed? What different birds do you find? What are their songs like? Can some interesting crafts be made from some woods found? Can certain grasses be woven? What do the waves of a river, bay, or ocean tell you?

The companionship of parents and children out with Nature can help to foster stronger love and help both to enjoy a more productive life, a more worthwhile feeling concerning self, and foster a happier, better understanding relationship with Nature and individuals throughout society. (JEANNE SATER MOEHN)

Two 4-year-olds using ordinary household materials.

Educational Toys

TWO-YEAR-OLD CRAIG smiles happily as he plays with pots and pans.

Charlotte, aged 4, is busy in her room dressing her dolls and getting them ready for bed.

Billy, a second grader, walks to school carrying some guppies to present at "show and tell."

Don and Eddie, 12 years old, are building a city. Small logs, blocks, and building sticks become stores, houses, and hotrods.

Although their age range is great, these children have several things in common. All are engaged in play.

Play is as important to the child as work is to the adult. In essence, play is the child's work. It is a way of life. It is primarily through play that the child builds early concepts about himself, his family, his playmates, and the world about him.

Play, first and foremost, is fun. There is enjoyment in painting and playing cowboys and Indians. There is satisfaction in building, collecting butterflies, and cooking a meal for your dolls.

Play can be an educational process. It contributes to all aspects of the child's growth and mental, physical, social, and emotional development. Solving a problem in block building, climbing a jungle gym, playing grocery store—all contribute to a child's total growth.

Toys and other play materials are the props that express or enhance the child's play. They may not be formally labeled "educational toys" by the professional educator or the public, but many of these materials have definite educational value.

At the start, I gave several examples of play materials. In each instance, the children were using the materials to serve a broad educational function.

My example shows that a wide variety of objects can be utilized in play. Some of the items I mentioned were purchased. Some were everyday household materials. Some were found out of doors. Some can be made in the home.

My example showed also that toys are where you find them—in the cupboard, the workbench, the sewing room, the yard, the discount house.

COMMERCIAL TOYS can be expensive, and you deserve the most from your investment.

Thought and planning before the actual purchase can save money and increase your chances of making an appropriate selection.

The following general guides will help you when you buy toys.

Is the toy appropriate to the child's interests and abilities?

This is the most important guideline. I offer some general suggestions in terms of ages and stages later.

A toy that does not hold the child's interest, or one used for a few moments, is a waste of time and money. A toy that is too advanced or too demanding also will be quickly discarded. A 25-dollar electric train bought for a 4-year-old boy is such an item. Children that young do not have the interest span nor the motor skills required for such complicated toys. Parents often buy musical instruments before a child has a genuine interest in music.

The reverse also holds true. Toys that are too simple do not challenge the child and soon are forgotten.

Observe your child and learn his interests. That rule is the best guide to purchasing toys.

Is the toy sturdy and well constructed?

Even an interesting toy has no value if it will not withstand some abuse.

Most children do not handle toys delicately. They play with them. Toys will be dropped, thrown, and left outside. Toys are shared, too: A lightweight slide may be all right when one child uses it, but it will not survive the normal wear and tear of several youngsters.

Check the construction of toys with moving parts. If the mechanism is delicate, doublecheck. Do the parts fit together? Do the gears mesh properly?

Many toys are to be used to make things. Examine them to see that they perform the function the manufacturer claims. Does the toy sewing machine really sew? Does the plastic toy factory really make plastic toys? You cannot expect a toy typewriter to perform as well as an IBM electric model, but it should be sufficiently well constructed

Teacher, 4-year-olds, blocks.

Three-year-old girl using a heavy-duty truck.

Two 5-year-olds using styrofoam, paint, and macaroni.

to provide maximum enjoyment and minimum frustration.

Some construction-type toys generally do not fit this requirement. One seldom finds toy saws, hammers, screwdrivers, and pliers that perform as they should. They are cheaply made and unsatisfactory. Should you wish to encourage carpentry skills in your child, buy tools of good quality that will do the job and withstand hard use.

Note, however: With young children there is some danger, and the use of these tools (not "toys") should be supervised. I feel that the time is worth the effort. A knowledge of tools and techniques of handling them is important in helping the child achieve a full, satisfying experience.

Is the toy safe?

Every year, thousands of children are injured by "safe, harmless" toys. Examine toys for sharp edges, splintering, and faulty mechanisms that can cause injury. Examine the way in which a toy is put together. Watch for nails, unprotected bolts, staples, and other sharp objects.

Be particularly careful of toys that are made of flammable materials and electric toys, which may well be fire hazards.

Federal laws prohibit the use of toxic materials in toys manufactured in the United States, but some toys of foreign manufacture have contained paints or plastics with toxic ingredients. Since a young child often places toys in his mouth, play materials containing toxic ingredients are dangerous and can cause serious disability or

death. If you have doubts about a toy, investigate further. If any doubt still exists, do not buy the item.

Is the toy functional?

Some toys are not toys at all. A 50-dollar hand-painted miniature doll is not a toy—it is a collector's item. Some model cars and trains are designed for adult hobbyists and not for children.

Ask: "Will the toy serve its function? Is the function worth the price?" Some toys are very expensive, particularly if their function is limited.

For young children it is advisable to buy serviceable toys that can serve many functions. Unit blocks are an example.

Unit blocks, or kindergarten blocks, are wooden blocks constructed on a standard unit. They come in single units (about 1.5 by 2.5 by 5.5 inches), double units (1.5 by 2.5 by 11 inches), quadruple units, cylinders, curves, arches, and so on. You can get them at large department stores, mail-order houses, and stores that specialize in toys.

We purchased a set for our boy when he was 2 years old. At 2, he stacked the blocks in his wagon and carried them from place to place. At 4 years, he used the blocks to make simple roads and one-story houses. At 6, he made the houses more complex. At 10, he used the blocks to make expressways and cities. The original cost was about 10 dollars; the set was later doubled. The blocks are more than 8 years old and are still being used.

Wagons can be used for many years as carryalls, trailers, trains, and planes.

Now some general ideas for different ages.

Since children vary, my ideas should be viewed as suggestive. Remember: The best rule in selecting toys is to know your own child's interests and abilities.

Cost is not a valid basis for choosing toys. Household articles often serve as toys, which may become more treasured than commercial products.

Five-year-old playing out a role of doctor.

One year: Play is just beginning for the 1-year-old, who usually manipulates toys simply via hand and mouth. My suggestions include items that are easy to grasp, have smooth edges, and are of one piece. Toys should be easy to clean with soap and water. Rattles and soft toys are examples. Homemade soft toys can be stuffed with old nylon stockings; they are easily washed. Infants generally prefer bright colors. Toys should be so large they cannot be swallowed.

Two to three years: This is the time of the senses. Children enjoy experimenting with smell, taste, textures. The attention span is short; avoid toys that require concentration over long periods. Play is new; the immediate world is fascinating. Look around the home for ideas for playthings.

Consult your librarian for simple picture books that contain stories about the here and now—animals, children, plants, houses, and familiar things and places.

Some suggestions:

Cardboard boxes of all sizes and shapes are fun to explore.

Pots and pans are fun in the kitchen and for water play.

Sandbox toys include wooden spoons, painted tin cans (remove the sharp edges), and a colander.

Texture experiences, like tearing paper or feeling various textures of cloth, paper, dirt, sand.

Toys: Pull toys, picture books, building blocks, dolls, soft toys, outdoor play equipment, simple cars and trucks, crayons and paints, tricycles, a wagon,

pedal cars, rhythm instruments, simple puzzles, balls, large beads to string, phonograph records.

Four and five years: Four- and five-year-olds are more aware of other children. Games, toys, and play experiences that include other children are fun for youngsters of this age.

Fours are curious, and toys and playthings that encourage inquiry are appropriate. Walks that show the immediate world and short excursions to the grocery store, airport, and fire station can be exciting.

Since 4's and 5's still have a relatively short attention span, trips usually should not exceed an hour.

Consult your librarian for picture books that tell about animals, people at work, people in other lands. Fantasy, too.

Suggestions:

Boards and boxes—all sizes and shapes can be used for simple construction of trains and houses. Use old clothes for dressing up.

Rainy-day box—with odds and ends of construction paper, yarn, cloth, scissors, buttons, thread, pipe cleaners. They are fun for simple sewing, cutting, pasting, and puppetmaking.

Tin cans and plastic containers can be painted and used in sand play and water play. Retain the labels and use them to play grocery store.

Nature study—trips to the woods to collect material for an aquarium or terrarium. Obtain a large thermometer and help the child keep track of the temperature. Use other simple devices for science experiences. Cooking, under supervision, is exciting.

Toys: Materials for creative play include telephones, toy iron and ironing board, doctor-and-nurse sets, tea sets, and dolls; building blocks; art materials; cars and trucks; power shovels; service station or farm sets; phonograph records; simple games; easy science kits; pets; tricycles and wagons; pedal cars; carpentry tools; hand puppets; and rhythm instruments.

Six to nine years: By 6 years, sex typ-

Block play (4-year-old) with a different type of blocks.

Four-year-old wiring a bell and buzzer in series with dry cell batteries.

ing has occurred, and a parent needs to concentrate more on "boylike" or "girllike" toys. The interest span is much greater, particularly as children advance toward 9, and more serious toys can be provided.

With more expensive and more delicate toys, the parent should also encourage and expect better care of equipment.

Collections are popular among children of this group, and they often collect in five or six categories at one time—rocks, butterflies, seashells, stamps, bottle caps, baseball cards.

By 7 or 8 years, boys begin to participate more in active group games like football and baseball. Girls may concentrate on domestic activities in group play. The family is still the major influence in the child's life, and family participation is important.

All-family activities (camping, games, trips) are meaningful to children of this age.

Suggestions:

Pets—if not earlier, an excellent time to introduce pets and help the child take a large share of the responsibility in care.

Boxes and boards are materials for active group play; for girls, materials for houses; for boys, stores, rocket ships.

Cooking experiences can be more advanced than earlier and is enjoyed by boys and girls.

Toys and other items: Roller skates, bicycles, science and nature toys, dolls and home equipment, musical instruments, service station and farm sets, books (consult your librarian), stamp and coin collections, sports equipment (badminton, croquet), simple model cars and planes, mechanical toys and equipment, puzzles, field-glasses, games (checkers, old maid).

Nine to twelve years: Just before adolescence, the interest in games is at its height. Children are active and enjoy being together in peer (but of the same sex) groups. Making things is still important. Boys and girls enjoy arts and crafts.

If not earlier, youngsters may now indicate an interest in learning to play a musical instrument.

Consult a librarian for biographies, adventure stories, and fantasy. Carefully selected books compete favorably with comics and television.

Suggestions:

Dramatic play—little theater; use household props. Fairs and carnivals, with games and prizes.

Group games—active outdoor games. Kick-the-can, Chinese tag, croquet, badminton.

Outings—visits to interesting historical places, factories, hobby shows; camping; group picnics.

Toys and materials: Items for leather, bead, and metal craft; painting; soap carving; bicycles; science and nature sets; sports equipment; games (Monopoly, hearts); Erector sets; shell and stamp collections; typewriter (adult model); printing press; miniature dolls and accessories; models (boats and cars); flying models; puppet theater; camping equipment; tape recorder. (D. KEITH OSBORN)

Books

BOOKS HAVE GONE UP in price, but their value has gone up, too, in terms of each person's need to know more about more subjects in this complex day.

Books are more useful, more available, more eagerly read, more beautiful, and better able to meet anyone's needs than ever before.

Their abiding values remain, of course. Books educate, sensitize, pleasure, and inspire us. They give a background of knowledge with perspectives and insights. They can spark imagination and develop our judgment. They give information that helps us keep, change, or advance on the job and face personal problems.

Books inform us about health, intelligent buying, technical and homemaking skills, differences between fact and propaganda, and our obligations in a democracy.

Many people want to own their own books, to keep them nearby as friends, mentors, and instructors. School and public libraries are fine, and we need more of them, but borrowing a book (and having to return it) is not the same as possessing one's own books.

Many a home library began with a collection of favorites from childhood and schooldays. Then comes the time for purposeful buying. The start may be a reference collection, which will be of continuous use and may have priority in the annual book allotment that will need to be built into the family budget. Consider together the reading needs, enthusiasms, and abilities of the adults and young people in the family when you choose books for the home library.

Basic reference books you may consider buying for home libraries include a Bible, dictionary, world atlas, almanac, book of quotations, a book on mythology, an anthology of poetry, and a cookbook.

In *The Booklist and Subscription Books Bulletin; a Guide to Current Books*, published semimonthly by the American Library Association (50 East Huron Street, Chicago, Ill., 60611; 6 dollars a year), reference books are evaluated as they are published. Consult back issues for reviews of older books. The Enoch Pratt Free Library in Baltimore, Md., has published *Reference Books for Branch Libraries; a Checklist of Recommended Titles* (second edition, 1964; 50 cents), which provides a choice for each type of reference book. These publications are available in larger libraries.

You will do well to consult your public librarian or State library agency about the purchase of an encyclopedia for children or adults, because an encyclopedia is a major investment. Each encyclopedia has special features to consider before purchasing. Accuracy and updating of facts are essential. Form and price vary from a single-volume publication at 32.50 dollars to a 30-volume set at 319.50 dollars.

Personal examination with the librarian's guidance is recommended. Compare the treatment of the same subject—one you know best—in several encyclopedias and note whether the person who wrote the entry is identified and is an authority.

WHAT MAKES a book important for one reader may make it meaningless for another. Bestseller lists may reflect the publishers' sales efforts as much as the popularity of the books. Handling and sampling a book is the best way to know whether you should invest the time to read it and the money to buy it.

Critical reviews in newspapers and magazines are helpful. In reacting to the content and qualities of each book, critics do have personal points of view; that being the essence of literary criticism. Compare the reviews, therefore, before you buy a book, especially an expensive book that is not in the local library or bookstore.

We have found book reviews in these periodicals especially deserving of attention:

Book Week. Weekly. New York Herald Tribune, Inc., 230 West 41st Street, New York, N.Y., 10036 (7 dollars a year; distributed with the Sunday editions of a number of newspapers).

New York Review of Books. Biweekly. A. Whitney Elsworth, 117 Broad Street, Milford, Conn., 06460 (6 dollars a year).

The New York Times Book Review. Weekly. New York Times Co., 229 West 43d Street, New York, N.Y., 10036 (7.50 dollars a year).

Saturday Review. Weekly. Saturday Review, Inc., 380 Madison Avenue, New York, N.Y., 10017 (7 dollars a year).

Atlantic Monthly, Harper's, The Reporter, Time, Newsweek, New Republic, and Yale Review are among the American periodicals that provide critical book reviews.

SOME READERS find that subscriptions to book clubs help build their libraries. Of the various kinds of book-buying clubs, some distribute newly published books; others, classics in fine bindings; still others, paperback editions. There are clubs for different age groups and for special interests, such as religion, public affairs, history, science.

Subscriptions usually require a guarantee that a stated number of books will be purchased each year and offer a book bonus to members. Be sure to retain the privilege of examining books before purchasing or of having a choice in the ones you will buy. Otherwise, the selection for your home library will be in the hands of those who do not know your tastes and needs.

PAPERBACKS (or soft-cover books) can stretch a book dollar. Their publishers offer a wide and good choice of fiction

and nonfiction. The 9,287 paperback titles published in 1964 were 32.6 percent of the total number of titles produced in the United States.

It is wise to buy the paperback of your choice as soon as it appears in the bookstore, department store, drugstore, market, or newsstand. Once out of stock, a paperback may be difficult to locate or order.

Reading a library copy of the book first will help you decide whether to own it in a paperback or hard-cover edition. The durability of a paperback cannot be judged by its price; a 35-cent book may withstand as much use as one that costs much more.

Studies and magazine articles on paperbounds abound. They offer interesting comments on the runaway popularity and remarkable variety of today's paperbacks, which are indeed a major contribution to our national cultural, literary, and educational life.

Paperbacks are published mainly as reprints and appear usually within a year after the original edition. Sometimes they may share the same publication date as the hard-cover edition or be the original and only edition.

How important paperbacks have become is discussed by Harry Gilroy in The New York Times Book Review of January 10, 1965. Three billion paperbacks have been sold in the past quarter century, he said. The economical price of the paperback—as low as 40 cents in the mass market, as low as 1.45 dollars for the small, finely printed editions—has placed virtually all the good writing of the world in the reach of the great part of the American public. He quoted the estimate that sales of paperbacks totaled 200 million dollars in 1964.

A useful paperbound described as a "comprehensive, annotated guide to more than 900 paperbound science books" is *A Guide to Science Reading,* compiled and edited by Hilary J. Deason, American Association for the Advancement of Science. It is a Signet Science Library book, published by the New American Library of World Literature, Inc. (501 Madison Avenue, New York, N.Y., 10022). It sells for 60 cents; add 5 cents for postage if you order from the publisher. In 54 scientific and mathematical categories, books are classified, described, and placed in one of four levels, indicating the reader level from the uninformed to the advanced college student.

Some public libraries prepare booklists for purposeful adult reading on such subjects as politics and government, child care, human relations, and regional writings.

The State library agency and local library can suggest reading guides for special needs.

For persons with "tired eyes," there are such lists as *Easy on your Eyes; a Listing of Books Printed in Large, Clear Type*, compiled by Adult Education Committee, Massachusetts Library Association (The New England Council of Optometrists, Inc., 101 Tremont Street, Boston, 02108).

The American Library Association in cooperation with the Public Affairs Committee, Inc. (22 East 38th Street, New York, N.Y., 10016), has published a series, *Reading for an Age of Change*. Each of the guides has an essay by an authority that surveys the subject and provides background for the descriptive lists of some 12 books that follow. Available at 60 cents each, or 2.50 dollars for the five titles, are *Space Science*, by Ralph E. Lapp; *Contemporary Arts*, by Bartlett H. Hayes, Jr.; *The Expanding Population in a Shrinking World*, by Marston Bates; *Freedom of the Mind*, by William O. Douglas; *The World of Economics*, by Robert L. Heilbroner. Five more have been planned.

Early each year, the American Library Association announces the selection by national vote of public librarians of notable books published the preceding year. The list is distributed by public libraries.

Organizations and associations bring to the attention of their members good reading in their special interest. An example: The National Recreation Association (8 West Eighth Street, New York, N.Y., 10011) publishes at 25 cents an annual annotated *Guide to Books on Recreation*.

PARENTS who enjoy reading reap a double harvest. They are likely to find that their children also are at home with books and take to reading easily. An early sharing of books, reading aloud, and relating books to the child's day-to-day experiences prepares a child for the reading experience, for learning, expressing himself, thinking, and imagining.

This sharing can begin when the child is about 8 months old, when he can respond to the sounds and rhythms of nursery songs and Mother Goose rhymes.

Helpful from this time on through age 12 is *A Parent's Guide to Children's Reading*, by Nancy Larrick. It was published by Doubleday in 1964 at 3.95 dollars and by Pocket Books at 50 cents. Dr. Larrick offers practical aid in selecting specific books for reading and reference and discusses such subjects as magazines children enjoy, the use of libraries and booklists, the pull of comics and TV, how reading is being taught.

Educators agree on the importance of reading aloud to youngsters. To help find the right book for read aloud sessions, try *Let's Read Together; Books for Family Enjoyment;* second edition, selected and annotated by a Joint Committee of the National Congress of Parents & Teachers and the American Library Association (American Library Association, Chicago, 1964; 1.50 dollars).

Each year we have a new crop of books for young people. The 2,808 juveniles published in 1964 represented an increase of 72.7 percent over the number published in 1961. Many are remarkably good and beautiful, but it becomes more and more difficult to select children's books for owning and giving.

The temptation to buy a complete

series of books should be resisted. Each title in a series should be judged individually for quality and need.

A literary set for children with stories, poems, and excerpts may attract mother or father, but a child likes stories individually presented. He long remembers each book for its story and by its feel, design, dimensions, and identity. Say no to the set, if it will cost your child his individual storybooks.

"Lists of good books for children are almost as numerous as children," writes May Hill Arbuthnot in the introduction to the third edition of her *Children's Books Too Good To Miss* (Press of Western Reserve University, Cleveland, 1963; 1.25 dollars). She lists more than 200 books by age (under 6 through early teens), with lively descriptions and illustrations. Every child should at least have a look at these books; their appeal to children has been proved; they have high literary quality; all offer wisdom or merriment or appreciation of beauty.

Two attractive lists of award-winning books and one annual publication are distributed by the Children's Services Division of the American Library Association. "Newbery Medal Books" lists the winners of the award since 1922 for an outstanding contribution to American literature for children. "Caldecott Medal Books" features those judged the most distinguished picture books for children since 1938. The third is "Notable Children's Books of the Year." These three folders may be available at your public library or State library agency. You may choose to request a single copy of each free from the American Library Association with the enclosure of a stamped, self-addressed envelope.

Many public libraries prepare gift lists, such as New York Public Library's "Children's Books Suggested as Holiday Gifts" (Fifth Avenue at 42d Street, New York, N.Y., 10018; 25 cents).

Book Week in November affords libraries, publishers, and bookshops the chance to exhibit and publicize the newly published books. At this and other times, children should have the pleasure of helping select the books they would love to own, weighing an old favorite against a new delight.

The book-reviewing periodicals I mentioned previously have sections and occasional articles on children's reading. *The Horn Book* (585 Boylston Street, Boston, Mass., 02116) is the only magazine devoted to books and reading for children and young people. Those books that deserve honors for fineness and permanence and for qualities that meet the tests of children—"sincerity, joy in writing, the power to give adventure which could not otherwise be had or that offer experiences worth reliving"—receive the "fanfare of trumpets" symbol. You may want to request *Five Year Fanfare:* Horn Book's Honor List (10 cents) and *Thirty Twentieth Century Children's Books Every Adult Should Know* (5 cents).

Several special booklists are necessities to librarians and teachers and may be used or owned by parents whose children have these interests or need guidance in developing them. *Reading Ladders for Human Relations;* fourth edition, edited by Muriel Crosby (American Council on Education, Washington, D.C., 1963; 4 dollars; paper edition, 2.50 dollars), describes some thousand books for children from elementary through senior high school grades. These books can help young people grow up, search for values, feel themselves a part of the family and group, and strengthen their link with people of different backgrounds.

The AAAS Science Book List for Children (second edition, compiled under the direction of Hilary J. Deason) is published by the American Association for the Advancement of Science and the National Science Foundation (Washington, 1963, 2.50 dollars; paper 1.50 dollars). It is a guide to selecting recreational and supplementary reading on the sciences and mathematics as well as to selecting reference books. For the science minded in the primary, intermediate, and advanced levels, the choices and descriptions will point to the right book on each subject.

The editor of *The Horn Book*, Ruth Hill Viguers, believes: "If children are going to find the excellent, more adults must set themselves to find it."

The encouragement and enthusiasm of parents for books, their practice of looking up words and information in books, good talk at home about writers and their ideas and real people and people made real in stories, and instances of the compassion and laughter and excitement and wonder in books—these will make children want to read all their lives.

THE TEENAGER in high school is going through the ordeal and satisfaction of growing up, of becoming a unique person. In rebelling against the dependence of childhood and in grasping at adulthood, he needs direction, support, knowledge—self-knowledge and much knowledge of this, his world. Books can give him answers.

If the adolescent reads, he will read hungrily and widely. Interests may change, as he may change, almost from day to day. Then again, some young people will read only one kind of book; they become specialists, respected for their information on, say, Civil War battles, herpetology, jazz, or batting averages. Others will read only what is assigned at school, if that.

The teenager who reads reluctantly may yield more easily to a suspense story, a book for laughs, the life story of his sports hero, of her romantic heroine. Paperbounds persuade young people to read.

If you are hopefully helping the teenager discover the pleasures of reading, you should know *Gateways to Readable Books; An Annotated Graded List of Books in Many Fields for Adolescents Who Find Reading Difficult;* third edition (H. W. Wilson, New York, 1958; 3 dollars). Most of the books, grouped by interest, are on the fifth-, sixth-, and seventh-grade reading levels. Find a book here on his true interest (what does he talk about with his friends? watch on TV? snatch the paper to see? tinker with in the toolshed?) and you have the best chance of drawing him into enjoyable reading.

If your young adult knows what he likes—and it happens to be science—you can give him *The AAAS Science Book List for Young Adults;* second edition, compiled under the direction of Hilary J. Deason, and published by the American Association for the Advancement of Science and the National Science Foundation (Washington, 1964; 3.50 dollars; paper, 2.50 dollars).

High-schoolers concerned with their future vocations, and this is a sizable worry for many, will find facts and inspiration in *Vocations in Biography and Fiction; An annotated List of Books for Young People,* compiled by Kathryn A. Haebich (American Library Association, Chicago, 1962; 1.75 dollars). Most of the 1,070 books listed are life stories. A section, "Vocations for Handicapped Persons," offers example and motivation to this group of young people.

Outstanding Biographies for College-Bound Students and *Outstanding Fiction for College-Bound Students* are leaflets prepared by the Young Adult Services Division of the American Library Association and available for 5 cents each on request with a stamped, self-addressed envelope.

The College Preparatory Reading List, by Flora Webb, is an especially stimulating selection of books from all fields that can build background and judgment in reading (Nioga Library System, Pine Avenue and Ninth Street, Niagara Falls, N.Y.; 10 cents with stamped, self-addressed envelope).

Something for everyone is found in the New York Public Library's *Books for the Teen Age,* published January of each year (50 cents). Chosen for leisure-time reading and grouped by subjects of interest to young adults, these books—whether fiction or fact—are clear, vivid, and appealing. Most of the 1,700 titles are adult books. The aim of reading specialists who work with young adults is to begin wherever they may be and guide them toward maturity in reading and understanding.

A briefer list is *Adult Books Significant for Young People*, an annual selection by librarians across the country, publicized by school and public libraries and State library agencies (American Library Association; 5 cents with a stamped, self-addressed envelope).

Young adults will find the printed resources that adults use to select their reading—the booklists, reviews, magazines, newspapers. We must not underestimate their curiosity, ingenuity, idealism, drive, and accomplishment as the years mount.

NONE OF US loses his ability to learn on his 21st birthday. We can learn even when we are old. In fact, the best time for liberal learning is after age 50.

Many opportunities for adult education are available throughout the country. The purpose is to assist adults to understand themselves, their families, society, and the world.

The basic purpose of adult education, as of education in general, is to help people gain knowledge, insights, and skills that will enable them to make the wisest possible decisions in their social, economic, and political lives, as well as to contribute to their personal enrichment. In our growing and changing society, education must be constantly updated, tested, and refreshed.

Adult education has many parts. One of the most accessible is the public library. Besides the books, records, and periodicals that are their usual stock in trade, many libraries offer rich resources to persons who wish to enlarge their horizons.

They can tell you about correspondence schools, museums and art institutes, and music and theater programs in your community. Many libraries also sponsor educational programs on their own—lectures, concerts, discussion groups, and films.

A large number of public school systems offer evening courses for adults.

For information on adult education, you may write to these sources: State Director of Adult Education of your State Department of Education; Local University Extension or Evening College Division; Adult Education Association of U.S.A., 1225 19th Street NW., Washington, D.C., 20036; National Association of Public School Adult Education, 1201 16th Street NW., Washington, D.C., 20036; Adult Basic Education Section, Office of Education, United States Department of Health, Education, and Welfare, Washington, D.C., 20202.

WITH THIS SAMPLING of booklists for adults, children, and young adults, we may look forward to more reading with more pleasure and profit.

Borrow books from the public library, add books to your home library, swap paperbacks, borrow books from your friends and organizations, join a book club.

Visit the nearest bookstores and paperback stores.

Talk books with your family, friends, colleagues; that can give new perspective to reading.

Elizabeth Barrett Browning in *Aurora Leigh* offers good advice to book readers:

We get no good
By being ungenerous, even to a book,
And calculating profits,—so much help
By so much reading. It is rather when
We gloriously forget ourselves and plunge
Soul-forward, headlong, into a book's profound,
Impassioned for its beauty and salt of truth—
'Tis then we get the right good from a book. (PAULINE WINNICK)

Where

Vision Is

CULTURAL ACTIVITIES form the loom on which talents, skills, and dreams of individuals can be woven into something colorful and distinctive—a play, pageant, art center, music festival, museum, library, garden, park—to enrich community life.

Cultural activities are central to rural areas development, a nationwide effort of rural people and those in public service and private endeavors who work with them to enrich the quality of life.

What may not be recognized by area leaders whose primary interest is in economic development is that cultural activities can be a part of the steam that supplies the drive.

The first heritage festival of Lawrence County in Arkansas illustrates how a cultural activity may emerge from a ferment of economic and social development and in turn spawn new ideas for further social and economic gain and other cultural activities.

Lawrence County, a mainly rural area in northeastern Arkansas, had a population of 17,000 in 1960.

Its eastern half is fertile. Wooded hills in the western half mark the beginning of the Ozark Range. The Black River runs between the delta, planted to rice, soybeans, and cotton, and the hills, where the farms are in livestock and poultry. Family-type farms employ a third of its work force.

Farmers thus made up the largest occupational group in the Lawrence County Development Council when it was organized in 1962.

Seventeen members of the council were farmers—nine in general farming, six livestock and poultry producers, one a dairyman, another a ricegrower. Also on the council were an industrial worker, two bankers, the manager of a production credit office, the manager of the power company, a druggist, the operator of a small general store, the president of Southern Baptist College, the superintendent of schools, two teachers, the county judge, a mayor, a postmaster, and five homemakers.

During the first 2 years the council addressed itself to the economic advancement of the county. It supported a 1-mill tax to guarantee construction of an industrial building in Walnut Ridge, the county seat and largest town. It helped organize the Cooper Creek watershed project. It was instrumental in getting a comprehensive manpower inventory and economic base study of the area. It arranged for workshops in farm management. It set up projects to train sewing machine operators and farm machinery operators. It helped the towns of Hoxie, Walnut Ridge, Black Rock, Portia, and Sedgwick begin steps leading to new or expanded water and sewage systems. It helped leaders of Imboden initiate a housing project for 20 elderly persons.

The milestone that gave the council deepest satisfaction was the consolidation of two political districts—districts formed shortly after the Civil War when it was more practical to construct two courthouses than to bridge the Black River and build roads.

The courthouse at Powhatan served the west side of the county. Although only two stories high, the stone building of Gothic architecture appears large and imposing because of its site on the brow of a hill overlooking the Black River. When the courthouse was built in 1888, Powhatan was a small inland port for cotton, corn, livestock.

But when the Iron Mountain Railroad was built, it bypassed Powhatan. The chief engineer of the railroad laid out another town, Walnut Ridge, which later was also designated as a county seat. A second courthouse was built in 1900.

Over the next half-century the railroad took the place of river transportation, and Powhatan gradually became a ghost town. The county continued to use the courthouse, where records dating back to 1815 had been maintained.

It had become clear to most people by 1962 that two courthouses were not needed. The county development council took the lead in surveying opinion. The results showed strong support for consolidation and foreshadowed the election. Votes favoring consolidation outnumbered those against by 10 to 1. A much needed new courthouse could now be planned.

Perhaps it was a sense of thanksgiving that inspired the idea of a rally, festival, and homecoming to be sponsored by the council. The chairman made the proposal at the quarterly meeting in November. His first thought was to organize a lively show that would emphasize sports. The council agreed that the idea should be explored and suggested the assignment be given to the committee on family living.

That committee, taking note of people whose gifts were in the arts as well as those whose abilities were in athletics, decided that a festival could be a memorable event.

The test would be to identify leaders with special gifts for cultural activities, choose a variety of activities, involve a high proportion of the people at every stage of the project, select a theme that focused on the uniqueness of the area, draw up comprehensive plans, and set a schedule and hold to it.

Four people agreed to take major responsibility—a housewife of Walnut Ridge; the principal of Hoxie High School; his wife, a teacher of speech and dramatics at the school; and a young minister, who served churches in three small towns.

The woman who chaired the committee had always lived in Lawrence County. The speech teacher and the minister grew up in nearby counties. The principal, a Kentuckian by birth, trained in mathematics and physics and with experience in industry, managed a radio station in Florida before he and his wife decided teaching was the field that most appealed to them. Her experience included little theater work, radio writing and broadcasting, and work as producer of pageants for churches in a large city. Thus, when the minister suggested a pageant be the major event of the festival, the committee found it had exceptional resources in technical skills and leadership.

These four knew something about the history of Lawrence County. It was named for the naval hero who said, "Don't give up the ship!" It was carved out of Louisiana Territory in 1815, two decades before Arkansas became a State. In fact, Lawrence County covered an area as large as a State. The original boundaries extended to within a few miles of what is now the Oklahoma line. As settlers moved into the region, Lawrence County was divided into other counties. The area that at one period in history was known as Lawrence County now forms 31 counties in Arkansas and Missouri.

"It's the mother of counties," said the principal, and that was the name selected for the pageant—"Mother of Counties."

A stately theme song was composed by the speech teacher, set to music by a member of the music department of Southern Baptist College, and published by the college print shop. It would be sung by a choir selected from the two high schools with music departments and from church choirs.

At least 300 persons helped produce "Mother of Counties." Helping the pageant directors were a stage manager, building director, lighting director, sound director, art director, costume director, and properties director, each with a technical crew, a casting director, music director, and a director from each of the 17 communities which took part. Each community director named a costume chairman, property chairman, and casting crew to assist in organizing the segment of the pageant selected by or assigned to the community.

PEOPLE ARE DRAWN to a program such as the heritage festival by a diversity of offerings in which they can participate and enjoy.

The planning committee in Lawrence County invited suggestions from everyone. The response showed strong interests in an arts and crafts exhibit, antiques of all kinds, a parade of old cars, folk singing, gospel singing, oldtime games, and contests and games for horseback riders. In every instance, there was someone in the area who could take charge of one of these segments. The Saddle Club, for example, arranged the contests involving horses.

A site for cultural activity is apt to be one of the most difficult decisions. The planners in Lawrence County drew up specifications for the site to be chosen: It must be an area in which there was a natural amphitheater; it must be accessible; there would need to be ample room for parking and concessions and several platforms for entertainers. It would need to be near buildings where the exhibits could be housed and where there were restrooms and near powerlines, so the platforms could be wired for electricity.

The little town of Lynn (population 263) met these specifications. A place near the Lynn school formed a natural amphitheater. The cafeteria was transformed into "Heritage Inn." Operators of the inn were members of the Hoxie Booster Club, who served as cooks and waiters under the supervision of the hospital dietitian. The income from the concession helped the club meet a pledge of funds for the Boy Scouts.

An unexpected bonus from the choice of Lynn was the effect on the citizens. They were galvanized to ac-

tion; they painted their homes, landscaped the churchyard, paved the streets, renovated stores, and cleaned the highway entrances.

As one observer remarked, the festival lifted the spirits of the people of Lynn to a new high. They had help from county officials. Early in the spring, road machinery was sent to Lynn to prepare the site. A little later, the grounds were fertilized and planted to grass. A few days before the festival, the area was treated with pesticides to control insects.

A SPECIAL EFFORT is required to reach wide audiences for cultural activities.

Lawrence County planners began immediately to set up a mailing list of former residents and visitors who could arrange to attend the festival. There were announcements and progress reports, and the final mailing to the 5,000 persons on the list was an attractive folder outlining the program. On the cover was a sketch of the Powhatan courthouse drawn by the speech teacher. The minister drew the figures heading the announcement of the parade, oldtime games, folk music, and the pageant.

This brochure carried an order blank for the special medals struck to commemorate the festival and designed by a talented woman who collects coins as a hobby.

When it came time to develop the program booklet, the people of Lawrence County were fully involved in the festival. Businessmen did not need to be urged to buy advertising space. That meant ample room for articles telling the history and recent industrial and recreational developments and a booklet to interest visitors, help finance the festival, and serve as a useful reference.

The people of Lawrence County had come alive to their heritage. They formed a historical society. They began plans to restore the old, dilapidated courthouse at Powhatan as a museum.

Then the question was raised: Why

not restore the old river port town as it was in the 1880's? Some of the old buildings were still standing. So were the piers to what had once been a fine swinging bridge. The setting was lovely. What the people visualized was a point of historic interest that would add a dimension to the recreational facilities in prospect with the development of the Flat River and Cooper Creek watersheds. Families who came for outdoor recreation would also enjoy visiting the town as it was in another day.

And the pageant, a capsule of history in music and drama, should not end with one night's performance. A color movie made by the Arkansas Parks and Publicity Commission showed a durable drama in "Mother of Counties." Could a permanent amphitheater be developed and a staff organized to produce this pageant all through the summer? Within a few weeks after the first performance, the committee and other interested persons had begun to study community organization involved in restorations and pageants across the Nation.

Old Irelandville in New York consists of an interesting group of old buildings and reproductions on the site of the 150-year-old village of Irelandville. Many antiques and collections of early Americana are contained in the 1747 tavern museum, the 1838 manor house, restored schoolhouse, country church, and old country store and ice cream parlor.

Hopewell Village in Pennsylvania preserves the remains of one of the finest examples of American 18th-century ironmaking villages on an 848-acre site about 14 miles southeast of Reading on the Birdsboro-Warwick road.

The Pennsylvania Farm Museum of Landis Valley contains an extensive collection of early farm implements and oldtime crafts illustrating early Pennsylvania farm and home life.

A Kansas museum, recreated "Stage Station No. 15" at Norton, where Horace Greeley and other historical personalities stopped, is one of several buildings in Kansas important to pioneer transportation.

"Unto These Hills," presented in Mountainside Theater in the Great Smoky Mountains of North Carolina, is the drama story of the Cherokees, misunderstood, forced back into the hills, driven west by military power, and of a handful who braved mighty wrath to stay in the Smoky homeland and develop into a race of useful American citizens. It is a tragic, triumphant, gay, and tearful story, staged with original music and dances.

"Let Freedom Ring," a historical drama of Hopewell and Prince George County, Virginia, is an exciting movement of scenes, in which the cast and chorus tell of the meeting at Jordan's Point in 1674, which ended in the selection of Nathaniel Bacon by acclamation to lead the now famous rebellion, an early torch to the spirit of independence.

The Lincoln Heritage Trail of Illinois has stops at the Lincoln log cabin, the furnished, reconstructed cabin home of Lincoln's father and stepmother, and Lincoln's New Salem, the famous historic reconstruction of the village where Abraham Lincoln lived (1831–37). The cabins and shops have many original items.

"LOOKING at the American scene," said President Kennedy, "one is impressed by its diversity and vitality . . . . In the midst of all this activity, it is only natural that people should be more active in the pursuit of the arts."

And as the people of Lawrence County found, these activities satisfy and renew the creative spirit of the individuals who take part in them, and they bind the people together. They light new pathways. They help people see fresh possibilities for making their communities more interesting and beautiful. The people are inspired to turn their dreams and hopes into reality. (MARGUERITE GILSTRAP AND C. B. GILLILAND)

CLOTHING

Clothing the Family

THE MONEY you spend for clothing for the family may be small compared with other spending, but the way you use it bears directly on the well-being of the whole family.

Total income and the family situation may determine what is spent for clothing, but needs of each family member will decide the way it is spent.

How do you decide what each individual needs?

Consider the father's occupation and the type and number of his social activities. The kind of work he does and the standard of dress he must maintain determine his clothing needs.

The daily activities of the wife and mother are reflected in her wardrobe. She takes into account her home, work, and social life.

Children need many different kinds of clothes, and it is not always easy to meet all those needs.

Generally it is best to buy clothing that fits the child at the time of purchase rather than to buy clothes for the child to grow into. Avoid buying too many clothes lest they are outgrown before they are worn out. Consider sturdy workmanship and self-help features when you buy for young children.

After deciding on individual needs for work, school, play, and social events, take a good look at what you already have on hand.

Decide whether the clothing is wearable as it is; whether it needs some alteration, cleaning, or mending to put it in use; or whether it should be discarded.

When you have made that decision, you can determine more easily which additional items are needed for each family member, what is needed immediately, and which garments can be bought later. Few people buy a completely new wardrobe at one time.

Planning your buying over a period should help you avoid overspending and impulse buying. Too often we need something in a hurry or see something we cannot resist because it is a bargain or lifts our spirits. This type of buying is an ever-present danger to a spending plan. If you plan your purchases, you will be able to take advantage of sales and still buy only the things you need and plan for.

It takes advance planning and some reliable information to shop wisely. Printed information on the item you plan to buy may not be readily available, but guides for consumers have been written for some items of clothing. Ask about them in your local library before you go to buy.

Before you go shopping, decide on a price limit for each item. This helps to keep you from overspending and cuts down on shopping time.

Be alert to what items are available in the stores. Shop in stores that have a reputation for good quality and fairness to customers.

Spend some time shopping around comparing quality and price. When you want the longest wear possible from a garment, you need to plan to buy the best quality available at the price you can afford. For certain items, things that will be worn only a few times and not subjected to hard wear, however, price may come first.

Learn the signs of good workmanship. You are then better able to make selections that give longer wear. Workmanship is how the garment is cut, sewn, and finished.

The general signs of good workmanship are: Seams wide enough to allow for letting out and finished to prevent fraying; garment cut with the grain of the goods; close and even machine stitching; hems and facings firmly attached but not showing on the right side of garment; weak points reinforced; and machine-made buttonholes firm and evenly stitched.

Be sure you know what fiber is used in the fabric. You need to know all you can about the material you are buying, regardless of whether it is in ready-to-wear or yard goods for home sewing.

Feel and appearance have been the shopper's guide to quality of fabric, but neither is adequate or dependable today. Your best helps are factual tags or labels. Read them carefully.

A label giving the fiber content is required by the Textile Fiber Products Identification Act and the Wool Products Labeling Act. You thus have reliable information about the fiber content, which is helpful if you prefer one fiber over another or if you need

additional information on how to care for the garment.

Some garments carry labels that tell about the workmanship, whether there is a special finish on the fabric (wash-and-wear, preshrunk, crease-resistant, water-repellent) and how to care for the garment (whether it can be laundered and, if so, the proper method to use, or whether it should be drycleaned only).

Some labels contain the manufacturer's name and address. Reliable firms want their name associated with their product.

How the garment is to be cared for is important. The cost of upkeep is greater for clothes that should be drycleaned only.

If fabrics have a finish that requires special handling when they are laundered, you should consider the additional time needed to care for them.

When you shop, consider the fit of the garment. A garment that fits correctly is more comfortable, more attractive, and will give longer wear. Extensive alterations may be expensive and add considerably to the original cost. Making your own alterations is one way of saving money, but be sure to attempt only the alterations that you know you can do easily and well.

IN TIMES when every young girl was taught to sew and the ready-to-wear market was small and expensive, the homemaker did not have to decide whether she would sew or buy clothing. Now she does. What influences her decisions?

Of the many types of shops available, the homemaker can patronize the specialty shop, department store, chain store, or discount store or order by mail.

Where you choose to shop depends, as you well know, on the availability of goods, the sizes needed, and the time and energy you have for shopping. For example, if you have small children, you may find it easier to select from a catalog and order by mail, rather than take the children on a shopping trip.

Before you decide to make a garment, ask yourself: Do I have the speed and accuracy so that my time is used wisely? Can my time be better spent doing something else for my family? Does the general appearance and fit of the clothing satisfy me and the person for whom it is made? Can I make a garment of better quality at a lower cost than I can afford to buy? Do I enjoy sewing?

Sewing is a creative and relaxing activity for many women. Knitting and other forms of handiwork and needlework are, too—but that is another story.

Certain things—the simple dresses, housecoats, little girls' dresses, playclothes, men's and boys' sportswear, and sport shirts, for example—are more successfully made at home than more complicated garments.

Heavy outerwear, such as coats, suits (men's and women's), and standard items in undergarments are usually purchased ready-to-wear even by the woman who sews for her family.

In deciding whether to buy or sew, consider that clothing costs involve (besides money paid out) an investment of time and energy in shopping or sewing.

The purchase of such accessories as hats, gloves, belts, scarves, neckties, and socks should be planned along with the rest of the wardrobe. The indiscriminate buying of accessories may ruin your clothing budget.

Accessories should complement and not detract from the overall appearance. One accessory, properly chosen, can be used with several outfits or may give the finishing touch to a particular outfit. (SHIRLEY J. MOTT)

For further reading, consult the following Department of Agriculture publications:
Fitting Coats and Suits, Home and Garden Bulletin No. 11; *How to Tailor A Woman's Suit*, Home and Garden Bulletin No. 20; *Mending Men's Suits*, Home and Garden Bulletin No. 39; *Men's Suits: How to Judge Quality*, Home and Garden Bulletin No. 54; *Pattern Alteration*, Farmers' Bulletin No. 1968; *Simplified Clothing Construction*, Home and Garden Bulletin No. 59.

Clothes That Fit

NOTHING GOOD can be said of clothing that fits poorly. It is unattractive and uncomfortable. Strains may develop in seams and fabrics that shorten the life of the garment.

Manufacturers and retailers of garments whose fit does not satisfy the consumer suffer through loss of goodwill and the return of merchandise.

Poor fit may mean a garment or pattern is a size too small or too large. Often it means the pattern or garment is not properly proportioned to fit the wearer.

Getting a good fit was a serious problem a generation ago. Each manufacturer then used his own system of sizing. Those systems had been developed by trial and error from measurements taken on a few individuals according to poorly defined and inaccurate procedures. Garments labeled the same size by different manufacturers differed greatly. Few fit without alterations.

NOW YOU HAVE A GOOD chance of buying clothes that fit with little or no alteration. The woman who sews usually can make well-fitting clothes by using commercial patterns with only minor adjustments—if any.

The change came about after scientists in the Department of Agriculture conducted a comprehensive study of the body dimensions of American women and children. They consulted manufacturers of patterns and garments in deciding which body measurements were needed.

Educational institutions helped ob-

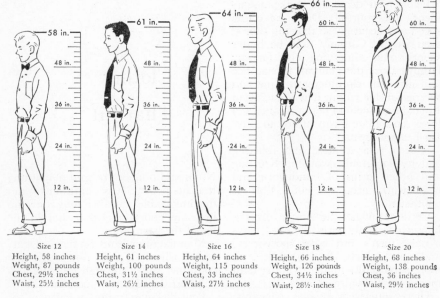

Size 12	Size 14	Size 16	Size 18	Size 20
Height, 58 inches	Height, 61 inches	Height, 64 inches	Height, 66 inches	Height, 68 inches
Weight, 87 pounds	Weight, 100 pounds	Weight, 115 pounds	Weight, 126 pounds	Weight, 138 pounds
Chest, 29½ inches	Chest, 31½ inches	Chest, 33 inches	Chest, 34½ inches	Chest, 36 inches
Waist, 25½ inches	Waist, 26½ inches	Waist, 27½ inches	Waist, 28½ inches	Waist, 29½ inches

Age is not a size. The size designation shown below each boy refers to his dimensions, not his age. (Source: Department Store Economist, September 1955.)

COMMERCIAL BODY MEASUREMENT STANDARDS*

Number	Title	Size range
CS 151–50	Body measurements for the sizing of apparel for infants, babies, toddlers, and children.	Up to 6X
CS 153–48	Body measurements for the sizing of apparel for girls.	7 to 12
CS 155–50	Body measurements for the sizing of boys' apparel.	2 to 20
CS 215–58	Body measurements for the sizing of women's patterns and apparel.	

Misses'
8R   to 22R
10T   to 20T
8S   to 18S
10R— to 22R—
12T— to 18T—
12S— to 18S—
8R+ to 16R+
10T+ to 14T+
8S+ to 12S+

Women's
30R   to 42R
32T   to 40T
32R— to 42R—
28R+ to 38R+
30T+ to 36T+

Half-sizes
10½   to 24½
12½— to 22½—
8½+ to 20½+

Juniors'
7R   to 19R
9T   to 17T
9S   to 15S

*All standards except CS 151–50 are based entirely on USDA data on body measurements. Data for infants, babies, and toddlers were obtained from the literature.

tain 36 measurements of 147,088 children (age 4 to 17) and 58 measurements of each of 14,698 women. Standards for sizing patterns and apparel were developed from the measurements through the joint efforts of industry and the Departments of Commerce and Agriculture.

THE STANDARDS are known as commercial standards.

They are of three types: Body measurement standards, which represent the body clothed in underwear or foundation garments; model form standards, which represent special length and girth modifications of body measurement standards for apparel-fitting purposes; and garment-size standards, which give dimensions for specific garments and are also based on the body measurement standards.

Because the body measurement standards are of more general interest, I discuss them in some detail. A table gives the titles of these standards and the range of sizes covered by them.

BODY MEASUREMENT standard CS 215–58 covers four classifications of women and nine different body types and is the most comprehensive of the standards we have.

The classifications are Misses', Women's, Half-sizes (shorter women), and Juniors'.

The body types are divided into three height groups (tall, regular, and short), with three bust-hip groups for each height group. The bust is the same in the three bust-hip groups; the hip types are slender (designated as minus), regular, and full (designated as plus).

The size number is based on the bust measurement but is not numerically equal to it. The number is combined with symbols to give the complete size designation.

Thus, 14R refers to a size 14 bust, regular or average height and hips; 14T− refers to a size 14 bust, tall in height, slender-hip type; and 14S+

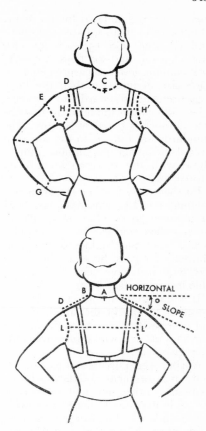

Location of some of the actual body measurements taken during the U.S. Department of Agriculture study on which the Commercial Standard for the Sizing of Women's Patterns and Apparel is based. Front view of woman: Cross-chest width; neck base, armscye, upper arm, elbow, and wrist girths. Back view of woman: Cross-back width; neck base and armscye; girths; shoulder length and slope.

refers to a size 14 bust, short in height, full-hip type.

The standard includes tables that give the weight and 47 measurements for each of 111 size designations. These designations include 46 Misses', 28 Women's, 21 Half-sizes, and 16 Juniors'.

The standard explains the various measurements and includes drawings showing how some of the more important ones are taken.

As would be expected, the body

measurement standards for the sizing of apparel for infants, babies, toddlers, and children (CS 151–50), for girls (CS 153–48), and for boys (CS 155–50) contain fewer measurements for each size designation than the body measurement standard for women. They differ from the latter in that the size number is based on stature. The standards are limited to the so-called "regulars" in the population; that is, those with the most common body proportions.

Further analysis of the Department's original measurement data has been undertaken to develop standards for the so-called "outsizes" in the population, as slims and huskies for boys and chubbies for girls. Some of these outsize standards have been made available in preliminary form.

It is important to note that the size numbers in any of the standards are not necessarily the same as the ages of the boys or girls whose measurements they give.

Anyone can purchase copies of the body measurement standards. Information on prices and how to order is available from the Office of Engineering Standards, Institute of Applied Technology, National Bureau of Standards, Washington, D.C., 20234.

Issuance as a commercial standard indicates that a standard has been accepted by a substantial segment of the trade. Firms and other organizations who accept a standard before it is issued as a commercial standard are listed in the printed standard.

Others may agree to accept it later, but no one is required to do so. All who are concerned with the manufacture and distribution of garments and patterns for women and children are encouraged to use the standards, with or without formal acceptance.

Anyone who accepts one of the standards agrees to use it insofar as practicable in the production, distribution, and purchase of patterns and apparel, but he reserves the right to depart from the standard as he deems advisable.

It is asked that products that comply with a standard in all respects be regularly identified or labeled as conforming to it. Such labeling is not mandatory. However, the use of labels or advertisements that indicate that a product conforms to a standard makes conformance mandatory. Thus, the absence of a label indicating that the sizing of a garment conforms to the appropriate standard does not necessarily mean that it does not conform. On the other hand, presence of such a label is assurance that it does.

In actual practice, labels and advertisements that mention the commercial standards for the sizing of garments and patterns are rare. Industry nevertheless has made extensive use of the information on body proportions contained in the standards in designing and sizing garments and patterns. As a result, women and children have a greater number of sizes to choose from and a much better chance than formerly of finding garments and patterns that give a good fit.

When the standards were developed, it was suggested that the size designations listed in them be used by all manufacturers and distributors for all types of garments. That would greatly simplify the shopper's problem.

For example, if a woman found that her proportions most closely checked those given in CS 215–58 for a size 12R in the Misses' classification, she would buy a size 12 Misses' garment, regardless of what garment she was buying or who manufactured it.

As most of us know, this system of designating sizes is not always followed. A shopper will find that she takes a size 12 Misses' dress in most lines. In some, she may find that it is the size 10 that fits her. She will also find that most manufacturers label some garments according to specific body measurements rather than by the size designations listed in the standard. Nevertheless, the chances are that the proportions of the garment are based on those given in the standard.

Several mail-order companies are

among the most enthusiastic users of the body measurement standards.

The consumer who shops by mail will find that their catalogs give the more important body measurements for the various sizes and illustrate the proper method for taking the measurements.

The manufacturers of patterns for women who sew at home also include certain key body dimensions in their catalogs and on pattern envelopes as guides to selection of patterns. The values given for these dimensions differ somewhat from those given in the standards. Thus, when you shop for patterns, check your measurements against those in the pattern book. Do not assume that you take the same size in patterns and ready-to-wear.

Whether the consumer shops by mail or in person, her problem is to select patterns and garments proportioned to fit her figure. Only by doing so can she benefit fully from the improvement in garment sizing. (FLORENCE H. FORZIATI)

Shoes

FEET AND SHOES travel many miles. An average, healthy 7-year-old boy may take 30 thousand steps every day. That adds up to about 10 miles a day and more than 300 miles a month. His mother, on a busy shopping day, may walk 10 miles. A policeman walks about 15 miles on his beat.

Feet carry the weight of your body and provide means to propel you when you walk, climb, and jump. As you step off, your body's weight travels down through the heel, along the outside of the foot to the ball, across the heads of the long bones to the first

metatarsal, and to the big toe. The big toe launches the walking motion. Each foot in turn bears the total weight of your body.

Feet are important to posture—the way you hold your body in sitting, standing, dancing, walking. Good posture has social and hygienic value. Ask your child's doctor to check feet, posture, and gait during his physical examinations.

The foot is a complicated structure of 26 small bones linked by many joints, held together and to the leg bones by numerous ligaments, moved by muscles and tendons, nourished by blood vessels, controlled by nerves, and protected by a covering of skin.

In a newborn child, some of the bones are merely bone-shaped pieces of cartilage, a gristlelike substance. As a child grows, real bone appears within and gradually spreads throughout the cartilage form. His heel, the largest bone, is not completed until he is about 20 years old.

SHOEMAKING is a complex process.

All shoes are made over lasts—wooden forms—which give the shoe its shape, size, and style.

Shoemakers in 1887 approved a chart of standard measurements for lasts. Successive changes in styling and mass production have introduced variations in the original measurements. Two lasts, marked 13C, for example, may differ considerably in their shape and dimensions.

More than 50 kinds of materials and more than 85 hand and machine operations are used in making a shoe.

Shoes consist of outsole (bottom), insole (if used), upper, and heel.

The insole, of leather or other materials, forms the foundation of the shoe. The front part of the upper is the vamp. The back part is the quarter.

A hidden counter—stiffened material between quarter and lining—keeps the back in shape. The insole is fastened to the last. The finished upper is drawn over the last and securely joined to the insole. The outsole is

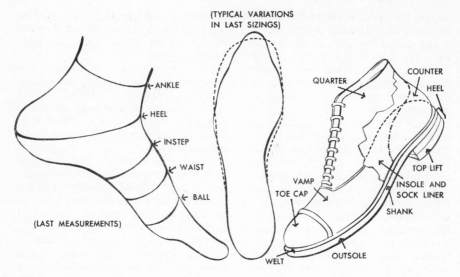

(TYPICAL VARIATIONS IN LAST SIZINGS)

(LAST MEASUREMENTS)

ANKLE / HEEL / INSTEP / WAIST / BALL

QUARTER / COUNTER / HEEL / TOP LIFT / VAMP / TOE CAP / INSOLE AND SOCK LINER / SHANK / WELT / OUTSOLE

permanently attached to the insole-upper components. Heels are attached. Finally the shoes are given several finishing touches.

Sewed, cemented, and nailed are names of three major shoemaking processes.

Welt shoes made without stitching inside are sturdy and flexible. The Goodyear welt process produces high-quality men's, women's, and children's oxfords.

In the stitchdown process, uppers are turned out and stitched directly to the outsole. This provides a smooth inner surface and resembles Goodyear welt.

Advantages of cemented shoes are their lighter weight, greater flexibility, and greater variety in styling.

Many grades of shoes can be made with the same method of construction. Many grades of materials are used.

Almost all rubber-canvas footwear is made by the vulcanizing process. By applying heat and pressure to an unvulcanized rubber mixture, a complete sole and heel are formed and permanently attached to the upper.

The newest method, similar to vulcanizing, is the injection-molded process. A vinyl (liquid plastic) is poured into a mold shaped like the finished product. Sole and heel are quickly attached to the finished upper.

Shoes have been made from almost everything—paper, raffia, felt, fur-skins, bark, and fabric.

Leather, the tanned skin or hide of an animal, is the traditional material. It is a favorite because of its toughness, durability, flexibility, shape retention, insulation, ability to absorb and pass off moisture from the foot, permeability to air, and attractive looks.

A new tanning process using glutaraldehyde, a chemical, makes leathers more resistant to breakdown by water, sweat, acids, and alkalies. Such leathers make better work shoes for farmwear. Use of other chemicals provides scuff resistance, improved wear, and water resistance.

Cotton and linen fabrics, nylon, straws, and plastics also are used for uppers.

Industry in 1964 announced many new manmade materials for shoe uppers, designated by coined or trade names. In general, the classes of new materials are poromeric, expanded vinyls, and nonexpanded vinyls.

Poromeric refers to a porous, permeable, leatherlike sheet material made up of a group of chemical compounds. An example is Corfam.

Expanded vinyl is a plastic sheet with tiny air cells evenly spaced in it to allow passage of air. One example is Pervel.

The nonexpanded is described as a flat sheet coated with vinyl to resemble patent leather.

The new materials are said to resist scuffing, be easy to care for, need no polishing, hold their shape, keep out moisture, show no water spots, be light in weight, and have clear colors that will not rub off. Some shoes of the new materials have leather linings.

Even newer are vinyl and fabric uppers bonded to cowhide splits—hides horizontally cut into layers. These uppers are said to combine long wear with easy care.

SOLES of children's shoes should preferably be slip resistant, lightweight, and flexible, but firm. Avoid boardlike soles.

Solings may be of leather, natural rubber, or manmade materials.

Synthetic rubber applies to any vulcanizable synthetic polymer having rubberlike properties. Solings of styrene-butadiene (synthetic) rubber are termed nuclear. Neolite is an example. Cellular designates a nuclear sole filled with blown air cells. Synthetic crepe soles are in this group.

The Children's Bureau recommends that for children up to age 6, shoe heels be one-fourth to one-half inch. After age 6, heel height may gradually be increased to 1 inch. Rubber heels or toplifts help prevent jarring when a child walks.

ONE COBBLER, Wilbur Gardner, of Medford, Oreg., became exasperated some years ago over the growing number of shoddy shoes people brought to his repair shop. He started a campaign for the labeling of materials in shoes. Through the support of Oregon's representatives in the Congress and interested organizations, his efforts gathered force and resulted in the Federal Trade Commission's Guides for Shoe Content Labeling and Advertising, adopted in October 1962.

Its main purpose is to insure that the consumer is not deceived. Shoe materials must be precisely identified.

Manufacturers and retailers cannot claim that a shoe is made of leather if part of it is some other material.

All labeling must be in the form of stamps, tags, or labels embedded in or attached to the product itself. The guides do not offer opinions or information as to the relative merits of various materials.

SHOE SIZES usually are designated by numbers for length and letters for width (based on girth at ball, waist, and instep).

With each half-size increase in length, there is a consistent increase in each of the basic measurements. Infants' sizes start at 0 (length of last is $3^{11}\!/_{12}$ inches) and run to 8 ($6^{7}\!/_{12}$ inches).

Other classifications of size are: Children, 8½ to 11; misses and youths, 11 to 2; growing girls and boys, 2½ to 5 or 6.

Do not ask for shoes by size. Ask the clerk to measure both feet. Have your child stand with his weight evenly divided between feet. The foot alters slightly in length and width when it takes the body's weight.

New shoes should be comfortable without alterations. Have your child walk in the shoes before you buy them.

Examine the edge trim of the shoe. Shoes of good quality have smooth, clean sole edges.

Examine the "break" of leather uppers at the ball of the shoe. Break refers to the tiny wrinkles formed on the grain (outer) surface when you bend the leather. Many fine wrinkles per inch indicate high-quality leather. A few large wrinkles indicate a poorer quality.

THINK ABOUT shoe needs before you shop.

Infants sometimes need foot coverings for warmth. Their shoes should be soft and loose. Bootees are mostly for appearance; babies quickly kick them off.

Most children do not need shoes until they begin to walk. Ask your doctor to recommend the type of first walking shoes.

Check the length, width, and height of instep to see that nothing restricts or cramps the toes and foot.

Enough toe height at the tip of the shoes is most important.

Buy shoes to fit the present foot size. Do not buy shoes too small or too large.

Sloppy fit may harm feet as much as tight shoes.

Check your child's shoes for fit about once a month.

Children need and want shoes for school, play, and dress. Up to about 6 years, children (especially little girls) tend to outgrow shoes before wearing them out.

After about 6 years, most children wear out even the best shoes before they outgrow them.

At school, a child sits a great deal. Laced oxfords make good school shoes.

Between school and bedtime, his active feet need good shoes. Have his sneakers or other play shoes fitted as carefully as his school shoes.

Let children go barefoot only in clean sand or grass. Protect their feet by sandals or shoes in places where there is apt to be broken glass, splinters, insects, hard floorings, or pavements.

If your 7-year-old boy weighs 55 pounds, he puts more than 800 tons of weight on his shoes every day (55 pounds times 30 thousand steps), or about 24 thousand tons a month. But a boy does more than walk. He jumps, kicks, and wades through puddles. His shoes lead a rough life. Estimates of the active life of shoes range from 20 days to 7 or 9 months, and average about 10 weeks.

No single component or characteristic determines the life of a shoe. Fit is most important. Only the wearer can tell if a shoe fits. Price does not guarantee good fit. Comfort, materials used, flexibility, weight of shoe, ability to hold its original shape and appear-ance influence shoe life. Length of service depends also on the wearer, where he wears his shoes, and his activities.

Wornout shoes may harm the feet. Ripped seams or soles with holes should be repaired promptly and worn toplifts replaced.

Half soles or resoling may change the size or shape of shoes and result in a poor fit.

Costs of repairs have risen. Sometimes it is better money management to buy new shoes to fit rapidly growing feet.

Lack of proper care, willful misuse, and perspiration can cause breakdown of shoes. Thousands of small sweat glands are located in the skin of the feet. The soles perspire a great deal to regulate foot temperature. When you walk briskly, each foot pours out about a tablespoon of sweat an hour. Accumulated sweat is hard on leather uppers, insoles, and linings.

Tight fitting, closed, sweaty shoes are ideal places for growth of micro-organisms. Micro-organisms contribute to bad foot odors and irritated skin and to breakdown of shoes.

If you can afford two pairs of shoes, wear one pair every other day to allow the shoes to dry out. Bathe the feet daily. Dry them carefully, especially between the toes.

Wear a clean pair of comfortable, well-fitted hose every day to protect foot health and footwear. (ROWENA P. DOWLEN)

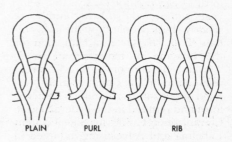

PLAIN   PURL   RIB

Plain and purl stitches and the rib.

Knitted

Fabrics

A KNITTED FABRIC, a structure of rows of loops hanging on other rows of loops, is made by pulling loops through loops.

Each vertical or lengthwise row of loops is called a wale. Each crosswise row of loops is called a course.

If the loops are stretched in any direction, they tend to return to their normal or relaxed shape. Knit goods therefore are elastic and have an advantage over woven goods.

Knitting is a craft that dates from antiquity. Master knitters made exquisite carpets, berets, shirts, afghans, shawls, and hosiery, some of which now, centuries later, are on exhibit in museums. The beginning of the machine age in the 19th century brought the decline of hand knitting as an industry.

Knitting continued in the home, however. More and more women (and men, too) knit now.

They consider knitting a rewarding, creative, relaxing, and inexpensive hobby and a productive undertaking for the odd moments at the hairdresser, say, or during longer periods.

Knitting is easy. One needs only two needles and some yarn. Pattern books and books on knitting give enough information for you to get started, but it is best to have some instruction at first. The needlework sections of department stores often give free lessons. In many communities you can get professional help in classes or schools.

The two classes of knitted fabrics are the filling knit and the warp knit.

Filling knit fabrics are quickly identified. They can be raveled readily, and they easily develop runs, or ladders, when a yarn is broken. In a flat piece, the yarn is raveled back and forth; in a circular fabric, around and around, as in a hand-knitted sock.

In filling knitting, the two basic stitches are the plain (jersey or stockinette) and the purl. The rib is made by alternating the plain and purl stitches. The way the loops are meshed determines the kind of stitch.

In the plain stitch, all the loops are drawn through others to the same side of the fabric. The face of the fabric is characterized by the wales running lengthwise; the back, by crosswise ridges.

In the purl stitch, also called the links-and-links stitch, the loops of alternate courses are drawn to opposite sides of the fabric. Both sides of the fabric look the same; the ridges run widthwise.

In rib knitting, the loops of the same course are drawn to both sides of the fabric. A rib fabric is the same on both sides. If the loops alternate one on one side and one on the other, it is called 1 x 1 rib. A 2 x 2 rib is called a Swiss rib.

Hand- and machine-filling knit fabrics may be circular or flat knitted. The circular knit comes off the knitting needles in a tubular form; the yarns run continuously in one direction across the fabric. The flat knit is a flat form in which the yarns run alternately back and forth.

Filling knit comprises a large part of the knit goods manufactured by machine and is organized around four major knitting systems: Plain, rib, purl, and interlock.

Of these, the plain knit comprises the largest yardage and is used in hosiery, underwear, and outerwear. It can be knit of the finest of yarns with as many as 50 wales per inch or with coarse yarns with as few as 3 loops per inch. Plain knit has considerable elasticity in both directions.

Rib knitting has much more elas-

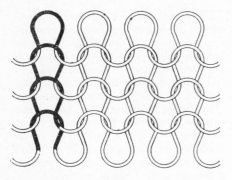

WALE

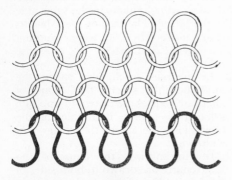

COURSE

Knitted structure showing wale and course.

ticity in the width than the plain because loops in certain wales are meshed in opposite directions to those in remaining wales.

Rib fabrics are used for slim-fit lingerie, half hose, and welts for pullovers. Rib fabrics are used in an unstretched form for many garments in which double thickness is desired.

Purl knitting is used largely in the manufacture of infants' and children's garments, as it more closely resembles hand knitting and produces the desired characteristics of softness and loftiness.

Interlock is a circular filling knitted material. This type of construction may be thought of as a double cloth made of two separate 1 x 1 rib fabrics so that the wales of one fabric lie between those of the other on both the face and back. The yarn forms loops on both sides of the fabric. Both sides have the appearance of a plain knit fabric.

Interlock is ideal for high-quality garments, such as T-shirts, sport shirts, pajamas, children's play clothes, and gloves.

Many double-knit fabrics that are variations of the plain interlock constructions are manufactured. Many are fabrics used by the garment trade for women's high-fashion dresses and suits. The double knits most commonly used for outerwear are the French and Swiss double piques. In each, alternate yarns form loops on the back and not on the face of the cloth. These fabrics do not stretch so much and hold their shape better than the plain interlock.

Unlimited variations in designs in filling knit fabrics are produced by using stitches other than plain, purl, and rib. Three of the commonest are the tuck, lace, and float stitches.

WARP KNITTING is one of the major knitting systems. Fabrics made by this system can be identified by determining the direction of the yarns that run lengthwise instead of crosswise. These fabrics do not readily develop runs when a yarn is broken and cannot be easily raveled. Most must be raveled on three or more yarns.

Warp-knit fabrics range in design from tight constructions to open structures similar to laces. The cloth is finished in widths from 80 inches or less up to 160 inches and is sold as piece goods, which is cut and made into garments.

Warp-knit fabrics are not so elastic and cannot compete with the production of circular filling knit fabrics, but designs of greater variety can be made.

Warp-knit fabrics must have at least one yarn for each wale of the fabric. Filling knit fabrics need but one yarn to form all the wales. A thousand or more yarns from a beam are fed into the knitting machine at the same time and are laid on needles. By the knitting action of the needle, each warp yarn is formed into loops, which are interlocked with adjacent loops made by warp yarns on either side.

The primary stitches in warp knit-

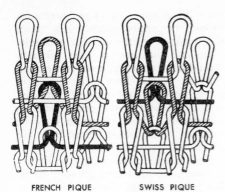

FRENCH PIQUE   SWISS PIQUE

Double-knit fabrics.

THE INHERENT characteristics of knitted fabrics make them desirable for many purposes. They will stretch under tension and recover their dimensions to a considerable extent when tensions are released.

Knitted garments conform to the shape of the body and are comfortable to wear. Knitted fabrics are more absorbent and warmer than woven fabrics of comparable weight. It is not always necessary to iron them after they are laundered. These materials are especially desirable for underwear and for sport and travel outerwear.

The most distinctive characteristic of a knitted fabric is its ability to take up the shape of the wearer and to recover its original shape—elasticity—after being worn.

ting are ordinary, chain, inlay, and float. In one of the drawings, the ordinary stitch is shown with the open loop, *a*, and the closed loop, *b*. The loop may mesh with a loop in an adjacent wale or with a loop in another wale. This stitch when used alone forms the simplest of warp fabrics.

The chain stitch may have open loop, *a* and *b*, or closed loop, *c*. The loops of one yarn mesh in only one wale. Therefore, unlike the ordinary stitch, it cannot form a fabric when it is used alone, but it imparts a great deal of stability to the structure when it is combined with other stitches.

The inlay and float stitches do not form loops. They impart bulk and stability to the fabric. The float extends lengthwise of the fabric without changing direction, while the inlay extends over one or more wales.

By far the greater portion of warp-knit materials is made on the tricot machine. The most popular fabric knit on this machine is made of two sets of warp yarns and is commonly called a two-bar tricot. The face of the tricot fabric shows vertical rows of loops and has the same appearance as the face of a plain knit fabric. The back shows horizontal rows of laps or floats. The fabric may be made in stripes, mesh, and elaborate designs. Examples of this fabric are the rayon and nylon jerseys used for women's dresses, blouses, and lingerie.

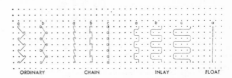

ORDINARY   CHAIN   INLAY   FLOAT

Primary stitches used in warp knitting.

Knitted fabrics are elastic because of their loop construction. Each loop behaves like a tiny spring, which tends to return to its normal or relaxed shape if stretched in any direction. Fabrics vary in their elasticity because of the fiber of which the yarn is spun and of the way the yarn is knit.

A wool fiber is more elastic than a cotton fiber. A fabric knit of wool therefore will hold its shape better than a fabric knit of cotton in the same construction. If cotton yarn is firmly knit, however, the fabric will hold its shape.

Some knitted garments shrink in length and stretch in width in laundering. The cause of the excessive change in dimensions is the distortion of the shape of the knitted loop, which has been elongated in the finishing operations. In laundering, the loop is relaxed and returns to its natural round shape.

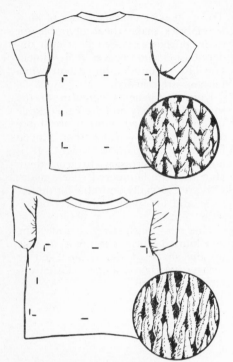

knit, the number of loops lengthwise should be approximately 1.1 times the number widthwise. For example, plain knit that has 30 wales per inch should have about 33 courses per inch.

Much of the knit piece goods in retail stores is not properly finished and hence will shrink and stretch in laundering. These materials may be relaxed in the home before they are made into garments.

Knit fabrics of wool may be lightly steamed, pressed, and allowed to lie flat before cutting.

Piece goods knit of cotton as well as other fibers may be relaxed by wetting out thoroughly, extracting or drying in a towel, and tumbler dried. If you do not tumble dry it, lay the fabric flat without distorting it for drying. (HAZEL M. FLETCHER)

T-shirts after 20 washes with tumble drying. Inserts show closeup of knit fabric before laundering; ink marks on shirts originally marked a 10-inch square.

Stretch
Fabrics

Because of distortion in finishing, many knit garments are unsatisfactory in size and in appearance after laundering.

For example, the plain knit cotton T-shirt in one of the drawings made of the fabric with elongated loops shrank in length and stretched in width and has ruffled sleeve seams and a stretched neckband. The T-shirt made of the fabric with round loops held its shape in laundering and maintained its attractive appearance.

How CAN ONE select knit garments that will not shrink or stretch?

Choose those with the round loops. This is not always easy, especially in a finely knit fabric. A sure way is to count the number of loops in a 1-inch distance both lengthwise and widthwise of the fabric. In case of a plain

STRETCH FABRICS are the sort of thing that leads one to ask, "Why didn't somebody think of it before?"

They provide better fit for many items, from baby clothes to upholstery. They come in many weights, fibers, colors, and finishes. Some have little stretch; others, much. Some give ease of movement or a smooth fit; others, forceful control.

We can classify their stretch in two ways.

One is the power stretch, of the kind built into foundation garments, swimsuits, men's tummy-restraining shorts and briefs, and so on.

The other is the comfort, or action, stretch. It is used in children's garments, sport and casual clothes, men's shirts, and other items in which movement is involved and a smooth fit is desired.

Many people know about power stretch. Comfort stretch is a newer idea, and it is the one I discuss here.

You cannot tell by looking at cloth whether or not it is a stretch fabric. It probably looks just like a similar fabric—gabardine, batiste, taffeta, or print cloth—which has only a normal stretch.

The amount of stretch in the finished fabric depends somewhat on the fiber and the method of producing the stretch.

THREE BASIC METHODS are used in making stretch materials.

Spandex—a fiber with rubberlike elasticity—is made from polyurethane. Spandex lasts longer than rubber and requires no special care.

Spandex is seldom used alone, but forms the core around which other fibers are spun. The amount of stretch is determined by the amount of elongation used during the spinning process. The treatment of the fabric is determined by the other fibers used.

Many of the power stretch fabrics are made from spandex. It also is used for comfort stretch, sometimes alone and sometimes as the core for spun yarn.

The second method is thermoplastic, or the heat setting of yarns. Any method for producing texturized or crimped yarns may be used. A common procedure for manmade fibers is to twist the yarn to the desired amount; heatset it; then twist it in the opposite direction.

This process gives a tight curl that uncurls and returns to a less tense position when forces are removed.

Cotton may be processed by this method, if resin is applied before the heat treatment. Again, the amount of stretch is predetermined by the manufacturer.

When stretch yarns are woven or knitted into fabrics, some of the stretch may be lost in the manufacturing.

The type of fibers, the original amount of stretch in the yarn, the tensions of the yarn during fabric construction, the temperatures and chemicals used in making, dyeing, and finishing, all affect the amount of stretch in the finished fabric, the amount of shrinkage to be expected, and the care required.

Slack mercerization, the third method, is a treatment applied to fabric. Cotton fabric is treated with sodium hydroxide while there is no tension in the direction that is to stretch. The fabric is then washed and finished to the chosen stretch, which may be 20 percent or less. Stretch may be lengthwise, widthwise, or both.

No industry standards for comfort stretch had been set in early 1965. In fact, according to one manufacturer, there were as many definitions for stretch as persons defining it.

As a result, some fabrics labeled "stretch" have little more stretch than a good-quality fabric of the same type that is not labeled "stretch."

In general, however, the trade has agreed that stretch in the widthwise direction (also called east-west, horizontal, or filling stretch) should be about 20 percent; in the lengthwise direction (called north-south, vertical, or warp stretch), 50 percent or more.

Sometimes a fabric stretches in both directions (but usually only in one), and garments are cut lengthwise or crosswise, depending on the type of garment.

Pants and slacks usually are cut with the stretch lengthwise; other garments, with the stretch widthwise.

ALTHOUGH I have discussed stretch only, fully as important to you is whether or not the material returns to its original size and shape after the forces are removed. If not, the material is said to "grow."

Growth is the percentage of increase in length after the fabric has been stretched and released. If the fabric grows, a garment made of it may become wrinkled and baggy.

The ideal fabric would have zero-percent growth. Some fabrics have a large amount of growth—20 percent or more. But the aim of reliable manufacturers is 2 inches per yard (about 5 percent) or less for children's and sports wear and less than 1 inch per yard (2 percent) for dressier wear.

Of course, the farther you stretch the fabric, the more it will grow. You therefore should select a fabric which has much more stretch than you actually need.

Since there are no labels to tell you how much a fabric stretches or grows, it will be necessary to check both to see if they are sufficient for your purpose. A test at the store does not guarantee that the material will wear well or that growth will not increase with wear. All that you are doing is assuring yourself that adequate stretch and minimum growth are in the fabric at the time you buy it.

As you can see, there are many places where mistakes can occur in making or selecting the right fabric for the purpose. It is more important than usual, therefore, that you consider before buying what you want and what you expect it to do.

The manufacturer of garments makes them so that the same garment will fit more different shapes of the same general size more comfortably and more attractively than a nonstretch fabric can. His judgment may vary from yours.

So, first consider carefully what the advantages to you will be if you choose a stretch fabric. You may not need stretch at all. A sleeveless blouse or a full skirt of stretch would be a waste of money. Why pay extra for stretch you will not use?

On the other hand, slacks or a blouse with sleeves may be much more comfortable in a stretch material. Certainly, a stretch slipcover would be much easier to fit around the corners of a chair than would a nonstretch fabric.

Having decided what you need, you next examine the cloth. Does it stretch any more than the same type of fabric not labeled stretch? Does it stretch enough to give a smooth, comfortable feeling in the use you plan for it? Does it stretch less than 20 percent? Perhaps a good knit which may be less expensive would serve as well for your purpose.

How much is 20 percent stretch? If you grasp the cloth at two points 5 inches apart, you should be able to stretch it 1 inch, or one-fifth of the original length.

If you are planning a garment to stretch widthwise, 20 percent is enough. If it is lengthwise stretch you want, better look for 50-percent elongation or more.

Does the fabric spring back to its original length after you have pulled it out the desired amount? Is there a bulge or a stripe of puckered threads? Only a slight ripple should appear.

If the answers are satisfactory, the cloth should be suitable.

Another thing to check in garments is whether lining, interlining, and lace (if any) stretch, too. If not, why use stretch for the part of the garment to which they are attached? It will neither wear nor clean satisfactorily. On the other hand, are shoulder seams, buttonholes, front opening, and other parts of the garment which should not stretch, properly reinforced?

Stretch will not prevent shrinkage. Read the label. Unless the manufacturer guarantees a shrinkage of less than 2 percent, you should probably buy a larger size in order to assure a good fit after the garment is laundered. Or, in the case of cloth, you should shrink it before you make it up. Dry-cleaning does not cause as much shrinkage as washing, but there may be some dimensional change, and you should plan accordingly.

Stretch may take care of some of the fitting problems, but it will not be an advantage if you force something into a space that is too small, so that there will be no chance for expanding and contracting. Just as well buy a nonstretch—it is cheaper.

BEFORE YOU PURCHASE stretch fabric, be sure that you know how to handle it. Stretch fabrics require special sewing techniques.

The fabric should be laid flat at least overnight so that folds and bumps can relax, and the material will be smooth before cutting.

No special patterns are needed, but each piece should be placed so that the stretch will be in the chosen direction.

Make test stitchings before sewing on the garment.

In general, fine needles and fine stitches are required. Fine zigzagging may make the seam more elastic. Seams may need machine overcasting to prevent fraying.

As I mentioned in connection with purchase of readymade items, linings, interlinings, trimmings, laces, and such should be as elastic as the outer fabric to which they attach or the purpose of the stretch will be lost. Tape stays, however, should be applied at shoulder, waist, and other places where no stretch is desired. Buttonholes need reinforcement.

Press the seams lightly with a cool iron and a press cloth.

As styles or manufacturing methods change, fabrics may change too, and the sewing instructions also may change. More detailed up-to-date instructions for sewing with stretch fabrics may be obtained from the thread or pattern companies.

As FOR THE CARE of stretch materials: As a rule, follow the same procedure for washing or drycleaning that you would use for any other fabric made from the same kind of fibers.

Read the labels, mark them for identification, and save them, if there are special instructions about care.

Most stretch fabrics can be washed, but the kind of fiber, weave (or knit), colors, and finishes may affect the method and temperature of cleaning.

Washing may bring back to shape a fabric that has stretched too much. If the garment is too small, however, the time will come when it will be poorly shaped, no matter what the treatment.

The best method for drying stretch fabrics is tumbler drying, with the dryer set at the correct temperature for the fiber. If you cannot use a dryer, the garment should be laid flat and blocked, if necessary, to insure the correct size in the dry garment.

Under no circumstances should an article with lengthwise stretch be hung up for drying—it will stretch.

Whatever method you use, be sure that the fabric is thoroughly dry before you use the article. Otherwise, it may lose its shape.

Usually no ironing is required, but if pressing is necessary, use a press cloth, a cool iron, and a light touch. Slack-mercerized fabrics are especially sensitive to a hot iron and pressure; overpressing may destroy the stretch or make the garment too large.

Stretch fabrics, wet or dry, should not be hung for long periods of time. Store the cloth flat in a drawer or on a shelf. Hanging in the closet is especially undesirable for lengthwise stretch, because the weight of the garment will cause it to lengthen an inch or more.

SINCE LABELS do not list stretch properties, you will probably always have to check the amount of stretch and growth in any fabric you buy to be sure that it is suitable for the use you plan. You will need to check garments and household articles to be sure that they stretch enough and that the manufacturer has not decided to use a less elastic fabric in order to cut costs. A cheaper product that does not perform properly is not an economic buy—why pay for stretch you do not get?

In short, a careful examination of each item you buy will be the best way to obtain the performance you expect. If the material does not live up to its guarantee, it should be returned for adjustment. Stretch is a "magic" word today, but be sure you receive the magic you pay for. (S. HELEN ROBERTS)

New Cotton

Textiles

COTTON ALWAYS has been a good material for clothing. Now it is even better. It is modified chemically to make textiles with such chemical and physical properties as wash-wear, stretch, and resistance to water, stains, mildew, shrinking, flame, glow, and heat.

Wash-wear fabrics and garments dry smooth after laundering and resist wrinkling during use. Improvements in the first wash-wear methods have led to the domestic use of more than 2 billion yards of fabric a year.

The smooth-drying and wrinkle-resistant properties are put into cotton by imparting memory to fabric, so that once the fabric is set flat and smooth, it will return to the original condition despite external influences, much as curls put in by a permanent wave return after the hair is washed.

A chemist imparts memory to cotton by reacting the long cellulose molecules with compounds having low molecular weight. The compounds must penetrate the fiber and crosslink the cellulose.

When crosslinking agents tie together adjacent lamellae in the fiber, the fabric exhibits good wrinkle recovery whether wet or dry.

White fabric treated with some of the earlier wash-wear finishes sometimes became yellow or the fibers became weak when it was bleached with common hypochlorite solution. Some of the fabrics tended to soil easily.

The finishes now used on white fabrics are not affected adversely by hypochlorite bleach, and the newer special additives—polyethylene, for example—do not appreciably attract soil. Many of the fabrics do not have to be ironed, but if ironing is considered desirable, the job is quick and easy.

Wash-wear finishes also produce other durable dividends: Very little shrinkage during use, quick drying, and resistance to many micro-organisms.

You can dryclean wash-wear goods and launder them at home with detergents, but repeated severe laundering can destroy the wash-wear characteristics of many fabrics. The acid rinse used in commercial laundering does most of the damage.

Some of the better finishes, such as those used on men's white shirts, can withstand commercial laundering. Wash-wear cotton fabrics can be tumble dried with generally fewer wrinkles than drying them on a line.

Since wash-wear garments tumble dry in about half the time needed for untreated cotton garments, it is more efficient to dry them in a separate load. You therefore should remove the clothes from the dryer as soon as they are dry and hang them so that any wrinkles can straighten out.

Tumbling hot garments after they are dry causes excessive linting and much more abrasion than when wet goods are tumbled.

Durable creases and pleats can be put into wash-wear clothing. Manufacturers have several methods of producing such garments, but they are not suitable for use by the home seamstress. In each method, creases, shape-holding, and wash-wear properties are imparted to the cotton by crosslinking cellulose molecules. The creases are put in after the garments are made.

STRETCH COTTON garments have become popular because of their comfort, ease of fitting, and neat appearance.

Commercial methods for producing stretch goods include slack mercerization of fabric; mechanical compaction of fabric, followed by resin finishing; elastic core yarns of spandex fiber; a blend of spandex fiber with cotton; and torque-crimp thermoplastic yarn with cotton yarn.

The slack (or tensionless) mercerization method of producing stretch cotton goods, developed by scientists in the Department of Agriculture, is inexpensive and effective. It is used for many types of outer garments, slipcovers, other household items, and industrial commodities.

Woven stretch fabrics are suitable for some household and industrial uses without additional chemical treatment. For use in apparel, however, a wash-wear finish is applied to produce better recovery from stretch as well as smooth drying and wrinkle resistance.

Stretch knit goods, especially cotton socks, can also be made by the slack mercerization process. Such socks have all the desired qualities of cotton and also have good stretch and recovery properties.

Stretch fabrics produced by mechanical compaction followed by a resin treatment have the stretch in the warp (length) in contrast to those produced by slack mercerization, which generally have the stretch in the filling (width), although they can have both warp and filling stretch.

Fabrics produced with about equal amounts of torque-crimp thermoplastic yarns and cotton yarns may have either warp or filling stretch. Fabrics made of yarns containing a spandex fiber core with a cotton sheath or of yarns containing a blend of cotton and spandex can have warp and filling stretch.

These fabrics generally contain at least 90 percent cotton, but their content of elastic spandex fiber requires that they be carefully laundered. Water for washing should be about 100° F. Chlorine bleaches must not be used, because they turn the spandex yellow or brown and degrade the fiber.

COTTON exposed to conditions of high humidity and warmth is readily at-

tacked and destroyed by certain micro-organisms (fungi and bacteria) unless they are protected by chemicals.

Mildew is a common term for the fungi responsible for most cotton degradation.

Micro-organisms do not subsist on cotton itself. Instead, they secrete enzymes that hydrolyze cotton cellulose to produce water-soluble products and then feed upon the soluble material.

Most of the spores from fungi do not germinate when the temperature is below 65° and the relative humidity is less than 40 percent.

Bacteria can flourish and rot cotton only when it is nearly soaking wet.

Cotton is subject to degradation by micro-organisms in end uses that include tents, tarpaulins, shoe linings, sandbags, boat covers, ditch liners for irrigation, and fishing equipment. The degradation can be retarded or prevented by treatment with additive finishes, such as copper-quinolinolate, copper naphthenate, and phenyl mercury esters.

Workers in the Department of Agriculture discovered that zirconium acetate and zirconium ammonium carbonate solutions solubilize many biocides and make it easier (and sometimes more effective) to apply them to cotton.

Other useful additives are pentachlorophenol and quarternary ammonium compounds. The most effective and durable treatments for cotton include acetylation, cyanoethylation, and deposition of polymers of melamine or of acrylonitrile. These agents give excellent rot resistance in sandbags, ditch liners, and other products in which the fabric touches soil.

COTTON has some natural resistance to degradation by sunlight, but it must be protected when it is exposed for long periods, as in tents, tarpaulins, awnings, truck covers, and beach umbrellas.

The damage to cotton by solar radiation is largely through photosensitization. In this process, some substance in the cotton—an impurity or an additive, such as a dye—absorbs light and then makes the absorbed energy available for rupture of the cellulose molecules. These degrading effects of sunlight vary with temperature, season, latitude, humidity, and contaminants in the air.

Cotton is protected from degradation by sunlight by removing or deactivating photosensitizers. To do that, materials are used that screen or scatter light or by substances that utilize solar energy themselves without transmitting degrading effects to the cotton.

Protective materials include certain pigments, inorganic compounds, and amino resins.

Pigments are the most effective and generally are inexpensive. Some of them provide outstanding protection. A weight increase as little as 2 to 4 percent can more than double the life of a fabric. Larger amounts often extend the life up to fourfold.

Pigments and some inorganic compounds must be bound to fabric with a polymeric substance that penetrates the interstices of the fabric or merely coats one side, as for awnings.

Fabrics protected against sunlight are also generally treated to make them resistant to mildew, rot, and water and sometimes resistant to flame.

WATER- and stain-repellent fabrics are used widely.

A fabric is termed water-repellent if it resists wetting and penetration. Water-repellent fabrics are needed for raincoats, sport coats, jackets, umbrellas, and other items.

Stain repellency is desired in some of these items but is especially needed for tablecloths, upholstery, and party dresses.

Water and stain repellency are imparted to cotton by chemicals that interact with the surface of the individual fibers and lower the surface energy of the fabric.

Three general classes of water repellents are those based on metallic salts and oxides, those based on polymers deposited on or in the fibers, and

those based on some chemical in which there is union between the repellent and the cotton.

A water-repellent fabric is different from a waterproof fabric in that its interstices are not closed, so that it is permeable to air and water vapor.

In waterproof fabrics, the interstices are filled and function like plastic films in that they do not allow free passage of water vapor and air. Waterproof fabrics and plastic films thus are less comfortable than water-repellent fabrics in garments.

An easy test for water repellency is to place a drop of water on a flat surface of the fabric. If it takes on a spherical shape, it has not wet the surface. If it flattens out, it has wet the surface, and the fabric is not water repellent.

Most water-repellent fabrics are also repellent to waterborne stains and spots, such as those caused by coffee, tea, fruit juices, and soft drinks. The repellents containing silicones or fluorocarbons are most effective against waterborne stains.

Fabrics containing fluorocarbons may also be resistant to greasy stains. A test is to place a drop of cooking oil on the surface of the fabric. If it takes on a spherical shape, the fabric has repellency to grease.

OILY OR GREASY PRODUCTS should be removed from a garment by blotting with an absorbent cloth. Rubbing causes greater penetration and makes removal difficult.

Water- and stain-repellent finishes applied to fabrics used in garments are durable to at least three to seven mild launderings or drycleanings.

Sometimes silicone-finished garments appear to have lost their water repellency during laundering, but generally it can be revived by a more thorough rinsing to remove all the detergent. Ironing also helps revive the repellency. The water and stain repellents generally used on upholstery fabrics are not durable to repeated laundering, however.

A FLAME-RESISTANT fabric is one that does not continue to flame when it is removed from the source of ignition.

Such fabrics are needed in garments worn by workers exposed to flames or sparks; in combat clothing, tents, awnings, draperies, and upholsteries used in places of public assembly; hospital bed linens; and in clothing for children and elderly persons who live in homes that are heated with open flames.

When cotton burns, the cellulose is broken down into volatile liquids or tar and gases that support the flame.

Cotton is made flame resistant by chemicals that alter the course of the decomposition and produce less flammable volatile material and more char.

A flame-resistant fabric should also be glow-resistant, but all are not. Certain phosphorous compounds are outstanding antiglow agents for cellulose as well as excellent flame retardants. A good flame and glow retardant should not reduce the strength of fabric or adversely affect drape, color, or abrasion resistance.

FLAME RETARDANTS are nondurable or durable. The nondurable ones must be reapplied after treated fabrics are laundered, drycleaned, or exposed to water leaching.

Two good nondurable flame-retardant formulations are 7 ounces of borax and 3 ounces of boric acid dissolved in 2 quarts of warm water; 12 ounces of diammonium phosphate dissolved in 2 quarts of water. Flame resistance is imparted by wetting cotton fabrics with either solution and then drying them.

(Details for the preparation and application of nondurable flame retardants can be obtained from the Department of Agriculture by writing for leaflet number 454.)

A type of durable flame retardant used extensively for tents and tarpaulins contains antimony oxide and chlorinated paraffins. They generally glow for about a minute or longer unless a phosphorous compound is added. The formulations also generally contain pigments to provide color and screen light, a biocide, and a water repellent. Flame retardants of this type increase the weight of the fabric about 60 percent or more.

Scientists in the Department of Agriculture developed a number of durable flame retardants based on the use of tetrakis (hydroxymethyl) phosphonium chloride, which is usually referred to as THPC.

Processes based on THPC are suitable for cotton apparel, such as uniforms, work clothes, ladies' and children's clothes, and for household and institutional products, such as draperies, sheets, and pajamas.

In the best processes, a nitrogenous compound is used to react with THPC to improve the efficiency and durability of the flame-retardant finish. These flame retardants are durable to laundering and to drycleaning. Some impart a moderate degree of dimensional stability and wash-wear properties. Most impart mildew and rot resistance. All of them have antiglow properties.

An outstanding flame retardant is based on THPC in combination with tris (1-aziridinyl) phosphine oxide (APO), referred to as APO–THPC flame retardant. Some fabrics, such as those in work uniforms, can be made flame resistant with as little as 12 percent weight increase of APO–THPC, whereas about 16 percent is required on the same type of fabric for the THPC finish. APO–THPC can also be used on lightweight goods, such as fabrics used in pajamas or sheets.

HEAT-RESISTANT cotton fabrics resist scorching when heated at temperatures that normally scorch cotton fabrics, but they are not flame resistant. Moist heat causes more degradation than dry heat, but a completely wet fabric is degraded least of all.

Heat-resistant fabrics are needed for ironing board covers, for hot-head presses, and for other industrial uses. One way of making cotton resistant to heat is by chemically blocking some of the hydroxyl groups in the cellulose.

At present, this method provides two chemically modified cottons with outstanding heat resistance. One is acetylated cotton. The other modified cotton is cyanoethylated cotton. Ironing board and commercial laundry press covers made of acetylated cotton fabric last three to five times longer than covers made from untreated cotton. The acetylated cotton does not stick to an iron and does not require special care.

Moderate heat resistance is exhibited by most easy-care or wash-wear cottons and by fabric treated with various additive-type chemicals, such as dicyandiamide. They are generally less expensive than the acetylated cotton but wear out sooner.

WARM GARMENTS that weigh less are welcomed by almost everyone. This advantage is one of several provided by foamback fabrics.

Textile goods composed of a rubbery foam, usually polyurethane, bonded to a fabric or between two fabrics are called foamback fabrics. Because of the construction, they are sometimes called two-faced fabrics, sandwich laminates, and bonded foam fabrics.

The polyurethane foam can vary in density, flexibility, and thickness. It is resilient and elastic. It is dimensionally stable.

Cotton, cotton blends, and almost any other textile fiber may be bonded to polyurethane foam. The fabrics may be knit or woven goods. They are bonded to the foam by an adhesive or by the foam itself after it is softened by heating.

Foamback fabrics have great possibilities, particularly for winter garments. They generally have wrinkle resistance, dimensional stability, shape retention, and insulating properties and can provide additional body without much increase in weight.

Some of the sandwich-type structures have a knit fabric on one side and a woven fabric on the other, with the foam in between. One side may even be a fleece fabric. Bonding stretch fabrics to the elastic foam produces particularly attractive apparel.

Polyurethane foams have been used as backing for carpets and rugs. Newer uses for foambacks include tablecloths, mats, and slipcovers for furniture.

YOU MAY have noticed the new and brighter colors of apparel. They are produced by new classes of dyes that can react with cellulose to form primary valence bonds. Older coloring substances are held in the cotton by various other means, such as by hydrogen bonds, by deposition of insoluble particles, and by resin bonding of pigments.

The new colors are used extensively. They are less resistant to fading by light than some of the older and duller colors are, but they have adequate resistance for the life of most garments.

Fluorescent brightening agents, which are chemicals closely related to dyes, are used on cotton fabrics to make white fabric whiter and colored clothes brighter. These brightening agents are added to most laundry detergents. They reduce the amount of bleach needed in the laundering of white goods.

STRETCH COTTON LACE can be made by slack mercerization, which converts inexpensive lace into goods having much more three-dimensional character as well as good stretch and recovery. This is a timely development for cotton, because lace is again becoming fashionable.

Laboratory methods have been developed for the production of stretch yarn that can be woven or knit into items such as sweaters.

Fabrics that soil less and are more easily cleaned are being developed to make household chores easier. For example, the factor most conducive to reduced soiling and easier soil removal is the attachment of anionic groups to cellulose.

Also of value to most consumers is

cotton with more luster. Progress has been made: New laboratory products exhibit a desirable degree of luster, but more basic research and developmental work must be completed before we can expect to see this development in wide use.

Fabrics with bactericidal properties are becoming available, especially for apparel and bed linens used in hospitals. This property is imparted by treating fabrics with bactericides that are slowly released during use.

Research has begun to develop bulky, warm cotton fabrics for fall and winter use. The bulk would be obtained by modifying yarn and fabric structures rather than by bonding the fabric to a polyurethane foam. (WILSON A. REEVES)

Wool

CLOTH AND CLOTHING made of wool are good looking, soft, comfortable, relatively soil resistant, easy to clean and tailor, and flame resistant.

Nevertheless, manmade—synthetic— fibers have become popular because they are easy to care for, resistant to shrinkage and moths, more resistant to wear, and quick to dry.

Because wool is a major agricultural product, we in the Department of Agriculture naturally would like to see wool keep its proper share of the textile market. We therefore have developed new knowledge of the structure and properties of wool. We have developed ways to treat and modify it with new and cheaper chemicals that build superior and durable properties into wool with relatively little treatment and little sacrifice of its natural qualities.

One development is the Wurlan treatment, which was designed primarily to reduce the amount of shrinkage in machine laundering. The treated fabrics also are more resistant to pilling and abrasive wear. They are stronger and more dye-fast than wools treated by earlier shrink-proofing treatments.

The first part of the word "Wurlan" are the initials of the Western Utilization Research and Development Division of the Department of Agriculture, where the process was discovered.

Wurlan-treated woven fabrics have come into large-scale commercial use as machine launderable yard goods, men's sport shirts, and women's and children's wear. The name "Wurlan" does not appear on any wool product on the market, because manufacturers prefer to use their own labels.

Like chemically modified cottons, Wurlan-treated fabrics are slightly altered in the feel to the hand. The change is described as "slightly more crisp." The amount of change depends on the level of treatment given, and that depends on the weave of the fabric.

The Wurlan treatment employs the same chemicals used to make nylon fibers. The basic principle used is called interfacial polymerization.

The chemicals react to form ultrathin resin films, surrounding and chemically grafted to each wool fiber so that they withstand washing and drycleaning.

Even though the total weight added to the wool by the film is generally 1 percent or less, the resistance to felting shrinkage on laundering of the treated wools is comparable to that of blends containing at least 50 percent of manmade fibers.

Obviously, the small amount of chemicals in the modified wools is an advantage for wool. Since the films anchored to the wool are so thin, there is relatively little change in the desirable properties of wool. For example, the moisture uptake of treated wools is essentially the same as that of normal wool.

Garments made from treated goods

go through many machine washings and drycleanings satisfactorily. Socks, for example, have been machine washed for as long as 5 hours without shrinkage, and the hand has remained good.

The procedure in machine washing garments made of Wurlan-treated fabrics may depend on the particular fabric and garment. In that case, the manufacturer recommends a method. For example, for Wurlan-treated men's sport shirts, the advice of one manufacturer is: "Wash at warm setting and spin dry; before pressing, hang to dry; do not tumble dry; press with a steam iron on the reverse side."

The rates of drying of the treated fabrics are the same as those of the untreated materials. The treated fabrics soil slightly less than untreated controls. They show no change in flammability. They may be steam pressed or dry pressed at 250° F.

Durable pleats and creases can be set as desired into the treated goods. In this case, the Wurlan fabrics may be treated as ordinary wools with chemical setting agents—such as sodium bisulfite, ammonium thioglycollate, or ethanolamine, or ethanolamine sulfite. These treatments are not recommended for home use. The ethanolamine treatment of the Department of Agriculture has been accepted for large-scale durable pleating treatment of military uniforms.

The wrinkling properties of Wurlan-treated wools are altered only slightly. The treated goods recover from wrinkling under wet conditions somewhat faster than do untreated wools and hence dry smoother. Under dry conditions, the wrinkle recovery and the draping properties of the treated materials are essentially unchanged.

Manufacturers have had no special problems in sewing the cloth. They use shrink-resistant thread and linings.

The Wurlan treatment can be applied to wool before it is spun into the yarns from which knit goods are made. Knit goods are harder to treat chemically than woven materials because they are distorted more easily in handling.

Wurlan-treated knit garments and treated woven goods are sold in stores across the country.

The interfacial polymerization principle employed for the Wurlan treatment can be used to apply a variety of chemically different resin films to wool. The research indicates potentialities for adding further desirable and durable properties to wool.

SCIENTISTS in the Department's wool laboratory have undertaken investigations to develop treated wools with even greater resistance to wear, with more durable resistance to moths and mildew, resistance to yellowing, higher luster, and greater resistance to wrinkling.

They seek quicker drying fabrics; durable resistance to soiling, acid, and alkali, and bacteria; and fabrics with greater pilling resistance and less scratchiness.

As the result of growing knowledge of wool and its modification, you can buy all-wool fabrics that are repellent to oil and water-carried soils.

Research promises to make these treatments permanent.

Also available are new types of wool fabrics—for example, foam-backed wool fabrics in which an undercoating foam plastic is bonded to the fabric to give firmness and wrinkle resistance; and stretch all-wool fabrics, in which the component yarns and fibers are chemically set into a highly crimped condition, which gives extra elasticity to the treated fabrics.

The day is at hand when scientifically designed, superior man-modified wools provide the answer to the threat to wool by the manmade fibers. (HAROLD P. LUNDGREN)

For further reading:
Lundgren, Harold P. and DuPré, Mason, Jr., "Cotton and Wool for Today," in *After a Hundred Years*, 1962 Yearbook of Agriculture.
Porter, Horace G. and Hornbeck, Bernice M., "Wool and Other Animal Fibers," in *Farmer's World*, 1964 Yearbook of Agriculture.

Blends of Fibers

THE VEGETABLE FIBERS (cotton and linen), animal fibers (wool, silk, mohair, and cashmere), furs, and pelts once provided most of the raw material for fabrics for clothing and household furnishings. Now, a variety of new fibers from the chemist's laboratory make up at least 35 percent of the total of textile fibers used in the United States.

Thus the textile industry has many fibers from which to create many fabrics—so many and so different that the consumer may not know which to buy for apparel, drapery, and other uses.

The labels and hang tags on garments contain not only general names for the manmade fibers, such as acetate, nylon, and polyester, but also the names of the companies that produce them, such as Celanese Fibers Co., Chemstrand Co., E. I. du Pont de Nemours & Co.

Further, registered trade names, such as Arnel, Avril, Dacron, Estron, Fortrel, Kodel, and Orlon, also appear on hang tags or labels, and handling instructions and claims may be printed on the hang tags.

These tags and labels are our most important guides to proper handling and claims as to performance.

A table (p. 366) gives a partial list of the major manmade fibers produced and distributed in the United States, with their generic (general) name, trade name, the producer of the fiber, the chemical class of the giant molecules that make up the fiber, and the major uses for each group.

The fibers are used alone or in combinations or blends with each other or with the vegetable and animal fibers.

Although we are primarily concerned here with fabrics made from blends or mixtures, we must remember that all-cotton fabrics are still a major source of textile fabrics. Slightly more than 4 billion pounds of cotton and about 500 million pounds of wool were used in 1965 by the American textile industry.

A TEXTILE FIBER may be a short, thin structure about an inch long, like cotton; 3 to 6 inches long, like wool; several hundred yards long, like silk; or several miles long on a single package, like a continuous filament acetate or nylon.

Very short fibers are called staple fibers. They are combed or carded and twisted by modern machinery to accomplish what our grandmothers did on their spinning wheels in order to produce a spun yarn.

All manmade fibers may be produced as staple fibers or as very long strands or bundles of fibers, which are referred to as continuous filament yarns.

Yarns spun from staple fibers usually are woven into fabrics that have subdued luster and a fuzzy surface. Continuous filament yarns are woven into smooth, lustrous fabrics.

Two or more staple fibers mixed together before they are spun into yarn form a blend of fibers. Some of the more important blends, which I discuss later, are the polyester blend with cotton and the acrylic blend with wool.

When 100 percent of a given fiber is spun into yarns, and these yarns, made up of different fibers, are arranged as stripes or checks in the fabric, it is called a combination fabric. A fabric woven with a 100-percent cotton warp and a 100-percent triacetate continuous filament filling is an example.

Knitting acetate and nylon continuous filament yarns together produces a combination tricot fabric for use in lingerie and dress goods.

Upholstery fabrics may have four or more fiber combinations of cotton, rayon, acetate, nylon, or other fibers to achieve various properties and color effects.

MANY FACTORS contribute to the consumer's satisfaction in using a garment, drapery, or upholstery material.

The Textile Fiber Products Identification Act was approved and made a part of the Federal Trade Commission's rules in July 1960. Its objective is to protect producers and consumers against misbranding and false advertising of the fiber content of textile fiber products. The fiber name and the generic or family name of all fibers present in amounts above 5 percent and the content of each as percentage by weight must be listed in the order of predominance.

Thus a label may read 100 percent combed cotton, 100 percent virgin wool, 100 percent Du Pont nylon, or 100 percent Celanese acetate. The label on blends or combination fabrics may read 65 percent Dacron polyester-35 percent cotton, or 50 percent Fortrel polyester-50 percent Avril rayon, or 50 percent Arnel triacetate-50 percent cotton.

This labeling program, however, gives no assurance that the garment will perform to your satisfaction in the specific end use, such as washable shirting; drycleanable printed dress; hand washable, lace-trimmed lingerie; machine washable-"no iron" slacks, and so on.

HOME ECONOMISTS, RETAIL store buyers, and consumers realize that the fiber composition of a fabric or garment is only one factor involved in producing a satisfactory product. Among the requirements are esthetic appeal, ease of handling, form stability, physiological aspects, special functional needs, retention of esthetic appeal, resistance to chemical degradation, resistance to mechanical fatigue

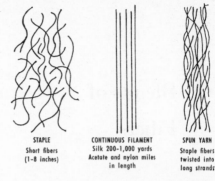

STAPLE	CONTINUOUS FILAMENT	SPUN YARN
Short fibers (1-8 inches)	Silk 200-1,000 yards Acetate and nylon miles in length	Staple fibers twisted into long strands

and wear, and ultimate strength and resistance to wear and tear.

Even when the best possible fibers are spun into proper yarns, woven and knit into well-designed fabrics, dyed to mode shades, finished to the desired feel and drape, and cut and sewn into fashionable styles, the product still can be displeasing to the consumer because the seams may pucker on washing, or the color may fade on exposure to excessive sunlight, or the cuffs, collars, or pockets may fray or wear out, or the crisp, firm feel may become soft and mushy after the first wash or drycleaning.

TEN OR SO major natural and manmade fibers account for more than 95 percent of the 7.5 billion pounds of textile fibers consumed in the United States in 1964.

Each has properties that make it suitable for one or several specific uses, but no one fiber is satisfactory for all of the dozens of garments and homefurnishings for which textiles are used.

All-cotton or all-rayon fabrics absorb moisture well, but manufacturers blend cotton and rayon with polyester fiber to achieve resistance to wrinkling and greater durability. All-cotton fabrics lose about 40 percent in strength and abrasion resistance when they are chemically treated for wash-and-wear performance.

A major development in blends has been the mixing of 65 percent polyester staple with 35 percent cotton fibers in lightweight batiste, broadcloth, and print fabrics for shirt and women's wear. Half-and-half blends of polyester and cotton are used in mediumweight fabrics of poplin, twill, gabardine, and sharkskin cloth for sportswear, rainwear, slacks, and sports jackets.

The cotton fiber contributes moisture absorption, comfort, a familiar touch or feel, antistatic properties, economical processing, and low fiber cost. The polyester fiber, because of its strength and resistance to abrasion, permits the construction of serviceable lighter weight fabrics.

For wash-and-wear garments, all-cotton fabrics are chemically treated to improve resistance to wrinkling. The treatment reduces the strength and abrasion resistance of the cotton fiber, but the addition of polyester fiber to the cotton increases the durability of collars and cuffs.

Because the polyester fiber absorbs little water, the polyester/cotton-blended fabrics dry faster than all-cotton fabrics of equal weight and build.

Fabrics woven or knitted of 100 percent wool fiber have become standard in men's and women's suiting, dress and casual slacks and trousers, and sweaters and other knit outerwear. Although great improvements have been made in the washability, shrinkage resistance, and the mothproofing of wool, this wonderful natural fiber still has to be handled with care in service and cleaning.

Blends of 55 percent wool and 45 percent of the polyester or acrylic fibers have improved the washability and "ease-of-care" properties. The polyester fiber, in particular, increases the resistance of the fabric to creasing.

Because the polyester fiber is so strong, blends with wool may show a tendency to pill. Firm, densely woven fabrics will pill much less than loosely woven or flannel fabrics.

Acetate and rayon fibers, the first manmade fibers, became available in the twenties. Nylon became available in the forties. Fifty percent blends of acetate and rayon are used extensively in women's suitings and dresses, men's and women's slacks, and in outerwear that can be drycleaned. The garments drape well, have an excellent feel, and are comfortable and inexpensive.

Nylon, which is highly resistant to abrasion, often is blended in 10 to 25 percent amounts with cotton or wool to improve the durability of the garments. Cotton work clothing containing 15 percent nylon staple will have two to three times the wear resistance around the pockets and cuffs.

Some fabrics are made up of arrangements of yarns, each of which is of only one fiber. These combination fabrics may use spun yarns of two different fibers or arrangements of spun and continuous filament yarns.

A variety of check and stripe fabrics is woven with six yarns of 100 percent cotton followed by six yarns of 100 percent continuous filament triacetate. When the fabrics are dyed with selected dyes for the cotton only, the resultant fabrics will have colored stripes or checks of cotton surrounded by white undyed triacetate stripes.

Because cotton shrinks and triacetate does not, puckered or seersucker fabrics can be produced. By stabilization of the two fibers by chemical and thermal treatments, washable, flat fabrics can be prepared.

Tens of millions of pounds of continuous filament acetate, triacetate, and nylon are warp knit into tricot fabrics for use in lingerie, bedwear, shirting, and dress goods. Frequently, fine yarns of nylon are warp knit together with continuous filament acetate or triacetate. The nylon contributes considerable strength and reinforces the acetate or triacetate yarn, which contributes drape, cover, and comfort to the fabric.

For stretch garments, particularly ski pants, specially textured nylon and polyester filament yarns have been used in combination with cotton or wool yarns. The textured strong yarns behave like springs, and permit a stretch of 25 to 35 percent in sports clothing. (FRED FORTESS)

MAJOR MANMADE FIBERS

Generic name	Manufacturer's trade name	Manufacturer	Fiber type	Major end uses
Acetate	Celanese* Estron* Avisco* Acele*	Celanese Fibers Co. Eastman Chemical Products, Inc. American Viscose Div. (FMC). E. I. du Pont de Nemours & Co.	Secondary cellulose acetate, filament and staple.	Lingerie, dress goods, drapery, sports and casual wear. Fiberfil.
Triacetate	Arnel*	Celanese Fibers Co.	Cellulose triacetate, filament and staple.	Tricot lingerie and outerwear dress goods, sports and casual wear.
Acrylic	Orlon* Acrilan* Creslan*	E. I. du Pont de Nemours & Co. Chemstrand Co. American Cyanamid Co.	Polyacrylonitrile (primarily staple).	Sweaters, knit goods, men's and women's slacks, carpets, blankets.
Nylon 66	Du Pont* Chemstrand* Celanese Beaunit	E. I. du Pont de Nemours & Co. Chemstrand Co. Celanese Fibers Co. Beaunit Fibers.	Polyamide (primarily continuous filament).	Hosiery and socks, lingerie, dress goods, blouses, upholstery, carpets, knit sports goods, uniforms and work clothing, and industrial yarns.
Nylon 6	Caprolan* Enka* Beaunit Firestone*	Allied Chemical Corp. American Enka Corp. Beaunit Fibers. Firestone Synthetic Fibers Co.	Same as for Nylon 66.	Same as for Nylon 66.
Polyester	Dacron* Fortrel* Kodel* Vycron*	E. I. du Pont de Nemours & Co. Fiber Industries, Inc. Eastman Chemical Products, Inc. Beaunit Fibers.	Polyester (primarily staple, filament for special applications).	Blends with cotton for shirting, sports clothing, dress goods, slacks. Blends with wool for suitings. Knit goods for shirting and sports wear. Fiberfil.
Rayon	Avril* Zantrel* Cuprammonium Fibro*	American Viscose Div. (FMC). American Enka Corp. Beaunit Fibers. Courtaulds North America, Inc.	Regenerated cellulose filament and staple.	Men's and women's slacks and suitings. Women's wear. Linings and drapery. Blankets, carpets, industrial yarns.
Glass	Fiberglas* Beta Fiberglas* PPG* Garon* Vitron*	Owens-Corning Fiberglas Corp. Owens-Corning Fiberglas Corp. Pittsburgh Plate Glass Co. Johns-Manville Fiber Glass, Inc. Johns-Manville Fiber Glass, Inc.	Silicon dioxide (sand) plus fluxes to lower melting point.	Nonflammable drapes, curtains, bedspreads, industrial fabrics.

*Registered trademark.

A FEW OF THE IMPORTANT BLENDS AND THEIR APPLICATIONS

End use	Fiber blends	Fabric construction	Important properties
Dress shirts	65/35 polyester/cotton.	Batiste. Broadcloth. Oxford.	Ease of care, fast drying, wrinkle resistant, durability.
Blouse	65/35 polyester/cotton.	Broadcloth. Crepe Combinations. Taffetas. Failles.	Ease of care, lightweight, appearance retention, fast drying, durability.
Dress goods. Printed and plain. Dyed.	65/35 polyester/cotton. 50/50 polyester/cotton. 50/50 polyester/rayon. 50/50 triacetate/cotton.	Broadcloth. Challis. Checks. Crepes. Twills. Linens.	Washability, ease of care, color styling, shape retention.
Sportswear. Shirting. Circular knit goods. Slacks.	65/35 polyester/cotton. 50/50 polyester/cotton. 55/45 acrylic/wool. 50/50 acrylic/rayon.	Sharkskin. Serge. Twills. Linens. Poplins. Sateens. Oxfords. Flannels.	Ease of care, durability, appearance retention, color styling, pleatability.
Slacks. Casual. Dress.	65/35 polyester/cotton. 50/50 polyester/cotton. 55/45 polyester/wool. 55/45 acrylic/wool. 70/30 polyester/acrylic. 50/50 triacetate/rayon. 50/50 acetate/rayon.	Gabardine. Twills. Tropicals. Denims. Sharkskin.	Appearance retention, washable or drycleanable (wool), ease of care.
Lightweight	55/45 polyester/wool. 50/50 acrylic/wool.	Gabardine. Tropical worsted. Twills. Flannels. Serge.	Durability, shape retention, ease of care.

IMPORTANT NATURAL FIBERS AND THEIR PROPERTIES AND END USES

Fiber	Fiber characteristics	Important end-use properties	Major end uses
Cotton	Very short lengths—⅞" to 1.5". Strong, low elongation. High moisture absorbing.	Excellent washability and comfort. Can be made "ease-of-care" by chemical finishing but loses strength and abrasion resistance. Slow drying.	Sheets and pillowcases, toweling, dress goods, work clothing, shirting. Blended with polyester fibers.
Wool	Short length, 1" to 8". Coarsest of the natural fibers. High moisture absorbency. Low strength.	High moisture absorbency. Comfort at high relative humidity. Fabric can be felted and fulled. Excellent wrinkle performance and crush resistance dry. Drycleanable. Careful washing and ironing.	Suitings, coating, blankets, carpets, sweaters and knit goods. Women's suiting, slacks, dress goods. Blended with polyester or acrylic fibers.
Silk	Long filamentous fibers 300–1,000 yards. Very fine, strong, and elastic.	Semilustrous and crisp feel. High strength makes possible sheer fabrics. Careful washing and ironing, drycleaning preferred.	Dresses, scarfs, hosiery, blouses. Combined with acetate, nylon, etc.
Linen	6–18 inches. Very coarse, strong, stiff fiber.	Silky luster, very strong and durable, poor wrinkling properties.	Tablecloths. Satin damask, dress goods, lace (blended with polyester fibers).

Soap and Syndets

YOU CAN BUY soap and synthetic detergents in liquid, powder, premeasured packet, and tablet forms, with or without pigments and with and without bleach. Some produce many suds. Some make few suds.

We can simplify the selection somewhat if we separate the products according to their general characteristics and intended purpose.

Soaps and synthetic detergents act as cleansing agents by aiding in removing soil from fabrics and by holding it in the water until the washing is finished.

Soap, the oldest and most familiar laundering product, is formed from animal fat and caustic soda (lye).

Synthetic detergents (sometimes shortened to "syndets") are made by processes in which petroleum products or animal and vegetable fats and oils are converted by chemical reactions into many complex products suited for a variety of cleaning tasks.

WE LAUNDER things to remove inert or insoluble material, such as sand, dirt particles, and oily soil (either by itself or in combination with other insoluble soil).

Soap and syndets remove the soils by wetting the fabrics and the soil; promoting emulsification (surrounding the insoluble oily substances with a film of detergent solution and thus separating it from the article); dispersing, or breaking, the soil into small particles that are more easily removed from the fibers; and holding the finely divided soil in suspension until the wash is completed, so that the soil is carried away with the wash water and does not become redeposited on the fabric.

Soap is most effective when it is used in a slightly alkaline solution. It undergoes decomposition in acid solutions, which may occur in large wash loads of heavily soiled articles. Manufacturers therefore add mildly alkaline substances to some soaps and to some syndets to increase their cleaning power.

Such soaps and syndets are referred to as "all-purpose," "heavy-duty," or "built" products, as contrasted to the "light-duty" or "unbuilt" products that are intended for lightly soiled articles and for special items, such as hose, lingerie, and other articles of delicate construction.

Light-duty soap and syndets are suited especially for use in laundering by hand, where mildness to the skin is important.

Labels indicate whether the products are for all-purpose or special use.

Most soap and syndets also contain small amounts of optical whiteners— colorless fluorescent dyes that increase the reflectance of light and so make the laundered articles look whiter and brighter.

The whiteners vary in their effectiveness on different fibers and in their ability to withstand different laundering and drying procedures.

Various pigments are added to some syndets, mostly to make them look more attractive. Pigments have no effect on cleaning effectiveness.

SEVERAL POINTS should be considered when you choose a soap or syndet.

Heavily soiled articles require a heavy-duty or all-purpose product.

You get good results when you launder lightly soiled fabrics with a light-duty or unbuilt product.

Use a mild or neutral soap or an unbuilt synthetic detergent for fabrics containing silk or wool, which are damaged by alkaline soaps and built syndets.

White or colorfast cottons, linens, and manmade fibers can be laundered safely with either soaps or synthetic detergents. If the fabric is not colorfast, an unbuilt soap or synthetic detergent generally causes less fading than a built soap or syndet.

Sometimes, as when you launder a heavily soiled article of delicate construction or poor colorfastness, you must choose between maximum cleanliness with a heavy-duty product and safeguarding the fabric with an unbuilt soap or syndet.

A DISADVANTAGE of soap is that it forms insoluble curds when it is used with hard water containing salts of calcium or magnesium. Until the soap precipitates all the calcium or magnesium or both from solution in the water, no suds will form and no soap will be available for cleaning.

Also, fabric grayness and stiffness result when the insoluble soap curd combines with particles of soil from the wash load and settles into the clothes being laundered.

Since the lime soap curd will not dissolve in water, the grayness will not be removed by subsequent launderings.

Results are good, however, when you use soap in naturally soft water (water that contains few mineral impurities) or when the water has been softened.

If the water is of only moderate hardness, you can choose to use a synthetic detergent or to soften the water and use soap.

Unless the water is extremely hard, you should have no great difficulties when you use synthetic detergents. Some ingredients of the syndets do react with calcium and magnesium salts, but the resulting compounds remain in solution and do not interfere seriously with cleaning ability of the product.

Slightly more syndet is required for comparable cleaning tasks in hard water than in soft or softened water. If the water is extremely hard, you may have to increase the amount of syndet or combine the use of synthetic detergents with the use of water softeners.

Water may be softened at home in two ways. A water-softening system that softens all the water coming into the house from the supply line is convenient, but you may decide to soften only the water you need for special tasks, such as laundering. Then you add water-softening chemicals to the wash water.

The chemicals are of two types, precipitating and nonprecipitating.

The precipitating water softeners settle out the minerals in the water, making the water cloudy or turbid as the minerals are removed from solution.

Nonprecipitating products combine with the minerals in such a way that they remain dissolved and do not react with soap to form insoluble soap curds. Nonprecipitating softeners also can be used to dissolve soap curd from fabrics.

How MUCH soap or syndet should you use?

Soap provides its own guide as to the amount needed. When a good suds is formed and maintained throughout the washing period, enough soap is present to overcome any hardness in the water and to be effective in removing and suspending soil. A drop in the suds level indicates that the soap has picked up all the soil it can hold and that you should add more soap to complete the removal of soil and to prevent redeposition of the soil held in the wash water.

Because synthetic detergents differ in amount of suds, it is not quite so easy to judge the correct amount to use.

You should be able to determine the amount of syndet needed for good cleaning if you use the manufacturer's directions on the container as a guide and take into consideration the size of the wash load, the degree of soiling, and the volume and hardness of the water.

The concentration of detergent, not the amount of suds, is the major factor in laundering when you use synthetic detergents, because the presence of suds is not an indication of cleaning power. Some syndets have been formulated with ingredients to increase and stabilize foaming. Others contain suds suppressors and form few suds.

Too much or too little soap or syndet can give poor results. If too little, the fabric is not thoroughly cleaned, and the chances for soil redeposition are greater. Redeposited soil is harder to remove than the original soil, because the fibers hold the smaller redeposited particles more firmly. The clothes become gray.

If too much is used, there is the chance of suds overflow, consequent difficulty with the machine, less free agitation of the fabrics, and the problem of rinsing clothes free of suds. High-sudsing syndets cause more difficulty of this sort than low-sudsing products or soap. Low-sudsing products therefore have become popular for use in automatic washers, especially front-loading machines.

BY THE EARLY SIXTIES, considerable publicity was being given to a major disadvantage of the syndets then available to consumers. These products were degraded so slowly by the bacteria in sewer systems that they got into streams and water supplies.

Detergents were by no means the only contributors to water pollution, but the fact that they produced foam made their presence more noticeable.

To overcome this difficulty, manufacturers developed new formulations, known as "soft" or "bio-degradable" detergents, which can be broken down more easily in sewer systems. As of 1965, the changeover to these biodegradable detergents is in progress. Most manufacturers are expected to continue use of their present brand names, and indications are that there will be no change in laundering performance.

Soaps cause no problems of water pollution; they are broken down readily by bacteria. (MARY L. WALSH)

Laundry

Hygiene

BACTERIA can remain alive on fabrics a long time. *Staphylococcus* ("staph") can live on wool blankets for 18 weeks and on muslin sheets for 12 weeks.

Contaminated clothing and household textiles thus can become carriers of disease-producing micro-organisms.

Micro-organisms—microbes—include bacteria (examples: *Staphylococcus, Pseudomonas*); viruses (examples: influenza, poliomyelitis); fungi (examples: those causing mildew and ringworm); protozoa (examples: those causing amebic dysentery and malaria).

Used clothing and textiles often contain large numbers of microbes. We have isolated as many as 5 million bacteria per square inch from the underarm parts of a T-shirt, and 53 million bacteria and 900 thousand fungi per square inch from a washcloth.

Even at the end of the spin-dry cycle of home laundering, the fabric may contain 25 thousand bacteria per square inch.

Many of these microbes are harmless, but some are harmful: *Staphylococcus aureus*, for example, can cause skin lesions (boils), pneumonia, or kidney infections. *Pseudomonas* also can cause skin infections (green pus producer), infections of the middle ear, and kidney infections. Paracolon bacteria can cause intestinal infections.

Whenever beds are made, towels are used, clothing is put on or taken off, and dirty clothes are sorted in the laundry, the fabrics are shaken enough to release microbes from them into the air. The microbes may then settle on other surfaces or may enter the body through the nose or through breaks in the skin.

Bacteria from one article may be transferred to another article during laundering. Harmful types that are present on the clothing or bedding of one person may be deposited on the clothing or bedding of another person.

Many bacteria can remain alive on the inner surface of the washing machine for at least 24 hours.

These are not, of course, the only ways in which microbes are spread. They do form one link in a chain of ways. If this one link can be broken, the whole chain is weaker.

IF WE HAVE ever thought about the problem of microbes in fabrics, most of us have probably assumed that laundering would solve the problem.

In former days it probably did, because many people used very hot wash water, and heat is one of the best ways to destroy micro-organisms. They sometimes even boiled the clothes, especially if there was sickness in the family.

But most people now use wash water at much lower temperatures. The average in home-type laundering in the United States is now 125° to 130° F. That is lower than the 160° to 180° used by commercial and institutional laundries and very much lower than boiling (212°).

A factor often overlooked in home laundering is the drop in temperature between the hot water tank and the washing machines and after several wash loads.

Most machines also have a warm-water setting, which delivers water at approximately body temperature and is used oftenest when the wash includes manmade fibers or certain dyed fabrics.

Furthermore, cold-water laundering has been introduced, in which special detergents are used. Water is used as it comes from the cold-water tap; the temperature could be 35° to 85°.

Why do people use these lower tem-

DISINFECTANTS FOR USE DURING LAUNDERING

Type	Examples* of available products	To be used in—	Amount to be used	Active ingredients
Chlorine (hypochlorite)	Clorox. Fyne-Tex Liquid Bleach. King Liquid Bleach. Purex Liquid Bleach.	Wash cycle.	As directed on label for bleaching. Usually: Front loading machines—4 oz. Top loading machines—8 oz.	Should contain 5-25% sodium hypochlorite. (Cannot be used on silk, wool, spandex, and certain dyed fabrics.)
Phenolic..........	Al-Pine. Pine-Sol.	Either wash or rinse cycle.	Front loading machines—5 oz. Top loading machines—8 oz.	3% orthobenzyl para chlorophenol or 3% chloro-o-phenylphenol.
Pine oil..........	Fyne-Tex. King Pine. Pine-O-Pine. White Cap.	Either wash or rinse cycle.	Front loading machines—4 oz. Top loading machines—6 oz.	Product must contain at least 80 percent pine oil.
Quaternary..........	Co-op Sanitizer. Roccal.	Rinse cycle.	Front loading machines—3 oz. Top loading machines—4 oz.	10% solution of alkyldimethylbenzyl ammonium chloride.

*Trade names are used in this publication solely for the purpose of providing specific information. Mention of a trade name does not constitute a guarantee or warranty of the product by the United States Department of Agriculture or an endorsement over products not mentioned.

peratures for wash water? Probably there are many reasons. Some are lower fuel costs, possible danger to children of very hot water, the use of new fibers and finishes, and lack of facilities for boiling clothes.

At any rate, whatever the reasons and however valid they may be, the use of lower laundering temperatures is an established practice in home management. In a program of household hygiene we cannot depend therefore on heat to control the problem of microbes in home-type laundering.

Another change is the greater use of coin-operated washing machines. Or, to put it another way, many of us use each other's laundry facilities. Since some microbes remain alive on the inside of the machines and since we do not use water that is hot enough to kill them, they can be transferred from the laundry of one family to the laundry of another family.

You cannot depend on the dryer to kill all bacteria that are still alive in the clothing. Some things are removed before they are really dry— to avoid wrinkling, perhaps, or because the timer on the dryer has stopped the machine, and all articles are removed, even though some are not dry. Dryers do, however, reduce the numbers of bacteria.

During drying, many bacteria are released from the fabrics, and the air movements force them out of the machine. Dryers therefore should be vented to the outside to prevent this atomizing of the bacteria back into the room.

We are asked about the effectiveness of outdoor line drying. Ultraviolet light has germicidal activity, but the amounts of it in the atmosphere vary in different parts of the country and may be reduced by clouds, smog, and smoke.

I have noted a considerable interest in making fabrics "self-sanitizing" or "resistant to microbes." This is also called "residual" disinfection, because if fabrics are soaked in solutions containing certain disinfectants, some of the disinfectant clings to the fibers even after drying and is therefore a residue.

When the fabrics are wet again, some of the disinfectant washes off and kills some of the microbes with which it comes in contact.

Such products often are used in the final rinse of diaper laundering to aid in the control of diaper rash. They have been used also on bedding and clothing of bedridden patients to aid in the prevention of bedsores.

Cloth that is to be made into tents, awnings, sails, and such often is treated with disinfectants to prevent rotting by fungi.

Considerable moisture is present under the special in-use conditions I mentioned (urine, perspiration, rain). Blankets and certain articles of clothing that have been treated with disinfectants can be bought.

Final judgment as to the usefulness of such treated articles under the relatively dry conditions of normal use must await further research and improved test procedures.

I should emphasize, however, that treated fabrics are not the solution to the problem of laundry hygiene. When disinfectants were added in the rinse cycle during in-use experiments on home laundering, a residue was left on the fabrics. When the clothes were used and laundered again, there was no discernible reduction in the number of bacteria found on them.

Research, carried out under in-use conditions, has demonstrated that the most effective solution to the problem is to add a sufficient amount of a suitable disinfectant directly to the wash water or the rinse water.

To be suitable for use in home laundering, a disinfectant must not discolor or injure the fabrics; it must not leave a residue on the fabrics that is toxic to the user or wearer; it must not leave a disagreeable odor on the fabrics; it must kill many kinds of microbes; it must be available on the consumer market; and the cost must not be prohibitive.

These four types of disinfectants have been found to be effective: Chlorine (hypochlorite), phenolic, pine oil, and quaternary.

I summarize examples of products available on the consumer market, their active ingredients, and suggestions for use in a table on page 372.

It is important to read the label on the bottles in order to be sure of the name and amount of disinfectant in any product. To insure effectiveness, it is also important to measure the amount to be used.

Future research may, of course, demonstrate the effectiveness of still other types of disinfectants.

When used as directed during home laundering, the four types of disinfectants I list reduce the numbers of bacteria to a safe level. (ETHEL McNEIL)

Removing

Stains

USUALLY it is easier to remove fresh stains than old ones. Identify the stain, if possible, or determine whether it is a greasy stain, a nongreasy stain, or a combination of the two.

The kind of stain remover you select should not harm the fabric on which you use it. Test the stain remover on a sample of the material or on a seam allowance, hem, the inside of a pocket, or the tail of a blouse or shirt.

Absorbent powders, such as cornstarch, cornmeal, talc, and powdered chalk, are used to remove some fresh stains, such as spattered grease. Spread the powder over the stain before it dries. Then remove it, as it absorbs the stain, by shaking or brushing.

Other absorbent materials, such as

absorbent cotton, sponges, white or fast-colored paper towels, facial tissues, and soft cloths, are used to soak up staining liquids before they soak into a fabric and to absorb stains as they are rinsed out of the fabric. This will work only on fabrics that absorb the staining liquid slowly.

Soap and synthetic detergents are used to remove many nongreasy and some greasy stains. Either can be rubbed into the stained place and rinsed out with water.

Solvents for nongreasy stains: Water alone or water and a detergent will remove many nongreasy stains. Rubbing alcohol can be used on some stains, such as those caused by medicine dissolved in alcohol, shellac, alcoholic beverages, and duplicating carbon paper, if it does not cause the dye on the fabric to bleed.

Acetone and amyl acetate (amyl acetate for fabrics of acetate, and Dynel and Verel modacrylic fibers) are used to remove such stains as fingernail polish and ballpoint-pen ink. Turpentine is used on oil-based paint stains.

Acetone, alcohol, amyl acetate, and turpentine may be purchased at drug or hardware stores. They are poisonous and flammable and should not be used near an open flame.

SOLVENTS for greasy stains are known as grease solvents, drycleaning fluids, and spot removers. Some are flammable. Some are nonflammable.

All are poisonous and should always be used in a well-ventilated area. Do not allow small children to play on the floor in a room where solvents are being used.

Arrange your working space so that the fumes are blown away from you by a fan or breeze from an open door or window. Use small amounts at a time. Keep the solvent bottle stoppered when you are not using it. Do not pour solvent into an open bowl unless you are working outdoors.

Never use your washing machine as a drycleaning machine. Flammable solvents can cause fires. With non-flammable solvents, the large amount needed to provide adequate coverage of a garment in the washing machine could produce enough poisonous fumes to be fatal.

The same hazards are present when drying articles damp from cleaning solvents in the clothes dryer.

Many of the stain removers sold in grocery and drug stores are mixtures of solvents. It is best to read the label on the bottle or can to see which solvents are used in the mixture, and then follow the manufacturer's directions for safe usage.

To remove greasy and nongreasy stains, place the stained place on a pad of soft cloth or other absorbent material with the stained side down, if possible. Dampen a piece of cotton or soft cloth with the solvent and sponge the back of the stain. Use small amounts of solvent repeatedly rather than large amounts fewer times. Work from the center of the stain toward the outer edge. Use light brushing or tamping motions. Change the pad or cloth as soon as it is soiled so the fabric will not reabsorb the stain. Sponge the stain irregularly around the edge so that no definite line will be present when the fabric dries.

CHEMICAL STAIN REMOVERS include bleaches, acetic acid, ammonia, iodine, oxalic acid, and sodium thiosulfate.

Three kinds of bleaches are recommended for home use—chlorine bleaches, peroxygen bleaches, and color removers. Test dyed fabrics for colorfastness when you use either type of bleach.

Chlorine and peroxygen bleaches remove the same types of stains.

The two cannot always be used interchangeably because of damage to some fabrics and some colors.

Do not use chlorine bleaches on fabrics containing silk, wool, or spandex fibers, on polyurethane foams, and on fabrics with special finishes (wash-wear, wrinkle resistant, et cetera) unless the label on the fabric or textile article clearly states that chlorine bleach is safe.

The peroxygen bleaches act quickly when used in hot water. Fabrics that contain wool, silk, or Dynel modacrylic fiber are sensitive to hot water and must be treated at lower temperatures; it therefore takes a longer time for the bleach to act.

Color removers generally are used for stains on which chlorine and peroxygen bleaches are not effective, such as dye stains, yellow stains caused by the use of chlorine bleaches on fabrics with some types of resin finishes, and a few types of ink. They are safe for all fibers but will fade or remove many dyes.

Acetic acid (or vinegar) is used for neutralizing alkalies and restoring colors changed by action of alkalies.

Ammonia is used for neutralizing acids and restoring colors changed by the action of acids.

Iodine is used only for silver nitrate stains.

Oxalic acid is used for rust and other metallic stains.

Sodium thiosulfate is used for removing iodine and chlorine stains.

Ammonia, iodine, and oxalic acid are poisonous.

TO APPLY CHEMICAL STAIN removers, dampen the stain with cool water and stretch the stained place over a bowl or place on an absorbent pad.

Try a mild treatment first; then strengthen the treatment if the stain is not removed.

Apply liquid removers with a medicine dropper. If you use dry removers, sprinkle them over the dampened spot. If the article is washable, the stained area or the whole article can be soaked in a solution of the remover. Do not let the remover dry on the fabric. Keep the stain wet with cotton dampened with the remover (or with water if a dry remover is used) until the stain is removed.

Remover may be rinsed from washable articles either by sponging the area repeatedly with water, rinsing the area, or rinsing the whole article in clear water.

Nonwashable articles may be rinsed by sponging the area repeatedly with water or placing the treated area over a bowl or sponge and forcing water through the spot with a syringe.

Some greasy stains in washable articles can be removed from clothing and linens by usual laundering procedures, by hand or machine. Others can be removed by rubbing detergent into the stain, then rinsing with hot water.

It often is necessary to use a grease solvent. This is effective even after an article has been washed. Sponge the stain thoroughly with grease solvent and dry. Repeat as often as necessary. Fabrics with a special finish often require extra time to remove greasy stains.

Greasy stains in nonwashable articles can be removed with the use of a grease solvent. Sponge the stain with a grease solvent and dry. Repeat as often as necessary.

Some nongreasy stains are removed from washable articles by regular laundering procedures. Other stains are set by them. For example, protein types, such as egg, blood, meat juices, and fish slime are set by hot water. Sponge the stain with cool water or soak it in cool water for 30 minutes or more.

Certain stains that have become set through aging may require soaking overnight. If the stain remains after soaking or sponging, work a detergent into it; then rinse. If a stain remains after the detergent treatment, use a chlorine or peroxygen bleach after you have tested them to see which bleach is safe for the fabric.

Nongreasy stains from nonwashable articles can be sponged with cool water, or cool water can be forced through the stain with a small syringe. A sponge under the stain absorbs the water. If the stain remains after this treatment, rub some detergent onto the stain and work it into the fabric; then rinse with clear water. After the final rinse, a sponging with alcohol helps to remove the detergent and dry the fabric more quickly. The alcohol should be tested on the fabric, in a hidden spot, to make sure it does not cause the dye to bleed. Alcohol should be diluted before use on acetate. Any stain remaining after the detergent treatment can be treated with a chlorine or peroxygen bleach after tests show which bleach is safe for the fabric.

For the combination stains (greasy and nongreasy substances), use the directions given for both greasy and nongreasy stains. (FLORENCE M. RICHARDSON)

Hidden
Damage

YOU CAN SEE what ordinary wear and tear does to clothing. Sometimes you cannot account for holes in fabrics or changes in color of dyes that appear suddenly.

Certain chemicals used in homes can make holes in fabrics or change the color.

Among them are strong alkalies, such as those in products sold for cleaning drains and ovens; strong acids, such as those in storage batteries, brick and mortar cleaners, and some toilet bowl cleaners; and oxidizing and reducing agents, such as those in fabric, hair, and wood bleaches and in home permanent-wave solutions.

The damage may appear instantly, so you have no doubt as to the cause, but often it does not appear until later—perhaps during washing or drycleaning—when you have forgotten the culprit.

If damage does not appear im-

mediately, quickly rinse out the spilled substance. Otherwise the chemical reaction may continue until a hole or color change appears.

Fibers themselves are chemical compounds, and different types of fibers react in different ways.

The speed with which they react with other chemicals (and thus the danger of fabric damage) usually increases at higher temperatures and when more of the chemical touches the fiber.

Wool and silk are damaged more easily than cotton is by oxidizing bleaches and alkalies, but are less readily damaged by acids.

Rayon reacts in much the same way as cotton does to acids, alkalies, and bleaches, but is somewhat more easily damaged.

The manmade fibers generally are less reactive chemically than the natural fibers and therefore less likely to be damaged by chemicals used in the home. Among the exceptions are nylon, which is damaged easily by acids, and most spandex fibers, which may be damaged by chlorine bleaches. Some fabrics with wash-wear finishes turn yellow when a chlorine bleach is used on them. Others do not turn yellow immediately, but may be discolored or destroyed when ironed.

Not all finishes are affected by chlorine bleaches. Fabrics with chlorine-retentive finishes should have a warning, "Do not use a chlorine bleach," on the label.

A hot lye solution can make a hole in wool or silk quickly. A cold solution of the same strength, if rinsed out promptly, may do little damage.

A concentrated acid solution that instantly makes a hole in nylon, acetate, rayon, or cotton produces no immediate effect if it is used in a more dilute solution. Concentrated solutions of bleaches are more likely to harm fabrics than dilute solutions.

Combinations of some chemicals, such as chlorine bleaches and acids, can do more damage than either used separately. A mixture of a strong acid with a chlorine bleach, in fact, can produce highly poisonous fumes as well as damage fabrics.

A dilute solution of a chemical, which causes little damage, becomes concentrated if it is allowed to dry on a fabric, and may cause damage—another reason for promptly washing out spilled chemicals.

A TRICKY KIND of acid damage occurs when the acid is formed from some other substance.

For example, aluminum chloride, sometimes used in deodorants, can react with water (this can come from perspiration) to form hydrochloric acid, which damages the underarm area of garments.

Nylon hose may disintegrate on your legs when soot particles, contaminated with sulfuric acid, settle on the hose. The acid can be formed by oxidation of sulfur compounds, formed when coal is burned and water vapor is present. Similar damage sometimes occurs in clothes dried outdoors in industrial areas or in winter in places where homes are heated with coal.

Neoprene synthetic rubber, sometimes used in shoulder pads or bonded wool interlinings, unless carefully compounded, can break down in time to form hydrochloric acid.

Celluloid articles, such as collar stays, combs, and knitting needles, also may decompose and give off acid fumes when they are left in a closed space for a long time. Fabrics in contact with these materials can be damaged.

I have heard of similar damage in laundry establishments in which washers, dryers, and drycleaning machines are in one room. If perchloroethylene fumes from the drycleaning machines are not properly vented and get into a dryer, hydrochloric acid can be formed by the combination of heat, moisture, and perchloroethylene vapor.

BROWN SPOTS or holes may appear suddenly in a garment that is being ironed, usually a dampened, starched dress with a zipper.

They are caused by the formation of a simple electrochemical cell—a battery, so to speak—in the garment. Two different metals in the zipper—usually aluminum in the teeth and copper or nickel-plated copper in the slide—act as the two electrodes. The salt used in many liquid starches acts as the carrier of the electric current in the wet garment. The small amount of acid formed in such a cell causes no apparent damage until it is concentrated by the heat of the iron.

Metals from other sources also can cause similar damage—impurities in a metal can act as the second electrode, as when dampened, starched clothes are stored in aluminum containers before they are ironed. Salt from liquid starches may act as the carrier of the current; but in some sections the water contains enough minerals to cause this type of damage.

The number of instances of electrolytic damage has been decreasing, no doubt because wash-wear fabrics seldom are dampened before ironing. Nylon zippers are also replacing the bimetallic zippers.

SUNLIGHT, that age-old bleaching agent, can weaken fibers and cause colors to fade.

The resistance of fibers and dyes to sunlight varies with the kind of fiber and dye. Only glass fibers are completely unaffected.

Other conditions, such as the amount of ultraviolet radiation in the light and the amount of moisture in the atmosphere, influence the reaction.

Some dyes, particularly yellow and orange vat dyes, make fabrics especially sensitive to photochemical damage. Yellow or orange figures in curtains may disintegrate, while other parts are still strong.

Drycleaners often are blamed wrongly for this damage, because the weakened spots may not show any visible change before drycleaning.

Most of us recognize that many dyes

fade on exposure to sunlight and select "light-fast" dyes for draperies.

Some other color changes in dyes are more difficult to predict or explain. It is not uncommon, for example, for a blue acetate dress to change to a reddish shade while hanging in a dark closet.

This kind of color change is called "fume fading" and has been traced to a reaction between certain dyes and oxides of nitrogen in the atmosphere. Minute amounts of these oxides (less than 1 part per million in the air) can cause fume fading.

Dyed acetate and triacetate fabrics are more likely to be affected, but fume fading also occurs in cotton, rayon, nylon, and wool.

Oxides of nitrogen in the atmosphere come from natural sources, such as electrical storms, but the main source of this type of pollution is from burning fuels, such as gasoline, natural gas, and oil. Automobile exhausts are a major source of such pollution.

Inside the home, oxides of nitrogen can come from unvented gas heaters and from gas-fired appliances, such as stoves and clothes dryers. Fabrics colored with dyes sensitive to oxides of nitrogen sometimes change color after being dried only a few times in a gas dryer. Some yellowing of used and laundered white cotton articles has also been traced to reactions with oxides of nitrogen in dryers.

OZONE, ANOTHER GAS, is present in very small amounts in the air. It can cause color changes in dyes. In contrast to oxides of nitrogen, which are present in higher amounts in cities, ozone may be present in significant amounts in both rural and urban areas.

Humidity is a factor in the reaction between dyed fabrics and atmospheric pollutants. Color changes in acetate and triacetate are not dependent on humidity, but high humidity usually increases color changes in fabrics made of other fibers.

A different kind of damage is this:

A homemaker hung the family's winter clothes on plastic hangers in closed garment bags with paradichlorobenzene (a moth preventive) in a hot attic. When she removed the clothing in the fall she discovered that the hangers had apparently melted into the fabric and then hardened. The temperature was not high enough to melt the plastic, however.

The trouble was traced to the combination of paradichlorobenzene vapor and the plastic. Plastics in some buttons, storage boxes, and in coatings on wires in electric blankets may also be affected by this vapor.

The perchloroethylene used in coin-operated drycleaning machines can also cause plastic hangers to soften and stick to clothes. Be sure that all solvent has evaporated from drycleaned garments before placing them on plastic hangers.

DRYING ARTICLES containing foam rubber in tumble dryers has been known to cause fires. Foam rubber oxidizes when it is heated, and this reaction produces considerable heat. The heat continues to build up and, together with the heat from the dryer, sometimes causes the rubber to burst into flame. A fire can also start outside the dryer if an article containing foam rubber happens to be on the bottom of a pile of hot clothes taken out of a dryer.

Heat can also damage fabrics even if they do not burn. All fabrics can be scorched by too hot an iron, but some of the manmade fiber fabrics have a very low sticking point. Blends of cotton and manmade fibers are especially vulnerable, because they look like cotton and are more likely to be ironed at the temperature used for cotton.

Sparks from burning cigarettes and fireplaces will quickly melt a hole in heat-sensitive fibers. Hot ashes from a fireplace, for example, may melt a hole in a nylon rug, although a wool rug would not be damaged. (VERDA MCLENDON)

The larvae of both species remain on the material they feed on throughout their lifespan of 30 to 45 days.

Insect

Damage

THE LARVA, or worm, stage of two species of clothes moths and four species of carpet beetles cause most of the insect damage to clothing, furs, blankets, pillows, carpets, rugs, upholstery, and furniture padding that contain animal fibers or feathers.

Those items can be a complete diet for the entire life of any of the fabric insects, but the damage they do can be prevented by using protective fabric treatments, proper storage procedures, good housekeeping practices, and effective insect-control measures.

THE TWO COMMON species of clothes moths found in the home are the webbing clothes moth and the casemaking clothes moth. They look much alike.

The adult moths are yellowish or buff colored and have a wingspread of about one-half inch. They usually stay in dark, secluded places but may come out and fly aimlessly about. The small eggs are white or cream colored and are laid directly on fabrics suitable as food for the hatched larvae.

The larvae look like worms and are white with dark heads. When they first emerge, they are very small, but under favorable conditions they grow to a length of about one-half inch.

The larvae of the webbing clothes moth move about freely, spinning a silken web as they feed. The larvae of the casemaking clothes moth build a protective case around themselves, which they drag from one spot to another as they feed.

THE FOUR COMMON species of carpet beetles found in homes are the common carpet beetle, the furniture carpet beetle, the varied carpet beetle, and the black carpet beetle.

The first three look much alike. The adults are small, round beetles, usually less than one-eighth inch long. They fly freely and, since they are attracted to light, may be found on window sills. They are mottled with white, yellow, brown, and black.

Each female lays about 100 tiny eggs directly on material the larvae feed on. The eggs hatch in 8 to 15 days.

The larvae are the feeding stage. Their oval bodies are covered with brownish or black bristles that give them a fuzzy appearance, from which they get their common name, "buffalo moths." As the carpet beetle larvae grow, they shed their skins several times. In 45 to 60 days they are full grown and about one-fourth inch long.

The black carpet beetle is easily distinguished from the other three species. The adults are black. The larvae are golden to dark brown and reach a length of about one-half inch. They are slender and tapered, with a characteristic tuft of long, brown hairs at the end of the body. They live considerably longer as larvae (9 to 12 months) than do the other carpet beetles.

THE EASIEST and most effective way to protect wool clothing, rugs, blankets, and other susceptible items against fabric insects is to have them treated with a moth-resistant compound.

The simplest way of getting this built-in protection is to purchase items treated for moth resistance. Select items already treated by the manufacturer with a permanent-type, moth-resistant compound.

Some treatments resist aging, dry-cleaning, and several washings and are usually guaranteed by the manufac-

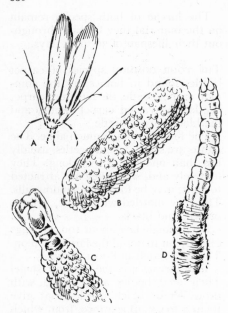

WEBBING CLOTHES MOTH
A, Adult; B, Cocoon; C, Cocoon with cast
pupal skin protruding;
D, Larva and silken feeding tube

turer for the life of the item. Others provide only temporary protection, which may disappear soon after you purchase the item. Read the label carefully.

You undoubtedly have many susceptible articles that have not been treated to withstand moths. You can have a moth-resistant treatment applied to wool clothing, blankets, and sweaters when you have them drycleaned and to your rugs and carpets when they are shampooed.

Such treatments are temporary and must be repeated each time the articles are cleaned.

You can treat some items yourself. There are a number of approved mothproofing solutions you can buy and apply yourself to clothing, rugs, and other items. Mothproofers are sold as liquid sprays or aerosols.

Regardless of which one you select, apply it as directed on the label.

Some labels specify that the treated garment should be drycleaned before

wearing. If you have no intention of doing so, or if there is a possibility that you may overlook having the treated suit, sweater, or blanket cleaned before it is worn, then do not select such a mothproofing compound. Pick one that will permit you to wear the treated garment either with or without drycleaning. Some of the mothproofers in this category are DDT, methoxychlor, Strobane, and Perthane.

PROPER STORAGE can be used effectively to protect woolens and other susceptible items. It is important to store only clean items and in insect-tight containers.

Soiled clothing attracts fabric insects more than clean clothing, and clothes that have been hanging around for some time may be infested. Therefore, before storing your materials, have them drycleaned or laundered.

If that is not possible, hang them outdoors, brush very thoroughly, especially the seams, folds, and pockets, and let them hang in the direct sun for several hours. Thorough brushing and exposure to sunlight are effective methods of ridding woolen articles of insects.

Well-constructed chests and closets and airtight garment bags make good storage containers. Before using any of them, however, make sure they are insect tight when closed. Seal all cracks or openings with masking tape.

Cedar chests and cedar-lined closets provide little or no protection against insects unless they are made with red cedar heartwood three-fourths inch thick, are tightly constructed, and are less than 3 or 4 years old. To be safe, use them as any other container or closet.

For added protection, place paradichlorobenzene crystals or naphthalene flakes or balls in the storage containers before sealing the lid or door.

In a trunk-size container, use 1 pound of these chemicals. In a closet, use 1 pound for each 100 cubic feet of space. Place them high in the

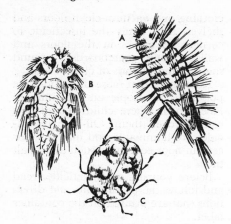

FURNITURE CARPET BEETLE
A, Larva; B, Pupa; C, Adult

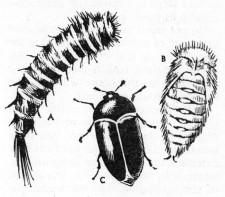

BLACK CARPET BEETLE
A, Larva; B, Pupa; C, Adult

storage container, because the vapors are heavier then air.

Large, bulky items can be wrapped in heavy kraft paper. Sprinkle naphthalene or paradichlorobenzene around the article as it is being wrapped. Then seal all edges of the wrapping paper with masking tape to make the package insect tight.

GOOD HOUSEKEEPING practices are important in preventing insect damage and in controlling insects in the home.

One of the most important practices is to get rid of old wool clothing, furs, feather pillows, and other susceptible items. Do not stick them in the attic or in the basement.

Old wool clothing and soiled wool rugs are the commonest haven of fabric insects in the home. If you must save some old garment for sentimental or other reasons, have it cleaned, and then treat it with one of the recommended protective sprays before you put it away.

The insects also live in the lint and hair that accumulate in corners; in cracks in the floor, baseboards, and molding; behind radiators; in heating or ventilator ducts and wells; and in other such places.

Thorough and frequent vacuum cleaning of all these places is recom-

mended. Cleaning removes the food on which fabric pests feed and picks up insect eggs and larvae that happen to be there. In this way you stop an infestation before it becomes serious.

Wool rugs and carpets become infested under heavy pieces of furniture, along the walls, and in places where there is little or no traffic. Pay particular attention to vacuum cleaning these places thoroughly and frequently.

After each vacuum cleaning, dispose of the sweepings carefully. They may contain insect eggs and larvae. Sweepings that stay in your cleaner for any length of time may spread the infestation throughout the house.

Inspect your rugs periodically. If you see any bare spots or if the nap of the rug seems to have been clipped down to the base, you may have the beginning of an infestation of clothes moths or carpet beetles.

Look for clothes moth webbing, for live carpet beetle larvae, or for cast skins. If you find signs of insects or insect damage, spray the rug with one of the recommended protective sprays or have it done by a commercial carpet cleaner or pest-control operator.

IF YOU FIND damage or actually see fabric insects in your home, it is best to take steps to control the infestation as soon as possible.

Do not panic and run to the nearest drugstore or hardware store to buy the first bottle or can of insecticide you see on the shelf, rush home, and cover everything in the house with it. The spraying should come last.

First, inspect the susceptible items in your house, especially in the room or part of the house where you have found insects or damage. Find out how extensive the damage or infestation is, where it is, and, if possible, the source of the infestation. Do not forget the attic and the basement.

Discard old clothing, rugs, stuffed furniture, feather pillows, and other articles that may be sources for the infestation. For your good clothes, rugs, and other susceptible items, follow the suggestions I gave for protective treatments.

Give your house a good cleaning.

Then you are ready to spray to control the insects.

Select an insecticide that is effective in killing fabric insects and is safe to use in the home.

Some of the insecticides that have been approved for this purpose are 3 to 6 percent DDT, 2 percent chlordane, 3 to 5 percent of premium-grade malathion, and one-half percent of lindane. These insecticides can be purchased as oil solutions, water emulsion concentrates, or as pressurized sprays. Aerosols are not recommended for this purpose.

Apply liquid sprays with a sprayer that produces a continuous coarse mist. If only a small area is to be covered, the insecticide can be applied with a paintbrush about 2 inches wide.

Do not apply the insecticide indiscriminately.

It should be applied only on the surfaces where the insects may be or are likely to crawl—along the edges of wall-to-wall carpets; in closets; behind radiators, baseboards, and moldings; and in corners, cracks, and other hard-to-clean places.

Before treating the closets, take the clothing out, vacuum-clean floors and shelves, then apply the insecticide to corners, to cracks in the floors and walls, along baseboards, around shelves, and at ends of clothes rods.

Remember that most insecticides are poisonous to people and to animals. Keep them where children and pets cannot reach them. Oil-base insecticides are flammable and may discolor certain floor coverings, such as asphalt tile.

Before you use an insecticide, read and follow the precautions and directions that are printed on the container label.

If the infestation persists, repeat the procedure every 3 months until it is cleared up. If the infestation is heavy and widespread, a professional pest-control operator may be needed. (HAMILTON LAUDANI)

Drycleaning

As THE DIRECTOR of Consumer Relations of the National Institute of Drycleaning, I give some reasons why an article should be drycleaned by a professional drycleaner.

Many types of soil are not removed from fabrics by water. Drycleaning solvents remove oily and greasy soil more readily than water.

The removal of spots and stains requires a knowledge of fabrics, dyes, and finishes in relation to the spotting reagent used, and the methods and techniques required to effect removal.

Specialized finishing equipment used by drycleaners is designed to accommodate the intricate garment details that cannot be pressed by hand iron on the home ironing board.

Cleaning a garment in a drycleaning solvent rather than water has the advantage of minimizing shrinkage, preserving tailoring details, and preserving many of the colors and finishes applied to modern fabrics.

When garments and household items are received for drycleaning, they are marked for identification and inspected. Notation is made of any rips, tears, unusual stains, and fabrics or construction that require special handling in drycleaning. Breakable articles such as buckles, buttons, and ornaments are removed and sent to the sewing department, where they are replaced on the cleaned and finished garment.

The items or articles are then sorted according to types. The woolen and worsted garments are separated from the silks and synthetics. Then they are classified further according to white, light, and dark colors. Items that require special handling are separated from those cleaned by regular procedures.

Pockets, cuffs, and seams are brushed to remove loose soil and lint to eliminate the possibility of shine or seam impressions.

Any soil, spots, or stains that have water as an integral part must be removed by a prespotting or prebrushing treatment or by spotting after cleaning. Some stains are set more tenaciously if they are not removed before they are drycleaned. Grass stains, gutter splash, and paint stains, for example, are removed before drycleaning.

The sequence and method of processing depend on the many classifications of items to be cleaned. The fundamental process for all items involves the immersion and agitation of the garment in solvents, which are of two general classifications: Petroleum (Stoddard, 140 F.) and synthetic (perchlorethylene, trichloro-trifluoro-ethane).

To remove soil and dirt from fabrics, there must be a certain amount of action, as in the washing cylinder of a drycleaning machine or, in some types of equipment, through reverse action of the washing cylinder. The cylinder may have a number of holes to allow the proper amount of solvent to flow through it. Ribs may be built inside the cylinder to aid in picking the garments up and then dropping them down gently to provide the action necessary for removal of soil.

Soaps and detergents used to get the dirt and soil from fabrics are different from those used at home, but they perform the same function when used with drycleaning solvents—they help to emulsify all loose soil and dissolve all oily and greasy soil.

When you wash a fabric that has oil or grease on it, you usually cannot remove the grease unless you have treated the stained area, because water and oil do not mix. But the reverse is true in drycleaning fabrics, and soil or stains that have water as an integral part of them are not removed by drycleaning solvents. Research has now made it possible to use methods that facilitate the removal of many of the water-soluble soils during the drycleaning operation proper.

Dirty solvent is drawn from washers continuously and replaced with clean solvent in order to prevent loose soil from redepositing on the cleaned items. The solvent is pumped out of the washer, through a filter, and then back into the washer, through the filter, and then back into the washer again. Depending on the size of the filter, solvent may be circulated at the rate of 2 thousand to 10 thousand gallons an hour. Various filtering aids, such as diatomaceous earths, clays, and absorbent powders, are used to keep it in condition.

After cleaning and rinsing, excessive solvent is removed from the garments by extraction. The last traces of solvent are removed in a special type of equipment called a tumbler. Here a carefully controlled current of warm, fresh air is circulated through the garments.

Some items, because of their construction, bulk, or size, are more effectively dried in a cabinet than in a tumbler. Here warm, fresh air is circulated through the fabric to remove any traces of solvent odor.

Up to this point, if a garment or household textile is not a specialty item, it has been processed together with a number of other articles. From now on it is handled individually. It goes to the spotting department where it is examined for spots and stains that require skill to effect removal.

A spotter has the responsibility of selecting the proper solvent, whether it be dry, wet, or semiwet; the proper lubricant; and the correct chemical for the particular fabric and stain involved.

The main problem in spot and stain removal is not that of finding the chemical reagent that will remove the stain, but, rather, the selection of a reagent that will remove the stain without resulting in damage to the fabric or dyestuff. You may get the identical stain on two different garments made of two different fabrics. In one case the spotter may be able to remove the stain; in the other, he may not be able to do so without damaging the fabric.

When garments or household items are thoroughly clean and free from spots and stains, they are sent to the proper finishing department. The term "finishing" is used rather than "pressing," because often no mechanical pressure is used. Only steam and air are applied. Pressure is not applied in the same manner as it is applied in home pressing. Presses have been built to accommodate every type of fabric. For example, men's and women's coats and suits are finished in the wool finishing department, and women's dresses and blouses are finished in the silk finishing department.

The modern drycleaning plant uses a variety of equipment to accommodate every size and shape of garment and every size and shape of household item.

Some items lend themselves readily to steam-air finishing so that an entire garment or household item may be finished on a form that is inflated with air. On this form, the fabric is softened with steam to remove the wrinkles. Then it is cooled to its original shape. Some parts of the article may require

touching up by hand pressing, as the lining of a coat.

Puff irons are perforated metal forms of various sizes and shapes that are padded and covered. They make it possible to finish the narrow frills, shirring, tucks, gathers, and darts of the most complicated bodice or waist of a garment.

The employees are trained to recognize what must be finished on the wool press in the wool finishing department and what must be finished on the type of presses found in the silk finishing department. Decisions are made on the basis of fabric and construction.

WHEN GARMENTS or household textiles get so badly soiled that drycleaning does not remove all the soil, general grime, and dirt, they must be further cleaned by a process known as wetcleaning. Items that may need bleaching and articles that are so stained that they may require the digestive action of enzymes, can be cleaned by wet processing. Some items are drycleaned first to remove all solvent-soluble soil.

Sometimes measurements are recorded before wetcleaning. Dyes are tested to determine if the item can be wetcleaned successfully, as some dyes bleed and run when wet with water.

Wetcleaning is not washing—rather, it is a hand-brushing operation. Quick drying is essential in wetcleaning. To accomplish this, a special piece of equipment, called a "windwhip," is heated to hasten quick drying and thus helps to eliminate the possibility of bleeding and streaking of the dye.

THE SELECTION and care of modern fabrics has become quite complicated.

Many properties combine to make a fabric or garment or household item perform satisfactorily in wear and in cleaning, whether laundering, wetcleaning, or drycleaning.

Among them are fiber content (an all-silk fabric does not have the same qualities as one made of 20 percent silk and 80 percent wool); yarn construction; fabric construction, whether simple or complex; dyeing or printing (dye chemistry and the proper application of dyes to fabrics are important); finish (of the many physical and chemical finishes applied to fabrics, a particular finish may cause limitations in use and care); decorative designs applied to a fabric surface or woven into the basic weave construction; they may give satisfactory performance in wear and in cleaning, but also may limit the wear of the fabric; and garment findings and trim (if the stitching thread shrinks or bleeds or the bias or stay tape and ribbon or embroidery trim do not perform satisfactorily in cleaning, the value of the entire garment is lost).

SELF-SERVICE coin machines provide only the cleaning part of drycleaning. After this has been completed, necessary pressing, shaping, ironing, or pleating is done at home.

Before using this service, you should check and follow cleaning instructions on garment labels and fabric tags; clean light-colored fabrics separately from dark, and fragile from heavy clothing; brush out the lint-catching areas, such as trouser cuffs and inside pockets; remove trimmings, fancy buttons, and belts, which are not suitable for cleaning; check the pockets for lipstick, fountain pens, and all loose articles; refer difficult stains to a professional cleaner; make necessary repairs; and follow the instructions for using the machine. It should not be overloaded.

Remove articles immediately after the cleaning and drying cycles. Hang on hangers to prevent wrinkling.

If there is a cleaning solvent odor in the articles, hang them in the open air or a well-ventilated room until they are thoroughly dry.

In coin-machine cleaning, the machines are automatically set so that all articles are cleaned the same length of time and with the same process.

In professional cleaning, sorting and classifying articles are part of the service. They are not cleaned the same

way, for the same length of time, or in the same cleaning machine.

Some garments, depending on the type, fabric, and extent of soil, need little or no touching up after drycleaning. However, most apparel requires pressing and shaping if the finished work is to look well.

Hard-wear wrinkles will not come out in any cleaning-only operation. Soft wrinkles ordinarily fall out during hanging. Hard wrinkles can be removed only through careful pressing.

Generally speaking, water removes only the stains that water has caused. Drycleaning solvents will remove some stains but have no effect on others.

Stubborn stains must be removed individually by the drycleaner with special treatments, called spotting. Paints, inks, dyes, and lipstick, beverage, and food stains are among this group. (DOROTHY SIEGERT LYLE)

Mending

YOU CAN MAKE many garments last longer if you repair breaks and tears in them and strengthen weak spots when you first notice them.

Choose the method of mending on the basis of the results you want. A durable repair, for example, is essential on garments that get hard wear or strain. On some garments, an inconspicuous repair may be more important than durability.

Some repairs that are both durable and inconspicuous are possible on many fabrics, however.

WHEN YOU REPLACE buttons: If the fabric under the button has become weakened, reinforce it by sewing a patch under the place where the button is to go.

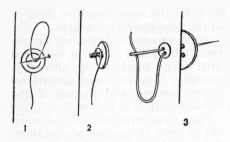

1	2	3

Replacing buttons.

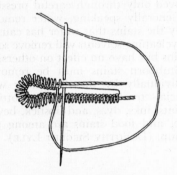

Worn buttonholes.

Sew buttons on with a shank so as not to be tight on the fabric. The shank should vary in length with the thickness of fabric.

To make a shank: Place a pin, toothpick, or match stem (depending on the desired length) across the button and between the eyes. Sew over this object as you sew the button on. Pull out the object, pull the button away from the cloth, wind the thread around the shank, and fasten off.

In some types of garments (such as topcoats and sports jackets, in which there is much strain on the button closing), it is wise to sew a tiny stay button directly under the top button on the inside of the garment. Sew through both buttons at the same time.

Some drycleaners sew on missing buttons on men's and boys' topcoats and suits as a special service. If they cannot match the button, they even may replace the entire set.

To repair worn buttonholes on lightweight garments where strain is great

on the buttonhole, you should reinforce the place that receives strain by sewing a patch on the underside of the hole. Rework the buttonhole by hand.

On coats and suit coats, use buttonhole twist thread or double regular thread. If the entire buttonhole is to be done over, reinforce with gimp or several strains of thread twisted together and waxed.

When you replace zippers, avoid stretching the fabric when you remove the old zipper. Steam-press the place from which the zipper was removed. Place the new zipper in place. Use a needle or pin to work the zipper ends under the facing or band at the top. Baste the zipper in place. Sew on the old line of stitching.

Snaps and hooks and eyes should be put in their original places. Use a buttonhole stitch for more lasting results.

THERE ARE SEVERAL ways to make patches.

The set-in patch is a good one to use on lightweight outer garments. On printed fabrics it can be inconspicuous and durable. Take the cloth for it from a pocket or hem or leftover scraps. If the garment has faded, the scrap should be shrunk and hung in the sun and faded to match the garment.

Prepare for the set-in patch by cutting a square or rectangle around the hole. Follow the weave of the fabric. Clip one-fourth inch diagonally in corners so that the raw edge can be turned under. Turn the seam under and crease. Place the patch under the hole and matching the design. Baste the patch in place. The patch should extend at least one-half inch beyond the hole on every side. With small thread (up to 100 for very fine fabrics) and a fine needle, make the smallest possible overhand stitch or blind stitch. Press the seams open on the wrong side and tack down as you see fit.

A darned-in patch is good for heavy and bulky fabrics. Trim the hole with the weave of the fabric, making it square or oblong. For woolens, place a

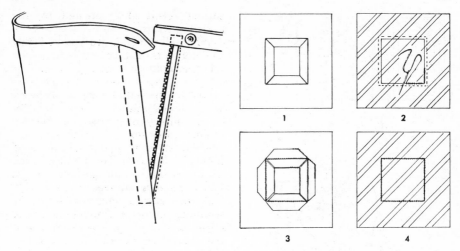

Replacing zippers.   *Set-in patch.*

lightweight fabric (lawn or organdie) on the underside of the hole and baste in place. For corduroy and some other napped fabrics, use fine net, since the darning stitch will be done from the underside and by hand. Cut the patch so that it fits exactly into the hole, matching the grain, the nap, and the pattern. Baste the patch to the reinforcing material. Hand-darn if the patch is to be as inconspicuous as possible. On some fabrics, the zigzag machine stitch may be satisfactory.

You can buy various kinds of press-on mending fabrics and patches. They will withstand drycleaning and careful laundering if they are applied with a hot iron as instructed on the package.

Press-on patches are of denim, corduroy, felt, cotton knits, and plain percale in a variety of colors. Suit the patch to the fabric of the garment.

These patches may be used to reinforce thin places and to hold together a cut place in a garment or as a substitute for stitching in the darned-in patch.

You can make almost invisible patches by using press-on plain percale mending fabric on the underside. To do this, shape the hole so the corners are square and the cut is with the weave of the cloth. Cut a piece of

fabric matching in design and size and nap from a seam, pocket flap, or facing. Fit this piece into the squared hole in the garment. With press-on mending tape on the wrong side, press the patch in place on the patch side with a warm (not hot) iron to insure perfect matching. Then carefully turn the garment over and press against the mending tape, as instructed on the package. Such patches may be reinforced by machine stitching along the plaid or stripe in matching thread.

The knees and elbows of sports clothes and children's play clothes may have decorative patches to extend their life. You can buy such patches (with adhesive backing) at notion counters, or you can make them from old hats, leather gloves, or leather purses. They may be applied by hand; a blanket stitch or a long machine stitch may be used.

Another type of patch, a rewoven one, is suitable only for material that is fairly coarsely woven. To do it, mark a square or rectangle around the hole to be covered. Clip and pull out one yarn on each side, thereby outlining the patch you want to make.

Cut a matched patch piece about one-half to 1 inch larger all around than the space to be covered. Fray the

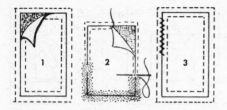

Darned-in patch.

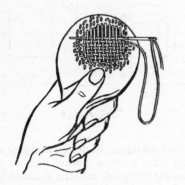

How to darn socks.

edges of the patch equally on all sides until it matches in size and design the outline you have made. Lay the matched patch on top of the hole on the right side of the material. Tack it in place.

With a very small crochet hook, draw the frayed yarns through the spaces left by the pulled-out yarns that formed the outline of the patch. If the patch is perfectly matched, there will be one frayed yarn on the patch to pull

through each space created by the pulled-out yarn.

When all the ends are pulled firmly to the underside, take little stitches, by hand, to hold the patch in place.

Holes in sweaters can be mended with a knit stitch.

Match the yarn as nearly as possible. To make the knit stitch, cut the knitting lengthwise to a point a little above and below the center of the hole. Then make two horizontal slits, one above and one below the hole.

Ravel out the lengthwise knitting within the cut area. Thread each loose crosswise end of the yarn and run it back into the underside of the knitting.

Place a piece of cardboard under the hole. With the matching yarn, zigzag lengthwise back and forth across the hole. Run the beginning and ending thread far enough into the corner of the knitting to prevent pulling out. These threads catch the loops of knitting at the top and bottom of the hole.

The knit stitch is made in horizontal rows, beginning from inside the loop at the lower right-hand corner of the cut hole. The knitting stitch is done over the lengthwise yarns. Keep the loops in line with the rows of knitting below and above the hole until the side of the hole is reached. Reverse, and continue back and forth until the hole is filled. Weave the end of the thread into the backside of the knitting to hold it in place.

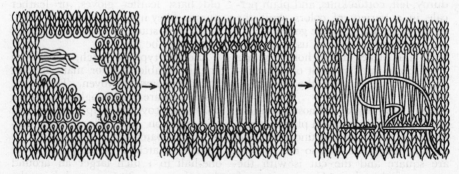

Mending sweaters.

To DARN lightweight socks, snip away ragged edges; leave the hole in the round shape it took as it developed. Insert a darner or firm cardboard to keep the soft knitted fabric in shape for working. Match the darning yarn to the weight of the stocking. (Hard-twist yarns may cause discomfort in wearing.)

Stitch in one direction, then the other, weaving in and out to make a plain weave. Do not try to bring the edges of the hole together when some of the fabric has been lost. That, too, will cause discomfort.

Press-on patches may be used to reinforce weak places before a hole appears. Turn the sock and put the patch on the inside.

To darn heavy knit socks, see the instructions for mending sweaters.

To TURN A COLLAR on a man's shirt, first find the center of the collar and neckband by bringing together the ends of the collar and neckband. Mark the center of both.

Remove the collar from the neckband by ripping the stitches carefully, so as not to tear or stretch the fabric.

Steam-press the collar and neckband carefully. Keep the seam edges turned in on the neckband.

Turn the collar over so the underside will be on top. Match the center markings. Insert the collar between the folded edges of the neckband as it had been. Pin and baste.

Be sure the old stitching lines are matched on both sides so that both edges of the neckband are caught in one stitching. Working from the neck side, machine stitch on the old stitching line.

WHEN CUFFS ON SHIRTS become too worn, the simplest thing is to make a short-sleeved shirt. Adjust the length to the wearer. Allow 1.5 inch for the hem.

To repair frayed cuffs: Carefully rip out all stitching on the lower edge of the cuff and into the curved ends. Steam-press the ripped seams. Turn the worn edges in on both sides of the cuff deeper than the old seam and worn edges. Pin and baste the edges together carefully. Stitch along edge from right side of sleeve.

To turn a folded cuff: Carefully rip the cuff from the sleeve. Steam-press the seam edges of the cuff. Turn the cuff over and replace it on sleeve as it was originally. This brings the worn edge to the inside fold of the cuff. Pin, baste, and stitch it in place to look like the original stitching.

ONE EASY WAY to take care of frayed sleeve edges on women's coats and jackets is to shorten the sleeve—various sleeve lengths are popular in women's wear.

On garments of soft fabrics, such as cashmere, where the nap has merely worn away, the sleeve edge may be rolled under about one-fourth inch, pressed, and tacked in the new position.

Worn cuffs may be removed and the

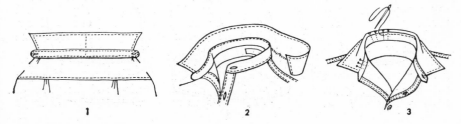

Turning a shirt collar.

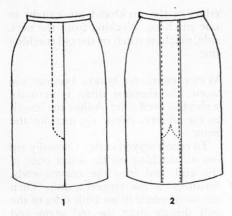

Ripped skirt pleats—knife pleat and box pleat.

sleeve edge refinished without them. Understitch the seam to the facing side.

To mend frayed places on sleeves of men's jackets, remove the sleeve buttons and detach the lining at the cuff. Press the crease out. Fold the facing to outside of the sleeve and press the crease on wrong side. Seam out the frayed part along this new crease. Trim to one-eighth inch seam. Understitch the seam to the facing side. Turn the facing back in the sleeve, press, and rejoin the lining and replace the buttons.

For RIPPED skirt pleats, if the fabric has been damaged, darn or apply press-on mending tape. Shorten the line of stitching (making the pleat longer) or lengthen the line of stitching (making the pleat shorter). End the line of stitching with a curve toward the fold of the pleat.

In box pleats, a curve toward each fold of the pleat is made, one at a time, after the pleat has been pressed open. The curved seam prevents undue strain on only a few threads, and it will not tear again.

YOU CAN MAKE DO with children's clothing in several ways.

Take advantage first of built-in expansion features, such as tucks for increasing sleeve and dress lengths, long straps, and extra lap for buttons. When you have exhausted those possibilities, consider these:

If the neck is too small, set the buttons over or cut out the neck opening and refinish with binding or facing.

If an armhole is too small, remove the sleeve or finish, enlarge the opening, and refinish by applying bias binding or a narrow bias facing. If a facing was used originally, you can make the armhole larger by turning and facing it to the outside, stitching around the armhole, and trimming the new seam, turning the facing back to the inside.

If the waist is too short, make a set-in belt with matching fabric or appropriate contrasting material.

Or, separate the blouse from the skirt at the waistline with matching fabric or contrasting material set in a band or belt.

If the skirt is too short, face it with matching or contrasting fabric; make the contrasting insertions a part of the design. (KATHLEEN THOMPSON)

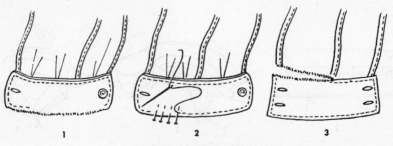

Repairing cuffs on shirts.

FOOD

The Foods

You Eat

THE FOODS you eat are more important to your health than the facts you know about nutrition. What you know may or may not influence what you eat, but what you eat does influence what you can do and how you feel.

It is easy to know more about nutrition than you may care to know, and it is easy to know more about it than you understand. Just as you can travel by air without being trained in aeronautics, you can be well nourished without being a specialist in nutrition science.

Nutrition does not mean eating food you do not like because it is good for you. Nutrition means how your body uses the food you eat for your well-being, health, vigor. Nutrition does not mean that eating should be a chore, a routine, a matter of bookkeeping and counting.

People may differ in how much they want to know about nutrition, but everyone needs to know a few facts about food and health as a basis for his decisions about the food he eats and thus the level of nutritional well-being he will have.

We need food to give us energy to move, breathe, keep the heart beating, keep warm, and help in growth and upkeep.

Energy is a necessity, but we need food for other reasons, too. Food supplies a complete variety of substances—nutrients—that are essential for building, upkeep, and repair and for keeping the body running in an efficient, orderly way.

Science knows at least 50 nutrients, each of which has special jobs to do in the body, jobs no other nutrient can do. Most nutrients do their jobs best when teamed with other nutrients working in the body at the same time.

EVERYBODY needs the same nutrients throughout life but in different amounts. Proportionately greater amounts are needed for growth of a body than just for its upkeep. Boys and men need more than girls and women. Large people need more than small people. Active people need more food energy than inactive ones. People recovering from illness need more than healthy people.

We can get all of the nutrients from foods, but no one food contains all of the nutrients. We must therefore eat a variety of different kinds of foods.

A diet that provides all the nutrients and energy in the amounts a person needs, we call a balanced diet or a well-balanced diet. Many kinds and combinations of food can form a balanced diet.

SUGGESTIONS for achieving a balanced diet are made by nutrition scientists. They translate the technical information about nutrient needs of people and the nutrient content of different kinds of food into a guide that is easy for everyone to use.

In the guide, the different foods are sorted into a few large groups on the basis of their similarity in nutrient content. Then suggestions are made for the number of servings from each food group that, with servings from the other groups, contribute the kinds and amounts of the many nutrients needed for good nutrition—a balanced diet.

An easy guide to follow is "A Daily Food Guide," on pages 394 and 395.

It gives us as wide a choice as possible among different foods while still assuring us of a balanced diet. It gives a good deal of free choice in selecting additional foods. If we are convinced of the importance of the food we eat to the way we feel, we will welcome a guide such as this one.

MANY PERSONS want to know why particular food groups are emphasized in the guide and the names of some of the important nutrients. Such information can make choosing food for ourselves and our families more rewarding.

Foods from the milk group are relied on to provide most of the mineral calcium needs for the day. They are also dependable sources of protein and contribute riboflavin and other vitamins and minerals.

Meat, poultry, fish, and eggs from the meat group are valued for the protein, iron, and the B vitamins—thiamine, riboflavin, and niacin—they provide. This is true also of their alternates, dry beans, dry peas, and nuts.

The vegetable-fruit group is de-pended on to supply most of the vita-min C and vitamin A value of the diet. Yet only a relatively small num-ber of foods are really good sources of either. To protect the nutritional value of your diet, your choices are directed toward the dark-green and deep-yellow ones for vitamin A value and to citrus fruit and a few others that are among the better sources of vitamin C.

The bread-cereal group, with its whole-grain and enriched bread and other cereal products, provides protein, iron, and the B vitamins.

Fats, oils, sugars, and sweets are not emphasized in the guide because all of them are common in every diet. Some of the fats and oils provide vitamin A, and some furnish essential fatty acids, but their chief nutritional contribution is energy value.

Some persons want to know more about foods than these general group-ings tell them.

They want to know the number of calories and the amounts of specific nutrients in individual foods. For them, a booklet, "Nutritive Value of Foods," is a mine of information. They will find in it figures for the amounts of the key nutrients in common measures or servings of more than 500 items. Single copies can be had without charge from the Office of Information, U.S. Department of Agriculture.

From the figures in its tables we can also locate the better food sources of the key nutrients provided by a food group. For example, it would take about 1.5 ounces of Cheddar cheese, 1.5 cups of cottage cheese, or nearly 2 cups of ice cream to provide the amount of calcium in a cup of milk.

A fund of accurate information makes the subject of food and nutrition more meaningful to some persons—perhaps to you. That is fine.

But knowledge beyond the basic facts about your food needs is neither a pre-requisite nor a guarantee to making wise food choices. A food guide can be that. Follow it. Here's to your health!
(RUTH M. LEVERTON)

Food To Satisfy

WE EAT FOOD to live, grow, keep well, and get energy for work and play. It is easy to learn to choose the kinds and amounts of food that help us achieve those purposes.

The daily food guide, which puts needed foods in four groups, is the beginning. It is on pages 394 and 395.

If you choose the specified amounts of food from each of the groups, you will have a good foundation, but you will want additional foods to complete your meals and to meet your need for food energy.

The number of combinations you can make is almost unlimited, so varied and abundant is our supply of food.

How much of these other foods you should eat to maintain a desirable weight will depend on your age, sex, size, activity, and state of health.

To illustrate the use of the food guide in planning the diet, I offer several examples.

SUSAN, 16 years old, attends a secondary school that participates in the national school lunch program. She allows little time for breakfast, but takes time to change her dress two or three times and fix her hair before she can face the world for the day.

"Breakfast makes me fat," she says, but to mollify her mother eats a little food before she leaves for school.

Susan eats the school lunch because the students are not permitted to leave the school grounds at noon. She could bring a bag lunch from home, but her parents insist that she have a warm meal. If cake, pie, or ice cream is served, she generally substitutes a piece of fruit she brings from home. (Menus are published a week in advance.) Susan requests and receives small portions.

Susan goes with friends after school to a soda fountain. She is hungry. She feels noble because she has eaten little all day. So she splurges on an ice cream creation (793 Calories).

At dinner, her parents are annoyed because she eats so little—she is again worrying about her weight. At bedtime, she raids the refrigerator.

The nutritional needs of teenage girls are great, and their emotional and psychological needs also are great. A girl may suspect there is inconsistency, maybe a lack of understanding, in this.

Susan, for example, knows she should eat a balanced diet. Like most teenagers, she wants to keep a slender figure and believes mistakenly that a balanced diet will make her fat.

So Susan tries to cut down or cut out the foods that have the nutrients she needs. Then she nibbles on foods that supply little besides calories or food energy. She does not gain weight, but she shortchanges herself nutritionally.

A teenager is more apt to make better choices of food if her daily routine pattern is not seriously involved—little time for breakfast; a stop after school at the soda fountain; a late evening snack.

By following the daily food guide, Susan can meet her daily nutritional needs without altering her activities very much. She can even eat the cake, pastry, or ice cream served in the school lunch if she chooses her snacks wisely.

A day's menu for a moderately active teenage girl like Susan may be:

Breakfast—orange juice, buttered toast, and skim milk.

School lunch—salmon loaf with cream sauce, green peas, bread and butter, perfection salad (jellied vegetable) with French dressing, an apple, and whole milk.

At the soda fountain—ice cream

A DAILY FOOD GUIDE

VEGETABLE-FRUIT GROUP

FOODS INCLUDED

All vegetables and fruit. This guide emphasizes those that are valuable as sources of vitamin C and vitamin A.

Sources of Vitamin C

Good sources.—Grapefruit or grapefruit juice; orange or orange juice; cantaloup; guava; mango; papaya; raw strawberries; broccoli; brussels sprouts; green pepper; sweet red pepper.

Fair sources.—Honeydew melon; lemon; tangerine or tangerine juice; watermelon; asparagus tips; raw cabbage; collards; garden cress; kale; kohlrabi; mustard greens; potatoes and sweetpotatoes cooked in the jacket; spinach; tomatoes or tomato juice; turnip greens.

Sources of Vitamin A

Dark-green and deep-yellow vegetables and a few fruits, namely: Apricots, broccoli, cantaloup, carrots, chard, collards, cress, kale, mango, persimmon, pumpkin, spinach, sweetpotatoes, turnip greens and other dark-green leaves, winter squash.

CONTRIBUTION TO DIET

Fruits and vegetables are valuable chiefly because of the vitamins and minerals they contain. In this plan, this group is counted on to supply nearly all the vitamin C needed and over half of the vitamin A.

Vitamin C is needed for healthy gums and body tissues. Vitamin A is needed for growth, normal vision, and healthy condition of skin and other body surfaces.

AMOUNTS RECOMMENDED

Choose 4 or more servings every day, including:

1 serving of a good source of vitamin C or 2 servings of a fair source.

1 serving, at least every other day, of a good source of vitamin A. If the food chosen for vitamin C is also a good source of vitamin A, the additional serving of a vitamin A food may be omitted.

The remaining 1 to 3 or more servings may be of any vegetable or fruit, including those that are valuable for vitamin C and vitamin A.

Count as 1 serving: ½ cup of vegetable or fruit; or a portion as ordinarily served, such as 1 medium apple, banana, orange, or potato, half a medium grapefruit or cantaloup, or the juice of 1 lemon.

MEAT GROUP

FOODS INCLUDED

Beef; veal; lamb; pork; variety meats, such as liver, heart, kidney.

Poultry and eggs.

Fish and shellfish.

As alternates—dry beans, dry peas, lentils, nuts, peanuts, peanut butter.

CONTRIBUTION TO DIET

Foods in this group are valued for their protein, which is needed for growth and repair of body tissues—muscle, organs, blood, skin, and hair. These foods also provide iron, thiamine, riboflavin, and niacin.

AMOUNTS RECOMMENDED

Choose 2 or more servings every day.

Count as a serving: 2 to 3 ounces of lean cooked meat, poultry, or fish—all without bone; 2 eggs; 1 cup cooked dry beans, dry peas, or lentils; 4 tablespoons peanut butter.

MILK GROUP

FOODS INCLUDED

Milk—fluid whole, evaporated, skim, dry, buttermilk. Cheese—cottage; cream; cheddar-type—natural or processed. Ice cream.

CONTRIBUTION TO DIET

Milk is our leading source of calcium, which is needed for bones and teeth. It also provides high-quality protein, riboflavin, vitamin A, and many other nutrients.

AMOUNTS RECOMMENDED

Some milk every day for everyone. Recommended amounts are given below in terms of whole fluid milk:

	8-ounce cups
Children under 9	2 to 3
Children 9 to 12	3 or more
Teenagers	4 or more
Adults	2 or more
Pregnant women	3 or more
Nursing mothers	4 or more

Part or all of the milk may be fluid skim milk, buttermilk, evaporated milk, or dry milk.

Cheese and ice cream may replace part of the milk. The amount of either it will take to replace a given amount of milk is figured on the basis of calcium content. Common portions of various kinds of cheese and of ice cream and their milk equivalents in calcium are:

1-inch cube cheddar-type cheese	= ½ cup milk
½ cup cottage cheese	= ⅓ cup milk
2 tablespoons cream cheese	= 1 tablespoon milk
½ cup ice cream	= ¼ cup milk

BREAD-CEREAL GROUP

FOODS INCLUDED

All breads and cereals that are whole grain, enriched, or restored; *check labels to be sure.*

Specifically, this group includes: Breads; cooked cereals; ready-to-eat cereals; cornmeal; crackers; flour; grits; macaroni and spaghetti; noodles; rice; rolled oats; and quick breads and other baked goods if made with whole-grain or enriched flour. Parboiled rice and wheat also may be included in this group.

CONTRIBUTION TO DIET

Foods in this group furnish worthwhile amounts of protein, iron, several of the B-vitamins, and food energy.

AMOUNTS RECOMMENDED

Choose 4 servings or more daily. Or, if no cereals are chosen, have an extra serving of breads or baked goods, which will make at least 5 servings from this group daily.

Count as 1 serving: 1 slice of bread; 1 ounce ready-to-eat cereal; ½ to ¾ cup cooked cereal, cornmeal, grits, macaroni, noodles, rice, or spaghetti.

OTHER FOODS

To round out meals and to satisfy the appetite everyone will use some foods not specified—butter, margarine, other fats, oils, sugars, or unenriched refined grain products. These are often ingredients in baked goods and mixed dishes. Fats, oils, and sugars are also added to foods during preparation or at the table.

These "other" foods supply calories and can add to total nutrients in meals.

soda. Dinner—meat loaf, baked potato, spinach, bread and butter, cup custard, and iced tea.

Evening snack—cheese and crackers and iced tea.

If you check the food guide, you see that the suggestions for the bread-cereal group were met in the day's menu with four slices of enriched bread and four crackers eaten during the day.

Susan had four glasses of milk or milk equivalent—milk for breakfast and lunch, cream sauce for lunch, cup custard for dinner, ice cream (in the soda), and cheese in the evening snack.

Fish for lunch and meat loaf for dinner provided two servings of meat.

The four servings of vegetables and fruit were peas and apple for lunch and baked potato and spinach for dinner. The orange juice for breakfast provided the vitamin C. The spinach for dinner is one of the dark-green vegetables that are valued sources of vitamin A.

The other foods added made the meals interesting and satisfying to Susan and provided approximately the 2,300 Calories of food energy a teenage girl of average activity needs daily.

A boy is different. His need for food energy—3,400 Calories for the moderately active boy—is greater than the girl's. He is not inclined to worry about his weight. He therefore eats more food and fares better nutritionally.

The food guide is a good way to check his meals to make sure he has enough of the foods included in the four basic groups.

GRANDMOTHER CARUSO came to the United States some years ago, but she likes best the food she had in the old country. Her daughter-in-law, with whom she lives, cooks many of the foods that Grandmother enjoys but has added many American dishes.

Grandmother prefers spaghetti and macaroni with various meats, seafood, or cheese and served with a rich tomato sauce. She likes fruits and vegetables. If she has raw vegetables, she usually serves them with oil and vine-

gar. If she cooks them, they are often served with a sauce. Her meals are not complete without Italian bread and coffee. She will eat the American-type prepared cereal and occasionally the milk puddings her daughter-in-law prepares for the children. When unfamiliar foods are served, however, she is inclined to make her meal of a macaroni dish, bread, and coffee.

The doctor has advised her that she should eat a greater variety of food and that she should watch her weight. He has frowned on the variety of spaghetti and other pasta dishes served with rich sauces she eats and on her preference for vegetables served with tomato and cheese sauces.

Grandmother has visions of her remaining days being filled with tasteless, uninteresting meals. The more she thinks of it, the more difficult it is to eat the food she believes she must have.

She occasionally can eat the food she enjoys, meet her nutritional needs, and keep her food energy down to the level suggested for women of her age. She will have to eat smaller portions than is her custom, however.

A day's menus for Grandmother Caruso may be:

Breakfast—orange juice, cornflakes, skim milk, Italian bread, enriched, coffee with milk and sugar.

Lunch—minestrone (vegetable soup with pasta), boiled beef (from soup), Italian bread, enriched, apple, cheese, coffee with milk and sugar.

Dinner—chicken, spaghetti, tomato sauce, mixed salad (romaine, tomato, green pepper, hard-cooked egg, oil and vinegar), Italian bread, enriched, tapioca pudding, coffee with milk and sugar.

A check of the menus with the food guide shows that Grandmother's need for foods from the bread-cereal group were met with three slices of Italian bread and a serving of cornflakes.

An elderly person needs two cups of milk daily. Grandmother's need for milk was met with the half cup of milk she used in coffee during the day, the half cup served with her breakfast cereal, the cheese in her lunch, and the half cup of milk in the tapioca pudding at dinner.

Her need for two servings of meat was met with beef at lunch and the chicken and hard-cooked egg at dinner.

The four servings of fruits and vegetables were met with orange juice (her vitamin C need was met here), apple, the vegetables in her soup at lunch, and in her dinner salad.

These menus will supply the 1,600 Calories of food energy recommended for the elderly woman. Grandmother will need to keep her portion of minestrone to 1.5 cups and her portion of spaghetti to 1 cup, served with a quarter of a 2-pound broiling chicken if she is to keep her food energy at the level of 1,600 Calories.

JOHN DOE, middle aged, is a strictly meat-and-potatoes man. He dislikes fancy salads, especially gelatin salads, and most casserole dishes. He will eat coleslaw and occasionally a tossed green salad, but he prefers his vegetables served as such—either cooked or raw.

He enjoys food. His doctor thinks he has reached the point where he enjoys eating more than exercising. His doctor has advised him to keep an eye on his physical condition, including his weight.

The prospect of forgoing the foods he enjoys most and the beer in the evening as he watches the ball game on TV does not appeal to Mr. Doe. He tried cottage cheese salads with crackers and milk for lunch; he even tried the highly advertised formula diets. After a few days, Mr. Doe concluded he could not work on such food. He decided he might as well be dead as persecuted and returned to his old pattern of eating whatever struck his fancy without giving a thought to the food combinations that made up his daily total intake of food.

Mr. Doe could meet his nutritional needs with foods that he enjoys, have his occasional glass of beer and a snack in the evening, and still keep his food energy intake to the recommended 2,600 Calories for a man of his age and activity.

A day's menus for Mr. Doe may be: Breakfast—grapefruit, bacon and scrambled eggs, toast, coffee with milk and sugar.

Lunch—stuffed green pepper (rice and meat) with tomato sauce, coleslaw, roll and butter, apple crisp, milk.

Dinner—swiss steak, mashed potatoes, glazed carrots, roll and butter, coconut custard pie, coffee with milk and sugar.

Evening snack—a can of beer, crackers, and cheese.

Mr. Doe's need for food from the bread-cereal group was more than met with two slices of toast for breakfast, rolls for lunch and dinner, and the rice in his lunch.

Two scrambled eggs for breakfast and swiss steak for dinner provided the two servings of meat or meat equivalent recommended in the guide.

Green pepper, cabbage (coleslaw), glazed carrots, and grapefruit made up the suggested four servings of fruits and vegetables. Grapefruit supplied the needed vitamin C and carrots the vitamin A.

Mr. Doe got his two cups of milk or milk equivalent in the milk he had for lunch, the custard of the pie, and the cheese in his evening snack.

Susan, Grandmother Caruso, and Mr. Doe are illustrations of the fact that with a reliable food pattern and a willingness to eat and enjoy the wide variety of food available in this country, you can eat what you need, like what you eat, and, barring accidents, expect to live to a pleasant old age. (MARY M. HILL)

For further reading, consult the following U.S. Department of Agriculture publications: *Eat a Good Breakfast to Start a Good Day*, Leaflet No. 268; *Food for Families with School Children*, Home and Garden Bulletin No. 13; *Food for Families with Young Children*, Home and Garden Bulletin No. 5; *Food for the Young Couple*, Home and Garden Bulletin No. 85; *Food Guide for Older Folks*, Home and Garden Bulletin No. 17; *Getting Enough Milk*, Home and Garden Bulletin No. 57.

Calories

and Weight

YOUR WEIGHT as an adult reflects how well you balance the energy—or calories—provided by the food you eat and that used by the body for work, for leisure activities, and for other needs.

Your weight stays the same when calories from food balance those used by the body.

You lose weight when you get fewer calories from food than the body uses.

You gain weight when you get more.

These facts point the way for weight control. Control the amount of food you eat, or your physical activity, or both so that the balance of calories is in the direction desired.

Children, of course, are expected to gain weight as they grow, but they should not gain more than is in keeping with normal growth.

A FIRST STEP in determining the number of calories needed to control your weight is to find out the best weight for you. Generally, the weight that is desirable for you in your midtwenties is the best weight for later years, too.

Take a woman of average height—5 feet 4 inches tall. She probably should weigh somewhere between 112 and 132 pounds. This range in weight takes into account the fact that bone structure and muscular development vary from person to person.

If this woman has an average frame, her desirable weight probably should be near the middle of the range, about 122 pounds. If she has a large frame, her weight probably should be between 122 and 132 pounds, and if her frame is small, between 112 and 122 pounds.

The range for a man of average height (5 feet 9 inches tall) is 141 to 169 pounds.

Height is measured without shoes and weight is without clothing.

BODY SIZE influences the amount of energy or the number of calories required from food.

For example, a man 25 years old whose activity is average and whose desirable weight is 150 pounds, needs 2,850 Calories a day to maintain that weight. One whose desirable weight is 180 pounds needs 3,250 Calories.

(The large Calorie, spelled with a capital C, is the measure commonly used in expressing the calorie need of individuals and the energy value of food.)

Physical activity is a big factor in determining calorie needs. The calorie allowances shown in the table are for individuals of average activity.

When a person is very active, the number of calories required may be as much as one-fourth higher than when activity is average. Inactivity, on the other hand, reduces calorie needs.

Average activity might be described as spending 8 hours a day asleep; 6 hours in activities while sitting, such as reading, driving a car, eating, watching television; 6 hours in activities while standing, such as personal care or moving from one room to another; 2 hours in purposeful walking, largely out of doors; and 2 hours in sports, exercises, and light physical work.

Age also affects calorie needs. A woman of average activity who weighs 130 pounds requires 2,100 Calories a day when she is 25 years old, 1,900 Calories when she reaches 45, and only 1,600 Calories at 65 years.

As adults grow older, fewer calories are required to keep the body functioning, and older people usually are less active physically than they were in earlier years.

To lose a pound of body fat, there

DESIRABLE WEIGHT FOR HEIGHT FOR
ADULTS

	Height (without shoes) Inches	Weight (without clothing) Pounds
Men:		
	64	122–144
	66	130–154
	68	137–165
	70	145–173
	72	152–182
	74	160–190
Women:		
	60	100–118
	62	106–124
	64	112–132
	66	119–139
	68	126–146
	70	133–155

CALORIE ALLOWANCES FOR ADULTS
OF AVERAGE PHYSICAL ACTIVITY

	Desirable weight Pounds	Calorie allowance		
		25 years	45 years	65 years
Men:				
	110	2,300	2,050	1,750
	120	2,400	2,200	1,850
	130	2,550	2,300	1,950
	140	2,700	2,450	2,050
	150	2,850	2,550	2,150
	160	3,000	2,700	2,250
	170	3,100	2,800	2,350
	180	3,250	2,950	2,450
	190	3,400	3,050	2,600
Women:				
	90	1,600	1,500	1,250
	100	1,750	1,600	1,350
	110	1,900	1,700	1,450
	120	2,000	1,800	1,500
	130	2,100	1,900	1,600
	140	2,250	2,050	1,700
	150	2,350	2,150	1,800
	160	2,500	2,250	1,900

need to be about 3,500 fewer Calories in the diet than the body uses.

If you want to lose 1 pound a week, your food should provide an average of 500 Calories a day fewer than are required to maintain weight (7 days × 500 Calories=3,500 Calories). For example, if you maintain weight on 2,300 Calories daily, this figures out to be 1,800 Calories a day for a reducing diet. If you have been gaining weight on the amount of food you customarily eat, you will need to cut down by more than 500 Calories a day.

A way to help create a shortage of calories while controlling your food intake is to increase physical activity. To illustrate: An extra half hour spent daily in purposeful walking and 30 minutes less spent sitting means that for an average-sized man or woman about 45 additional Calories will be used up. In a year's time, the calorie equivalent of 4 to 5 pounds of body fat will be expended.

If the shift is made from sitting to daily exercises, sports, or light physical work, the man would use up about 90 Calories more, the woman about 60 Calories more. That would be the equivalent in calories in a year to about 9 pounds of fat for the man and 6 pounds for the woman.

For many persons, particularly for those whose calorie needs are low to begin with, it probably would be best to increase activity *and* to reduce calorie intake below the level needed to maintain weight.

When diets have fewer than 1,200 Calories, it is difficult to get the minerals and vitamins needed from foods. With an increase in activity, calorie intake would not need to be reduced as much to bring about a weight loss.

If you are considerably overweight, you probably should reduce. Check with your doctor before you begin, to learn if you are in good enough physical condition for reducing. If you are, he can tell you how much weight to lose, the number of calories to include in your diet every day, and if exercise or other extra physical activity is desirable.

If you are only a little overweight, you may only need to watch your diet to avoid putting on more weight.

To PLAN a diet for weight control, you need to know the number of calories your daily food should supply.

Once you know what your calorie need is, you can refer to tables or charts listing calorie values of foods and make selections that will total to the desired number of calories. But it is wise to have a food guide as well as a table of calorie values as an aid in choosing food. Then you will be sure to include the kinds of foods in meals that are important for nutrients, such as proteins, vitamins, and minerals.

The Daily Food Guide, which is printed on pages 394 and 395, suggests that you have two or more cups of milk a day; two or more servings of meat, poultry, fish, eggs, or occasionally dry beans, dry peas, or nuts; four or more servings of vegetables and fruits, including a daily serving of citrus fruit or other source of vitamin C and a serving every other day of a dark-green or deep-yellow vegetable for vitamin A; and four or more servings of whole grain or enriched breads and cereals—plus additional foods to round out meals.

For a quick check of your food selections, the following calorie values can be used. In some instances foods have been grouped together, and a single calorie figure is given. However, if you customarily have little variety in what you eat of the kinds of foods I have grouped together, it would be best to use a table giving calorie values for individual foods.

Such a table can be found in the Department of Agriculture's Home and Garden Bulletin No. 72, "Nutritive Value of Foods," and in Home and Garden Bulletin No. 74, "Food and Your Weight."

Some of your milk can be in the form of cheese or ice cream. Skim milk and buttermilk and cheese made from skim milk are lower in calories than other types of milk and cheese.

	Calories
1 cup fluid skim milk or buttermilk....	90
1 cup fluid whole milk...............	160
1 ounce creamed cottage cheese.......	30
1 ounce of most cheeses other than cottage cheese	105
½ cup plain ice cream..............	150
1 large glass chocolate ice cream soda..	455

The calorie values for meat, poultry, fish, and eggs that follow do not include the calories from fat that might be used in cooking such as when these foods are fried. And it is assumed that

meat has been trimmed of visible fat; otherwise the calorie figure would be higher.

For example, on an average, a 2-ounce serving of beef pot roast that includes both fat and lean would add 165 Calories to the diet. The figure I have listed for 2 ounces of cooked lean meat is 130 Calories.

	Calories
2 ounces of cooked lean meat or poultry without bone.....................	130
2 ounces bologna, frankfurters........	170
2 ounces cooked fish................	105
2 ounces cooked shellfish.............	60
1 large egg........................	80
½ cup cooked dry beans or peas......	135
2 tablespoons peanut butter..........	190

Vegetables vary quite widely in the number of calories furnished.

5 Calories
    1 large leaf lettuce, 4 small radishes, 6 slices cucumber, 1 large stalk celery, ½ medium green pepper
20 Calories
    ½ cup cooked or canned vegetables like asparagus, snap beans, beets, broccoli, brussels sprouts, cabbage, carrots, cauliflower, greens, pumpkin, summer squash, tomatoes or turnips—or 1 small tomato
65 Calories
    ½ cup cooked or canned vegetables such as parsnips, peas, mashed potatoes and winter squash
90 Calories
    ½ cup cooked or canned lima beans or corn, 1 large ear of corn, 1 medium potato
110 Calories
    1 small sweetpotato

If you add butter, margarine, or bacon drippings to cooked vegetables for flavoring or if you fry vegetables, their calorie count would be higher than the figures given. For example, one-half cup of mashed potatoes without fat gives 65 Calories; one-half cup of hash-browned potatoes supplies 225 Calories.

Sauces added to vegetables would also increase their calorie value and so would dressing eaten with salads.

For fruits, use the following calorie figures:

40 Calories
    ½ cup unsweetened or artificially sweetened canned fruit
50 Calories
    Raw fruits in the portions indicated—1 small apple, banana, orange, pear; 1

CALORIES PROVIDED BY SOME "OTHER" FOODS

Desserts		Calories
Cooky	3-inch cooky	120
Doughnut, cake	1 doughnut	125
Cornstarch pudding	½ cup	140
Cupcake, iced	1 medium	185
Pie, such as apple, cherry, mince	⅐ of 9-inch pie	350
Chocolate layer cake	2-inch wedge from a 10-inch cake	445
Cream		
Half-and-half cream and milk	1 tablespoon	20
Coffee cream	1 tablespoon	30
Heavy whipping cream	1 tablespoon	55
Fats, oils, and related foods		
Butter, margarine	1 teaspoon	35
Other fats, oils	1 teaspoon	40
Boiled salad dressing	1 tablespoon	30
French dressing	1 tablespoon	60
Mayonnaise	1 tablespoon	110
Sugars and sweets		
Sugar	1 teaspoon	15
Jams, jellies, honey, sirup	1 tablespoon	55
Marshmallows	3 or 4	90
Hard candy	1 ounce	110
Caramels	3 medium	115
Fudge	1 ounce	115
Chocolate creams	2 or 3	125
Milk chocolate, plain or with almonds	1 ounce	150
Beverages		
Ginger ale	8-ounce cup	70
Regular cola-type drink	8-ounce cup	95
Beer, 3.6 percent alcohol	8-ounce cup	100
Whiskey, 90-proof	1½ ounces	110
Miscellaneous		
Olives, black	2 large	15
Pretzels	5 small sticks	20
Popcorn with added fat	1 cup	65
Potato chips	10 medium	115
Gravy	2 tablespoons	35
White sauce	¼ cup	110

large peach; 2 plums; ⅔ cup berries; ½ cup pineapple; ½ medium cantaloup or grapefruit

60 Calories
    ½ cup of most fruit juices
105 Calories
    ½ cup fruit canned in sirup

Sugar and cream eaten with fruits increase their calorie value.

When you select breads and cereals, choose those that are whole grain or enriched. Although they are not any lower in calories than the others, they are more nutritious.

	Calories
1 slice bread, regular slice	60
1 slice bread, thin-sliced	45
1 ounce of most ready-to-eat cereals	105
⅔ cup cooked breakfast cereals	95
⅔ cup cooked cereal products such as macaroni, spaghetti	105

Toast supplies the same number of calories as the slice of bread does before it is toasted.

There are also other foods that are commonly eaten as a part of meals, as additions to foods in cooking or in preparation for the table, or as snacks. They include desserts, such as pies, cakes, cookies, puddings; butter, margarine, cooking fats and oils, salad oils and dressings; cream; sugars and sweets; fried tidbits; soft drinks and alcoholic beverages. These foods often account for the "extra" calories in a diet. Cutting down on them is an excellent way to cut down on calories without shortchanging the body of its other needs.

In choosing a diet for weight control,

select first the foods suggested by the Daily Food Guide. Count the calories these selections furnish and subtract the total from your calorie quota. In this way you will know how many calories you can afford to have come from "other" foods.

For example:

	Calories
1⅔ cups skim milk	150
½ cup cottage cheese	120
3-ounce serving cooked lean meat	195
1 large egg	80
½ cup greens	20
½ cup orange juice	60
½ cup beets	20
1 small tomato	20
3 slices enriched bread	180
1 ounce ready-to-eat cereal	105
Total	950

If your daily quota is 1,200 Calories, you have 250 Calories left to come from additional choices. Some of the remaining calories probably will be used for a spread for the bread. Other choices may include more fruit and vegetables or meat, for example, or an occasional treat. With a quota larger than 1,200 Calories, a greater variety of selections would be possible.

Learn to enjoy the natural flavor of foods. Calories can be saved by avoiding added fat, sugar, sauces, cream, and so forth. For variety, foods can be seasoned with spices, herbs, vinegars, or tart fruit juices.

Eating regular meals each day is a good idea. Skipping breakfast or lunch leads to nibbling and an unplanned snacking and may cause you to exceed your calorie allowance.

Snacks can be a part of a diet for weight control, though, if they are planned. Save on calories from meals to allow for them. Or a piece of fruit, milk, or a simple dessert saved from mealtime can be eaten between meals.

You may find that small meals along with between-meal snacks planned to fit within your calorie allotment may work better for you than eating the customary three meals daily.

Once you have reached your desirable weight, continue to choose foods with an eye on their calorie con-

tent so that you will not go back to old eating habits that resulted in unwanted pounds.

Keep in mind that it is the calories in excess of your need that make you fat—not any one food. (LOUISE PAGE)

Nutrition Nonsense

ONE CONSUMER in 19 spends 50 dollars a year on unnecessary or falsely represented vitamin products and so-called health foods. All told, this type of consumer deception costs consumers more than 500 million dollars a year.

More than money is involved, however. Ignorant and unscrupulous promoters may distort the facts and claim benefits against diseases or symptoms that are not caused by dietary deficiencies of vitamins and minerals, and persons who may have serious medical problems are tricked into making their own diagnosis and thus delay getting proper attention.

Laws have been made to help protect the health and pocketbooks of consumers.

The Food and Drugs Act and the Meat Inspection Act of 1906 established the responsibility of the Federal and State Governments to protect consumers by barring foods that are hazardous, adulterated, or misbranded. The 1906 Food and Drugs Act has now been replaced with the Federal Food, Drug, and Cosmetic Act, passed by the Congress in 1938.

Before the Food and Drugs Act was passed, a variety of chemical preservatives and dyes that could be hazardous to health were being used indiscriminately in foods. The law prohibited the practice. Since then, levels of safety for all additives to foods must be established before they may be used.

At one time, the reported sales of "Vermont maple sirup" exceeded the production capacity of that State by about 10 times.

Another example of an adulterated food was butter that contained other fats, such as lard. These products were not harmful, but they were not what the consumer believed they were.

Today, all foods entering interstate commerce must have labels that inform the purchaser of the contents.

THE LABEL must not be false or misleading. It must be easily read and understood. Imitations must be prominently labeled.

If the food has two or more ingredients, they must be listed by their common or usual names and in the order of their amounts in the food. The net contents must be stated in common units of weight or measure.

The container must not mislead, either. Even though properly labeled, the product must fill the package at the processing plant. This presents difficulties with products such as cereals and crackers that shake down with handling.

Labels must also include the name and business address of the manufacturer, packer, or distributor.

When manufacturers label their products in compliance with the appropriate laws, consumers are furnished the information they need to be intelligent purchasers and protect the health of their families.

The final and necessary step that the consumer must take to benefit from these activities of both industry and Government, however, is to read and use the information on the label.

THE AMERICAN CONSUMER has become health conscious, diet conscious, vitamin conscious, mineral conscious, weight conscious, protein conscious, and fat conscious, but his ability to deal with all of these concepts may be limited.

He is aware that there are important nutritional factors and developments, but his knowledge does not permit him to distinguish always between sound nutritional advice and nutritional nonsense.

Words such as vitamins, minerals, protein, polyunsaturated fat, enriched, and fortified are rained upon him daily so that he feels much happier if he sees one or two of these words on the label of any food he buys.

At the same time he is constantly being told that if he wishes to enjoy good health, he must "improve" his diet with some type of supplement.

As a result, it is not surprising that some consumers find it difficult to make a rational choice of their foods.

It is a violation of Federal law to make false and misleading claims in the labeling or advertising of foods, drugs, and cosmetics. The Food and Drug Administration is responsible for the enforcement of the law against false and misleading labeling. The Federal Trade Commission and the Post Office Department enforce the laws relating to false advertising and the use of the mails to defraud.

It is of interest to note that several organizations that are foremost in spreading nutritional nonsense almost invariably have a stake in the sale of so-called natural foods and vitamins.

THE METHODS of promotion are so similar that the four chief selling points have been dubbed "the four myths" of nutrition.

These are:

The myth that almost all diseases are due to improper diets. The claim is made that chemical imbalance in the body because of a faulty diet is the primary reason for almost all diseases. The consumer is told that to correct this imbalance he must consume quantities of certain food supplements in addition to his regular diet.

The proponents of this myth fail to

state, however, that there are extremely few diseases in the United States today that are caused by dietary deficiencies. The American food supply is unsurpassed in volume, variety, and nutritional value. By patronizing all departments of a modern supermarket, the American consumer can easily supply all of his nutritional needs. In fact, he actually must go out of his way to avoid being well nourished.

Another myth is that soil depletion causes malnutrition. The nutrition nonsense purveyor, or faddist as he is commonly called, claims that almost all of our farmland has now been so depleted of minerals that our nutritional needs cannot be met by plants grown on such land and animals fed on crops grown on such soil. In order to counteract this "nutritional sterility," according to the faddist, one must supplement his usual food intake with a manufactured concoction containing all of the nutrients alleged to be missing from the soil.

What is not mentioned is that the composition of the soil has little significant effect upon the composition of the plants grown on it. Certain soil elements are needed for growth and reproduction of the plant, and the plant will not grow or reproduce unless these are available. Thus the quality of the soil on which food is grown has a definite effect on the quantity of the crop but very little on the nutritional quality of it.

That commercial food processing and cooking destroys the nutritive value of foods is another myth.

Foods such as white flour, refined cereal, canned food, and even pasteurized milk are condemned by the food faddist. He bemoans the supposed extensive loss in vitamins because of warehousing, storage, and exposure to daylight and insists that there is nothing left of any nutritional value after the food has been cooked.

In effect, the food faddist would seem to want us all to become grazing animals eating only foods *au naturel*.

He overlooks the fact, however, that grazing animals have digestive systems quite different from the human digestive system.

He does not tell you that modern food processing methods have been designed to produce foods of high nutritional value. Fruit and vegetables are canned or frozen at the peak of their nutritional value, and flour, bread, milk, and margarine are all nutritionally improved in accord with recommendations of authorities on nutrition.

A certain percentage of raw fruit and vegetables is desirable in the diet, but most of our common foods usually are served cooked because they are more palatable and because they are more easily digested.

The fourth myth is that most Americans suffer from "subclinical" deficiencies and therefore must supplement their diets with various concoctions. A "subclinical" deficiency is merely one that has no observable symptoms. Thus, almost any ailment from falling hair to tired blood could be called a "subclinical" deficiency because of a lack of sufficient vitamins and minerals in the diet.

The person with chronic aches and pains finds this an especially appealing argument. Even though his physician has examined him and told him there is nothing wrong with him, he "knows" that there is. So when a dietary supplement salesman says there are certain vitamin deficiencies that doctors cannot detect, our friend falls right into the trap.

What the consumer should realize is that no normal person can go through a small part of his life without experiencing an occasional wornout, tired feeling. There is no more basis for believing that this is due to a "subclinical" deficiency than attributing it to the number of children in one's family—although that could well be the cause of that tired feeling—or the phase of the moon. If such feelings persist, of course, the advice of one's physician should be obtained.

THE MAJOR function of the Food and Drug Administration is to enforce the Federal Food, Drug, and Cosmetic Act.

In the sphere of nutrition misinformation, however, the complete protection of the consumer through law enforcement alone is not possible.

The consumer himself must assume the responsibility for learning the facts about nutrition so that he is in a position to make a wise choice among the many items he encounters in the marketplace.

Many organizations other than the Food and Drug Administration are concerned with carrying effective nutrition education programs to the consumer. Other groups active in this are the Department of Agriculture, the American Medical Association, the National Better Business Bureau, the American Home Economics Association, the American Dietetic Association, the American Public Health Association, and the Nutrition Foundation.

The basic fact that our farming and food processing industries have provided the American consumer with an unequaled variety of wholesome and nutritious food was corroborated with information obtained from studies of the Food and Drug Administration.

The studies were made on market-basket samples collected from grocery stores in five major United States cities in 1961 and 1962. They showed that the average moderate-income diet recommended by the Department of Agriculture contained an abundance of nutritive value when prepared and cooked by usual home kitchen procedures.

The studies originally were planned to discover how much strontium 90 and cesium 137 were present in the daily diet. They were extended to include analyses for pesticide residues and protein and vitamin content.

Analytical examination of these diets as prepared for eating showed that in all cases the amounts of protein, vitamin A, thiamine, riboflavin, niacin, vitamin B_6, and vitamin B_{12} were well above the amounts required for good nutrition.

This certainly refutes the claim of the purveyors of food misinformation that the foods available at the grocery are of no nutritional value and that in order to achieve proper nutrition it is necessary to purchase specially grown foods or specially formulated diet supplements.

The study again shows that persons in good health who eat a variety of foods have no need to worry about dietary deficiencies. Foods, not pills, are the best sources of vitamins, minerals, and other nutrients.

The studies also showed that the pesticide residues present in the diet were well within safe tolerance limits.

They further showed that the radioactivity present was well within the amounts considered by the Federal Radiation Council as acceptable for lifetime consumption under normal peacetime conditions.

To PROVIDE some guidelines for consumers, I list several products and practices consumers should beware of.

"Shotgun" formulas. Food supplements that contain dozens of different ingredients are designed to impress the gullible. More than 40 recognized essential nutrients are required for metabolism in the body, but less than half that number are recognized by experts in nutrition as being appropriate for supplementation of the diet.

Loaded formulas. Many dietary supplements contain amounts of vitamins and minerals that are many times the quantities that can possibly be utilized by the body. The uninformed consumer thinks that because he is getting more of certain substances, the product must therefore be better for him— if a little is good, more is that much better.

Actually, the body requires only certain amounts of the essential nutrients for proper functioning. Any excess, with the exception of the fat-soluble vitamins A and D, is not utilized.

Natural and organic foods. These are

foods that are supposed to be grown and produced without the aid of chemical fertilizers, pesticides, or food additives of any type.

It is questionable, however, whether very many are actually grown and processed in the manner represented. They are frequently a very expensive source of nutritional factors that are readily available in ordinary foods that cost much less.

The human body cannot differentiate between vitamin C from an orange and vitamin C prepared synthetically. They are identical chemical compounds and will be so used in the human body.

There is certainly no justification for paying premium prices for "natural" vitamins when the source has nothing to do with their value to the body.

Miracle foods. Many common foods are offered by self-styled "experts" as cures for various serious conditions other than nutritional deficiencies. Examples are carrot juice for leukemia, apple vinegar as a general cure-all, garlic pills for high and low blood pressure, lecithin for heart disease, powdered grapefruit for diabetes, and royal jelly for sexual rejuvenation.

While the overall nutritional status of an individual will determine to a great extent his susceptibility to various diseases, no one food can be considered a cure or treatment for such diseases. One's physician is the only safe source of advice for proper treatment.

Reducing products. It has been shown time and again that the most effective reducing plan is the ability to push yourself away from the table before you eat too much.

Because they do not have sufficient willpower, many persons look for willpower in a pill, capsule, or elixir.

Most reducing products that can be bought without prescription today are merely food supplements along with which there is a diet plan. If the diet plan is followed, with or without the food supplement, one will reduce calo-

rie intake and therefore lose weight.

Mail-order products. Mail-order literature is particularly noted for the prevalence of exaggerated claims, especially in the area of nutrition. The Postmaster General has warned that this type of practice is at an alltime high.

"Doorbell doctors." House-to-house peddlers of food supplements are merely salesmen and are not qualified to discuss and give advice about health and dietary problems. Such advice should be obtained from one's physician.

Health food lecturers. Some sincere and many not-so-sincere persons are self-styled nutrition experts who offer one or more free lectures on health and nutrition as a come-on for a paid series that follows. Such a person usually has something to sell—a line of "natural" foods, special cooking utensils, or false and misleading literature, all at fantastic prices. The forewarned consumer can recognize such a person immediately.

Popular books on nutrition. The advice not to believe everything one reads is especially pertinent in the field of nutrition.

Many popular books on nutrition do contain good information, but many give medically and nutritionally unsound advice and encourage self-diagnosis. Thus, all too frequently, the unwary and uninformed resort to self-diagnosis, and a medical problem remains unchecked.

THE LATE President Kennedy stated the four rights of the consumer as: The right to safety, the right to be informed, the right to choose, and the right to be heard.

The four rights are inherent in the Federal Food, Drug, and Cosmetic Act. There are provisions for preventing the use in foods of untested and untried chemicals and of harmful and injurious substances; requiring accurate informative labeling so that the consumer has a basis for choice among many similar items; and providing opportunities for the consumer to make known his opinion at public hearings before food standards and regulations are established.

Consumers and industry are encouraged to express their opinions and ask questions through correspondence and personal visits.

Inherent in the consumer's right to choose, of course, is his right not to become informed and not to state his views to those who can take them under proper consideration.

The consumer who does not accept the protection of the law and its attendant responsibilities jeopardizes himself, his family, and his money. He also hinders the enforcement of a law designed for his benefit. (EUGENE H. STEVENSON)

Question,

Please

HUNDREDS OF LETTERS come to the Department of Agriculture every week from persons who want information about food and food values. The questions they ask oftenest and the answers we gladly give as a service to all consumers follow.

FOODS AND NUTRIENTS

Are all foods of the same importance in nutrition?

No. Many foods supply several nutrients; others but a few. Some foods we value mainly for the flavor, color, and texture they provide.

What is a nutrient?

A nutrient is a chemical substance that has its own specific function in the body and works with other nutrients for growth and for regulation of all body processes throughout the life cycle.

Are all the nutrients the body needs present in foods?

Yes, abundantly. Foods vary in the kinds and amounts of nutrients they contain, however.

What are the essential nutrients?

Essential nutrients for which needed amounts have been recommended include: Protein; calcium and iron; vitamin A; three vitamins of the B-complex group (thiamine, riboflavin, niacin); and ascorbic acid (vitamin C).

Fat (and fatty acids), carbohydrate, phosphorus, sodium, potassium, and other nutrients also are known to be important in the body, although no specific amounts of them have been recommended.

Is water classed as a nutrient?

Water once was classed as a non-nutrient, but it is recognized as a nutrient in current texts. A person usually needs the equivalent of 4 to 8 glasses of water daily as water or in beverages.

What is meant by an adequate diet?

It is one that supplies all the known essential nutrients in sufficient amounts for the maintenance of health in the normal individual.

Is appetite a safe guide in choosing a diet?

Not necessarily. A haphazard diet may lack certain nutrients and supply too much of others. A satisfactory diet can be obtained from well-selected foods in the different food groups.

What are food groups?

Nutritionists have made convenient groupings of foods according to their similarity of predominant nutrients. One such grouping lists: Milk group; meat group (meat, fish, poultry, eggs); vegetable-fruit group; bread-cereal group. See "Food for Fitness—a Daily Food Guide," Department of Agriculture Leaflet No. 424. It is reproduced in this book on pages 394 and 395.

Why is protein particularly important in nutrition?

Protein is an indispensable component of every cell in the body and, after water, comprises the greatest proportion of body tissues. Protein is needed to build, maintain, and repair body tissues and to fulfill regulatory functions. It may also provide energy when needed. Building materials for body protein must be supplied constantly to the body.

What are the building materials?

Proteins are made up of simpler units called amino acids.

What is meant by nonessential and essential amino acids?

Some amino acids the body can make from fragments made available in the breakdown of food following digestion. They are called nonessential (or dispensable) in the sense that it is not essential that they be supplied by the foods in the diet.

Eight amino acids cannot be made by the body and have to be supplied readymade from the diet. They are called essential or indispensable.

How is protein in food evaluated?

Protein in foods varies in quantity and in quality. Protein is considered of excellent quality, or high biological value, if it has the indispensable, or essential, amino acids in proportions needed by the body.

The kinds and amounts of amino acids provided by protein of one food often complement the kinds and amounts of amino acids in protein of another food. When foods that supplement each other are eaten together, as cereal with milk, the protein mixture has a better value to the body than if each food were eaten alone.

Why is fat necessary to well-being?

Fat, a component of all body tissues, is necessary in the diet. It is a source of energy, a carrier of fat-soluble vitamins, and a source of essential fatty acids. As fat is more slowly digested than protein or carbohydrate, it has satiety value and may help deter overeating. Fat layers help conserve body heat and cushion internal organs.

What are hydrogenated fats?

Hydrogenation is a process by which hydrogen is added to oils to obtain a solid fat product. Margarine and shortenings are examples of hydrogenated fats.

What are unsaturated and saturated fats?

A fat is described by the chemist as unsaturated if it can combine with more hydrogen and as saturated if it cannot. Generally, unsaturated fats are liquid at room temperature, as the oils extracted from cottonseed, soybean, corn, safflower seed. Most saturated fats are solid at room temperature, as beef suet, hydrogenated vegetable fats, mutton tallow.

Are fatty acids essential in nutrition?

Yes. Fats provide those fatty acids regarded as necessary in nutrition and many others whose roles in nutrition are not yet known.

From what foods can linoleic acid be obtained?

Richest sources of linoleic acid, an essential unsaturated fatty acid, are of plant origin.

How much fat should one eat daily?

Little is known about man's requirement for fat except that some is needed daily. No specific amounts have been recommended.

Does carbohydrate mean sugar or starch?

It includes both. Sugar, starch, and fiber (cellulose) are the principal carbohydrates.

Are carbohydrates of plant or animal origin?

Most carbohydrates are formed in plants from carbon dioxide of the air and from water, with the aid of sunlight and the green pigment, chlorophyll. Only a few foods of animal origin contain carbohydrate. Milk is one of these. More than one-third of the solid matter of milk is lactose, commonly called milk sugar.

Why is sugar sometimes called "quick energy"?

Ordinary sugar, sucrose, is quickly broken down into compounds that are readily absorbed and circulated to the various parts of the body by the blood.

What happens to sugar and starch eaten in excess of daily needs?

A limited amount is held for ready use as carbohydrate. The remainder is converted to fat and stored.

In what foods do carbohydrates occur?

Starch is found richly in cereal grains (rice, wheat, sorghum, corn, millet, rye). Potatoes and some other tubers and roots as well as seeds of legumes have a relatively high content of starch.

Sugars of several kinds are present in foods. Various sugars are naturally present in honey, fruit, vegetables, and milk. Sugar from sugarcane and sugarbeets may be highly refined for table use.

Does sugar have more calories than starch?

Weight for weight, the calorie values of sugar and starch are about the same.

How much carbohydrate should be in the average daily diet?

No daily amounts of carbohydrate have been recommended. Healthful diets may contain widely varying amounts of carbohydrate. In some countries where the food supply is mainly from plant foods, the proportion of carbohydrate in the average diet is much higher than in the United States and consists largely of starch.

Is food energy the same as calories?

No. The calorie is a standard unit of measure of energy produced in the metabolism of protein, fat, and carbohydrate in the body.

Do the sometimes-called energy nutrients (protein, fat, carbohydrate) yield the same amount of energy?

No. Weight for weight, fat yields about two and one-fourth times as many calories as protein or carbohydrates.

What are high-calorie and low-calorie foods?

There is no exact line of demarcation. The calorie value of a food depends on its composition. In general, foods highest in calorie value are those rich in fat and low in moisture. Other concentrated sources are foods composed mainly of carbohydrate or protein or a mixture of either or both with fat. Sugars, cereals, dried fruits, and cheese are among the relatively concentrated sources of energy.

Foods low in calorie value in general are those that contain large amounts of water and relatively little fat. These include many fruits and vegetables, particularly succulent vegetables.

What are vitamins? How do they work?

Vitamins are chemical compounds that occur in foods in minute amounts and must be supplied to the body for normal functioning and development. Vitamins take part in chemical reactions that release energy from foods for use by the body, promote normal growth of different kinds of tissue, and are essential to the proper functioning of nerves and muscle. Research is constantly adding to knowledge of the many capacities in which various vitamins function.

How many vitamins are there? How are they classified?

At least 13 vitamins are known at present to be needed in nutrition. They are sometimes classified in two groups as fat-soluble vitamins and water-soluble vitamins. The fat-soluble group includes vitamins A, D, E, and K. The water-soluble vitamins include ascorbic acid, thiamine, riboflavin, niacin, vitamin B_6, pantothenic acid, biotin, folic acid, and vitamin B_{12}. Choline and inositol are sometimes listed in the water-soluble group.

How are vitamins measured?

Today most vitamins are measured in units of weight, usually in milligrams or micrograms. One milligram is 1/1000 of a gram and one microgram is 1/1000 of a milligram, or one millionth of a gram. These are minute quantities, as 28.35 grams equal one ounce.

How many mineral elements are known to be needed as nutrients by the human body?

More than a dozen different minerals are known to have definite functions in the body. Those needed in appreciable amounts are calcium, phosphorus, iron, sodium, chlorine, potassium, magnesium, and sulfur.

What are trace elements?

They are minerals needed in very small amounts. They include iodine, manganese, copper, zinc, cobalt, fluorine, molybdenum, and perhaps others.

Are all the minerals the body needs present in foods?

Yes.

In what foods does sodium occur?

Sodium content of food varies widely. Ordinary table salt, baking soda, and monosodium glutamate are highly concentrated sources. Foods of animal origin (meat, fish, poultry, cheese) have more sodium than plant foods. Cured foods and other foods with salt added are generally high in sodium. Vegetables, with a few exceptions, are low in sodium. Fresh, frozen, and canned fruit is low in sodium unless it has been added in some form.

Are the same daily amounts of essential nutrients recommended for everyone?

No. Needed amounts vary according to age, size, stage of growth, and condition of the individual. In general, the amounts are higher for rapidly growing boys and girls and pregnant and lactating women; they are lower for young children as well as for older persons.

Are recommended daily dietary allowances the same as minimum daily requirements?

No. Recommended daily dietary allowances are amounts of nutrients that are judged to be adequate for the maintenance of good nutrition in the population of the United States. The amounts are changed from time to time as newer knowledge of nutritional needs becomes available.

Minimum daily requirements are amounts of various nutrients that have been established as standards for labeling food and pharmaceutical preparations for special dietary uses.

Is guidance available in planning an adequate diet from an ordinary variety of common foods?

Yes. A leaflet on a daily food guide, bulletins on foods needed for good nutrition of young children, schoolchildren, the young couple, and older people, and many other publications on food and nutrition are available from the Office of Information, U.S. Department of Agriculture, Washington, D.C., 20250.

RETAINING NUTRIENTS IN FOOD

Can "once a good source, always a good source" be said of nutrients in foods?

No. Losses occur in the many stages from site of origin to the consumer's plate.

What kinds of losses does food undergo?

The basic losses are of two kinds: The physical loss, when edible parts, such as outer leaves of plants, outer layers of grains, the fat of meat, and various cooking liquids, are discarded; and the chemical loss that occurs naturally when food is held at elevated temperatures, when food is cut, exposing greater surface, and when the tissues are bruised or dried.

Why is ascorbic acid so often cited in reporting the retention of nutrients in fruit and vegetables?

Ascorbic acid is lost more easily from most food than other important nutrients are. Means that protect ascorbic acid usually protect other water-soluble vitamins (thiamine, riboflavin, niacin) and other heat-sensitive vitamins (especially thiamine) as well.

Is ascorbic acid the same as vitamin C?

Ascorbic acid is the chemical name for vitamin C.

Are minerals in foods more stable than vitamins?

Yes. The minerals are not destroyed, but the portions that pass into solution will be lost if cooking water, meat drippings, and canning liquid are discarded.

How is ascorbic acid in roots and tubers affected by storage?

Prolonged storage increases the losses. For example, potatoes lose about one-half their ascorbic acid during the first 3 months in storage and about two-thirds during the first 6 months. Sweetpotatoes lose about 30 to 50 percent of their ascorbic acid during the first 3 months in storage and another 10 percent by the end of 6 months.

Are green spots on potatoes dangerous?

Exposure to light causes green areas to develop. It is advisable to remove the green parts, although we know of no instances in which ill effects from eating these parts have been reported. Sprouts have more of the green-containing substance (solanin) than the potato, and should not be eaten.

Does canning destroy the nutritive value of fruit and vegetables?

Good commercial canning methods cause relatively little loss.

Are home-canned foods as nutritious as commercially canned foods?

It depends. Foods of high quality canned at home under favorable conditions retain their nutrients well, but home operators and methods vary so much that it is not possible to make definite comparisons. See Home and Garden Bulletin No. 8, "Home Canning of Fruits and Vegetables."

In canned vegetables and fruit, are the nutrients in the food or in the liquid?

Soluble nutrients are about evenly distributed throughout the contents of the can. Drained solids make up about two-thirds of the contents; therefore, about two-thirds of the soluble nutrients would be in the food and one-third in the liquid.

Is it safe to leave canned foods in the can?

Yes. The can is an excellent container, but food in cans should have the same care as fresh-cooked foods and be kept in a refrigerator.

Do canned fruits and vegetables lose food value on the pantry shelf?

Very little, if the storage place is cool. In a year, foods stored at a temperature under 65° F. show a small loss of ascorbic acid and thiamine, ranging from 10 to 15 percent. However, when stored at temperatures up to 80°, the loss doubles, increasing to 25 percent. The loss continues as the storage period lengthens.

Does freezing affect the nutritive values of fruit and vegetables?

Foods of high quality, frozen by good methods, retain their nutrients well. Blanching before freezing causes some loss of vitamins and minerals.

How are the food values of meat, poultry, and fish affected by freezing?

These foods have about the same nutritive value, frozen or fresh.

Is freezer burn harmful?

Freezer burn (a change of color due to loss of moisture or dehydration) does not make the food unsafe to eat but results in some loss of quality. To prevent freezer burn, wrap the food in moisture-vapor-resistant wrapping material and seal the package tightly.

How should meat, fish, and poultry be thawed?

They should be thawed in the refrigerator, whenever possible. When time does not permit, they may be placed in a watertight wrapper and thawed in cold water. Direct exposure to water to hasten thawing results in some loss of flavor and nutritive value.

Is it safe to refreeze frozen foods?

Frozen fruit, vegetables, and red meat that have been thawed and appear in good condition can safely be used or refrozen if they have been thawed and held at recommended refrigerator temperatures for not more than a few days. Repeated thawing and refreezing may impair flavor, texture, and nutritive value, particularly of fruit and vegetables.

See Home and Garden Bulletin No. 10, "Home Freezing of Fruits and Vegetables," and Home and Garden Bulletin No. 93, "Freezing Meat and Fish in the Home."

How does cooking affect nutrients?

Some cooking procedures result in much greater losses than others. The "three R's" of cooking to retain nutrients are: Reduce the amount of water used; reduce the length of the cooking period; and reduce the amount of food surface exposed.

Is waterless cooking a superior method?

Not necessarily. Although the amount of cooking water is small, the longer cooking period required by this method may offset the advantage of the smaller amount of water used.

Is pressure cooking a desirable method?

This intensive method may overcook tender vegetables and result in loss of nutrients. If timing is carefully regulated, however, retention of nutrients may be as good by pressure cooking as by other methods.

Does cooking lock the nutrients in foods?
No. Losses continue to the end. Cooking for one meal at a time and serving quickly is the best assurance of maximum nutritive values.

What kind of cooking utensils best conserve the nutrients in foods?
Any cooking utensil with a well-fitting lid is satisfactory, whether made of aluminum, enamel, glass, stainless steel, or other materials ordinarily used.

Do aluminum cooking utensils cause cancer?
No. The American Medical Association stated that this rumor has been investigated thoroughly and that there is no scientific evidence that the use of aluminum ware causes cancer or is in any way injurious to health.

Is it safe to eat raw meat?
No.
Pork cooked to the well-done stage (185°) carries no danger of trichinosis—a disease caused by trichinae (small worms) embedding themselves in the intestinal tract and muscles.

Beef should be cooked at least to the rare done stage (internal temperature 140°) to avoid infestation by a form of tapeworm called cysticercus, which is sometimes present in raw beef.

Rabbit should be thoroughly cooked. Wild rabbits are often infected by *Bacterium tularense*, caused by certain tick bites that produce the disease, tularemia (rabbit fever), in man. Any bacteria remaining in the rabbit after skinning can be destroyed by cooking. Domestic rabbits are less likely to be affected, as their hutches are usually free from ticks.

Is it harmful to eat pork in summer?
No. With present-day refrigeration, pork, like other meats, may be enjoyed the year around.

What are meat tenderizers and are they safe to use?
Meat tenderizers have as a basic ingredient papain, a vegetable enzyme of the tropical papaya melon. The tenderizer product may be prepared either with or without the addition of salt, spices, dextrose, and seasonings.

The ingredients are harmless to the consumer when used as directed.

Is there a danger to health in raw eggs?
Raw eggs are not sterile and may carry Salmonella, one of the harmful bacteria. Eggs should be cooked. If the shells are cracked or badly soiled, the eggs must be thoroughly cooked.

Does cooking affect the nutrients in eggs?
Only slightly.

Are white-shell eggs higher in nutritive value than brown-shell eggs?
No. Color of shell is a characteristic of the breed of hen.

ADDING NUTRIENTS TO FOODS

Is whole-wheat flour more nutritious than plain white flour?
Yes. Whole-wheat flour is milled to include all parts of the wheat kernel, including the germ and outer layers, in which some nutrients are highly concentrated. White flour is milled from the endosperm, which is mainly starch. Enrichment of white flour is common now.

What is enriched flour?
Enriched flour is refined flour to which certain vitamins and minerals are added within limits stipulated by law. Enrichment has led to great improvement in the American diet.

Are there other foods with added nutrients?
Yes, many. The first important addition of an essential nutrient to a staple article of food was addition of iodine to table salt in 1924. Vitamin A may be added to margarine in amounts set by Federal law and vitamin D to milk according to Federal or State laws. Many other foods have nutrients added in amounts that are not regulated by law. Many breakfast cereals, particularly those in ready-to-serve form, have added nutrients. Ingredients added to foods for which there are no regulations as to amounts must be named on the label.

Are commercial breads as nutritious as the old-fashioned loaf?
Yes. In fact, today's commercial recipes have improved the nutritive value of white bread over that of the twenties.

SPECIAL DIETS

What is meant by a special diet?

Special diet is a broad term for diets planned to meet particular needs of individuals or groups. Most special diets can be based on an ordinary well-balanced diet for the normal person.

Can an individual safely plan a special diet for himself?

No. A self-prescribed diet may have imbalances among nutrients or shortages of essential nutrients and lead to more serious problems than it is intended to alleviate. Special dietary planning varies widely and should be prescribed by a physician who is familiar with the needs and problems of the individual.

Is it natural for an adult to put on weight as he grows older?

It may be natural, but it is not desirable. For best health it is recommended that a person maintain the weight that was right for his height and body build at 25 years of age. This requires gradual reduction of calorie intake to meet reduced energy requirements due largely to lessening of vigorous physical activities and decreasing metabolic rate. See Home and Garden Bulletin No. 74, "Food and Your Weight."

Is sodium necessary or harmful?

Sodium is a required nutrient in the body. The usual intake of sodium in this country is estimated as 3 to 7 grams a day. A person in normal health who follows good dietary practices need not be concerned about too much or too little sodium. A sodium-restricted diet should be supervised by a physician.

Are salt substitutes safe?

Yes, in general. However, salt substitutes vary in their chemical composition, and the kind and amount used should be determined by the physician who has evaluated both the individual's condition and the chemical composition of the salt substitute.

Are materials available in planning a sodium-restricted diet?

Yes. Besides the doctor's orders, material for dietary planning on different levels of sodium intake and general information on diet and heart disease are available from American Heart Association, 44 East 23d Street, New York, N.Y., 10010, or from State and county Heart Association offices and from the Public Health Service, United States Department of Health, Education, and Welfare, Washington, D.C., 20201.

Is cholesterol necessary in the body?

Yes. Cholesterol, a fatlike substance present in all animal (body) tissues, is synthesized within the body in normal metabolic processes and is also supplied by foods.

What is the significance of cholesterol in the diet?

This has not been clearly established. Low-cholesterol diets have received much attention in the treatment of atherosclerosis and cardiovascular diseases. Until more is known about possible relationships, however, foods should not be omitted from the diet because they contain cholesterol.

What are the food sources of cholesterol?

Cholesterol occurs only in products of animal origin. Concentrated sources are nerve tissue, as brains from calf, beef, lamb, hog; also egg yolk. Butter is a relatively concentrated source. Meat, poultry, fish and shellfish, and cheese have a fairly high content.

How can foods be selected for carbohydrate-restricted, fat-restricted, low-residue, bland, and other special diets?

The primary source of information is the doctor's order. General information on many special conditions may be obtained from Public Inquiries Branch, Public Health Service, United States Department of Health, Education, and Welfare, Washington, D.C., 20201; and the Department of Community Health and Health Education, American Medical Association, 535 N. Dearborn Street, Chicago, 60610.

Will a dietary supplement added to an adequate diet to supply extra amounts of the well-known vitamins provide extra health benefits to the normal, healthy person?

No. Furthermore, the practice of

taking large doses may be harmful.

FOOD QUACKERY

What can be said of the so-called "health foods," "wonder foods," "miracle foods," "organic foods," and such?

Food quackery is of great concern. It is often difficult for the consumer to know what is fact, fad, or falsity among the innumerable claims made for foods. The so-called "health foods" usually are ordinary foods.

No single food or combination of foods have any health-giving properties other than the nutrients they provide. An ample supply of nutrients is available from foods purchased in regular markets at ordinary, current prices.

What are the facts concerning the food and health values of the products to which some writers have ascribed unusual values?

Yogurt has the same nutritive and calorie values as the milk from which it is made. When made from partly skimmed milk, as is often the case, yogurt is lower in fat, vitamin A value, and calories than when made from whole milk. It is a good source of other nutrients in milk, particularly calcium, riboflavin, and protein.

Yogurt, like other fermented milks, has a fine curd which may permit it to be digested more quickly than plain milk. Yogurt has no food or health values other than those present in the kind of milk from which it is made.

Blackstrap molasses is the third and final extraction of sugarcane and has more of the B-vitamin complex and iron, along with its impurities, than refined molasses. Blackstrap has a strong flavor, and usually only small amounts are eaten.

Brewer's yeast is a good source of the B vitamins and of protein of high biological value. However, adequate amounts of these nutrients are present in the ordinary diet that includes meat, eggs, and whole-grain or enriched cereals.

Brewer's yeast should not be confused with baker's yeast, which is a live yeast that should not be eaten either directly or in powder form. Baker's yeast is a living organism and uses thiamine in the intestinal tract for its own growth, thus reducing the amount of thiamine from other foods that should be available to the body. Cooking renders the live property of baker's yeast inactive; in bakery products it is harmless.

Wheat germ is a part of the wheat kernel and composes 2 to 3 percent of the grain. The germ is a concentrated source of protein, iron, vitamin E, and some of the B vitamins. It has no health-promoting qualities other than the nutrients it contributes. It is usually eaten in small amounts added to other foods.

Alfalfa leaves, like many other green leaves, are rich in carotene (a precursor of vitamin A) and in some other nutrients, but their high fiber content makes them more suitable for animal feeding than for human use. Alfalfa tea, sometimes promoted as cure for certain disabilities, has been found in some experiments to be harmful.

Rose hips are the fruit of the rose (*Rosa rugosa*) and are high in ascorbic acid (vitamin C) content. When usual foods are in short supply, as in wartime, rose hips have been used in some countries to help overcome a scarcity of this nutrient. They have no unusual properties.

Sunflower, sesame, pumpkin, and squash seeds vary in nutritive value. They are relatively high in fat content and have more fiber than most foods. These seeds are used variously as appetizers, as garnish for prepared foods (sesame seed on bakery products), and in other ways. Sunflower seed is used mainly as feed for poultry. These seeds have no unique health-promoting properties.

Honey and vinegar is an imaginative combination, but these foods have no special nutritional merit, taken either singly or together. About four-fifths of the weight of honey is a mixture of sugars. The remaining one-fifth is water. Honey has only very small amounts of other nutrients.

Distilled vinegar has only a trace of mineral matter.

Safflower oil has no nutrients contributing to health that are not present in various other foods. Safflower oil is higher in linoleic acid than are other fats and oils, but adequate amounts of this fatty acid can be obtained from an ordinary mixed diet of commonly used foods.

False claims that capsules of safflower oil were effective in reducing weight regardless of calorie intake and that they were effective in lowering cholesterol level of the blood and in treating arteriosclerosis and heartburn, improving the complexion, increasing resistance to colds, promoting health, and increasing sexual drive led to Government seizure of the supply as being misbranded.

Juices made at home (usually with well-advertised, expensive blenders) have no unusual values. On the same weight basis, juices have about the same nutritive values as the foods from which they were extracted. Juices add variety to the diet and may be useful when one is unable to eat solid food. However, juicing is a wasteful practice of both food material and nutritive value. The strained juice of an orange, for example, comprises only two-thirds to three-fourths of the edible part of the orange. Nutrients present in the pulp are lost.

What are organic foods, and are they superior in nutritive value to other foods?

Organic and natural are terms that have been used by some groups to refer to foods grown in soil fertilized with only compost or manure. However, no sound scientific evidence demonstrates that such foods have nutritive values or health factors superior to foods produced with an appropriate combination of fertilizers.

Is it true that all chemicals used in the production, processing, and marketing of foods are harmful to the consumer?

No. Chemicals are necessary to insure a safe, wholesome, and abundant food supply. The Federal Government has responsibility for insuring that foods in interstate commerce are safe, pure, and wholesome and are produced under sanitary conditions.

The Department of Agriculture and the Department of Health, Education, and Welfare work together on the safe use of chemicals for food products. Foods that do not meet the standards of safety and wholesomeness are seized and condemned. When a harmful residue is found on food products, they cannot be marketed. Every effort is made to label chemical products with instructions and precautions to insure safe use. It is the responsibility of every user to follow directions and heed precautions.

Homemakers should, of course, observe commonsense precautions in the home, such as washing fruits to be eaten out of hand and caring for foods in appropriate ways.

Where may information on food and nutritional quackery be obtained?

Write to the Director of Information, Food and Drug Administration, United States Department of Health, Education, and Welfare, Washington, D.C., 20201.

How may one know which books on nutrition are based on sound scientific fact and which contain false, misleading, and harmful statements?

One such list is titled "Nutrition Books—Recommended and *Not* Recommended." Most of the books included in this list appeared in "Nutrition Books for Lay Readers—a Guide to the Reliable and the Unreliable" by Helen S. Mitchell, published in Library Journal, February 15, 1960, and in "Guide to Selected Nutrition Books," Supplement No. 1, October 1961 and Supplement No. 2, April 1962, Joint Committee on Nutrition Literature, Massachusetts Public Health Association, Boston, Mass.

A revised list, "Recommended and Non-Recommended Nutrition Books for Lay Readers" was issued in April 1964.

Inquiries about these lists may be addressed to Nutrition Section, Massachusetts Department of Public Health,

88 Broad Street, Boston, Mass., 02110; or Connecticut State Department of Health, Hartford, Conn., 06115.

Where may further information on foods and nutrition be obtained?

Food, the Yearbook of Agriculture, 1959, is an excellent one-volume reference. For sale ($2.25) by the Superintendent of Documents, U.S. Government Printing Office, Washington, D.C., 20402. This book may be available in a nearby library. The Department of Agriculture has no copies for general distribution.

A list of popular printed publications including those on food and nutrition may be obtained from the Office of Information, U.S. Department of Agriculture, Washington, D.C., 20250. (EDNA W. SOPER AND BERNICE K. WATT)

When You

Buy Food

YOU PROBABLY CAN feed your family better and cut your grocery bill if you do some planning—perhaps with paper and pencil—before you go to the store.

Plan meals ahead, with your family's needs and tastes in mind.

The daily food guide (pp. 394–395) will help you fit meals to your family's requirements.

From it, you will learn the number of servings of food in four groups—milk, meat, vegetables and fruit, and bread and cereals—that will provide the main part of the day's nutrient needs. In each of the groups, supermarkets offer many items with different price tags.

The family's approval is important. No food is a bargain or a body builder if it is not eaten. Keeping waste to a

minimum is a big step toward keeping food costs down.

Consider also your own time schedule. Almost every homemaker has to budget time as well as money. The convenience foods save the time of cleaning, squeezing, peeling, mixing, and sometimes even cooking.

As to their cost, compare that and the cost of preparing an equal amount of a similar product at home. You will find that some convenience foods cost about the same or less than similar foods prepared at home.

Examples may be frozen and canned orange juice, biscuit mix, cake mixes, and instant coffee. Others, such as frozen and ready-to-eat biscuits, rolls, cakes and pies, ready-to-eat cereals, and dehydrated and frozen potatoes, may cost more than similar products that you clean, peel, mix, and cook at home. You may find these services well worth the extra cost, particularly if your time is limited.

Since you think of food needs, preferences, time, and storage facilities as well as cost, you may have to compromise as you plan menus. For example, you decide to find time to make inexpensive breakfast rolls that the family likes. Joe's favorite T-bone steak gives way to the pork roast advertised as the weekend special. You forgo cantaloup until the price is lower. On the other hand, you spend a little more for a company meal, and you get the small and more expensive boxes of raisins rather than the 1-pound box because they are handier for packed lunches.

A list made from menus that you have planned and that takes into account the food on hand makes shopping easy. It can help you avoid the pitfall of impulse buying—the out-of-season fruit and the costly, ready-prepared items or snacks that add little to the diet and much to the grocery bill.

Do not hesitate to adjust the list to make way for specials and other suitable items that offer price advantage when you compare prices at the store.

In my shopping, I go first to the meat counter to select the main-dish items. The price per pound is of little help in comparing costs of meat for a meal, because some cuts contain only edible meat, while others contain fat, gristle, and bone. I generally buy a cut for the servings of cooked lean meat it provides. I have learned to spot the packages that give the servings needed for a family meal—or for more meals as planned. I compare the costs of amounts we need for a meal to see which cuts are the best buys.

Examples of costs of some popular cuts of meats are shown below. Prices are from a Washington, D.C., store in January of 1965. For this comparison, one serving equals a 3-ounce serving of cooked lean meat. I may serve more or less than that, depending on the amount one of the family wants or the size of pieces, such as chicken parts, chops, or steaks.

	Price per pound	Cost of 1 serving	4 servings
Hamburger, regular......	$0.54	$0.14	$0.56
Haddock, fillet..	.49	.14	.56
Beef liver, frozen.......	.65	.16	.64
Chicken, fryer..	.39	.16	.64
Special price..	(.29)	(.12)	(.48)
Turkey, roaster.	.45	.19	.76
Chuck roast, bone in......	.59	.27	1.08
Ham, whole....	.69	.30	1.20
Leg of lamb....	.79	.33	1.32
Pork roast, bone in....	.69	.35	1.40
Special price..	(.49)	(.25)	(1.00)
Round steak, bone out.....	1.29	.40	1.60
Sirloin steak....	1.29	.50	2.00
Special price.	(.99)	(.39)	(1.56)
Pork chops.....	1.09	.56	2.24
Lamb chops....	1.49	.69	2.76

An average serving of cooked lean meat at this store would have cost as little as 14 cents and as much as 69 cents if I chose from these selected items. Specials, such as those given for chicken, pork roast, and sirloin steak, may bring expensive cuts within my budget limits or make inexpensive items even better buys.

Regardless of cost, you can get about the same food value from equal-size servings of cooked lean from different types and cuts of meats. Exceptions are frankfurters, sausages, bacon, and some meats with breaded coatings. Amounts of these meats usually served may cost less than servings of average size of other meats but do not give as much in food value.

Eggs, dry beans, and peanut butter, often used as alternates for meat, usually are good buys in nutrients.

OTHER SAVINGS can be made on purchases of milk.

Let us say yours is a family of four— two adults and two teenagers—and you use 21 quarts of milk a week, the minimum suggested in the guide. By making a few changes in the way you buy and use milk, you could make the following savings each week in the Washington, D.C., area in January 1965:

$0.63 by getting your milk in half gallons at the store, not through home delivery. In some places, one can save even more by buying the gallon rather than the half-gallon container.

$0.63 if you buy skim milk instead of whole milk in half gallons at the store.

$1.64 if you mix one-half nonfat dry milk (reconstituted) with one-half whole milk bought in half gallons at the store.

$3.26 if you use all nonfat dry milk instead of whole milk bought at the store.

You could save 2 cents each time you use a cup of evaporated milk (reconstituted) in place of a cup of whole milk, or 4 cents if you use a cup of nonfat dry milk (reconstituted) instead of a cup of whole milk.

Reconstituted nonfat dry milk and fluid skim milk have only a little more than half the calories of whole milk— an advantage to weight-watchers but a disadvantage to persons needing more food energy. The vitamin A value in the fat of whole milk is lacking in these more economical nonfat products unless the manufacturer adds it.

A VEGETABLE or fruit may be expensive or not depending somewhat on the item, season, and supply and whether it is fresh, canned, frozen, or dehydrated. If it is canned, frozen, or dehydrated, the brand, type of process, and seasoning affect the cost.

Costs of a serving of selected vegetables and fruit, fresh, frozen, canned, and dehydrated—some 80 all told— were compared in a Washington supermarket in January.

(One serving was counted as one-half cup of vegetable or fruit or a portion as ordinarily served, such as a medium apple, banana, orange, potato, half a medium grapefruit or cantaloup.)

Costs varied from less than 3 cents a serving of fresh carrots, cabbage, or potatoes to more than 10 cents a serving of fresh tomatoes, asparagus, navel oranges, strawberries, or pears.

Note that all these examples (both the cheapest and the most expensive) are fresh products, rather than frozen, canned, or dehydrated.

Fresh fruit and vegetables are a tonic to dreary meals, and choosing them with care is important to the economy-minded shopper.

Prices change markedly from season to season for many items. Use these fresh foods generously when they are in peak supply and when they are offered at a good price.

Consider the condition of perishable fruit and vegetables and the facilities for storing at home in deciding how much to buy.

A can or a package of frozen fruit or vegetable or two cans or two packages sometimes are a little less or a little more than my family's appetite requires. I buy the container that best fits the needs for a meal (or more, as planned) and serve larger or smaller portions.

You may well compare the cost of the container of frozen or canned products and the cost of the amount of fresh produce needed for a meal. An example, for a family of four, may be: A pound can of peas (18 cents), a

10-ounce package of frozen peas (19.5 cents), and 2 pounds of fresh peas (38 cents).

In making such comparisons among different kinds of fruit and vegetables on the cost basis alone, differences in nutrient content are not considered. To be safest on this count, I choose a variety of fruit and vegetables, making sure to include a good source of vitamin C daily and a good source of vitamin A every other day.

Cost comparisons among some good and fair sources of vitamin C as listed in the food guide, at January prices in a Washington store, are given. One serving of a good source or two servings of a fair source are suggested daily. Therefore, costs are given for one serving for good sources and for two servings for fair sources.

	Cost of
Good sources of vitamin C:	*1 serving*
Orange juice, canned or frozen concentrate	$0. 05
Orange, navel, fresh.............	. 06
Grapefruit:	
Segments, canned..............	. 07
White, fresh....................	. 06
Broccoli, fresh or frozen..........	. 07
Strawberries:	
Frozen.......................	. 11
Fresh........................	. 14
Cantaloup................	not available

	Cost of
Fair sources of vitamin C:	*2 servings*
Cabbage served raw.............	$0. 03
Tomato juice, canned............	. 05
Tomatoes, canned...............	. 09
Potatoes, cooked in skins.........	. 09
Kale, frozen....................	. 09
Sweetpotatoes, cooked in skins.....	. 10
Spinach, frozen.................	. 12
Tomatoes, fresh.................	. 19
Watermelon....................	. 38

Similar comparisons of costs of servings of good sources of vitamin A are:

	Cost of
Good sources of vitamin A value:	*1 serving*
Carrots.......................	$0. 03
Kale, frozen....................	. 04
Sweetpotatoes..................	. 05
Spinach, frozen.................	. 06
Apricots, canned................	. 06
Broccoli, fresh or frozen.........	. 07
Winter squash, fresh.............	. 08
Cantaloup................	not available

BREADS AND CEREALS are an important part of each day's food because they give worthwhile amounts of many nutrients as well as food energy. They are well liked. They are easily fitted into meal plans. Many cost only a penny or two a serving.

To put these pennies to best use for good health, make sure that they are spent for whole-grain or enriched products.

Three and one-half loaves of unenriched white bread, costing about 75 cents, are needed to give the amount of thiamine (one of the B vitamins) in a loaf of enriched white bread, costing 21 cents, or a loaf of whole wheat bread, costing 24 cents.

Specialty breads, such as French, Italian, or raisin, often are not enriched. Check the wrapper to be sure.

Enriched spaghetti, macaroni, and noodles are superior to unenriched products in food value and sometimes cost less.

Parboiled rice is more nutritious than white milled rice. Even though parboiled rice costs more per serving, it is by far the best buy in food value.

Many ready-to-eat cereals give as much in nutrients and cost only a little more than cooked cereals. Small packages, coatings of sugar, and special flavorings add to the cost of the ready-to-eat kinds.

ASIDE FROM the four groups of foods, many other items find their way to your grocery cart, such as salad dressings, spreads for bread, sugar, beverages, pudding mixes, gelatin desserts, catsup and mustard, salt and pepper.

As a general rule, these foods add only calories (not necessarily nutrients) and spice to your meals. Calories and spice are needed, but in moderate amounts.

Sugar, sweets, fats, and oils often are used with other foods—sugar on cereals; margarine, butter, jam, and jelly as spreads on bread; and shortening for frying meat and seasoning vegetables and in salad dressing.

The cost of food energy from sugar and fat varies widely. One hundred Calories from granulated sugar may cost only a penny but as much as a dime from fancy candy. You get 100 Calories for less than a penny from margarine and other vegetable shortenings or for 2 cents or more from butter and fancy salad dressings.

Furthermore, weight-watchers will do well to forgo large amounts of sugar and fat in favor of other foods that give other nutrients needed for good nutrition.

What about savings from quantity buying? Be careful! The big economy size may mean only big waste at your house. If it can be used without waste, however, food in the large can or package is usually a good buy, but not always.

How can you tell? This is where the arithmetic comes in.

Look on the container for the net weight. It may be in small print, but it will be there. Divide the price on the container by the weight in ounces to find the cost of 1 ounce of food. The container with the lowest cost per ounce is the best buy.

For example, cornflakes are packaged in eight 1-ounce individual packs (32 cents), an 8-ounce pack (16 cents), and an 18-ounce pack (27 cents). By dividing the price by the number of ounces, we find the cornflakes in individual packs cost 4 cents an ounce; in the 8-ounce package, 2 cents an ounce; and in the 18-ounce package, 1.5 cents an ounce.

"Who cares about a 2-cent saving?" you may ask. But your family of four eating cornflakes every morning could save 70 cents a week by using the 18-ounce pack rather than individual packs.

So:

Plan meals to fit your family's nutrient needs, food likes, time schedule, and pocketbook.

Compare costs.

Know where your food dollars go.

Most of all, be proud of your job as food manager. (BETTY B. PETERKIN)

Plentiful

Foods

You can save up to 6 percent of your weekly food bill by buying meat, poultry, eggs, fruit, and vegetables when your local market has them in good supply and features them as sale items.

That means a sizable saving in a year. It is wise therefore to be flexible with your meal plans and serve the items that are in biggest supply.

Improvements in harvesting methods, packaging, transportation, and storage have extended the traditional season for most foods. But— especially for fresh fruit and vegetables—there is still a major harvest season when they are most plentiful in your locality.

Favorable weather or other crop and marketing conditions can bring about bumper harvests that overstock normal marketing channels. When there is a big supply of fresh produce on the market, prices tend to go down. That is the time to buy fresh fruit and vegetables.

For example, you may be tempted to serve fresh tomatoes and sweet corn in December, but unless they are in plentiful supply you may pay 14 cents a pound more for tomatoes and 29 cents more for six ears of corn in December than in peak harvest periods.

Another advantage is that fresh foods bought at harvest peak may be highest in flavor and nutritive value. A processed food in heavy supply probably was frozen, canned, or packed at the peak of quality.

Seasonal supply charts are good guides, but you should remember that they are guides and that supplies can vary year to year. Some years there is a short crop, and contrary to chart indications, the supply is limited.

Other years, the words "seasonally abundant" fail to describe the king-size harvests that exceed normal demands and may well cause problems of marketing. When that happens, the price to the grower drops, sometimes to levels below his cost of production.

At times you may have overbought something or purchased just the right amount but could not use it as you planned. On a large scale, that can happen to a producer, who harvests a larger crop than he expected or has the crop ready for market ahead of or behind schedule, and the deliveries overlap with those from other sections. Just like you, he has to revamp his plans to avoid waste. He tells people about the abundance.

This information is readily available. Through its plentiful foods program, the Department of Agriculture regularly issues reports about foods that are especially plentiful. Food editors of newspapers and magazines, retail merchants in advertisements and displays, and radio and TV broadcasters pass the information on to consumers.

Newspapers tell in articles, recipes, and pictures about an abundant food. Radio and television stations have spot announcements and other consumer service features. Extension consumer marketing and home agents make available interesting ideas. They are a product of cooperative endeavors of Government and private enterprise to help producers, sellers, and consumers.

An instance: Beef was especially plentiful during 1964 in the United States, which always has been a leading beef-consuming country. The producers, who raise these animals and feed them for market, had achieved the highest level of beef production ever recorded in this country. Beef was listed as a plentiful food.

Excellent beef was available in abundance in markets everywhere at good prices. The help of food editors and others was enlisted to develop new ways of serving beef. Suggestions for freezing it at home were made available. "Eat Beef" was added to the plethora of slogans that bombarded Americans, but it helped.

Consumers did eat beef and in so doing helped move a food abundance through the normal channels of trade, to the benefit of producers, packers, the food industry, and consumers, who were able to stretch their food budgets while beefing up their menus.

I offer some suggestions about the use of plentiful foods.

For some, turkey still means Thanksgiving and Christmas, but turkey now is available all year. Consumers willing to change their buying habits take advantage of summer turkey sales and serve turkey in new ways—stuffed and roasted, broiled, barbecued, fried, or served cold in sandwiches or salads.

The next time turkey is featured, do not look at the calendar but rather in the cookbook. Generally you pay less per pound for the larger turkeys, a 20-pound tom being cheaper per pound than 10-pounders. You get more meat in proportion to carcass on the big ones. Just be sure you can manage a big turkey.

Try this: Ask the meatman to saw a frozen turkey into halves or quarters. Wrap the pieces individually and place them in your homefreezer as soon as you can.

Modern methods of producing and processing keep the number of broiler-fryers that come to market in rather abundant supply all year. Grocers like to offer special sales on them to alternate with specials on other meats. If you find broilers on special sale, you may be able to save as much as 20 to 30 percent. Put them in your freezer.

Instead of roasting chickens, buy whole broiler-fryers of 2.5 pounds or more for stuffing and roasting. You may be able to save 10 cents a pound, or more.

For stewing, get a large broiler-fryer and simmer it to tenderness. The cooking time will be less, because these are young, tender birds. Stewed broiler-fryers are excellent in soups, stews, and casseroles.

Chicken necks can stretch your budget. Three pounds simmered slowly until the meat is easily removed from bones yield about three cups of dark meat, enough to serve six, for casseroles and croquettes.

The prices of beef vary because of greater demand for certain cuts, like porterhouse, rib, sirloin, and round steaks, as compared to chuck, brisket, plate, neck, and shank meat. Because ground beef usually is prepared from less popular cuts, it costs less.

Lean for lean and fat for fat, however, all cuts of beef are about the same in nutritional value. Variations in calories are related to the amount of fat that interlaces the lean meat. A well-balanced diet needs a certain amount of fat for proper digestion and utilization of the goodness in all foods.

Knowledge of the different cuts of beef helps one in buying beef. The demand for steaks and rib roasts is exceptionally high in some seasons. For example, summer cookouts create a heavy demand for steaks and barbecue meats. If roasts go on sale then, buy one, even if it is summer, or stock your freezer with several roasts.

Buying larger cuts of beef when they are featured can be a wise purchase, too. The trick is to have the meat cut into portions to suit your family needs. A rib roast five ribs thick may be too large for an average family; ask the meatman to remove the shortribs, cut off two or three rib steaks, and leave the two-rib roast. You now have the makings for three meals: A braised shortrib dish, broiled rib steaks, and a rib roast for a special dinner.

Small- and medium-size eggs sometimes sell for as much as one-fourth less than the large and extra-large size in the same grade, especially in late summer and early fall.

Always compare prices of eggs of different sizes within the same grade to see which is the best buy. It does vary. The size does not affect quality, but it does affect price. You should always judge egg quality by the grade, not by the size. There are Grade A Extra Large, Grade A Medium, and Grade A Small eggs as well as Grade B Extra Large, Grade B Medium, and so on.

To determine which eggs are the best buy, divide the cost of a dozen eggs by the number of ounces a dozen eggs weigh. That gives the cost per ounce, which, multiplied by 16 (ounces), gives the cost per pound, of the dozen eggs. The minimum weights per dozen are: Extra Large eggs, 27 ounces, or 1 pound 11 ounces; Large, 24 ounces, or 1 pound 8 ounces; Medium, 21 ounces, or 1 pound 5 ounces; Small, 18 ounces, or 1 pound 2 ounces.

For example, if Extra Large Grade A eggs sell for 86 cents a dozen, the price paid per pound is 51 cents. If Small Grade A eggs sell at 58 cents a dozen, the price per pound is 52 cents. The Extra Large eggs would be about 1 cent a pound cheaper. If, however, the Small Grade A eggs sell at 40 cents a dozen, the price per pound is 36 cents, or 15 cents a pound cheaper than the Extra Large Grade A eggs at 51 cents a dozen.

Fresh, frozen, canned, and dried fruits and vegetables are the mainstay of menus. The increase in processed foods makes it important for each consumer to keep a watchful eye on food advertisements. For many times the abundant supply is a processed food item rather than the fresh product.

Citrus fruit, root vegetables, cranberries, and apples generally are plentiful and more favorably priced in fall and winter. Fresh berries, melons, peaches, plums, and garden produce are in generous supply and lower in price during the late spring to fall harvest months. They are usually lowest in price in your community when it is harvesttime in the nearest growing district. Advances in transportation, however, make it possible for all to share in an abundant harvest miles away.

Budgets and appetites respond when plentiful fruits and vegetables are included in the shopping lists.

For example, if lettuce goes up in price (perhaps because of weather conditions that cut the size of the crop), consider using cabbage or endive for the salad or have a relish tray salad of carrot, green pepper, and celery.

Fresh oranges and grapefruit are most reasonably priced in January into April. In summer, the family can still enjoy citrus products in canned or frozen form. Many grocers feature frozen and canned orange, grapefruit, and lemon products in summer. Watch the advertisements so you can keep your freezer and cupboards well stocked.

You can also get vitamin C from tomatoes, raw cabbage, and some of the dark-green vegetables that may be in plentiful supply.

When a fresh product comes on the market, at the beginning of its harvest season, it may be higher in price than it will be after the harvest has been underway for awhile.

For instance, tomatoes may start coming onto the market in quantity in May, and prices may start dropping. But lowest prices usually do not come until midsummer, sometime in August, when the harvest is at its peak.

Keep checking the advertisements and keep a watchful eye on the various produce items when shopping, if you plan to buy in quantity for canning or stocking the freezer.

Canned and frozen foods often are bargains when grocers make their end-of-year inventory. January sales on odd lots of canned goods, discontinued lines, or lines that are moving slowly are good for stocking the cupboard.

Sometimes case-lot promotions are conducted in February and March. Fall by-the-case sales also are worth watching, especially if there is a generous new pack of the fruit or vegetable. It is important for the last year's pack to be moved in order to make room for the new. Sales of frozen food also gain momentum then.

Take advantage of special sales of salad and cooking oils. Buy by the quart, half gallon, or gallon for use in many ways, like these:

Add 1 tablespoon salad oil per layer when whipping up a packaged cake mix. The result is extra lightness.

Brush gelatin and candy molds lightly with oil before using. The molded creations will come out easily.

To keep macaroni, rice, noodles, and spaghetti separated during cooking and also to keep water from boiling over, add a tablespoon of oil per cup of boiling water.

Cakes, cupcakes, and breads will have evenly browned, unbroken crusts when the pans are brushed lightly with vegetable oil and then dusted lightly with flour before the batter or dough is added. (JOYCE SEARLES SHORT)

USDA Grades

USDA (United States Department of Agriculture) grades for food are a dependable, nationally uniform guide to quality and a means of making valid comparisons of quality and price.

Beef, lamb, butter, poultry, and eggs are the products most likely to carry the USDA grade shield.

This official emblem of quality is not so widely used on other foods, although it is available for use on many others.

The food that carries the USDA grade shield—usually with the designation U.S. Grade A or AA, or (for meat) U.S. Choice—measures up to a definite standard of quality, as determined by a Government grader who has examined it. It is clean and wholesome.

Processors and packers who wish to employ Government grading services and have their product carry the USDA grade shield must meet strict requirements for plant sanitation and operating procedure.

Meat and poultry must be inspected for wholesomeness if they are to be graded.

Products with the shield are not the only ones graded. Your grocery store may do most of its buying on the basis of USDA grades. Wholesale grades, such as U.S. No. 1, marked on containers of fresh fruit and vegetables often carry through to the retail level. They may appear on consumer packages of such commodities as potatoes, onions, apples, and citrus fruits.

THE DEPARTMENT OF AGRICULTURE performs three functions that have to do with the quality and wholesomeness of food—standardization, grading, and inspection.

Since food, as a product of Nature, comes in varying degrees of quality, some way of sorting it out—grading it—is needed.

Before you can grade a product, you have to have a standard measure of quality, in the same way you need a standard measure of quantity, such as a pound, a bushel, or a quart, before you can measure how much.

Standards for grades of quality cannot be quite so precise as measures of quantity. They are based on the attributes of a product that determine its value and its usefulness.

For instance, consumers have said they want tenderness, juiciness, and flavor in a beefsteak. In order to develop standards for grades of beef, then, it is necessary to identify the factors that indicate how tender, juicy, and flavorful the meat from a particular beef carcass will be.

The standards for beef accordingly take into account the amount of marbling (fat interspersed within the lean), the color, firmness, and texture of the meat, and the age of the animal.

Standards for each product describe the entire range of quality. The number of grades for a product depends upon its variability. It takes eight grades to span the range of beef quality, for example, but only three are required for frying chickens, since their quality varies less than beef does.

Specialists in the Department of Agriculture have developed and published grade standards for more than 300 farm products.

They develop new ones as they are needed and revise the established ones to reflect changes in production, use, and marketing practices.

The standards are widely used by processors and packers for their own quality-control programs. The use of the Department of Agriculture grading services, often operated in cooperation with State departments of agriculture, is voluntary, unless required under State or local law or an industry program. They are provided on a fee-for-service basis, not at Government expense.

Inspection for wholesomeness, on the other hand, is a Department service that is required under Federal law for meat and poultry destined for interstate or foreign trade and therefore is provided at Government expense. Inspection in this sense does not relate to the quality of the food—only to its fitness for human food.

Here, for use as a shopping guide, is a summary of the kinds of products graded, the grade names, and an explanation of what the grades mean in each case.

SIX KINDS OF MEAT are graded: Beef, veal, calf, lamb, yearling mutton, and mutton.

The grade names, U.S. Prime, U.S. Choice, and U.S. Good, can apply to all, except that mutton is not eligible for the Prime grade. There are lower grades for each of these meats, also, which differ slightly in terminology but are not likely to be seen in retail stores.

The next three lower grades for beef, U.S. Standard, U.S. Commercial, and U.S. Utility, may appear on occasion on retail counters. A store usually carries only one grade—the one it has found pleases most of its customers.

U.S. Prime, the top grade of beef, is produced from young and well-fed beef-type cattle. Meat of this grade is liberally marbled. Roasts and steaks are tender, juicy, and flavorful. Most of the supply of Prime beef is sold to restaurants and hotels.

U.S. Choice is the grade preferred by most consumers and is widely available at retail. It is of high quality and usually has less fat than Prime beef. Roasts and steaks from the loin, rib, and top round in this grade are tender and juicy. Other cuts, such as those from the bottom round or chuck, which are more suitable for pot roasting or braising, are juicy and have a well-developed flavor.

U.S. Good grade beef is lean but of fairly good quality. Although cuts of this grade lack the juiciness and flavor associated with a higher degree of fatness, their relative tenderness and high proportion of lean to fat please many thrifty shoppers.

U.S. Standard grade beef has very little fat and a mild flavor. It lacks juiciness but is relatively tender, since it comes from young animals.

U.S. Commercial beef comes from older cattle and therefore lacks tenderness. Long, slow cooking with moist heat is required for most cuts to develop the rich, full flavor of mature beef.

VEAL is produced from animals that are 3 months or less in age; calf from animals between 3 months and 8 months old. The higher grades of veal, U.S. Prime and Choice, are more thickly fleshed than the lower grades and have a higher proportion of meat to bone.

Also, they have more fat and therefore are more juicy and flavorful. No grade of veal, however, has enough fat intermingled with the lean to make cooking with dry heat practical. Moist heat is needed to insure juiciness and development of flavor. Calf is intermediate between veal and beef in its texture, flavor, and tenderness.

MEAT produced from sheep is divided into three classes, according to its age when slaughtered—lamb, yearling mutton, and mutton.

Most of the sheep produced in this country are marketed as lamb. Because lamb is produced from young animals, most of the cuts of the higher grades are tender enough to be cooked by dry heat—roasting, broiling, and pan broiling.

Yearling mutton comes from animals between 1 and 2 years old. It is produced in limited quantities, but is preferred by some people because it is more flavorful than lamb. Chops and legs of the higher grades are tender enough to be cooked by dry heat.

Mutton, which comes from mature animals, lacks natural tenderness and should be braised or pot roasted.

SIX KINDS OF POULTRY are graded: Turkey, chicken, duck, goose, guinea, squab.

The grade names are U.S. Grade A, U.S. Grade B, and U.S. Grade C.

Poultry grades are based on the conformation, or fleshing, of the bird—the proportion of meat to bone; the finish—the amount of fat in and under the skin, which tends to keep the meat moist and tender while cooking; and the absence or degree of defects such as cuts, tears, and bruises.

The "class" of the bird, which will appear on the label, is a guide to tenderness and to the appropriate cooking method. "Class" is indicated by the words "young," "mature," or "old," and by such terms as "broiler," "roaster," "stewing hen."

Much of the poultry produced is graded and is identified at retail with the USDA grade shield.

Usually only U.S. Grade A is identified. Lower grades are seldom, if ever, labeled as such.

EGGS ARE GRADED for size and for quality. There is no relation between size and quality.

The grade names for quality are Fresh Fancy Quality or U.S. Grade AA, U.S. Grade A, and U.S. Grade B.

For size, the names are U.S. Jumbo, Extra Large, Large, Medium, Small, and Peewee.

The two higher grades of quality have a large proportion of thick white, which stands up well around a firm, high yolk. They are delicate in flavor. Grade B eggs have a thinner white, which spreads over a wide area when broken. The yolk is rather flat and may break easily.

The term "Fresh Fancy Quality" is used only on eggs that have been produced under a special quality-control program designed to insure freshness as well as high quality.

Official egg sizes are based on weight per dozen, not size of the individual egg, although variation of sizes of individual eggs within a dozen is limited by the standards. Minimum weight of a dozen Large eggs is 24 ounces; Medium, 21 ounces; Small, 18 ounces, and so on. There is a 3-ounce difference between each weight class.

OF THE DAIRY PRODUCTS, butter, Cheddar and Swiss cheese, and nonfat dry milk are graded.

A quality-control program and "Quality Approved" rating is available for process cheese, cottage cheese, sour cream, and buttermilk.

Grade names: U.S. Grade AA, U.S. Grade A, and U.S. Grade B for both butter and Cheddar cheese. They are the same for Swiss cheese, except there is no U.S. Grade AA. (There is also a Grade C for Cheddar and C and D grades for Swiss cheese.)

Grades for nonfat dry milk are U.S. Extra Grade and U.S. Standard Grade.

The higher grades of butter have a pleasing and desirable sweet flavor and are made only from cream that has such flavor. Grade B butter is generally made from selected sour cream and therefore lacks the fresh flavor of the top grades.

The top grades of cheese indicate desirable and consistent flavor, body, and texture, as appropriate for the type of cheese, which in Cheddar includes sharp, mellow, and mild. Labeling of cheese with the U.S. grade shield is not widespread, though much of it is graded at wholesale.

The U.S. grade shield on a package of nonfat dry milk is assurance of dependable quality and compliance with sanitary requirements. It is also assurance, in the case of "instant" nonfat dry milk, that the milk powder will in fact dissolve instantly.

MOST FRESH FRUIT and vegetables are packed and sold on the wholesale market on the basis of U.S. grades. There are standards for 72 different kinds. Thirteen "consumer standards" have been developed for use at the retail level but are seldom used.

The typical range of grades used at wholesale for fresh fruit and vegetables includes U.S. Fancy, U.S. No. 1, U.S. No. 2. There are sometimes grades above and below that range. For instance, grades for apples are U.S. Extra Fancy, U.S. Fancy, U.S. No. 1, and U.S. Utility. The "consumer grades" are, generally, U.S. Grades A, B, and C.

Grades for fresh fruit and vegetables are determined on the basis of the product's color, size, shape, degree of maturity, and freedom from defects. Defects may be those caused by dirt, freezing, disease, insects, or mechanical injury.

GRADES have been developed for a great variety of processed fruits and vegetables, canned, dried, and frozen, and a number of related products, such as peanut butter, jams, jellies, pickles, olives, honey, and orange juice crystals.

The usual grade names are U.S. Grade A or U.S. Fancy; U.S. Grade B or U.S. Choice or U.S. Extra Standard; U.S. Grade C or U.S. Standard. There are few exceptions to this pattern.

U.S. Grade A (or Fancy) indicates an excellent quality in processed fruit and vegetables, uniformity in size and color, virtual freedom from defects, and the proper degree of maturity or tenderness. This grade is suited for special uses, as in desserts or salads, where appearance and texture are important.

U.S. Grade B is a good quality, just as nutritious as the top grade, but the product may be less uniform in size and color and less tender and free from blemishes. Most processed fruit and vegetables are of this grade. It is quite satisfactory for most uses.

U.S. Grade C indicates fairly good quality. The product is just as wholesome and may be as nutritious as the higher grades.

Only a limited amount of processed fruits and vegetables and related products are marked with the U.S. grade shield, which means that a Government grader has examined the product and certified that it is the quality stated.

Hundreds of processors, however, employ the grade standards in packing and selling processed fruit and vegetables. They may use the grade name, without the "U.S." in front of it, on their labels, even though the product has not been examined by a Government grader, as long as the quality actually is as good as indicated by the grade name.

If the quality does not measure up to the grade claimed, the processor is liable to prosecution under laws on mislabeling.

MILLED (white) and brown rice, dry edible beans, peas, and lentils are graded.

The grades are: For milled (white) rice, U.S. Grades 1, 2, 3, 4, 5, and 6; for brown rice, U.S. Grades 1, 2, 3, 4, and 5; for beans and peas, U.S. Grades 1, 2, and 3; for lentils, U.S. Grades 1 and 2.

For dry beans there are also special handpicked grades that are adapted to use at retail. They include U.S. No. 1 Choice Handpicked, U.S. No. 1 Handpicked, U.S. No. 2 Handpicked, and U.S. No. 3 Handpicked.

The grades for rice are based on such factors as the absence or degree of defective kernels (broken kernels or those damaged by heat, water, or insects); mixed varieties (which may affect cooking qualities); and objectionable foreign material. General appearance and color also are considered.

Grades for beans, peas, and lentils are based on factors such as color and absence or presence of defects, foreign material, and beans, peas, or lentils of different classes.

Grades for all of these products are widely used in the trade but seldom appear on retail packages. Some packages of rice are marked with the grade name. (ELEANOR FERRIS)

Wholesome

Meat and Poultry

YOU ALREADY KNOW—or take for granted—that you can buy federally inspected meat and poultry products with confidence that they are wholesome.

You can also be sure that they are truthfully labeled. If you read the label, you can learn what you are paying for and put the information on the label to work for you.

The law requires that the label on a federally inspected meat or poultry product carry five items of information:

The true name of the product, such as frankfurter, beef pot pie, kosher salami, or chicken cacciatore.

A list of the ingredients, beginning with the one greatest in weight or volume.

The name and address of the processor or distributor.

The weight, if it is shown, must be accurate.

The inspection stamp or mark.

ALL MEAT products prepared under Federal supervision must carry a "U.S. Inspected and Passed" stamp, and poultry products must carry the "Inspected for Wholesomeness" mark.

On meat, you may see this stamp (abbreviated to "U.S. INSP'D & P'S'D"), in purple on large cuts, although often the butcher trims it off at the retail market. (This purple color is safe. You need not trim it off, unless you dislike purple.)

On fresh poultry and uncooked frozen poultry, the stamp usually is attached as a tag to the wing of the bird, printed on the plastic film wrapper, or on the wrapper enclosing the giblets.

On prepared foods, such as frozen meat dinners, bologna, or chicken pies, the mark of inspection is printed on the package, can, or label.

This stamp, whether on fresh or prepared meats, is your assurance that the product is wholesome. It tells you that the animal or bird was healthy; the carcass and all its parts were examined individually; other ingredients, if any, are wholesome; and the product was handled in a clean plant, under sanitary conditions.

The stamp also assures you that the label is truthful. That is because the Department of Agriculture must approve all labels on products processed under its supervision before the labels are used. The Federal inspector in the plant makes sure that the labels are used properly.

HOW CAN THE LABEL help you get what you pay for?

Chile con carne, a cooked-meat product, is an example. If it is a federally inspected product, it must contain at least 40 percent meat on a fresh-weight basis. You can be sure that the inspector in the plant saw to it that the batch of chile met that requirement.

Since the meat is cooked, it would be hard for you to identify the kind of meat used if you had to depend on your own taste after it has been seasoned with chili and other spices. The Federal inspector is in the plant to make sure that if the label says beef, and if it has no other meat listed in the statement of ingredients, the chile does not contain meat from the head or heart.

Sometimes head, cheek, or heart meat are used. When they are, they cannot exceed 25 percent of the total meat, and they must be identified in the ingredients statement on the label. These are wholesome, nutritious meats, but generally less expensive than the beef cuts you may use at home. The statement of ingredients can help you judge the product that best suits your taste.

If the label says, "chile (or chili) con carne with beans," the meat content is less than in "chile con carne." Regulations specify that this product, if it bears the mark of Federal inspection, must contain at least 25 percent meat on a fresh-weight basis.

Whatever chile you decide to buy, if the Federal stamp is on it, you can know that ingredients other than meat are limited, too.

For instance, a chile con carne mixture may not contain more than 8 percent of such ingredients as cereals, flour, vegetable starch, and nonfat dry milk, either individually or altogether. The Federal inspector in the plant is there to see that no more of these ingredients, which are less expensive than meat, are used than permitted in the regulations.

THE LABELS on other products can help in the same way.

For instance, you can learn whether frankfurters are all beef, all meat, or meat with cereals or contain nonfat dry milk or other additives.

You can find out what kind of meat is in the bologna of your choice, the salami, luncheon loaf, and any other kind of sausage or meat food product

that comes from a federally inspected plant.

As to poultry, the label on one of the new frozen products—for example, turkey roll—tells whether the roll contains all breast meat, white and dark meat combined, or all dark meat. This information helps you to suit your taste and your pocketbook.

Federal regulations for both meat and poultry products limit the amounts of other ingredients used in their preparation, although these limits vary with the item.

In frankfurters, for instance, ingredients such as cereals or nonfat dry milk are limited to 3.5 percent of the weight of the finished product, regardless of whether those ingredients are used individually or in combination.

You can see why this is an important area in which Federal inspection offers you protection. Products, like frankfurters and chicken croquettes, that are made by grinding, chopping, and mixing, afford opportunity for the excessive use of the less-expensive ingredients if their production is not supervised.

Even though these other ingredients may be safe, you do not want to pay for more water or cereal or nonfat dry milk than is necessary to prepare the product properly.

FEDERAL inspection is required only in processing plants that ship in interstate trade. Not all plants engage in interstate commerce. Thus, only about 65 percent of prepared meat foods are handled under Federal supervision. The percentage is higher for animals inspected at the time of slaughter. About 84 percent of all commercial slaughter is conducted under Federal inspection.

Products prepared for sale only within a State are not subject to Federal inspection.

Some State and local governments require inspection. Some do not. Some States and municipalities have strict requirements for labels; some do not. About 90 percent of the slaughter and processing of poultry are handled under Federal inspection. Some plants that sell only within a State can qualify for and receive Federal inspection for poultry if they pay the cost.

The Federal program for both meat and poultry provides for continuous supervision in all plants operating under its jurisdiction, a standard that is met by few other systems.

Meat inspection is one of the oldest services provided by the Federal Government for the protection of consumers. The first Meat Inspection Act was passed in 1906. Meat inspection has been a continuous function of the United States Department of Agriculture ever since.

The Federal inspection of poultry came later and has been extended as the production of poultry has shifted to large-scale enterprises.

Both programs are geared to keep pace with new techniques, like freeze-drying and other packing processes, as they are developed by industry. (CLARENCE H. PALS)

Protecting

Quality

OUR LAWS contain many aids to help you in the economical and satisfying purchase and use of food.

In some fields—the safety and cleanliness of food, for instance—the law takes over to do what the consumer cannot do.

In others, the law is designed rather to help the informed consumer to help himself.

Commercially processed foods must be clean and wholesome and prepared under sanitary conditions. That is the law. Spoiled tomatoes may not be used in tomato catsup. Insect-infested and rodent-contaminated wheat may not be used for flour. Bakery employees who prepare creampuffs must take care to avoid contamination of the cream filling. Storage warehouses must see to it that foods are kept clean and sanitary. To fail in any of these respects is to violate the law.

The housewife therefore ordinarily need not worry about the cleanliness of the foods she buys.

Inspectors of the Food and Drug Administration (FDA) periodically visit all kinds of food processing and storage establishments to check on sanitary conditions.

When they find violations—rarely, considering the thousands of firms involved—the matter is taken to court. Unfit products can be removed from the market through Federal court seizure. Firms can be fined, and individuals can be put in jail.

You can be of help to FDA in enforcing the law by reporting suspected violations. Reports may be made to FDA regional offices or to headquarters in Washington. The report should give the brand name, the place and date of purchase, the name of the firm listed on the label, and any code marks on the top of the can or elsewhere on the package.

THE LAW says foods must not only be clean. They must also be safe to eat.

The housewife does not have the means and skills to examine fresh fruit and vegetables for residues of pesticides or to check processed food for harmful preservatives or other additives. She has, in effect, through the Congress, created rules to protect the safety of foods and Government agencies to enforce the rules.

The manufacturer of a pesticide must conduct research to show it safe before he can sell it. He must register (with the Department of Agriculture) the label he will use.

He must show how much residue will remain on the crop if his label directions are followed. He must submit to FDA (which is a unit of the Department of Health, Education, and Welfare) the results of tests to show that this amount of residue will not be harmful to persons, even if they eat the food for a lifetime.

The safety of food additives and color additives must also be proved to the Government (FDA) in advance of their use in foods. Inspections are made of growers and processors.

Thousands of samples are tested in FDA laboratories each year to see that the safety rules for pesticides and additives are followed.

This protection extends to the additives in animal feeds and to veterinary drugs to be sure that there is no harmful contamination of milk, meat, eggs, or other food byproduct for human use.

Thus when you read a list of ingredients on a food package and see something like "Butylated hydroxyanisole added to prevent rancidity," you need not worry about whether it is safe. If its safety were in question, FDA could and would stop its use.

If you prefer nevertheless to buy a product without the preservative, this is your prerogative, too. That is why the label must tell you the additive is there.

The food label must contain other useful information.

It must tell the common or usual name of the food, not just some fancy name the manufacturer might wish to use. If it is made from two or more ingredients, the label must name them (except for the standardized foods I discuss later).

The label must tell the amount of food in the package. It must give the name and address of the manufacturer, packer, or distributor. If the food is intended for use in weight control or the treatment or management of disease or other special dietary use, the label must give the special information the user needs.

The label must not give details that are false or misleading. The package must not deceive the consumer as to what or how much is in the package. Any picture or vignette on the label must be an honest representation of the food in the package.

The package must not deceive the consumer as to the amount of food in it, even though a correct statement of contents is given on the label.

Labels are the shopper's friend. Read them!

FOODS FOR SPECIAL dietary use must have additional labeling.

Examples are foods designed for use by infants, pregnant and lactating women, obese persons, and persons who must restrict their intake of sodium or of ordinary sweets.

To illustrate: If a food is intended for use, say, by a person on a low-sodium diet, the label must state how much sodium is in a specified amount of the food so the user can calculate his intake of sodium over a period of time.

If the food purports to have special value because of its nutrient content, the label must tell how much of the particular nutrients it contains.

A vitamin-mineral preparation, for example, must give the amount of each vitamin and mineral in terms of the proportion of the daily requirement of each it supplies. If the daily requirement has not been established, that fact must be stated. If there is no known need for the particular factor in human nutrition, that fact also must be stated.

A revision of the special dietary food regulations was begun in 1962. The Food and Drug Administration proposed, among other things, to establish standards for the kind and amounts of nutrients deemed appropriate for vitamin and mineral food supplements.

Here, again: The wise consumer looks for and uses the additional information on the labels of such foods.

MANY BASIC FOODS have been standardized by Government regulation. Consumers, manufacturers, and Government technicians help set the standards.

A definition and standard of identity is something like an official recipe for the food. All brands of such a standardized food must contain the important ingredients the consumer is entitled to expect in the amounts or proportions expected.

All brands thus will have the same nutritional value, although different brands may vary as to flavor, texture, or some other factor controlled by optional ingredients permitted by the standard.

CONSUMERS CAN USE this information about standardized foods to shop for the most economical buy, in the absence of a preference for some particular brand, recognizing that the basic ingredients and nutritional quality of all brands are the same.

In order to use the standards, however, it is essential to know the difference in major classes of standardized foods.

For example, if the housewife is to shop wisely for the macaroni-noodle type of product, she must at least know that macaroni, spaghetti, and vermicelli can all be made from the same dough, but noodles must contain egg yolk or whole eggs, which are not required in the macaroni-type product.

Before you can shop wisely for food dressings, you should know that mayonnaise contains a minimum of 65 percent of oil, but salad dressing need contain only 30 percent. The oil content is an important factor in the price.

Such standards are called standards of identity.

Minimum standards of quality also have been set for most canned fruit and vegetables to assure that the quality will not fall below that reasonably expected.

If the quality of a food falls below the minimum required by the standard, special labeling must tell the purchaser of this fact.

These standards of minimum quality are not to be confused with the quality grades administered by the Department of Agriculture or with the manufacturers' own brand-labeling systems to designate different degrees of quality above the minimum.

Standards of fill of container have also been set for certain foods, such as canned shrimp and oysters, canned tuna, and a number of canned fruit and vegetable products to assure reasonable uniformity in the amount of food in the container.

Such standards are particularly useful if the food is packed in a liquid that may or may not be consumed.

PROTECTION of consumers in a rapidly changing technology requires continuous research.

Research programs are carried on to investigate potential food contaminants, develop laboratory techniques for law enforcement, and improve methods of detecting and identifying the most minute contamination of milk and food crops by residues of pesticides.

The amount of pesticide residue and radioactivity in the total diet of a typical teenager is kept under continuing surveillance in several geographical locations throughout the country.

Such studies are an "early warning" system against the possibility that our food supply might become dangerously contaminated from excessive or unwise use of pesticides or as a result of radioactive fallout.

IMPORTANT ADVANCES have been achieved in the identification of potentially toxic materials produced by certain molds that grow on peanuts and cereal grains.

Methods for the rapid screening of new food ingredients for toxicity are under continuous study and improvement.

Training courses in the use of the most advanced scientific instruments are carried on for personnel of headquarters and regional offices of the Food and Drug Administration.

Such research underwrites continued consumer confidence in the safety and integrity of our food supply. (JAMES L. TRAWICK)

Saving
Food Values

THE ATTRACTIVE, flavorful, and nutritious foods you so carefully select for your family can lose their color, flavor, and texture and some of their vitamins and minerals before they reach the table. How much depends on how you store, trim, and cook them.

From harvest to table, some loss of nutrients is inevitable. Some nutrients, such as carbohydrates (sugars and starches), are well retained during storage and cooking.

Others, such as some of the vitamins and minerals, are easily lost from certain foods, although they are well retained in others.

Vitamin C and thiamine are among the least stable. Measures that protect them from destruction and loss usually will protect the more stable nutrients as well.

Methods of storage and preparation that conserve nutrients usually preserve the most appetizing color, flavor, and texture, too.

GOOD STORAGE conditions can slow down the loss and destruction of food values and retard spoilage. Many perishable foods need to be refrigerated.

In a drawing, "Guide to Refrigerator Storage," are tips on the kinds of foods to refrigerate, the placement of foods in the refrigerator, and the approximate length of storage.

Most fresh vegetables need refrigeration, but some keep better when stored outside the refrigerator.

Sweetpotatoes, mature onions, winter squash, turnips, and rutabagas should be stored at cool room temperatures, about 60° F. White potatoes need darkness and cool temperatures of 45° to 50°.

If storage at those temperatures is not possible, buy only a week's supply of those vegetables at one time.

Unripe tomatoes should be ripened in the light but not in direct sunlight. Temperatures of 60° to 75° are best to produce a full red color and to maintain high vitamin C content.

Bananas darken in the refrigerator. Store them at room temperature.

Unripe melons and pineapples ripen better at cool room temperature (60° to 70°) than at refrigerator temperature; after ripening, they can be stored a short time in the refrigerator.

Citrus fruit can be stored for a short time at cool room temperatures or in the refrigerator.

Bread stays fresher longer in a breadbox at room temperature than in the refrigerator, but storage in a refrigerator during hot, humid weather will prevent the formation of mold.

Cereals, flour, spices, and sugar can be stored at room temperature. The containers should be tightly covered to keep out dust, moisture, and insects.

Nonfat dry milk and unopened canned milk keep well at room temperature. Because dry milk takes up moisture and becomes lumpy and stale when exposed to air, close the package tightly. Reconstituted dry milk and opened canned milk should be refrigerated like fresh milk.

Canned foods should be kept in a cool, dry place. Because losses in food value do occur gradually with time, canned foods should be used and replaced within a year.

CAREFUL TRIMMING is necessary to improve the appearance, texture, and flavor of many foods, but too much trimming causes unnecessary loss of nutrients.

The dark-green leaves of vegetables are higher in most nutrients than the stems and midribs. When you discard the green outer leaves of cabbage and

GUIDE TO REFRIGERATOR STORAGE

FROZEN FOOD	**FREEZER AT 0° F.**

FRESH MEAT, POULTRY, FISH
Loosely wrapped
   Roasts, steaks, chops—
      3 to 5 days
   Ground meats, variety
    meats, poultry, fish—
      1 to 2 days

MILK, CREAM, CHEESE
Tightly covered
   Milk, cream, cottage
    cheese, cream cheese—
      3 to 5 days
   Hard cheese—
      Several weeks

COLDEST PART OF REFRIGERATOR

BUTTER, MARGARINE
Tightly covered — 2 weeks

EGGS
Covered — 1 week

MAYONNAISE AND OTHER SALAD DRESSINGS—*Covered*
   Refrigerate after opening

OPENED CANNED FOODS, FRESH OR RECONSTITUTED JUICE
Tightly covered

NUTS
Tightly covered
PEANUT BUTTER
   Refrigerate after opening

FRESH FRUITS, RIPE—*Uncovered*

Apples—1 week

Berries } 1 to 2 days
Cherries }

Apricots }
Grapes }
Pears } 3 to 5 days
Peaches }
Plums }
Rhubarb }

SOME FRESH VEGETABLES—*Uncovered*

Ripe tomatoes
Corn in husk

Lima beans } In pods
Peas }

OTHER PARTS OF REFRIGERATOR

MOST FRESH VEGETABLES

Leafy green vegetables	Beets	Cucumbers
Asparagus	Cabbage	Green onions
Brussels sprouts	Carrots	Peppers
Cauliflower	Broccoli	Radishes
Summer squash	Celery	Snap beans

CRISPER AND/OR PLASTIC BAG

lettuce and the leaves of broccoli, you are throwing away nutritious parts of the vegetables. On the other hand, removing the stems and midribs from kale and collard greens involves smaller losses of nutrients.

Some roots and tubers, such as carrots, potatoes, and turnips, can be cooked in their skins—a good way to conserve nutrients, color, and flavor. Beets usually are cooked before peeling to prevent excessive loss of color.

Cut surfaces of such fruit as apples, pears, and peaches darken rapidly when exposed to air. To prevent darkening, peel and cut the fruit just before use or sprinkle it with citrus fruit juice or pineapple juice.

When you peel vegetables, remove only a thin layer.

When trimming or shredding, always use a sharp blade to prevent bruising. Losses of vitamins A and C occur when tissues are bruised.

Wash and stem berries and cherries just before use. They lose vitamin C and spoil quickly if they are washed and stemmed before storage.

It is necessary to wash some foods before you use them. Fruit and vegetables always should be washed thoroughly. Washing rice before cooking is not recommended, however, because it causes loss of nutrients.

If meat needs surface cleaning, it should be wiped with a clean, damp cloth or paper towel. Dipping meat into water or soaking it causes loss of soluble nutrients and flavor.

Raw fruit and vegetables introduce variety in color, flavor, and texture to meals. Cooking changes color, flavor, and texture and causes some loss of nutrients, even when carefully done.

COOKING, however, is necessary to make some foods acceptable. Well-cooked foods look and taste good and retain most of their nutrients.

To help you make sure that the food you serve is both appetizing and nutritious, we give some suggestions.

Cook most foods at low to moderate temperatures. High temperatures cause meat and poultry to shrink excessively, fats to break down and smoke, and eggs and cheese to become rubbery.

At high temperatures, custards are likely to curdle, and milk may acquire a scorched taste. High temperatures also speed the destruction of thiamine (vitamin B_1) and vitamin C.

Use no more water than necessary for cooking vegetables, rice, spaghetti, macaroni, noodles, and other foods cooked in liquid.

When you cook food in a large amount of liquid and then discard the liquid, you are throwing away valuable water-soluble vitamins and minerals. Some of the flavor goes down the drain, too.

Cooking "strong-flavored" vegetables, such as cabbage, in a large amount of water was thought once to make them milder. That wastes nutrients. Even "strong-flavored" vegetables can be cooked in a small amount of water if they are cooked briefly—just long enough to make them tender.

Leafy vegetables often can be cooked in just the water clinging to the leaves after washing.

Rice simmered in approximately twice its volume of water should absorb all of the water by the time cooking is completed. It will retain nutrients better than rice cooked in a large amount of water. Rice should not be rinsed after cooking, because nutrients will be lost.

Use a pan with a tight-fitting lid when you boil, braise, or simmer food. A tight-fitting lid holds in most of the steam and shortens the cooking time. Escaping steam carries with it some of the flavor. Prolonged cooking destroys nutrients.

Even green vegetables cooked in a covered pan retain their natural color fairly well if cooked just until tender. They turn an unattractive olive color only if overcooked.

Do not overcook. Cooking too long makes meat, poultry, and fish dry and tough, eggs and cheese curdled or rubbery, baked products dry and crusty, and vegetables mushy and discolored. It also causes them to lose part of their thiamine and vitamin C, which are easily destroyed by too much heat.

Serve foods as soon as possible after cooking. Holding hot foods at serving temperature is like overcooking them.

Use, do not discard, liquids in which you cook vegetables, meat drippings, and liquids drained from canned foods. Add them to gravies, soups, sauces, and gelatin dishes to enhance nutritive value and flavor.

Refrigerate leftovers as soon as possible and use them within a day or two. Cooked vegetables lose part of their nutritive value and appeal during storage and reheating. Do not count on them to be as nutritious or appetizing as freshly prepared vegetables.

Serve leftover meats cold or reheat them briefly. (BARBARA H. BLUESTONE and PATRICIA K. VANDERSALL)

Storing
Frozen Foods

THE ORIGINAL fresh flavor, color, texture, and nutritive value of frozen foods will reach the table only if they are protected during storage.

Frozen foods need a temperature of 0° F. or lower if they are to keep their top quality longer than a few days or weeks.

At zero, frozen foods change slowly, and fresh qualities are preserved.

Extremely cold temperatures inhibit the growth of spoilage organisms and slow down chemical changes in the food itself and reactions between the food and oxygen in the air around the food.

At higher temperatures, changes speed up; foods may discolor, change texture, lose nutrients, and develop off-flavors.

The length of time a frozen food is stored is just as important as the temperature of storage. There will be eventual changes in all foods, even in those held at zero. Some foods may be kept longer than others before any change is noticeable.

Most fruit and vegetables, beef and lamb roasts, and whole chickens and turkeys are relatively stable when good storage practices are followed.

Other foods are more sensitive. Shorter holding periods are recommended for such foods as pork, cut-up poultry, ground meats, and prepared or precooked products.

The relationship between temperature of storage and the length of time foods are held is highly important.

Deterioration in frozen foods accelerates rapidly with a rise in storage temperature. For example, experienced food tasters were able to detect a change in flavor from the original freshness of frozen strawberries after a year's storage at 0°, after 2 months' storage at 10°, and after only 9 days' storage at 30°.

Proper packaging also is important. Moisture-vapor-proof and moisture-vapor-resistant materials prevent the food from drying out and protect it from contact with air, which may cause oxidized off-flavors to develop.

Information on the materials and methods for packaging different kinds of food for homefreezing is given in manuals available from the freezer industry, State extension services, and the Department of Agriculture.

Commercially frozen foods already have the packaging they need.

To give frozen foods the best environment possible, two basic rules should be followed.

First, know the capabilities and limitations of your equipment.

Second, tailor your storage and use of frozen foods to these capabilities and limitations.

In American homes, frozen foods are stored in separate freezers, in the freezer compartment of combination refrigerator-freezers, and in the ice-making and iceholding area of conventional refrigerators. This area often is called "frozen food compartment."

Sometimes it is difficult to distinguish between a combination refrigerator-freezer and a conventional refrigerator.

You may be sure it is a refrigerator-freezer if each compartment has its own exterior door. The refrigerator-freezer with a single exterior door has a solid piece separating the freezer section from the refrigerator area, and the inner door to the freezer section is insulated.

In the conventional refrigerator, a removable drip tray separates the frozen food compartment from the general storage area, and the door to the compartment is not insulated.

Homefreezers and most combination refrigerator-freezers can maintain a storage temperature of 0° or lower and are well suited for long-term storage of frozen foods. If you have this type of equipment, your first concern is to make sure that the temperature is actually zero in the storage area. The fact that packages are hard frozen to the touch is no assurance they have the storage temperature they need.

If the storage area in your freezer is not equipped with a thermometer, buy one so that you can check the temperature. Then adjust the thermostat or temperature control to attain 0° in the warmest spot in the storage area.

Door storage in some combination refrigerator-freezers is a few degrees warmer than the cold-storage area, and food kept there should not be stored as long as those in the zero area.

Zero storage space gives you latitude in selecting food for the freezer and planning for its use. Consider family preferences and the susceptibility of the food to change during storage.

It is sensible to store quantities of a variety of food especially liked and used often in family meals, but it does not make sense to store such a large amount that the food cannot be used while still in its prime.

A year's supply of favorite fruit frozen in season at the peak of quality and stored at zero will give you good eating throughout the year.

Ice cream, however, can be expected to keep its top quality for only about a month, and storing more than the family will use in that time means poorer eating quality.

Zero storage offers convenience in many ways to all users. Those who grow some of their own food save the most. Those of us who rely solely on market sources for food may save some money by freezing food in season when prices are low, by taking advantage of special sales, or by purchasing foods in quantity. Careful planning and careful pricing are needed to achieve appreciable savings, however.

SOME SUGGESTIONS for wise use of your zero storage space follow.

Store food of original high quality. When you buy food for storage, buy from a reputable dealer.

Use food often; replace food often. Long storage adds nothing to food value or eating quality, but it does add to cost. The more the freezer is used, the lower the cost per package for freezing and storing.

Keep a record, so that you know at all times what kinds of food and how much of each are in the freezer. Mark each package with the date stored.

Rotate the food. Place new packages at the bottom or back of the storage area. Keep unfrozen or warmed packages from touching those already in storage. Use the oldest food first.

For best eating quality, use frozen food before its suggested maximum storage period has expired. The home storage maximums are based on studies with commercially frozen foods but may also be used as a guide in planning length of storage for home-frozen foods. These maximums for well-packaged foods of original high quality held continuously at zero or below are (in months):

Fruit:
　Cherries, peaches, raspberries, straw-
　　berries........................ 12
Fruit juice concentrates:
　Apple, grape, orange.............. 12
Vegetables:
　Asparagus, beans, peas............ 8
　Cauliflower, corn, spinach.......... 8
Meat:
　Beef:
　　Roasts, steaks................... 12
　　Ground beef.................... 3
　Lamb:
　　Roasts........................ 12
　　Patties....................... 4
　Pork (fresh):
　　Roasts........................ 8
　　Sausage....................... 2
　Pork (cured)..................... 2
　Veal:
　　Roasts........................ 8
　　Chops, cutlets................. 6
　Cooked meats:
　　Meat dinners, meat pies, and swiss
　　　steak....................... 3
Poultry:
　Chicken:
　　Whole........................ 12
　　Cut-up....................... 9
　　Livers........................ 3
　Turkey:
　　Whole........................ 12
　　Cut-up....................... 6
　Duck, goose (whole).............. 6
　Cooked chicken and turkey:
　　Sliced meat and gravy........... 6
　　Pies......................... 12
　　Fried chicken................. 4
Bakery products:
　White bread, plain rolls............ 3
　Cakes:
　　Angel, chiffon................. 2
　　Chocolate layer................ 4
　　Pound, yellow................. 6
　　Fruit........................ 12
　Doughnuts...................... 3
　Pies (unbaked):
　　Apple, boysenberry, cherry, peach. 8
Ice cream, sherbet.................. 1

The ice-cube compartment of a conventional refrigerator usually cannot hold a temperature of 0° without freezing the perishable foods in the general storage area. This compartment is limited to storage for only a few days if fresh eating qualities and food values are to be preserved.

To use above-zero storage space:

Keep the temperature control at the setting for just-above-freezing in the general storage area;

buy frozen food just before checking out at the grocery store;

buy only what will be used within a few days;

ask the grocery packer to put frozen foods in an insulated bag or a double paper bag and take foods home as quickly as possible;

place frozen food in contact with the floor of the ice-cube compartment or the refrigerated ice tray shelf.

Home storage should not be an endurance test for frozen food. Although cheeses and wines benefit from aging, frozen food does not. Planning for their use within the framework of the capabilities of your home equipment to hold top quality is good storage practice. (RUTH A. REDSTROM)

Dairy Products

MILK is one of our best and most popular foods. It and food products made from it are so diverse that it is easy to include them in any type of balanced diet—whether high, medium, or low in calories—and in many special diets.

The sanitary quality of our milk supply is guaranteed by a program of protection in which Federal, State, and local agencies, and the dairy industry participate. Most American communities require the pasteurization of fluid milk products.

In pasteurization, the raw milk is heated quickly and promptly cooled to destroy harmful bacteria that may be present and to improve the keeping quality of the milk.

Pasteurization does not change the flavor or the essential nutritive value and goodness of milk.

Most of the fluid milk sold today is

homogenized—the fat globules in it are broken up in a special process.

The bottle cap or carton label will give name and grade of the product and tell whether it contains added vitamins, minerals, or nonfat milk solids and whether it is pasteurized, homogenized, or otherwise processed.

THE VARIETY of milk and dairy products is enough to satisfy your nutritional needs, personal tastes, and food budget.

Fluid whole milk contains both the fat and solids-not-fat parts of milk. The content of milk fat usually is standardized at 3.5 percent, although minimum requirements of States vary from 3.0 to 3.8 percent. Standards for milk solids-not-fat vary from 8.0 to 8.5 percent.

Homogenized milk has its fat globules broken into minute particles and dispersed throughout the liquid, so that it has a richer flavor and softer curd. A cream layer does not form in homogenized milk.

Skim milk has most of the milk fat removed. In some States, it is milk that has any amount of milk fat less than the amount required for whole milk. Skim milk is a good source of calcium, riboflavin, and protein. It lacks milk fat and vitamin A. Some skim milks are modified or fortified with added vitamins and minerals.

Low-fat, partly skimmed, and 2 percent milk are terms used in some markets to describe a fresh fluid product in which the content of milk fat is lowered and the nonfat milk solids content may or may not be increased. For example, the popular product known as 2 percent–10 percent contains 2 percent milk fat (instead of the usual 3.5 percent) and 10 percent nonfat milk solids (instead of the usual 8.5 percent); "2–10" has the appeal of a heavier consistency and richer taste than skim milk.

Chocolate milk is whole milk with added sugar and chocolate. Chocolate-flavored milk contains cocoa instead of chocolate.

Chocolate drink and chocolate-flavored drink use the same flavoring ingredients as chocolate milk, but are made from skim milk or from milk having less milk fat than whole milk.

Cultured milk products have smooth and mildly acid flavors produced by bacteria cultures, which convert the milk sugar into lactic acid. Cultured buttermilk is made from skim milk or partly skimmed milk.

Sour cream (or cultured sour cream) is usually made from light cream.

Yogurt, a specially cultured product, is made from concentrated whole milk or partly skimmed whole milk and may contain fruit or other flavoring.

These cultured (fermented) products have the same general food values as the products from which they were prepared.

Cream is the milk-fat part of milk. Cream containing about 18–20 percent milk fat is known as light cream, coffee cream, or table cream. It often is homogenized to improve consistency. Whipping cream contains 30–36 percent milk fat and is not homogenized.

Half-and-half is a mixture of milk and cream, usually containing 10–12 percent milk fat. It is used as a creaming agent in coffee and as a dessert topping.

Pressurized whipped cream is a mixture of cream, sugar, stabilizers, flavors, and emulsifiers packed in aerosol cans under pressure. The cream is whipped when the pressure is released through the nozzle.

Butter is churned cream. It contains, by law, not less than 80 percent milk fat. It may or may not contain salt. The butter of highest quality is made from sweet cream or may be made from sweet cream to which a culture, similar to that used in cultured milk products, has been added. Cultured butter has a pleasing, mildly acid flavor.

Most of the butter sold at retail bears a Department of Agriculture shield mark, with a letter grade that indicates the quality of the butter at the time of grading. U.S. AA and A are the grades usually sold at retail.

Whipped butter results when air or an inert gas is incorporated into the butter. This increases volume and makes the butter easier to spread. Most of the whipped butter sold in this country is unsalted.

Cheese is available in many forms, flavors, and textures to suit every taste and occasion.

Cheeses are natural or processed. Natural cheeses usually are made from whole cow's milk in this country, but some are made from skim milk, whey, or mixtures of all three.

Cheeses also are made from sheep's or goat's milk or cream.

Natural cheeses can be divided into four general classifications: Very hard, such as Parmesan; hard, as Cheddar and Swiss; semisoft, as Brick and Blue; and soft, as cream and cottage.

Cheddar cheese is our most popular hard cheese. It is sometimes called by the style in which it is made (Daisy, Longhorn, or Picnic) or by the locality where it is made—Wisconsin, New York, or Oregon. Natural Cheddar cheese is often labeled mild; medium cured or mellow aged; or cured, aged, or sharp, depending on the length of time the cheese is aged.

Cheddar and other closely related types of cheese are often called American or American-type cheese.

Process cheese is made by blending and pasteurizing fresh and aged natural cheeses with the aid of heat, water, and an emulsifier. Process cheese does not increase in flavor after manufacture. It melts easily when reheated. Pimientos, fruit, vegetables, or meat sometimes are added to process cheese.

Pasteurized processed American cheese contains at least 50 percent fat in the solids and may contain a maximum of 40 percent moisture.

Cheese food is made in much the same way as process cheese. It contains less cheese, though, and has added nonfat milk solids and moisture.

Cheese spreads are similar to cheese foods but contain less milk fat and more moisture.

Cold pack cheese or *club cheese* is a blend of one or more varieties of natural cheese mixed into a uniform product without heating. The flavor is about the same as the natural cheese used (usually aged or sharp), but the cheese is softer in texture than natural cheese and spreads easily.

Cottage cheese, a widely used unripened soft cheese, is produced by adding lactic-acid-producing bacteria to skim milk. It is sold in dry form or creamed.

Similar to cottage cheese are bakers, farmers, and pot cheeses.

Ice cream is made by freezing—while stirring—a pasteurized mixture of milk, cream, sugar, and stabilizer. It is flavored with extracts, fruit, chocolate, or nuts. Eggs are an optional ingredient.

Air is whipped into ice cream during freezing to increase its volume 80 to 100 percent.

Ice cream should have a fresh flavor, the body should be firm (neither fluffy nor soggy), and the texture should be fine grained (neither coarse nor icy).

Ice milk is made like ice cream and with the same ingredients as ice cream, except that it contains less milk fat and more nonfat milk solids. Ice milk may be sold in either soft- or hard-frozen form. It often is sold "soft" in cups and cones from freezers at refreshment stands and frozen on sticks and bars and in packages.

Sherbet is a low-fat, frozen mixture of sugar, milk solids, stabilizer, food acid, and water, with fruit, fruit juices, and extracts used for flavoring.

Evaporated milk is a sterilized, homogenized product that contains about 60 percent less water than whole milk. Most evaporated milk is fortified with vitamin D. It is easily transported and stored. It is cheaper than fresh whole milk and, when mixed with an equal volume of water, has about the same average composition of whole milk.

Sweetened condensed milk is milk from which about half of the water has been removed and about 44 percent sugar has been added as a preservative.

Dry whole milk is whole milk with the water removed. When reliquefied, it has about the same composition as fresh whole milk.

Nonfat dry milk is skim milk with water removed. Most nonfat dry milk on the consumer market today is "instant"—so named because it dissolves quickly in water. Nonfat dry milk contains the lactose, proteins, minerals, and water-soluble vitamins in the same relative proportions as fresh skim milk.

Goat's milk is similar to cow's milk in composition, but it has smaller fat globules and forms finer curds in the stomach. For these reasons, goat's milk has been used by infants, children, or adults troubled with digestive disturbances. Goat's milk is readily available in some communities. It should be produced and handled from farm to user with the same care as cow's milk.

A GOOD RULE to follow in handling dairy products in the home is to keep them cool, clean, and covered.

Fluid milk products should be refrigerated as soon as possible after purchase. Remove fluid milk products from the refrigerator only as needed, and put the containers back in the refrigerator promptly.

Because milk can absorb odors and flavors from other foods, the containers should be as tightly covered as possible.

Fluid milk products that have been on hand for some time—or have been allowed to stand at room temperature—should not be mixed with fresh milk products. Fluid milk products properly cared for in the home should keep good flavor for at least a week or 10 days after you buy them.

Nonfat dry milk, kept dry and cool, can be stored on the pantry shelf for several months without deterioration. As soon as you reconstitute nonfat dry milk, the liquid product needs refrigeration. Chilling the reconstituted product improves its flavor.

Dry whole milk should be stored in tightly covered, moistureproof containers. Reconstituted dry whole milk needs refrigeration.

Canned evaporated milk keeps well on the pantry shelf until opened. Once the can is opened, evaporated milk needs refrigeration and has about the same storage life as fresh milk.

Natural cheeses should be kept refrigerated.

Soft cheeses, such as cottage and cream cheese, are quite perishable and should be used soon after purchase.

Cured cheeses, such as Cheddar and Swiss, keep well in the refrigerator for up to several months if protected from drying out.

If possible, keep the cheese wrapped with its original wrapper. The cut surface of a cheese may be protected from drying out by covering with wax paper, foil, or plastic wrapping material.

If you wish to store large pieces of hard cheese for several weeks or more, dip the cut surfaces in hot paraffin. Small pieces should be rewrapped.

Any mold that may develop on natural cheeses is not harmful, but it may be scraped or cut off the surface.

Ends or pieces of cheese that have become dry may be grated and kept refrigerated in a clean, tightly covered glass jar. This cheese is excellent for garnishing or accenting other food.

Aromatic cheeses, such as Limburger, should be stored in a tightly covered jar or container. They are fast curing and taste best when used shortly after purchase.

Hard cheeses may be frozen, but freezing may change the characteristic body and texture and cause it to become crumbly and mealy. Many varieties of cheese cut into pieces weighing a pound or less and not over 1 inch thick may be frozen satisfactorily for as long as 6 months if the cheese is frozen quickly at a temperature of 0° F. or lower. Before you freeze cut cheese, wrap it carefully with moistureproof freezer wrap.

You can freeze the following varieties of cheese successfully in small pieces by following the foregoing directions: Brick, Cheddar, Edam, Gouda, Muenster, Swiss, Provolone, Mozzarella, and Camembert. Thaw frozen cheese in the refrigerator and use it as soon as possible. (ALEXANDER SWANTZ)

How To Cook Meat

ALL YOU NEED TO DO to be a celebrated cook is to apply a few basic principles in selecting and cooking meat and add originality to sauces and seasonings. The reputations of many famous chefs rest on how they cook meat.

Clues as to the best way to cook a particular cut are the amount of fat in the lean portion, the connective tissue, and the shape of the bone.

Heat causes toughening of muscle fibers, and toughening is less noticeable when flecks of fat are distributed throughout the lean—that is, when the meat is well marbled.

Connective tissue, which binds together muscle fibers in the lean meat, increases in amount with age of animal and exercise of the muscle. Cuts containing large amounts of connective tissue are less tender and require slow cooking with moisture in order to soften the connective tissue.

The T-bone, rib, and wedge bones appear in the more tender cuts, which included muscles along the backbone that received little exercise.

Tender cuts (which often are the most expensive) usually are best when roasted, broiled, panbroiled, or panfried.

The round bone in leg (round) and the round and blade bones of the shoulder (chuck) are signs of less tender cuts. Many cuts containing round bones may be roasted or panfried, but these less tender cuts, from the parts of the body that are exercised the most, often are better when they are braised or cooked with liquid, and the meat is surrounded by steam or the hot liquid.

You have to know more about the cuts and grades of beef than you do about veal, pork, or lamb, because beef comes from older animals; there are more cuts of beef and more ways to serve them; and the ranges in quality and price are wider.

BEEF CUTS from the round and chuck of low-grade carcasses (Commercial and Utility) are best braised or simmered for tenderness and development of the full, rich flavor of mature beef.

The cuts from the round and chuck of high-grade carcasses (Prime and Choice) may be roasted or broiled.

Other beef cuts to braise or simmer include shortribs, flank, brisket, and corned beef.

If you do not know the quality of a cut, it is best to braise or simmer it.

VEAL, LAMB, and pork cuts are tender. They come from young animals.

Because of its mild flavor, small amount of fat, and relatively large amounts of connective tissue, however, veal needs slow cooking to the well-done stage to develop flavor and to soften connective tissue. Large, meaty cuts of veal may be roasted. Thin cuts (chops and cutlets) may be braised or panfried. Bony cuts (riblets, breast, and shanks) should be braised or simmered.

Veal has too little fat for satisfactory broiling.

Most cuts of lamb are tender enough to be roasted, broiled, or cooked without added moisture. It is best to braise neck, breast, riblets, and other bony cuts, which contain large amounts of connective tissue.

Fresh cuts of pork are tender enough to be roasted or baked. Pork chops and steaks may be panfried or braised. Fresh pork requires a long cooking period to develop flavor. Broiling therefore is not recommended.

Smoked slices of ham and Canadian bacon may be broiled. Smoked hams and shoulders usually are roasted or baked, although, for milder flavor, it is best to simmer country-style hams.

IF YOU TRY to speed the cooking, you are apt to have tough, dry meat. So, choose meat that you can prepare properly in the time you have.

Roasting and braising usually require more than an hour. Broiling and panbroiling can be done in less than an hour.

For long or slow cooking, you have a variety of meat from which to choose.

Use low to moderate temperatures for cooking all meat. This basic principle may be the difference between a tough, dry product and a tender, juicy one. Too much heat can make even the tenderest meat tough.

Meat cooked at low temperatures will have less shrinkage and fewer cooking losses and therefore provide more servings. It will be tender and juicy and will be uniformly cooked. There is less spattering and less watching.

ROASTING is done in heated air (usually in an oven) in an uncovered pan with no additional liquid.

To roast meat, place it fat side up on a rack in an uncovered pan. Insert a meat thermometer in the center of cut. The tip of the thermometer should be in muscle, rather than fat, and it should not touch bone. A meat thermometer is the most accurate guide for determining doneness.

Place the meat in a slow oven (325° F.) and roast it to the desired degree of doneness.

Low to moderate cooking temperatures (300° to 350° F.) are particularly important for roasting the less tender cuts of the leg and shoulder.

Cooking time depends on the shape, size, and composition as well as degree of doneness of the meat.

Thick, chunky cuts take more time than thin cuts of the same weight. Allow an extra 10 minutes per pound for boneless or rolled roasts.

Frozen meat may be roasted satisfactorily either thawed or unthawed. The roasting time for frozen meat is about one and one-half times that of fresh or thawed meat.

BROILING is cooking by direct heat from a flame, electric unit, or glowing coals.

For broiling, use steaks and chops at least an inch thick and cured ham slices one-half inch thick. Slash the outside fat at intervals to keep the meat from curling, and place it on the broiler rack. Broil each side and turn the cut about midway during the cooking period.

To test doneness, cut a small slit in the lean and note the color and texture of the interior.

Allow 10 to 25 minutes for broiling 1-inch steaks—the shorter time for rare, the longer for well-done meat.

Lamb chops and cured ham slices require 12 to 20 minutes. Canadian bacon needs only 10 minutes.

Use low to moderate temperatures for broiling.

The broiling temperature may be regulated by changing the distance

ESTIMATED TIMES FOR ROASTING MEAT CONTAINING BONE IN AN OVEN 325° F.

5-pound cut	Internal temperature of meat when done (Fahrenheit)	Hours
Beef	140° (rare)	2 to 2½.
	160° (medium)	2½ to 3.
	180° (well)	3 to 3⅔.
Veal	170° (well)	2½ to 3½.
Lamb	180° (well)	2¾ to 3¼.
Fresh pork	185° (well)	3½ to 4.
Smoked pork:		
Cook before eating	160° to 170°	2½ to 3½.
Fully cooked	130°	1½ to 2.

between the meat and the source of the heat, altering the thermostat setting on some broilers, or adjusting the opening of the broiler door.

For frozen steaks and chops, use very low broiling temperatures and increase the broiling time about one-third.

PANBROILING and panfrying are variations of broiling wherein cooking is done by direct contact with a heated pan.

In panbroiling, no fat is added, and the fat is poured off or removed as it accumulates.

When fat is added to the pan or allowed to accumulate, the method is called frying, panfrying, or sauteing.

Cuts less than 1-inch thick may be used for panbroiling and panfrying.

To panbroil or panfry meat, slash the outer edge of the fat to keep meat from curling. Cook the meat slowly in a heavy frying pan, uncovered, over low to medium heat. Turn it occasionally. Gradual browning produces juicy meat.

Cooking time for panbroiling is about the same as that for broiling. Panfrying takes a little less time. The total cooking time for panbroiled patties or 1-inch beefsteaks or lamb chops is about 10 to 20 minutes, depending on doneness. For panfrying, 8 to 15 minutes are required.

To panfry chops and steaks (cutlets) from veal or pork carcasses, allow 25 to 30 minutes. Meat to be panfried may be dredged first in seasoned flour or crumbs to increase browning.

BRAISING is cooking in steam that is trapped and held in a covered container or foil wrap.

Pot roasting is braising large cuts of meat on top of range or in the oven.

First, brown the meat slowly on all sides in a heavy frying pan to develop color and flavor. Add fat for browning low-fat meats, such as veal, and for floured meats. Season the meat and add a small amount of liquid, such as water, vegetable juice, or diluted soy sauce (about one-half cup for a roast).

More liquid may be added if necessary.

Some cuts may be braised without any added liquid; the meat itself provides the moisture. Cover tightly and cook slowly until the meat is fork tender (well done).

Braising may be done on top of the range (simmer setting), in a moderate oven (350°), or in a pressure saucepan.

The cooking time depends on the kind, amount, and thickness of the meat. For 1-inch chops, allow 45 to 60 minutes; for 1-inch-thick steaks, 2 hours; for roasts, 2 to 4 hours.

Braising in a pressure saucepan reduces the cooking time, but more shrinkage and less juicy meat result.

STEWING (or simmering), a form of braising, refers to cooking meat in liquid just below the boiling point. For stews, the meat is cut into 1- to 2-inch cubes.

To stew or simmer meat, brown the meat in a heavy pan or kettle (except corned beef and smoked cuts, which usually are not browned). Dust the meat with flour before browning if a deep-brown color is desired. Barely cover the meat with liquid. Season. Cover the kettle tightly and cook slowly over low heat until the meat is tender. The time depends on the cut and its size. About 30 to 45 minutes before the meat is done, add carrots, potatoes, onions, and other vegetables as desired. Add liquid as necessary.

Overcooking shrinks meat and makes it dry, flavorless, stringy, and hard to carve. About 3 hours is required to simmer a 4- to 5-pound cut. Stew meat requires about 2 hours for the meat to become fork tender.

Allow 3 to 4 hours for simmering corned beef, oxtails, or ham hocks, but only 15 to 30 minutes for sweetbreads.

When liquid is the cooking medium, seasonings penetrate the meat and add variety to meat dishes. The possibilities are almost limitless, since flavor can be varied according to the liquid and seasonings used. The liquid may be water, soup stock, consomme, bouillon, fruit or vegetable juice, soy sauce, sour cream, or marinade. Seasonings may be herbs, spices, and vegetables.

Cookbooks, magazines, and newspapers often feature recipes for specialty meat dishes that use braising and simmering procedures.

Exotic or foreign titles frequently hide simple recipes that use inexpensive cuts—*boeuf à la mode*, for example, is French for pot roast.

Opportunities for applying your creative abilities are especially great with braised and simmered meats. Try braised meat seasoned delicately with a sprinkling of fresh or dried herbs, such as rosemary or marjoram. Add asparagus, okra, or parsnips to a stew. Or serve a tart fruit sauce of red cherries or cranberries with ham or pork.

A meat dish with a subtle, distinctive flavor that is simply prepared can be the basis for your reputation as an excellent cook. Just select the meat, cook it properly at low to moderate temperatures, and add seasonings with ingenuity. (OLIVE M. BATCHER)

Cooking

Poultry

THREE POINTERS to success in cooking poultry are:

Know the classes of poultry that are available.

Cook poultry at moderate temperatures with moist or dry heat, as may be required.

Serve poultry accented with seasonings at the peak of cooked quality.

The particular class of each kind of poultry—turkeys, chicken, ducks, geese, guineas, pigeons—is the index to the type of cooking.

The class is based on physical characteristics associated with age and sex. The classes of each kind progress from young and tender poultry to fully mature. The classes listed in the table as tender can be cooked by any method or used in any recipe. The more mature classes have less-tender flesh and require certain procedures.

THE SECOND POINTER is: Apply dry or moist cooking at moderate temperatures as required for the particular class of poultry. That is, vary the method of cooking according to the age of the poultry.

When you do this, it is easy to select the right class of poultry for a special recipe or, if necessary, to adapt a recipe to assure a tender, juicy product from a particular class of poultry.

Dry heating includes all methods in which dry air surrounds the poultry. Examples are cooking in an open pan in an oven, under the broiler, or over hot coals. Cooking poultry by hot fat also is considered to be a dry-heating method.

These methods are suitable only for the young, tender-meated classes.

The second way, by moist heating, modifies the dry methods so that the more mature classes can be cooked tender. Covering the pan to surround the bird with steam or adding varied amounts of liquids, such as water, sauces, or vegetable juices, and heating with moderate temperatures assures moist heating.

As basic cooking methods representative of dry heating you should know how to roast, fry, and broil. Modifications of these methods to moist heating methods, such as oven and pan braising or simmering, follow easily.

If you know of the basic cooking methods for dry and moist heating, you can extend your skill to more elaborate recipes.

A bird you select with a knowledge of its age can be dipped into the right seasonings or coating and roasted, fried, or simmered so that every time it is done to perfection.

ROASTING is a popular way to prepare 10- to 15-pound turkeys, but turkeys can also be roasted in sizes as small as 4 pounds or as big as 25 pounds or more.

Think of roasting as just placing the poultry in an open pan in an oven set at 325° F.

Then add to this a few preparation steps, some tips to follow during roasting, and important points when poultry is stuffed. With this, you can place roasting on your list of basic poultry cooking methods.

The steps in preparing poultry for roasting are: Rinse the bird with cool water; then pat it dry. Season the cavities with salt or fill with stuffing. Bind or truss the bird to assure even cooking by pinning the wings to the sides of body and tucking the drumsticks under the band of skin at the tail.

During roasting, keep the skin moist and tender by basting occasionally with pan drippings or melted fat. Cover the breast and drumsticks with a piece of foil when the skin is a rich, golden-brown color. This prevents overbrowning them while the other parts, such as the lower thighs, cook.

Although 325° is the best temperature for roasting all sizes of poultry, broiler chickens and small turkey halves or quarters can be roasted quickly and successfully at temperatures as high as 375° or 400°.

Most people like stuffing in roasted poultry.

A word of caution: Always combine the ingredients just before roasting. Place the stuffing into poultry neck and body cavities lightly, so it will heat rapidly. Choose an oven temperature for roasting (325°) that will let the stuffing pass quickly through the temperature range of 50° to 120° at which food-poisoning organisms, if present, grow and multiply. Be sure stuffing reaches a final temperature of 165° to assure destruction of any harmful organisms.

Some recipes for stuffing: Calculate the amount of stuffing needed by allowing one-half cup of bread cubes for each pound of poultry.

STUFFING

3 tablespoons butter, margarine, or poultry fat
¾ cup chopped celery
3 tablespoons chopped parsley
2 tablespoons chopped onion
1 quart bread cubes (2- to 4-day-old bread)
½ teaspoon savory seasoning
½ to ¾ teaspoon salt
Pepper to taste

TENDERNESS OF DIFFERENT CLASSES OF POULTRY

Kind	Class	Type of meat
Turkey	Fryer or roaster	Tender.
	Young hen or tom	Tender.
	Yearling hen or tom	Reasonably tender.
	Mature or old	Less tender.
Chicken	Fryer or broiler (includes Cornish Game hen)	Tender.
	Roaster	Tender.
	Capon	Tender.
	Stag	Reasonably tender.
	Hen or stewing chicken	Less tender.
	Cock or old rooster	Less tender.
Ducks	Fryer or broiler	Tender.
	Roaster duckling	Tender.
	Mature or old duck	Less tender.
Geese	Young	Tender.
	Mature or old	Less tender.
Guinea	Young	Tender.
	Mature or old	Less tender.
Pigeon	Squab	Tender.
	Pigeon	Less tender.

Melt the fat in a frypan; add celery, parsley, and onion; and cook a few minutes. Add to the bread with seasoning. Mix lightly.

For variety:

Oyster stuffing—omit celery, and reduce parsley and onion to 1 tablespoon each. Add 1 cup oysters, heated in their own liquid and drained.

Nut stuffing—omit parsley and savory seasoning, and add ½ cup chopped nut meats (pecans, roasted almonds, filberts, or cooked chestnuts).

To change roasting to oven braising, just cover the poultry during heating.

Oven braising surrounds the poultry with moistness from the cooking drippings or from a small amount of added liquid, and assures a tender, juicy product, particularly from mature poultry. It is possible to increase the oven temperature to 350° and speed up the cooking time. To give a golden-brown exterior, remove the cover during the last 30 to 45 minutes of braising.

Braising is an excellent way to cook game birds, such as grouse, quail, partridge, and pheasant, when the age is not known.

THE REMAINING basic methods are especially suitable for cut-up poultry—halves, quarters, or parts.

For frying, a type of dry heating, choose a young, tender bird. The poultry is cut up into serving-size pieces. Season the pieces with salt and pepper, then roll in flour, or dip pieces in a batter made by mixing 1 cup flour, 1 egg, ¾ cup milk, and ½ teaspoon salt.

To panfry, place the pieces skin-side down in about one-fourth inch of fat preheated in a heavy skillet. Cook uncovered 15 to 25 minutes on each side.

Oven frying is done in the same way by placing the fat and poultry in a shallow pan in an oven set at 425° for 30 minutes, then turning the pieces and cooking 20 to 30 minutes longer.

For french-frying or deep-frying poultry, place the coated poultry pieces in enough hot fat to cover. The poultry is cooked in 10 to 15 minutes.

Broiling is a quick and easy way to cook poultry pieces. The pieces are seasoned beforehand, or seasonings can be basted on during broiling along with melted fat, which keeps the skin from becoming tough and dry.

The pieces are placed on a broiler pan at a distance from the preheated broiler unit or hot coals so that it takes about 15 minutes for the pieces to begin to brown. The pieces should be golden brown and ready to turn after 25 minutes so the other side is cooked in about 15 minutes.

For moist heating, fry or broil poultry pieces just enough to brown. Then cover the pan and cook pieces gently on the top of the stove or in the oven at 350° for about 20 minutes. This additional step brings about moist heating and is a useful adaptation of frying or broiling to include all classes of poultry.

Many of the favorite United States regional recipes, like southern fried chicken, chicken Hawaiian, or chicken Maryland style, are combinations of frying to brown the outside and then cooking in a covered pan to tenderize and blend in seasonings.

Some recipes call for cooked and boned poultry—which may be meat remaining from roasted or braised poultry or meat from poultry that has been simmered whole or in pieces in water until tender.

Remove the meat from the bones and save the stock for use in a sauce or soup. Simmering is a moist-heating method and is a good way to cook mature birds. The meat can be smothered with vegetables in a sauce or combined with sour cream with paprika, orange-almond, or barbecue sauces.

THE FINAL POINTER: Serve poultry accented with seasonings at the peak of cooked quality.

Seasonings may be sprinkled on poultry before or during cooking.

For simple seasoning, use salt with a

little pepper. Add paprika, garlic or onion salt, tarragon, or rosemary to accent the bland flavor of poultry. Heat sauces with the poultry during the final 15 to 30 minutes of cooking to blend flavors. White or tomato sauces or sour cream are pleasing.

Cookbooks contain many variations: Add cheese and toasted crumbs; vegetables like onions, shallots, or celery; ingredients such as soy sauce and ginger to give an oriental touch; or an Indian influence with curry and chutney.

When is poultry cooked enough? Timetables that you see in cookbooks or often attached to the poultry when purchased are good guides.

For large birds that are cooked by roasting or oven braising, place a meat thermometer in the center of the inside thigh muscles. When they reach a temperature of 185°, the poultry usually is done to the peak of cooked quality.

Another way is to grasp the end of the drumsticks and see if drumstick and thigh joints move easily. Press the thickest part of the drumstick meat with protected fingers to see if it is soft.

For the other methods of cooking poultry, the time given on the recipe is the best guide. The meat should seem soft and tender when probed with a fork, and the joints should move easily. Meat will no longer adhere tightly to the bone. (IRMA M. HOKE)

For further reading, consult the following Department of Agriculture publications: *Cheese Buying Guide for Consumers*, Marketing Bulletin No. 17; *Conserving the Nutritive Values in Foods*, Home and Garden Bulletin No. 90; *Family Food Budgeting for Good Meals and Good Nutrition*, Home and Garden Bulletin No. 94; *Freezing Combination Main Dishes*, Home and Garden Bulletin No. 40; *Freezing Meat and Fish in the Home*, Home and Garden Bulletin No. 93; *Home Care of Purchased Frozen Foods*, Home and Garden Bulletin No. 69; *Home Freezing of Poultry*, Home and Garden Bulletin No. 70; *Shopper's Guide to U.S. Grades for Food*, Home and Garden Bulletin No. 58; *Storing Perishable Foods in the Home*, Home and Garden Bulletin No. 78; *Tips on Selecting Fruits and Vegetables*, Marketing Bulletin No. 13; *U.S. Grades for Beef*, Marketing Bulletin No. 15.

Basic Breads

SUCCESS IN BAKING yeast breads begins with the flour, the main ingredient in all kinds of bread.

White flour generally is used, but whole-wheat, rye, oatmeal, and other kinds of flour may replace part or all of the white flour in a bread recipe.

All-purpose, enriched flour is the type usually sold in American retail stores.

Standards established for enrichment per pound of flour of white flour (*Code of Federal Regulations*, Title 21, Part 15) are: Thiamine, 2.0–2.5 mg; riboflavin, 1.2–1.5 mg; niacin, 16–20 mg; iron, 13–16.5 mg.

In northern regions of the United States, all-purpose flours generally are blends of hard wheats. In the South and some States of the West, all-purpose flours usually are blends of soft wheats.

Hard-wheat flour absorbs more moisture, requires more mixing, and withstands more fermentation than soft-wheat flour.

The gluten of the hard-wheat flour tends to be more cohesive and elastic. The gluten of the soft-wheat types is more delicate and less elastic. That is why hard-wheat flour makes the best yeast breads, and soft-wheat flour the best muffins and biscuits. You can use all-purpose flour for making yeast bread successfully at home, however.

All-purpose flours contain enough of the gluten-forming proteins to make good yeast bread. Gluten, a protein complex that is gummy, cohesive, and elastic, develops as a colloidal network throughout batters and doughs as a result of beating, stirring, and kneading.

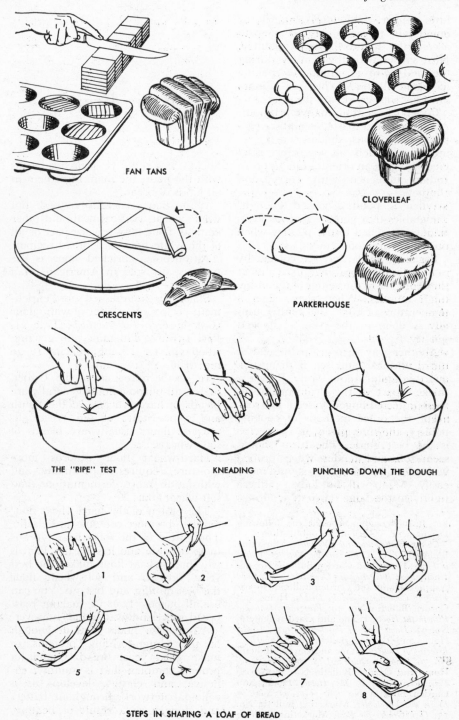

FAN TANS

CLOVERLEAF

CRESCENTS

PARKERHOUSE

THE "RIPE" TEST

KNEADING

PUNCHING DOWN THE DOUGH

STEPS IN SHAPING A LOAF OF BREAD

As the yeast acts to produce carbon dioxide, the gluten network stretches to form cells, which expand and hold the leavening gas in batters and doughs. The hardening of gluten during baking gives structure to the bread.

The liquid to use to make the dough may be milk, water, or water in which potatoes have been cooked.

MILK GIVES A GOOD FLAVOR and improves the nutritive value. Bread made with milk has a finer texture and better keeping qualities than bread made with water. The milk may be fresh, fluid milk, evaporated milk, or dry milk powder.

Scald fresh, fluid milk to destroy any substance that might produce undesirable changes in the bread during fermentation. Dilute evaporated milk with an equal amount of warm water.

You can substitute 1 cup of warm water and 3 tablespoonfuls of dry milk powder for each cup of milk the recipe calls for.

You may use active dry or compressed yeast, but either kind should be fresh.

The action of the yeast produces bubbles of carbon dioxide, which expand and cause doughs to rise. Yeast grows best at a temperature between 80° and 85°. High temperatures destroy the yeast. Low temperatures retard its growth. Active dry or compressed yeast must soften in lukewarm water 5 to 10 minutes to separate and activate the cells.

Fats add flavor and make the bread tender and the crumb moist, soft, and velvety. Lard, hydrogenated fats, oils, margarines or butter may be used.

Salt adds flavor and helps control action of the yeast.

Sugar starts activity of the yeast and gives flavor to the bread and a "bloom" to the crust.

Eggs add flavor and nutritive value. They also improve the color, texture, and structure of muffins, rich roll batters, and dough.

MAKING BREAD doughs by combining all the ingredients at one mixing saves time.

If you soften the yeast and scald fresh milk and cool it to lukewarm temperature, the order of adding ingredients is not too important. Adding the flour to the liquid ingredients helps control stiffness of the dough.

Beat the dough with a spoon or use the medium-low speed of a mixer until the gluten is stretchy and the dough forms circles around the bowl.

Continue to add flour until the dough is stiff and does not cling to sides of the bowl.

Turn out on a lightly floured board or pastry cloth.

Dry, stiff doughs have too much flour and do not make good bread. Neither do doughs that are too soft and sticky.

All flour needed to keep the dough from sticking should be added during the mixing and the first kneading. Flour added later forms streaks in the bread and coarsens the texture.

KNEAD the dough quickly and easily. Give the dough a one-quarter turn with each pushing motion. Keep the fingers curved, and lift and fold the dough over from far side toward you. Push the dough from you with heel of palms and keep an easy rhythm in your kneading.

Do not break or tear the dough, for that injures the gluten. If the dough seems hard to manage, let it rest 10 minutes.

The average kneading time is about 10 minutes. The actual kneading time depends on whether the flour is hard or soft, the amount of dough, and the way you manipulate the dough.

The dough is kneaded enough when its surface is smooth and satiny; many small blisters appear under the surface; and the dough does not stick to your hand if you hold it on the surface for 30 seconds.

NEXT COMES fermentation in the bowl.
Place the dough in a lightly greased

bowl and turn the dough upside down. Set the bowl in an unlighted oven above a pan of hot water. Allow the dough to rise until it is twice its bulk.

To test whether the dough is light enough, press the tip of the first finger into the dough to the second joint, quickly in and out. If the dent stays in the dough, it is ready to punch down. Plunge your fist into the middle of the dough. Fold the edges of the dough to the center. Then turn the ball of dough upside down. This releases excess gas, unites the gluten strands, and distributes the yeast and its nutrients more evenly.

A second fermentation period may be omitted, but if the flour is a hard-wheat type, the bread may not be as good as you desire.

A second, or even a third, fermentation period is recommended for bread dough prepared at high altitudes. Doughs double their size faster at high altitudes than at low altitudes. The higher the altitude, the shorter the time required for a dough to double its bulk.

Punching the dough down more times allows fermentation to continue long enough to produce good bread. This is because fermentation needs to go on long enough to cause changes in the gluten to develop "buttery" flavors and to make the bread tender, light, and good.

When fermentation is complete, the dough is ready for shaping as described in the various recipes.

PLAIN BREAD generally is baked in an oven preheated to a temperature of 400° to 450° for 40 to 45 minutes.

If you use the higher temperature, reduce the oven temperature to 350° after the first 15 minutes. Rich doughs are baked at temperatures of 350° to 375° to prevent overbrowning.

Remove the baked loaf from the oven and brush the crust with fat. Remove the loaf from the pan soon after baking and cool it on a rack. When the bread is cool, wrap and store it in a clean, dry place.

Roll doughs are softer and richer than bread doughs. They may be allowed to ferment only once, then punched down and shaped into rolls. You may want to experiment with making several kinds and shapes.

When rolls are light, they retain the dent when pressed lightly, and are ready to bake. Plain roll-types are baked in a preheated oven at 400° to 425° for 12 to 15 minutes. Rolls and coffeecakes that contain much sugar, honey, or molasses require lower oven temperatures of about 350°.

If you do not use all of a yeast dough immediately, you may store it in the refrigerator. Cover the dough to prevent formation of a crust, which makes streaks in the baked products. Warm doughs continue to rise even in the refrigerator and therefore must be punched down. Refrigerated doughs keep about 2 or 3 days.

No-knead, batter breads were developed to simplify making yeast breads and to save time of the homemaker. Coffeecakes and sweet rolls are the products usually made by this process.

The no-knead doughs are softer and contain more fat than kneaded doughs. These doughs are mixed in the same way as the kneaded types. Not quite so much flour is used, and the gluten is developed by beating.

A no-knead dough is allowed to rise in the pan until light and baked at temperatures from 375° to 425°. The baked products are more open in grain and less delicate in crumb and butterlike flavor than those made from kneaded doughs.

QUICK BREADS are leavened with air, steam, or carbon dioxide, which is released by the action of baking powder, or of soda with various sour milks.

Pancakes, waffles, muffins, gingerbread, and biscuits are examples of quick breads.

Techniques for making quick breads differ somewhat. Once you acquire the simple, but exact, skill for making muffins or biscuits, you will find it easier to make them right than wrong.

Good muffins are light and tender. The crusts are an even, golden-brown color, pebbly, and free from peaks. The texture of muffins is somewhat coarse and free from vertical tunnels.

The way you combine the liquid and dry ingredients really determines whether you will succeed or fail in your efforts to make good muffins. Only a few extra strokes of the mixing spoon may spoil your muffins. A muffin batter should look lumpy, not smooth. If the batter is smooth, it is overmixed, and overmixing is the commonest cause of poor results.

Oil the bottom of the pan, but not the sides. Hold the spoon close to the pan and push the batter out of the spoon with a spatula. Avoid stirring the batter during this process.

BISCUITS ARE QUICK and easy to make if you use a tested recipe, add the correct amount of milk for the flour you are using, and develop a deft hand for mixing and handling the dough.

Experiment to find the right amount of milk for your particular flour. Add all of the milk at once and stir quickly until the dry ingredients are thoroughly moistened.

The dough stiffens rather suddenly. Turn it out immediately on a lightly floured board or pastry cloth. Knead the dough quickly and gently about 10 to 15 times. The dough should be light and soft, not sticky. Neither sticky doughs nor solid, stiff doughs make good biscuits.

After slight kneading, roll or pat the dough to the desired thickness. Cut as many biscuits as possible from the first rolling, as rerolling results in overmixing.

Cut square biscuits to save time and eliminate the need of rerolling the scraps.

PREPARED MIXES provide a shortcut for mixing a variety of breads.

The savings in time and money depend on whether you prepare your own mix, the kind and amount of baking, way of shopping, and the ingredients.

Products prepared from boxed mixes may cost more than products made from basic recipes or homemade mixes, but the preparation time is shorter.

THE MANY KINDS of bread available in retail markets range from those that require some preparation to ready-to-serve items.

Frozen, unbaked bread and rolls, refrigerated biscuits and rolls, and brown-n-serve products must be baked. Many resemble home-prepared breads. Baked breads, rolls, and coffeecakes range from standard to foreign and specialty types.

Some markets sell day-old bread often at half the original price.

Either the home-baked or commercial breads freeze well and may be stored in a freezer up to 3 months. Cool home-baked bread thoroughly. Wrap, label, and freeze it immediately. Thaw the bread in the original wrapper at room temperature. Heat wrapped rolls, muffins, and biscuits in an oven at 275° to 300° for 10 to 15 minutes.

WHITE BREAD

6 cups sifted all-purpose flour
1¾ cups milk
¼ cup lukewarm water
1 package yeast
5 tablespoons sugar
2 teaspoons salt
¼ cup cooking oil or soft shortening

Pour the scalded milk over the sugar, salt, and oil or soft shortening, which you have measured into a mixing bowl.

Add half of the flour and beat well.

Soften the yeast in one-fourth cup of warm water. Add it to the batter and beat until smooth.

Add the remainder of flour, or enough to make a moderately soft dough, and mix thoroughly.

Turn the dough out on a lightly floured board or pastry cloth. Knead it until it is smooth and elastic.

Place the dough in a greased bowl;

cover and let rise at 80° to 85° until doubled in bulk (about 1 hour and 20 minutes).

Punch it down. Let it stand on the bread board for 5 minutes.

Divide the dough in half and shape each portion into a ball. Allow each to rest 10 minutes.

Flatten each ball and press into rectangles about 1 inch thick. Fold in half lengthwise and stretch dough gently until it is about three times the length of the baking pan. Fold the ends to the center until they overlap, and press down firmly.

Fold the dough in thirds lengthwise and seal by pressing down firmly. Roll the dough lightly with your hands and place in greased pans with seam side underneath.

Yield: Two loaves.

Each loaf should fill an 8½ x 4½ x 2½ inch pan half full.

Brush the tops of the loaves lightly with melted fat.

Set the pans in a warm place (80° to 85°) to rise (about 55 minutes). When the dough is doubled, it is ready to bake at 375° for 45 to 55 minutes.

Approximate fermentation times in minutes for high altitudes: First bowl fermentation—60 at 5 thousand feet, 45 at 7,500 feet, and 40 at 10 thousand feet; second bowl fermentation—30 at 5 thousand feet, 25 at 7,500 feet, and 20 at 10 thousand feet; pan fermentation—30 at 5 thousand feet, 25 at 7,500 feet and 20 at 10 thousand.

BASIC SWEET DOUGH

  2 packages yeast
  ¼ cup lukewarm water
  1 cup milk
  2 teaspoons salt
  ½ cup sugar
  ¼ cup oil or soft shortening
  5 cups sifted all-purpose flour (about)
  2 eggs
  1 teaspoon grated lemon rind or
½ teaspoon lemon extract (if desired)

Soften the yeast in lukewarm water.

Scald the milk and add sugar, salt, and oil or shortening. Cool to lukewarm.

Add enough flour to make a thick batter. Beat until smooth.

Add softened yeast, eggs, and lemon rind or lemon extract. Beat well.

Add the remaining flour—enough to make a soft dough. Turn on a lightly floured board or pastry cloth and knead until smooth and satiny.

Place in a greased bowl, cover, and let rise in a warm place (80° to 85°) until doubled (about 90 minutes).

When it is light, punch it down. Let rest 10 minutes.

Shape it into rolls or coffeecakes.

Let it rise until it has doubled (about 45 minutes). Bake in moderate oven (350°) 20 to 30 minutes.

Approximate yield: Three coffeecakes or about 3½ dozen rolls.

Approximate fermentation times in minutes for high altitudes: First bowl fermentation—75 at 5 thousand feet, 55 at 7,500 feet, and 45 at 10 thousand feet; pan fermentation—35 at 5 thousand feet, 35 at 7,500 feet, and 30 at 10 thousand feet.

ROLL VARIATIONS

Cloverleaf: Make balls of dough of a size that three balls half fill a cup of a muffin pan. Dip each ball in melted butter or other fat and place (fat side up) in greased cups of muffin pans.

Crescents: Roll or pat the dough into circles about 10 inches in diameter and one-fourth inch thick. Cut the dough into 12 pie-shaped pieces and brush with fat. Begin at the outer edge and roll the dough to the point and press together. Curve the rolled dough slightly to form a crescent and place it, pointed side underneath, on a greased baking sheet.

Fan-tans: Roll or pat the dough into a rectangle about one-fourth inch thick. Brush the top with melted fat. Cut the dough into strips 1 inch wide. Place five to eight strips one on top of another. Cut into pieces about one and one-half inches long. Place each short pile on end in greased muffin cups.

Parker House: Roll or pat the dough about one-half inch thick. Brush the top with soft butter or other fat and cut the dough with a biscuit cutter. Fold each circle over, fat side in, to form a half circle. Press the outer edges together firmly and place on a greased baking sheet.

No-knead batter bread

1 package yeast
¼ cup lukewarm water
1 cup milk, ¼ cup sugar, 1 egg
1 teaspoon salt
¼ cup oil or soft shortening
3¼ cups sifted all-purpose flour
Soften the yeast in warm water.

Add scalded milk to sugar, salt, and oil or soft shortening. Cool to lukewarm.

Add 2 cups of flour.

Beat well with a spoon or mix 1 minute on medium-low speed of mixer.

Add softened yeast and egg. Beat well again with a spoon or 1 minute on medium-low speed of mixer.

Add remaining flour to make a thick batter. Beat until smooth.

Cover and let rise in a warm place 80° to 85° until doubled.

Stir down and smooth into two greased 8 x 8 x 2 inch pans.

Topping, if used, is added here.

Cover and let rise until almost doubled (about 50 minutes). Bake 25 to 35 minutes at 375°.

When you use topping, the baking time is usually about 35 minutes.

Variations

Coconut pineapple coffeecake: Melt 3 tablespoons margarine or butter in an 8 x 8 x 2 inch pan. Spread evenly over the bottom of the pan 2 tablespoons dark-brown sugar and one-half cup shredded coconut. Arrange one-third cup pineapple tidbits on the sugar-coconut mixture. After it has risen in the bowl, turn the batter into the pan. Let rise about 50 minutes. Bake at 350°.

Orange coffeecake: Melt 3 tablespoons margarine or butter in a pan 8 x 8 x 2 inches. Spread one-fourth cup dark-brown sugar evenly over the bottom of the pan. Arrange sections of mandarin orange on the sugar-butter mixture. Pour the batter into prepared pans after it has risen the first time in a bowl. Let rise about 50 minutes. Bake at 350°.

Sesame seed bread: Brush the top of the batter in each 8 x 8 x 2 inch pan with one and one-fourth teaspoons of melted butter. Sprinkle with one-fourth cup of sesame seeds, and allow to rise about 50 minutes. Bake at 350°.

Crumble squares:
¼ cup flour
¼ cup breadcrumbs
2 tablespoons sugar
½ teaspoon cinnamon
2 tablespoons butter or margarine
Combine the flour, crumbs, sugar, and cinnamon. Cut or rub in butter or margarine until the mixture is crumbly. Spread evenly over the batter in an 8 x 8 x 2 inch pan. Divide into nine squares by pressing lines deep into the batter with floured finger tips. Let rise 50 minutes. Bake at 350°.

Sugar crumb topping:
¼ cup flour
¼ cup sugar (white or brown or part of each)
1 teaspoon cinnamon
2 tablespoons butter or margarine
¼ cup chopped nuts (if desired)
Mix the flour, sugar, and cinnamon. Cut in margarine or butter until the mixture is crumbly. Stir in nuts. Sprinkle over top of no-knead bread. Let rise in the pan about 50 minutes. Bake at 350°.

Approximate fermentation times in minutes for high altitudes: Bowl fermentation—50 at 5 thousand feet, 40 at 7,500 feet, and 35 at 10 thousand feet; pan fermentation—30 at 5 thousand feet, 25 at 7,500 feet, and 20 at 10 thousand feet.

Muffins

2 cups sifted all-purpose flour
2 to 4 tablespoons sugar
2½ teaspoons baking powder
½ teaspoon salt
2 to 4 tablespoons melted shortening or cooking oil
1 egg, well beaten
1 cup milk

Sift dry ingredients together into a mixing bowl. Combine the beaten egg, milk, and cooled melted shortening or oil. Make a well in the dry ingredients. Add the liquid mixture and stir just enough to combine. The mixture should have a rough appearance. Fill greased muffin pans two-thirds full. Bake at 400° to 425° until golden brown (about 20 to 30 minutes). No changes are required for preparation at altitudes up to 10 thousand feet.

Approximate yield: 12 muffins.

VARIATIONS

Bacon muffins: Substitute bacon fat for melted shortening or oil. Add one-fourth to one-half cup chopped cooked bacon to dry ingredients.

Blueberry muffins: Use one-fourth cup sugar and one-fourth cup shortening. Add three-fourths to 1 cup of frozen or well-drained, canned blueberries to the batter and stir in carefully.

Cheese muffins: Add 1 cup grated Cheddar cheese and one-fourth cup milk.

Date-nut muffins: Add one-half cup chopped dates, one-half cup chopped nuts, and one tablespoon milk.

Whole-wheat muffins: Substitute two-thirds cup whole-wheat flour for two-thirds cup all-purpose flour.

BAKING POWDER BISCUITS

2 cups sifted all-purpose flour
2½ teaspoons baking powder
½ teaspoon salt
¼ cup shortening
¾ cup milk (about)

Sift the dry ingredients into mixing bowl. Cut the shortening into dry ingredients until the mixture looks like coarse cornmeal.

Make a well in the center. Add milk and stir quickly and lightly until well blended. The mixture should be soft but not sticky. Turn onto a lightly floured board or pastry cloth. Knead lightly about 10 to 15 strokes.

Pat or roll out to desired thickness (one-fourth inch for crusty biscuits; one-half inch for soft biscuits).

Cut with floured biscuit cutter and place on ungreased baking sheet. Bake at 450° for 12 to 15 minutes or until golden brown.

Yield: About 16 biscuits cut ½ inch thick and 2 inches in diameter.

No changes are required for preparation at altitudes up to 10 thousand feet.

VARIATIONS

Cheese biscuits: Add one-half cup grated Cheddar cheese to the sifted dry ingredients.

Orange biscuits: Add one and one-half teaspoons grated orange rind and substitute orange juice for the liquid.

Whole-wheat biscuits: Substitute one-half cup whole-wheat flour for one-half cup of all-purpose flour. (FERNE BOWMAN)

Vegetables

AMONG the many attributes of vegetables is one you may not have thought of—the ability of their different colors, flavors, textures, shapes, and temperatures to brighten meals.

A meal looks better and maybe tastes better if it has a variety of colors—not, for example, a yellow omelet, yellow corn, and yellow pineapple.

Instead, try combining vegetables so that you have at least two of these color groups: White, green, red, and yellow or orange.

Be careful not to have more than one food in the same color group in the same meal—such as beets and tomatoes or carrots and corn.

Consider also the color of the serving dish. Choose colors that complement the food—for instance, put sliced tomatoes on a pale yellow or white plate. Sliced tomatoes on a violet plate—no.

As to the shape of food: A dinner of parsleyed new potatoes, green peas, hamburger, and melon ball salad may be colorful, but the shapes of all are the same.

Looks are not all, of course. Food must taste good. Flavor, texture, and temperature are factors that make food pleasing to us.

A balance of sweet and sour, salty and bitter, and mild and strong is desirable in a meal. Too much of one is too much.

For more flavor, try a sauce, such as sweet-sour, cheese, vinaigrette, mushroom, sour cream, or hollandaise, or drop a bouillon cube in the cooking water.

Some lemon or orange juice in the cooking water of white, yellow, or red vegetables adds a new flavor.

You can dress up buttered vegetables by a pinch of celery seeds, snipped chives or snipped scallions, curry powder, horseradish, lemon juice or rind, prepared mustard, or grated cheese.

Or try one or another of the unusual spices and herbs like cumin, tarragon, dill, chervil, nutmeg, ginger, cardamom, allspice, and oregano.

A meal in which there is more than one texture is most pleasing. A meal of mashed potatoes, soft rolls, meat loaf, stewed tomatoes, and apple betty is pretty dull. Raw carrots or lettuce, in place of the tomatoes, or Melba toast, instead of the rolls, would help.

Or, on soft or mushy vegetables, try a topping of slivered almonds, bacon bits, chow mein noodles, peanuts, water chestnuts, french-fried onion rings, toasted crumbs, or crushed dry cereal.

Other toppings of another texture are sauteed mushrooms, buttered croutons, chopped hard-cooked eggs, diced pimiento, onion or green pepper rings, carrot curls, and cheese cubes. Relishes are good, too.

Most of us are used to cooked vegetables that are served hot, but no law says they must be.

A reminder (since surely you have tried it): Cook green beans, peas, asparagus, zucchini, okra, green pepper, broccoli, carrots, celery, or corn. Then marinate the vegetables and toss them with mayonnaise or a salad dressing you like. Or, combine the vegetables with salad greens or other cooked vegetables.

Or, try adding other salad ingredients, such as cheese cubes, buttered croutons, onions, bacon, chopped egg, cooked meat or fish, and serve them in a tossed salad or a gelatin salad.

A nice start in a summer meal may be a chilled vegetable soup—borsch, vichyssoise, or gazpacho. Chilled avocado, cucumber, seafood bisque, tomato, or mixed-vegetable soup also is a nice addition to a meal.

VEGETABLES make excellent appetizers and snacks because of their variety in texture, color, flavor, and nutritive value.

Vegetables eaten plain or dipped in low-calorie dressings and sauces contain nutrients but few calories. Otherwise, sauces and dips such as cream cheese with chives, bacon or onion, hollandaise or cocktail sauce can be used. They can be served hot or cold and as finger food or fork food.

Carrots, celery, and radishes generally are served raw as snacks. Cauliflower, cabbage, green peppers, tomatoes, and pickled vegetables also may be offered raw as appetizers and snacks.

Some of the cooked vegetables that make good appetizers are artichokes, eggplant, mushrooms, leeks, onions, green peppers, tomatoes, asparagus, broccoli, green beans, and cabbage.

Vegetables can also be stuffed or used in fritters, puddings, souffles, soups, sauces, cakes, cookies, pies and breads.

Tomatoes, green and red peppers, mushrooms, cabbage, kohlrabi, artichokes, potatoes, sweetpotatoes, onions, cucumbers, zucchini and other squashes are especially good when stuffed.

The stuffings can be made of mixtures of rice, meat, bread, cheese, and other vegetables.

Corn, carrots, asparagus, mushrooms, and spinach are good in custards. Chopped spinach, broccoli, asparagus, onion, and corn are good in souffles.

Many creamed vegetable soups make excellent sauces for meat and main dishes or for other vegetables.

Onions, sweetpotatoes, spinach, corn, potatoes, and sauerkraut can be used in stuffings for meat, fish, and poultry. Squash, sweetpotatoes, and pumpkin can be used in dessert cakes, puddings, and pies.

Spinach pie, a Greek specialty, is served with the main course.

Carrots can be used in cakes, puddings, cookies, and bread. Peas, carrots, potatoes, cabbage, and cauliflower are some of the vegetables you can use in Indian curries or pilafs, which are oriental dishes made of rice boiled with meat, fowl, or fish and spice and vegetables.

ON YOUR OUTDOOR grill, you can cook vegetables in aluminum foil or put them directly on the grill or in the coals.

The fresh vegetables that can be cooked in foil are beets, corn, eggplant, mushrooms, onions, potatoes, sweetpotatoes, and squashes. They also can be cooked directly on the grill along with carrots, peppers, and tomatoes. Potatoes can be cooked in the coals.

Vegetable shish kabobs can be made of onions, carrots, tomatoes, potatoes, sweetpotatoes, and peppers.

Vegetables that can be roasted whole on the spit are white potatoes, yams, eggplant, green peppers, onions, and summer squashes.

Fresh vegetables can also be marinated or basted with various sauces during roasting.

Canned and frozen vegetables and vegetable casseroles also can be cooked on a grill. The frozen vegetables can be dotted with butter, wrapped in foil, and placed on the grill.

Canned vegetables in their opened cans and vegetable casseroles can be placed directly on the grill for heating.

To RETAIN their color and texture, vegetables must be properly cooked.

Overcooking green vegetables or cooking them with acid (such as lemon juice or vinegar) turns the bright green color to an olive green. On the other hand, a bit of acid in the cooking liquid of the white and red vegetables helps them retain their color.

To boil fresh vegetables, cook them in as little water as possible. Add salt to the water, if desired. Bring the salted water to a boil and add the vegetable. Return to boil, cover the pan, and reduce the heat. Cook gently until the vegetable is just tender.

Fresh carrots, onions, potatoes, sweetpotatoes, squash, and tomatoes also make excellent baked vegetables. They can be baked at 375° F. about 15 minutes for the onions and tomatoes and about 60 to 90 minutes for the others, depending on their size.

For frozen vegetables, follow the directions for boiling given on the package. You can also cook them in the oven while other foods are baking at a moderate temperature. Partly defrost the vegetable to separate the pieces, spread it into a greased casserole, season, and cover. Bake them until just tender (about 45 minutes at 350°). The length of time will vary with the size of the pieces and the amount of thawing.

Canned vegetables need only reheating. Drain the liquid from the vegetable into a saucepan; boil it down to about one-half its original volume. Add the vegetable and heat to serving temperature.

You no longer need to soak some dried vegetables overnight before cooking them. Up-to-date methods have shortened the preparation time for dried vegetables such as beans, peas, and lentils.

Dried beans and whole peas still need soaking before cooking, but a 2-minute boil before soaking softens the skins so that an hour of soaking is enough.

In preparing dehydrated or freeze-dried vegetables, follow the directions on the package. (KAREN L. BERKE)

New Ways
With Fruit

BESIDES COLOR and flavor, fruit adds health to meals.

Yellow and orange fruit—peaches, apricots, oranges—contribute vitamin A, which promotes normal vision, especially in dim light, and helps to keep the skin and linings of the nose, mouth, and inner organs in good condition and resistant to infection.

Most kinds of fruit are fair sources of the B-complex vitamins, which help with steady nerves, normal appetite, good digestion, good morale, and healthy skin.

Most of all, fruit is important as a source of vitamin C, which helps cement body cells, keeps tissues in good condition and resistant to infection, and helps in the healing of wounds. The familiar citrus fruit—oranges, grapefruit, and lemons—furnish bountiful amounts of vitamin C. A 4-ounce glass of orange or grapefruit juice, fresh, canned, or frozen, goes a long way toward meeting one's daily need for vitamin C.

The same is true of half a grapefruit, a whole orange, or a couple of tangerines and lemons. Other worthwhile sources of vitamin C are fresh strawberries and cantaloup.

Although most varieties are not rich sources of iron, which helps to build red blood, blackberries, apricots, peaches, oranges, prunes, figs, raisins, and dates, used in liberal amounts, are fair sources.

Fruit also contains cellulose. Because people cannot digest it, it adds bulk to the intestines and stimulates peristalsis, thus helping to avoid or overcome constipation.

Another virtue of fruit, particularly the acid varieties, is that in digestion they supply base-forming substances (the opposite of acids), which neutralize acid substances from other foods, such as meat, fish, poultry, eggs, cheese, cereals, and some nuts.

MAKE THE MOST, then, of fruit.

One way is to drink, first thing in the morning, a glass of chilled orange, grapefruit, prune, apricot, pineapple, or cranberry juice or a tropical blend.

Or, to start breakfast, have juice or fruit, whole, sliced, or chunked, canned, frozen, or fresh. To finish breakfast, have peaches, pears, plums, apricots, or applesauce. Another time, serve the dried form stewed. At other breakfasts, include fresh fruit in season, strawberries, other berries, and cantaloup.

High in water content and therefore comparatively low in calories, fruit is ideal for snacktime. Fruit juices, fresh, frozen, canned, or bottled, are anytime-of-day beverages.

A bowl of fresh fruit is a ready-to-eat snack and is decorative as well.

For lunch or dinner, use fresh or processed fruit or juices as appetizers, accompaniments to the main course, or dessert.

As an appetizer, serve the juices plain or blended and the fruits as salads or fruit cups.

Fruit soups may be an appetizer or dessert; we give a recipe later.

Used with cheese, fruit makes a hearty salad main course for lunch. As a salad with a sandwich lunch, fruit provides contrasting succulence.

Baked apples, bananas, and pears and stewed or spiced, dried prunes, peaches, and apricots go well with meat. Canned and frozen fruit needs no preparation for such uses. They also are readymade desserts as they are or when garnished with mincemeat, jelly, jam, cranberry sauce, or chopped candied ginger.

Fresh fruit makes a good dessert,

served on individual fruit plates with a fruit fork and knife.

To GET THE MOST for the money when you buy fresh fruit:

Make your own inspections and selections, asking yourself, "What is best for my purposes?"

Consider fruit in season in nearby fruitgrowing sections. The price in season usually is lower, but do not buy it merely because the price is low.

Do not buy more than you can store or refrigerate or use without waste.

Avoid selections that show deterioration, as waste offsets any reduction in price.

The largest is not always the best. Heft the fruit to weigh it, particularly oranges and melons; and if they are light for size, they may lack juiciness.

Learn the difference between defects that affect appearance only and those that affect edible quality. Many blemishes can be removed in normal preparation.

Watch for full measure of containers. Examine containers in which the best specimens are on top and ordinary or poor fruit is underneath.

Consider the commodities designated as plentiful foods by the Department of Agriculture.

Do not handle fruits unnecessarily. Rough handling causes spoilage and waste, for which consumers as a group must pay.

When you select fresh fruit, look for these desirable characteristics in each kind:

Apples—proper variety for intended purpose; fresh and firm; well colored for the variety; free from bruises.

Bananas—bright, fresh appearance; firm, unscarred; full yellow or brown-flecked yellow color if they are for immediate use.

Berries—fresh, clean, firm, with bright appearance; well colored for the type.

Cherries—fresh, bright, plump; good color for the variety.

Grapefruit—firm; heavy for size, relatively smooth, well shaped.

Grapes—plump, fresh, highly colored for the variety, firmly attached to stems.

Oranges—firm, heavy for size, reasonably fine-textured skin for the variety, good color for the variety.

Peaches—bright, plump, fresh appearance, yellowish or creamy background color with overlying blush or red, fairly firm to firm, free from bruises.

Pears—clean, plump, fairly firm to firm, free from bruises.

Cantaloups—well netted, "full slip" stem scar, color changing to yellowish-buff or gray; characteristic aroma.

Watermelons—good red flesh which appears firm and fresh, is not stringy, not watery or mealy, and contains dark-colored seeds.

If fresh fruit is to be kept for several days, store it in the area of the refrigerator designated by the manufacturer. Usually there is a bin for such products.

WHEN YOU BUY frozen fruit:

Choose a reputable dealer who buys quality frozen fruits from refrigerated trucks and keeps the packages frozen solidly until the consumer buys them.

Select packages that are clean and firm. Make sure that the packages are not torn, crushed, or juice stained.

When buying many groceries, select the frozen fruit last. For the trip home, protect them with an insulated bag or a double paper bag.

When you buy frozen fruit in quantity, check one package for quality soon after you buy it. If the fruit is not frozen solidly and of bright appearance, plan to store it for a short time only or return it to the store.

To check for quality when the package is opened, note whether frost has formed inside (large amounts may indicate impaired quality) and whether the color is normal and bright. Color changes indicate long holding periods or high temperatures. Some fruit held at too high temperatures first darken and then turn brown. Note also whether any undesirable change in texture has occurred, such as excessive softness or flabbiness.

Store in the freezing unit of the refrigerator for not more than a week. For longer periods, keep in a freezer at 0° F. or lower.

When you buy canned fruit:
Read the label to determine grade or quality.

Select the quality that best suits the purpose.

Choose the highest quality for salads and fruit cups and for serving as is. Second quality, which is fully as flavorful, will serve the purpose well in shortcakes, puddings, pies, and cobblers.

Store in a dry place at room temperature, preferably not above 70° and in a dark place to prevent color loss if canned in glass. Dampness causes rust, which in time may perforate the metal. To prevent breakdown of texture, avoid freezing canned fruit.

Lime Frost

1 cup fresh lime juice
2 tablespoons lemon juice
¾ cup canned pineapple juice
¾ cup sugar
¼ cup water
Ginger ale

Add the sugar to the fruit juices and water. Stir until dissolved. Freeze in ice cube trays that have dividers. Place two cubes in a glass, add the ginger ale and serve as appetizer or between-meal snack beverage. Serves 9.

Fruit Soup

12 oz. can apricot nectar
12 oz. can pear nectar
12 oz. can cranberry juice
1 tablespoon cornstarch
1 pint can or jar of apple-raspberry sauce.
½ tablespoon lemon juice
1 teaspoon grated lemon rind
⅛ teaspoon cinnamon
⅛ teaspoon salt
Few drops red food coloring

Combine the first three ingredients in a saucepan. Add the cornstarch.

Cook over low heat until slightly thickened. Add the remaining ingredients and heat to simmering point. Garnish with lemon slices. Serve hot or chilled. Serves 8.

Citrus Cooler

Add 1 cup sugar to 1 cup fresh, frozen, or canned lemon juice and stir until completely dissolved. Add 4 cups orange juice (fresh, canned, or frozen) and 8 cups chilled ginger ale or sparkling water. Pour into tall glasses. Just before serving, top with scoops of ice cream or sherbet. Garnish with orange and lemon slices or fresh strawberries. 12 servings.

With Main Dishes

Glazed apricots with ham slices.
Pineapple tidbits with curried shrimp or baked fish fillets.
Hot minted pears with lamb.
Cinnamon apple slices with pork.
Spiced peaches, plums, or cherries with poultry.
Canned peach halves broiled with hamburgers or chops on the grill.
Chunks of pineapple, peaches, or bananas alternated with meats as kabobs.

Baked Fruit Flambé

1 cup orange marmalade
4 teaspoons grated lemon peel
½ cup lemon juice
3 cups light-brown sugar, firmly packed
3 teaspoons cinnamon
2 cans (1 lb. size) peach halves, drained
2 cans (1 lb. size) pear halves, drained
2 jars (9½ oz. size) pineapple sticks, drained
4 bananas, peeled and quartered
2 teaspoons rum flavoring
2 cubes sugar
Lemon extract

Preheat oven to 400°. In small saucepan, combine marmalade, lemon peel, and lemon juice; mix well. Bring just to simmering over low heat. Add rum flavoring and set aside.

Meanwhile, in a medium bowl, combine brown sugar and cinnamon; mix well.

Dry the fruit (except the banana quarters) well on paper towels. Dip all pieces of fruit in marmalade mixture, then in sugar mixture, coating completely.

Arrange the fruit in two 13½ x 9 x 2 inch baking dishes. Bake 15 minutes.

Just before serving, place the sugar cubes on top of fruit, wet thoroughly with lemon extract, ignite, and serve. Makes 12 servings.

STIR-AND-BAKE FRUIT COBBLER

1 cup sugar
1 cup plain flour
1 cup milk
2 teaspoons baking powder
½ teaspoon salt
1 teaspoon nutmeg or cinnamon
½ stick butter or margarine
1 pint of canned fruit and juice (cherries, pears, apricots, peaches, fruit cocktail, or stewed dried fruits)

Make batter of first six ingredients. Cut butter or margarine into 3 or 4 pieces and add. Pour into a greased baking dish. Add fruit and juice. Bake at 325° until brown (about 45 minutes). Serves 6 to 8.

PERSIAN PEACHES

4 cups sliced peaches
1 cup orange juice
6 tablespoons honey
2 to 3 tablespoons finely chopped candied ginger
Dash salt

Combine all ingredients, mixing gently. Cover; chill thoroughly. Spoon into chilled sherbet glasses. Makes 5 servings.

CANTALOUP RING SALAD

Peel cantaloup and slice one-half inch thick. Remove seeds from slices and place on bed of lettuce. Fill the center of each cantaloup ring with fresh seedless grapes, cubed peaches,

pears, or bananas dipped in lemon juice, and garnish with strawberries, cherries, or blueberries.

APPLE-FIG SALAD

Wash, core, and slice red apples. Arrange apple slices and canned Kadota figs on bed of salad greens.

Garnish with seedless raisins or chopped dates. Serve immediately.

DESSERT FRUIT AND CHEESE TRAY

1 No. 2½ can whole apricots, drained
2 1-lb. cans blueberries, drained
2 oranges, peeled and sectioned

Assorted cheeses (Edam or Gouda; Camembert, Port du Salut are good selections)

Put the chilled apricots in one bowl and blueberries in another. Garnish blueberries with orange sections. Arrange the fruit and cheese on a large tray, with assorted crackers at hand. Serve with both dessert plates and sauce dishes convenient to the tray. Serves 6.

PLUM SORBET

1 quart can greengage plums
Juice from canned plums

Drain the plums, mash, and put through a coarse sieve, and recombine with juice. Freeze in refrigerator tray or ice cream freezer to mushy stage. Serve in chilled sherbet glasses. Garnish with fresh strawberries, maraschino cherries, or orange wedges. Serves 4 to 6.

RASPBERRY SORBET

1 10-oz. package of frozen raspberries

In a mixer, blend frozen raspberries to a semiliquid stage. Serve in chilled sherbet or cocktail glasses. Garnish with grated coconut or sprig of mint. Serves 3 or 4. (SUSAN C. CAMP AND IZOLA F. WILLIAMS)

Beverages

BEVERAGES, which are any fluids we drink, may be hot, cold, thick, thin, nourishing or not, stimulating or not, and pleasant or unpleasant. They may quench thirst, appease hunger, or refresh or do all three.

Beverages include water, milk, fruit and vegetable juices, coffee, tea, soup, cocoa, chocolate, carbonated drinks, and drinks made from fruit and cereal grains. Nobody could live very long without a goodly amount of liquid every day.

Beverages may be fresh, frozen, canned, low in calories, natural, synthetic, or a combination of natural and synthetic.

Generally we prefer the natural, fresh flavor, but personal likes, time and ease of preparation, flavor, availability, storage space, and cost are factors that determine the form of beverage we choose.

Beverages can be used in various ways and for various purposes.

A beverage high in vitamin C (such as orange and grapefruit juice) can be served at breakfast and provide all or most of the vitamin C needed for the day.

Beverages served as the first course of a meal may stimulate the appetite. At a party, they may be served before the guests are seated at the dining table.

One or more beverages, such as coffee, tea, or fruit punch, are usually served at teas and receptions, often with some food such as cakes or sandwiches, suitable to the guests and the hour.

Beverages that are used as snacks by themselves or with other food should be selected carefully. Snacks may be high in fat and sugar and low or lacking in other nutrients. Fruit and vegetable juices and fruit drinks can provide nutrients and relatively few calories if they are not highly sweetened. Fruit juices and drinks may be combined with milk for added flavor and food value.

Water, the most important beverage, is next to oxygen in importance to our survival. It is the base of most other beverages. It should come from a safe, dependable source.

FRUIT JUICES may be fresh, frozen, refrigerated, bottled, and canned.

Frozen fruit juices are concentrates of the fruit juice. Mixed with the suggested amount of water, they are similar to the same fresh fruit juice. The frozen concentrates save time and space.

Bottled and canned fruit juices include lemon, lime, grapefruit, orange, pineapple, prune, grape, apple, cranberry, fig, apricot, peach, pear, and papaya. They are natural fruit juices and can be used in any way fresh juices are used.

Vegetable juices include tomato, sauerkraut, and carrot juices and combinations of two or more.

The average values of the various forms of orange juice are similar. A cup of fresh, canned (unsweetened), frozen concentrate (water added), and dehydrated (water added) orange juice has 100, 120, 110, and 115 Calories, respectively, and 112, 100, 112, and 108 milligrams, respectively, of vitamin C.

Usually the flavor and nutritive value of juices are better if they are prepared from high-quality fruit or vegetables as soon as possible after harvest. Most commercially canned and frozen juices are prepared under these conditions—in fact, it is possible that canned and frozen juices could be better in flavor and food value than juices made from fresh fruit and vegetables that are not of high quality or are not handled properly.

Much of the nutritive value is lost when the juice—whether juice freshly squeezed from fruit or from a can—comes in contact with heat and air. Keep it cold and covered, therefore, to retain as much food value as possible.

Only citrus fruit juices, tomato juice, and fruit and vegetable juices to which the processor has added extra amounts of vitamin C are dependable sources of vitamin C.

When you serve fruit juices cold, it is better to put the ice in the glass and pour the thoroughly chilled juice over it so as not to dilute the juice unduly.

Tea and plain-flavored carbonated beverages give body and variety to fruit-juice beverages. When you mix tea and fruit juices, be sure that the combination will be an attractive color. When carbonated beverages are used, the drink should be served quickly.

Fruit beverages can also be made more attractive by adding scoops of sherbet, mint leaves, and pieces of fruit.

Fruit juices frozen in ice cube trays that have release levers add flavor and help make the beverage more attractive.

Fruit juices served hot may be made especially tasty with spices, such as spiced cider or spiced tea.

Vegetable juices can be served hot or cold.

COFFEE is a popular drink almost everywhere. The many available blends vary according to brand and the place where the beans were grown.

Most coffee is purchased ground, although many coffee lovers insist the only way is to grind it themselves fresh every day.

Grinds of coffee you can buy include percolator, regular, drip, fine, and extra fine to be used in those kinds of coffeemakers used.

You have a choice of a great number of kinds of coffee. Each one has its own special flavor. The most common ones are Santos and Rio coffees, which come from Brazil. Milder coffees, such as Java, Mocha, Bogota, and Puerto Rican, usually are added to the Brazil coffees.

Instant coffee saves time and space and is convenient when coffee is prepared in small amounts. A new product is freeze-dried coffee.

When you make coffee, use a thoroughly clean coffeemaker. Use freshly drawn, cold water.

Measure coffee and water accurately.

For weak coffee, use 1 tablespoon coffee to three-fourths cup water.

For medium coffee, use 2 tablespoons coffee to three-fourths cup water.

For strong coffee, use 3 or 4 tablespoons coffee to three-fourths cup water.

Use the proper grind for your coffeemaker.

If your percolator is not automatic, perk coffee 5 to 10 minutes for the strength you want. After doing this you will know the exact amount of time so you can time it accurately. Avoid boiling.

Serve the coffee fresh or keep it at the serving temperature. Do not reheat cold coffee.

Coffeemakers include percolators, dripolators, vacuum types, and the "boiled" coffee pots. Good coffee can be made with any of them if you follow directions.

If the coffee grind is smaller than the openings in the basket in the percolator or dripolator, a filter paper will help keep the grounds from going through.

Besides the usual way of serving coffee hot and black or with cream and sugar, some people like it with whipped cream that has been flavored with cinnamon, cocoa, grated orange, or crushed peppermint candy. In some countries it is made strong and served half and half with hot milk—café au lait.

For iced coffee, the coffee is made stronger than usual.

THE THREE TYPES of tea are green, black, and oolong. The green is not fermented, the black is fermented, and the oolong is half-fermented.

Black teas made from the youngest leaves are designated as flowery pekoe, flowery orange pekoe, broken orange pekoe, and orange pekoe.

Since the younger leaves are considered to give the finest quality of tea, black teas that carry those names are regarded as the best grades.

Black teas made from older and larger leaves are called pekoe and souchong. Most black tea on the market is a combination of orange pekoe and pekoe.

Special blends available in some markets or specialty shops include flavors such as smoke, jasmine or other flowers, and spices.

You can buy tea in bulk or in bags and as instant. Some instant teas are flavored with lemon and sugar.

Tea should be made from freshly drawn cold water, which is brought just to the boil and poured promptly over the tea. Avoid boiling. Instant tea may be made with hot or cold water.

A clear iced tea may be made by putting tea in a glass or pottery container and covering with cold water. Put a lid on the container and place in the refrigerator for 24 hours.

Cocoa AND CHOCOLATE are used as beverage bases. Their main difference is the amount of fat.

Of the many grades of cocoa and chocolate, the higher quality generally is less harsh and bitter.

Chocolate is at least 50 percent fat, and breakfast cocoa has at least 22 percent fat.

Dutch-process cocoa has been treated so that it dissolves more easily and has a darker color and a bland flavor.

Instant and regular cocoa are usually made with milk, but some have dried milk added and are made with water. Milk increases the food value.

Instant malted milk, chocolate flavored drinks, and chocolate syrup can be used to make hot or cold chocolate drinks.

Hot broth consommé or hot or cold creamed soups can be used as beverages. They may be homemade or purchased. Broth is available in cans or in cubes, to which you need add only hot water.

FRUIT DRINKS—powdered, bottled, canned, refrigerated, and frozen— may be made from natural or synthetic fruit juice or a combination of the two. Some contain pulp of the fruit. Other ingredients may include natural or artificial flavoring, coloring and sweetening, added vitamins, and a preservative.

Carbonated beverages in bottles and cans include cola, fruit-flavored, or plain concoctions. They may be artificially sweetened so that the calorie value has been lowered.

FOUNDATION PUNCH

3 cups strained orange juice
1½ to 2 cups strained lemon juice
2 cups sugar
Water to make 1 gallon

Make the sugar into a syrup with 2 cups of the water. Cool. Combine with fruit juice and remaining water. Pour a small amount into a punch bowl; add a block of ice; pour the rest of the punch over ice. Tea may be substituted for part of the water.

VARIATIONS

For cranberry, grape, raspberry, pineapple, or cherry punch: Allow 3 parts of foundation punch to 1 to 2 parts grape, raspberry, cranberry, pineapple, or cherry juice.

Tea punch: Allow 3 parts of foundation punch or lemonade to 2 parts tea.

Mint punch: One gallon of foundation punch and 1 dozen small sprigs of fresh mint. Pour the hot syrup used in making foundation punch over the mint. Let stand 5 minutes. Strain and cool before adding to fruit juice. A garnish of fresh mint is good.

Ginger ale punch: Use the foundation punch, substituting 1 bottle of ginger ale for an equal amount of water.

SPICED TEA

Juice of 1 lemon
Juice and grated rind of 2 oranges
1 teaspoon cloves
2 qts. boiling water
Grated rind of ½ lemon
2 cups sugar
2 sticks cinnamon
¼ cup tea
Steep for 20 minutes. Strain and serve hot.

LEMON COOLER

2 lemons
½ cup sugar
1 pint milk
Sweet soda or ginger ale
Grate and squeeze the lemons. Combine sugar and the lemon juice and rind with milk and beat until foamy. Pour one-fourth cup into a glass. Add ice and soda.   (JOSEPHINE FLORY)

Cooking Out

MENUS for outdoor cookery need not be confined to a few foods. Steaks and hamburgers are delicious—but so are chicken, turkey, fish, seafoods, stew, and barbecued beans.

First decide on the meat or main dish. Then select salad, vegetables, bread, beverages, and dessert to complement it. A meal cooked outdoors can be just as nutritious, colorful, and appealing as one served inside.

Plan your menu with a variety of flavors. Accent one or two of the dishes with smoky, spicy flavor. Have others with bland flavor.

Simplicity is the key to successful cookouts. Limit the number of items you actually will cook outdoors. When you are feeding a crowd, be sure your facilities for cooking are adequate for serving all the guests at one time.

Before an outdoor meal, make a list of everything you need and assemble the items.

Be sure to have working space near the fire for the chef.

A buffet table set a reasonable distance from the cooking area—on the side away from the smoke—is best for serving.

Heavy paper plates and napkins reduce the dishwashing.

Plan how you will keep hot foods hot and cold foods cold. Vacuum jugs and picnic chests can be a help. Food can be prepared in the kitchen and brought out in a casserole. Some of your electrical appliances can be put to good use outside, too.

Have plenty of food. The outdoors stimulates appetites.

ALTHOUGH outdoor cooking can be done with the simplest of grills—even a long stick over a fire—many outdoor chefs now have the convenience of supermodel barbecue equipment.

If you have no firsthand experience with open-fire cookery, better resist the temptation to build an elaborate fireplace or buy expensive equipment—at least to start with.

All that is necessary is a portable grill—one that is adjustable and has a durable firebox.

The most commonly used accessories are: Asbestos gloves (you may also want cotton gloves); two pairs of long-handled tongs (one for meat, one for charcoal); long-handled salt and pepper shakers; long-handled spatula, fork, spoon, basting brush; cutting board for carving and carving knife and fork; and rolls of paper toweling near the grill.

FOR THE FIRE, the chances are you will be using charcoal briquets.

A base of gravel or similar material about an inch thick in the firebox permits the fire to breathe by drawing in air from below. Wash the gravel after using it several times.

The firebox may be lined with heavy aluminum foil, which will increase the radiant heat and also make for easier cleaning.

Use lighter fluid to help ignite the charcoal. Do not use kerosene as a starter; it produces undesirable flavor. Never use gasoline; it is much too dangerous. Put the lighter fluid on only a few pieces of charcoal. Stack them in the form of a pyramid before igniting.

A chimney is a help. You can make one from a tall can by cutting off both ends. Cut holes at the bottom of the can about an inch apart to allow draft.

After the fire starts, spread the briquets and add as many more as you will need to cook for the crowd.

Do not start cooking before the fire has burned down to gray coals with no flame. Novice outdoor cooks may use too much fuel; the food burns before it is done inside.

Even though you have trimmed excess fat from the meat, you may still get flareups from drippings. Control the heat and flareups with water in a plastic squirt bottle or clothes sprinkler. Use just enough water for control of the fire; do not soak the coals.

SOME TIPS on charcoal broiling, beginning with steaks:

Meat is the hub of your meal; everyone should have a portion from the first grilling.

Select your steak carefully. Have it cut to 1.5 to 2 inches thick. A thick steak, which can be carved into serving portions, is better than several thin ones.

Tender cuts are best—sirloin, club, T-bone, porterhouse. Round or flank steak should be marinated or treated with tenderizer. Trim the excess fat so drippings will not blaze up. Slash the edge of steak at 2-inch intervals to prevent buckling.

Spear some of the steak trimmings with a long-handled fork and rub them over the hot grill to keep the steak from sticking.

When the coals have burned down to a glow with a gray film over the top, it is time to start cooking the steak. Arrange the steak 3 to 5 inches from

the hot coals. Broil the first side until brown. Turn with tongs instead of a fork to avoid losing juices.

Salt and pepper the browned side.

Continue broiling until the steak is done the way you like it.

For a 1-inch steak (starting with the meat at room temperature), the approximate cooking time for each side is 6 to 8 minutes for rare and 10 to 15 minutes for medium to well done.

For a steak 2 inches thick, the approximate cooking time for each side is 10 to 15 minutes for rare and 15 to 20 minutes for medium to well done.

If you like, brush the steak with barbecue sauce from time to time during the cooking.

For a quick smoke flavor, toss a few damp hickory chips over the coals near the end of the cooking time.

As to hamburgers: Look for bright red meat, with some fat for flavor.

If you have beef ground to order, choose round steak, chuck, flank, or sirloin tip. Medium-ground or coarsely ground meat gives a light-textured hamburger.

Handle the meat lightly. The more gently you handle the patties, the more tender your hamburgers will be.

If the grids of the grill are too widely spaced to hold the hamburgers, place heavy aluminum foil on the grill.

Turn the meat only once while you are broiling it—do not flip it back and forth.

Brush the patties with your favorite barbecue sauce if desired.

For lamb chops, select thick (1 to 1.5 inches) loin or rib chops. Slash the fat around the edges. Grill about 3 to 5 inches from the heat to the desired doneness (10 to 20 minutes). Turn once. Season and serve.

Ham slices: Select a cooked ham slice 1 inch thick. Trim off the fat and cut the edge to prevent curling. Place on the slightly greased grill about 4 to 6 inches from the coals. Grill until brown (about 5 minutes). Turn and continue grilling until brown.

Uncooked ham will require about double the time.

Choose a chicken weighing about 2.5 pounds when ready to cook, split in half lengthwise or quartered. Some may prefer chicken pieces.

Break the joints of the leg, hip, and wings, so the bird will lie flat during grilling.

Chicken may be marinated in barbecue sauce. Drain off the excess sauce before grilling.

Place the chicken on the grill 6 to 8 inches from coals with the bone side nearest the heat. Turn every 3 to 5 minutes. Baste with sauce. Do not let the chicken burn or blister. Cooking takes 40 to 60 minutes, depending on size. A larger size may take close to 90 minutes. Chicken is done when the joints move easily.

Turkey can be grilled in the same way. The time you must allow depends on the size of the pieces.

Fish or shellfish cooked over charcoal has a delicious flavor. All fish may be cooked out of doors by any of the basic cooking methods. Overcooking toughens it, dries it out, and destroys its delicate flavor.

Cut fillets, steaks, or pan-dressed fish into serving-size portions and place in a single layer in a shallow baking dish. Pour your favorite barbecue sauce or French dressing over the fish and let it stand for 30 minutes, turning once. Remove the fish, reserving the sauce for basting.

Place the fish in a well-greased, hinged-wire toaster-basket. Cook it about 4 inches from moderately hot coals for about 8 minutes. Baste with sauce. Turn and cook 7 to 10 minutes longer, or until the fish flakes easily when you test it with a fork.

SKEWERS, you know, are thin sticks of wood or metal on which you spear pieces of food, including meat, for cooking.

Thread on a skewer the items that cook in a reasonable time. Alternate pieces of meat and a vegetable or fruit. Use cubes of tender cuts of meat, such as sirloin. Some vegetables should be parboiled. Bacon strips wrapped around other foods are used to add flavor as well as fat.

For shish kabob, squares of meat from a leg of lamb are soaked in a marinade of oil, food acid, such as lemon juice or vinegar, and seasonings.

Less-tender cuts of beef, like round steak, also are marinated. Thin strips of round steak cut across the grain are preferable to cubes, since round is a less-tender cut of meat.

Additional oil or butter is added to the marinade to use as a basting sauce. Have the basting sauce hot so it will not cool the foods.

From Hawaii, we have learned to use short skewers for bite-sized, highly seasoned foods used as appetizers. These are often cooked on a hibachi, a small tabletop charcoal-burning stove introduced from the Orient.

Skewer cooking requires a slow fire and careful watching. This is just as true for grilling a hotdog as for the many other kabobs.

Here are some combinations to try:

Wrap bacon around wiener pieces which have been cut in fourths. Alternate with chunks of dill pickle.

Alternate onion slices, marinated lamb cubes, and green peppers.

Combine cherry tomatoes, beef sirloin cubes, mushrooms, and onions.

ROTISSERIE ROASTING, an ancient form of spit cookery, owes its revived popularity to the electric spit. Enthusiasts think that no other method cooks meat so evenly.

Select tender cuts of meat, which are regular in shape. Truss and tie chickens and turkeys so the wings and legs are tight against the body, in order to make the food as compact as possible.

Meat must be speared through the middle to balance the weight and insure that the meat will turn with the rod.

The spit should turn away from the cook. Then the fat drops off on the upswing, and the fire can be placed toward the back of the firebox. Place a drip pan, which can be made of foil, under the meat.

Basting is optional unless the meat is very lean. Meat that is properly spitted will baste itself automatically with its own juices.

The time of cooking will depend on the size of the piece, the beginning temperature of the meats, and the temperature of the fire and whether the spit is shielded from the wind.

The satisfactory way to determine doneness is to use a meat thermometer. Beef is done rare at 130°–135° F., medium at 145°–155°, and well done at 160°–180°. Pork should be cooked to 185°.

WHEN YOU MARINATE meat, you soak it in an oil-acid mixture, which usually is seasoned with sugar, spices, and herbs. The acid may be supplied by vinegar, tomato juice, or lemon juice. The marinade flavors meat and tenderizes it.

Be sure to soak the meat in the liquid at least 1 hour before grilling. The marinade may be brushed on during grilling as a barbecue sauce.

Barbecue sauces also are an oil-acid mixture seasoned with spices, herbs, and various additions, like catsup, Worcestershire sauce, tabasco, horseradish, chopped onion, garlic, or brown sugar.

Most outdoor chefs agree that barbecue sauces should be spicy but not necessarily fiery. The purpose is to enhance—not overpower—the meat flavor.

Barbecue sauces are a matter of taste. Some like them hot and spicy. Others prefer them mild, with a hint of herb. Recipes for them are endless. Find one that suits your taste or concoct your own. A commercial oil-type salad dressing, such as Italian or French, is an easy barbecue sauce.

For lemon barbecue sauce, stir in one-half cup oil, one-half cup lemon juice, 2 tablespoons chopped onion, one-half teaspoon salt, one-half teaspoon pepper, and one-half teaspoon dried thyme. Allow to stand at least 1 hour to blend flavors. This recipe makes three-fourths cup of sauce and is particularly good with fish and fowl.

An all-purpose barbecue sauce can be made by adding one-third cup catsup, one-third cup tomato juice, one-half teaspoon Worcestershire sauce, three-fourths teaspoon paprika, and two-thirds cup water to the lemon barbecue sauce. The thyme may be omitted. Crushed garlic or garlic salt may be added. Vinegar may be used instead of lemon juice. Heat to boiling and keep hot for basting.

Opinions vary on the best time to use the sauce for basting. Some use it before and throughout the cooking period. Others prefer to brown the meat before starting the basting.

TWO POPULAR baked vegetables to accompany a barbecue are baked potatoes and roasted corn. You may prefer your potato baked in the coals and your corn roasted in the husks. A practical way is to wrap them in heavy-duty aluminum foil.

Choose firm, medium-size baking potatoes (or yams or sweetpotatoes). Scrub the potatoes and brush them with salad oil. Wrap each in a square of aluminum foil, overlapping the ends.

Bake them 45 to 60 minutes on the grill or on top of the coals. Turn the potatoes occasionally.

Give them the pinch test for doneness. When ready, fork open and push ends to fluff. Season and serve.

Toppings for baked potatoes may be sour cream, pats of butter, chopped chives, green onions, crumbled Blue cheese, and grated Parmesan cheese. Some like to crumble crisp bacon on baked potatoes.

For roasted corn, select young, tender ears. Remove the husks and silk. Spread the corn with butter, sprinkle with salt and pepper, and then wrap it securely in aluminum foil. Roast for 15 to 20 minutes over hot coals or on the grill. Turn several times.

Frozen vegetables are fine for outdoor cooking because they cook quickly. Thaw the vegetables until they can be broken into chunks. Place the chunks on a large sheet of heavy foil or two sheets of light foil, or make individual packets. Add salt, pepper, butter. Shape into a long, flat package, with edges of foil tucked under. Place on the grill and cook about 5 minutes longer than the printed directions. Serve from the foil; fold the edges back.

You may like to have a relish tray arranged with crisp vegetables in place of a more conventional salad. Help-yourself combinations may include celery sticks, sliced cucumbers, carrot strips, tomato wedges, young green onions, radishes, peppers, and cauliflower. Crushed ice under the vegetables will help keep them crisp.

Vegetables with a robust dressing complement the barbecue. If your salad must travel, pack it at the last minute into refrigerator bags, foil, or vegetable crisper. Add the dressing just before serving the salad.

FOR DESSERT, the best advice is keep it simple.

Have it kitchen cooked and carried outside or not cooked at all.

Cheese and fruit are ample to complete the outdoor meal. Trays of grapes, apples, pears, pineapple chunks, melon slices, and berries are colorful and nutritious. Add to this your favorite kind of cheese.

Fruit kabobs, made of chunks of firm fruit threaded on skewers, are another possibility. Various flavors, colors, and textures of the fruit add interest.

Cookies, cupcakes, and brownies are easy to serve. They are adequate alone, but they team up well with ice cream. (FERN S. KELLEY AND EVELYN B. SPINDLER)

For further reading, consult the following Department of Agriculture publications:
Eggs in Family Meals, A Guide for Consumers, Home and Garden Bulletin No. 103; *Family Fare, Food Management and Recipes,* Home and Garden Bulletin No. 1; *Meat for Thrifty Meals,* Home and Garden Bulletin No. 27; *Potatoes in Popular Ways,* Home and Garden Bulletin No. 55; *Tomatoes on Your Table,* Leaflet No. 278.

Timesaving Tricks

WORKING WIVES, full-time home-makers, single girls, and even bachelors all need at some time or other to prepare a meal quickly.

My most helpful suggestion is: Plan ahead. A little thought can save a lot of steps and time.

Keep on hand a supply of quickly prepared foods for unexpected guests and for days you are late and have to prepare a meal in a hurry. You can prepare quick and good meals with canned and frozen meat, vegetables, and fruit; mixes; and canned and dehydrated soup.

Know well a few tried-and-true quick recipes that you can trust in an emergency.

Plan for leftovers. Buy a roast that will do for two or three meals. The cooked meat can be used in casseroles, salads, sandwiches, and other quickly prepared dishes.

Prepare some foods in advance if you know company is coming and you will not have much time to prepare dinner that evening.

Get ingredients ready to go together—salad greens washed and refrigerated in a plastic bag; onion, green pepper, and other raw vegetables prepared and stored in tightly covered containers; seasonings measured into a small jar.

Some casseroles can be prepared and refrigerated one day and baked the next day.

Desserts, such as pie and cake, and gelatin salads can be made a day ahead of time.

FROM SOUP MIXES to chopped nuts, the array of foods that are partly or fully prepared is amazing. They provide an excellent way of speeding things up.

Does your recipe call for a sauce? Try canned sauce, dehydrated sauce mix, or undiluted canned cream soup.

Need a crumb topping for a casserole? Combine herb-seasoned stuffing mix with melted fat.

Want onion, garlic, mushroom, or parsley flavor without peeling or chopping? Use dehydrated onion or parsley flakes, bottled onion juice, instant garlic powder, freeze-dried mushrooms.

THE LABELS on packages of mixes and refrigerated doughs often suggest variations, but your own ideas may be even better.

From biscuit mix or refrigerated dough, for example, you can make sweet rolls, coffeecake, doughnuts, shortcake, cobblers, bread sticks, turnovers, fruit or meat rollups, miniature pizzas, and more.

You can use cake mixes for upsidedown cakes, coffeecake, cupcakes, baked Alaska, and Boston cream pie. Or serve the cake warm from the oven with a hot sauce made from a pudding mix.

Homemade mixes for biscuits, pastry, and other quick breads are easy to make.

Pastry mix usually contains flour, salt, and fat; biscuit mix contains those ingredients plus baking powder. Nonfat dry milk can be included in the biscuit mix if desired.

Use the proportion of ingredients in a basic recipe for pastry or biscuits. Blend the dry ingredients thoroughly; then cut in the fat.

If you make the mixes with hydrogenated vegetable shortening and double-acting baking powder, they will keep several weeks in a tightly closed container at room temperature. When you are ready to bake, just add the liquid ingredients and blend.

Homemade mixes can be varied in the same way as commercial mixes.

Homemade refrigerated doughs that you can keep on hand include cooky dough and yeast roll dough. Use any recipe for "refrigerator cookies" or "refrigerator rolls."

If it is tightly wrapped, cooky dough will keep up to a week in the refrigerator or 4 to 6 months in a freezer at 0° F. Yeast roll dough will keep 4 to 5 days in the refrigerator.

If you want to freeze yeast roll dough, make a rich dough with twice the usual amount of yeast and freeze it immediately after kneading. Do not allow it to rise first. Yeast dough prepared this way can be stored up to 2 months in a freezer at 0°.

OVEN, pressure cooker, electric mixer, electric blender, electric frypan, freezer—all can make your life easier.

You can prepare a complete meal in your oven (except salad and beverage), if you plan carefully. Select foods that require about the same baking temperature. At 375°, for example, you can bake meat loaf, potatoes (they will require 10 to 20 minutes longer than at 425°), tomatoes, and apples. When the meat loaf comes out of the oven, boost the temperature to 400° and put in a pan of muffins. Make a salad and a beverage, and dinner is ready.

A good broiler meal may include shish kabobs (meat cubes, green pepper pieces, mushrooms, and tiny onions threaded on skewers), broiled tomatoes, and canned whole potatoes brushed with melted fat and broiled.

One-dish meals baked in the oven are timesavers. An example is a casserole that combines meat or poultry, vegetables, and biscuit topping.

A pressure cooker can cut hours from the cooking time for such slow-cooking meats as pot roasts, swiss steak, shortribs, corned beef, and spareribs. Beets, dry beans, and potatoes also can be cooked in much less time than they ordinarily need. Follow the manufacturer's directions exactly. Even a minute or two of overcooking may be too much.

An electric mixer saves time and

energy in mixing cakes, cookies, and other batters and doughs and in preparing meringues and whipped toppings. Keep your mixer ready to use in a handy place. You will use it oftener if it is convenient.

An electric blender can quickly puree foods; make soups smooth; whip up drinks, such as milkshakes; chop nuts; blend salad dressings, sauces, and sandwich spreads; and grate cheese, breadcrumbs, and raw vegetables.

An electric frypan is good for frying, panbroiling, braising, and grilling because it produces an even, controlled heat. Perhaps its most timesaving use is to prepare one-dish combinations of meat and vegetables cooked together. A good combination is ham slices with glazed sweetpotatoes and pineapple. Another is pork chops braised with tomatoes and rice.

WHEN YOU HAVE A FREEZER, you can keep on hand a supply of prepared foods that need only to be thawed or heated before serving. You can save time by preparing two or three times the amount you need for one meal and freezing the extra. When you are planning a party, you can avoid some of the last-minute rush by preparing foods in advance and freezing them.

Main dishes that freeze well include cooked meat and poultry, stews, meat or poultry pies, meat loaves, chile con carne, meatballs in sauce, stuffed peppers, various casserole dishes, and creamed meat, poultry, and fish. Cool the food quickly; then package and freeze it at once.

Casserole dishes can be frozen right in the baking dish. If you need the container for another use, line it with foil, add the food, and freeze. Then you can lift out the contents and wrap tightly in foil.

For best quality, plan to use frozen cooked main dishes within a few weeks.

Baked products that freeze well include yeast breads, quick breads, cakes, cookies, and pies (except meringue and custard pies).

Cakes can be frozen either unfrosted

or frosted, but boiled or 7-minute frostings do not freeze well.

You can package and freeze individual portions of cake, cookies, and pies and store them in a plastic bag. They will be handy for packed lunches.

Sandwiches of many kinds freeze well. It saves time to make lunch-box sandwiches weekly instead of daily. Party sandwiches, too, can be made several days ahead of time.

Use soft butter, margarine, cream cheese, or peanut butter as a spread—not mayonnaise or salad dressing, which soak into the bread. And omit egg white (which toughens), raw tomatoes and crisp greens, and very moist fillings.

Well-wrapped sandwiches keep up to a month in a freezer at $0°$; they thaw in 3 to 4 hours at room temperature.

FOR BUSY DAYS when you have to prepare a meal in minutes, here are some suggestions:

The kinds of meat that cook quickly include hamburgers (shape them before storing in refrigerator or freezer), cubed or minute steaks, liver, ham slices, thin pork chops (one-half inch thick), Canadian-type bacon, and frankfurters.

Meat loaf bakes in less than half the time it ordinarily requires if you press it into muffin pans instead of shaping into a large loaf.

Leftover roast meat or poultry (or canned tuna) heated with undiluted canned cream soup and served over biscuits or toast makes another quick main dish.

CANNED AND FROZEN vegetables save time because they need not be washed, pared, or shelled.

Solidly packed frozen vegetables, such as spinach and chopped broccoli, cook in less time if they are broken into small chunks before cooking.

You can shorten the cooking time of fresh vegetables by slicing, dicing, or coarsely shredding them.

To speed the slicing or dicing of

carrots, celery, potatoes, or onions, line up several on a cutting board and cut across all of them at once with a sharp knife.

Slice small cooked or canned potatoes or beets with an egg slicer.

Potatoes can be baked in half the time it usually takes if they are first boiled for 15 minutes.

Try this for a quick-setting gelatin salad: Empty the contents of a 3-ounce package of fruit-flavored gelatin into a 4-cup measure, add boiling water to the 1-cup mark, and stir to dissolve. Then add ice cubes to the 2-cup mark. Stir often until the mixture begins to thicken. Then stir in fruit, vegetables, or cottage cheese. Chill until set. If you use frozen fruit, use cold water instead of ice cubes and add the fruit without thawing; it will chill the mixture enough to hasten setting.

If you have a few minutes early in the day, make an ice cream pie or cake.

For pie: Make a crumb crust by mixing graham cracker or cooky crumbs with melted butter or margarine. Press the mixture into a pie pan. Chill it. Fill the crust with softened ice cream, rippled with sauce or crushed fruit if desired. Freeze until firm.

For cake: Slice a baked, unfrosted cake into three layers and spread softened ice cream between the layers. Top with sifted confectioners' sugar or whipped dessert topping; freeze.

For a last-minute dessert, top sherbet with fruit: Raspberry sherbet topped with raspberries, pineapple sherbet topped with pineapple, lemon sherbet topped with strawberries.

THESE ARE JUST a few suggestions to help you save time. You can think of others. Above all, careful planning and efficient use of modern foods and equipment will help you make the most of your time in the kitchen. (PATRICIA K. VANDERSALL)

For further reading:
U.S. Department of Agriculture, *Money-saving Main Dishes*. Home and Garden Bulletin No. 43, 1962.

Exotic Food

YOU CAN BECOME a world traveler of sorts by a trip no longer than one to your supermarket, where in full array are food items that not many years ago were prized as exotic, strange, mysterious.

By bringing some of the fine food of other countries to your table, you can give your family and friends new experiences in eating.

The recipes and details for foreign cookery you read in cookbooks and magazines may call for ingredients not available in the market, but you can make substitutions easily without destroying the quality of the dish.

The possibilities are almost endless, but we limit ourselves here to gustative journeys to a few countries.

WE TRAVEL FIRST to Italy to enjoy at firsthand Italian pizza and spaghetti.

Pizza means pie, so saying "pizza pie" is like saying "pie pie." The Italian pizza is made of a thin round of leavened dough worked up after leavening with a small amount of olive oil.

On this round, small depressions are made, and the whole is covered with one of a variety of mixtures. These may be only tomatoes and oregano or may include grated cheese, anchovies, or ground meat. Sometimes one-half of the round is covered with one mixture and the other with a different one.

Then the round of dough is placed in a hot oven and baked until the dough has become crusty. This, with a green salad, makes a good snack or lunch.

Pasta makes the meal for many Italians. Pasta includes spaghetti, macaroni, and lasagna. The Italians do not limit themselves to two or three, as we do, but use dozens of varieties. Try some of the more unusual ones on the grocery shelves the next time you want an Italian dish.

Minestrone soup, made thick with a variety of vegetables and spaghetti, is easy to make, hearty, and excellent for lunch.

Italians like vegetables—greens, artichokes, zucchini, cauliflower, asparagus, and many others. They often combine a variety of greens in fresh salads and use olive oil dressing.

Other vegetables they may stuff, prepare with tomato sauce, deep-fry, bake, or top with cheese sauce. Rarely are they merely boiled.

A popular dessert in Italy is fruit and cheese. A tray with a variety of cheeses on it and a bowl of fruit brought to the table where family or guests can make their own selection makes a fitting end, along with coffee, to a meal.

WE GO NEXT to Nigeria in Africa. Many dishes there may be too highly spiced for the average American palate, but you can control the amount of spice.

Many dishes are of the one-pot variety, in which several items are cooked together, like our stews and casseroles.

One such is jolliff rice, which combines such meats as chicken, pork, and ham with shrimp, vegetables, and rice. It is cooked on top of the stove.

Africans can give us new ideas about using peanuts, or groundnuts, in cooking. One cookbook from Nigeria lists 10 recipes that call for peanuts, including groundnut soup and groundnut biscuits. For most, the nuts are pounded to a paste. You can substitute peanut butter.

Groundnut soup made with chicken is delicious. For it, the chicken is cut in pieces and generally cooked with tomatoes, onions, and peppers, along with the groundnuts. The mixture is served over rice. With a salad, it makes a tasty meal.

Coconut, as used in African cooking, adds an interesting flavor to many dishes. For example, rice may be cooked in coconut milk rather than water; coconut milk may form the base for a soup.

THE NEAR EAST is the home of many spices, yet the food is not excessively hot.

One feature of its cookery is the wide use of vegetables, such as eggplant, cauliflower, asparagus, squash, and tomato.

Eggplant stuffed with a mixture of lamb or other meat, rice, and spices and simmered in tomato sauce makes a satisfying one-dish meal.

Leaves are used to wrap mixtures of rice, meat, and seasonings. Stuffed grape and cabbage leaves are famous. Either kind is first cooked until it is tender enough to shape. A mixture of rice, meat, and seasonings, such as onion, chopped parsley, cinnamon, allspice, and lemon, is placed on the leaf. The leaf is then folded around the mixture and placed in a pan lined with leaves. When all the stuffed leaves are in the pan, they are covered with liquid (water, tomato sauce, or sweet-sour sauce) and cooked until tender.

Yogurt, an ingredient of many dishes, may be eaten as it is or used with cucumbers or eggplant for appetizers or salads; in soups; for marinating meat; and with fruit, sugar, honey, or preserves as a dessert.

Apricots, prunes, pomegranates, and other kinds of fruit are combined with meat or poultry in soup or main dishes.

Bulgur, or pilaf, is a basic cereal. It is a wheat product and has a nutty flavor. It is available in American markets in a dry form and as ready-to-use canned bulgur.

Bulgur can add variations to any part of the meal from soup to dessert, but a starting place may be as an accompaniment to the meat in place of rice or potatoes. When recipes call for rice or noodles in soup, bulgur can be substituted.

The shish kabob, from the Turkish

words for skewer and broiling, is made of meat cut in small pieces and marinated. The pieces are seasoned and placed on a skewer alternately with green pepper, onion, and tomato, and broiled.

A range of herbs and spices includes allspice, bay leaves, cardamom seeds, cinnamon, curry powder, dill, garlic, mint, nutmeg, oregano, paprika, saffron, sumac, tarragon, thyme, and tumeric. Many spices are used, but the flavors are combined subtly to make a dish that is not hot.

FROM INDIA we learned about curry, which is easy to prepare and gives a cook wide scope.

Curry, served with rice, is a delectable main dish. It can be prepared a day ahead of time.

A curry is a food—meat, poultry, seafood, eggs, vegetables—cooked in a spiced sauce. In India many spices are ground and blended to make curry. Ginger, tumeric, red pepper, and coriander are considered essential, but as many as 20 different spices may be used. Curry powder is available in American stores. It can be used alone, or other spices may be added.

Various condiments may accompany the curry. They are served in small, separate dishes arranged around the main dish of curry. They may include chutney, bananas, sliced gherkins, crystallized ginger, grated orange rind, kumquats, raisins, currants, chopped onion, tomato, green pepper, nuts, or hard-cooked eggs. If imports are available, Bombay duck (a dried fish) and pappadums may be added. The diner selects condiments to sprinkle over his curry.

CHINESE RESTAURANTS in American cities are evidence that Americans like Chinese food.

Chinese food is characterized by a few features.

Most foods are cut into small pieces so they can be eaten with chopsticks and will cook quickly with a minimum loss of flavor and nutrients. They may be sliced, diced, cubed, minced, or shredded.

Three seasonings give Chinese dishes their flavoring—soy sauce, ginger root, and monosodium glutamate.

Sauces are thickened with cornstarch, rather than flour.

Food is braised, semifried, deep fried, or roasted (except rice)—never just boiled.

Vegetables are never cooked until soft. Many recipes give cooking time in terms of a few minutes or even seconds.

There is a maximum of preparation and a minimum of cooking for most dishes. Because of the shortness of cooking time, everything should be ready before the cooking itself begins. An ancient Chinese proverb says: "Better that a man should wait for his meal than the meal wait for the man."

Vegetables are cooked with little or no liquid by a method called stir frying. Our adaptation is panning.

To pan (or stir-fry), a tablespoon or two of oil is placed in a large, heavy frying pan or dutch oven. Prepared vegetables cut into small pieces are added to the hot fat. They are cooked for a few minutes with constant stirring (or tossed, as one would toss a salad) to prevent burning. They are cooked to a tender, but crisp, stage.

The real pleasure in exploring Chinese cooking can come from using the stir-frying method of preparing vegetables for some of the familiar dishes, such as chow mein, or venturing to some other popular dishes, such as fried rice, sweet-sour pork, and beef and peppers.

Chop suey is not a true Chinese dish but is made according to a Chinese pattern. The term means "small bits."

THE JAPANESE WAYS of cooking and serving food are among the most beautiful in the world: The dishes on which the food is served and the arrangement and color of the food are considered carefully to appeal to the eye as well as the appetite.

As in Chinese cookery, the preparation time is longer than the actual cooking time. All foods are prepared before the cooking begins to avoid delays that may spoil the end results.

Many dishes are cooked at the table. An electric frypan makes it possible for us to copy this method with ease.

Sukiyaki, the best known of Japanese dishes, along with rice, is a meal in itself. It is nutritious, partly because of the variety of ingredients and partly because it is cooked quickly. Essential food values are not lost.

Four keys to success with sukiyaki are: A combination of a large number of vegetables with a meat; the combination of flavors in the cooking liquid; quick cooking; and cooking enough for one serving only at a time.

As many as 10 ingredients may be used—thin sliced beef; celery sliced diagonally; a leafy vegetable, such as spinach; a root vegetable, such as carrot, turnip, radish, or sliced potato; sliced onions; scallions or green onions; sliced mushrooms; and bean sprouts. To a combination of these may be added bamboo shoots, soybean curd cut in cubes, and dried mushrooms.

The cooking liquid is a combination of soy sauce, a broth, and Japanese wine. The latter can be omitted.

The vegetables and meat, prepared in small pieces, are arranged in separate piles on a tray or plate so the whole is attractive. There is no time for last-minute preparations, so all ingredients should be ready before the guests are summoned to the table.

Only enough for one serving is included in the pan at a time. While the first serving is being eaten, the second is started. None of the sukiyaki is served overcooked.

The cooking begins with the meat, which is just heated through. Then the vegetables are added in order of cooking time. Genuine Japanese cooking calls for each vegetable to be kept in separate piles in the pan and tossed with chopsticks, but for the American it is easier to let them be mixed in the stirring. The effect is not quite so artistic, but the taste is unimpaired. It does not take long to cook sukiyaki—not more than 10 minutes.

FROM MEXICO we have the tortilla, a thin, flat, unleavened "pancake" of corn baked on a heated iron or stove. It is the bread of Mexico and is used in soups, sandwiches, and chili specialties and as toasted crisps to serve with dips and salads. You can buy tortillas canned or frozen in many markets.

Tacos, the Mexican sandwich, is usually made by rolling or folding a tortilla around a mixture of beans, cheese, eggs, meat, and shredded lettuce. This mixture may be fried, baked, or grilled and served plain or with a sauce made of tomatoes, onion, garlic, chili powder, oregano, and ground cumin.

Enchiladas, also made of tortillas, may be prepared in different ways. They are usually rolled, but they may be folded or stacked. To make them, the tortillas are fried and then dipped in a chili mixture. Shredded cheese and chopped onion are placed on each tortilla, then rolled and arranged on a baking disk. The enchiladas are covered with chili sauce, more cheese, and baked.

Tamales are really stuffed corn husks, the chief ingredient of which is masa. Masa is corn that has been soaked in limewater and ground. The masa is wrapped around a mixture of meat, beans, or dried fruit and placed on a corn husk, which is folded around the mixture to hold it. Then the tamales are arranged carefully in a pan for steaming. There are many forms, some of which are sweet. Miniature tamales are served as appetizers. (HELEN STROW)

For further reading, consult the following Department of Agriculture publications:

Apples in Appealing Ways, Leaflet No. 312; *Green Vegetables for Good Eating*, Home and Garden Bulletin No. 41; *Honey . . . Some Ways to Use It*, Home and Garden Bulletin No. 37; *Peanut and Peanut Butter Recipes*, Home and Garden Bulletin No. 36; *Root Vegetables in Everyday Meals*, Home and Garden Bulletin No. 33.

School Lunches

COMMUNITIES and parents and producers of food, almost as much as the children themselves, gain in the national school lunch program.

Figures, impressive as they are, reveal only part of the balance sheet of the project, which was authorized by the National School Lunch Act of 1946: Sixteen million children (one out of every three schoolchildren in the United States) in 68,500 public and nonprofit private schools in 1964 had balanced, nutritious lunches, at an average national cost to the child of 27 cents a day. Needy children, about one in ten, paid 5 or 10 cents or nothing.

The full balance sheet would bring out that two-thirds of American children do not receive lunches from the program. About half of those children are in schools that have the benefits of the program, but for one reason or another many of those in attendance do not participate. The other half of those children are in schools which have not become part of the program. Many of them are in sections where the need is greatest.

Federal, State, and local authorities stand ready to help communities and schools provide lunch service for children. For additional information, school officials should write to the State educational agency in their capital city. Since some States are able to administer the program only in public schools, private schools may be referred to an appropriate field office of the Department of Agriculture.

The community gains in the health of its children and, therefore, in time, in community health, which are matters that can be measured and proved.

For those who want another kind of assessment, I point out that 883 million dollars' worth of food was used in preparing lunches in 1964; nearly four-fifths of that amount was spent by the schools in obtaining the food in local markets. Thus the program provides good markets for local businesses, food industries, and farmers.

Employment is provided also for some 300 thousand local workers who operate the individual programs.

LOCAL LUNCHROOMS participating in the program receive Federal donations of abundant agricultural products and cash assistance, which amounts to more than 23 percent of the total cost of the program. Children's payments take care of more than 50 percent of the cost. State and local sources pay the rest.

Federal funds for the school lunch programs are apportioned among the States to be used in reimbursing schools for part of the cost of the foods they purchase. The amount of money each State receives is determined by two factors: School lunch participation in the State, and per capita income for the State.

Federal funds used in a State for reimbursing school lunches must be matched with funds within the State at the rate of 3 dollars for each Federal dollar. State and locally appropriated funds, children's payments, and donated goods and services may be used as matching sources.

Under this program, any nonprofit public or private school is eligible to participate. Local schools may enter into agreements with State departments of education to operate lunch programs in accordance with certain standards and regulations. They are reimbursed at the rate of 1 to 9 cents per lunch for a portion of their food expenditures.

An especially needy school, having a high proportion of children unable to pay for their lunches, may be reimbursed up to 15 cents per lunch.

THE MOST IMPORTANT operating standards established for the program are: The lunches shall meet the minimum requirements of a nutritional standard based on research, and established by the Department of Agriculture; the lunch program shall be operated on a nonprofit basis; and children who are unable to pay the full price of the lunch shall be served free or at a reduced cost.

The United States Department of Agriculture is authorized by the act to purchase foods that are in plentiful supply for distribution to schools participating in the national school lunch program. These foods usually include meat and poultry items, either frozen or canned, and a variety of canned fruits and vegetables which will help to assure nutritional adequacy.

Schools also receive foods acquired in the operation of surplus-removal and price support programs.

Distribution of these foods helps the farmer by removing surpluses from the market and providing increased consumption outside of normal market channels. These foods vary in kind from time to time according to crop and market conditions.

The foods received through the various distribution programs in the Department of Agriculture provide about 7 cents' worth of food per lunch. The other foods used are purchased by the schools in local markets throughout the country.

Each month the United States Department of Agriculture supplies a list of foods which are in plentiful supply. Local schools are encouraged to use these foods in their menus.

THE FIRST of the standards—the so-called Type A pattern—guides the planning of well-balanced lunches and helps to assure the nutritional quality of the lunches. It is based on the amount of food needed to provide at least one-third of the daily nutritive requirements of 10-year-old children.

The lunches have five basic components: One-half pint of whole fluid milk; 2 ounces of meat or other protein-rich food; three-fourths cup of fruit or vegetable in at least two items; a serving of whole-grain or enriched bread; and 2 teaspoons of butter or fortified margarine.

Those five basic components form the foundation of the lunch. When those foods are used in the amounts specified and in combination with other foods needed to satisfy the appetite, the lunches generally will meet one-third of the daily nutritional needs of a child about 10 years old. Larger portions or seconds are recommended to meet the nutritional needs of teenagers. The regulations permit serving lesser amounts of certain foods in the lunch to younger children, provided the adjustment of portion is based on the lesser food needs of these children.

All schools that participate in the national school lunch program must meet the minimum requirements of the Type A pattern daily.

Besides, those who plan the lunches consider other factors, like the esthetic value of foods, the food habits of the community, the foods available in local markets, and the equipment available to produce the meal.

COMMUNITIES, schools, and parents derive benefit from the education in nutrition that accompanies the food service. Nutritionists tell us that a large part of the population have diets that furnish less than the recommended amounts of various nutrients. Sometimes inadequate diets reflect a lack of knowledge of what constitutes good nutrition or of good food habits.

The lunch program helps children form good food habits and increase their knowledge of the importance of food to good health. Teachers and lunch supervisors work together to encourage children to learn to eat and enjoy a variety of foods. (ANNE G. EIFLER)

One New Product

IT BECAME APPARENT in 1953 that some new, convenient form of potatoes was needed, for per capita consumption of potatoes, an important commodity, had been declining steadily. In the United States, more potatoes are eaten mashed than in other forms. Why not develop a good instant mashed potato?

It was, and I tell about its development as an example of research in the Department of Agriculture that benefits farmers and consumers and as an example of the work, skill, and success that are behind many new products on your grocery shelf.

Dehydrated mashed potatoes were not new. Several types were being made commercially in 1953. Some of them left much to be desired.

Department of Agriculture chemical engineers engaged in developing food processes thought a good product might be made by drying mashed potatoes on the surface of a steam-heated, rotating cylinder—that is, by drum drying.

It is an efficient and economical method of drying. Cooked potatoes had been dried in that way in Germany and the Netherlands for at least 50 years for cattle feed. Good feed it was, but unfit for people, because it became a pasty mess when it was reconstituted with liquid.

The pasty characteristic was due to the release of starch granules from plant cells, many of which were broken during the process.

The problem the research scientists had, then, was to reduce the breakage of the cells and alter the starch to change its tendency to form paste.

Research and development went hand in hand in this case, for there was no laboratory counterpart for a process of this type. The entire research from the start was carried out on a pilot-plant scale, with due regard for factors of engineering and costs.

Biochemists in the Department of Agriculture and elsewhere had shown the effect of temperature on potato starch and how monoglycerides—certain types of fats suitable for food—altered the properties of starch. This basic knowledge was put to practical use in the development of a commercial process.

Within 2 years, a process was developed. It consisted of the following steps.

Potatoes from the field were washed, lye peeled, and trimmed by the methods common in potato processing plants. They were cut into slabs about one-half inch thick and then immersed briefly in warm water to gelatinize the starch.

A cold-water dip, which altered the gelatinized starch to make it less pasty, followed. The precooked and cooled slabs were then cooked in steam until soft. Then they were riced to a mash.

A small amount of glycerolmonostearate was added to the mash to contribute fluffiness. An antioxidant—a substance that prevents changes in the small amount of fat in potatoes—was incorporated at this stage to preserve good flavor. This mash was then fed to a drum drier of exactly the same type used in making cattle feed.

The product, however, was quite different. It came off the drum as a continuous sheet and was then mechanically broken to small flakes. Upon the addition of hot water and milk, mashed potatoes of good texture and flavor could be made.

The potato flakes of commerce now on grocery shelves almost everywhere are made by this basic process.

All the equipment needed for commercialization was readily available. The steps in the process were simple, but the conditions under which they had to be carried out to give a good product required hundreds of experiments.

An integrated pilot plant was built to demonstrate the process and to try out the many varieties of potatoes from different growing areas.

Good flakes could be made from all of the some 12 varieties tested, whether they were grown in Maine, Washington, or places in between. Naturally, the varieties of higher solids were preferable, as they yielded more.

How would the public accept the new product? An actual market test had to be made. That was done in the area of Binghamton, Endicott, and Johnson City, New York, in both large and small stores. It was a cooperative enterprise of the Maine Potato Growers Association, the Maine Agricultural Experiment Station, the Marketing Service of the State of Maine, the Eastern Utilization Research and Development Division of the Agricultural Research Service, and the Market Development Branch, Marketing Research Division, Agricultural Marketing Service.

A carload of potatoes was made into flakes in the pilot plant of the Eastern Utilization Research and Development Division of the Department at Wyndmoor, Pa., where the process was developed.

An advertising program and demonstrations of the product in stores during the early part of the test informed the public of the new product. Public acceptance was good. Notably, sales of fresh potatoes did not fall off.

About a year later, the first commercial runs were made in Maine. New plants began springing up in New York, Michigan, North Dakota, Idaho, and Oregon. Before long, 12 plants with a total production of 50 million pounds of flakes from about 6 million bushels of potatoes annually were in operation.

In the summer of 1959 the Institute of Food Technologists presented its first Industrial Achievement Award to the Department engineers who developed potato flakes for their contribution to the food industry.

Potato flakes, along with potato granules, frozen French fries, slices, and chips, have become staples on kitchen shelves. These developments have reversed the downward per capita consumption of potatoes.

Today the production of potato flakes is worldwide. You will find them nearly everywhere that packaged foods are sold. They may be labeled Kvikk Poteter, Snabb Potatis, Potatismos, Minutt Poteter, Kartoffelbrei, Pure de Papas, Purée de Pommes de Terre en Flocons, but they are still potato flakes and are good to eat. (RODERICK K. ESKEW)

Why Process Food?

EACH OF US eats nearly 30 pounds of food a week: 10 pounds of vegetables and fruit, 8 pounds of milk and dairy products, 4 pounds of meat, 3 pounds of cereal products, 1 pound of eggs, 1 pound of fat, and 1.5 pounds of sugar.

We eat about the same food each week of the year, thanks to modern developments in agriculture and in storage, shipping, and processing.

Sweet corn, for example, used to be available for a month or two in the late summer. Canned cream-style corn was one of the early major canned items; now we have sweet corn canned and frozen in a number of ways and field-chilled fresh sweet corn is available also nearly all of the year.

Lettuce and other salad vegetables are always in our refrigerators, yet not many years ago we could not have them for more than 9 months of the year.

Fresh meat and processed meat products, milk, and an increasing variety of dairy products are always available in our stores.

To achieve this continual availability and variety, food processing must do three basic things: Control spoilage and toxic microbes; control the enzymes, the natural biochemical catalysts present in all living tissue; and control the oxidation of the constituents of food.

Processing makes it possible to take vegetables and fruit fresh from the field, at the height of ripeness, and stabilize them to keep their quality.

For example, peas are harvested by mowing the entire plant and quickly transporting it to the factory where the pods are removed and shelled and the peas are frozen or canned in a few minutes. In this same way, many processed vegetables and fruit come to your table with less opportunity for biochemical change to take place after ripening than fresh products have. (The research on processing of peas was carried out in a Department of Agriculture laboratory in the Western Utilization Research and Development Division, Albany, Calif.)

Food preservation methods can be classified by their effectiveness in controlling the factors I listed earlier.

Canning and irradiation destroy the micro-organisms present; the other three methods stop their growth.

Packaging becomes of primary importance in preventing recontamination and subsequent growth of organisms in sterilized foods. The tin can and glass container are still the basic protection for our processed foods, but we can look forward to major changes as the use of plastic films and foils is accelerated.

CHEMICAL METHODS of preservation are varied, but they share common principles on which their effectiveness is based.

Meat curing, salting, pickling of vegetables, and preservation of fruit in sugar sirup all work because they inhibit biochemical processes, most notably the growth of several microorganisms.

Pickles, sauerkraut, and cheese are preserved because the fermentation process produces an acid—acetic acid for the first two and lactic acid for cheese, yogurt, sour cream, and other fermented milk products. These acids inhibit the spoilage bacteria.

Salting works in a somewhat similar manner. Common spoilage bacteria cannot grow in a salt brine of 15 percent. Therefore, if the salt concentration in the water present can prevent the growth of these bacteria, the food will be preserved. It also can be air-dried to make it quite stable. Salt meat, the stable food of navies for many centuries, was preserved by packing meat in dry salt so as to prevent bacterial attack.

Pepper and other spices have an effective antibacterial action. This is the basis of pepper-cured hams.

SUGAR SIRUPS OF ABOVE 62.5 percent have such an osmotic pressure that they draw the water from bacteria and yeasts and thus prevent their growth.

How this fact was discovered is lost in the years, but fruit was kept as jellies and jams long before modern food

	Effectiveness in control of—		
Processing principle	*Microbes*	*Enzymes*	*Oxidation*
Canning	Destroys	Destroys	Prevents
Freezing	Inhibits	Inhibits	Retards
Dehydration	Inhibits	Inhibits	Permits
Chemical	Inhibits	Inhibits	Inhibits
Irradiation	Destroys	Slight	Slight

technology was developed. Today, the volatile flavors boiled off are caught and returned to the products, so that the fresh flavor that grandmother could not achieve is restored. This is another development of the Department of Agriculture that makes our modern processed foods taste better. (The pioneering studies on recovery of flavor were carried out in the Eastern Utilization Research and Development Division, Wyndmoor, Pa.)

Tissue enzymes are destroyed by the heat necessary for sterilization of canned foods, but they constitute a problem in irradiated foods, especially meat, for their continued action affects all three quality factors I cited. Some heat treatment to destroy enzymes therefore probably will be necessary in irradiation-sterilized foods. Both freezing and dehydration slow up the action of tissue enzymes. Chemical methods of preservation inhibit tissue enzymes by changing the acidity or by osmotic effects.

The third requirement of food processing methods, the control of chemical reactions between constituents and control of the serious effects of atmospheric oxygen, is of equal importance.

Until now, irradiated, dried, and frozen foods have all had such problems and probably will continue to have them. Here again, packaging in an oxygen-free atmosphere is possible and probably will be the method of choice.

Now AS TO THE question that is often asked me: Why do we process food?

The historical purpose of food processing was to preserve food. That was followed by the conversion of natural products to different and more useful forms and treatments to produce new and desirable flavors and textures. Many processes fulfill all three of these functions.

You cannot make a loaf of bread from a bushel of wheat. It must be made into flour by a miller; the more carefully controlled the milling process, the more uniform will be the success of the baker in the home or in an industrial bakery.

SUGAR IN THE CANE or the beet is not of much use to us. It must be extracted and purified, and it comes to us as refined sugar or sirup.

Oilseeds are processed to yield liquid food oils, which are processed further to give us solid shortenings.

Frozen orange juice concentrate, developed by cooperative research of the Department of Agriculture and the Florida Citrus Commission, puts orange juice into our homes all year. These are processing methods that change the farm product into a more useful form.

Frequently we process foods to produce different flavors and textures that we like—more than 400 varieties of cheese, dill pickles, sauerkraut, many types of salami and bologna, coffee, and tea. You can think of others.

We seldom realize how many of our foods must be processed before we eat them. The faddist, who is really consistent in demanding "natural" foods, will eat a limited diet, restricted essentially to raw fruits, vegetables, and nuts.

I NEXT COME TO THE reason for food processing that many people would put first—convenience. Our food processing industry is a part of our very pattern of living, for the time saved by the housewife, as a result of the continually higher degree of processing of the foods she purchases, enables her to do many things she could not otherwise do.

A study showed that use of processed foods can save up to 4 hours a day and that the housewife who, for example, makes her own french-fried potatoes can consider that she has earned 4 cents an hour for her time. This figure, on the other hand, is as high as 3 dollars an hour for making waffles. It was also shown that the convenience food items are, on the whole, less expensive than if they were purchased fresh. (SAM R. HOOVER)

THE CONTRIBUTORS

TESSIE AGAN, *Associate Home Economist*, Kansas State University, Manhattan, Kans.

L. O. ANDERSON, *Engineer*, Forest Products Laboratory, Forest Service, Madison, Wis.

B. A. APP, *Assistant Chief*, Grain and Forage Insects Research Branch, Entomology Research Division, Agricultural Research Service.

MILDRED G. ARNOLD, *Assistant Professor*, Consumer Services and Equipment, College of Home Economics, The Pennsylvania State University, University Park, Pa.

GLENN D. BARQUEST, *Assistant Professor and Extension Specialist*, Agricultural Engineering Department, University of Wisconsin, Madison, Wis.

OLIVE M. BATCHER, *Research Food Specialist*, Human Nutrition Research Division, Agricultural Research Service.

HELEN L. BECKER, *Health Education Specialist*, Cooperative Extension Service, University of Nebraska, Lincoln, Nebr.

KAREN L. BERKE, *Home Economist*, Food Distribution Area Office, Consumer and Marketing Service, New York, N.Y.

ELIZABETH BEVERIDGE, *Department of Household Equipment*, College of Home Economics, Iowa State University, Ames, Iowa.

THURLOW J. BIDDLE, *Safety Officer*, Personnel Division, Agricultural Research Service.

ARCHIE A. BIGGS, *Architect*, Agricultural Engineering Research Division, Agricultural Research Service.

BARBARA H. BLUESTONE, *Nutrition Analyst*, Consumer and Food Economics Research Division, Agricultural Research Service.

VICTOR R. BOSWELL, *Chief*, Vegetables and Ornamentals Research Branch, Crops Research Division, Agricultural Research Service.

FERNE BOWMAN, *Head of the Department of Food Science and Nutrition*, Agricultural Experiment Station, Colorado State University, Fort Collins, Colo.

THOMAS P. BRANCH, *Electrical Engineer*, Electrical Standards Division, Rural Electrification Administration.

G. S. BURDEN, *Entomologist*, Entomology Research Division, Agricultural Research Service, Gainesville, Fla.

LOUISE BUSH-BROWN, Ambler, Pa., *President*, The Neighborhood Garden Association of Philadelphia.

SUSAN C. CAMP, *Nutritionist*, Florida State University, Tallahassee, Fla.

HENRY M. CATHEY, *Horticulturist*, Crops Research Division, Agricultural Research Service.

E. GARTH CHAMPAGNE, *Chief*, Division of Forest Products, Economics, and Marketing Research, Central States Forest Experiment Station, Forest Service, Columbus, Ohio.

L. C. COCHRAN, *Chief*, Fruit and Nut Crops Research Branch, Crops Research Division, Agricultural Research Service.

LAWRENCE V. COMPTON, *Head Biologist*, Plant Sciences Division, Soil Conservation Service.

RICHARD D. CRAMER, *Associate Professor of Design*, Department of Home Economics, University of California, Davis, Calif.

L. L. DANIELSON, *Leader*, Weed Investigations-Horticultural Crops, Crops Research Division, Agricultural Research Service.

SAVANNAH S. DAY, *Assistant Research Professor*, School of Home Economics, University of North Carolina, Greensboro, N.C.

ROWENA P. DOWLEN, *Textile Specialist*, Clothing and Housing Research Division, Agricultural Research Service.

R. S. DYAL, *Soil Scientist*, Soil and Water Conservation Research Division, Agricultural Research Service.

FLORENCE EHRENKRANZ, *Professor and Chairman*, Division of Household Equipment, School of Home Economics, University of Minnesota, St. Paul, Minn.

ANNE G. EIFLER, *Supervisor*, School Lunch and Nutrition, Pennsylvania Department of Public Instruction, Harrisburg, Pa.

RODERICK K. ESKEW, *Chief*, Engineering and Development Laboratory, Eastern Utilization Research and Development Division, Agricultural Research Service, Philadelphia, Pa.

ELEANOR FERRIS, *Writer*, Marketing Information Division, Consumer and Marketing Service.

HAZEL M. FLETCHER, *Textile Physicist*, Clothing and Housing Research Division, Agricultural Research Service.

JOSEPHINE FLORY, *Food and Nutrition Specialist*, Extension Division, University of Missouri, Columbia, Mo.

JOHN A. FLUNO, *Assistant to the Chief*, Insects Affecting Man and Animals Research Branch, Entomology Research Division, Agricultural Research Service.

FRED FORTESS, *Manager*, Textile Products Development, Celanese Fibers Company, Charlotte, N.C.

FLORENCE H. FORZIATI, *Chief*, Clothing and Textiles Laboratory, Clothing and Housing Research Division, Agricultural Research Service.

ADRIAN C. FOX, *Head*, Education Relations Section, Information Division, Soil Conservation Service.

D. L. GILL, *Plant Pathologist*, Crops Research Division, Agricultural Research Service, Georgia Coastal Plain Experiment Station, Tifton, Ga.

C. B. GILLILAND, *Deputy Director*, Rural Community Development Service.

MARGUERITE GILSTRAP, *Field Representative*, Rural Community Development Service.

JANE GRAFF, *Extension Specialist*, Department of Related Art, University of Wisconsin, Madison, Wis.

A. A. HANSON, *Research Agronomist*, Crops Research Division, Agricultural Research Service.

MARTHA L. HENSLEY, *Home Economist*, Clothing and Housing Research Division, Agricultural Research Service.

O. C. HEYER, *Engineer*, Forest Products Laboratory, Forest Service, Madison, Wis.

MARY M. HILL, *Nutritionist*, Consumer and Food Economics Research Division, Agricultural Research Service.

IRMA M. HOKE, *Research Food Specialist*, Human Nutrition Research Division, Agricultural Research Service.

EMMA G. HOLMES, *Family Economist*, Consumer and Food Economics Research Division, Agricultural Research Service.

SAM R. HOOVER, *Assistant Administrator*, Agricultural Research Service.

MILDRED HOWARD, *Housing Specialist*, Clothing and Housing Research Division, Agricultural Research Service.

LYDIA INMAN, *Department of Household Equipment*, College of Home Economics, Iowa State University, Ames, Iowa.

SETH JACKSON, *Chief*, Employee Relations Branch, Division of Personnel Management, Forest Service.

MARILYN H. JOHNSON, *Landscape Architect*, U.S. National Arboretum, Crops Research Division, Agricultural Research Service.

HARMON R. JOHNSTON, *Wood Products Insect Laboratory*, Southern Forest Experiment Station, Forest Service, Gulfport, Miss.

FAYE C. JONES, *Associate Housing Specialist*, Agricultural Experiment Station, University of Arizona, Tucson, Ariz.

LAWRENCE A. JONES, *Leader*, Agricultural Risk and Insurance Group, Farm Production Economics Division, Economic Research Service.

BEATRICE A. JUDKINS, *Program Leader*, Division of Home Economics, Federal Extension Service.

F. V. JUSKA, *Turf-Research Agronomist*, Crops Research Division, Agricultural Research Service.

HARRY L. KEIL, *Research Plant Pathologist*, Crops Research Division, Agricultural Research Service.

FERN S. KELLEY, *Assistant Director*, Division of 4-H and Youth Development, Federal Extension Service.

D. L. KLINGMAN, *Leader*, Weed Investigations-Grazing Lands, Crops Research Division, Agricultural Research Service.

K. W. KREITLOW, *Assistant Chief*, Forage and Range Research Branch, Crops Research Division, Agricultural Research Service.

HAMILTON LAUDANI, *Director*, Stored-Product Insects Research and Development Laboratory, Market Quality Research Division, Agricultural Research Service, Savannah, Ga.

R. E. LEE, *Professor*, Floriculture Department, Cornell University, Ithaca, N.Y.

CARLTON B. LEES, *Executive Secretary and Director of Publications*, Massachusetts Horticultural Society, Boston, Mass.

RUTH M. LEVERTON, *Assistant Administrator*, Agricultural Research Service.

MARION W. LONGBOTHAM, *Associate Professor and Home Management Specialist*, Home Management and Family Living Department, University of Wisconsin, Madison, Wis.

HAROLD P. LUNDGREN, *Chief*, Wool and Mohair Laboratory, Western Utilization Research and Development Division, Agricultural Research Service, Albany, Calif.

DOROTHY SIEGERT LYLE, *Director of Consumer Relations*, National Institute of Drycleaning, Silver Spring, Md.

MINNIE BELLE MCINTOSH, *Family Economist*, Consumer and Food Economics Research Division, Agricultural Research Service.

VERDA MCLENDON, *Textile Chemist*, Clothing and Housing Research Division, Agricultural Research Service.

ETHEL MCNEIL, *Microbiologist*, Clothing and Housing Research Division, Agricultural Research Service.

LOUIS D. MALOTKY, *Director*, Rural Housing Loan Division, Farmers Home Administration.

LOUISAN MAMER, *Member Services Officer*, Office of Member Services Coordinator, Rural Electrification Administration.

LYLE M. MAMER, *Associate Professor*, Home Management, Equipment, and Family Economics, University of Tennessee, Knoxville, Tenn.

RICHARD H. MANVILLE, *Director*, Bird and Mammal Laboratories, Bureau of Sport Fisheries and Wildlife, U.S. Department of the Interior.

DOROTHY M. MARTIN, *Public Information Specialist*, Division of Information and Education, Forest Service.

VICTOR P. MINIUTTI, *Technologist*, Forest Products Laboratory, Forest Service, Madison, Wis.

STELLA L. MITCHELL, *Home Management Specialist*, Division of Home Economics, Federal Extension Service.

JESSIE J. MIZE, *Head*, Department of Housing and Home Management, School of Home Economics, University of Georgia, Athens, Ga.

JEANNE SATER MOEHN, *formerly Extension Family Life Specialist*, University of Maryland, College Park, Md.

LUCILE F. MORK, *Family Economist*, Consumer and Food Economics Research Division, Agricultural Research Service.

SHIRLEY J. MOTT, *Clothing Specialist*, Clothing and Housing Research Division, Agricultural Research Service.

LOUISE N. MUMM, *Staff Consultant*, National Social Welfare Assembly, New York, N.Y.

GERTRUDE NYGREN, *Program Assistant*, Cooperative Extension Service, Michigan State University, East Lansing, Mich.

DOLORES L. NYHUS, *Nutrition Consultant*, Bureau of Public Health Nutrition, California State Department of Public Health, Berkeley, Calif.

CONSTANCE D. O'BRIEN, *Housing Specialist*, Clothing and Housing Research Division, Agricultural Research Service.

D. KEITH OSBORN, *Chairman*, Community Services Area, The Merrill-Palmer Institute, Detroit, Mich.

LOUISE PAGE, *Nutrition Analyst*, Consumer and Food Economics Research Division, Agricultural Research Service.

CLARENCE H. PALS, *Director*, Meat Inspection Division, Consumer and Marketing Service.

W. RUSSELL PARKER, *Architect*, Clothing and Housing Research Division, Agricultural Research Service.

LLOYD E. PARTAIN, *Assistant to the Administrator on Recreation*, Soil Conservation Service.

ALICE PEAVY, *Extension Economist*, Home Furnishing, Auburn University, Auburn, Ala.

JEAN L. PENNOCK, *Chief*, Family Economics Branch, Consumer and Food Economics Research Division, Agricultural Research Service.

BETTY B. PETERKIN, *Food Economist*, Consumer and Food Economics Research Division, Agricultural Research Service.

NADA D. POOLE, *Household Equipment Specialist*, Clothing and Housing Research Division, Agricultural Research Service.

EDWARD V. POPE, *Human Development and Human Relations Specialist*, Division of Home Economics, Federal Extension Service.

RUTH A. REDSTROM, *Food Economist*, Consumer and Food Economics Research Division, Agricultural Research Service.

WILSON A. REEVES, *Chief*, Cotton Finishes Laboratory, Southern Utilization Research and Development Division, Agricultural Research Service, New Orleans, La.

FLORENCE M. RICHARDSON, *Chemist*, Clothing and Housing Research Division, Agricultural Research Service.

MARTHA RICHARDSON, *Research Home Economist*, Clothing and Housing Research Division, Agricultural Research Service.

S. HELEN ROBERTS, *Textile Physicist*, Clothing and Housing Research Division, Agricultural Research Service.

R. R. ROBINSON, *Soil Scientist*, Soil and Water Conservation Research Division, Agricultural Research Service.

JOHN W. ROCKEY, *Assistant Chief*, Agricultural Engineering Research Division, Agricultural Research Service.

S. F. ROLLIN, *Chief*, Seed Branch, Grain Division, Consumer and Marketing Service.

JOYCE SEARLES SHORT, *Home Economist*, Food Distribution Division, Consumer and Marketing Service.

JOSEPH W. SIMONS, *Leader*, Farmhousing Investigations, Agricultural Engineering Research Division, Agricultural Research Service, The University of Georgia, Athens, Ga.

HENRY T. SKINNER, *Director*, U.S. National Arboretum, Crops Research Division, Agricultural Research Service.

WALTON R. SMITH, *Assistant Director*, Southeastern Forest Experiment Station, Forest Service, Asheville, N.C.

B. J. SMITTLE, *Entomologist*, Entomology Research Division, Agricultural Research Service, Gainesville, Fla.

EDNA W. SOPER, *Assistant in Research*, Consumer and Food Economics Research Division, Agricultural Research Service.

EVELYN B. SPINDLER, *Nutritionist*, Division of Home Economics, Federal Extension Service.

EUGENE H. STEVENSON, *Assistant to Director*, Division of Nutrition, Food and Drug Administration, U.S. Department of Health, Education, and Welfare.

HELEN STROW, *Education Specialist-International*, Division of Extension Research and Training, Federal Extension Service.

ALEXANDER SWANTZ, *Deputy Director*, Dairy Division, Consumer and Marketing Service.

R. KATHERINE TAUBE, *Household Equipment Specialist*, Clothing and Housing Research Division, Agricultural Research Service.

GENEVIEVE K. TAYLOE, *Housing Specialist*, Clothing and Housing Research Division, Agricultural Research Service.

LUTHER L. TERRY, *Surgeon General*, Public Health Service, U.S. Department of Health, Education, and Welfare.

NORMAN C. TETER, *Agricultural Engineer*, Agricultural Engineering Research Division, Agricultural Research Service.

KATHLEEN THOMPSON, *Specialist in Clothing and Handicraft*, Cooperative Extension Service, Auburn University, Auburn, Ala.

JAMES L. TRAWICK, *Director*, Division of Consumer Education, Bureau of Education and Voluntary Compliance, Food and Drug Administration, U.S. Department of Health, Education, and Welfare.

PATRICIA K. VANDERSALL, *Food Specialist*, Human Nutrition Research Division, Agricultural Research Service.

ARTHUR F. VERRALL, *Principal Pathologist*, Southern Forest Experiment Station, Forest Service, New Orleans, La.

REBECCA F. WAGONER, *Instructor*, School of Home Economics, University of North Carolina, Greensboro, N.C.

MARY L. WALSH, *Textile Specialist*, Clothing and Housing Research Division, Agricultural Research Service.

GEORGE H. WALTER, *Assistant-Emergency Programs*, Office of The Secretary.

BERNICE K. WATT, *Nutrition Analyst*, Consumer and Food Economics Research Division, Agricultural Research Service.

D. E. WEIDHAAS, *Acting Chief*, Insects Affecting Man and Animals Research Branch, Entomology Research Division, Agricultural Research Service.

NANCY WHITE, *Assistant Professor*, Child Development Area, School of Home Economics, The University of North Carolina, Greensboro, N.C.

IZOLA F. WILLIAMS, *Specialist in Nutrition*, Florida State University, Tallahassee, Fla.

PAULINE WINNICK, *Public Library Specialist*, Office of Education, U.S. Department of Health, Education, and Welfare.

L. W. WOOD, *Engineer*, Forest Products Laboratory, Forest Service, Madison, Wis.

DONALD WYMAN, *Horticulturist*, Arnold Arboretum of Harvard University, Jamaica Plain, Mass.

ROBERT G. YECK, *Chief*, Livestock Engineering and Farm Structures Research Branch, Agricultural Engineering Research Division, Agricultural Research Service.

491